Joining the Conversation

A Guide for Writers

Second Edition

Mike Palmquist

Colorado State University

Bedford/St. Martin's   Boston ✱ New York

For Bedford/St. Martin's

Publisher for Composition: Leasa Burton
Developmental Editors: Rachel Goldberg, Sarah Macomber
Production Editor: Kendra LeFleur
Production Supervisor: Steven Cestaro
Executive Marketing Manager: Molly Parke
Editorial Assistants: Rachel Childs, Sherry Mooney
Indexer: Jake Kawatski
Photo Researcher: Sheri Blaney
Senior Art Director: Anna Palchik
Text Design: Lisa Garbutt, Claire Seng-Niemoeller
Cover Design: Donna Dennison
Composition: Jouve
Printing and Binding: RR Donnelley and Sons

President, Bedford/St. Martin's: Denise B. Wydra
Editor in Chief: Karen S. Henry
Director of Marketing: Karen R. Soeltz
Production Director: Susan W. Brown
Director of Rights and Permissions: Hilary Newman

Manufactured in the United States of America.

8   7   6   5   4   3

f   e   d   c   b   a

For information, write: Bedford/St. Martin's, 75 Arlington Street, Boston, MA 02116
   (617-399-4000)

ISBN   978–1–4576–5316–2

Acknowledgments
Acknowledgments and copyrights are continued at the back of the book on pages 691–93, which constitute an extension of the copyright page. It is a violation of the law to reproduce these selections by any means whatsoever without the written permission of the copyright holder.

Preface for Instructors

Since the first edition of *Joining the Conversation* was published, I've spent time working with colleagues who have used the textbook in their courses. In campus visits and at conferences, in e-mail and phone conversations, and through the careful peer-review process that shaped work on this new edition, I've learned about the assignments they've developed, the activities they've used in class, and the strategies they've adopted to address student questions. I've learned what has worked well — and where improvements could be made. I've also reflected on my experiences in the classroom, asking where my thinking has changed and how some of my most recent ideas about using the conversation metaphor might be brought into this new edition.

The result is a book that deepens the first edition's emphasis on rhetorical situation and argument, expands its emphasis on genre and design, and continues to offer a clear and accessible discussion of writing processes. This new edition of *Joining the Conversation*, like the first, relies heavily on Kenneth Burke's notion of the parlor (although admittedly one that is both less confrontational and more collaborative than Burke's early vision) to help students build on their experiences with spoken conversation and grow as writers. It also maintains its commitment to viewing the composing process as necessarily shaped by technology, reflecting the ways in which computers, tablets, and smartphones allow us to access information, ideas, and argument and shape our interactions with readers and peers.

In this edition, you'll find a more comprehensive introduction to the conversation metaphor, one that not only helps students understand how the experiences they bring to the classroom can help them develop their writing skills but also discusses how to use sources to engage with the issues they encounter in their academic, civic, and personal lives. You'll also find expanded treatments of critical reading and source evaluation, peer review and collaborative work, rhetorical analysis, argumentation, presentations, and genre and design.

New to the Second Edition

This edition of *Joining the Conversation* includes the following new features:

New technology resources that help students reflect, research, write, and revise. Technology has changed the kinds of writing students do, the genres they read, the tools they use, and the processes they follow. This edition of *Joining the Conversation* discusses the use of new and widely-used technologies (from smartphones to tablets to Twitter and other social-networking venues) as natural parts of the writing process. New **Tech Tips** help students apply what they already know about technology to the challenges of academic writing, and readings throughout the book reflect a range of online and visual genres.

Tech Tips help students connect what they know about technology to their academic writing.

🖋 **TECH TIP: TAKING PHOTOS, MAKING RECORDINGS, AND SAVING NOTES**

If you have a smartphone or a tablet, you can record conversations with others, record voice memos that contain ideas about your project, save video, take photos of sources you find in the periodical room (see p. 474), and surf the Web to locate sources. Most smartphone and tablet operating systems provide access to "apps"

A note lists relevant authors

A photo records a location

Voice recording apps can be used to conduct interviews or record ideas

(or applications), often at no or low cost, that allow you to collect and organize information in the same way you would on a laptop or desktop computer.

As you save information with these tools, keep your work well organized. Use descriptive names, save work in folders or albums, and include notes about where and when you found the information. Talk with other writers about the apps they've found useful. and if they're free. try them out yourself.

▲ **See pages 445–446.**

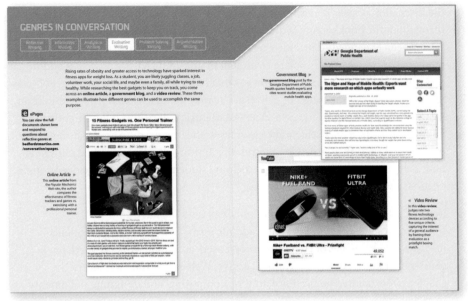

GENRES IN CONVERSATION

▲ **See pages 274–275.**

Genres in Conversation chapter openers help students analyze design choices.

e Now with Bedford Integrated Media for even more engaging readings

The Bedford Integrated Media for *Joining the Conversation,* Second Edition, extends your book beyond the printed page, with e-Pages that offer eighteen additional readings with engaging media such as video, audio, and animation. The e-Pages also provide access to the full documents included in the **Genres in Conversation** feature, allowing students to compare purposes and genre across three different selections on the same substantive topic, such as identity theft, veterans' issues, and athletes with disabilities. Access to the Bedford Integrated Media for *Joining the Conversation* is available, for free, in every new book and can be purchased separately for students with used or rented books. Visit bedfordstmartins.com /conversation.

Deeper coverage of key composing processes, including clearer integration of genre and design into planning, drafting, and revising. In response to suggestions from instructors who have used the book in their classes, the second edition of *Joining the Conversation* offers tailored advice on composing processes, from critical reading to peer review to argument and analysis. The book's treatment of critical reading includes greater attention to understanding writers' arguments, while the discussion of peer review has been expanded significantly — and reinforced throughout the book's many **Working Together** features. The discussion of analysis has been expanded to include rhetorical analysis, and the discussion of argument includes a clear and concise treatment of Toulmin analysis as well as additional coverage of appeals. Calling attention to what has been an overlooked aspect of modern rhetoric — the canon of delivery — *Joining the Conversation,* Second Edition, treats genre and design choices as essential rhetorical decisions bound tightly to issues ranging from our selection of sources to the organization and drafting of our documents. With this principle in mind, the drafting chapter in the first edition is now a chapter on drafting and design, helping students understand the deep connections between these two processes.

New "Working with Genres" chapter provides targeted advice for writing in specific genres. Going beyond the academic essay, Chapter 17 helps students navigate the challenges of creating source-based, academic work across the genres, including articles, multimodal essays, Web pages, and blog posts. The chapter offers tailored advice for planning, composing, and designing documents in each genre.

New "Presenting Your Work" chapter helps students take the next step in the writing process. Students now have multiple opportunities to present their ideas in a range of contexts and media. Chapter 18 addresses oral presentations, multimedia presentations, and the latest platforms for student portfolios. The text provides clear guidance on issues ranging from composition and presentation strategies to choices of presentation tools and technologies.

Now in two versions — one with a handbook. The full version of *Joining the Conversation,* Second Edition, includes a new handbook section that uses student-friendly language and lively examples to explore matters of style, grammar, punctuation, and mechanics. Written by Barbara Wallraff of the *Atlantic Monthly* magazine, the handbook serves as both a quick reference and a foundation for in-depth revision and editing. Embracing the conversation metaphor that shapes the book, the handbook builds naturally from the rest of *Joining the Conversation.* And in keeping with the overall book's approach, it provides a new take on the handbook genre, grounding its advice in the writer's purpose, relationship with readers, and context.

Key Features of *Joining the Conversation*

Writing Is a Social Act

Students are reading, writing, and collaborating now more than ever before. Some estimates, in fact, suggest that our students are writing five to ten times more on their own than they are in their courses. As teachers, we can build on these experiences. Online and face-to-face, students already know how to listen to what others have to say, how to acknowledge contributions made by others, and how to advance the discussion by adding something new. *Joining the Conversation* recognizes this and helps students connect these familiar everyday practices to the kinds of inquiry-based and collaborative work that they will be asked to do in writing for college and in their professional lives. In Parts One and Two **Working Together** boxes offer more group activities, and **Peer Review** boxes provide guidelines and prompts for

Peer Review: Improve Your Reflective Essay

One of the biggest challenges writers face is reading a draft of their own work as a reader rather than as the writer. Because you know what you're trying to say, you find it easy to understand your draft. To determine how you should revise your draft, ask a friend or classmate to read your essay and to consider how well you've adopted the role of observer (see p. 102).

Purpose	
	1. Did you understand the significance of my observations? Do I need to state my main idea more directly or say anything more to clarify what's important about my subject?
	2. Does my subject seem relevant to you personally? Why or why not? Is there anything I can do to forge a better connection with readers?
	3. How did you respond to my reflections and observations? Do you accept what I had to say? Have I left you with something to think about?
Readers	4. Did the story of my experiences and insights make sense to you? Do you want to know anything else about them?
	5. Does my personality come through in my writing? Should I put more (or less) of myself into the essay?
	6. Have I offered you a fresh or unusual perspective on my subject?
Sources	7. Is it clear which experiences and observations are my own and which I brought in from other sources?
	8. If I have referred to any published works or cited my source(s) appropriately?
	9. How well does my use of details show, rather than significance of my subject? Should I add o
	10. Have I used dialogue effectively? Is there t
Context	11. Did you understand any references I made social contexts? Do I need to explain anyth
	12. Is the physical appearance of my essay ap the font easy to read? Did you have enoug comments? Did I use illustrations effective

For each of the points listed above, ask your reviewers to offer improving your essay. You might want to ask them to adopt th someone who is working with you to improve your draft. You peer review in Chapter 4.

Working Together: Try It Out Loud

Before you start writing a reflective essay, try having a conversation with your classmates about a common experience. Form small groups, and list the subjects each of you is considering writing about. Choose one that most people in the group can relate to (such as an embarrassing moment, a fight with a friend, or the first day of class). Take turns sharing your memories about the experience while the other members of the group listen, respond, and ask questions. Your purpose is to connect with the other members of your group, so try to present an honest, personal view of the event.

When you are finished, take a few minutes to reflect on the exercise. What did you learn about your audience? Did you have to adapt what you said based on their interest level or on those parts of your story they didn't understand? What did you discover about what you have in common and what you do not?

Working Together and Peer Review boxes emphasize collaborative writing.

◄ See page 149.

▲ See page 135.

specific assignments. By emphasizing the importance of working with other writers on individual and collaborative projects, *Joining the Conversation* encourages students to become active participants in the exchange of ideas.

Writers Respond to All Kinds of Readings and Sources

Joining the Conversation recognizes that the volume and variety of information that students are likely to come across as they develop their ideas can be overwhelming. Writers need sharply honed critical reading skills in order to recognize and analyze the differences among conversations and readers' expectations. To this end, Chapter 3, "Reading to Write," suggests specific strategies for reading actively and evaluating sources, and introduces the concept of "reading like a writer" with in-depth student examples and opportunities for practice.

To illustrate the variety of genre, tone, and style within each writing purpose, assignment chapters include a diverse selection of professional readings by authors such as Cheryl Strayed, George Chauncey, Atul Gawande, Brooke Gladstone, Sito Negron,

Diverse reading selections reflect a range of print, online, and visual genres.

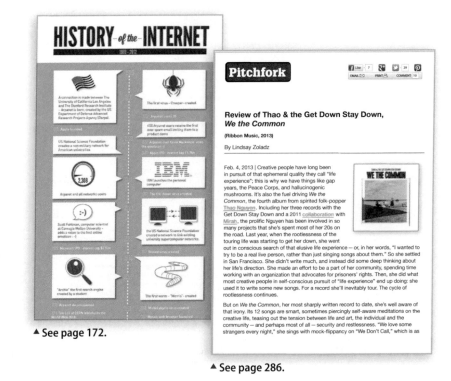

▲ See page 172.

▲ See page 286.

Anu Partanen, and Christina Hoff Sommers. Readings not only serve as examples of admirable writing but also demonstrate successful design choices, whether traditional print essays or real-world genres, such as brochures, blogs, and multimedia presentations. The layout of the textual readings has also been carefully designed to vary by genre in order to give students a realistic sense of the original source. Each selection is accompanied by questions for critical reading that ask students to consider both the piece's writing situation and genre.

Purpose and Genre Are Critical to the Writing Situation

The six assignment chapters in *Joining the Conversation* introduce students to the most common purposes for writing: to reflect, to inform, to analyze, to evaluate, to solve problems, and to convince or persuade. *Joining the Conversation* also emphasizes that purpose and genre are inextricably linked, by showing how a variety of genres can serve the same purpose and consequently how genres change and respond to a writer's purpose or role.

To help make the concept of purpose even more tangible for students, each assignment chapter also identifies a related role that writers adopt in written conversations and personifies each role with an avatar — the Observer reflects, the Reporter informs, the Interpreter analyzes, the Evaluator evaluates, the Problem Solver solves

---

What Is Writing to Inform?

Many of the documents you encounter on a regular basis are informative: newspaper and magazine articles, manuals, brochures, and books (including this textbook) are among the genres — or types of documents — that allow writers to add information to conversations about a wide range of subjects. In writing and writing-intensive courses, typical informative-writing assignments include essays, reports, and Web sites. You might also be asked to create pamphlets, multimedia presentations, memos, or posters.

Writing to inform involves adopting the role of reporter. Reporters make others aware of the facts central to a written conversation. They might provide background information for people just starting to learn about a subject or might present new information to those with a long-standing interest in it. One reporter, for example, might describe the events leading to elections in a new democracy, while another might explain the United Nations' role in monitoring those elections.

Reporters typically refrain from interpreting or analyz-

The Writer's Role: Reporter

PURPOSE
- To share information
- To answer questions

READERS
- Want to be informed
- Expect a fair and reasonable presentation of information, ideas, and arguments
- Need clear explanations of important ideas and concepts

▲ See page 162.

Avatars and icons help students consider their purposes and rhetorical situations.

problems, and the Advocate convinces or persuades. As students become familiar with the different writers' roles, they learn to recognize how specific writing situations affect their choice of genre, their relationship with their readers, and the content of their documents.

Students Still Need Support as They Write

The true measure of a textbook should be how well it works for student writers. Just because students can type, search, and read the news at the same time doesn't mean they can juggle all the skills they need to engage readers with their ideas and make a contribution to a meaningful conversation. *Joining the Conversation* lays out a clear process for inquiry-based writing that asks students to listen in on the conversations happening around them, to consider carefully their readers' expectations, and to focus on their roles as writers as they choose their topics, develop their ideas, and draft and design their documents. Part One introduces students to the rhetorical concepts that make the book tick and includes chapters on critical reading and working together through collaborative writing and peer review. The Part Two assignment chapters first show students what purpose-based writing looks like, with three readings in different genres. The assignment chapters then guide students step by step as they write their own documents. Parts Three and Four provide thorough information about researching and composing processes, and Part Five explains the MLA and APA documentation systems, with numerous citation examples. In the

In Process boxes offer insight into the writing processes of featured student writers.

In Process

Searching Databases

Ali Bizzul used her interpretive question — *Why do so many football players risk their health by adding extra weight?* — to develop search terms for searches of her library's databases. She knew from exploring her subject that it had been addressed in newspapers and magazines, so she searched databases such as LexisNexis Academic and Newspaper Source. Because she also wondered whether scientific studies had been conducted on the subject, she also searched the MedLine and PubMed databases.

Ali used the search terms *football, health,* and *weight.* She searched all fields in the database and used the Boolean operator AND to require that all three words be present (see Chapter 12).

Search	Ovid MEDLINE(R) and Ovid OLDMEDLINE(R) 1948 to Present with Daily Update

Basic Search	Find Citation	Search Tools	Search Fields	Advanced Ovid Search	**Multi-Field Search**

Enter a search term, select a specific field to search in, and click 'Search'. Click 'Add New Row' to add more terms.

	football	All Fields	▾
AND ▾	health	All Fields	▾
AND ▾	weight	All Fields	▾

Search ▸   Add New Row

▸ Limits (Click to expand)

▲ Ali's search of the MedLine database

▲ See page 236.

full version of the book, Part Six offers a useful handbook for coverage of style, grammar, punctuation, and mechanics.

Joining the Conversation not only reflects a new kind of writing process for students, it also supports students as they work through their own writing processes, reminding them constantly to reflect on — and reconsider — their writing situations. **Practice** boxes offer specific, accessible strategies for finding a conversation to join, gathering information from sources, and preparing a draft — tall tailored to each writing purpose.

Because students learn from listening to each other, each assignment chapter includes an essay by a featured student writer and follows that student's process throughout the chapter. **In Process** boxes highlight specific points in the featured writers' processes, showing the materials they used and created, including database searches, brainstorming notes, outlines, survey questions, and peer-review materials. Examples throughout the book illustrate how real students solve problems as they work with sources, draft, and design their documents — all with the goal of putting students at the center of the writing process and helping them to apply concepts in the book to their own writing.

Acknowledgments

This project represents another year of weekends and evenings that might otherwise have been spent with my family. For their patience and support, I offer my deepest thanks to my wife, Jessica, and our children, Ellen and Reid.

I offer my thanks as well to the colleagues who have inspired me as I worked on this book. David Kaufer and Chris Neuwirth helped me understand the power of the conversation metaphor and provided valuable advice as I entered the discipline. Richard Young not only inspired me but also provided me with the tools to think carefully and productively about the role of textbooks within the discipline. I owe much to the colleagues with whom I regularly discuss the teaching of writing: Will Hochman, Nick Carbone, Lynda Haas, Kate Kiefer, Sue Doe, Janice Walker, Michael Pemberton, Michael Day, and Lisa Langstraat.

A project like this necessarily involves the contributions of a wide range of colleagues who worked on key resources for the book. I am grateful to Barbara Wallraff, for her work on the handbook included with some editions of this book; to Michelle McSweeney, for her expertise during the editorial development of the handbook; to Heather Landers, for her contributions to the materials on oral and multimedia presentations; to Sue Doe, for updating and substantially expanding the instructor's manual that she wrote for the first edition; to Shannon Walsh, for researching potential reading selections; and to Kate Mayhew, for updating the citation models.

I am also indebted to the following reviewers who offered careful critiques of drafts of this book: Angela Bartlett, Chaffey College; Polly Buckingham, Eastern Washington University; Susan Butterworth, Salem State University; Misty Dawn Carmichael, Hawaii Community College; Michael Catrillo, Northampton Community College; Joseph Couch, Montgomery Community College; Donna Craine, Front Range Community College; Cherie Dargan, Hawkeye Community College; Anthony Di Renzo, Ithaca College; Kevin Ferns, Woodland Community College; Don Foster, University of Massachusetts Dartmouth; Margaret Gillio, Finger Lakes Community College; Audley Hall, NorthWest Arkansas Community College; Barbara Heifferon, Louisiana State University; Mark Houston, York College; Sara McCurry, Shasta College; Trista Merrill, Finger Lakes Community College; Deborah Miller, University of Georgia; Leanne Doornbos Nagel, Calvin College; Cynthia Ostrom, University of South Dakota; Martha Payne, Ball State University; Jason Pickavance, Salt Lake Community College; Wayne Ross, College of Western Idaho; Paul Skinner, University of Nebraska at Kearney; Andrea Spofford, University of Southern Mississippi; Betty Stack, Rowan Cabarrus Community College; Greg Wilson, College of Western Idaho; Rita Wisdom, Tarrant County College–Northeast; Carole Yee, Los Angeles Valley College. Their reactions and thoughtful suggestions helped me understand where the first edition of the book had been successful and where it could be improved, and I thank them for the time and care they took in their reviews.

Once again, I have been extraordinarily fortunate to find, in my colleagues at Bedford/St. Martin's, a group of editors and assistants who care deeply about producing the best possible textbooks. For their support, encouragement, and generous approach to editing, I thank my developmental editors, Rachel Goldberg and Sarah Macomber. Their good ideas, thoughtful feedback, and willingness to entertain even the most offbeat thoughts about where we might take this new edition — all the while keeping me more or less on task — made the preparation of this edition a pleasant and satisfying experience. I thank them for their patience, support, intelligence, and good sense. I am also grateful to editorial assistants, Sherry Mooney and Rachel Childs, for their many contributions to this project, from finding additional readings to tracking down sources to responding quickly and well to the unexpected tasks that came up so often. I am indebted, as well, to Anna Palchik and Claire Seng-Niemoller for the outstanding design of this book; to my production editor, Kendra LeFleur, for her attention to detail in directing its complex production; and to Linda McLatchie for her careful copy editing. I also offer my thanks to editor in chief Karen Henry for her leadership throughout both editions of this book, and to Molly Parke, Jimmy Fleming, and Karita Dos Santos for their work in helping instructors understand how *Joining the Conversation* might make a contribution in their classrooms.

Many years ago, Rory Baruth introduced me to the editors at Bedford/St. Martin's. I am grateful not only for the introduction but for the good advice he has offered since. Thanks as well to Joan Feinberg and Denise Wydra for their support of *Joining the Conversation* and for their good ideas during this revision. I offer particular thanks to Leasa Burton for her contributions to this project. From her ideas about the overall direction of the book to her feedback on the revision plan, Leasa's investment of time and effort into this book has been a continuing source of inspiration to me.

Finally, I offer my thanks to the six student writers whose work is featured in this book and on the companion Web site: Alison Bizzul, Caitlin Guariglia, Dwight Haynes, Ellen Page, Vince Reid, and Jennie Tillson. I deeply appreciate their willingness to share their work and their insights about their writing processes with other student writers. I hope that their superb examples inspire the students who use this book to join and contribute to their own written conversations.

Mike Palmquist
Colorado State University

You get more choices for *Joining the Conversation*

Bedford/St. Martin's offers resources and format choices that help you and your students get even more out of the book and your course. To learn more about or order any of the following products, contact your Bedford/St. Martin's sales representative, e-mail sales support (sales_support@bfwpub.com), or visit the Web site at bedfordstmartins.com/conversation/catalog.

Choose from Alternative Formats of *Joining the Conversation*

Bedford/St. Martin's offers a range of affordable formats, allowing students to choose the one that works for them. For details, visit bedfordstmartins.com/conversation /catalog/formats.

- *Paperback version with handbook or brief version* To order *Joining the Conversation* with the handbook use ISBN 978–1–4576–2928–0. To order the brief version, use ISBN 978–1–4576–5316–2.

- *Loose-leaf edition* The loose-leaf edition does not have a traditional binding; its pages are loose and two-hole punched to provide flexibility and a low price to students. To order the loose-leaf edition with the handbook, use ISBN 978–1–4576–8180–6. To order the brief loose-leaf edition, use ISBN 978–1–4576–8164–6.

- *Bedford e-Book to Go* A portable, downloadable e-book at about half the price of the print book.

- *Other popular e-book formats* For details, visit bedfordstmartins.com/ebooks.

Select Value Packages

Add value to your text by packaging one of the following resources with *Joining the Conversation*, Second Edition. To learn more about package options for any of the following products, contact your Bedford/St. Martin's sales representative or visit bedfordstmartins.com/conversation/catalog.

LearningCurve for Readers and Writers, Bedford/St. Martin's adaptive quizzing program, quickly learns what students already know and helps them practice what they don't yet understand. Gamelike quizzing motivates students to engage with their course, and reporting tools help teachers discern their students' needs. *LearningCurve for Readers and Writers* can be packaged with *Joining the Conversation* at a significant discount. An activation code is required. See Ordering Information on page xvii for the ISBN to order LearningCurve packaged with the print book. For details, visit bedfordstmartins.com/englishlearningcurve.

VideoCentral is a growing collection of videos for the writing class that captures real-world, academic, and student writers talking about how and why they write. Writer and teacher Peter Berkow interviewed hundreds of people — from Michael Moore to Cynthia Selfe — to produce over 140 brief videos about topics such as revising and getting feedback. VideoCentral can be packaged with *Joining the Conversation* at a significant discount. An activation code is required. See Ordering Information on page xviii for the ISBN to order VideoCentral packaged with the print book.

i-series This popular series presents multimedia tutorials in a flexible format — because there are things you can't do in a book.

- *ix visualizing composition 2.0* helps students put into practice key rhetorical and visual concepts. See Ordering Information on page xxv for the ISBN to order *ix visualizing composition 2.0* packaged with the print book.

- *i-claim: visualizing argument* offers a new way to see argument — with six multimedia tutorials, an illustrated glossary, and a wide array of multimedia arguments. See Ordering Information on page xviii for the ISBN to order *i-claim: visualizing argument* packaged with the print book.

Portfolio Keeping, **Third Edition,** by Nedra Reynolds and Elizabeth Davis, provides all the information students need to use the portfolio method successfully in a writing course. *Portfolio Teaching*, a companion guide for instructors, provides the practical information instructors and writing program administrators need to use the portfolio method successfully in a writing course. See Ordering Information on page xviii for the ISBN to order *Portfolio Keeping* packaged with the print book.

Bedford Select for *Joining the Conversation* For a wider array of academic readings, package a Bedford Select reader in print or digital form with *Joining the Conversation* at a discount. A pre-built Quick Select table of contents, "Joining the Academic Conversation," includes academic readings that complement the book. Use it as is or customize it for your students. For more information, visit bedfordstmartins.com /select/catalog.

Discover What LaunchPad Can Do for Your Course

Bedford's new course space, LaunchPad, combines an interactive e-book with high-quality multimedia content and ready-made assessment options, including LearningCurve adaptive quizzing. Pre-built units are easy to assign or adapt with your own material, such as readings, videos, quizzes, discussion groups, and more. While a streamlined interface helps students focus on what's due next, social commenting tools let them engage, make connections, and learn from each other. Use LaunchPad on its own or integrate it with your school's learning management system so your class is always on the same page. *LaunchPad for Joining the Conversation* can be purchased separately or packaged with the print book at a significant discount. An activation code is required. See Ordering Information on page xvii for the ISBN to order *LaunchPad for Joining the Conversation* with the print book.

Choose the Flexible *Bedford e-Portfolio*

Students can collect, select, and reflect on their coursework and personalize and share their e-portfolios for any audience — instructors, peers, potential employers, or family and friends. Instructors can provide as much or as little structure as they see fit. Rubrics and learning outcomes can be aligned to student work, so instructors and programs can gather reliable and useful assessment data. Every *Bedford e-Portfolio* comes preloaded with *Portfolio Keeping* and *Portfolio Teaching*, by Nedra Reynolds and Elizabeth Davis. *Bedford e-Portfolio* can be purchased separately or packaged with the print book at a significant discount. An activation code is required. See Ordering Information on page xvii for the ISBN to order *Bedford e-Portfolio* with the print book. For more information, visit bedfordstmartins.com/eportfolio.

Watch Peer Review Work

Eli Review lets instructors scaffold their assignments in a clearer, more effective way for students — making peer review more visible and teachable. Because teachers get real-time analytics about how well students have met criteria in a writing task *and* about how helpful peer comments have been, they can intervene in real time to teach how to give good feedback and how to shape writing to meet criteria. When students can instantly see which comments are endorsed by their teacher and how their feedback has been rated by their peers, they're motivated to give the best reviews, get the best ratings, think like writers and revise with a plan. *Eli Review* can be purchased separately or packaged with the print book at a significant discount. An activation code is required. See Ordering Information on page xvii for the ISBN to order *Eli Review* with the print book. For more information, visit bedfordstmartins .com/eli.

Try *Re: Writing* 2 for Fun

bedfordstmartins.com/rewriting

What's the fun of teaching writing if you can't try something new? The best collection of free writing resources on the Web, *Re:Writing 2* gives you and your students even more ways to think, watch, practice, and learn about writing concepts. Listen to Nancy Sommers on using a teacher's comments to revise. Try a logic puzzle. Consult our resources for writing centers. All free for the fun of trying it. For more information, visit bedfordstmartins.com/rewriting.

Instructor Resources

bedfordstmartins.com/conversation/catalog

You have a lot to do in your course. Bedford/St. Martin's wants to make it easy for you to find the support you need — and to get it quickly.

Teaching with Joining the Conversation is available as a PDF that can be downloaded from the Bedford/St. Martin's online catalog. In addition to chapter overviews and teaching tips, the instructor's manual includes sample syllabi, correlations to the Council of Writing Program Administrators' Outcomes Statement, and classroom activities.

Teaching Central offers the entire list of Bedford/St. Martin's print and online professional resources in one place. You'll find landmark reference works, sourcebooks on pedagogical issues, award-winning collections, and practical advice for the classroom — all free for instructors.

Bits collects creative ideas for teaching a range of composition topics in an easily searchable blog format. A community of teachers — leading scholars, authors, and editors — discuss revision, research, grammar and style, technology, peer review, and much more. Take, use, adapt, and pass the ideas around. Then, come back to the site to comment or share your own suggestions.

To order any of the ancillaries, please contact your Bedford/St. Martin's sales representative, e-mail sales support at sales_support@bfwpub.com, or visit our Web site at bedfordstmartins.com. Note that activation codes are required for LearningCurve, *ix visualizing composition 2.0*, *i-claim*, VideoCentral, *Eli Review*, and *Bedford e-Portfolio*. Codes can be purchased separately or packaged with the print book at a significant discount.

Ordering Information

To order the ***Bedford e-Portfolio* access card** with the print book, use these ISBNs:

- 978–1–4576–7621–5 (*Joining the Conversation: A Guide and Handbook for Writers*)
- 978–1–4576–7624–6 (*Joining the Conversation: A Guide for Writers*)

To order the ***Eli Review* access card** with the print book, use these ISBNs:

- 978–1–4576–7612–3 (*Joining the Conversation: A Guide and Handbook for Writers*)
- 978–1–4576–7611–6 (*Joining the Conversation: A Guide for Writers*)

To order the ***LaunchPad for Joining the Conversation* access card** with the print book, use this ISBN:

- 978–1–4576–5321–6 (*Joining the Conversation: A Guide and Handbook for Writers*)

To order the **LearningCurve access card** with the print book, use these ISBNs:

- 978–1–4576–7651–2 (*Joining the Conversation: A Guide and Handbook for Writers*)
- 978–1–4576–7653–6 (*Joining the Conversation: A Guide for Writers*)

To order the **VideoCentral access card** with the print book, use these ISBNs:

- 978–1–4576–7587–4 (*Joining the Conversation: A Guide and Handbook for Writers*)

- 978–1–4576–7588–1 (*Joining the Conversation: A Guide for Writers*)

To order the *ix visualizing composition 2.0* **access card** with the print book, use these ISBNs:

- 978–1–4576–7601–7 (*Joining the Conversation: A Guide and Handbook for Writers*)

- 978–1–4576–7600–0 (*Joining the Conversation: A Guide for Writers*)

To order the *i-claim* **access card** with the print book, use these ISBNs:

- 978–1–4576–7631–4 (*Joining the Conversation: A Guide and Handbook for Writers*)

- 978–1–4576–7632–1 (*Joining the Conversation: A Guide for Writers*)

To order the ***Portfolio Keeping,*** **Third Edition,** with the print book, use these ISBNs:

- 978–1–4576–7579–9 (*Joining the Conversation: A Guide and Handbook for Writers*)

- 978–1–4576–7578–2 (*Joining the Conversation: A Guide for Writers*)

Joining the Conversation Works with the Council of Writing Program Administrators' (WPA) Outcomes

The Council of Writing Program Administrators established a set of desired outcomes for first-year composition courses across the country. As an inquiry-based rhetoric focusing on purpose and genre, *Joining the Conversation* helps instructors and students accomplish these teaching and learning goals. The following table provides detailed information on how *Joining the Conversation* supports each outcome.

DESIRED OUTCOMES	RELEVANT FEATURES IN *JOINING THE CONVERSATION*
Rhetorical Knowledge	
Focus on a purpose	**Chapter 1** introduces the concept of writing for particular purposes. **Chapter 2** invites students to determine their purposes as they assess their writing situations. **Chapters 5–10** present the most common purposes for writing—to reflect, to inform, to analyze, to evaluate, to solve problems, and to convince or persuade. **Avatars** in these chapters (see p. 10, for example) personify writers' roles to make the concept of purpose more concrete.
Respond to the needs of different audiences	**Chapter 1** explains that readers' needs affect how they read documents, while **Chapter 2** helps students identify their readers. **Chapters 15, 16, 17, and 18** continue to help students respond to readers' needs as they organize, draft, design, and present their documents.
Respond appropriately to different kinds of rhetorical situations	Each of the assignment chapters **(Chapters 5–10)** focuses on a different rhetorical situation that students are likely to encounter. **The Writer's Role boxes** in these chapters analyze the purpose, readers, sources, and context for each rhetorical situation (see p. 102, for example), and each chapter offers advice for reading, responding, drafting, and revising that is specific to the writer's situation, purpose, and audience.
Use conventions of format and structure appropriate to the rhetorical situation	**Chapter 1** introduces the concepts of genre and design and shows how they relate to the writer's purpose. Advice about writing in **Chapters 5–10** helps students make effective genre and design choices for their documents. **Chapters 16, 17, and 18** provide advice and **Checklists** (see p. 556, for example) for following the design conventions of academic essays, multimodal essays, articles, and Web sites.
Adopt appropriate voice, tone, and level of formality	Readings in **Chapters 5–10** demonstrate how various audiences, genres, and rhetorical situations call for different levels of formality, and **essays by featured student writers** (see p. 150, for example) model appropriate tone for academic work. **Chapter 20 and the Handbook (Part Six in some versions of this book)** provide practical advice for writing with style and using appropriate voice, tone, language, and formality.
Understand how genres shape reading and writing	**Chapter 1** introduces the concept of genre as linked to purpose and design and provides a practice activity on analyzing genre. **Chapters 5–10** open with a **Genres in Conversation** feature that invites students to analyze how genre and writing situation influence design choices (see pp. 100–101, for example). Readings in those chapters are designed to reflect the various genres in which they were originally published. **Chapters 16 and 17** address the composing processes and design conventions of popular and academic genres.
Write in several genres	**Chapter 17** focuses on writing in various genres, including guidance on composing processes, writing conventions, and design features. Each genre is accompanied by a **Checklist** and **Annotated Example** (see p. 565, for example). Readings in **Chapters 5–10** cover thirty-six genres, including memoirs, audio essays, literacy narratives, brochures, Web sites, infographics, news analyses, multimedia presentations, rhetorical analyses, progress reports, speeches, proposals, editorials, and advertisements. Each assignment chapter also ends with **Project Ideas** for essays and other genres suited to that chapter's purpose (see p. 156, for example).
Critical Thinking, Reading, and Writing	
Use writing and reading for inquiry, learning, thinking, and communicating	Throughout the text, the metaphor of writing as conversation emphasizes writing as a tool for inquiry and the exchange of ideas. **Chapter 2** covers inquiry extensively, establishing reading and writing as part of written conversations that in turn inspire and inform further discourse. **Chapter 3** provides advice and strategies for reading critically and actively, evaluating sources, and reading for a purpose. **Starting a Conversation questions** (see p. 112, for example) enable students to engage critically with each reading in **Chapters 5–10**.

(continued on next page)

Critical Thinking, Reading, and Writing (cont.)

Understand a writing assignment as a series of tasks, including finding, evaluating, analyzing, and synthesizing appropriate primary and secondary sources	**Chapter 2** breaks down the steps of analyzing an assignment and assessing the writing situation. **Chapter 3** explains how to evaluate sources based on relevance, use of evidence, author, publisher, timeliness, comprehensiveness, and genre, as well as how to quote, paraphrase, and summarize sources. **Chapters 5–10** discuss the kinds of sources best suited to each type of assignment, from print and electronic sources to interviews, observations, and surveys. **Chapters 11–13** offer strategies for developing a search plan, locating print and electronic sources, conducting field research, and avoiding plagiarism.
Integrate their own ideas with those of others	**Chapter 19** provides specific advice for integrating sources effectively; summarizing, paraphrasing, and quoting strategically; and avoiding plagiarism. **Chapters 21 and 22** help students document sources in MLA and APA style correctly and provide models for dozens of source types.
Understand the relationships among language, knowledge, and power	**Chapter 1** introduces the idea of writing as a conversation in which writers share information, ideas, and arguments. Readings in **Chapters 5–10,** from Sito Negron's analysis of drug violence in Juarez, Mexico, to a commencement speech about the civil rights movement by Michelle Obama, illustrate the profound effects of writing on readers. Furthermore, **Chapter 10** provides detailed coverage of claims, evidence, and counterarguments.

Processes

Be aware that it usually takes multiple drafts to create and complete a successful text	Writing processes based on multiple drafts are demonstrated throughout **Chapters 5–10**. **Chapter 20** emphasizes the importance of revising and editing and offers specific advice for working with multiple drafts.
Develop flexible strategies for generating ideas, revising, editing, and proofreading	**Chapter 2** suggests different ways to generate ideas, including brainstorming, freewriting, looping, clustering, and mapping. Demonstrating that writing processes must vary with each writing situation, **Chapters 5–10** provide purpose-specific guidance for generating ideas, preparing drafts, and reviewing and improving drafts. **Chapter 20** offers practical advice and **Checklists** for revising and editing.
Understand writing as an open process that permits writers to use later invention and re-thinking to revise their work	**Chapter 2** introduces the concept of writing as a process that requires revision. **In Process boxes in Chapters 5–10** (see p. 133, for example) follow featured student writers through their writing processes from the early stages to the final draft. **"Review and Improve Your Draft" sections** in each of those chapters offer purpose-specific advice for revising different types of assignments (see p. 146, for example). **Chapter 20** provides guidance on revising and editing.
Understand the collaborative and social aspects of writing processes	By framing writing as conversation, the book underscores writing as a social act. **Chapter 4** explains the value of working with other writers and offers specific guidance for both individual and collaborative projects. **Peer Review boxes in Chapters 5–10** help students work together to review and improve drafts (see p. 149, for example). **Working Together boxes throughout Chapters 1–10** suggest group activities to help students work through assignments.
Learn to critique their own and others' works	**Chapter 4** focuses on peer review and offers guidelines for giving and receiving feedback on written work. **Peer Review boxes in Chapters 5–10** help students work together to review and improve drafts (see p. 149, for example).
Learn to balance the advantages of relying on others with the responsibility of doing their part	**Chapter 4** explains how working with others can benefit a writing project. **Working Together boxes** help students develop solutions to potential problems (p. 348), establish ground rules (p. 601), and create a project plan (p. 603).

Processes (cont.)

Use a variety of technologies to address a range of audiences	Readings in **Chapters 5–10** model a variety of technologies and media, with examples drawn from photo essays, Web sites, multimedia presentations, and blogs. **Chapters 12 and 19** provide advice for finding and integrating electronic sources, images, video, and audio. **Chapter 17** covers design conventions for multimodal essays and Web sites. **Chapter 18** discusses how technology can help you present your work effectively through a multimedia presentation or online portfolio tool.

Knowledge of Conventions

Learn common formats for different kinds of texts	The concept of genre-specific design and formatting is foregrounded in **Chapter 1**. Readings in **Chapters 5–10** are designed to reflect the various genres in which they were originally published to familiarize students with common formats and design conventions. **Genres in Conversation chapter openers** (see pp. 100–101, for example) help students analyze the reasons for various design choices as they relate to purpose and the writing situation. **Chapters 16, 17, and 18** provide advice and **Checklists** for following appropriate conventions for academic essays, multimodal essays, articles, and Web sites.
Develop knowledge of genre conventions ranging from structure to tone	**Chapter 17** focuses on choosing the right genre and composing effectively in that genre. **Starting a Conversation questions** following each reading in **Chapters 5–10** focus on genre to help students analyze the structure, style, tone, and conventions of various types of writing.
Practice appropriate means of documenting their work	**Chapter 13** is devoted to questions of plagiarism and research ethics. **Chapter 19** provides specific advice for integrating sources effectively and avoiding plagiarism. **Chapters 21 and 22** help students correctly document sources in MLA and APA style.
Control surface features (syntax, grammar, punctuation, spelling)	**Chapter 16** addresses syntax, effective transitions, and consistent point of view, and **the Handbook (Part Six in some versions of this book)** helps with the finer points of grammar, spelling, and punctuation as part of the drafting and editing process.

Composing in Electronic Environments

Use electronic environments for drafting, reviewing, revising, editing, and sharing texts	**Chapter 4** explains how to use chat sessions, e-mail discussion lists, Web discussion forums, wikis, and blogs to generate and refine ideas; file-sharing Web sites to share documents; and word-processing programs to conduct peer review.
Locate, evaluate, organize, and use research material collected from electronic sources	**Chapters 6, 7, 8, and 10** integrate examples of students' online research practices into advice about the writing process. **In Process boxes** in these chapters illustrate library catalog, database, and Web searches. **Chapter 11** offers detailed advice on managing digital source material. **Chapter 12** explains how to perform effective searches using electronic library catalogs, scholarly and other subject databases, the Web, and media search sites. It also demonstrates how to use Boolean terms and define search limits for more targeted results.
Understand and exploit the differences in the rhetorical strategies and in the affordances available for both print and electronic composing processes and texts	Readings in **Chapters 5–10** illustrate a variety of print and multimodal genres, from memoirs, essays, and letters to advertisements, Web sites, and multimedia presentations. **Chapters 16, 17, and 18** address effective and appropriate design for academic essays, multimodal essays, articles, and Web sites.

Contents

e Your book goes beyond the printed page: bedfordstmartins.com/conversation.

6 WRITING TO INFORM   159
GENRES IN CONVERSATION: INFORMATIVE WRITING   160

What is writing to inform?   162

What kinds of documents are used to inform?   163

e-Pages

How can I write an informative essay?   180

Your book goes beyond the printed page: bedfordstmartins.com/conversation.

7 WRITING TO ANALYZE   213
GENRES IN CONVERSATION: ANALYTICAL WRITING   214

What is writing to analyze?   216
The Writer's Role: Interpreter   216

What kinds of documents are used to present an analysis?   217
MAGAZINE ARTICLES   218
Sito Negron, *Baghdad, Mexico*   218
RHETORICAL ANALYSES   223
Brooke Gladstone, *The Goldilocks Number*   224
ANALYTICAL BLOG POSTS   228
Nick Bilton, *Disruptions: Digital Era Redefining Etiquette*   228

e-Pages
NEWS ANALYSES
Chicago Tribune, *The Drone Future*
DOCUMENTARY FILMS
Adriana Barbaro and Jeremy Earp, *Consuming Kids: The Commercialization of Childhood*
ANALYTICAL ESSAYS
Marlene Zuk, *Misguided Nostalgia for Our Paleo Past*

How can I write an analytical essay?   232
○ In Process: An Analytical Essay about Football & Health   232

8   WRITING TO EVALUATE   274

e Your book goes beyond the printed page: bedfordstmartins.com/conversation.

9 WRITING TO SOLVE PROBLEMS   325
GENRES IN CONVERSATION: PROBLEM-SOLVING WRITING   326

---

e Your book goes beyond the printed page: bedfordstmartins.com/conversation.

PART THREE: WORKING WITH SOURCES   433

11 BEGINNING YOUR SEARCH   435

18 PRESENTING YOUR WORK   583

PART ONE

Joining a
Conversation

Making Connections

Writing is often referred to as a mysterious process. Some people even consider the ability to write well a rare and special gift. Well . . . perhaps. But only if you're talking about the ability to write a prize-winning novel or a poem that will be celebrated for generations. If, on the other hand, you're talking about conveying information, ideas, and arguments clearly and convincingly, the writing process is anything but mysterious.

In fact, once you realize that writing shares a surprising number of similarities with participating in a conversation, you'll find that writing is an activity you can approach with confidence.

Why Think of Writing as Conversation?

Learning to write is similar to learning other complex processes, such as playing a musical instrument, taking up a new sport, or figuring out how to work with people.

- Learning to write takes time and effort.
- It helps if you can turn to others for guidance and advice.
- Most important, it helps if you can connect what you're learning to what you already know.

In this book, writing is treated as an activity similar to conversation. The documents you'll write are contributions that move a conversation forward. The designs you'll choose reflect your purposes and those of your readers. And the processes you'll use to write are similar to those used to participate in a discussion. By thinking of writing as conversation, you'll be able to use your already extensive understanding of how conversations work to become a confident, effective writer.

You Already Know How Conversations Work — Online and Off

Imagine yourself at a party. When you arrived, you said hello to friends and found something to eat or drink. Then you walked around, listening briefly to several conversations. Eventually, you joined a group that was talking about something you found interesting.

If you're like most people, you didn't jump right into the conversation. Instead, you listened for a few minutes and thought about what was being said. Perhaps you learned something new. Eventually, you added your voice to the conversation, other members of the group picked up on what you said, and the conversation moved along. The same thing happens when you join a new group online. Whether you join a discussion board or a Facebook group, more than likely you listen in (or read what's been posted) to learn about the group's interests before you make any posts.

You can use your understanding of how conversations work to become a better writer. By thinking of writing as a conversation, you'll realize that good writing involves more than simply stating what you know. You'll see writing, instead, as a process of joining, reflecting on, and contributing to a conversation about a topic or an issue.

Thinking of writing as a form of conversation allows you to build on skills you already possess. In addition, because written conversations take place over much longer periods of time than spoken conversations do, you can use your conversational skills to far greater advantage. You can thoroughly consider your purposes and analyze your readers' needs, interests, and backgrounds. And you can explore the contexts — physical, social, and cultural — that will shape how your document is written and read.

Today, many of us are as likely to engage in conversations through writing as through speaking. Some of us prefer a text message to a phone call. Some of us spend more time using e-mail than talking with friends. Some of us spend entire evenings on Web discussion forums, sharing information or arguing about the best new games, music, or movies. Some of us post, read, and reply to blogs on a regular basis. And some of us spend more time keeping up with friends on Facebook, Twitter, or Tumblr than we do hanging out together.

Interestingly, if you ask people who spend significant amounts of time online whether they do much writing, they'll often say they don't. They don't think of creating text messages, e-mail messages, status updates, comments, notes, forum posts,

Practice: Inventory Your Writing Life

We all have writing lives. Even if you think yours is on life support, you probably do much more writing than you think. Conduct an inventory of your writing activities, and reflect on how your experiences might enhance the writing you'll do for class assignments. To get started, use the following prompts:

1. **Create a list of everything you do that involves typing.** Be sure to include typing on phones, tablets, and computers.

2. **List everything you do that involves handwriting.** Include everything from grocery lists to notes taken in class to personal letters.

3. **Identify the purposes and audiences of each activity you've listed.** For each item, indicate why you do it or what you hope to accomplish by doing it (purpose). Then indicate who reads it (audience). In some cases,

such as shopping lists or class notes, your audience will most likely be yourself.

4. **Identify activities that involve locating information.** For each activity on your list, indicate whether you read sources (such as newspaper or magazine articles, Web sites, blogs, or books), search the Web, collect information through observation, or talk to others in the course of carrying out the activity.

5. **Review your list to identify writing activities that might prepare you for academic writing.** Look for activities that involve accomplishing a purpose; thinking about the needs, interests, and experiences of your readers; or collecting information. Consider how carrying out these activities might help you succeed at academic writing assignments.

or blog entries as writing. Yet it is. And the writing you've done in these settings can help prepare you for the writing you'll be asked to do in class or at a job.

Of course, there are differences between the writing you do online and the writing you do in an academic essay. Using abbreviations such as OMG or LOL in an essay might go over just about as well as writing "In summary, the available evidence suggests" in a text message. Despite these differences, you can build on your experiences as a writer in a wide range of settings. Just as you will adapt your tone or level of formality in a spoken conversation to the people involved in the conversation — for example, treating new acquaintances differently than you treat old friends — you're likely to adapt your writing to the situation in which you find yourself. Just as you'll tailor your comments to friends when you write on their Facebook pages, you can consider the interests and experiences of the people who will read your next academic essay. And just as you've learned to be critical — even suspicious — of what you read online, you can apply the same caution to your reading of the sources you encounter as you work on assignments.

Conversations Help You Share Information, Ideas, and Arguments

Much like a spoken conversation, a written conversation involves an exchange of information, ideas, and arguments among readers and writers. Instead of spoken words, however, the people engaged in the conversation communicate through written documents. Just as most people listen to what's being said before contributing to a conversation, most writers begin the process of writing about a topic by reading.

After they've read about a topic, most writers reflect on what they've learned and search for something new to offer to the other members of the conversation. Then they contribute to the conversation by writing their own document. In turn, that document will be read by other participants in the conversation. If these participants are interested, concerned, or even offended by what another writer has added to the conversation, they might write their own documents in response. In this sense, a conversation among writers and readers becomes a circular process in which the information, ideas, and arguments shared through documents lead to the creation of new documents.

Consider the experiences of Mia Jackson, a college student taking a first-year writing course at a community college in the Colorado Springs area. Since the college is near a large military base and many members of the campus community have connections to the military, Mia's instructor decided to focus the first major assignment on veterans' issues. Mia wanted to investigate the experiences of veterans who had returned from the wars in Iraq and Afghanistan. She knew from news reports and personal experience — two of her cousins and a close friend from high school had served in the wars — that the return to the United States could be far from smooth. But she didn't know how widespread the challenges were. To learn more, Mia started to listen in on written conversations about the issue, reading articles, news reports, and blogs. Some of what she read was written by veterans themselves. Other sources were written by journalists or by people who hoped to help them. Mia found herself drawn to discussions of employment for veterans and began to focus her reading on discussions of "green" jobs, or jobs that help the environment. Eventually, she would write an analytical essay that responded to what she had read.

After reading widely about the issue of green jobs for veterans, Mia realized that she wanted to encourage others to support efforts to train veterans for these jobs. She decided to share her ideas with friends and family, as well as with others who were interested in the issue. To get started, she posted on Tumblr and shared her post on Facebook. Some of Mia's friends responded by posting comments on her Facebook page. Some "liked" her Tumblr posts and shared them with their friends. Eventually, a student reporter for her college newspaper commented on her ideas in an article about green jobs in Colorado.

You can see conversational exchanges among readers and writers in a number of contexts. Articles in scholarly and professional journals almost always refer to previously published work. Similarly, in the letters-to-the-editor section of newspapers

Writers learn about a topic through reading.

articles

news reports

blogs

Mia

and magazines, you'll frequently see references to earlier letters. You can even see this process in writing classes. As writers share their work with classmates and instructors, they receive feedback that often leads to important changes in their final drafts. In turn, as writers read the work of their classmates, they often refine their thinking about their own writing projects.

As you work on your own writing projects, keep in mind the circular nature of written conversations. Remember: just as when you join a group of friends who are chatting at a party, you'll be entering a situation in which others have already contributed their observations and ideas to the conversation. Your contribution should build on what has already been written. In turn, other members of the conversation will read what you've written and build on the ideas, information, and arguments you've shared with them.

Conversations Allow You to Adopt Roles

In spoken conversations, we often take on roles. A speaker might explain something to someone else, in a sense becoming a guide through the conversation. Another speaker might advance an argument, taking on the role of an advocate for a particular position. These roles shift and change as the conversation moves along. Depending on the flow of the conversation, a person who explained something at one point in the conversation might make an argument later on.

Practice: Find a Written Conversation

We're surrounded by written conversations. Some focus on politics, others on sports, and still others on issues in an academic discipline. You'll find contributions to conversations on the front page of newspapers, on Web sites such as CNN .com and Foxnews.com, in academic and professional journals, and in the blogs at Tumblr or Blogger.com. Spend some time locating a conversation about a topic that interests you. Use the following prompts to find the conversation:

1. **List a topic that interests you.** Because you'll be searching for sources, jot down a list of search terms, or keywords (see p. 454), that you can use to locate sources on the topic.

2. **Choose a newspaper or magazine or search for sources.** Browse the newspaper or magazine or search for sources on a Web search site (see p. 465), a library database (see p. 461), or a library catalog (see p. 457) using the keywords you jotted down about your topic.

3. **Identify sources that seem to address the topic.** Skim each source (see p. 53) to get a sense of how it addresses your topic.

4. **Decide whether the sources are engaged in the same conversation.** Ask whether the sources are addressing the same topic. If they are, list the ways in which they are "talking" to one another about the topic. Identify any agreements, disagreements, or differences in their approach to the topic.

5. **Reflect on the conversation.** Ask whether the sources you've identified tell you enough to understand the conversation. Consider whether you might need to locate more sources to give you a fuller picture of the conversation.

OBSERVERS (Chapter 5) focus on learning about and exploring the implications of a person, an event, an object, an idea, or an issue. They typically reflect on their subject and often trace their thinking about it.

> I wonder what my life would be like if I majored in advertising.

REPORTERS (Chapter 6) present themselves as experts and present detailed but neutral information. A reporter might also provide an overview of competing ideas about a topic, such as a guide to the positions of candidates for public office.

> I'm focusing on the advertising dollars generated by sites like Facebook and Amazon.

INTERPRETERS (Chapter 7) analyze and explain the significance of ideas or events.

> I have to wonder about the truthfulness of the ads aired during this year's Super Bowl. I think I'll check a few of them out.

EVALUATORS (Chapter 8) consider how well something meets a given set of criteria. Their judgments are usually balanced, and they offer evidence and reasoning to support their evaluation.

> Who cares about the truth? I wonder which ads were most effective. Did sales actually go up as a result of the ads? Did people view the products more favorably?

PROBLEM SOLVERS (Chapter 9) identify and define a problem, discuss its impact, and offer solutions based on evidence and reasoning.

> The problem I'm wrestling with is how smaller companies can benefit from events like the Super Bowl. How can they get their message out when the ads are so expensive?

ADVOCATES (Chapter 10) present evidence in favor of their side of an argument and, in many cases, offer evidence that undermines opposing views.

> If anybody cares about the truth, it's me. And I'm sure I'm not alone. We need to do something about deceptive advertising. And I know just what that is.

A similar form of role-playing — and shifting — takes place in written conversation. The roles writers take on reflect their purpose, their understanding of their readers, and the types of documents they plan to write. To help them achieve their purpose, writers typically adopt one or more of the roles you'll learn about in later chapters of this book.

As in spoken conversations, the roles writers play are not mutually exclusive. In an introduction to an argumentative essay, you might find yourself adopting the role of reporter, helping your readers understand an issue so that they will be better positioned to understand the argument you'll advance later. Similarly, you might find yourself adopting the role of advocate in a problem-solving essay as you shift from explaining a potential solution to arguing that it should be put into effect. To understand how this fluid shifting of roles can take place — and make sense — reflect on your experiences in spoken conversations. You'll find that thinking of writing as a conversation will make it easier to understand how, and when, to shift roles.

Working Together: Explore Roles

Work together with your classmates to explore roles during a conversation. In a group of five, ask three people to talk about a topic that has recently been in the news or that has been the focus of attention on campus. As the conversation unfolds, the other two members of the group should listen and write down the different roles that are adopted during the conversation, noting when and why the roles were adopted. After five minutes of conversation, respond to the following prompts:

1. **What roles were adopted?** The two observers should share their list of roles. Ask whether the observers saw the same roles. If there are differences, discuss them.

2. **When were different roles adopted?** Ask when each role was adopted. Which roles were adopted at the beginning of the conversation? Did the members of the conversation shift roles during the conversation? If so, when?

3. **Why were different roles adopted?** Explore the reasons for adopting each role. For example, ask whether people who knew more about the topic adopted different roles than did those who knew less. If you saw shifts in role, ask why those shifts occurred.

4. **Connect the activity to your work as a writer.** Consider how the idea of roles might play out in your own writing. As a group, discuss roles you've adopted in the past, and consider how you might use the idea of roles in your future writing.

What Should I Know about Writing Situations?

When people participate in a spoken conversation, they pay attention to a wide range of factors: why they've joined the conversation, who's involved in the conversation, and what's already been said. They also notice the mood of the people they're speaking with, their facial expressions and body language, and physical factors such as background noise. In short, they consider the situation as they listen and speak. Similarly, when writers engage in written conversation, they become part of a **writing situation** — the setting in which writers and readers communicate with one another. Writing situations — the phrase we'll use in this book to refer to rhetorical situations — are shaped by these and other important factors, including the sources you use and the type of document you decide to write.

Writing Situations Are Rhetorical Situations

A writing situation is another name for a **rhetorical situation**, a concept that has been studied for thousands of years. The ancient Greeks, particularly Plato, Socrates, and Aristotle, contributed in important ways to our understanding of rhetorical situations. So did rhetoricians in China, Japan, India, Africa, Rome, the Arab world, and other cultures. Viewing writing as a rhetorical act helps us understand how writers or speakers pursue their purposes, consider the needs and interests of their audiences, adapt to the conditions in which they address their audiences, and present, organize, or design their documents or speeches.

This book is based strongly on a "rhetorical approach" to writing. Throughout the book, you'll find yourself considering why writers pursue particular purposes and the roles they adopt; how readers' reactions are affected by their needs, interests, knowledge, and backgrounds; and how the contexts in which documents are written and read shape the experience of reading them. You'll also find yourself considering not only the opportunities you can take advantage of as you create your contribution to the conversation but also the limitations that will reduce your choices about how to craft your document.

Writing Has a Purpose

As is the case with spoken conversations, writers join written conversations for particular **purposes**, which in turn affect the roles they adopt (see pp. 9–11). Writers hoping to persuade or convince their readers, for example, take on the role of advocate, while those hoping to inform readers take on the role of reporter. You can read more about the roles writers adopt in Chapters 5 through 10.

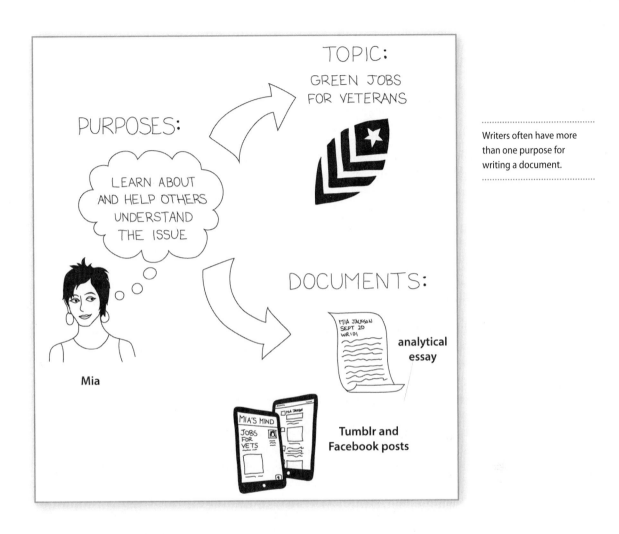

Writers often have more than one purpose for writing a document.

Writers often have more than one purpose for writing a document. Writers of academic essays, for instance, might complete their essays not only to earn a grade and pass the course but also to learn about a particular topic or improve their composition skills. Similarly, writers of newspaper and magazine articles usually write because an editor has given them an assignment. But they often find themselves interested in their subjects and end up writing as much for themselves as for their readers.

Writers' purposes for joining a conversation are shaped by their **needs**, **interests**, and **backgrounds**. For example, a person who suffers from asthma might need to ensure that plans to build a coal-powered electrical generating plant near his neighborhood will take health concerns into account. Another person with a strong interest in the use of clean coal technologies might want to support proposed legislation on reducing power-plant emissions. Still others, such as those employed by the power industry, might be concerned about how proposed legislation on power-plant emissions might affect their employment.

Your purposes will affect what you choose to write about and how you compose a document. Mia Jackson, the student who posted on Tumblr and Facebook about green jobs for military veterans, wanted not only to learn about the issue but also to call attention to a need to expand employment opportunities for others. As she wrote in her posts, her purposes affected her choice of what to write about, which information to use as supporting evidence for her points, and how to address the information, ideas, and arguments she encountered in her reading.

Readers Have Purposes, Needs, Interests, Knowledge, and Backgrounds

Just as writers have purposes, so do readers. Among other purposes, readers often want to learn about a subject, assess or evaluate ideas and arguments, or understand opposing perspectives. And like writers' purposes, readers' purposes are strongly affected by their own needs, interests, and backgrounds. Mia's needs and interests regarding green jobs for military veterans, for example, were driven by her awareness of the challenges faced by friends and family members who had served in the military. Her readers were probably drawn to her post by similar personal experiences — knowing unemployed veterans, working in green jobs themselves, living in a region with many unemployed veterans, or simply having read an article or having heard a radio report about the issue.

As writers craft their contributions to a written conversation, they ask who their readers are likely to be. They reflect on their readers' values and beliefs, determine what their readers are likely to know about a subject, and take into account their readers' likely experiences — if any — with the subject. They consider what readers need to know about a subject, and what readers might be interested in knowing. They ask why potential readers would want to read their document — and what might cause readers to stop reading. In short, writers try to understand and connect with their readers.

Writing Builds on the Work of Others

One of the most important ways in which writing situations resemble spoken conversations is their reliance on taking turns. In spoken conversations — at least in those that are productive — people take turns sharing their ideas. To move the conversation forward, speakers build on what has been said, often referring to specific ideas or arguments and identifying the speakers who raised them. Comments such as "As Ellen said . . ." and "Reid made a good point earlier when he pointed out that . . ." are frequently made in spoken conversations. They show respect for the contributions made by others and help speakers align themselves with or distance themselves from other members of the conversation.

Written conversations also build on earlier contributions. Writers refer to the work of other authors to support their arguments, to provide a context for their own contributions, or to differentiate their ideas from those advanced by other authors. For example, an opinion columnist might show how her ideas differ from those offered by other members of the conversation by quoting a statement made by another columnist. Later in the same column, she might use a statement made by yet another author to support her argument.

Writers also use sources to introduce new ideas, information, and arguments to a conversation. A blogger concerned with the challenges faced by young families wishing to purchase a home, for example, might share information from a congressional hearing on lending practices with readers. Similarly, a reporter might conduct research on market trends and use what she learns to compare the conditions home buyers faced twenty years ago with those of today. When writers use sources in this way, they provide citations to indicate that the information is provided by other authors and to help readers locate the sources in case they wish to review them.

Even when writers do not refer directly to other sources, the work of other writers is likely to influence their thinking about a subject. As you compose your contribution to a conversation, be aware that what you've read, heard, seen, and experienced will shape your thinking about the subject — and by doing so, these sources will affect the information, ideas, and arguments in your document.

Writing Takes Place in Context

Just as in spoken conversations, written conversations are affected by the contexts — or settings — in which they take place.

- **Physical context** affects how you read and write (on paper or on a computer screen) and how well you can concentrate (for example, consider the differences between trying to read in a noisy, crowded, jolting bus and in a quiet, well-lit room).

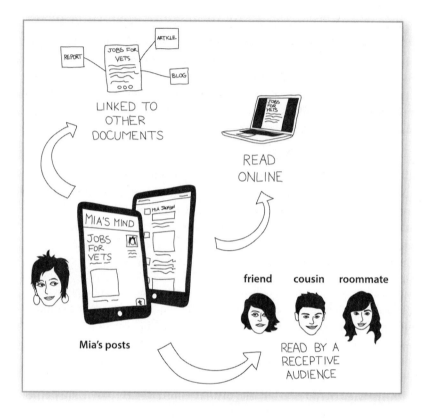

Physical, social, disciplinary, and cultural contexts affect the writing and reading of documents.

- **Social context** affects how easily writers and readers can understand one another. Readers familiar with topics such as violence in American secondary schools, for example, will not need to be educated about them — they will already know the key points. This reduces the amount of time and effort writers need to devote to providing background information.

- **Disciplinary context** refers to the shared writing practices, general agreements about appropriate types of documents, and shared assumptions about what is worth writing about common to a particular profession or academic discipline, such as history, accounting, construction management, or chemistry.

- **Cultural context** refers to a larger set of similarities and differences among readers. For instance, readers from the American Midwest might find it easier to understand the allusions and metaphors used in a document written by someone from Oregon than those in a document written by someone from Peru or Sri Lanka. Similarly, today's teenagers might find it easier to follow what's being said in a document written one month ago by a high school senior in Milwaukee than a document written in 1897 by a retired railroad engineer from Saskatchewan.

For students, one of the most important social and cultural contexts shaping their written work is academic life itself, that complex mix of instructors, fellow students, classes, tests, labs, and writing assignments that they negotiate on a daily basis. Academic culture — and U.S. and Canadian academic culture in particular — is the product of hundreds of years of arguments, decisions, revisions, and reinventions of a way of thinking and behaving. Academic culture affects far more than how you behave in class, although that's certainly an important element of it. It also shapes the writing you'll do during and after your time in college.

In nearly every instance, what you say and how you say it will reflect a combination of contexts. For example, the fact that Mia's posts were both written and read online allowed her to link directly to other digital documents, such as Facebook, other Web sites, and blogs. At the same time, because her work would be read on a computer monitor, she was cautious about readers having to scroll through multiple screens. As a result, her posts tended to be brief. Because she was writing to an audience that knew her well (friends and family), she didn't need to provide a great deal of

Working Together: Analyze a Writing Situation

Work together with your classmates to analyze a writing situation. Generate a list of documents that members of the group have written recently. Then choose one and analyze its writing situation. To conduct your analysis, respond to the following prompts:

1. **What was written?** Describe the document in enough detail to allow other members of the class to understand its main point.

2. **What were the writer's purposes?** List the purpose or purposes that drove the writer's work on the document. Why did he or she write it? What did he or she hope to gain by writing it? How was the writer's purpose shaped by his or her needs, interests, values, beliefs, knowledge, and experience?

3. **Who were the intended readers?** Describe the people who might have been expected to read the document, and list their purpose or purposes for reading it. How would their reading of the document have been shaped by their needs, interests, values, beliefs, knowledge, and experience?

4. **What sources were used in the document?** Identify the sources of information, ideas, and arguments used in the document. Indicate how the sources were used (for example, to support a point or to differentiate the writer's ideas from those of another author).

5. **What contexts shaped the writing and reading of the document?** Identify the physical, social, disciplinary, and cultural contexts that shaped the writer's work on the document and the readers' reading of it.

information about her background. And because many of her friends and family shared her connection to the military, she did not feel that she had to justify her beliefs as strongly as she might have were she writing to another group of readers.

What Should I Know about Genre and Design?

As you craft your contribution to a written conversation, you can draw on two powerful tools to create an effective document: genre and design. Genre and design are closely related. In fact, the characteristic design of a particular type of document — for example, the use of columns, headings, and photographs in a newspaper article — can help you distinguish one type of document from another.

Genres Are General Categories of Documents

You're probably familiar with generic drugs. If you have a headache, for example, you can take a pain reliever. You might choose a brand-name pain reliever based on the chemical compound acetaminophen, such as Tylenol or Anacin III. Or you might choose a less expensive, generic equivalent based on the same compound.

In the same way that generic drugs refer to general categories of pharmaceuticals, genres refer to general categories of documents. When you use the word *novel*, for example, you're referring to a general category of long fiction. If you say that you like to read novels, you aren't talking about reading a particular book; instead, you're expressing a preference for a general type of document.

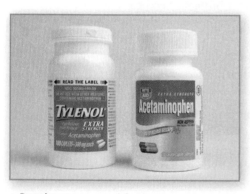

▲ Brand name or generic?

Opinion columns, academic essays, scholarly articles, and personal Web pages are all genres. So are personal journals, thank-you letters, and entries on personal blogs. In fact, there are a wide variety of genres, and the number seems to grow larger every few years. Until the 1990s, for example, personal home pages didn't exist. Nor did blogs. Nor, for that matter, did phone-based text-messaging, tweets, or Facebook posts. Yet all these have become important genres.

Although the word *genre* is typically used to refer to general categories of documents, such as novels or Web pages, it can also be used to refer to more specific categories. For example, you might refer not simply to novels but also to romance novels, mystery novels, and historical novels. Or you might refer to different types of academic essays, such as reflective essays, argumentative essays, or analytical essays. The word *genre*, in this sense, is somewhat imprecise. Sometimes it's used in the largest possible sense, and sometimes it refers to highly specific categories of documents.

Design Is a Writing Tool

Document design is the use of visual elements — such as fonts, colors, page layout, and illustrations — to enhance the effectiveness of written documents. A well-designed chart, for example, can be far more effective at conveying complex information to a reader than even the most clearly written paragraph can. Similarly, the emotional impact of a well-chosen illustration, such as a photograph of a starving child or a video clip of aid workers rushing to help victims of a natural disaster, can do far more than words alone to persuade a reader to take action. By understanding and applying the principles of document design, you can increase the likelihood that you'll achieve your purposes as a writer and address the needs and interests of your readers. Throughout this book, you'll find design treated as a central writing

MCC's Veteran Green Corps provides veterans of OEF and OIF the opportunity to learn the necessary skills to pursue jobs within land management agencies such as USFS, NPS, USFWS, and BLM.

2012 Veteran Corps Program Dates:
late May - August and August - October

Participants receive:
300+ hours of skills training/practice
S212 Wildland Fire Chainsaw training/certification
Basic Wildland Firefighter training
First Aid & CPR training
Networking with land management employers
After service networking with Veterans Green Jobs
Instruction on applying for federal jobs with
veteran and non-competitive options
PLACE based education
Living stipend and education award

Applicants must have served in the U.S. Armed Forces and have a DD214. Qualified individuals with disabilities and those from diverse backgrounds are strongly encouraged to apply. We provide reasonable accommodations for qualified individuals.

Including an empowering photograph makes this document even more persuasive than text alone might have.

New Skills for a New Career
MCC Veterans Green Corps

MONTANA
CONSERVATION
CORPS
Tools for Living. Experience for Life.

1-866-JOIN MCC • www.mtcorps.org
fb.com/MontanaConservationCorps

Limited Space - Apply Today!

strategy, and you'll find numerous examples of the design characteristics of the genres discussed in each chapter. You'll also find an in-depth discussion of design in Chapters 16, 17, and 18.

Genre and Design Are Related

Think about a Web site you visited recently. Now picture an article in a print newspaper or magazine. The differences that come to mind reflect how genre and design are intertwined. You can tell genres apart by focusing on why they are written, how they are written, and what they look like. When you read a document, you'll probably recognize it as a particular genre. The style in which it's written, its organization and use of sources, and its appearance work together to help you understand that a document is, for example, a scholarly journal article, a blog entry, a letter to the editor, or a brochure. On the basis of design alone, it's usually quite easy to tell the difference between an academic essay and an article in a popular magazine. As you read a document (and often without really thinking about it), you'll notice characteristic features of a genre, such as the use of boldface headlines or detailed footnotes. And once you've identified the genre, you'll find that it's easier to read the document. For example, understanding how a document is organized can make it easier to locate information. Similarly, if you recognize a document as an advertisement, you're less likely to be swayed by questionable reasoning.

The following documents illustrate a wide range of genres that might be used to write about a topic. Each document addresses the topic of support services for

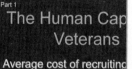

A PowerPoint presentation uses bulleted lists, images, graphs, and charts to summarize large amounts of information.

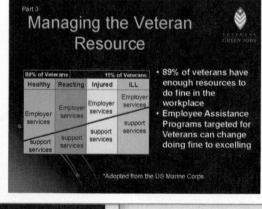

Brochures provide information by using large, descriptive titles and colorful images to draw the reader's eye to important information.

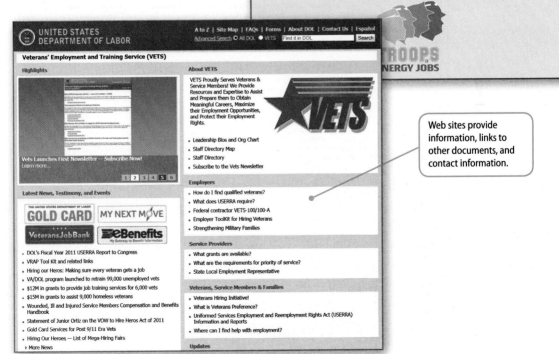

TROOPS to ENERGY JOBS

Connecting Veterans to Rewarding Energy Careers

Program Overview

Energy jobs offer promising opportunities to both experienced workers and those just starting their careers. These jobs are active, hands-on, rewarding, and available in every state, in an industry that is stable and growing.

With nearly 40 percent of the nation's energy workforce either eligible for retirement or departing their jobs because of attrition during the next five years, the energy industry is working now to develop programs to attract and train new workers for energy-related generation, transmission, and distribution careers.

Troops to Energy Jobs will accelerate the training and employability of Veterans for key energy positions. With their extensive military training and experience, many Veterans already have the skills and knowledge required for energy careers. They just need a pathway to successful job placement and career advancement.

Managed by the Center for Energy Workforce Development (CEWD), Troops to Energy Jobs will work with the U.S. Departments of Defense, Labor, and Energy and their state agencies, as well as community colleges, unions, the American Council on Education, ACT, Inc., and Kuder, Inc., to create a unique partnership between the U.S. military and the energy industry.

Initially, Troops to Energy Jobs will include selected "pilot" utilities that have been recognized as part of the elite group of Top Military Employers and that work in states with strong State Energy Workforce Consortia. The goal is to expand the program beyond the pilot companies to the entire energy industry.

> "Their extensive military training, strong work ethic, and leadership skills make military Veterans highly desirable employees for energy companies. I am proud that Troops to Energy Jobs will help connect these Veterans to rewarding energy careers."
>
> – Tom Farrell, Chairman, President and CEO, Dominion, and Chairman, Edison Electric Institute

continued ▶

TROOPS ENERGY JOBS

UNITED STATES DEPARTMENT OF LABOR

A to Z | Site Map | FAQs | Forms | About DOL | Contact Us | Español
Advanced Search ○ All DOL ● VETS   Find it in DOL   Search

Veterans' Employment and Training Service (VETS)

Highlights

Vets Launches First Newsletter — Subscribe Now!
Learn more...

1 2 3 4 5 6

Latest News, Testimony, and Events

GOLD CARD | MY NEXT MOVE
VeteransJobBank | eBenefits

- DOL's Fiscal Year 2011 USERRA Report to Congress
- VRAP Tool Kit and related links
- Hiring our Heros: Making sure every veteran gets a job
- VA/DOL program launched to retrain 99,000 unemployed vets
- $12M in grants to provide job training services for 6,000 vets
- $15M in grants to assist 9,000 homeless veterans
- Wounded, Ill and Injured Service Members Compensation and Benefits Handbook
- Statement of Junior Ortiz on the VOW to Hire Heros Act of 2011
- Gold Card Services for Post 9/11 Era Vets
- Hiring Our Heroes — List of Mega-Hiring Fairs
▸ More News

About VETS

VETS Proudly Serves Veterans & Service Members! We Provide Resources and Expertise to Assist and Prepare them to Obtain Meaningful Careers, Maximize their Employment Opportunities, and Protect their Employment Rights.

- Leadership Bios and Org Chart
- Staff Directory Map
- Staff Directory
- Subscribe to the Vets Newsletter

Employers

- How do I find qualified veterans?
- What does USERRA require?
- Federal contractor VETS-100/100-A
- Employer ToolKit for Hiring Veterans
- Strengthening Military Families

Service Providers

- What grants are available?
- What are the requirements for priority of service?
- State Local Employment Representative

Veterans, Service Members & Families

- Veterans Hiring Initiative!
- What is Veterans Preference?
- Uniformed Services Employment and Reemployment Rights Act (USERRA) Information and Reports
- Where can I find help with employment?

Updates

Web sites provide information, links to other documents, and contact information.

An article published in a scholarly journal is directed to readers who are familiar with research on a topic. It offers an abstract, keywords, and headings to help readers quickly identify important information and ideas.

Contemporary Issues In Education Research – January 2010   *Volume 3, Number 1*

Veterans Returning From War Into The Classroom: How Can Colleges Be Better Prepared To Meet Their Needs

Lana Zinger, Queensborough Community College, USA
Andrea Cohen, Queensborough Community College, USA

ABSTRACT

Colleges throughout the country are bracing for a large influx of returning veterans over the next couple of years and the question is whether they can meet the needs of this population. There is a paucity of empirical literature on Iraqi and/or Afghan veterans' adjustment in the college arena and the factors that mitigate the attrition rate and facilitate success. This research offers a glimpse into the lives of the veterans returning into college life. An important implication of this research is to better inform educators, mental health professionals and administrators with regard to policy making, program development and restructuring efforts. A qualitative research design using structured interviews to obtain information about returning veterans from Afghanistan and/or Iraq was used in this study. This study discusses the many challenges that soldiers face when they return into the classroom. Experiencing symptoms of PTSD is an issue exacerbating the transition into student life. Campus health and counseling officials should have knowledge regarding symptoms and treatment strategies for PTSD and have an extensive referral list for veterans.

Keywords: Veterans as college students, PTSD

INTRODUCTION

Colleges throughout the country are bracing for a large influx of returning veterans over the next couple of years and the question is whether they can meet the needs of this population. There is a paucity of empirical literature on Iraqi and/or Afghan veterans' adjustment in the college arena and the factors that mitigate the attrition rate and facilitate success. The research literature primarily focuses on student veterans' adjustment post WWII and Vietnam (Ritchie, 1945; Berry, 1977; O'Neill & Fontaine, 1971; Morris, 1947; Moore, 1948; Williamson, 1944; Aaronson, 1949), but not on the more recent wars in Iraq and Afghanistan.

The wars being fought in Afghanistan and Iraq are the most sustained combat operations since the Vietnam War (Litz, 2006). Soldiers are exposed to multiple deployments and extended tours of duty and often pushed beyond their emotional and physical limits. The frequency and length of deployments increases soldiers' vulnerability to combat stress. Other factors affecting this vulnerability are related to the unique circumstances of the war in Iraq which is characterized by unpredictability and no recognizable front line. (Usher, 2006).

This research offers a glimpse into the lives of the veterans returning into college life. An important implication of this research is to better inform educators, mental health professionals and administrators with regard to policy making, program development and restructuring efforts. Although the results of qualitative studies have limited generalizability, clarification of issues and needs of veterans through this study can begin the process of helping colleges be better prepared with regard to veteran programs. A study of this nature is particularly pertinent because of the limited research to date on this very timely issue.

Many Iraqi and Afghan veterans are pursuing vocational and educational interests to build a secure future. The college setting has become the new front line for many of these returning veterans. Military members returning veterans. The documents range from a brochure and a journal article to a PowerPoint presentation and a Web site. As you look at each document, think about the purpose for which it was written, the readers it addresses, the genre conventions it follows, and the design it uses.

Genres Help Writers Achieve Their Goals

Typically, genres develop to help writers accomplish a general purpose. Informative essays, for example, help writers demonstrate their knowledge to an instructor, while informative articles in newspapers, magazines, and newsletters help writers share information and ideas with their readers. Opinion columns and letters to the editor, in contrast, are often used by writers to advance arguments.

Documents in a particular genre are usually written for the same general purpose. Documents that follow a particular genre also tend to use similar writing conventions, such as level of formality or the type of evidence used to support a point. For example, newspaper obituaries are usually formal and serious, while e-mail messages are often relaxed and informal. Scholarly articles almost always refer to the source of evidence offered to support their points, while letters to the editor sometimes offer no evidence at all. In addition, documents in a particular genre often use similar design elements. Academic essays, for example, are usually written with wide margins and double-spaced lines, while magazine articles often use columns and make extensive use of color and illustrations.

In most cases, genres are social inventions, shaped by the social, cultural, and disciplinary contexts from which they emerge. When writers and readers form a community — such as an academic discipline, a professional association, or a group that shares an interest in a particular topic or activity — they begin to develop characteristic ways of communicating with one another. Over time, members of a community will come to agreement about the type of evidence that is generally accepted to support arguments, the style in which sources should be cited, and how documents should be designed and organized. Over time, the specific needs of a community will result in subtle but important changes to a genre. If you've ever read informative articles in magazines for automobile or motorcycle enthusiasts, for example, you'll notice that they differ in important ways from informative articles in magazines about contemporary music. Similarly, you'll find important differences in the organization and evidence used in scholarly articles written by such diverse groups of scholars as sociologists, civil engineers, and chemists.

As the needs and interests of a community change, genres will change to reflect those needs and interests. In some cases, a genre will change. Academic essays, for example, might begin to make greater use of color and illustrations. In other cases, a single genre might evolve into several distinct genres. For an example of this, take a look at the Web. As the number of readers on the Web has exploded over the past two decades, Web sites have become far more specialized. In the mid-1990s, most Web sites looked alike. Today, you'll find characteristic differences among personal blogs, commercial Web sites, government agency Web sites, and entertainment Web sites.

Practice: Analyze a Genre

For this exercise, analyze the Veterans Green Jobs newsletter, *The Call*, and respond to the following prompts:

The newsletter informs readers of news and initiatives related to the program.

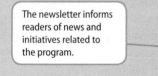

THE CALL

Issue 2, Spring 2012

Visit from the White House

In January, Veterans Green Jobs was honored to host Nancy Sutley, President Obama's principal environmental advisor and Chair of the White House Council on Environmental Quality, for a visit and tour of the Veterans Green Jobs facilities. Ms. Sutley was interested in learning about Veterans Green Jobs' programs to employ veterans.

White House CEQ Chair Nancy Sutley and VGJ CEO Dr. Bill Doe

She toured the Go Green Warehouse and the weatherization warehouse, met several staff members, and learned more about Veterans Green Jobs programs. The visit was on the heels of President Obama's State of the Union address and his announcement of a commitment to grow clean energy industries and jobs. We shared details about our work preparing Iraq and Afghanistan veterans for careers in the natural resources field through our Veterans Green Corps program in eight western states, and the home energy efficiency work our team members are doing in Colorado. We look forward to future conversations with the CEQ about creating green job opportunities for our nation's servicemen and women. View a photo gallery of the visit on our Facebook page.

Veterans Green Force: Connecting Veterans with Jobs

John Toth

With key startup funding from the Call of Duty Endowment, Walmart and Northrop Grumman, Veterans Green Jobs recently launched its signature initiative, Veterans Green Force. This is an outreach, recruitment and placement program exclusively for military veterans. Veterans Green Force aims to connect with 1,000 veterans and place 30 percent, or 300, of them into full-time, green-sector jobs by mid-2013.

Veterans Green Force is forging strategic partnerships with private businesses, government agencies, nonprofit organizations, professional associations and higher education institutions that offer jobs or training to former U.S. servicemen and women.

To lead this strategic program, Veterans Green Jobs hired Lieutenant Colonel (Retired, U.S. Army) John Toth as senior director of Veterans Programs. A decorated airborne-ranger infantry officer and combat veteran of Operation Iraqi Freedom, Toth recently completed his military career as professor of military science at the University of Colorado-Boulder. He brings a wealth of experience working with post-9/11 soldiers and cadets. *Welcome, John Toth!*

Mike Bremer

MIKE BREMER, 2012 CORPSMEMBER OF THE YEAR

Veterans Green Jobs congratulates Mike Bremer, recently named a 2012 Corpsmember of the Year by The Corps Network, a national organization representing the nation's 158 Service and Conservation Corps. In 2010, this U.S. Army veteran joined the Southwest Conservation Corps' Veterans Fire Corps, then went on to secure a job with the U.S. Forest Service as a wildland firefighter and sawyer for the San Juan National Forest.

VETERANS GREEN JOBS

Kynnie Martin Honored

Kynnie Martin, CPT, MI, OIF III Veteran, Veterans Green Jobs' volunteer program manager, was selected as one of five winners of the Call of Duty Endowment's Outstanding Female Veteran Award. She was nominated because of her extraordinary service to our country. As one of the five winners, the Endowment has made a $1,000 donation in Kynnie's name to Veterans Green Jobs, her veteran organization of choice. Two other CODE award recipients (female veterans) are donating their $1,000 winnings to VGJ, as well.

SEE INSIDE

Colorado Governor Hickenlooper thanks veterans at our 2011 Veterans Day Breakfast, page 6.

Go Green Warehouse celebrates one year, page 7.

We've built a Wall of Honor, page 8.

Running for a Reason: The Colfax Marathon May 20, page 8.

To learn more about genre and design, pay attention to the wide range of documents you encounter in your reading. The most important part of this process is simply being aware that genres exist. By thinking about how writers use different types of documents, you'll take the first steps toward using genres to achieve your own purposes and consider your readers.

3. **Organization.** How is the newsletter organized? Did you find it easy to follow? Difficult? Somewhere in between? Why?

4. **Citation style.** Are sources cited in the newsletter? If so, how are the sources cited — in a works cited list, in footnotes, or in the text itself? Why do you think the author cites (or doesn't cite) sources in this way?

1. **Writing style.** Is the newsletter written in a formal or an informal style? Somewhere in between? How would you describe the relationship that the authors of the newsletter's articles attempt to establish with readers?

2. **Evidence.** What sort of evidence is used in the newsletter? Why do you think articles in the newsletter use this kind of evidence?

5. **Design.** Briefly identify the design elements used in the document, such as columns, photographs, and text formatting. (For more information on design elements, see Chapter 16.) How does the design of the document set up expectations about its content? To what extent does the design help or hinder your ability to read and understand the document?

In Summary: Making Connections

✳ **Think of writing as a form of conversation (p. 4).**

✳ **Understand the rhetorical nature of writing situations (p. 12).**

✳ **Learn about genre and design (p. 18).**

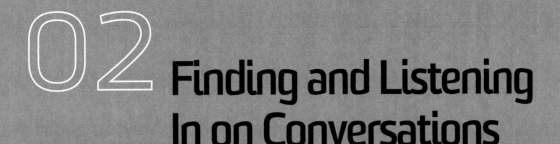

02 Finding and Listening In on Conversations

▶▶ In the most general sense, getting started on a writing project involves "listening in" on conversations and choosing one that interests you. To begin this process, analyze your assignment and generate ideas about potential topics. Then spend time learning about the conversations that interest you most.

How Can I Analyze an Assignment?

Writers in academic and professional settings usually work in response to an assignment. You might be given general guidelines; you might be asked to choose a topic within a general subject area; or you might be given complete freedom. However, no matter how much freedom you have, your assignment will provide important clues about what your instructor and your other readers will expect.

A close reading of an assignment can reveal not only its basic requirements and goals but also useful information about your purpose, readers, sources, and context. Most important, a close reading can help you develop a successful response to the assignment.

Assess Your Writing Situation

What you write about depends on your writing situation — your purpose, readers, sources, and context. In many cases, your assignment will identify or suggest these elements for you. If it doesn't, take some time to think about the situation that will shape your work.

DETERMINE YOUR PURPOSE

Every writer has a purpose, or reason, for writing. In fact, most writers have multiple purposes (see pp. 12–14). In Chapters 5 through 10, you'll explore a range of goals that you might be asked to pursue: to reflect, to inform, to analyze, to evaluate, to solve problems, and to convince or persuade. You will also bring your personal goals to a writing project, such as learning something new, improving your writing skills, convincing others to adopt your point of view, earning respect from others, getting a good grade, or earning a promotion.

DETERMINE WHO YOUR READERS ARE AND WHY THEY WOULD READ YOUR DOCUMENT

Your assignment might identify your readers, or audience, for you. If you are working on a project for a class, one of your most important readers will be your instructor. Other readers might include your classmates, people who have a professional or personal interest in your topic, or, if your project will be published, the readers of a particular newspaper, magazine, or Web site. If you are writing in a business or professional setting, your readers might include supervisors, customers, or other people associated with the organization. You can read more about readers on page 14.

Essay Assignment

For this assignment, you'll identify and describe a problem that affects veterans as they return from active duty. Your purpose will be to inform members of your community about how the problem affects them, the consequences of not addressing the problem, and the costs of addressing it effectively.

> The choice of topic is left to the writer, although some general guidelines are provided. The purpose is discussed here and in the requirements section.

Due Date: October 1, at the beginning of class

Your Readers: Your audience will be the members of your community. I will also be a reader, but my primary role will be to consider how well you've addressed the members of your community.

> The assignment specifies the readers and defines the role the instructor will play as a reader.

Essay Requirements: Your essay should be between 750 and 1,000 words in length. Your essay should

> The genre is identified as a standard academic essay.

- introduce the problem you are addressing

- describe the potential effects of the problem

- propose a solution to the problem

- estimate the costs of putting the solution into effect

- support your points with evidence (personal experience, information from sources)

- clearly document your sources following MLA style

> The repeated use of the words *problem* and *solution* indicates that the writer's purpose is to write a problem-solving essay.

Conclude your essay by doing more than simply summarizing what you've said so far. In general, try to leave your readers with something to think about after they've read your essay. Finally, revise to clarify and strengthen your argument, and edit to remove errors in spelling, grammar, and mechanics so that your writing is clear and readable.

> Aside from the due date, requirements are listed in a separate section. Key requirements include length, content, and documentation system.

Format: Please submit your essay in a folder clearly labeled with your name and e-mail address. Your folder should contain the following:

- the final draft of your essay, formatted with one-inch margins, double-spaced lines, and a readable (e.g., not italic or script) 12-point font

- rough drafts of your essay

- a list of additional sources you consulted as you created your essay

- the homework you completed as you worked on your essay

- the workshop comments you received from your classmates on drafts of your essay

- your workshop comments on your classmates' essays

> The assignment requires students to turn in not only the final essay but also rough drafts, homework, and comments on classmates' drafts.

▲ Essay assignment

CONSIDER THE ROLE OF SOURCES

Most documents are influenced by the work of other writers (see p. 14). As you analyze an assignment, determine whether you'll need to draw on information from other sources, such as magazine or journal articles, Web sites, or scholarly books. Ask whether you'll need to cite a minimum or a maximum number of sources and whether you're required to use a specific documentation system, such as the system created by the Modern Language Association (MLA) or the American Psychological Association (APA).

Working Together: Analyze an Assignment

Work together with your classmates to analyze your assignment. Use the following prompts to guide your analysis:

1. **Determine whether a topic has been assigned.** If a topic has been assigned, look for indications of how you should address the topic. If you are allowed to choose your own topic, look for indications of what the instructor considers an appropriate topic.

2. **Examine the assignment for discussions of purpose.** What purposes might a writer pursue through this assignment? Identify your own purposes — personal, professional, academic — and those of your classmates for working on this assignment.

3. **Identify and describe potential readers.** Describe their likely needs, interests, backgrounds, and knowledge of the topic. Ask why readers would want to read your document.

4. **Determine the role of sources in your document.** Identify potential sources of information that will help you learn about your topic. Then determine whether you need to cite a minimum number of sources or use a specific documentation system, such as MLA or APA.

5. **Identify the context in which the document will be written and read.** For example, will your document be read in print or online? How have historic or recent events shaped your readers' understanding of and attitudes toward your topic?

6. **Identify the genre, if any, defined by the assignment.** If the assignment leaves the choice of genre open, identify genres that are well suited to the assignment.

7. **Understand requirements and limitations.** Look for specific requirements and limitations, such as document length and due date, that will affect your ability to address a particular topic. Identify other requirements, such as number of sources, document structure, documentation system, and intermediate assignments or rough drafts.

8. **List potential opportunities.** Identify opportunities that might save time or enhance the quality of the document.

Whether or not an assignment provides guidelines for sources, ask what you'll need to learn to complete your project, and then identify potential information resources. You can read more about finding and using sources in Part Three of this book.

IDENTIFY THE GENRE AND CONTEXT

Context refers to the physical, social, disciplinary, and cultural settings that shape the writing and reading of a document (see p. 15). To identify the context for your writing project, ask whether your document will be read in print or online. Ask whether it will need to take the form of a particular genre (or type of document), such as a report, an opinion column, a blog post, or a multimedia presentation. Consider how social and cultural contexts — such as recent events and shared history — will shape the attitudes and understanding of your readers. Consider as well how the genre and context will influence your decisions as a writer.

Note Requirements, Limitations, and Opportunities

As you analyze your assignment, identify its requirements, consider potential limitations, and look for opportunities. Being aware of these factors will help you weigh the potential drawbacks of choosing a particular topic. In the face of a looming due date or a limited word length, for example, you might find that you need to narrow the scope of a topic significantly.

Requirements can include

- required length or word count
- due date
- number and type of sources you must use (electronic, print, and field)
- suggested or required resources
- document organization (title page, introduction, body, conclusion, works cited list, and so on)
- documentation format (such as MLA, APA, *Chicago*, or CSE)
- intermediate reports or activities due before you turn in the final document (such as thesis statements, notes, outlines, and rough drafts)

Limitations might include lack of access to sources, lack of time to work on a project, or limited access to software or hardware (such as printers or video cameras) that would help you produce a quality document.

Sometimes writers get so wrapped up in the requirements and limitations of an assignment that they overlook their opportunities. As you think about possible topics, ask whether you can take advantage of opportunities such as

- access to a specialized or particularly good library
- personal experience with and knowledge about a topic
- access to experts on a topic

How Can I Find Interesting Conversations?

Writers aren't mindless robots who create documents without emotion or conviction — or at least they shouldn't be. One of the most important things you can do as a writer is to look for a conversation that will hold your interest as you work on your writing project.

Analyzing an assignment will help you think of general topics that interest you and that fit your writing situation. Even if you are assigned a specific topic, you can almost always find an approach that will engage you and still accomplish the goals of the assignment. In fact, most successful writers have learned to deal with "boring" topics by creating personal or professional connections to them. Essentially, they try to convince themselves that they actually care about a topic — and in many cases, they end up developing a genuine interest. You can do this by generating ideas and asking questions about potential topics, taking care not to rule out any topics until you've given them a chance.

Generate Ideas

You can generate ideas about possible topics of conversation by using prewriting activities such as brainstorming, freewriting, blindwriting or dictating, looping, clustering, and mapping. These activities are useful not only for deciding which topics interest you most but also for identifying a focus that is well suited to your writing situation.

BRAINSTORM

Brainstorming involves making a list of ideas as they occur to you. This list should not consist of complete sentences — in fact, brainstorming is most successful when you avoid censoring yourself. Although you'll end up using only a few of the ideas you generate during brainstorming, don't worry about weeding out the less promising ideas until later.

Brainstorming sessions usually respond to a specific question, such as "What interests me personally about this project?" or "Why would anyone care about _____?" For example, Bob Miller, a student in the same writing course as Mia Jackson (see p. 7), had recently returned from serving a year-long tour of duty in Afghanistan and had used his GI benefits to enroll in college. He drew on his experience as a returning veteran as he brainstormed the following list in response to the question "What factors have helped me return to civilian life?"

> Getting healthy, starting running again
> Taking my dog on long hikes in the hills outside of town
> Working with a career counselor to figure out my career plan

This brainstorming list helped Bob recognize that he might take a reflective approach to the assignment, contemplating his own experiences alongside other sources that address his topic.

FREEWRITE

Freewriting involves writing full sentences quickly, without stopping and — most important — without editing what you write. You might want to start with one of the ideas you generated in your brainstorming activity, or you could begin your freewriting session with a prompt, such as "I am interested in _____ because . . ." Some writers set a timer and freewrite for five, ten, or fifteen minutes; others set a goal of a certain number of pages and keep writing until they meet that goal.

After brainstorming about factors that helped him adjust when he returned home, Bob freewrote about his readers' purposes and interests.

> No one in this town is a stranger to the military life. With Fort Carson nearby, so many of us — in school and in the Springs — have served in the military or have friends and relatives who did, or who are serving right now. I think people would want to know what it's like, so they can support veterans better. A lot of people want to help veterans adjust to life after war, but they don't really know what to do.

To freewrite, write as much as you can, don't pause to consider whether your sentences are "good" or "bad," and don't pay attention to details such as spelling and grammar. If all this work results in a single good idea, your freewriting session will be a success.

Writers consider the needs, interests, and backgrounds of their readers.

BLINDWRITE OR DICTATE

If you find it difficult to freewrite without editing, try blindwriting — freewriting on a computer with the monitor turned off. Or consider dictating. Many smartphones and tablets allow you to speak your thoughts aloud and convert them immediately to text. These forms of freewriting can take your focus away from generating text, largely because you can carry them out without looking at the screen.

LOOP

Looping is yet another form of freewriting. During a looping session, you write (or dictate) for a set amount of time (five minutes works well) and then read what you've written. As you read, identify one key idea in what you've written, and then repeat the process with this new idea as your starting point. If you're using a word-processing program, you can copy the sentence and paste it below your freewriting;

if you are writing by hand, highlight or draw a circle around the sentence. Repeat the looping process as needed to refine your ideas.

Bob's looping session built on the last sentence of his freewriting exercise.

> A lot of people want to help veterans adjust to life after war, but they don't really know what to do. Unemployment can be tough on anyone, but for veterans who have had a purpose and a mission, it can be especially hard. And well-meaning friends and family might ask a lot of questions about what it was like being at war, but veterans usually want to put those experiences behind them.

CLUSTER

Clustering involves putting your ideas about a topic into graphic form. As you map out the relationships among your ideas, clustering can help you gain a different perspective on a topic. It can also help you generate new ideas.

Bob created the cluster on page 36 to explore the topic of helping veterans return to civilian life.

To cluster ideas about a topic, place your main idea, or a general topic that interests you, at the center of a page. Jot down key ideas — such as subcategories, causes and effects, or reasons supporting an argument — around the main idea. Then create clusters of ideas that branch out from the key ideas. In these clusters, list groups of related ideas, evidence, effects, causes, consequences — in short, ideas that are related to your key ideas.

MAP

Mapping is similar to clustering in that it places related ideas about a topic in graphic form. Unlike clustering, however, mapping helps you define the relationships among your ideas. The practice is especially helpful if you are exploring a topic in terms of causes and effects, sequences of events, costs and benefits, or advantages and disadvantages. For example, you might create a map to predict what would happen if cigarette taxes were doubled. Or you might create a map to identify factors that led to an oil spill along the Oregon coast.

Bob used his word-processing program to create a map that explored the costs and benefits of a program that could help veterans return to civilian life (see p. 37).

To map a topic, place your main idea at the top of a page. If you are looking at more than one aspect of a topic, such as costs and benefits, list as many relationships as you can think of. If you are looking at causes and effects, start with a single effect.

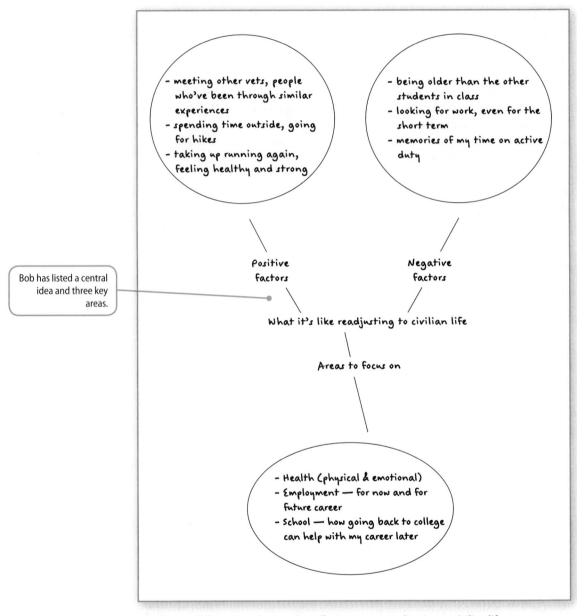

Bob has listed a central idea and three key areas.

▲ A cluster of ideas about factors that affect veterans readjusting to civilian life

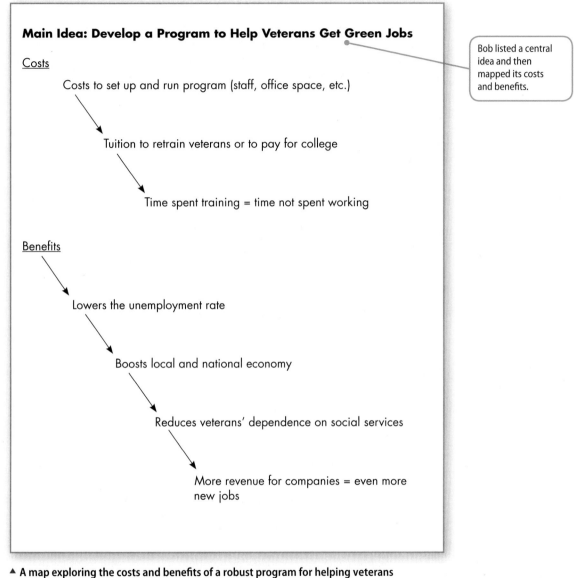

Main Idea: Develop a Program to Help Veterans Get Green Jobs

Costs

Costs to set up and run program (staff, office space, etc.)

Tuition to retrain veterans or to pay for college

Time spent training = time not spent working

Benefits

Lowers the unemployment rate

Boosts local and national economy

Reduces veterans' dependence on social services

More revenue for companies = even more new jobs

Bob listed a central idea and then mapped its costs and benefits.

▲ A map exploring the costs and benefits of a robust program for helping veterans reintegrate into society

Then explore the topic by identifying related causes and effects, costs and benefits, advantages and disadvantages, and so on. For example, if you are mapping a topic using causes and effects, treat each effect as a new cause by asking yourself, "If this happened, what would happen next?" Then use arrows to show the consequences. If you are mapping a topic using costs and benefits, show groups of costs and identify the relationships among them.

Ask Questions

When you have completed your brainstorming, freewriting, blindwriting or dictating, looping, clustering, or mapping activities, review what you've written. In all likelihood, these idea-generating techniques have provided you with a useful list of ideas for a topic. You can select the strongest candidate and generate additional ideas by asking questions. Writers often ask questions to

- define a topic
- evaluate a topic
- consider goals
- explore potential outcomes
- consider appropriate courses of action
- compare and contrast topics
- understand causes and effects
- solve problems

Each of the chapters in Part Two provides a series of questions that will help you narrow your focus and explore ideas for a particular kind of writing project. You can create your own exploratory questions by pairing question words — *what, why, when, where, who, how, would, could, should* — with words and phrases that focus on different aspects of a topic.

For example, Bob generated the following questions to explore and focus his topic on what helps veterans readjust to civilian life:

What are the biggest challenges facing veterans?
What has been helpful to me as I adjust to life back home?
What kinds of support can families, friends, schools, and communities give to veterans?

Which situations have helped and which have hurt my readjustment?

When and where do veterans have success readjusting to civilian life?

How can we minimize the emotional and physical effects of being at war?

Is it possible for workplaces to be sensitive to veterans' needs?

Should the state be involved in encouraging employment opportunities for veterans?

Are there jobs that would allow veterans to work but still get the benefits of being outdoors?

As you ask questions, be aware of the role you are adopting as a writer. If you are writing an informative essay, for example, the words *what*, *when*, and *where* are appropriate. If you are conducting an analysis, you might use the words *why* and *how*. If you are interested in goals and outcomes, try the words *would* and *could*. If you want to determine an appropriate course of action, ask questions using the word *should*.

Practice: Find a Topic That Interests You

Generate ideas for possible writing topics by conducting at least three of the prewriting activities described on pages 32–39: brainstorming, freewriting, blindwriting or dictating, looping, clustering, mapping, and asking questions. Then use your responses to the following prompts to decide which topic interests you most.

1. What are the three most important topics I have identified so far?

2. Of these topics, which one will best sustain my interest in this project?

3. Which one will best help me achieve my purposes as a writer?

4. Which one will best address my readers' needs, interests, and backgrounds?

5. Which one best fits the requirements of my assignment?

6. Which one is most appropriate for the type of document I plan to write?

7. Which one has the fewest limitations?

8. Which one allows me to best take advantage of opportunities?

9. Based on these answers, the topic I want to choose is _____ .

The questions you ask will probably change as you learn more about a topic, so it's best to think of them as flexible and open-ended. By continuing to ask questions that reflect your growing understanding of a topic, you can build a solid foundation for your own contribution to the conversation.

How Can I "Listen In" on Written Conversations?

If you've chosen a topic that appeals to more than a few individuals, it is almost certainly the subject of several ongoing conversations. Listening in on these conversations allows you to become familiar with various aspects of the topic. Written conversations about the broad topic of federal regulation of new drugs, for example, might focus on issues such as childhood vaccination, prevention of birth defects, and the treatment of diseases such as AIDS and Alzheimer's. Each of these issues, in turn, might be addressed by different groups of people, often for quite different purposes. Childhood vaccination, for instance, might draw the attention of parents worried about potential side effects, health officials concerned about epidemics, and researchers interested in the growth of drug-resistant diseases. In other words, not only do conversations focus on different aspects of a topic, but the same aspect of a topic can also be discussed by different groups of people.

Listening in on these conversations allows you to determine which group you want to join. To make that decision, you don't have to engage in a full-blown research project. You simply have to invest enough time to determine whether you want to learn more. At this early stage in your writing project, you are essentially eavesdropping in order to find the conversation you want to join.

To learn more about each of the conversations you've identified and to figure out what — or whether — you might contribute to it, "listen in" by discussing your ideas with others, observing a situation firsthand, and finding and reviewing published sources.

Discuss the Topic with Others

Discussing your writing project can provide insights you might not find on your own. Identify resources by talking with an instructor, a supervisor, or a librarian. Learn what other people think about a topic by conducting interviews (see p. 478). Gather information and insights by corresponding with experts or with people who have been affected by a topic (see p. 479). Get a sense of how readers might respond to your ideas by posting on Facebook, Tumblr, or Twitter and seeing how your friends respond to your ideas (see p. 41).

Observe the Topic Firsthand

Observing something for yourself allows you to learn about a topic without filtering it through the interpretation of other writers. If you are considering a topic that focuses on a particular place, event, or activity, you might want to conduct one or more observations. If you're interested in a local issue, for example, you might attend a community meeting and listen to what people have to say. If you're interested in the impact of parental involvement in youth sports, you might spend time at a youth soccer game. If you're interested in connections between fast food and health issues, you might spend time watching people place their orders at a fast-food restaurant. For more on planning and conducting observations, see page 479.

Read What Others Have Written

Even if you are familiar with a topic, you need to learn as much about it as you can before you begin to write. Reading what others have written about a topic will help you gather new information and ideas; it is also an important step in identifying conversations and determining which ones interest you.

- **Search online library catalogs** for sources using title, author, and subject words. Before you begin your search, generate a list of words and phrases that are related to the topic you want to explore.

- **Browse library shelves** to find sources related to those you've already located. Review the works cited lists, footnotes, endnotes, or in-text citations or particularly useful sources. Then find and review these cited sources.

- **Visit the periodicals room** to find the latest magazines, newspapers, and scholarly journals.

- **Search databases** just as you would search an online library catalog. To identify relevant databases, ask a reference librarian for assistance.

- **Search the Web** using the search terms you used for your catalog and database searches. Remember, though, that many Web-based sources will not have undergone the same review process applied to sources in library catalogs and databases.

- **Browse the Web** by following useful links from one site to another.

- **Use social media** since Tweets, Facebook updates, or blog posts on your topic can lead to other relevant sources.

- **Visit online discussion venues**, such as e-mail lists, newsgroups, and Web discussion forums to find everything from expert opinions to the musings of people who know little or nothing about a topic. If you read posted messages with a bit of skepticism, however, you can begin to learn about the issues surrounding a topic.

Review Your Sources

As you learn about a topic, you'll begin the process of focusing your attention on a specific issue — a point of disagreement, uncertainty, concern, or curiosity that is being discussed by a community of readers and writers. Look for patterns in the information, ideas, and arguments you encounter.

- **Notice central concepts.** When several sources refer to the same idea, you can assume that this information is central to the topic.

- **Find broad themes.** Sources that discuss the same general theme are most likely involved in the same conversation. By recognizing these broad themes, you can identify some of the key issues addressed in the conversations about your topic.

- **Look for disagreements.** Some sources will explicitly indicate that they disagree with the arguments, ideas, or information in other sources. If you look for explicit statements of disagreement, you can identify a group of sources that are engaged in conversation with one another.

- **Recognize recurring voices.** You might find that some authors write frequently about your topic or that some are cited frequently. These authors might have significant experience or expertise related to the topic, or they might represent particular perspectives on the topic.

Practice: Choose a Conversation

Take the topic you selected at the end of the activity on page 39, and listen in on a few of the conversations taking place about it. You might discuss this topic with other people, conduct an observation, or read a few sources that address your topic. Identify the three most promising conversations you've found. To choose among the conversations, ask the following questions about each one:

1. Will joining this conversation help me accomplish my purpose?

2. Do my readers need to be exposed to this conversation?

3. Do my readers want to be exposed to this conversation?

4. How will my readers' backgrounds affect their reactions to this conversation?

As you review the conversations you've identified, ask what interests you most about each one. At a minimum, you'll want to choose a focus that interests you and is appropriate for your assignment. Ideally, this focus will also match up well with the purposes, needs, interests, and backgrounds of your readers.

How Can I Prepare for a Successful Writing Project?

You can improve your chances of successfully completing a writing project by taking ownership of your writing project, familiarizing yourself with the writing process, and learning to manage your sources and your time.

Take Ownership

Successful writers have a strong personal investment in what they write. Sometimes this investment comes naturally. You might be interested in a topic, committed to achieving your purposes as a writer, intrigued by the demands of writing for a particular audience, or looking forward to the challenges of writing a new type of document, such as a Web site or a magazine article. At times, however, you need to create a sense of personal investment by looking for connections between your interests and your writing project. This can be a challenge, particularly when you've been assigned a project that normally wouldn't interest you.

The key to investing yourself in a project you wouldn't normally care about is to make it your own. Look for ways in which your project can help you pursue your personal, professional, and academic interests. Consider how it might help you meet new people or develop new skills. Or look for opportunities associated with the project, such as learning how to build arguments or how to design documents. Your goal is to find something that appeals to your interests and helps you grow as a writer.

To take ownership of a writing project, carry out the following activities:

- **Explore academic connections.** Is the writing project relevant to work you are doing in other classes or, more generally, in your major or minor? Look for ways that working on this project might help you develop useful academic skills or might expose you to information, ideas, or arguments that allow you to make progress as a student.
- **Consider personal connections.** Sometimes your personal interests — such as hobbies and other activities — can spark an interest in the writing project. Do

any of your experiences relate to the project in some way? Will working on this project allow you to develop skills and abilities that might help you in your personal life?

- **Look for professional connections.** Does the writing project have any relevance to the job you currently have or one day hope to have? Will working on this project help you develop skills or expose you to information, ideas, or arguments that might be relevant to your professional goals?

Understand That Writing Is a Process

Few writers complete a major writing project in a single sitting. In fact, most writers spend more time learning about and reflecting on a topic than they do drafting, reviewing, and revising a document. You can avoid frustration and increase your chances of success by understanding the writing processes that experienced writers typically use: finding and listening in on a conversation, developing ideas, preparing a draft, and reviewing and rewriting.

You can also avoid frustration by recognizing that every writer approaches his or her writing situation in a manner that reflects the unique demands of that situation. In fact, writers seldom follow precisely the same process each time they write. As you work on your writing, you will no doubt find yourself moving from one process to another, and then back again. In a given composing session, you might move from reading to collecting sources to drafting to experimenting with a new idea. It's best, as a result, to think of the composing processes described here as a set of guidelines rather than a fixed sequence of steps.

You can see this process in action in Chapters 5 through 10. The documents in these chapters demonstrate how writers share their reflections, inform their readers, report their analyses of a subject, share their evaluations, define and solve problems, and make arguments. Each chapter follows the writing process of a featured student writer who found, listened in on, reflected on, and made a contribution to a written conversation. You'll see selections of the work they carried out as they generated and refined their ideas, developed their arguments, and worked with sources. You'll also see the final drafts of their essays.

FIND A CONVERSATION AND LISTEN IN

Settling on a topic is often the most challenging part of a writing project. If you are assigned a general topic, consider which aspect of that topic might help you accomplish your purposes and those of your readers. If you can choose your own topic, spend some time thinking about your writing situation before deciding what you'll write about. In either case, be sure to listen in on written conversations about potential topics. You'll almost certainly find that some conversations are better suited to your writing situation than others. Some conversations, for example, might seem to be largely settled, and you'll have little to offer to further the discussion. Others might require a deeper knowledge of a subject than you currently possess or could develop before the due date for your assignment. Still others, however, might intrigue and surprise you and, as a result, might be good candidates for exploration.

Narrowing your focus is a critical point in your writing process. Once you've chosen a general conversation and identified a specific aspect of it that intrigues you, you can begin to collect information in earnest, read with a purpose, and take notes. See pages 40–42 for tips on generating ideas and listening in on written conversations. In Chapter 3, you'll learn how to read actively and evaluate sources. Part Three discusses strategies for gathering information and working with your sources.

DEVELOP YOUR IDEAS

After you have listened in and reflected on a conversation, you'll begin the process of developing your own contribution to the conversation. Depending on your purposes and the role you've adopted as a writer (see pp. 9–11), you'll find that different kinds of activities come into play as you shape your ideas. Each of the chapters in Part Two helps you work through these activities: observing and reflecting on a subject (Chapter 5), determining how to inform your readers (Chapter 6), analyzing a subject (Chapter 7), evaluating a subject (Chapter 8), defining and solving problems (Chapter 9), or convincing or persuading your readers (Chapter 10).

PREPARE A DRAFT

Drafting involves expressing your thoughts in written form. That process begins with defining your main point and organizing the relationships among the information, ideas, and arguments you've located in sources and formed on your own. In general, writers use all the initial work they've done — collecting sources, reading critically, and developing ideas — as the basis for a first rough draft. Each chapter in Part Two guides you through the process of preparing a draft for a given writing project, and Part Four offers strategies for specific elements of drafting — such as forming a thesis, crafting paragraphs, integrating sources, writing introductions and conclusions, outlining, and writing with style.

Preparing your draft also involves planning its design. By understanding and applying the principles of document design — the use of visual elements such as fonts, color, page layout, and illustrations — you can make your writing project more effective and easier to understand. You can also ensure that any document you create is consistent with the conventions of a particular genre. Chapters 16, 17, and 18 offer strategies for using design effectively in several important genres.

REVIEW AND REWRITE

After you have completed a rough draft, you can begin the process of revision. Revising involves rethinking and re-envisioning your document. It focuses on such big-picture issues as whether the document you've drafted is appropriate for your writing situation, whether your argument is sound and well supported, and whether you've organized and presented your information, ideas, and arguments clearly.

Polishing and editing, the final stages of a writing project, focus on improving your style and assessing the effectiveness, accuracy, and appropriateness of the words and sentences in your document. During these final stages, you'll also make sure that you've given credit to the writers whose ideas you've used in your work and that you have fully documented your sources. Chapter 20 offers strategies for revising and editing your writing. Chapters 21 and 22 provide information about documenting sources.

Revising your essay often relies on peer-review activities conducted in collaboration with other writers. Chapter 4 discusses peer review and other collaborative activities. You'll also find peer-review guidelines in Chapters 5 through 10, as well as a wide range of Working Together activities throughout this book.

Create a Writer's Notebook

A writer's notebook — where you can keep the sources you collect along the way and record your thoughts, observations, and progress — can help you keep track of what you find and think about as you work on your project. A writer's notebook can take many forms:

- a notebook
- a word-processing file or a folder on your computer
- a folder or binder
- a set of note cards
- notes taken on a smartphone or a tablet
- a tape recorder or voice recorder

Although it might seem like extra work now, creating a writer's notebook at the beginning of your project will save you time in the long run.

Manage Your Time

Time management should be a high priority as you begin your writing project. Without adequate time management, you might, for example, spend far too much time collecting information and far too little time working with it. As you begin to think about your writing project, consider creating a project timeline. A project timeline can help you identify important milestones in your project and determine when you need to meet them.

Practice: Create a Project Timeline

In your writer's notebook, create a project timeline like the one shown here. The steps in your process might be slightly different, but most writing projects involve these general stages. As you create your timeline, keep in mind any specific deadlines given in your assignment, such as the dates when you must hand in first drafts and revised drafts.

Project Timeline

Activity	Start date	Completion date
• Analyze your assignment		
• Generate ideas		
• Collect and read potential sources		
• Choose a focus		
• Develop your ideas		
• Write a first draft		
• Review and revise your first draft		
• Write and revise additional drafts		
• Polish your final draft		
• Edit for accuracy and correctness		
• Finalize in-text citations and works cited list		

In Summary: Finding and Listening In on Conversations

* Get started by analyzing your assignment and assessing your writing situation (p. 28).

* Generate ideas for finding conversations about interesting topics (p. 32).

* Ask questions about the conversations you've found (p. 38).

* Listen in on promising conversations by discussing your topic with others, observing the topic firsthand, and reading what others have written (p. 40).

* Review what you've learned to determine which conversation to join (p. 42).

* Lay the foundation for a successful writing project by taking ownership of your project, understanding writing processes, creating a writer's notebook, and managing your time (p. 43).

Reading to Write

As you join a written conversation, you'll "listen in" to find out what other writers have already contributed to the discussion and begin developing your own thoughts about the subject. In this chapter, you'll learn how to read these contributions critically and actively. You'll also learn how to take notes and how to evaluate and respond to the information, ideas, and arguments you encounter as you read.

How Can I Read Critically?

Reading critically means reading with an attitude. It also means reading with your writing situation in mind. Through critical reading, you can quickly recognize the questions — points of disagreement, uncertainty, concern, or curiosity — that are under discussion in a written conversation as well as think about how you'll respond to one of these questions.

Read with an Attitude

As you learn about and prepare to contribute to a written conversation, both your point of view and your attitude are likely to change. Initially, your attitude might be one of curiosity. You'll note new information in your sources and mark key passages that provide insights. You'll adopt a more questioning attitude as you determine whether sources fit into the conversation or are reliable. Later, after you begin to draw conclusions about the conversation, you might take on a more skeptical attitude, becoming more aggressive in challenging the arguments made in sources than you were at first.

Growing familiarity with and understanding of an issue ⟶

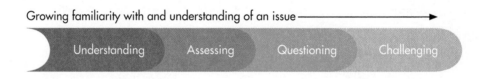

Understanding   Assessing   Questioning   Challenging

Regardless of where you are in your writing process, you should always adopt a critical attitude. Accept nothing at face value; ask questions; look for similarities and differences among the sources you read; examine the implications of what you read for your writing project; be on the alert for unusual information; and note relevant sources and information. Most important, be open to ideas and arguments, even if you don't agree with them. Give them a chance to affect how you think about the conversation you've decided to join.

Be Aware of Writing Situations

Reading critically involves approaching each source with an awareness not only of your own writing situation but also of the writing situation that shaped the source. Keep in mind that each document you read was written to accomplish a particular purpose and was intended for a particular group of readers. Realize that the physical, social, disciplinary, and cultural settings in which the document was produced affected how the writer presented information, ideas, and arguments. And remember that the writing situation that helped produce the source might differ significantly from your own writing situation.

As you read, remember what you are trying to accomplish. Your purpose will affect your assessment of the information, ideas, and arguments you encounter. Moreover, your readers' purposes, needs, interests, and backgrounds will affect your assessment of what you read.

Finally, and perhaps most important, remember that you are working on your writing project to make a contribution, to shape your readers' thinking about your subject. Avoid being overly deferential to the authors who have written before you. You should respect their work, but don't assume that their conclusions about the subject are the last word. Be prepared to challenge their ideas and arguments. If you don't do this, there's little point in writing, for you'll simply repeat the ideas of others instead of advancing your own.

What Strategies Can I Use to Read Actively?

Once you've thought about your writing situation and the writing situations that shaped your sources, you're ready to start reading actively. Reading actively means interacting with sources and considering them in light of the conversation you've decided to join. When you read actively, you might do one or more of the following:

- skim the source to get a general sense of what it's about
- write questions in the margins
- jot down your reactions
- identify key information, ideas, and arguments
- note how you might use information, ideas, and arguments in your document
- visually link one part of the source to another
- identify important passages for later rereading

To read actively, focus on three strategies: skimming, marking and annotating, and examining sources closely.

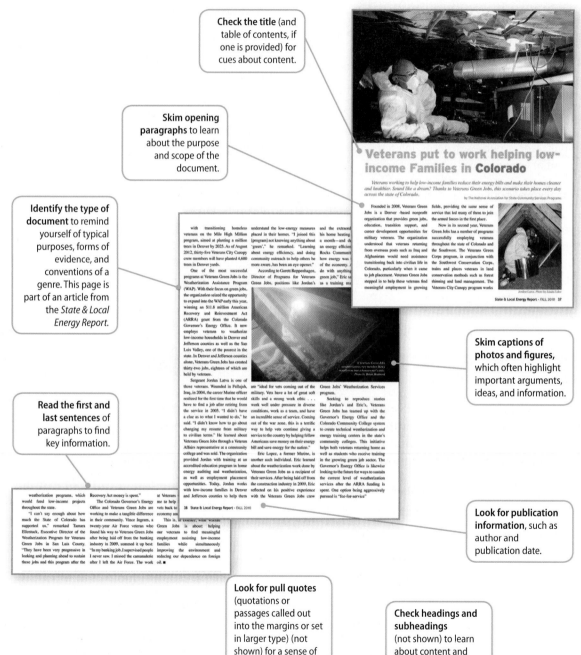

Check the title (and table of contents, if one is provided) for cues about content.

Skim opening paragraphs to learn about the purpose and scope of the document.

Identify the type of document to remind yourself of typical purposes, forms of evidence, and conventions of a genre. This page is part of an article from the *State & Local Energy Report*.

Read the first and last sentences of paragraphs to find key information.

Skim captions of photos and figures, which often highlight important arguments, ideas, and information.

Look for publication information, such as author and publication date.

Look for pull quotes (quotations or passages called out into the margins or set in larger type) (not shown) for a sense of the writer's main idea.

Check headings and subheadings (not shown) to learn about content and organization.

▲ How to skim a print document

Skim for an Overview

Before investing too much time in a source, skim it. Skimming — reading just enough to get the general idea of what a source is about — can tell you a great deal in a short amount of time and is an important first step in reading a source critically. To skim sources, glance at surface elements without delving too deeply into the content.

Megan Martinez, a student working on the same assignment about returning veterans as Mia Jackson (see p. 7) and Bob Miller (see p. 33), used skimming to gain a quick overview of a *State & Local Energy Report* that mentioned Veterans Green Jobs, a Colorado nonprofit organization that helps veterans find employment that benefits them and the environment. She also skimmed the organization's Web site.

Veterans Put to Work Helping Low-Income Families in Colorado

Veterans working to help low-income families reduce their energy bills and make their homes cleaner and healthier. Sound like a dream? Thanks to Veterans Green Jobs, this scenario takes place every day across the state of Colorado.

by The National Association for State Community Services Programs

Founded in 2008, Veterans Green Jobs is a Denver-based nonprofit organization that provides green jobs, education, transition support, and career development opportunities for military veterans. The organization understood that veterans returning from overseas posts such as Iraq and Afghanistan would need assistance transitioning back into civilian life in Colorado, particularly when it came to job placement. Veterans Green Jobs stepped in to help those veterans find meaningful employment in growing fields, providing the same sense of service that led many of them to join the armed forces in the first place.

Now in its second year, Veterans Green Jobs has a number of programs successfully employing veterans throughout the state of Colorado and the Southwest. The Veterans Green Corps program, in conjunction with the Southwest Conservation Corps, trains and places veterans in land conservation methods such as forest thinning and land management. The Veterans City Canopy program works with transitioning homeless veterans on the Mile High Million program, aimed at planting a million trees in Denver by 2025. As of August 2012, thirty-five Veterans City Canopy crew members will have planted 4,600 trees in Denver yards.

One of the most successful programs at Veterans Green Jobs is the Weatherization Assistance Program (WAP). With their focus on green jobs, the organization seized the opportunity to expand into the WAP early this year, winning an $11.8 million American Recovery and Reinvestment Act (ARRA) grant from the Colorado Governor's Energy Office. It now employs veterans to weatherize low-income households in Denver and Jefferson counties as well as the San Luis Valley, one of the poorest in the state. In Denver and Jefferson counties alone, Veterans Green Jobs has created thirty-two jobs, eighteen of which are held by veterans.

Sergeant Jordan Latva is one of those veterans. Wounded in Fallujah, Iraq, in 2004, the career Marine officer realized for the first time that he would have to find a job after retiring from the service in 2005. "I didn't have a clue as to what I wanted to do," he said. "I didn't know how to go about changing my resume from military to civilian terms." He learned about Veterans Green Jobs through a Veteran Affairs representative at a community college and was sold. The organization provided Jordan with training at an accredited education program in home energy auditing and weatherization, as well as employment placement opportunities. Today, Jordan works with low-income families in Denver and Jefferson counties to help them understand the low-energy measures placed in their homes. "I joined this [program] not knowing anything about 'green,'" he remarked. "Learning about energy efficiency, and doing community outreach to help others be more aware, has been an eye opener."

According to Garett Reppenhagen, Director of Programs for Veterans Green Jobs, positions like Jordan's are "ideal for vets coming out of the military. Vets have a lot of great soft skills and a strong work ethic . . . work well under pressure in diverse conditions, work as a team, and have an incredible sense of service. Coming out of the war zone, this is a terrific way to help vets continue giving a service to the country by helping fellow Americans save money on their energy bill and save energy for the nation."

Eric Lopez, a former Marine, is another such individual. Eric learned about the weatherization work done by Veterans Green Jobs as a recipient of their services. After being laid off from the construction industry in 2009, Eric reflected on his positive experience with the Veterans Green Jobs crew and the extraordinary reduction in his home heating bills — almost $140 a month — and decided to enroll in an energy efficient program at Red Rocks Community College. "I saw how energy was taking the forefront of the economy. Any job that had to do with anything important was a green job," Eric said. Today, he works as a training manager for Veterans Green Jobs' Weatherization Services program.

Seeking to reproduce stories like Jordan's and Eric's, Veterans Green Jobs has teamed up with the Governor's Energy Office and the Colorado Community College system to create technical weatherization and energy training centers in the state's community colleges. This initiative helps both veterans returning home as well as students who receive training in the growing green job sector. The Governor's Energy Office is likewise looking to the future for ways to sustain the current level of weatherization services after the ARRA funding is spent. One option being aggressively pursued is "fee-for-service" weatherization programs, which would fund low-income projects throughout the state.

"I can't say enough about how much the State of Colorado has supported us," remarked Tamara Ellentuck, Executive Director of the

Weatherization Program for Veterans Green Jobs in San Luis County. "They have been very progressive in looking and planning ahead to sustain these jobs and this program after the Recovery Act money is spent."

The Colorado Governor's Energy Office and Veterans Green Jobs are working to make a tangible difference in their community. Vince Ingram, a twenty-year Air Force veteran who found his way to Veterans Green Jobs after being laid off from the banking industry in 2009, summed it up best: "In my banking job, I supervised people I never saw. I missed the camaraderie after I left the Air Force. The work at Veterans Green Jobs would allow me to help low-income families, put vets back to work, and help green the economy and the environment."

This is, in essence, what Veterans Green Jobs is about: helping our veterans to find meaningful employment assisting low-income families while simultaneously improving the environment and reducing our dependence on foreign oil.

Mark and Annotate

Marking and annotating are simple yet powerful active-reading strategies. Mark a source to identify key information, ideas, and arguments. Annotate a source to note agreements and disagreements, to identify support for your argument, or to remind yourself about alternative positions on your issue. Common techniques include

- using a highlighter, a pen, or a pencil to identify key passages in a print source
- attaching notes or flags to printed pages
- highlighting passages in digital texts with your word-processing program
- writing reactions and notes in the margins of print sources
- creating comments in digital texts

Pay Attention

Although writing projects can differ greatly, you'll want to examine at least some documents closely for key information, ideas, and arguments. Noting various aspects of a written work during your active reading will help you better understand the source, its role in the conversation you've decided to join, and how you might use it in your own writing.

Check the page title in the title bar of the browser for information about the purpose and content of the page.

Check the URL to learn about the purpose of a Web page — for instance, whether the page is part of a larger site. Extensions such as .com (for business), .edu (for education), .org (for nonprofit organizations), and .gov (for government) can provide clues about the site's purpose.

Check the navigation headers and menus to learn about the site's content and organization.

Check for information about the author to learn about the author's background, interests, and purposes for writing the document.

Check the title.

Skim captions of photos and figures, which often highlight important arguments, ideas, and information.

Read the first and last sentences of paragraphs to find key information.

Scan for boldface, colored, or italic text, which might be used to emphasize important information.

Check for links to other sites to learn more about the issue.

▲ **How to skim a web page**

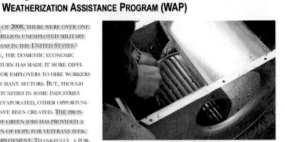

What's the number now?

Check on what happened after the Recovery Act funds ran out.

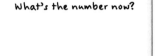

Megan highlighted key passages and wrote notes in the margin.

Is $12 an hour enough to live on if you have a family?

SIERRA CLUB
FOUNDED 1892
Explore, enjoy and protect the planet

Green Jobs for Veterans in Colorado

WEATHERIZATION ASSISTANCE PROGRAM (WAP)

AS OF 2008, THERE WERE OVER ONE MILLION UNEMPLOYED MILITARY VETERANS IN THE UNITED STATES.[1] WORSE, THE DOMESTIC ECONOMIC DOWNTURN HAS MADE IT MORE DIFFICULT FOR EMPLOYERS TO HIRE WORKERS ACROSS MANY SECTORS. BUT, THOUGH OPPORTUNITIES IN SOME INDUSTRIES HAVE EVAPORATED, OTHER OPPORTUNITIES HAVE BEEN CREATED. THE PROSPECT OF GREEN JOBS HAS PROVIDED A BEACON OF HOPE FOR VETERANS SEEKING EMPLOYMENT. THANKFULLY, A PORTION OF THE FUNDING FROM THE AMERICAN RECOVERY AND REINVESTMENT ACT WILL SEEK TO PUT VETERANS BACK TO WORK FOR THE BETTERMENT OF THE ENVIRONMENT IN THE STATE OF COLORADO.

As veterans served the nation in war, they will continue to serve the nation through the Weatherization Assistance Program, a part of the Recovery Act, in Colorado. The Governor's Energy Office has teamed up with the organization Veterans Green Jobs to weatherize homes in the San Luis Valley of southern Colorado. The program offers job trainings to become energy auditors and energy efficiency specialists. The training costs are largely covered by stipends and revenue from on-site work. Veterans Green Jobs will receive over $1 million from the state's Recovery Act WAP allocations to make 240 homes in six counties more energy efficient.[2] The veterans will be paid good wages of $12 to $24 per hour depending on the county, and will gain expertise in energy efficiency. These skills will give veterans a strong grip on the first rungs of the promising green economy career ladder, a ladder that the Recovery Act's investments in America is starting to build.

Photo: A veteran repairs a heater in the San Luis Valley (Credit: Veterans Green Jobs)

This initiative will not only provide jobs for the brave men and women who served our country, but it will also cut energy consumption statewide, reduce energy bills for low-income consumers, and avoid harmful greenhouse gas pollution. By providing employment opportunities for veterans living in Colorado, veterans will be on the front lines of economic and environmental recovery in the state of Colorado.

ACTION:

In addition to Veterans Green Jobs, ten other non-profit organizations will administer the Weatherization Assistance Program in Colorado. Colorado plans to use the $80 million in Recovery Act WAP funds to weatherize 16,280 homes.[3] Colorado's portion under the Recovery Act represents a four-fold yearly increase from its 2008 allocation, providing the opportunity to reach more homeowners.

Along with an increase in funding, there has also been an increase in eligibility requirements, making it possible for more

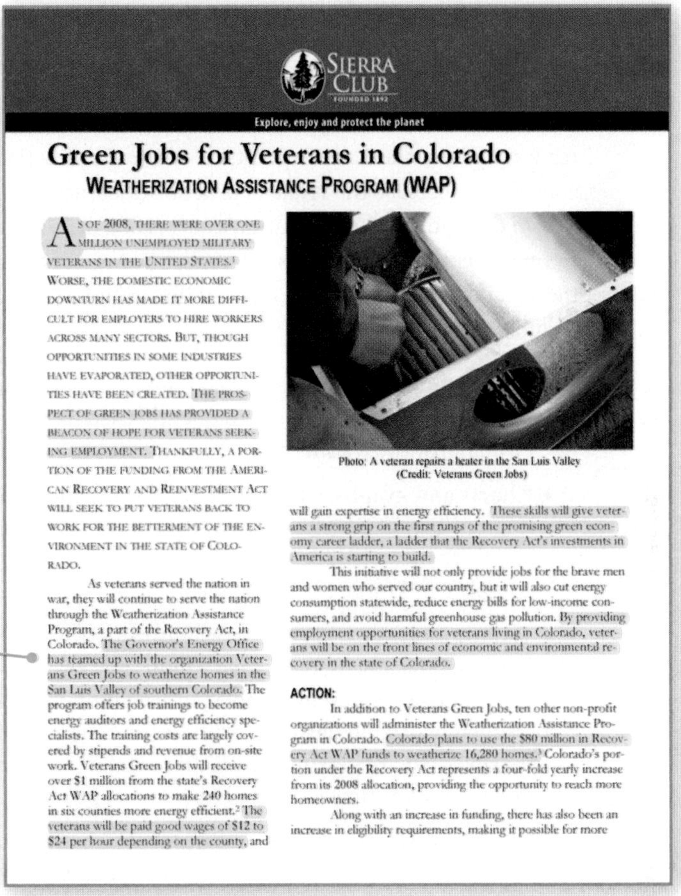

▲ **Marking and annotating a source**

RECOGNIZE THE GENRE

One of the most important things to pay attention to is the type of document — or genre — you are reading. For example, if a source is an opinion column rather than an objective summary of an argument, you're more likely to watch for a questionable use of logic or analysis. If you are reading an article in a company newsletter or an annual report, you'll recognize that one of the writer's most important concerns is to present the company in a positive light. If an article comes from a peer-reviewed scholarly journal, you'll know that it's been judged by experts in the field as well founded and worthy of publication.

Recognizing the type of document you are reading will help you create a context for understanding and questioning the information, ideas, and arguments presented in a source.

CONSIDER ILLUSTRATIONS

A growing number of documents are using illustrations — photographs and other images, charts, graphs, tables, animations, audio clips, and video clips — in addition to text. Illustrations are typically used to demonstrate or emphasize a point, help readers better understand a point, clarify or simplify the presentation of a complex concept, or increase the visual appeal of a document. Illustrations can also serve as a form of argument by presenting a surprising or even shocking set of statistics or setting an emotional tone. As you read, be aware of the types of illustrations and the effects they produce. The types of illustrations you are likely to encounter include the following:

- **Photographs and images.** Photographs and other images, such as drawings, paintings, and sketches, are frequently used to set a mood, emphasize a point, or demonstrate a point more fully than is possible with text alone.

- **Charts and graphs.** Charts and graphs provide a visual representation of information. They are typically used to present numerical information more succinctly than is possible with text alone or to present complex information in a compact and more accessible form.

- **Tables.** Tables provide categorical lists of information. Like charts and graphs, they are typically used to make a point more succinctly than is possible with text alone or to present complex information in a compact form. Tables are frequently used to illustrate contrasts among groups, relationships among variables (such as income, educational attainment, and voting preferences), or change over time (such as growth in population during the past century).

- **Digital illustrations.** Digital documents, such as PowerPoint presentations, Web pages, and word-processing documents intended for reading on computers, tablets, or phones, can include a wider range of illustrations than print documents can. Illustrations such as audio, video, and animations differ from photographs, images, charts, graphs, and tables in that they don't just appear on the page — they do things.

You can read more about the uses of illustrations in Chapter 16.

RECORD NEW INFORMATION AND CHALLENGING IDEAS

As you read, mark and annotate passages that contain information that is new to you. In your writer's notebook, record new information in the form of a list or as a series of brief descriptions of what you've learned and where you learned it.

You might be tempted to ignore material that's hard to understand, but if you do, you could miss critical information. When you encounter something difficult, mark it and make a brief annotation reminding yourself to check it out later. Sometimes you'll learn enough from your continued reading that the passage won't seem as challenging when you come back to it. Sometimes, however, you won't be able to figure out a passage on your own. In that case, turn to someone else for help — your instructor, a librarian, members of an online forum or a newsgroup — or try searching a database, library catalog, or the Web using key words or phrases you didn't understand.

IDENTIFY SIMILARITIES AND DIFFERENCES

You can learn a lot by looking for similarities and differences among the sources you read. For example, you might identify a group of authors who take a similar approach to an issue, such as favoring increased government support for wind energy. You could then contrast this group with other groups of authors, such as those who believe that market forces should be the primary factor encouraging wind power and those who believe we should focus on other forms of energy. Similarly, you can make note of information in one source that agrees or disagrees with information in another. These notes can help you build your own argument or identify information that will allow you (and potentially your readers) to better understand the issue.

Understand the Writer's Argument

Written conversations typically include a range of positions on an issue. Determining where authors agree and disagree can help you understand the conversation as a whole. Similarly, identifying the reasons and evidence authors offer to support their positions can help you gain insights into the conversation.

IDENTIFY THE MAIN POINT

Most sources make a main point that you should pay attention to. An editorial in a local newspaper, for example, might urge voters to approve financing for a new school. An article might report a new advance in automobile emissions testing, or a Web page might emphasize the benefits of a new technique for treating a sports injury. Often the main point will be expressed in the form of a thesis statement. As you read critically, make sure you understand what the writer wants readers to accept, believe, or do as a result of reading the document.

FIND REASONS AND EVIDENCE THAT SUPPORT THE MAIN POINT

Once you've identified the main point, look for the reasons given to accept it. If an author is arguing, for instance, that English should be the only language used for official government business in the United States, that author might support his or her argument with the following reasons:

The use of multiple languages erodes patriotism.

The use of multiple languages keeps people apart — if they can't talk to one another, they won't learn to respect one another.

The use of multiple languages in government business costs taxpayers money because so many alternative forms need to be printed.

Reasons can take a wide range of forms and are often presented in forms that appeal to emotions, logic, principles, values, or beliefs (see p. 415 in Chapter 10). As persuasive as these reasons might seem, they are only as good as the evidence offered to support them. In some cases, evidence is offered in the form of statements from experts on a subject or from people in positions of authority. In other cases, evidence might include personal experience. In still other cases, evidence might include firsthand observations, excerpts from an interview, or statistical data.

When you find empirical evidence used in a source, consider where the evidence comes from and how it is being used. If the information appears to be presented fairly, ask whether you might be able to use it to support your own ideas, and try to verify its accuracy by consulting additional sources.

Working Together: Identify Information in a Source

Working with a group of classmates, identify the main point, reasons, and evidence in the report "Veterans Put to Work Helping Low-Income Families in Colorado," 53.

1. List the main point at the top of your page. Determine what the author is asking you to know, believe, or do.

2. Briefly list each reason to accept the main point in the order in which it appears in the source. You might want to brainstorm lists individually based on your reading of the article and then share your ideas to create the group's list.

3. Determine the most important evidence offered as proof for each reason. Once you've agreed on the reasons, work together to identify the evidence used to support each reason.

How Can I Take Notes?

Notes — in the form of direct quotations, paraphrases, and summaries — provide you with a collection of important information, ideas, and arguments from your sources, as well as a record of your reactions to your sources. Taking notes early in your work allows you to keep track of the information, ideas, and arguments you encounter in your sources. Later, as you begin to plan and write your document, review your notes to determine whether to reread a source or set it aside for other, more relevant sources.

You should take notes when a source

- features an idea that surprises or interests you or that you think you might want to argue for or against
- provides a statement that would enhance your understanding of the issue
- offers insights into how an authority or expert understands the issue
- provides an understanding of someone else's firsthand experience with an issue or event

As you take notes, remember that they should reflect your purpose for working on a project and should provide direction for quoting, paraphrasing, and summarizing information, ideas, and arguments.

Quote Directly

A direct quotation is an exact copy of words found in a source. Taking notes that contain quotations can help you accurately keep track of the information, ideas, and arguments you encounter as you learn about a conversation.

When you use quotations in your notes, be sure to place quotation marks around any quoted passage. If you don't, you might later think that the passage is a paraphrase or summary and might unintentionally plagiarize it when you draft your document (see Chapter 13 and Chapter 16). The solution to this problem is simple: ensure that you take notes carefully and accurately. Be sure to do the following:

- Enclose quoted passages in quotation marks.
- Identify the author and title of the source for every quotation.
- List the page number (or paragraph number, if you are using a source that does not have page numbers) where the quotation can be found.
- Proofread what you have written to make sure it matches the original source exactly — including wording, punctuation, and spelling.

Source: Felicity Barringer, "Veterans Discover Allure of Jobs in Western Wilderness," p. A16

"This initiative will not only provide jobs for the brave men and women who served our country, but it will also cut energy consumption statewide, reduce energy bills for low-income consumers, and avoid harmful greenhouse gas pollution. By providing employment opportunities for veterans living in Colorado, veterans will be on the front lines of economic and environmental recovery in the state of Colorado."

▲ **A direct quotation**

Megan Martinez decided to quote from an article that appeared in the *New York Times* about Veterans Green Jobs. The article, written by Felicity Barringer, described a project that put veterans to work preserving public lands.

Paraphrase

When you restate a passage from a source in your own words, you are paraphrasing. Using paraphrases in your notes serves three purposes. First, restating a passage in your own words can help you remember it better than if you simply copy and paste a quotation. Second, because paraphrases are written in your own words, they're usually easier to understand later, when you're drafting. Third, paraphrasing as you take notes will help you save time during drafting, particularly if you find — as many writers do — that you don't want to rely exclusively on quotations from your sources.

Paraphrasing is a useful skill that takes practice. One of the most common problems writers have as they paraphrase is mirroring the source material too closely — that is, making such minor changes to the wording and sentence structure of a source that the paraphrase remains nearly identical to the original passage. Another common problem is distorting the meaning of the source.

Consider the differences among the original passage (shown in the note above) and the appropriate and inappropriate paraphrases on the next page.

Appropriate Paraphrase

Not only will veterans living in Colorado find employment but they will also contribute directly to efforts to help the state's economy and improve its environment.

> Preserves the meaning of the original passage without replicating the sentence structure and wording.

Inappropriate Paraphrase

The initiative will not only give jobs to the brave veterans who served our country, but it will also reduce energy use across the state, lower energy bills for poorer residents, and avoid the production of greenhouse gases. By helping Colorado veterans find jobs, veterans will be in the forefront of the state's fiscal and environmental recovery.

> Does not differ sufficiently from the original; uses the same sentence structure and changes only some key words.

Inappropriate Paraphrase

This initiative will help veterans lower their energy use, thus reducing the production of greenhouse gases and reducing their monthly energy bills.

> Distorts the meaning of the original passage.

When paraphrasing, focus on understanding the key ideas in the passage, and then restate them in your own words. Begin a paraphrase with the phrase "In other words." This strategy reminds you that it's important to do more than simply change a few words in the passage. In addition, you might want to set the original source aside while you paraphrase so that you won't be tempted to copy sentences directly from it.

In your note, identify the author and title of the source, and list the page number (or paragraph number, if you are using a source that does not have page numbers) where the passage you have paraphrased can be found. After you've completed your paraphrase, check it for accuracy and ensure that the wording and sentence structure differ from the original passage.

Summarize

A summary is a concise statement of the information, ideas, and arguments in a source. Including summaries in your notes can help you identify important arguments in the conversation you are about to join. You can write summaries to capture the overall argument and information in a source or to record a writer's main idea so that you can respond to it later. The following notes contain appropriate and inappropriate summaries of the Sierra Club article, "Green Jobs for Veterans in Colorado," on p. 57.

Appropriate Summary

> In the article "Green Jobs for Veterans in Colorado," the Sierra Club reports on an innovative partnership between the state of Colorado and Veterans Green Jobs, a nonprofit organization founded in 2009 to help veterans make the transition from war to civilian life while benefiting the environment. Funded through the Weatherization Assistance Program, a Federal program, the project will result in weatherizing hundreds of homes across the state of Colorado — and, with continued funding and the involvement of other nonprofit groups in the state, that total is expected to rise into the thousands. Veterans participating in the project not only will receive competitive wages (from $12 to $24 per hour, depending on the county in which the work is performed) but also will gain an advantage in climbing what the Sierra Club calls "the promising green economy career ladder" (p. 1).

The summary gives a broad overview of the article's argument and avoids close paraphrases of key points.

Problems can arise when a writer fails to summarize ideas and instead either creates a close paraphrase or writes a patchwork summary that is little more than a series of passages copied from the source.

Inappropriate Summary

> In Colorado, veterans who served the nation in the Iraq and Afghanistan wars are continuing to serve the nation through the Weatherization Assistance Program. The nonprofit organization Veterans Green Jobs has entered into a partnership with the Governor's Energy Office to weatherize homes in Colorado's San Luis Valley. The program helps veterans gain training in jobs such as energy auditors and energy efficiency specialists. The veterans will be paid competitive wages of $12 to $24 per hour depending on the county in which they work, and will gain expertise in energy efficiency. The skills they gain will help veterans be competitive in the promising green economy career area.

The summary consists of a series of unattributed quotations and close paraphrases of important parts of the article.

In your note, identify the author, the title, and, if you are summarizing only part of a source, the pages or paragraphs where the information can be found. To avoid mirroring the language and sentence structure of the source, begin your summary with "The author argues that" or "The author found that." You might want to set aside the original source while you write your summary so that you won't be tempted to copy sentences directly from it. After you've completed your summary, check it for accuracy and unintentional plagiarism.

Use Notes to Connect Sources

Paying attention to your sources as a group — not just to individual sources — helps you see connections among them and allows you to gain a more complete understanding of your subject. Review your notes to identify aspects of arguments that seem to build on points raised in other sources as well as differences in how sources address a subject.

As she read articles and Web sites about green jobs for veterans, Megan Martinez noticed that several of her sources referred to a Colorado nonprofit organization, Veterans Green Jobs. She made a note of one such instance and wrote a reminder to herself.

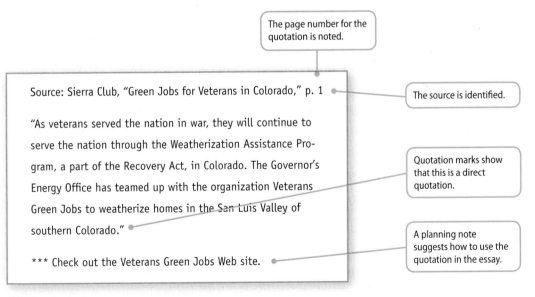

The page number for the quotation is noted.

Source: Sierra Club, "Green Jobs for Veterans in Colorado," p. 1

The source is identified.

"As veterans served the nation in war, they will continue to serve the nation through the Weatherization Assistance Program, a part of the Recovery Act, in Colorado. The Governor's Energy Office has teamed up with the organization Veterans Green Jobs to weatherize homes in the San Luis Valley of southern Colorado."

Quotation marks show that this is a direct quotation.

*** Check out the Veterans Green Jobs Web site.

A planning note suggests how to use the quotation in the essay.

▲ **A planning note**

As you learn more about your conversation, think about how the authors of your sources might respond to one another. In particular, look for disagreements, which provide good indications of how writers align themselves.

How Can I Evaluate Sources?

At the beginning of a writing project, you'll usually make quick judgments about the sources you come across. Skimming an article, a book, or a Web site (see p. 53) might be enough to tell you that spending more time with the document would be wasted effort. As you prepare to write, however, you should evaluate potential sources in light of your writing situation and your needs as a writer. Evaluating a source means examining its relevance, evidence, author, publisher, timeliness, comprehensiveness, and genre.

Determine Relevance

Relevance is the extent to which a source provides information you can use in your writing project. Remember your purpose when you evaluate potential sources. Even if a source provides a great deal of information, it might not meet your needs. For example, an analysis of the printing features in word-processing programs might contain a great deal of accurate and up-to-date information — but it won't be of much use if you're writing about color laser printers for college students.

Your readers will expect information that meets their needs as well. If they want to read about personal printers for college students, for instance, pass up sources that focus on high-capacity office printers.

Consider the Use of Evidence

Evidence is information offered to support a point. Statistics, facts, expert opinions, and firsthand accounts are among the many types of evidence you'll find. As a writer, you can evaluate not only the kinds of evidence in a source but also the quality, amount, and appropriateness of that evidence. Ask yourself the following questions:

- **Is enough evidence offered?** A lack of evidence might indicate fundamental flaws in the author's argument.

- **Is the right kind of evidence offered?** More evidence isn't always better evidence. Ask whether the evidence is appropriate for the reasons being offered and whether more than one type of evidence is being used. Many sources rely far too heavily on a single type of evidence, such as personal experience or quotations from experts.

- **Is the evidence used fairly?** Look for reasonable alternative interpretations, questionable or inappropriate use of evidence, and evidence that seems to contradict points made elsewhere in a source. If statistics are included, are they interpreted fairly or presented clearly? If a quotation is offered to support a point, is the quotation used appropriately?

- **Are sources identified?** Knowing the origins of evidence can make a significant difference in your evaluation of a source. For example, if a writer quotes a political poll but doesn't say which organization conducted the poll, you might reasonably question the reliability of the source.

Identify the Author

The significance of authorship is affected by context. For example, take two editorials that make similar arguments and offer similar evidence. Both are published in your local newspaper. One is written by a fourteen-year-old middle school student, the other by a U.S. senator. You would certainly favor the senator's editorial if the subject was U.S. foreign policy. If the subject was student perceptions about drug abuse prevention in schools, however, you might value the middle school student's opinion more highly.

Ask the following questions about the author of a source:

- **Is the author knowledgeable?** An author might be an acknowledged expert in a field, a reporter who has written extensively about an issue, or someone with firsthand experience. Then again, an author might have little or no experience with a subject beyond a desire to say something about it. How can you tell the difference? Look for a description of the author in the source. If none is provided, look for biographical information on the Web or in a reference such as *Who's Who*.

- **What are the author's biases?** We all have biases — a set of interests that shapes our perceptions. Try to learn about the author's affiliations so that you determine the extent to which his or her biases affect the presentation of arguments, ideas, and information in a source. For instance, you might infer a bias if you know that an author writes frequently about gun control and works as a regional director for the National Handgun Manufacturers Association.

Learn about the Publisher

Publishers are the groups that produce and provide access to sources, including books, newspapers, journals, Web sites, sound and video files, and databases. Like authors, publishers have biases. Unlike authors, they often advertise them. Many publishers have a mission statement on their Web sites, while others provide information that can help you figure out their priorities. You might already be familiar with a publisher, particularly in the case of major newspapers or magazines, such as the *New York Times* (regarded as liberal) or *U.S. News and World Report* (regarded as conservative). If the publisher is a scholarly or professional journal, you can often figure out its biases by looking over the contents of several issues or by reading a few of its editorials.

Establish Timeliness

The importance of a source's date of publication varies according to your writing situation. For example, if you're writing a feature article on the use of superconducting materials in new mass-transportation projects, you probably won't want to spend a lot of time with articles published in 1968. However, if you're writing about the 1968 presidential contest between Hubert Humphrey and Richard Nixon, then sources published during that time period will take on greater importance.

Print sources usually list a publication date. However, it can be difficult to tell when Web sources were created. When in doubt, back up undated information found on the Web with a dated source.

Assess Comprehensiveness

Comprehensiveness is the extent to which a source provides a complete and balanced view of a subject. Like timeliness, the importance of comprehensiveness varies according to the demands of your writing situation. If you are working on a narrowly focused project, such as the role played by shifts in Pacific Ocean currents on snowfall patterns in Colorado last winter, comprehensiveness in a source might not be important — or even possible. However, if you are considering a broader issue, such as the potential effects of global climate change on agricultural production in North America, or if you are still learning as much as you can about your subject, give preference to sources that provide full treatment.

Recognize Genre

Knowing the genre of a source can help you understand a great deal about its intended readers, the kind of evidence it is likely to use, and the kind of argument it is likely to make. An article in a professional journal, for example, will almost certainly rely on published sources or original research, and it will carefully cite its sources so that readers can easily locate related documents. In contrast, a blog entry is more likely to rely on personal observation and reflection.

By understanding the conventions of a particular genre, you can understand whether the information, ideas, and arguments found in it might be of use to you as you work on your writing project. To evaluate a genre, carry out the following activities:

- **Analyze the writing style.** Determine how formally (or informally) the document is written. Check for the use of specialized terms that might be unfamiliar to general readers. Try to understand how the writer views himself or herself in relation to readers.

- **Consider how evidence is used.** Identify numerical information; quotations and paraphrases; summaries of other documents; charts, graphs, and tables; and images and other illustrations. Ask yourself why the writer chose the types of evidence you've found in the document.

- **Look at the organization.** Try to break the document into major sections. Ask whether you've seen this type of organization used in other documents, and think about the purposes of those documents. Documents within a genre often follow a similar structure.

- **Identify citation styles.** Determine whether the sources of information, ideas, and arguments are identified in the document.

- **Consider design.** A document's appearance can tell you a lot about its purpose, intended readers, and likely means of distribution. Is the document's medium print or digital? Does it use color, columns of text, and images or other illustrations? What types of readers might appreciate the use of these design elements? And what effect might these elements have on potential readers?

Examine Digital Sources Closely

You can apply the general evaluative criteria discussed above to most types of sources. However, digital sources can pose special challenges. Because anyone can create a Web site, start a blog, put a video on YouTube, or post a message to a newsgroup, e-mail list, or Web discussion forum, approach these sources with more caution than you would reserve for print sources such as books and journal articles, which are typically published only after a lengthy editorial review process.

WEB SITES AND BLOGS

To assess the credibility of a Web site or a blog, consider its domain (.edu, .com, and so on), and look for information about the site (often available on the "About This Site" or "Site Information" page).

NEWSGROUPS, E-MAIL LISTS, AND DISCUSSION FORUMS

To assess the relevance and credibility of a message on a newsgroup, an e-mail list, or a Web discussion forum, check for a "signature" at the end of the message, and try to locate a Frequently Asked Questions (FAQ) list. A signature can provide information about the sender, such as a professional title, and the URL for a personal home page where you can learn more about the author. FAQs can tell you about the purpose of a newsgroup, an e-mail list, or a discussion forum; whether messages are moderated (reviewed before being posted); and whether membership is open or restricted to a particular group.

WIKIS

Wikis are Web sites that can be added to or edited by visitors to the site. Reference sites such as Wikipedia (en.wikipedia.org) have grown in importance on the Web, and many are highly ranked by search sites such as Ask, Yahoo!, and Google. Unfortunately, it can be difficult to evaluate the credibility of wiki pages because changes occur quickly and repeatedly, with no guarantee of accuracy or credibility. You might want to use wikis when you are beginning to learn about a topic, but avoid citing them as the "last word" on a topic. In fact, those "last words" might change before you submit your final draft.

Check the domain to learn about the site's purpose and publisher:

.biz, .com, .coop: business .mil: military
.edu: higher education .gov: government
.org: nonprofit organization .net: network organization

Check the title bar and page headers or titles to learn about the site's purpose, relevance, and publisher.

Check the site's timeliness by looking for publication and "last modified" dates.

Search for information about the author or publisher.

Read the body text and review illustrations to evaluate relevance, evidence, and comprehensiveness.

Check page footers for information about the publisher and author. Look for About or Contact links.

▲ How to evaluate a Web site

How Can I Read Like a Writer?

When you read like a writer, you prepare yourself to become an active member of the conversation you've decided to join. You learn where the conversation has been — and where it is at the moment. In short, reading like a writer helps you think critically about what you've read and prepares you to write your own document.

To engage more fully with the information, ideas, and arguments you encounter in your reading, you'll want to go beyond simply knowing what others have written. By reading to understand, reading to respond, and reading to make connections — and putting your thoughts into words — you can begin to find your voice.

Read to Understand

Reading to understand involves gaining an overview of the most important information, ideas, and arguments in a source. When writers read to understand, they often create summaries — brief descriptions of the main idea, reasons, and supporting evidence in a source. Depending on the complexity of the source, summaries can range from a brief statement about the argument found in a source to a detailed description of the key points and evidence it provides.

Practice: Evaluate a Source

Select a source you have found as you've learned about a topic. In your writer's notebook, respond to the following questions:

1. Is the source relevant to your writing project?

2. Does the source present evidence and use it appropriately?

3. What can you learn about the author?

4. What can you learn about the publisher?

5. Is the source timely?

6. Is the source comprehensive enough?

7. What type of document is it?

Many writers believe that a summary should be objective. It would be more precise to say that a summary should be accurate and fair. That is, you should not misrepresent the information, ideas, or arguments in a source. Achieving accuracy and fairness, however, does not necessarily mean that your summary will be an objective presentation of the source. Instead, your summary will reflect your purpose, needs, and interests and — if you're writing for an audience — those of your readers. You'll focus on information, ideas, and arguments that are relevant to your writing situation. As a result, your summary is likely to differ from one written by another writer. Both summaries might be accurate and fair, but each one will reflect its writer's writing situation.

As you read to understand, highlight key points in the source, and note passages that include useful quotations or information you might use to add detail to your summary. If you are writing a summary for a class, it will typically take one of three forms: a main-point summary, a key-point summary, or an outline summary.

In doing research for her argumentative essay, Megan Martinez found the opinion column on page 74 during her search for information about green jobs for veterans. Published by the *Denver Post*, a newspaper, the column argued for increased awareness of and solutions for the severe problem of unemployment among veterans.

Guest Commentary: Green Jobs for Veterans

By Bill Doe and BG James "Spider" Marks
The Denver Post

More bad news may be looming on the horizon regarding the number of unemployed veterans in this country. This week the Bureau of Labor Statistics (BLS) will release its annual Veterans' Unemployment Summary. In 2009, BLS found that 21.1 percent of veterans ages 18–24 were unemployed, higher than non-veterans of the same age. The same statistics reveal female veterans were unemployed at the rate of 13.5 percent, almost twice that of female non-veterans. The only other cohort group in our society facing these levels of unemployment is high school dropouts.

No, your calendar is set correctly — today is not Veterans' Day or the Fourth of July — it is indeed March. So why bring these startling facts to your attention? As Americans, we must begin to first acknowledge our veterans are struggling to transition into this bleak job market at home and second, we must work together to create more solutions to make their lives and their families' lives easier. Suicide and homelessness among recent returning veterans are rising at alarming rates. Our service members make enormous sacrifices to ensure our freedom and security. The right thing to do is ensure they receive the proper attention for job training and career placement after their return.

Unfortunately, too many of our service members are coming home to a beleaguered economy that holds little hope for career placement. They must also deal with the stigma associated with "signature" wounds of our wars in Iraq and Afghanistan. They face a complex array of federal services and institutions that they are expected to navigate to receive their due benefits, all while trying to readjust to home with loved ones who have been growing and developing both personally and professionally. Make no mistake, the path for successful integration is a difficult road to navigate.

Our nation's leaders, including President Obama and Chairman of the Joints Chief of Staff, Admiral Mullen, have ardently addressed this national and complex dilemma in front of business, military, and community audiences. Admiral Mullen has emphasized that there is a "Sea of Goodwill" in society for returning service members and their families, but that support must be linked around common objectives aimed at what he calls the "Reintegration Trinity" for veterans—envisioned as a triangle with the three sides representing (1) access to health care for life, (2) education, and (3) employment. The successful integration and application of these three components will ensure a seamless transition back into society and improved quality of life for veterans and their families.

The solution to successful integration of veterans and their families is partnership and funding support amongst the many organizations seeking to help them—businesses, government, educational institutions, professional organizations, veterans' services organizations, and non-profits.

For example, Activision Blizzard started The Call of Duty Endowment in October of 2009 to raise awareness about the astonishing number of unemployed veterans and support those organizations that are in the field working with former service members to help them start their next career. With the support of a successful corporation, and the devotion of Activision's CEO Bobby Kotick, to keep the issue on the public's radar, the Endowment is raising millions of dollars to help combat the issue. Those dollars can allow innovative programs like Veterans Green Jobs, a national non-profit headquartered in Denver, to flourish, and allow more of our heroes to gain the tools, training, and resources needed to secure a lasting career track.

The responsibility to honor our heroes upon their return must be shared by everyone: the employers, the employees that can encourage their boss to hire them, and local and state governments that can provide incentives to hire our veterans. The fact is our veterans are likely to be among the best employees an employer could ever hire. These men and women return with valuable technical skills, leadership experiences, and a sense of mission and teamwork that can be repurposed into our economy and society. They simply need an opportunity to show those qualities in the workforce. Do your part and find out ways you can help our returning service members transition smoothly into civilian life. They deserve nothing less.

Lieutenant Colonel William W. "Bill" Doe III (USA-Ret), Ph.D., is the Chief Executive Officer of Veterans Green Jobs, a national, Denver-based non-profit connecting military veterans to employment opportunities that serve both the community and environment.

Brigadier General James "Spider" Marks (USA-Ret.) is an advisory board member to Activision's Call of Duty Endowment and CEO to InVisM, a Denver-based firm that develops simulation products for global education and training markets.

MAIN-POINT SUMMARIES

A main-point summary reports the most important information, idea, or argument presented in a source. You can use main-point summaries to keep track of the overall claim made in a source, to introduce your readers to a source, and to place the main point of that source into the context of an argument or a discussion of a subject. Megan might have written the following main-point summary of Bill Doe and Spider Marks' column:

> In their column "Green Jobs for Veterans," Bill Doe and Spider Marks argue that we all share a responsibility to help our veterans find employment when they return to civilian life.

Main-point summaries are brief. They identify the source and its main point.

KEY-POINT SUMMARIES

Like a main-point summary, a key-point summary reports the most important information, idea, or argument presented in a source. However, it also includes the reasons (key points) and evidence the author uses to support his or her main point. Key-point summaries are useful when you want to keep track of a complex argument or understand an elaborate process.

> In their column "Green Jobs for Veterans," Bill Doe and Spider Marks argue that we all share a responsibility to help our veterans find employment when they return to civilian life. Pointing to high rates of unemployment among younger veterans (21.1 percent of veterans ages 18–24 are unemployed, as are 13.5 percent of female veterans of all ages), they express concern over the rising rate of suicides and homelessness among recently returned veterans. Noting the sacrifices veterans have made to safeguard our freedom and security, Doe and Marks write, "The right thing to do is ensure they receive the proper attention for job training and career placement after their return" (para. 2). Unfortunately, they report, economic conditions and the challenges of reintegrating into civilian life have worked against veterans' efforts to secure employment. Doe and Marks identify a few initiatives, including those launched by Veterans Green Jobs (a Colorado nonprofit organization), as examples of how we might support our veterans.

The authors, source, and main point are identified.

Statistical evidence is provided.

The challenges faced by veterans are defined.

Potential solutions are included.

OUTLINE SUMMARIES

Sometimes called a plot summary, an outline summary reports the information, ideas, and arguments in a source in the same order used in the source. In a sense, an outline summary presents the overall "plot" of the source by reporting what was written in the order in which it was written. Outline summaries are useful when you need to keep track of the sequence of information, ideas, and arguments in a source.

The authors, source, and main point are identified.

In their column "Green Jobs for Veterans," Bill Doe and Spider Marks argue that we all share a responsibility to help our veterans find employment when they return to civilian life. Pointing to high rates of unemployment among younger veterans (21.1 percent of veterans ages 18–24 are unemployed, as are 13.5 percent of female veterans of all ages), they express concern over the rising rate of suicides and homelessness among recently returned veterans.

The summary identifies each of the major points made in the article in the order in which they were made.

Given such "alarming rates" of suicide and homelessness among our newest veterans, Doe and Marks call for an acknowledgment that our veterans are struggling to find work in a tough economy. As a society, they argue, "The right thing to do is ensure they receive the proper attention for job training and career placement after their return" (para. 2). Yet doing the right thing has its own challenges, from an economy that has been producing too few jobs, to the challenges of readjusting to civilian life, to "a complex array of federal services and institutions that they are expected to navigate to receive their due benefits" (para. 3).

The authors' names are mentioned whenever information from the source is used.

The key to success, they believe, is to focus on what has been referred to by Admiral Mullen, Chairman of the Joint Chiefs of Staff, as the "Reintegration Trinity" for veterans: "(1) access to health care for life, (2) education, and (3) employment" (para. 4). To achieve this, Doe and Marks call for building partnerships among the groups trying to help veterans, including business, government, veterans groups, and various organizations, including nonprofits. Doe and Marks identify a few initiatives, such as those launched by Veterans Green Jobs (a Colorado nonprofit organization that draws support from business and government), as examples of how we might support our veterans.

Doe and Marks conclude by reminding us not only that we owe our veterans a
debt of gratitude but also that they possess the qualities that will make them
outstanding employees and strong contributors to society.

> Phrases and terms such as "pointing to" and "conclude" provide a sense of movement through the source.

Read to Respond

Reading to respond allows you to begin forming your own contribution to a conversation. Your response will help you focus your reactions to the information, ideas, and arguments you've encountered in a source. To prepare to write a response to a source, note passages with which you agree or disagree, reflect on interesting information and ideas, and record your thoughts about the effectiveness of the argument advanced in the source.

AGREE/DISAGREE RESPONSES

If you want to explore an idea or argument in a source, try freewriting about why you agree or disagree with it. In your response, clearly define the idea or argument to which you are responding. Then explain whether you agree or disagree with the idea or argument — or whether you find yourself in partial agreement with it — and why.

Practice: Summarize a Source

Using the following guidelines, write an outline summary of the *State & Local Energy Report* article "Veterans Put to Work Helping Low-Income Families in Colorado" (p. 53):

1. Record the authors and title of the source.

2. Identify the main point and key points made by the writers. Present the main point and key points in the order in which they appear

in the source. For each point, briefly describe the evidence provided to back it up.

3. Clearly credit the authors for any information, ideas, and arguments you include in your summary: use quotation marks for direct quotations, and identify the page from which you've drawn a paraphrase or quotation. (See Chapter 19 for guidelines on citing sources.)

REFLECTIVE RESPONSES

A reflective response allows you to consider the meaning or implications of what you read. You might focus on a key passage or idea from a source, explaining or elaborating on it. Or you might reflect on your own experiences, attitudes, or observations in relation to a piece of information, an idea, or an argument. You can also use a reflective response to consider how an idea or argument might be interpreted by other readers, how it might be applied in a new context, or how it might be misunderstood.

ANALYTIC RESPONSES

An analytic response focuses on the important elements of a source, such as its purpose, ideas, argument, organization, focus, evidence, and style. For example, you might ask whether the main point is stated clearly, or whether appropriate types of evidence are used to support an argument. You might also analyze the logic of an argument or map its organization. Or you might offer suggestions about how an author could have made the source more effective.

Even when writers choose a particular type of response, they often draw on the other types to flesh out their ideas. For example, you might consider why you disagree

Practice: Respond to a Source

Putting your response into words can help you sort out your reactions to the ideas, information, and arguments in a source. Use the following guidelines to write an informal response to Bill Doe and Spider Marks' column (p. 74) or the *State & Local Energy Report* article (p. 53):

1. Identify a focus for your response. You might select important information, an intriguing idea, or the author's overall argument.

2. Decide what type of response you are going to write: agree/disagree, reflective, analytical, or some combination of the three types.

3. Write an introduction that identifies the information, idea, argument, or source to which you are responding, lays out your overall response (your main point), and identifies the source's author and title.

4. Provide reasons to support your main point and evidence to support your reasons.

5. Clearly credit the sources of any information, ideas, or arguments you use to support your response: use quotation marks for direct quotations, and identify the page or paragraph from which you've drawn a paraphrase or quotation. (See Chapter 19 for guidelines on documenting sources.)

with an argument by analyzing how effectively the source presents the argument. Or you might shift from agreeing with an idea to reflecting on its implications.

Read to Make Connections

You can learn a lot by looking for similarities and differences among the sources you read. For example, you might identify a group of authors with a similar approach to a subject, such as favoring increased government support for wind energy. You could then contrast this group with other groups of authors, such as those who believe that market forces should be the primary factor encouraging wind power, or those who believe we should focus on other forms of energy. Similarly, you can take note of information in one source that supports or contradicts information in another. These notes can help you build your own argument or identify information that will allow you (and your readers) to better understand a conversation.

As you read more and more about a subject, you'll start to notice common themes and shared ideas. Recognizing these connections among groups of authors can help

Working Together: Make Connections among Sources

Work together with a group of classmates to identify general approaches to the subject of returning veterans. To prepare for the group activity, each member should read, mark, and annotate the articles, Web pages, and reports on veterans in this chapter. During class, you should carry out the following activities:

1. Members of the group should take turns reporting what they've learned about one of the sources.

2. As each report is made, the other members of the group should take notes on the key ideas highlighted by the reporter.

3. When the reports have been completed, the group should create an overall list of the key ideas discussed in the individual reports.

4. Identify sources that seem to share similar approaches to the issue. Give each group of sources a name, and provide a brief description of the ideas its authors have in common.

5. Describe each group in detail. Explain what makes the authors part of the same group (their similarities) and how each group differs from the others you've defined.

Once you've completed the activity, consider how you would respond to each group of authors. Ask whether you agree or disagree with their approaches, and describe the extent to which you agree or disagree. Consider whether you would want to join a group, whether you would want to refine a particular approach to better fit your understanding of the subject, or whether you would rather develop a new approach.

you understand the scope of the conversation. For example, knowing that people involved in your conversation agree on the overall definition of a problem might lead you to focus your efforts on either challenging that definition with an alternative one or suggesting a possible solution. If you find yourself agreeing with one group of authors, you might start to think of yourself as a member of that group — as someone who shares their approach to the subject. If you don't agree with any of the groups you've identified, perhaps you are ready to develop a new approach to the subject.

To make connections among authors, jot down notes in the margins of your sources or in your writer's notebook. Each time you read a new source, keep in mind what you've already read, and make note of similarities and differences among your sources. When you notice similar themes in some of your sources, review the sources you've already read to see whether they've addressed those themes.

Beyond a collection of notes and annotations, reading to make connections might also result in longer pieces of freewriting (see p. 33). In some cases, you might spend time creating a brief essay that defines each group, identifies which authors belong to each group, and reflects on the strengths, weaknesses, and appropriateness of the approach taken by each group.

In Summary: Reading to Write

* Read with a purpose (p. 50).

* Read actively (p. 51).

* Take notes carefully (p. 60).

* Evaluate potential sources in light of your writing situation (p. 66).

* Summarize useful ideas, information, and arguments (p. 63).

* Respond to what you read (p. 78).

* Explore connections among sources (p. 79).

Working Together

With rare exceptions, writing is a social act. We write to inform, to entertain, to bring about change. We write to share ideas. We write to make a difference. Most important, we write *to someone* and *for a purpose*. To write more effective documents, writers frequently turn to other writers for feedback and advice. The skills required to give useful feedback and advice — and to use that feedback and advice effectively — are among the most important a writer can have. In fact, they're strongly related to the skills you draw on when you engage in any form of conversation — listening carefully, treating others with respect, and deciding how to make a useful contribution. In this chapter, you'll learn how to benefit from working with other writers and how to do so effectively and efficiently.

How Can Collaborative Activities Improve My Writing?

Writers frequently solicit support from other writers as they work on individual projects. In some cases, they seek this support independently, most often by asking for advice about the choice of a topic or by requesting feedback on a draft. In other cases, a writing instructor might direct students to work together to generate ideas, collect sources on a common topic, engage in peer review, and develop and refine arguments.

Work Together to Generate Ideas

Writers often collaborate to generate ideas. Common strategies for generating ideas with other writers include group brainstorming and role-playing activities.

GROUP BRAINSTORMING

Group brainstorming draws on the differing backgrounds and experiences of the members of a group to generate ideas for a writing project. For example, you might work with a group to create a list of ideas for an essay about new advances in communication technologies or social media, or you might collaborate to generate possible solutions to a problem with funding for a local school district.

To engage in group brainstorming, follow these guidelines:

- **Take notes.** Ask someone to record ideas.
- **Encourage everyone in the group to participate.** Consider taking turns. If your group chooses to contribute ideas as they occur to members, establish a ground rule that no one should cut off other group members as they're speaking.
- **Be polite.** Avoid criticisms and compliments. Treat every idea, no matter how odd or useless it might seem, as worthy of consideration.
- **Build on one another's ideas.** Try to expand on ideas that have already been generated, and see where they take you.
- **Generate as many ideas as possible.** If you get stuck, try asking questions about ideas that have already been suggested.
- **Review the results.** Once you've stopped brainstorming, look over the list of ideas, and identify the most promising ones.

ROLE-PLAYING

Role-playing activities are frequently used to generate and refine ideas. By asking the members of a group to take on roles, you can apply a variety of perspectives to a subject. For example, you might ask one person to play the role of a "doubting Thomas," someone who demands evidence from a writer for every assertion, or a devil's advocate, who responds to a writer's arguments with counterarguments. Role-playing activities that are useful for generating and refining ideas include staging debates, conducting inquiries, and offering first-person explanations.

Staging a debate. In a debate, speakers who represent different perspectives argue politely with one another about an issue. You might try one or more of the following role-playing activities:

- **Adopt the role of the authors of readings used in a class.** Each "author" presents his or her perspective on the issue.

- **Adopt the role of a political commentator or celebrity who has taken a strong stand on an issue.** One member of a group might adopt the role of Rachel Maddow, for example, while another might adopt the role of Rush Limbaugh, and still others might adopt the roles of Candy Crowley, Joe Scarborough, or Bill O'Reilly. Each "commentator" or "celebrity" presents his or her perspective on the issue. To prepare for the debate, watch or listen to commentaries on a site such as YouTube.com to learn about the positions these commentators have taken in the past.

- **Adopt the role of an authority on an issue,** such as a scientific adviser to a local zoning commission, the manager of a small business, or the director of a nonprofit organization. To prepare for the debate, conduct research in your library's databases or on the Web about the person whose role you are adopting.

- **Adopt the role of someone affected by an issue or event.** For example, if you were generating ideas about a natural disaster, such as the effects of a flood in the Mississippi River valley, you might take on the roles of people who lost their homes and were forced to move, health care workers and police officers who stayed on duty, students who lost their schools, or small business owners who lost their livelihoods, all of whom could discuss the impact of this natural disaster on their lives. To prepare for the debate, conduct research on how the community was affected by the event.

Conducting an inquiry. An inquiry is an attempt to understand a situation or an event. For example, a military tribunal might review soldiers' actions during a military operation, while a medical inquiry might focus on the causes of a problem that occurred during a medical procedure. To conduct an inquiry, try the following role-playing activities:

- **Defend a contemporary or historical figure.** The writer presents a case for this person, and the other group members ask questions about the person's actions or ideas.

- **Review a proposal.** The writer presents a proposal to address an issue or a problem. The other members of the group raise questions about the merits of the proposal and suggest alternatives.

Giving testimony. First-person explanations offer insights into the causes of, effects of, or solutions to a particular issue or problem. Role-playing activities that involve giving testimony include the following:

- **Adopt the role of devil's advocate.** The writer offers an explanation, and one or more respondents offer reasonable objections. Each devil's advocate — the term is drawn from the process by which the Roman Catholic Church confers sainthood, in which an advocate of the devil argues that the candidate is not worthy of sainthood — asks for clarification of the points made by the writer and suggests alternative explanations.

Working Together: Role-Play

Work together with your classmates to generate and refine ideas for your writing project. Choose one of the categories of role-playing activities — staging a debate, conducting an inquiry, or giving testimony — and assign roles to the members of your group. Then do the following:

1. Appoint a member of your group — ideally, someone who is not involved in the role-playing activity — to record the ideas.

2. Create a framework for the role-playing. Decide who will speak first, how long that person will speak, and what sort of responses are appropriate.

3. As you conduct the role-playing, be polite (within bounds, of course — some political commentators are far from polite to their opponents).

4. If you are responding to a writer's ideas, ask for evidence to support his or her arguments or explanations.

5. If you are adopting a role that requires you to disagree, don't overdo it. Be willing to accept a reasonable explanation or argument.

Once you've completed the activity, review the notes taken by your recorder, and assess what you've learned.

- **Adopt the role of a person affected by an issue.** The writer takes on the role of someone who has been affected by the issue. After the writer explains the effects, the other members of the group ask questions about the writer's experiences with this issue.

Work Together to Collect and Work with Information

You might be asked — by an instructor or by another writer — to work together to collect, critically read, evaluate, and take notes on information from sources. Common collaborative activities for collecting and working with information include the following:

- **Develop a search strategy for published sources.** Depending on the scope of a writing project, creating a plan for finding sources can be quite challenging. Working with other writers can improve the odds of developing an effective and appropriate plan. You can learn more about developing a search plan on page 439.

- **Assign responsibility for locating sources.** When a group is working on a shared topic, instructors often encourage the group to collaboratively compile a collection of sources. For example, one member of the group might search for sources through a library catalog, another through full-text databases, and still another through searches on the Web. Each person locates promising sources and makes copies for other members of the group. See Chapter 12 for more information about locating sources.

Need a refresher on evaluating sources? See Chapter 3.

- **Assign responsibility for field research.** In writing projects that involve surveys, interviews, observation, or correspondence (see p. 478), a group might develop a plan to conduct a particular type of field research. After reviewing the plan, each member of the group carries out his or her assigned research task and shares it with the group.

- **Create shared annotated bibliographies.** Members of a group working on a shared topic can create citations and annotations (brief summaries) for each source they collect. You can learn more about creating annotated bibliographies on page 448.

- **Share evaluations of sources.** Writers working on a shared topic meet to discuss the merits of the sources they've collected and read. For more information on evaluating sources, see page 66.

- **Share notes on sources.** Writers working on a shared topic compile their notes on the sources they have read. You can learn more about taking notes on page 60.

Work Together to Refine Your Argument

As you learn about and reflect on the conversation you've decided to join, you'll begin planning what you will contribute to the conversation. Feedback from other writers can help you develop and refine the main point you'll share with your readers and the reasoning and evidence you'll use to persuade them to accept your main point.

Writers usually express their main point through a thesis statement (see Chapter 14). A good thesis statement invites readers to learn something new, suggests that they change their attitudes or beliefs, or advocates taking action of some kind. In effect, your thesis statement serves as a brief summary of the overall argument you want to make to your readers. To determine whether your thesis statement conveys your main point clearly and effectively, ask for feedback from other writers. You might ask friends or family members to read your thesis statement and tell you what they think it means, as Megan Martinez did with an early draft of a thesis statement she developed for an argumentative essay about supporting returning military veterans. You might ask them to offer counterarguments or alternative perspectives on your issue. You might ask them to engage in a role-playing activity, in which they pretend to be someone who disagrees with your perspective. Or you might ask for feedback during a peer-review session in class. Regardless of where it comes from, listen carefully to the feedback you receive. Your thesis statement plays a central role in shaping the decisions you'll make about the reasons and evidence you'll offer to support your main point, and it can also affect the organization and design of your document.

> Do you have any ideas about what "doing more" would involve? Are you thinking about government programs? Private-sector programs?

> We need to do more to help returning veterans become contributing members of society.

> I'm not sure what you mean by "contributing members of society." Haven't they already made a pretty major contribution? Do you mean that you want them to have jobs? Go to school?

▲ **Feedback on a draft of Megan Martinez's thesis statement**

As you develop a set of reasons to accept your main point, ask for feedback on them as well. You might create an outline of your argument (see p. 512) or write a rough draft (see Chapter 16). Friends, family, and classmates should be able to provide their reactions to the reasons you are offering. They can give you feedback on the appropriateness and effectiveness of the evidence you've selected to support your reasons and the order in which you present your reasons and evidence. And they can help you generate ideas for new and potentially more effective reasons and sources of evidence. Just as you can with a thesis statement, you can ask people to offer counterarguments or to adopt roles. And, of course, you can solicit feedback on your reasons and evidence from classmates during peer-review or idea-generation sessions.

Federal and state governments, in partnership with business and nonprofit organizations, should create programs to prepare returning veterans for green jobs.

Reason 1. Society needs to focus on green jobs to save energy, produce new sources of energy, and preserve the environment.

Reason 2. Veterans need jobs and a sense of purpose, similar to what they had in the military.

Reason 3. Veterans have the skills and attitudes that can help them succeed in green jobs.

Evidence: Barringer's *New York Times* article, Sierra Club article, Doe and Marks column

> Who would fund these programs? Is this financially viable?

> Seems like they'd have the right attitude, but what kind of skills are you thinking about?

> How does your evidence support these reasons?

▲ **Feedback on an informal outline**

Your argument — your main point, reasons, and evidence — is the heart of your contribution to the conversation you've decided to join. By working with other writers, you can gain valuable feedback on your argument, feedback that can help you refine it and make it more effective.

How Can I Use Peer Review to Improve My Writing?

Writers frequently engage in peer review, an activity in which writers give feedback to each other on rough drafts. When designed effectively and treated seriously, peer review can provide valuable information to writers about the effectiveness, clarity, organization, and design of their drafts. Few experienced writers, in fact, produce major documents without asking for feedback on their drafts. They've learned that it can help them enhance their composing processes, improve their documents, and increase the likelihood of successfully completing a major writing project.

Use Peer Review to Enhance Your Writing Process

In addition to the direct benefits you can gain through assistance and feedback from other writers, you can benefit from providing assistance or feedback to other writers. By helping another writer generate ideas, you can practice effective brainstorming strategies. By participating in a planning session, you can learn something new about planning your own documents. By reading and responding to documents written by other writers, you might pick up some new strategies for organizing an essay, crafting an introduction, incorporating illustrations, or using evidence effectively. Perhaps most important, learning how to analyze other people's work can help you assess your own writing more productively.

Use Peer Review to Improve Your Document

Peer review gives you the benefit of multiple perspectives. The feedback you receive from other writers can help you learn whether your main point is conveyed clearly, whether sufficient evidence is offered, whether your document is organized effectively, and whether readers are likely to react favorably to the information, ideas, and arguments you have presented in a draft. Feedback from other writers can also help you identify passages in a draft that might benefit from additional revision, polishing, or editing.

To increase your chances of creating an effective document, you might ask for feedback on your overall argument, your reasoning about an issue, and your use of evidence. You might ask a friend or classmate, "What do you know about . . . ?" or "Do you think it would be effective if . . . ?" or "Does this seem convincing to you?" You might ask a reviewer to pretend to be part of the intended audience for your document, or you might ask for feedback on specific aspects of your document, such as its organization, style, or design.

Use Peer Review to Succeed on a Major Project

Working on collaborative projects has become common in many writing and writing-intensive courses. In engineering courses, for example, teams of students often carry out a complex project and produce presentations and written reports. Web design courses frequently involve students in team projects. Similarly, first-year writing courses often include a collaborative writing project. Typically, these projects are far more ambitious than those assigned to individual students. It is only through the contributions of all the members of the group that they can be completed at all.

How Can I Conduct an Effective Peer Review?

As you engage in peer review, either as a writer or as a reviewer, consider what stage the project is in. Early in a writing project, a writer is likely to be most interested in feedback about the overall direction of the project. Big-picture concerns such as the overall purpose of the document, the general soundness of an argument, and how readers are likely to react to that argument will probably be more important than issues such as style and tone. Later, questions about the integration of evidence from sources, style and tone, and design will grow in importance, particularly in terms of how they help the writer pursue his or her purpose and goals. Consider, too, the contexts in which a peer review takes place and the technologies that might be used to carry out the review.

Consider Context

As you begin a peer review, consider the context in which it is taking place. If you are conducting a peer review in a classroom, you might have limited time to read and reflect on a document. Try to focus specifically on a few primary concerns — either those defined by your instructor, perhaps through a rubric or a set of key questions, or those defined by the writer, who might help in particular areas. If you are conducting a peer review outside of class, you might have more time to consider a fuller range of issues related to the document. If so, think carefully about the kind of feedback that would help the writer, and then read the document — ideally more than once — with those concerns in mind.

Consider Technology

Peer review often calls to mind images of students hunched over desks in a classroom, marking paper drafts with pens or pencils before they offer feedback to one another. Increasingly, however, peer review takes place on computers, tablets, or even phones, both inside and outside of the classroom. If you are conducting a peer review using a word-processing program, a commenting program, a class discussion forum, an ePortfolio tool, a wiki, or a blog, think about the kinds of tools you have available to support your peer review. (For more information about these tools, see p. 94.) You'll almost certainly be able to save comments and revise them before you return the draft to the writer. You'll probably have access to tools for highlighting text and suggesting edits to the document. You'll be able to make links to related documents, Web sites, and databases. And you will certainly be able to share your comments not only with the writer but also with other members of the class, including your instructor. Some instructors, in fact, ask to see the feedback writers give to one another, not only as a means of ensuring greater attention to the peer-review process but also to get a sense of the kinds of writing issues members of the class are struggling to address.

Consider Your Needs as a Writer

Whenever you ask for feedback from other writers, keep the following guidelines in mind.

When you ask for feedback on a draft:

- **Be clear.** Tell your reviewers where you'd like them to focus. For example, let them know that you are struggling with the transition from one point to another or that you would appreciate feedback on your conclusion.

- **Be reasonable.** Your reviewers have more to do in life than review your draft. Don't expect — or ask — them to spend more time reviewing a draft than you spent writing it. For that matter, don't expect them to put more than half an hour into a review — if that.

- **Be prepared.** Provide a draft that is easy to review. If you are asking the writer to comment on a printed draft, format it with double-spaced lines and wide margins. If you are providing a digital draft, make sure the reviewer can access, read, and comment on your file easily.

When you receive feedback on a draft:

- **Be open to criticism.** Don't dismiss constructive criticism as a problem with the reviewer's comprehension. A reviewer might make poor suggestions for revision, but it's more likely that he or she is reacting to a problem in the draft. Even when the suggested revision is inappropriate, it might point to an area that needs attention.

- **Be willing to ask questions.** If you aren't sure what a reviewer's comments mean, ask for clarification.

- **Be willing to change.** If a reviewer offers a critique of your argument or ideas, consider addressing it in your document. You will make a stronger argument if you tell readers about alternative ways of looking at an issue — particularly when you can counter the alternatives effectively.

- **Be fair to yourself.** It's your draft. Don't feel obligated to incorporate every suggested change into your draft.

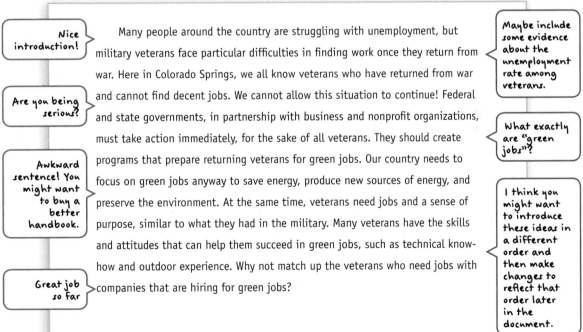

▲ **Ineffective** and **effective** feedback on Megan Martinez's first draft

Consider Your Role as a Reviewer

When you provide feedback to another writer, consider the following guidelines.

To prepare for a peer-review session:

- **Be certain you understand the assignment.** Ask the writer to describe the draft's purpose and audience, and read the assignment sheet, if there is one.

- **Be certain you understand the writer's needs.** Ask the writer what type of response you should provide. If you are reviewing an early draft that will be revised before it's submitted for a grade, focus on larger writing concerns such as the overall argument, evidence, and organization. If the writer wants help with proofreading and editing, focus on accuracy, economy, consistency, biased language, style, spelling, grammar, and punctuation (see pp. 641–642).

- **Be certain you understand any peer-review guidelines.** If you are using a feedback form or a set of questions provided by your instructor, make sure you understand these guidelines. If you don't, ask the instructor or the writer for clarification.

- **Set aside sufficient time to review the draft.** Take your job seriously, and give the draft the time it deserves. You'll want the same courtesy when your draft is reviewed.

Before you make comments:

- **Be prepared.** Read the draft all the way through at least once before making any comments. This will help you understand its overall structure and argument.

- **Be organized.** Take a few minutes to identify the areas most in need of work. On a first draft, for instance, you might identify three main areas that need the writer's attention, such as thesis statement, organization, and effective use of sources.

As you make comments:

- **Be positive.** Identify the strengths of the draft. Be specific in your praise: "This quotation really drives home your point about veterans' struggles after deployment" is more helpful, for instance, than "Nice quotation" because the first comment allows the writer to see why a certain strategy is effective.

- **Be judicious.** Focus on the areas of the draft most in need of improvement. Avoid commenting on everything that might be improved. In most cases, a limited set of suggested changes — particularly those that focus on bigger-picture concerns such as purpose, audience, argument, and organization — will ripple through a document in ways that make many of the other changes you might have suggested irrelevant.

- **Be clear.** If you are addressing an overall issue such as structure or integration of evidence from sources, discuss it thoroughly enough that the writer will understand your concerns. If you are addressing a specific passage, indicate where it can be found.

- **Be specific.** Avoid general comments, such as "This draft suffers from a lack of clarity." This kind of statement doesn't give the writer direction for improving the draft. Instead, offer specific comments, such as "I found it difficult to understand your explanation of the issue in the second paragraph." Similarly, focus your questions. Instead of asking, "What are you trying to do here?", ask a question such as "It seems as though you are trying to build on what you stated in the previous paragraph. Can you show the connection more clearly?"

- **Be constructive.** Offer concrete suggestions about how the draft might be improved, rather than just criticizing what you didn't like. Being constructive can also mean encouraging the writer to continue doing what you see as effective.

- **Be reasonable.** Keep the writing assignment in mind as you make suggestions for improvement. Don't hold the draft to a higher standard than the instructor's.

- **Be kind.** Be polite. Don't put down the writer simply because you find a draft inadequate, confusing, or annoying.

- **Be responsible.** Review your comments before you give them to the writer.

Understanding how to conduct and use feedback from peer review not only will help you improve a particular document but also will help you become a better writer. As you consider the type of document you'll write to contribute to a written conversation, keep these principles in mind. Also keep in mind the distinctive characteristics of writing for particular purposes, such as writing to inform or writing to solve problems. Chapters 5 through 10 provide carefully designed peer-review activities that will help you get feedback on drafts for the kinds of writing projects featured in those chapters.

What Resources Can I Draw on as I Review and Collaborate?

Resources that support peer review and other forms of collaborative work include technological tools as well as your instructor, classmates, family, and friends.

Use Technological Tools

For many writers, the phrase "working together" implies face-to-face meetings, often during class. In fact, many collaborative activities can be carried out without the need to meet in person.

- If you are working with other writers to generate and refine ideas, you might use chat programs to meet online. At the end of the chat session, you might want to save a transcript of the session for later review. If your class is supported by Web discussion forums, you can carry out your discussion in that format. Similarly, you can refine and generate ideas by using an e-mail distribution list (or by sending each message to all of the people in your group). You might also post ideas on a blog and then use the blog's Comments tool to generate responses to each idea.

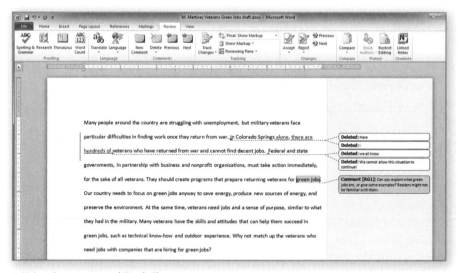

▲ **Using Comments and Track Changes**

- If you are collaborating with other writers to collect and work with sources for a shared topic, you can use discussion forums, wikis, cloud-based folders (such as Dropbox, iCloud, and SkyDrive), and e-mail to distribute sources, source citations, source evaluations, and source notes.

- If you are conducting a peer review, you can share your drafts by sending them as e-mail attachments. Reviewers can open the attachments in a word-processing program, comment on them using the program's Comment and Track Changes tools, save the file with a new name, and return them to you.

- If your class is supported by a course management system, you can ask your instructor to create discussion forums, wikis, and file-sharing folders to support your group work. You can take advantage of e-mail to share ideas, schedule meetings, and exchange files. You might also have access to electronic whiteboard programs that allow you to meet online and work on drafts of your document.

To learn more about blogs, see page 469. If you have questions about the technological tools that are available to support collaborative writing, ask your instructor.

Consult Instructors, Classmates, Friends, and Family

The most important resources for peer review and collaboration are your instructor, your classmates, and your friends and family. Not only can family and friends provide honest feedback on the quality of your drafts, but they can also be resources for generating ideas about and planning a writing project. Simply discussing a writing project with sympathetic friends or family members can help you make progress on the project. They might remind you of something you'd forgotten about the topic; they might share new information with you; or they might respond in a way that sparks a new idea.

Similarly, classmates and instructors can help you fine-tune a draft by serving as a sounding board for your ideas and by responding to it. Instructors can also show you how to work with peer-review forms and can provide feedback on the quality of the comments you offer to your classmates. Finally, and perhaps most important, instructors can help you understand your assignment — but only if you ask them for advice.

In Summary: Working Together

* Understand how collaborative activities can improve your writing (p. 82).

* Use peer review to enhance your writing process, improve your document, and succeed on writing projects (p. 88).

* Take advantage of resources that help writers work together (p. 94).

PART TWO

Contributing to a
Conversation

Writing to Reflect

I write as an **observer** when I reflect on a topic.

GENRES IN CONVERSATION

| Reflective Writing | Informative Writing | Analytical Writing | Evaluative Writing | Problem-Solving Writing | Argumentative Writing |

In the post-9/11 era, stories of returning home from war are gaining attention as more and more veterans decide to speak out and share their experiences. In the documents shown here — a **memoir**, an **interview**, and a **journal article** — writers use three distinct genres to reflect on the lasting effects of the trauma of war, regardless of one's life predeployment. Although all three genres focus on veterans' experiences, they employ distinct visual forms and follow specific genre conventions.

e-Pages

You can view the full documents shown here and respond to questions about reflective genres at **bedfordstmartins.com /conversation/epages**.

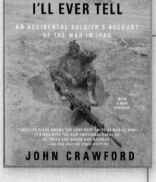

Memoir ▶

This best-selling **memoir**, in standard paperback form, recounts the experiences of John Crawford, who joined the Florida National Guard to pay for his college education, not expecting he would be called to serve in Baghdad.

PREFACE

TWO YEARS AGO I was a newlywed and a college student only a few classes away from graduation. The world seemed uncomplicated. Now, all I can say for sure is that I am no longer a college student, no longer illusioned by new love, and I don't feel young anymore. My quiet optimism has been replaced by something darker, a kind of hatred—of what, I cannot even grasp or imagine.

I was raised in a small town in northeast Florida. I spent my summers playing war in the swamps behind my parents' house, listening eagerly at my father's side as he told me about his war, and I yearned. I grew larger every year, filling out, my

Interview ▶

In this **interview**, part of the Library of Congress Veterans History Project, a veteran reflects on her experiences in boot camp and during her deployment in Afghanistan.

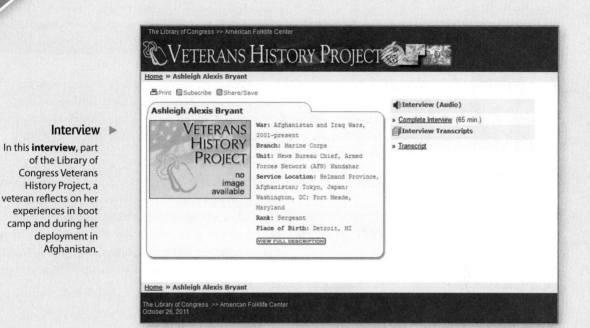

VETERANS HISTORY PROJECT

Home » Ashleigh Alexis Bryant

🖨 Print 📡 Subscribe 💾 Share/Save

Ashleigh Alexis Bryant

VETERANS HISTORY PROJECT

no image available

War: Afghanistan and Iraq Wars, 2001-present
Branch: Marine Corps
Unit: News Bureau Chief, Armed Forces Network (AFN) Kandahar
Service Location: Helmand Province, Afghanistan; Tokyo, Japan; Washington, DC; Fort Meade, Maryland
Rank: Sergeant
Place of Birth: Detroit, MI

VIEW FULL DESCRIPTION

🔊 **Interview (Audio)**

» **Complete Interview** (65 min.)
📄 **Interview Transcripts**

» **Transcript**

Home » Ashleigh Alexis Bryant

The Library of Congress >> American Folklife Center
October 26, 2011

▼ Journal Article

A scholarly **journal article** by an English professor uses literary sources to reflect on the transition from military to academic life and the links between rehabilitation and composition.

RECONSIDERATIONS:
"Brave Words": Rehabilitating the Veteran-Writer

Liam Corley

From September 2008 to July 2009, I traded academic robes for the Army Combat Uniform issued to US Navy personnel deploying to Afghanistan. Along with using the ceramic and Kevlar body armor I learned to don at Fort Jackson, South Carolina, I metaphorically defended myself from the disruption to my personal and professional life that would result from this mobilization by calling it a fully funded overseas federal fellowship. "War as sabbatical" became a way of making my departure from a tenure-track job as an English professor seem less unusual, less concerning to senior faculty, and, ultimately, less perilous, especially for me and my family. Optimistic even up to my last trip to the state university where I taught American literature, I grabbed a number of unread scholarly books from my office shelves, intending to shoehorn them into one of my overfull seabags.

Although I thought of myself as the man inside the uniform, photographs posted on my deployment blog gave the lie to the sabbatical charade. Who can see a professor behind ballistic eyewear, seventy pounds of armor, and an M16 swinging on a three-point sling? There's no insignia for PhD, no patch that portrays a pen rampant over a field of swords. What I had negotiated and what my university had given was a stop on my tenure clock, a lacuna in the vitae that would document my campaign for tenure, a silent fit of laughter that any of this could ever occur. My last month of interactions with university colleagues, administrators, and staff oscillated between professional nullity and personal concern: tender eyes and words even as minds accepted that I was hurtling away on a trajectory that might have no returning.

And so for 293 days I carried a gun instead of a textbook, a journal article, or a pile of ungraded essays. I jockeyed four computers instead of one; knowledge passed up instead of down. I slept alone, ate curry prepared by Indian contractors, and made

Liam Corley is assistant professor of English at California State Polytechnic University-Pomona, where he teaches courses in American literature and poetry. His work has appeared in such journals as *Studies in the Literary Imagination*, *War, Literature, and the Arts*, and *Christianity and Literature*. He was commissioned in the US Navy Reserve in 2004.

College English, Volume 74, Number 4, March 2012

new friends. The one academic piece of writing I completed while deployed was turned down by three publications.[1] One kindly editor suggested I would be better able to convey my experiences after I gained some distance from them. Seeing now how the opposite is true, I marvel at her tact. The essay I wrote on the way to war was infected by denial, the tyro prophet's willful avoidance of the fact that he lives in a city slated for destruction. I strained to put this interlude of violence into a civilized context, a literary heritage, a moralizing space. I made an aesthetic of war, and the effect was a lie, another step farther off the path toward tenure, security, and normalcy. Like many veterans, I decided, at least provisionally, that silence would be better than mouthing conventional lies about an experience I could not articulate. Academic books stayed on the shelf. When I packed my belongings into a Gorilla box for the long-awaited shipment home, I noted the outline left by three volumes of history and criticism, furred with the ash and dust of an Afghan summer, fall, winter, and spring. Alone among my possessions, the pages of these books were clean.

*****

In the first few months after I returned from Afghanistan, I was plagued during my walk from the faculty parking lot past the library and up to my office with fits of muscle memory. My right hand slapped the thigh where it used to reassure itself with the grip of an M9 pistol. My gait remained awkward from the phantom weight of a drop holster and magazines, despite having left them in Kuwait at a "Warrior Transition Course." Sitting in my quiet office, surrounded by old, familiar books, I compulsively searched the Web for news articles about my last duty station, reading between the lines for a glimpse of what was really going on in Kabul, Herat, and Farah. Mentally, I was struggling to detoxify from switching between four computer systems, each with a separate email account, unique capabilities, and classification level. More than anything else, I had to relearn how to concentrate without the adrenaline rush of hourly deadlines, abrasive colonels, and the acid anxiety of overlooking the one deadly needle in a relentlessly replenished haystack of daily communications and intelligence reports.

I was more blunt than usual in conversations with colleagues and students, accustomed as I was to pounding urgent points home to hardheaded army leaders befuddled by lack of sleep, past experience, and professional prejudice against "the Navy." Terse and ironic, I left first-years reeling. I held no hands, changed no grades, and always said I was adjusting fine. In 1946, W. H. Auden wrote, "Professors back from secret missions / Resume their proper erudition, / Though some regret it" ("Under Which Lyre" 333–34). I marveled at his concise expression of the emotional withdrawals I felt now that I was cut off from the daily morphine drip of significance conveyed by relentless deadlines and the endlessly reinforced message that *lives depended on the accuracy and clarity of my work*. I struggled with self-loathing as I engaged in academic tasks less evidently meaningful.

What Is Writing to Reflect?

Writing to reflect is one of the most common activities writers undertake. At the beginning of almost every writing project, writers spend time exploring and deepening their understanding of their subject. In this sense, writing to reflect provides a foundation for documents that inform, analyze, evaluate, solve problems, and convey arguments.

Reflection can also be the primary purpose for writing a document. In journals and diaries, writers reflect on a subject for personal reasons, often with the expectation that no one else will read their words. In more public documents — such as memoirs, letters, opinion columns, and blogs — writers also use reflection to share their thoughts in ways that benefit others.

Reflective writing is carried out by writers who adopt the role of *observer*. These writers spend time learning about and considering a subject. Sometimes they explore the implications of putting a particular idea into practice. Sometimes they trace relationships among ideas and information. Sometimes they ask whether or how an author's words might help them better understand their own lives. Sometimes they ask whether their understanding of one situation can help them better understand another.

Readers of reflective documents usually share the writer's interest in a subject. They want to learn what another person thinks about the subject, and often they'll use what they've read as the basis for their own reflections. In general, readers of reflective documents expect writers to provide a personal treatment of a subject, and they are willing to accept — and are likely to welcome — an unusual perspective.

To gather details for their observations, writers of reflective documents use sources, including their personal experiences and expertise, reports of recent

The Writer's Role: Observer

PURPOSE
- To share a writer's insights about a subject
- To connect with readers

READERS

- Want to learn about other people's ideas and experiences
- Expect a personal treatment of the subject
- Welcome an unusual perspective

SOURCES
- Personal experiences and observations are often the major sources for reflective writing.
- Published sources might provide additional information to support a reflection.
- Cultural productions, such as music, art, movies, plays, and literature, can inspire reflection.

CONTEXT

- Reflections often draw on readers' knowledge of social events and their awareness of cultural context.
- Design choices anticipate the physical context in which the document is likely to be read.

events, and cultural materials such as music, art, movies, plays, books, short stories, and poems. These sources can also provide the inspiration for a reflective document. For example, a writer might reflect on an experience, a book, a poem, or a song.

Writers of reflective documents often connect their observations to the social, cultural, and historical contexts they share with their readers. For example, they might refer to events or people who have recently received attention in the news media. In addition, they might refer to works of art, such as the *Mona Lisa*, or quotations from well-known works of literature, such as Hamlet's question "To be, or not to be?" Writers of reflective documents are also aware of the physical contexts in which their documents are likely to be read, and they design their documents to meet the needs of those contexts: for instance, a short essay for a writing class will typically feature double-spaced text with wide margins and few, if any, adornments, while a blog entry might include animated graphics, audio and video clips, or links to related Web sites.

Whether writing for themselves or others, writers use reflective writing to connect ideas and information, often in new and intriguing ways. Through reflection, writers can create new ways of understanding the world in which we live.

What Kinds of Documents Are Used to Share Reflections?

As a writer, you can use the reflections of other writers in many ways. Among other purposes, they can help you gain firsthand impressions from people who have been affected by an event. They can allow you to learn more about a particular historical period. They can help you understand the motivations and experiences of key figures in a political, cultural, or social movement. And they can help you develop a fuller understanding of your own experiences as you prepare your own reflective document.

You can begin to understand the contributions made by reflective documents by learning about the purposes, readers, sources, and contexts that have influenced other writers. In the following sections, you'll find discussions and examples of reflective essays, humorous reflections, and photo essays. In the e-Pages for this chapter (available online at bedfordstmartins.com/conversation/epages), you'll find discussions and examples of literacy essays, memoirs, and audio essays.

View the e-Pages for reflective writing at **bedfordstmartins.com/conversation/epages.**

Reflective Essays

Reflective essays convey a writer's observations and thoughts on a subject to the members of a written conversation. Like memoirs and literacy narratives, reflective essays draw on personal experience and are often written from a first-person (*I, me, my*) point of view. However, writers of reflective essays generally move beyond themselves as the primary focus of their essays, typically by using personal experience as a foundation for exploring more abstract ideas. In doing so, they show the significance of their experiences in a broader context.

In academic settings, such as writing and writing-intensive classes, reflective essays are often written in response to the information, ideas, or arguments found in another document, such as an article, an opinion column, or a personal essay. (If writers refer to another source, they cite it in the body of the essay and in a works cited or references list using a documentation system such as MLA or APA; see Chapters 21 and 22.) Because instructors and classmates will review and comment on them, reflective essays written for college courses are usually designed with wide margins, readable fonts, and double-spaced lines. In some cases, writers use illustrations, such as photographs and drawings, to set a mood or illustrate a point.

 Cheryl Strayed
What Kind of Woman Are You?

"What Kind of Woman Are You?" is an excerpt from the book *Wild: From Lost to Found on the Pacific Crest Trail* (2012), a #1 *New York Times* best seller. Cheryl Strayed, also the author of *Torch* (2006) and the advice columnist behind *The Rumpus*'s "Dear Sugar," set off as a novice hiker on a life-changing trek after her mother's death and the end of her marriage. In this excerpt, Strayed reflects on her progress, setbacks, motivation, and challenges both on and off the trail, eventually seeking help from "three men of unknown intent." As you read, pay attention to how Strayed weaves moments of reflection into an otherwise chronological narrative.

WHAT KIND OF WOMAN ARE YOU?

I spent the day at Golden Oak Springs with my compass in hand, reading *Staying Found*. I found north, south, east, and west. I walked jubilantly without my pack down a jeep road that came up to the springs to see what I could see. It was spectacular to walk without my pack on even in the state my feet were in, sore as my muscles were. I felt not only upright, but lifted, as if two elastic bands were attached to my shoulders from above. Each step was a leap, light as air.

When I reached an overlook, I stopped and gazed across the expanse. It was only more desert mountains, beautiful and austere, and more rows of white angular wind turbines in the distance. I returned to my camp, set up my stove, and attempted to make myself a hot meal, my first on the trail, but I couldn't get my stove to sustain a flame, no matter what I tried. I pulled the little instruction book out, read the troubleshooting section, and learned that I'd filled the stove's canister with the wrong kind of gas. I'd filled it with unleaded fuel instead of the special white gas that it was meant to have, and now the generator was clogged, its tiny pan blackened with soot by my efforts.

I wasn't hungry anyway. My hunger was a numb finger, barely prodding. I ate a handful of tuna jerky flakes and fell asleep by 6:15.

Before I set out on the fourth day, I doctored my wounds. An REI worker had encouraged me to buy a box of Spenco 2nd Skin—gel patches meant to treat burns that also happened to be great for blisters. I plastered them in all the places my skin was bleeding or blistered or red with rash—on the tips of my toes and the backs of my heels, over my hip bones and across the front of my shoulders and lower back. When I was done, I shook my socks out, trying to soften them before I put them on. I had two pair, but each had become stiff with dirt and dried sweat. It seemed they were made of cardboard rather than cloth, though I switched them out every few hours, wearing one pair while the other air-dried, dangling from the bungee cords on my pack.

After I hiked away from the springs that morning, fully loaded down with 24.5 pounds of water again, I realized I was having a kind of strange, abstract, retrospective fun. In moments among my various agonies, I noticed the beauty that surrounded me, the wonder of things both small and large: the color of a desert flower that brushed against me on the trail or the grand sweep of sky as the sun faded over the mountains. I was in the midst of such a reverie when I skidded on pebbles and fell, landing on the hard trail facedown with a force that took my breath away. I lay unmoving for a good minute, from both the searing pain in my leg and the colossal weight on my back, which pinned me to the ground. When I crawled out from beneath my pack and assessed the damage, I saw that a gash in my shin was seeping copious blood, a knot the size of a fist already forming beneath the gash. I poured a tiny bit of my precious water over it, flicking the dirt and pebbles out the best I could, then pressed a lump of gauze against it until the bleeding slowed and I limped on.

I walked the rest of the afternoon with my eyes fixed on the trail immediately in front of me, afraid I'd lose my footing again and fall. It was then that I spotted what I'd searched for days before: mountain lion tracks. It had walked along the trail not long before me in the same direction as I was walking—its paw prints clearly legible in the dirt for a quarter mile. I stopped every few minutes to look around. Aside from small patches of green, the landscape was mostly a range of blonds and browns, the same colors as a mountain lion. I walked on, thinking about the newspaper article I'd recently come across about three women in California—each one had been killed by a mountain lion on separate occasions in the past year—and about all those nature shows I'd watched as a kid in which the predators go after the one they judge to be the weakest in the pack. There was no question that was me: the one most likely to be ripped limb from limb. I sang aloud the little songs that came into my head—"Twinkle, Twinkle, Little Star" and "Take Me Home, Country Roads"—hoping that my terrified voice would scare the lion away, while at the same time fearing it would alert her to my presence, as if the blood crusted on my leg and the days-old stench of my body weren't enough to lure her.

As I scrutinized the land, I realized that I'd come far enough by now that the terrain had begun to change. The landscape around me was still arid, dominated by the same chaparral and sagebrush as it had been all along, but now the Joshua trees that defined the Mojave Desert appeared only sporadically. More common were the juniper trees, piñon pines, and scrub oaks. Occasionally, I passed through shady meadows thick with grass. The grass and the reasonably large trees were a comfort to me. They suggested water and life. They intimated that I could do this.

Until, that is, a tree stopped me in my path. It had fallen across the trail, its thick trunk held aloft by branches just low enough that I couldn't pass beneath it, yet so high that climbing over it was impossible, especially given the weight of my pack. Walking around it was also out of the question: the trail dropped off too steeply on one side and the brush was too dense on the other. I stood for a long while, trying to map out a way past the tree. I had to do it, no matter how impossible it seemed. It was either that or turn around and go back to the motel in Mojave. I thought of my eighteen-dollar room with a deep swooning desire, the yearning to return to it flooding my body. I backed up to the tree, unbuckled my pack, and pushed it up and over its rough trunk, doing my best to drop it over the other side without letting it fall so hard on the ground that my dromedary bag would pop from the impact. Then I climbed over the tree after it, scraping my hands that were already tender from my fall. In the next mile I encountered three other blown-down trees. By the time I made it past them all, the scab on my shin had torn open and was bleeding anew.

On the afternoon of the fifth day, as I made my way along a narrow and steep stretch of trail, I looked up to see an enormous brown horned animal charging at me.

"Moose!" I hollered, though I knew that it wasn't a moose. In the panic of the moment, my mind couldn't wrap around what I was seeing and a moose was the closest thing to it. "Moose!" I hollered more desperately as it neared. I scrambled into the manzanitas and scrub oaks that bordered the trail, pulling myself into their sharp branches as best I could, stymied by the weight of my pack.

As I did this, the species of the beast came to me and I understood that I was about to be mauled by a Texas longhorn bull.

"Mooooose!" I shouted louder as I grabbed for the yellow cord tied to the frame of my pack that held the world's loudest whistle. I found it, brought it to my lips, closed my eyes, and blew with all my might, until I had to stop to get a breath of air.

When I opened my eyes, the bull was gone.

So was all the skin on the top of my right index finger, scraped off on the manzanitas' jagged branches in my frenzy.

The thing about hiking the Pacific Crest Trail, the thing that was so profound to me that summer—and yet also, like most things, so very simple—was how few choices I had and how often I had to do the thing I least wanted to do. How there was no escape or denial. No numbing it down with a martini or covering it up with a roll in the hay. As I clung to the chaparral that day, attempted to patch up my bleeding finger, terrified by every sound that the bull was coming back, I considered my options. There were only two and they were essentially the same. I could go back in the direction I had come from, or I could go forward in the direction I intended to go. The bull, I acknowledged grimly, could be in either direction, since I hadn't seen where he'd run once I closed my eyes. I could only choose between the bull that would take me back and the bull that would take me forward.

And so I walked on.

It took all I had to cover nine miles a day. To cover nine miles a day was a physical achievement far beyond anything I'd ever done. Every part of my body hurt.

Except my heart. I saw no one, but, strange as it was, I missed no one. I longed for nothing but food and water and to be able to put my backpack down. I kept carrying my backpack anyway. Up and down and around the dry mountains, where Jeffrey pines and black oaks lined the trail, crossing jeep roads that bore the tracks of big trucks, though none were in sight.

On the morning of the eighth day I got hungry and dumped all my food out on the ground to assess the situation, my desire for a hot meal suddenly fierce. Even in my exhausted, appetite-suppressed state, by then I'd eaten most of what I didn't have to cook—my granola and nuts, my dried fruit and turkey and tuna jerky, my protein bars and chocolate and Better Than Milk powder. Most of the food I had left needed to be cooked and I had no working stove. I didn't have a resupply box waiting for me until I reached Kennedy Meadows, 135 trail miles into my journey. A well-seasoned hiker would have traversed those 135 miles in the time I'd been on the trail. At the rate I was moving, I wasn't even halfway there. And even if I did make it through to Kennedy Meadows on the food I had, I still needed to have my stove repaired and filled with the proper fuel—and Kennedy Meadows, being more of a high-elevation base for hunters and hikers and fishers than a town, was no place to do it. As I sat in the dirt, ziplock bags of dehydrated food that I couldn't cook scattered all around me, I decided to veer off the trail. Not far from where I sat, the PCT crossed a network of jeep roads that ran in various directions.

I began walking down one, reasoning that I'd eventually find civilization in the form of a highway that paralleled the trail approximately twenty miles to the east. I walked not knowing exactly what road I was on, going only on faith that I would find something, walking and walking in the bright hot sun. I could smell myself as I moved. I'd packed deodorant and each morning I'd swabbed it under my arms, but it made no difference anymore. I hadn't bathed in over a week. My body was covered with dirt and blood, my hair, dense with dust and dried sweat plastered to my head underneath my hat. I could feel the muscles in my body growing stronger by the day and at the same time, in equal measure, my tendons and joints breaking down. My feet hurt both inside and out, their flesh rubbed raw with blisters, their bones and muscles fatigued from the miles. The road was blissfully level or gently descending, a welcome break from the relentless up and down of the trail, but still I suffered. For long stretches I tried to imagine that I didn't actually have feet, that instead my legs ended in two impervious stumps that could endure anything.

After four hours I began to regret my decision. I might starve to death out there or be killed by marauding longhorn bulls, but on the PCT at least I knew where I was. I reread my guidebook, uncertain by now that I was even on one of the roads they'd described in a cursory way. I took out my map and compass every hour to assess and reassess my position. I pulled out *Staying Found* to read again how exactly to use a map and compass. I studied the sun. I passed a small herd of cows that were unbound by a fence and my heart leapt at the sight of them, though none moved in my direction. They only stopped eating to lift their heads and watch me pass while I delicately chanted to them, "Cow, cow, cow."

The land through which the road passed was surprisingly green in places, dry and rocky in others, and twice I passed tractors parked silent and eerie by the side of the road. I walked in a state of wonder at the beauty and the silence, but by late afternoon, apprehension rose in my throat.

I was on a road, but I had not seen a human being in eight days. This was civilization and yet, aside from the free-range cows and the two abandoned tractors, and the road itself, there was no sign of it. I felt as if I were starring in a science fiction movie, as if I were the only person left on the planet, and for the first time in my journey, I felt like I might cry. I took a deep breath to push away my tears and took off my pack and set it in the dirt to regroup. There was a bend in the road ahead and I walked around it without my pack to see what I could.

What I saw was three men sitting in the cab of a yellow pickup truck.

One was white. One was black. One was Latino.

It took perhaps sixty seconds for me to reach them on foot. They watched me with the same expression on their faces as I'd had when I saw the longhorn bull the day before. As if any moment they might yell "Moose!" My relief at the sight of them was enormous. Yet as I strode toward them my whole body tingled with the complicated knowledge that I was no longer the sole star in a film about a planet devoid of people. Now I was in a different kind of movie entirely: I was the sole woman with three men of unknown intent, character, and origin watching me from the shade of the yellow truck.

When I explained my situation to them through the open driver's-side window, they gazed at me silently, their eyes shifting from startled to stunned to scoffing until they all burst out laughing.

"Do you know what you walked into, honey?" the white man asked me when he'd recovered, and I shook my head. He and the black man looked to be in their sixties, the Latino barely out of his teens.

"You see this here mountain?" he asked. He pointed straight ahead through the windshield from his position behind the wheel. "We're getting ready to blow that mountain up." He explained to me that a mining operation had bought rights to this patch of land and they were mining for decorative rock that people use in their yards. "My name's Frank," he said, tapping the brim of his cowboy hat. "And technically you're trespassing, young lady, but we won't hold that against you." He looked at me and winked. "We're just miners. We don't own the land or else we'd have to shoot you."

He laughed again and then gestured to the Latino in the middle and told me his name was Carlos.

"I'm Walter," said the black man sitting by the passenger window.

They were the first people I'd seen since the two guys in the minivan with the Colorado plates who'd dropped me by the side of the road more than a week before. When I spoke, my voice sounded funny to me, seemed to be higher and faster than I'd remembered, as if it were something I couldn't quite catch and hold on to, as if every word were a small bird fluttering away. They told me to get in the back of the truck, and we drove the short distance around the bend to retrieve my pack. Frank stopped and they all got out. Walter picked up my pack and was shocked at the weight.

"I was in Korea," he said, hoisting it into the truck's metal bed with considerable effort. "And we ain't never carried a pack that heavy. Or maybe once I carried one that heavy, but that was when I was being punished."

Quickly, without my being much involved, it was decided I'd go home with Frank, where his wife would feed me dinner and I could bathe and sleep in a bed. In the morning, he'd help me get someplace where I could have my stove repaired.

"Now explain all this to me again?" Frank asked a few times, and each time all three of them listened with confused and rapt attention. They lived perhaps twenty miles from the Pacific Crest Trail and yet none of them had ever heard of it. None could fathom what business a woman had hiking it by herself, and Frank and Walter told me so, in jovial, gentlemanly terms.

"I think it's kind of cool," said Carlos after a while. He was eighteen, he told me, about to join the military.

"Maybe you should do this instead," I suggested.

"Nah," he said.

The men got into the truck again and I rode in the back for a couple of miles by myself, until we reached the spot where Walter had parked his truck. He and Carlos drove off in it and left me alone with Frank, who had another hour of work to do.

I sat in the cab of the yellow truck watching Frank go back and forth on a tractor, grading the road. Each time he passed, he waved to me, and as he rode away I surreptitiously explored the contents of his truck. In the glove compartment there was a silver flask of whiskey. I took a shallow swig, and quickly put it back, my lips on fire. I reached under the seat and pulled out a slim black case and opened it up and saw a gun as silver as the whiskey flask and shut it again and shoved it beneath the seat. The keys to the truck dangled from the ignition, and I thought idly about what would happen if I started it up and drove away. I took off my boots and massaged my feet. The little bruise on my ankle that I'd gotten from shooting heroin in Portland was still there, but faded to a faint morose yellow now. I ran my finger over it, over the bump of the tiny track mark still detectable at its core, amazed at my own ludicrousness, and then put my socks back on so I wouldn't have to see it anymore.

"What kind of woman are you?" Frank asked when he was done with his work and he'd climbed into the truck beside me.

"What kind?" I asked. Our eyes locked and something in his unveiled itself, and I looked away.

"Are you like Jane? Like the kind of woman Tarzan would like?"

"I guess so," I said, and laughed, though I felt a creeping anxiety, wishing that Frank would start the truck and drive. He was a big man, rangy and chiseled and tan. A miner who looked to me like a cowboy. His hands reminded me of all the hands of the men I'd known growing up, men who worked their bodies for a living, men whose hands would never get clean no matter how hard they scrubbed. As I sat there with him, I felt the way I always do when alone in certain circumstances with certain men—that anything could happen. That he could go about his business, mannerly and kind, or he could grab me and change the course of things entirely in an instant. With Frank in his truck, I watched his hands, his every move, each cell in my body on high alert, though I appeared as relaxed as if I'd just woken from a nap.

"I've got a little something for us," he said, reaching into the glove compartment to remove the flask of whiskey. "It's my reward for a hard day's work." He unscrewed the cap and handed it to me. "Ladies first."

I took it from him and held it to my lips and let the whiskey wash into my mouth.

"Yep. That's the kind of woman you are. That's what I'm going to call you: Jane." He took the flask from me and had a long drink.

"You know I'm not actually out here completely alone," I blurted, making up the lie as I spoke. "My husband—his name is Paul—he's also hiking. He started at Kennedy Meadows. Do you know where that is? We each wanted the experience of hiking alone, so he's hiking south and I'm hiking north and we're meeting in the middle, and then we'll go the rest of the summer together."

Frank nodded and took another sip from the flask. "Well, then he's crazier than you," he said, after thinking about it for a while. "It's one thing to be a woman crazy enough to do what you're doing. Another thing to be a man letting his own wife go off and do this."

"Yeah," I said as if I agreed with him. "So anyway. We'll be reunited in a few days." I said it with such conviction that I felt convinced of it myself—that Paul that very minute was making his way toward me. That in fact we hadn't filed for divorce two months before, on a snowy day in April. That he was coming for me. Or that he would know if I didn't make it further down the trail. That my disappearance would be noted in a matter of days.

But the opposite was true. The people in my life were like the Band-Aids that had blown away in the desert wind that first day on the trail. They scattered and then they were gone. No one expected me to even so much as call when I reached my first stop. Or the second or third.

Frank leaned back in his seat and adjusted his big metal belt buckle. "There's something else I like to reward myself with after a hard day's work," he said.

"What's that?" I asked, with a tentative smile, my heart hammering in my chest. My hands on my lap felt tingly. I was acutely aware of my backpack, too far away in the bed of the truck. In a flash, I decided I'd leave it behind if I had to push the truck door open and run.

Frank reached under the seat, where the gun resided in its little black case.

He came up with a clear plastic bag. Inside, there were long thin ropes of red licorice, each bunch wound like a lasso. He held the bag out to me and asked, "You want some, Miss Jane?"

Starting a Conversation: Respond to "What Kind of Woman Are You?"

In your writer's notebook, reflect on the meaning and implications of Strayed's essay by responding to the following questions:

1. What do you think are the most significant ideas in this essay? Why do you think they are significant?

2. As a reflective document, "What Kind of Woman Are You?" not only relates a series of events from the narrator's point of view but also explains and interprets her experiences. At what specific points in the story can you see the narrator moving between — or blending—the roles of observer and interpreter? (For an overview of writers' roles, see p. 101.)

3. From evidence in the essay (such as her use of language, the events she refers to in her narrative, and her use of imagery), how do you think Strayed imagines her readers? What makes the essay accessible to a general audience?

4. Reflective essays often rely on observation and careful description to familiarize readers with a subject. How does Strayed take advantage of the five senses (sight, sound, touch, taste, and smell) to describe her experiences on and off the Pacific Crest Trail? Try to find examples of at least one of each among her descriptions. What do they contribute to the overall impression Strayed is trying to make?

5. Strayed makes ample use of reflection both as she hikes the trail and as she interacts with Frank, Carlos, and Walter. What do those moments of reflection contribute to her essay? How do you think her readers would have responded to her essay if it had included less reflection?

Humor

"Humor can be dissected, as a frog can," wrote the essayist E. B. White, "but the thing dies in the process and the innards are discouraging to any but the pure scientific mind." Humor is difficult to explain and define, because our perceptions of what's "funny" are so subjective. One thing is certain, however: comic writers are careful writers, regardless of the genre in which they are working. All comic forms require a sensitivity to the sound, rhythm, and suggestiveness of words. Moreover, humorous writing can take on serious subjects as well as light ones. If that seems contradictory, consider the comic "fools" in the works of Shakespeare, who are usually the bearers of uncomfortable and sobering truths. Similarly, the writers of reflective essays can use humor to deepen our understanding, make surprising connections, or startle us into viewing familiar things from unfamiliar angles.

In reflective essays, comic writers frequently assume the role of observers and interpreters. The subjects—and objects—of humor can be sobering, even as they make us laugh: human fallibility, the disparity between the "ideal" and the "real," the incongruities and ironies of everyday life. Sometimes they try to make sense of obviously absurd or comic situations; at other times, they reveal the subtle absurdity of day-to-day life. In both cases, they make connections and share insights with readers, almost always from an eccentric, original, and profoundly personal point of view. When they succeed, our own point of view may be altered—permanently.

David Sedaris
Keeping Up

"Keeping Up" first appeared in the *New Yorker* and was later published in *When You Are Engulfed in Flames*, David Sedaris's 2008 book of essays. Here, Sedaris considers his experience of traveling with and living with his partner, Hugh. Yet the essay ultimately highlights Sedaris's own unusual behavior, even as it touches on foreign travel, language, and dysfunctional relationships—all filtered through the writer's comic sensibility. Sedaris is the author of several books, including *Dress Your Family in Corduroy and Denim* (2004). He also contributes regularly to Public Radio International's *This American Life.*

Keeping Up
by David Sedaris

My street in Paris is named for a surgeon who taught at the nearby medical school and discovered an abnormal skin condition, a contracture that causes the fingers to bend inward, eventually turning the hand into a full-time fist. It's short, this street, no more or less attractive than anything else in the area, yet vacationing Americans are drawn here, compelled for some reason to stand under my office window and scream at each other.

For some, the arguments are about language. A wife had made certain claims regarding her abilities. "I've been listening to tapes," she said, or, perhaps, "All those romance languages are pretty much alike, so what with my Spanish we should be fine." But then people use slang, or ask unexpected questions, and things begin to fall apart: "*You're* the one who claimed to speak French." I hear this all the time, and look out my window to see a couple standing toe to toe on the sidewalk.

"Yeah," the woman will say. "At least *I* try."

"Well, try *harder*, damn it. Nobody knows what the hell you're saying."

Geographical arguments are the second most common. People notice that they've been on my street before, maybe half an hour ago, when they only thought they were tired and hungry and needed a bathroom.

"For God's sake, Philip, would it kill you to just ask somebody?"

I lie on my couch thinking, *Why don't you ask? How come Philip has to do it?* But these things are often more complicated than they seem. Maybe Philip was here twenty years ago and has been claiming to know his way around. Maybe he's one of those who refuse to hand over the map, or refuse to pull it out, lest he look like a tourist.

The desire to pass is loaded territory and can lead to the ugliest sort of argument there is. "You want to *be* French, Mary Frances, that's your problem, but instead you're just another American!" I went to the window for that one and saw a marriage disintegrate before my eyes. Poor Mary Frances in her beige beret. Back at the hotel it had probably seemed like a good idea, but now it was ruined and ridiculous, a cheap felt pancake sliding off the back of her head. She'd done the little scarf thing, too, not caring that it was summer. It could've been worse, I thought. She could have been wearing one of those striped boater's shirts, but, as it was, it was pretty bad, a costume, really.

Some vacationers raise the roof—they don't care who hears them—but Mary Francis spoke in a whisper. This, too, was seen as pretension and made her husband even angrier. "Americans," he repeated. "We don't live in France, we live in Virginia. Vienna, Virginia. Got it?"

I looked at this guy and knew for certain that if we'd met at a party he'd claim to live in Washington, D.C. Ask for a street address, and he'd look away mumbling, "Well, just outside D.C."

When fighting at home, an injured party can retreat to a separate part of the house, or step into the backyard to shoot at cans, but outside my window the options are limited to crying, sulking, or storming back to the hotel. "Oh, for Christ's sake," I hear. "Can we please just try to have a good time?" This is like ordering someone to find you attractive, and it doesn't work. I've tried it.

Most of Hugh's and my travel arguments have to do with pace. I'm a fast walker, but he has longer legs and likes to maintain a good twenty-foot lead. To the casual observer, he would appear to be running from me, darting around corners, intentionally trying to lose himself. When asked about my latest vacation, the answer is always the same. In Bangkok, in Ljubljana, in Budapest and

Bonn: What did I see? Hugh's back, just briefly, as he disappeared into a crowd. I'm convinced that before we go anywhere he calls the board of tourism and asks what style and color of coat is most popular among the locals. If they say, for example, a navy windbreaker, he'll go with that. It's uncanny the way he blends in. When we're in an Asian city, I swear he actually makes himself shorter. I don't know how, but he does. There's a store in London that sells travel guides alongside novels that take place in this or that given country. The idea is that you'll read the guide for facts and read the novel for atmosphere—a nice thought, but the only book I'll ever need is *Where's Waldo*? All my energy goes into keeping track of Hugh, and as a result I don't get to enjoy anything.

> All my energy goes into keeping track of Hugh, and as a result I don't get to enjoy anything.

The last time this happened we were in Australia, where I'd gone to attend a conference. Hugh had all the free time in the world, but mine was limited to four hours on a Saturday morning. There's a lot to do in Sydney, but first on my list was a visit to the Turanga Zoo, where I'd hoped to see a dingo. I never saw that Meryl Streep movie, and as a result the creature was a complete mystery to me. Were someone to say, "I left my window open and a dingo flew in," I would have believed it, and if he said, "Dingoes! Our pond is completely overrun with them," I would've believed that as well. Two-legged, four-legged, finned, or feathered: I simply had no idea, which was exciting, actually, a rarity in the age of twenty-four-hour nature channels. Hugh offered to draw me a picture, but, having come this far, I wanted to extend my ignorance just a little bit longer, to stand before the cage or tank and see this thing for myself. It would be a glorious occasion, and I didn't want to spoil it at the eleventh hour. I also didn't want to go alone, and this was where our problem started.

Hugh had spent most of his week swimming and had dark circles beneath his eyes, twin impressions left by his goggles. When in the ocean, he goes out for hours, passing the lifeguard buoys and moving into international waters. It looks as though he's trying to swim home, which is embarrassing when you're the one left on shore with your hosts. "He honestly does like it here," I say. "Really."

Had it been raining, he might have willingly joined me, but, as it was, Hugh had no interest in dingoes. It took a solid hour of whining to change his mind, but even then his heart wasn't in it. Anyone could see that. We took a ferry to the zoo, and while on board he stared longingly at the water and made little paddling motions with his hands. Every second wound him tighter, and when we landed I literally had to run to keep up with him. The koala bears were just a blur, as were the visitors that stood before them, posing for photos. "Can't we just . . . ," I wheezed, but Hugh was rounding the emus and couldn't hear me.

He has the most extraordinary sense of direction I've seen in a mammal. Even in Venice, where the streets were seemingly designed by ants, he left the train station, looked once at a map, and led us straight to our hotel. An hour after checking in he was giving directions to strangers, and by the time we left he was suggesting shortcuts to gondoliers. Maybe he smelled the dingoes. Maybe he'd seen their pen from the window of the plane, but, whatever his secret, he ran right to them. I caught up a minute later and bent from the waist to catch my breath. Then I covered my face, stood upright, and slowly parted my fingers, seeing first the fence and then, behind it, a shallow moat with water. I saw some trees — and a tail — and then I couldn't stand it anymore and dropped my hands.

"Why, they look just like dogs," I said. "Are you sure we're in the right place?"

Nobody answered, and I turned to find myself standing beside an embarrassed Japanese woman. "I'm sorry," I said. "I thought you were the person I brought halfway around the world. First-class."

A zoo is a good place to make a spectacle of yourself, as the people around you have creepier, more photogenic things to look at. A gorilla pleasures himself while eating a head of iceberg lettuce, and it's much more entertaining than the forty-something-year-old man who dashes around talking to himself. For me, that talk is always the same, a rehearsal of my farewell speech: ". . . because this time, buddy, it's over. I mean it." I imagine myself packing a suitcase, throwing stuff in without bothering to fold it. "If you find yourself missing me, you might want to get a dog, an old, fat one that can run to catch up and make that distant panting sound you've grown so accustomed to. Me, though, I'm finished."

I will walk out the door and never look back, never return his calls, never even open his letters. The pots and pans, all the things that we acquired together, he can have them, that's how unfeeling I will be. "Clean start," that's my motto, so what do I need with a shoe box full of photographs, or the tan-colored belt he gave me for my thirty-third birthday, back when we first met and he did not yet understand that a belt is something you get from your aunt, and not your boyfriend, I don't care who made it. After that, though, he got pretty good in the gift-giving department: a lifelike mechanical hog covered in real pigskin, a professional microscope offered at the height of my arachnology phase, and, best of all, a seventeenth-century painting of a Dutch peasant changing a dirty diaper. Those things I would keep—and why not? I'd also take the desk he gave me, and the fireplace mantle, and, just on principle, the drafting table, which he clearly bought for himself and tried to pass off as a Christmas present.

Now it seemed that I would be leaving in a van rather than on foot, but, still, I was going to do it, so help me. I pictured myself pulling away from the front of our building, and then I remembered that I don't drive. Hugh would have to do it for me, and well he should after everything he'd put me through. Another problem was where this van might go. An apartment, obviously, but how would I get it? It's all I can do to open my mouth at the post office, so how am I going to talk to a real estate agent? The language aspect has nothing to do with it, as I'm no more likely to house-hunt in New York than I am in Paris. When discussing sums over sixty dollars, I tend to sweat. Not just on my forehead, but all over. Five minutes at the bank, and my shirt is transparent. Ten minutes, and I'm stuck to my seat. I lost twelve pounds getting the last apartment, and all I had to do was sign my name. Hugh handled the rest of it.

On the bright side, I have money, though I'm not exactly sure how to get my hands on it. Bank statements arrive regularly, but I don't open anything that's not personally addressed or doesn't look like a free sample. Hugh takes care of all that, opening the icky mail and actually reading it. He knows when our insurance payments are due, when it's time to renew our visas, when the warranty on the washer is about to expire. "I don't think we need to extend this," he'll say, knowing that if the machine stops working he'll fix it himself, the way he fixes everything. But not me. If I lived alone and something broke, I'd just work around it: use a paint bucket instead of a toilet, buy an ice chest and turn the dead refrigerator into an armoire. Call a repairman? Never. Do it myself? That'll be the day.

I've been around for nearly half a century, yet still I'm afraid of everything and everyone. A child sits beside me on a plane and I make conversation, thinking how stupid I must sound. The downstairs neighbors invite me to a party and, after claiming that I have a previous engagement, I spend the entire evening confined to my bed, afraid to walk around because they might hear my footsteps. I do not know how to turn up the heat, send an e-mail, call the answering machine for my messages, or do anything even remotely creative with a chicken. Hugh takes care of all that, and when he's out of town I eat like a wild animal, the meat still pink, with hair or feathers clinging to it. So is it any wonder that he runs from me? No matter how angry I get, it always comes down to this: I'm going to leave and then what? Move in with my dad? Thirty minutes of pure rage, and when I finally spot him I realize that I've never been so happy to see anyone in my life.

"There you are," I say. And when he asks where I have been, I answer honestly and tell him I was lost.

Starting a Conversation: Respond to "Keeping Up"

In your writer's notebook, analyze how Sedaris's writing strategies contribute to his humorous reflection by responding to the following questions:

1. What roles does Sedaris take on in this piece? At what points in the reading would you describe him as an observer, an interpreter, or a problem solver?

2. In paragraph 21, Sedaris muses, "It's all I can do to open my mouth at the post office, so how am I going to talk to a real estate agent?" How does his self-deprecating tone throughout the essay affect your view of him and his reflections?

3. How does Sedaris connect his observations of traveling couples early in the reading to his own relationship with Hugh later on? What kind of context does he set up for his own personal story?

4. "Keeping Up" originally appeared in the *New Yorker*, which generally has an educated and relatively affluent audience. What aspects of this essay reflect that readership and the assumptions Sedaris makes about them?

5. Although much of what Sedaris publishes is rightly considered humor, what other genres might you use to classify this reading? What elements of his writing make the "humor" label suitable?

Photo Essays

A photo essay combines text and photographs to create a dominant impression of a subject, often suggesting the author's main idea rather than stating it outright. As a visual document, a photo essay offers a powerful and refreshing opportunity to convey thoughts and emotions that might not easily be put into words and to present complex concepts in a way that readers can grasp almost intuitively.

Many reflective photo essays visually explore subjects that have spurred debate, seem misunderstood, or are relatively unknown to readers. Others are deeply personal, highlighting images and experiences intimately connected to the writer's life. Writers might rely on published images from historical and contemporary sources or present original photographs. In either case, the pictures serve a central role in the author's reflection because they contribute to the meaning of the document. Text and image play off each other to reinforce ideas and to clarify what the writer has to say. Readers are invited to draw their own conclusions from what they see, although the author typically uses the surrounding text to nudge them in a particular direction.

James Mollison
Where Children Sleep

The photos reprinted on pages 120–131 are from *Where Children Sleep* (2010), a collection of photographer James Mollison's portraits of children from around the world and the rooms in which they sleep. When he embarked on the project, Mollison says, "I soon realized that my own experience of having a 'bedroom' simply doesn't apply to so many kids." Along with each set of photographs, he includes biographical details about each child to provide context for the portraits. Born in Kenya, Mollison grew up in England and currently lives with his family in Venice, and his work has been featured in many international publications.

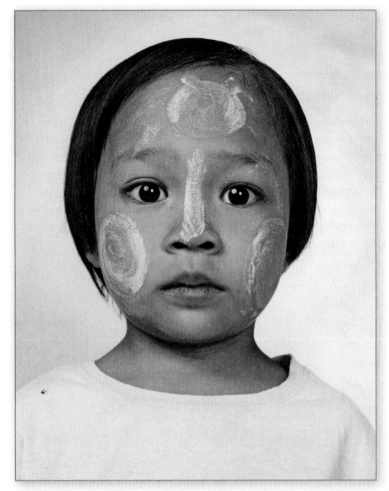

Lay Lay is four years old. The cream she has on her face is made from the bark of the thanaka tree, used to condition and protect the skin. Lay Lay lives in Mae Sot, Thailand, close to the border with Burma. When her mother died, no other members of her family came to claim her, so she was placed in an orphanage. She shares this home with twenty-one other nursery-aged children. The orphanage consists of two rooms. During the day, one room is the classroom and the other is a dining room. At night, these rooms become bedrooms. The tables are pushed to one side and mats are rolled out for the children to sleep on. Each child has one drawer in which to keep their belongings. Lay Lay does not have many belongings—just a few clothes. All that is known of her background is that she is from an ethnic group of people called the Karen, one of the persecuted minority ethnic groups which make up about forty percent of the Burmese population. Lay Lay and her mother fled from the brutal Burmese military dictatorship and arrived in Thailand as refugees.

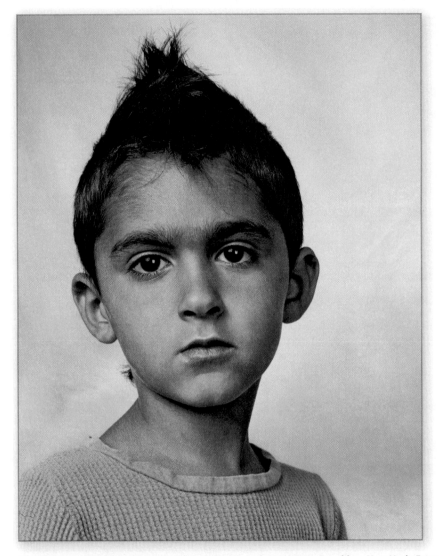

Jivan is four years old. He lives with his parents in a skyscraper in Brooklyn, New York. From his bedroom window, he can see across the East River to New York's Manhattan Island and the Williamsburg Suspension Bridge, which connects it to Brooklyn. Jivan has his own bedroom with an en-suite bathroom and a toy cupboard. The room was designed by Jivan's mother, who is an interior designer. His father is a DJ and music producer. Jivan's school is only a ten minute walk away. To gain a place at his school, Jivan had to take a test to prove that he can mix socially with other children. He found this quite stressful as he is a very shy boy. His parents were also interviewed before he was accepted by the school. Jivan's favorite foods are steak and chocolate. He would like to be a fireman when he grows up.

Kaya is four years old. She lives with her parents in a small apartment in Tokyo, Japan. Most apartments in Japan are small because land is very expensive to buy and there is such a large population to accommodate. Kaya's bedroom is every little girl's dream. It is lined from floor to ceiling with clothes and dolls. Kaya's mother makes all Kaya's dresses—up to three a month, usually. Now Kaya has thirty dresses and coats, thirty pairs of shoes, sandals and boots, and numerous wigs. (The pigtails in this picture are made from hairpieces.) Her friends love to come around to try on her clothes. When she goes to school, however, she has to wear a school uniform. Her favorite foods are meat, potatoes, strawberries, and peaches. She wants to be a cartoonist when she grows up, drawing Japanese anime cartoons.

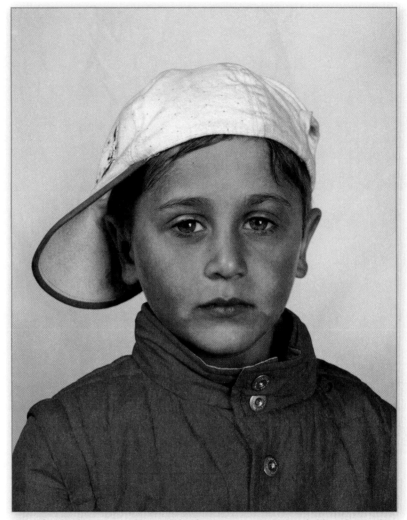

Home for this four-year-old boy and his family is a mattress in a field on the outskirts of Rome, Italy. The family came from Romania by bus, after begging on the streets for enough money to pay for their tickets (€100 per adult and €80 per child). When they first arrived in Rome, they camped in a tent, but the police threw them off the site because they were trespassing on private land and did not have the correct documents. Now the family sleeps together on the mattress in the open. When it rains, they hastily erect a tent and use umbrellas for shelter, hoping they will not be spotted by the police. They left Romania without identity documents or work papers and so are unable to obtain legal employment. This boy sits by the curbside while his parents clean car windshields at traffic lights, to earn thirty to fifty cents a time. No one from the boy's family has ever been to school. His parents cannot read or write.

Indira lives with her parents, brother and sister near Kathmandu in Nepal. Her house has only one room, with one bed and one mattress. At bedtime, the children share the mattress on the floor. Indira is seven years old and has worked at the local granite quarry since she was three. The family is very poor so everyone has to work. There are 150 other children working at the quarry, some of whom will lose their sight because they do not have goggles to protect their eyes from stone splinters. Indira works five or six hours a day and then helps her mother with household chores such as cleaning and cooking. Her favorite food is noodles. She also attends school, which is a thirty minute walk away. She does not mind working at the quarry but would prefer to be playing. She would like to be a Nepalese dancer when she grows up.

Li is ten years old and lives in an apartment block in Beijing, China, with her parents. She is an only child—as a result of the Chinese government's "one child per family" policy, introduced to control population growth. Families with more than one child are usually penalized. Li goes to a school nearby, where she enjoys learning math, singing, and music. She is a perfectionist and will spend up to three hours each night completing her homework to the highest standard. She also attends ballet classes twice a week after school. Three times during her school life, she will have to attend a compulsory army summer camp organized by the People's Liberation Army. In preparation for this she has to attend army training. Li does not want to be in the army when she grows up. She wants to be a policewoman so that she can protect people.

**Starting a
Conversation:
Respond to
"Where
Children
Sleep"**

In your writer's notebook, reflect on the ideas presented in Mollison's photo essay by responding to the following questions:

1. A reflective photo essay such as this one might not have a strictly defined thesis statement. But how would you describe the main idea of Mollison's work? What is the dominant impression created by his mix of words and pictures?

2. While he acknowledges the issues of poverty and wealth that inform his photos, Mollison says, "There is no agenda to the book other than my own journey and curiosity, and wanting to share in pictures and words the stories that I found interesting, or that moved me." In what ways does this statement fit with the purpose of a reflective document? What changes do you think Mollison would have made to his approach if he had, in fact, been creating an analytical or argumentative photo essay?

3. As you look at the photographs and their accompanying text, consider this statement from Mollison: "The book is written and presented for an audience of 9–13 year olds . . . intended to interest and engage children in the details of the lives of other children around the world, and the social issues affecting them, while also being a serious photographic essay for an adult audience." How successfully do you think Mollison's work reaches each of those audiences? What do you see in Mollison's writing style and in the composition of his photographs that would appeal to adults and to older children? What do you think members of each audience — 9–13 year olds, older teens, and adults — would take away from his work?

4. Why do you suppose that Mollison chose to use color images? Would black-and-white photographs have had as much impact, more impact, or less impact? Why do you think so?

5. Consider how Mollison's photographs might have been different if he had chosen to focus on one country or region of the world. How would his audience and their expectations of his work have changed, and how would they have remained the same?

How Can I Write a Reflective Essay?

For some writers, the greatest challenge in writing a reflective essay is getting past the idea that no one would be interested in reading their reflections on a subject. In fact, readers show a great deal of interest in reflective writing. They buy memoirs and autobiographies, visit blogs, and read opinion columns. They read articles and essays in which writers share their thoughts about their experiences and ideas. Some readers even try to pick the locks on their sisters' diaries.

Reflective writing is popular not only among readers but also among writers. Reflective essays allow you to share your insights with instructors and classmates, people who are likely to have an interest in your perspective on a subject.

Writing a reflective essay involves choosing and reflecting on a subject, preparing a draft, and reviewing and improving what you've written. As you work on your essay, you'll follow the work of Caitlin Guariglia, an Italian American student who wrote a reflective essay about a family trip to Italy.

Find a Conversation and Listen In

Reflective essays allow you to share your thoughts about a subject with readers who might have a common interest in it. You might reflect on a personal experience, an idea you've encountered in a book or a blog, a photograph or other physical object that holds special meaning for you, a person you've met or read about, a troubling conversation with a friend, or a recent event. In fact, you can reflect on almost anything. To get started on your reflective essay, spend some time thinking about your purpose, your readers, and the context in which your writing will be read (see p. 102). Then generate some ideas about possible subjects for your reflection, choose one that seems promising, and learn more about it by observing it closely or discussing it with others.

In Process

A Reflective Essay about a Family Vacation

Caitlin Guariglia wrote a reflective essay for her introductory composition course. Caitlin based her reflection on a family trip to Italy, using her observations of the people she met in Rome to consider how cultural influences affect her Italian American family's behavior. Follow her efforts to write the essay as you read the In Process boxes throughout this chapter.

EXPLORE YOUR EXPERIENCES

Brainstorming (see p. 32) provides a good way to generate ideas for the subject of a reflective essay. Start by asking questions about your past or recent experiences, such as the following:

- Why is my favorite childhood memory so special to me?

- Did I learn anything about myself this weekend?

- What surprised me in my history class this week?

- What story that is currently in the news annoys me the most?

- What is the last thing that made me laugh?

- What do I worry about most?

- What in my life do I wish had gone differently?

- What am I most proud of, and why?

Use your imagination to come up with questions about your personal, academic, and professional experiences. Quickly jot down answers to your questions. Then review your answers to identify a subject that will meet your purpose, interest your readers, and be suitable for the context, requirements, and limitations of your writing assignment. If you're still not sure you've found the right inspiration for a topic, check the writing project ideas at the end of this chapter for additional suggestions (p. 156).

ASK QUESTIONS ABOUT PROMISING SUBJECTS

You can begin to focus on a subject by asking questions about it (see p. 38). If you were considering writing a reflective essay about online communities such as Facebook or Twitter, for example, you might use the following strategies to identify interesting aspects of the subject.

- **Ask *why, why not, when, where,* and *who.*** You might ask why so many parents react negatively to social-networking sites such as Facebook, or you might ask who is likely to cause difficulties for members of online communities.

- **Ask how your subject functions as a whole.** You might ask how Web sites such as Facebook are changing how people communicate, whether they represent a distinctly different kind of community, or why they're so popular with a particular age group.

- **Ask about parts of a whole.** You might ask which aspects of online communities are more attractive than others or whether one subgroup in an online community is likely to behave differently than another subgroup.

- **Ask questions about degree and extent.** You can ask about the degree to which something affects something else or about the extent of a problem. For instance, you might ask how friendships formed at a school direct the formation of online communities or whether the dangers associated with teenage use of social-networking sites are as widespread as reported.

CONDUCT AN OBSERVATION

If you've chosen a subject that lends itself to observation, you might find it useful to conduct one. Observing a subject firsthand can provide you with valuable insights that simply aren't possible when you're learning about the subject secondhand — for example, through discussion or through reading a book, magazine, or Web page. In addition, conducting an observation can increase your credibility as a writer. A reflective essay usually carries more weight if the writer has taken the time to observe the subject personally.

Although some observations can involve a significant amount of time and effort, an observation need not be complicated to be useful. Effective observations usually involve the following activities.

Decide whether to conduct an observation. Before you take the time to conduct an observation, ask yourself what kind of results you expect to gain, what those results will contribute to your writing project, and whether you could obtain comparable support for your ideas more effectively and efficiently in another way.

Want to know more about field research? See Chapter 12.

Some subjects are more suited for observation than others. For example, a reflective essay about how parents behave during soccer games would lend itself well to

Working Together: Try It Out Loud

Before you start writing a reflective essay, try having a conversation with your classmates about a common experience. Form small groups, and list the subjects each of you is considering writing about. Choose one that most people in the group can relate to (such as an embarrassing moment, a fight with a friend, or the first day of class). Take turns sharing your memories about the experience while the other members of the group listen, respond, and ask questions. Your purpose is to connect with the other members of your group, so try to present an honest, personal view of the event.

When you are finished, take a few minutes to reflect on the exercise. What did you learn about your audience? Did you have to adapt what you said based on their interest level or on those parts of your story they didn't understand? What did you discover about what you have in common and what you do not?

observation. On the other hand, a writer would be more likely to turn to interviews (see Chapter 6) or published sources for an essay on community resistance to new federal education reforms.

Decide what you should observe and how often to observe it. Your decision will depend largely on the role your observations will play in your essay. If you want to learn more about a subject but don't plan to include what you observe as part of your reflection, a fairly limited observation should suffice. The same holds true if you hope to gather a few details but will base your reflection on your own experience. However, if your subject is complex, or if you expect to use details from what you observe throughout your essay, you might need to conduct multiple observations, possibly in more than one setting.

Decide what to look for. The biggest limitation of observation is that you can see only one thing at a time. Experienced observers focus on activities that are most relevant to their writing projects. As a result, their observations are somewhat selective. Spreading yourself too thin will result in fairly "thin" results. Then again, narrowing in too quickly can cause you to miss important aspects of a setting or an event. Your reasons for conducting an observation and what you hope to gain from it are probably your best guide to what to focus on.

Find out whether you need permission to observe. Seeking permission to observe an individual or a group can be complicated. People have expectations about privacy even in public settings, but people can (and often do) change their behavior when they know they are being watched. As you consider whether to ask for permission, imagine yourself in the position of someone who is being observed. If you are still uncertain, ask your instructor for advice.

Conduct your observation. To conduct your observation, follow these steps:

1. Arrive early.

2. Review your planning notes.

3. If appropriate, introduce yourself.

4. If you are using recording equipment, set it up. Make sure you have a notepad and pens or pencils nearby.

5. Take notes, even if you are using recording equipment.

6. If you have asked for permission to observe, leave your contact information and send a thank-you note.

Reflect on Your Subject

Perhaps you've had the opportunity to listen to musicians jamming during a concert, or perhaps you're a musician yourself. If so, you know about the ebb and flow of the music, how one line of melody plays off another, how the music circles and

In Process

Conducting an Observation

Caitlin Guariglia's reflective essay was based on a series of informal observations of strangers in Rome and family members at home. She recorded her observations in a journal.

> 5-24
>
> Saw the funniest thing today — Dad and I were waiting for Mom to come out of a shop by Piazza di Spagna, so we got to stand on a side street for a while and watch people go by. There was water in the street by this one restaurant, and the guy who owned the place was pacing around the sidewalk. Practically everyone walking by felt like they had to stop and put in their two cents about the problem! And they would all wind up gesturing and pointing. Dad and I just kept trying not to laugh. Dad said it was the same way where he grew up — if something went wrong, everyone tried to help, even though half the time they just ended up getting in the way.

▲ Caitlin reviewed her notes as she planned and then began to draft her essay.

builds. Reflection is similar to this process. As you reflect on a subject, your thinking moves from one aspect to another, flowing smoothly forward at some times and circling back at others. Reflection can involve seeking understanding, making connections, and exploring contrasts. In the same way that a jam session offers surprises not only to listeners but also to the musicians, reflection can lead you in unexpected directions. The key to reflecting productively is a willingness to be open to those directions.

Reflection is most effective when you record your thoughts. Writing them down as notes in a writer's notebook or as entries in a journal allows you to keep track of your thinking. As you make decisions about your writing project, you can turn to your notes to review your reflections.

Reflection begins with viewing your subject from a particular perspective. It also involves collecting details and finding significance. To prepare to reflect, place yourself in a relaxing situation that will allow you to think. Take a walk, ride a bike, go for a run, enjoy a good meal, listen to music, lie down — do whatever you think will free you from distractions.

EXAMINE YOUR SUBJECT

Begin to reflect on your subject by viewing it through a particular lens, such as how it compares to something else, what caused it or what effects it might have, or what challenges and difficulties you associate with it. Although some perspectives are likely to be better suited to your subject than others, try to look at your subject from more than one angle.

Explore processes. Thinking of something as a process can help you understand how it works as well as how it contributes to the context in which it takes place. For example, instead of reflecting on text-messaging as a social phenomenon, reflect on the processes involved in text-messaging. Ask how it works, what steps are involved in composing and sending a message, and how people understand and respond to messages.

Consider implications. Considering the implications of a subject can help you understand its impact and importance. You can ask questions such as what is likely to happen, what if such-and-such happens, what will happen when, and so on. As you reflect on implications, stay grounded: don't get so carried away by speculation that you lose track of your reason for reflecting.

Examine similarities and differences. Use comparison and contrast to find points of connection for your subject. You might examine, for example, the similarities and differences between new communication technologies, such as e-mail and text-messaging, and older means of staying in touch, such as letter writing and passing notes in class. Or you might compare and contrast the ways in which people get to know one another, such as hanging out together, joining organizations, and dating.

Trace causes and effects. Thinking about causes and effects can help you better understand a subject. For example, you might reflect on the origins of complaints — some dating back to the ancient Greeks — that the latest generation of young people is not only impolite and uncultured but also likely to undo the accomplishments of previous generations. You might also reflect on the effects that this attitude has on relationships between the old and the young.

Consider value. Reflection often involves considering factors such as strengths and weaknesses, costs and benefits, and limitations and opportunities. For example, you might reflect on the relative strengths and weaknesses of a candidate for political office. Or you might weigh the costs and benefits of a proposed law to make the Internet safer for children. Similarly, you might consider the limitations and opportunities associated with proposals to increase funding for higher education.

Identify challenges and difficulties. Getting to the heart of an issue or idea often involves determining how it challenges your assumptions or values or identifying the nature of the difficulties it poses for you. For example, ask yourself why an idea bothers you, or ask why it might bother someone else.

Reflect on your experiences. As you reflect on your subject, search for connections to your own life. Ask whether your personal experiences would lead you to act in a particular way. Ask how they are likely to influence your reactions and attitudes. Ask whether you've found yourself in situations that are relevant to your subject.

COLLECT DETAILS

People are fond of saying, "It's all in the details." Although this is true for nearly all types of writing, it's especially true for reflective essays. Without details, even the best essay can fall flat. You might get a laugh out of the following story, for example, but few people will find it truly satisfying:

> Once upon a time, they all lived happily ever after.

To collect details for a reflective essay, use the following strategies.

Describe your subject. If you can, use observation to collect details about your subject (see p. 102). If you have firsthand experience with the subject, freewrite or brainstorm about it to refresh your memory: write down what you saw and heard, what you felt, even what you smelled. Provide as much detail as possible.

Compare your subject with something else. Many subjects are best understood in relation to others. Darkness, for example, is difficult to understand without comparing it to light. Success is best understood in the context of its alternatives. And for those who live in colder climates, spring is all the more welcome because it follows winter. To find useful points of comparison, create a two-column log: place your subject at the top of one column and a contrasting subject at the top of the other, and then record your reflections on the similarities and differences between the two subjects in each column. Use the results to provide details for your essay.

Discuss your ideas. If you talk about your subject with other people, you might be able to use their comments to add detail to your essay. You might want to set up a formal interview with someone who is an expert on the subject or with someone who has been affected by it (see Chapter 6), but you can also simply bring up your subject in casual conversations to learn what others think. If they tell a story about their experiences with your subject, ask whether you might add their anecdote to your reflection. Similarly, if you hear an interesting turn of phrase or a startling statement related to your subject, consider quoting it. (See Chapter 19 to learn more about integrating quotations into an essay.)

Learn more about your subject. As you gain a better idea of how you'll focus your essay, look for opportunities to add to your understanding of the subject. Browse newspapers and magazines in your library's periodical room to pick up bits of information that will add depth to your essay, or see what's been written recently about your subject on news sites and in blogs (see Chapter 12). As you read about your subject, take note of interesting details that might grab your readers' attention.

FIND SIGNIFICANCE

Every good story has a point. Every good joke has a punch line. Every good reflective essay leaves its readers with something to think about. As you reflect on your subject, consider why it's important to you, and think about how you can make it important for your readers. Then ask whether they'll care about what you've decided to share with them. The main idea of your reflective essay should hold some significance for your readers. Ideally, after reading your essay, they'll continue to think about what you've written.

By now, you'll have reflected a great deal on your subject, and you'll be in a good position to identify the most significant aspects of what you've learned. To find significance, freewrite or brainstorm about your subject for ten or fifteen minutes. Ask yourself what your readers will need or want to know about it. Ask what will spark their imaginations. Ask what will stir their emotions. Then ask whether the ideas you've come up with will help you accomplish your goals as a writer.

In Process

Making Comparisons

Caitlin Guariglia used comparison to reflect on her experiences with strangers in Rome and with her family. She used a two-column table to make direct comparisons.

Strangers in Rome	Family in America
get involved in other people's business if they feel like they know how to do it better and can help	get involved in your business, whether you like it or not!
cool, confident, witty, LOUD	not always so cool, but definitely loud, full of themselves, and usually really funny
passionate about their city, its history, and its food	love NY, but not all are passionate about it, definitely opinionated about Italian food
beautiful Italian accents	only speak a little Italian, NY accents
really big on family, and like to make you feel like part of theirs	exactly the same

▲ Caitlin used her notes to shape a point in her final essay:

> Our ancestors may have brought the food, the expressions, and the attitudes with them to the United States a few generations ago, but it is safe to say that over the years we have lost some of the style and the musical language that Italians seem to possess from birth.

Prepare a Draft

As you prepare to draft your reflective essay, you'll think about how to convey your main idea, how to shape your reflection, which details to include, and what point of view to take. You'll also make decisions about how to design and craft your essay. You can read about other strategies related to drafting academic essays, such as writing strong paragraphs and integrating information from sources, in Part Four.

CONVEY YOUR MAIN IDEA

Reflective essays, like other kinds of academic essays, should have a point. Before you begin writing, try to express your main idea in the form of a tentative thesis statement, a single sentence that articulates the most significant aspect of your reflections on your subject. By framing your main idea in a particular way, you can focus your efforts and help your readers see why your reflection should matter to them.

Consider the differences among the following tentative thesis statements about pursuing a career as a writer:

> Without commitment and discipline, pursuing a career as a writer would be a waste of time.

> Without a genuine love of words and a desire to share your ideas with others, pursuing a career as a writer would be a waste of time.

> The paths that lead to a career in writing are as varied as the writers who follow them.

Each of these statements would lead to significantly different reflective essays. The first frames becoming a writer as a test of character. It implies that writers can't succeed unless they are prepared to dedicate themselves to the hard work of writing. The second thesis statement shifts the focus from discipline and commitment to the writer's relationship with words and readers. It paints a warmer, less intimidating picture of what it takes to become a writer. The third thesis statement shifts the focus completely away from the qualities shared by successful writers, suggesting instead that each writer has different reasons for pursuing a career in writing. You can read more about developing a thesis statement in Chapter 14.

Need help with main ideas? See Chapter 14.

Even though having a main idea is necessary, the final draft of a reflective essay doesn't always include a formal thesis statement. Depending on the nature of the reflection, writers sometimes choose to use their observations to create a dominant impression of a subject. That is, they tell a story or build up details to show — rather than state outright — why the subject is significant.

TELL A STORY

Almost every type of writing — at least, writing that's interesting — tells a story. An autobiography tells readers about events in the writer's life. An opinion column uses an anecdote — a brief description of an event or experience — to personalize an abstract issue. An article on ESPN.com describes what happened in a game — and speculates about what it means for the playoffs. In fact, some people have said that everything we do can be understood as a story.

If the subject of your reflection is an event in your past, shaping your essay as a story (that is, a chronological narrative with a beginning, a middle, and an end) is a natural way to proceed. But other kinds of subjects also lend themselves to storytelling. For example, because writers of reflective essays often share their thinking about a subject by explaining how they arrived at their conclusions, they essentially tell a story about their reflections.

As you draft, think about what kind of story you want to share. Will it be a tale of triumph against all odds? Will it lead to a surprising discovery? Will it have a happy ending? Will it be a tragedy? A comedy? A farce?

To create a story, consider the following elements:

- **Setting.** Where does your story take place? What are the characteristics of the setting? How does the setting affect the story?

- **Character.** Who is involved in your story? What motivates them? What do they want to accomplish? What are their hopes and dreams?

- **Plot.** What happens in your story? In what order do the events take place?

- **Conflict.** Do the characters in your story disagree about something? What do they disagree about? Why do they disagree?

- **Climax.** What is the defining event in the story? What does the story lead the reader toward?

- **Resolution.** How is the conflict resolved in your story?

- **Point of view.** Who is telling this story? How is it told?

Even if you don't present your reflection as a traditional story, the elements of storytelling can help you shape your observations in a more concrete manner. For example, by asking who is involved in your subject and how they have dealt with conflicts, you can decide whether you should focus on a character's actions or on the reasons leading to a conflict. By asking about the climax of your story, you can decide whether to focus your reflection on a single event or on the results of that event.

GO INTO DETAIL

Experienced writers are familiar with the advice "Show. Don't tell." This advice, more often applied to creative writing than to academic writing, is founded on the belief that characters' words and actions should be used to convey a story. Simply explaining what happened is far less satisfying for readers than viewing it through a series of unfolding events.

In the sense that a reflective essay conveys the story of your thinking about a subject, showing how you came to your main idea can be preferable to telling readers what it is. As you reflect, consider sharing what you've seen and heard about your subject that places others — the characters in your story — at the center of your essay. Use details to convey their actions. Use dialogue to convey their words.

Each point you present in your essay, each event you describe, and each observation you make should be illustrated with details. As you reflected on your subject, you collected details that helped you understand the subject. Now, return to those details, and decide which ones to include in your essay. You can go over your notes, reread your brainstorming and freewriting, and review the events and experiences associated with your subject. As you do so, select those details that will best help your readers understand your subject and grasp its significance, and add new ones as they occur to you.

CHOOSE YOUR POINT OF VIEW

In academic writing, point of view refers to the perspective the writer takes. Sometimes a writer will choose to reflect on a subject as a *detached observer*. Rather than participating in the action, the writer stands outside it, making observations or showing what happened without becoming a part of the story. This detached point of view is characterized by the use of third-person pronouns (*he, she, they*) and a seemingly objective relationship with the subject. James Mollison, for example, adopts a detached point of view for his photo essay "Where Children Sleep" (p. 119). By distancing himself from the lives of the children he has photographed, Mollison enables readers to consider his observations in a broader context.

At other times, a writer will reflect on a subject as a *participant observer*, someone who is centrally involved in the story being told. In this case, the writer shares experiences and observations from a personal perspective. This participatory point of view is characterized by the use of first-person pronouns (*I, me, we*) and a more personally involved relationship with the subject. By adopting this perspective, writers become key players in their own stories and can connect with their readers on a more intimate level. Consider, for example, "What Kind of Woman Are You?" (p. 104), in which Cheryl Strayed uses the first-person point of view to personalize her reflections on the Pacific Crest Trail and the people she encounters while hiking it.

Your decision about point of view will depend on the subject of your reflection, your relationship to the subject, and the amount of information you want to reveal about yourself. If you are reflecting on a subject with which you have little or no personal experience, or if you want to downplay your involvement, it's usually more effective to adopt the role of a detached observer. If, on the other hand, you want to directly convey your experiences with and perceptions of an event, or if you want to make an abstract subject more personal for readers, writing as a participant observer is often the better choice.

CONSIDER GENRE AND DESIGN

Reflective essays, like other academic essays, use design elements to make it easier for instructors and classmates to read and comment on drafts. As you draft your essay, consider how decisions about fonts, line-spacing, margins, and illustrations will help your readers respond to your ideas.

- **Choose a readable font.** If you've ever read a document formatted with a decorative font, such as **MAVERICK** or Felt Tip Woman, you know how difficult it can be to read. Now imagine that you're an instructor reading twenty-five, fifty, or even a hundred essays over a weekend. Think about how you would feel if you found yet another essay printed in a decorative script, in a bright color, in CAPITAL LETTERS, or in an *italic* face. It's generally best to choose a simple font that's easy to read, such as Times New Roman or Helvetica.

- **Provide generous margins and double-spacing.** If you are asked to submit your essay on paper, your instructor will usually make comments in the margins. Leave plenty of room for handwritten comments. Your margins should be at least one inch wide, and lines should be double-spaced.

- **Consider using illustrations.** Depending on your subject, your reflective essay might benefit from illustrations. Photographs and other images can set a mood and help your readers understand the subject more completely. If you do decide to include illustrations, be sure that they contribute to your reflection; purely decorative images are usually more distracting than helpful.

You can learn more about these and other elements of document design in Chapter 16.

FRAME YOUR REFLECTIONS

Once you've made decisions about the content and design of your essay, consider how you'll frame it, or direct your readers' attention to particular aspects of your reflections rather than to others. Framing your reflections allows you to influence your readers' understanding of, and attitudes toward, what's most important to you.

Organization. The organization of a reflective essay is typically determined by the nature of the subject. Most stories, for instance, are arranged chronologically so that readers can easily follow the sequence of events. Reflections on a place or an object, on the other hand, might be arranged spatially, tracing the way a reader's eyes would take in the subject in person: top to bottom, left to right, near to far, and so on. If your reflections consider similarities and differences between your subject and something else, ordering your ideas by points of comparison and contrast might be most effective. (For more on these and other organizing patterns, see Chapter 15.)

Introduction and conclusion. Your introduction and conclusion provide the framework within which your readers will understand and interpret your reflections, so spend some time experimenting with them until they feel right. (Because these elements of an essay often prove the most challenging to draft, you might want to put them off until you finish the rest of the essay.) Several strategies are available for writing introductions and conclusions, but a few are particularly useful for reflective essays. For instance, you might open with a surprising statement or an anecdote — a brief, pointed story — that sets the stage for your main idea. As you close your essay, consider circling back to a detail from the beginning or reiterating the significance of your reflections. (For advice on drafting introductions and conclusions, see Chapter 16.)

Review and Improve Your Draft

Completing your first draft is a major milestone. However, additional consideration of your subject and a careful review of your draft will no doubt provide numerous opportunities to improve your essay. As you review your draft, pay particular attention to how you've presented and framed your main idea, the order in which you've presented your reflections, any use of dialogue, and your inclusion of details that show rather than tell.

ENSURE THAT YOUR MAIN IDEA IS CLEAR

Readers should be able to identify the point of your essay, even if you haven't provided a thesis statement. As you review your essay, ask whether your reflections support the tentative thesis statement you drafted before writing (see p. 142), and ask if everything you wrote helps your readers understand your subject in the way you intended. You might find that you need to revise your thesis statement to reflect your draft, or that you need to adapt your draft to better support your main idea.

EXAMINE THE PRESENTATION OF YOUR OBSERVATIONS

Reflective essays frequently rely on narrative, or storytelling. Review your draft to find out whether the order in which you've told your story makes sense and whether the details you have included will lead readers to be sympathetic to your observations. Upon review, you might decide that you should change the order, add important ideas or observations, or remove details that seem unnecessary or irrelevant.

REVIEW DIALOGUE

Many reflective essays use dialogue — spoken exchanges between key figures in a story — to help readers better understand a subject. Dialogue can underscore the significance of your subject and help readers gain insight into how people are affected by or react to the subject. Dialogue can also add interest to a story or allow others to make a point that you might not want to state outright. If you've included

In Process

Adding Dialogue

As she reviewed her first draft, Caitlin worried that a particularly important passage felt less interesting than it should:

> Anytime our group slowed down or started to get tired, Marco would yell to us to keep going, and suddenly we were revived. He knew everything about Rome, and everywhere we went, he knew someone. He loved his city and loved sharing it with all of us.

By adding dialogue, she created a better sense of Marco's personality and helped readers imagine themselves on a tour with him:

> Anytime our group slowed down or started to get tired, Marco would yell, "Andiamo! (Let's go!)," and suddenly we were revived. He knew everything about Rome, and everywhere we went, he knew someone. All day he was calling out to friends, "Ciao bella!" or "Come stai?" He loved his city and loved sharing it with all of us.

dialogue, ask whether you've used it effectively. For example, have you relied too heavily on other people's words? Are the right people engaged in dialogue? Does what they say make sense in the context of your story? If you haven't used dialogue, ask yourself where you might include it to liven up your essay or engage readers with your subject.

SHOW, DON'T TELL

As you review your draft, think about how you can bring your observations to life by placing the people and events involved with your subject at the center of your essay. Have you done more than simply summarize your points? Will adding details help your readers better understand and connect to your subject? Can you make your points more effectively by quoting dialogue among the characters in your story? Can you illustrate key ideas by showing characters in action?

After reviewing your essay, ask yourself how you might polish and edit it so that your readers will find it easy to read (see Chapter 20).

Finally, if you've drawn on ideas, information, or examples from written works such as essays or stories or cultural productions such as movies or concerts, make sure that you've documented those sources in the body of your essay and in a works cited or references list.

Do you know why you should document sources? See Chapter 13.

For guidelines on the MLA and APA documentation systems, see Chapters 21 and 22.

Peer Review: Improve Your Reflective Essay

One of the biggest challenges writers face is reading a draft of their own work as a reader rather than as the writer. Because you know what you're trying to say, you find it easy to understand your draft. To determine how you should revise your draft, ask a friend or classmate to read your essay and to consider how well you've adopted the role of observer (see p. 102).

Purpose	1. Did you understand the significance of my observations? Do I need to state my main idea more directly or say anything more to clarify what's important about my subject?
	2. Does my subject seem relevant to you personally? Why or why not? Is there anything I can do to forge a better connection with readers?
	3. How did you respond to my reflections and observations? Do you accept what I had to say? Have I left you with something to think about?
Readers	4. Did the story of my experiences and insights make sense to you? Do you want to know anything else about them?
	5. Does my personality come through in my writing? Should I put more (or less) of myself into the essay?
	6. Have I offered you a fresh or unusual perspective on my subject?
Sources	7. Is it clear which experiences and observations are my own and which I brought in from other sources?
	8. If I have referred to any published works or recent events, have I cited my source(s) appropriately?
	9. How well does my use of details show, rather than tell, the significance of my subject? Should I add or remove any details?
	10. Have I used dialogue effectively? Is there too little or too much?
Context	11. Did you understand any references I made to cultural, political, or social contexts? Do I need to explain anything more directly?
	12. Is the physical appearance of my essay appropriate? Did you find the font easy to read? Did you have enough room to write down comments? Did I use illustrations effectively?

For each of the points listed above, ask your reviewers to offer concrete suggestions for improving your essay. You might want to ask them to adopt the role of an editor — someone who is working with you to improve your draft. You can read more about peer review in Chapter 4.

✱ Student Essay

Caitlin Guariglia, "Mi Famiglia"

The following reflective essay was written by featured writer Caitlin Guariglia.

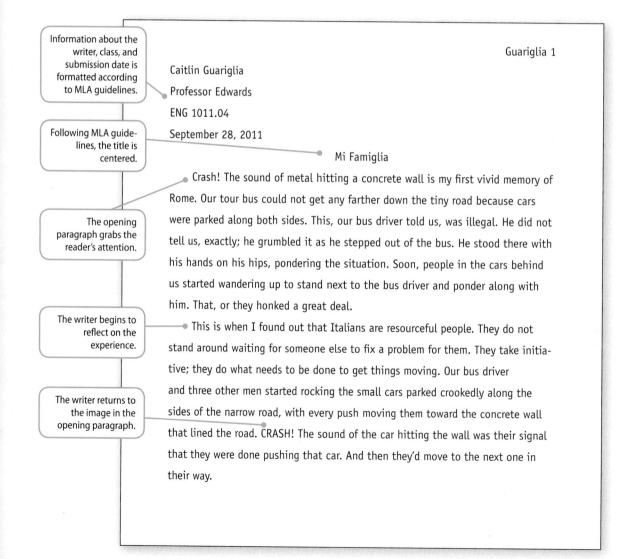

Information about the writer, class, and submission date is formatted according to MLA guidelines.

Following MLA guidelines, the title is centered.

The opening paragraph grabs the reader's attention.

The writer begins to reflect on the experience.

The writer returns to the image in the opening paragraph.

Guariglia 1

Caitlin Guariglia

Professor Edwards

ENG 1011.04

September 28, 2011

Mi Famiglia

Crash! The sound of metal hitting a concrete wall is my first vivid memory of Rome. Our tour bus could not get any farther down the tiny road because cars were parked along both sides. This, our bus driver told us, was illegal. He did not tell us, exactly; he grumbled it as he stepped out of the bus. He stood there with his hands on his hips, pondering the situation. Soon, people in the cars behind us started wandering up to stand next to the bus driver and ponder along with him. That, or they honked a great deal.

This is when I found out that Italians are resourceful people. They do not stand around waiting for someone else to fix a problem for them. They take initiative; they do what needs to be done to get things moving. Our bus driver and three other men started rocking the small cars parked crookedly along the sides of the narrow road, with every push moving them toward the concrete wall that lined the road. CRASH! The sound of the car hitting the wall was their signal that they were done pushing that car. And then they'd move to the next one in their way.

Guariglia 2

Angry people on Vespas sped by, making various hand gestures; some I knew and understood, but others I did not. The bus driver boarded the bus, his sleeves rolled up, sweat pouring down his face, and told us that these kind people on their Vespas were wishing us good luck. He moved the bus up about ten feet before he encountered another car he could not pass. The process repeated itself. CRASH! Another car moved. Soon a police officer walked up, talked to the bus driver, looked around, shrugged, and helped them shove the cars into the wall. People who had parked there began to come back and move their cars before it was done for them. When we finally made it the hundred feet down the rest of the road, everyone on our tour bus cheered. Our bus driver smiled sheepishly, as if to say, "Eh, it was nothing."

> Details help the reader visualize the writer's experience.

This was the sort of thing I hoped to see in Italy. I wanted to see how Italians live. My dad's side of the family is Italian, so I wanted to understand more about our heritage and our family traits, like why my family is so loud and concerned with everyone else's business. Was it a cultural thing? Or was it a family thing? Was it just something about the region of Italy where my family is from? I smiled when I read Elizabeth Gilbert's memoir *Eat, Pray, Love*. Gilbert writes, "The Neapolitan women in particular are such a gang of tough-voiced, loud-mouthed, generous, nosy dames, all bossy and annoyed and right up in your face just trying to friggin' help you for chrissake, you dope — *why they gotta do everything around here?*" (78). This sounds exactly like almost all of my great-aunts, and I was curious to find out if the women in Rome would have the same attitude.

> The writer explains what she hoped to gain from traveling to Italy.

> A quotation from another writer places the writer's questions about her heritage in a larger context.

And the obsession with eating! My grandmother feeds us constantly. My dad and I always laugh at that scene in *Goodfellas* where the mobsters show up at two in the morning after killing someone, and one mobster's mother whips up a full pasta meal for them. We know that my grandmother would do the same thing: "Are you hungry? Here, sit, eat!" Grandma holds interventions over pasta. If she is unhappy with something someone in the family is doing, she invites everyone over for pasta, and we hash it out together. Was this something all Italians do?

> The page number for the quotation is provided, following MLA guidelines.

Guariglia 3

The writer connects questions about her heritage to her trip to Italy.

Or was my idea of a typical Italian person all wrong? Our time in Rome clarified some of these questions for me.

When we finally got to our hotel, we met our tour guide Maresa. This small, stout, sweet Italian woman said we could call her Mama. Mama looked up our reservation, glanced at it, and said our last name. Normally, that would be nothing to celebrate. But she said our last name perfectly. Actually, not just perfectly, she said it *beautifully*. After listening to Americans butcher my difficult Italian last name my entire life, hearing this Italian woman say it was music to my ears. My grandfather would have given her a standing ovation.

The writer uses text formatting (italics) to emphasize her point.

A transition indicates that time has passed.

The next morning we met our tour guide Marco. A large, sturdy man who looked like my grandmother cooked for him, he was confident and full of life. He took us to the main historical sites that day: the Vatican, the Colosseum, the Pantheon, the Roman Forum. While all of that was spectacular, I enjoyed listening to Marco more than anything we saw. He was a true Roman, big, proud, and loud. The Italian accent made it seem like he was singing everything he said, making it all seem that much more beautiful. Anytime our group slowed down or started to get tired, Marco would yell, "Andiamo! (Let's go!)," and suddenly we were revived. He knew everything about Rome, and everywhere we went, he knew someone. All day he was calling out to friends, "Ciao bella!" or "Come stai?" He loved his city and loved sharing it with all of us. He had such a passion for Rome, and it made me passionate about it, too. He was also an entertainer; he enjoyed making us laugh. When our group reached a crosswalk near the Vatican, he knew all of us would not make it across in one light, so he told us to try to hurry up across the street. He told us if we did not make it before the light changed, it's okay, the cars won't hit us. "And if they beep at you," he added, "it's because they like-a the music."

The writer uses dialogue to make the scene more vivid.

The writer returns to her reflections about the connections between her family and her Italian heritage.

Marco fit into what my family came to know as the image of the quintessential Roman man. All of the men have two-day stubble, enough to look chic and sophisticated, but not so much as to look scruffy or messy. They also have half-smoked cigarettes hanging from their mouths. It is never a freshly lit

Guariglia 4

cigarette, or a little butt, but right at that perfect halfway mark. There is a confidence, but not arrogance, in their walk. In essence, Roman men are eternally cool. In *Eat, Pray, Love*, Elizabeth Gilbert remembers watching a group of Roman men outside a bakery on their way home from a soccer game. They are "leaning up against their motorcycles, talking about the game, looking macho as anything, and eating *cream puffs*" (Gilbert 70). She is surprised at how cool they can look while eating something like cream puffs, but I have definitely seen what she means. Somehow they are manly without even having to try.

> The writer draws on a source to illustrate a point.

Romans, like many Italian Americans I've known, also have an opinion on everything and want you to know what that opinion is. Walking by the Spanish Steps on our second day in Rome, we saw a restaurant with a water leak that had spilled out into the street. It was a narrow street with mostly pedestrian traffic. As the water trickled between the cobblestones, the restaurant owner stood over the mess, looking a lot like our bus driver with his hands on his hips. Every Italian walking by had to stop and talk to this man, and then give him advice on how to go about fixing it. The two would wave their hands at each other, sometimes nodding in agreement, sometimes yelling and waving their hands harder. This reminded me of many of my own family. When any problem arises, all the men in the house stand around looking at it saying, "No! What you gotta do is . . ." None of them are listening to each other, but each of them wants their point to be heard. It felt like déjà vu watching the same thing happen on this street in Rome. It was funny that they were all being stubborn and acting like know-it-alls, but I saw underneath it that the people stopping by really thought they were helping. They were not being rude or bossy in their minds; they were just looking out for their fellow Roman.

The last morning, Mama herded our tour group onto a bus to take us to the train station. When she got to my family, she gave us all a kiss on the cheek and a hug. She told us, "You must come back again and visit!" Then she looked at my sister and me, winked, and said, "And bring some husbands!" She must have channeled my grandmother at that moment, telling us to settle down

Guariglia 5

with a nice Italian boy. We laughed and thanked Mama for her kindness during our visit.

The writer begins her conclusion by sharing her thoughts as her trip comes to a close.

As we pulled away from the station, I thought of all the wonderful people we met in Rome. I imagined them coming to our family reunion barbecue that takes place every summer. I think they'd fit right in. Mama would sit with Grandma and my father's aunts and talk about how beautiful their family is. Marco would sit with my dad and his cousins, drinking scotch and smoking cigars and cigarettes. Everyone would have a place.

The conclusion offers reflections on differences between Italians and Italian Americans.

But then I thought of my cousin with two-day stubble, sitting on a Vespa, and I giggled. The image was ridiculous. Our ancestors may have brought the food, the expressions, and the attitudes with them to the United States a few generations ago, but it is safe to say that, over the years, we have lost some of the style and the musical language that Italians seem to possess from birth. Then why did so much of what I saw and heard in Italy feel strangely familiar? It seems that for Italians and Italian Americans, the traits we share are not just a cultural thing or just a family thing; they are both. It is impossible to separate the two. My time in Rome showed me that to Italians, a shared culture is a kind of family, one that extends even across the ocean.

Guariglia 6

Works Cited

Gilbert, Elizabeth. *Eat, Pray, Love: One Woman's Search for Everything across Italy, India and Indonesia.* New York: Viking, 2006. Print.

Goodfellas. Dir. Martin Scorsese. Perf. Robert De Niro, Ray Liotta, Joe Pesci, and Lorraine Bracco. Warner Bros., 1990. DVD.

> Following MLA guidelines, the title of the Works Cited section is centered on its own line.

> Sources used in the essay are cited and formatted according to MLA guidelines.

✳ Project Ideas

The following suggestions provide ways to focus your work on a reflective essay or another type of reflective document.

Suggestions for Essays

1. REFLECT ON A PERSONAL EXPERIENCE

Write a reflective essay about something you've done, or something that happened to you, within the last month or so. Support your reflections with personal observation and reasoning. You might also consider discussing the experience with friends or family members to gain their perspectives on it. If the experience was of a public nature or was related to a public event, consult news reports for background information and alternate perspectives.

2. REFLECT ON A PUBLIC EVENT

Reflect on a recent event covered in your local newspaper. In your essay, describe the event, and offer your reflections on its significance for you and your readers. Support your reflection with examples from personal experience, information published in the newspaper, or an interview with someone associated with the event (see Chapter 6). If you participated in the event yourself, be sure to include your observations of what happened.

3. REFLECT ON A POEM, SHORT STORY, OR NOVEL

Respond to a work of literature that you've read recently. Support your reflection by describing your reactions to and understanding of the work. You might also read published reviews or analyses to get an idea of other readers' reactions. In your essay, briefly describe the work to which you're responding. Then offer your reflections on it: share with your readers why it affected you the way it did, and consider how it relates to your own experiences or beliefs.

4. REFLECT ON A PLAY OR MOVIE

Attend a play or movie and reflect on it. Support your reflection by drawing on your reactions to the play or movie, relevant personal experiences, and your own reasoning. You might also discuss the play or movie with a friend, a family member, a classmate, or an instructor who has seen it, or read other viewers' responses posted to online forums. In your essay, identify the subject of the play or movie, briefly summarize the plot and any key themes, and offer your reflections on the meaning or emotional impact of what you viewed.

5. REFLECT ON AN ISSUE OF INTEREST

Reflect on an issue in a discipline or profession in which you have an interest. For example, a writer interested in nuclear technology might reflect on the political or environmental implications of plans to store nuclear waste in Nevada. Support your reflection by drawing on your personal knowledge, experiences, and concerns, referring to information or arguments from published sources as necessary to inform your readers of the issue at hand. If appropriate, you might also interview an expert on the issue or conduct an observation to get a firsthand look at your subject. In your essay, introduce the issue and offer your reflections on it, but don't compose an argument. Instead, focus on how the issue affects you and your readers.

Suggestions for Other Genres

6. WRITE A MEMOIR

Write a brief memoir that reflects on a key event in your life. Carefully describe the event and offer your insights into its meaning and significance, keeping in mind the need to help readers understand, connect to, and benefit from your reflections. Your memoir should be based primarily on your memories. If you like, you might also discuss the event with a friend or family member and include some of their recollections and insights, or draw on published sources to give readers background information and context.

7. CREATE A PHOTO ESSAY

Take or gather several photographs that illustrate an important aspect of your life or a public issue that intrigues you. The pictures might be from your personal collection of photographs or from published sources such as history books, magazines, or Web sites. Select five to seven images that create a dominant impression of your subject. Then introduce them with a few paragraphs that reflect on what they show, or else write an introduction along with a sentence-length caption for each image. The final mix of images and words should lead your readers to think about the subject from a perspective they wouldn't have developed on their own.

8. WRITE A SHORT STORY

Choose a personal experience or a recent public event, and write a fictional story about it. You can use real-life episodes and examples, or you can make up elements (the characters, the specifics of what happened, the dialogue) as necessary to make the story lively and to draw readers in. Build your story around a central conflict and its resolution, and give readers a main idea to think about when they've finished reading the tale.

9. WRITE A COMPREHENSIVE LITERACY NARRATIVE

Write a literacy narrative that reflects on your overall attitudes toward literacy. Do you enjoy reading and writing, avoid them, struggle with them, find strength from engaging with them? Support your reflections by drawing on your personal experiences and insights into several events that have shaped your attitudes, as well as an assessment of your current relationship with writing and reading. To support your reflections, try to include a few telling comments made by family members or teachers about your experiences with literacy.

10. WRITE A LITERACY NARRATIVE ABOUT A KEY EXPERIENCE

Write a focused literacy narrative that identifies and reflects on a personal experience (or a series of closely related experiences) that strongly influenced you as a writer or reader. Shape your reflection as a story, building to a moment of insight to which your readers will relate. Conclude with a brief assessment of your current relationship with literacy.

In Summary: Writing a Reflective Essay

✳ **Find a conversation and listen in.**

- Explore your experiences (p. 134).
- Ask questions about promising subjects (p. 134).
- Conduct an observation (p. 135).

✳ **Reflect on your subject.**

- Examine your subject (p. 138).
- Collect details (p. 139).
- Find significance (p. 140).

✳ **Prepare your draft.**

- Convey your main idea (p. 142).
- Tell a story (p. 143).

- Go into detail (p. 144).
- Choose your point of view (p. 144).
- Consider genre and design (p. 145).
- Frame your reflections (p. 146).

✳ **Review and improve your draft.**

- Ensure that your main idea is clear (p. 146).
- Examine the presentation of your observations (p. 147).
- Review dialogue (p. 147).
- Show, don't tell (p. 148).

06 Writing to Inform

> When I take on the role of a reporter, I focus on informing my readers about a topic.

Readers of informative documents often have a specific purpose or interest in the subject. Able-bodied athletes, Paralympic hopefuls, and spectators alike can benefit from information on the current state of parasports, from equipment to competition. The documents that follow — **an infographic**, **a press release**, and **a Web site** — show how writers have used different genres to shed light on the regulations and classifications that shape sports for athletes with disabilities.

e-Pages

You can view the full documents shown here and respond to questions about reflective genres at **bedfordstmartins.com /conversation/epages.**

Infographic ▶

This **infographic** released by Allianz, a partner of the International Paralympic Committee, uses diagrams to illustrate for the general public how athletes are matched with proper cycling equipment depending on their type of impairment.

Information Graphic
Cycling

Mark Rohan
Handcycling, Ireland
"My training is varying depending on the time of the year, but standard is six sessions per week. In winter, I am not on the road but on an indoor cycling trainer and complement my training with weights and recovery sessions. From early spring, I spend 350 km per week on my handbike while also working on flexibility."
http://sponsoring.allianz.com

Allianz ⑪   Allianz ⑪   Allianz ⑪

80 km/h top speed downhill

Classification
Depending on the impairment, athletes are allowed to compete in bicycle, tricycle, tandem or handcycling events. The lower the number of each athlete's class, the greater the impact of his impairment on his ability to cycle.

Bicycle (Road and Track)
Classes C1-C5: Ambulant athletes with different levels of amputations and other impairments

Tricycle (Road)
Classes T1-T2: Athletes with different levels of cerebral palsy

Tandem (Road and Track)
Class B: Athletes with different levels of visual impairment

Handcycling (Road)
Classes H1-H4: Athletes with different levels of spinal-cord injuries and amputations

Handbike
Each handbike is tailored to its athlete's needs allowing to ride in a sitting or lying position.

Adjustable Crank
Disk Brake
Adjustable Backrest
Ultra-light Frame
Footrest

Press Release ▶

This **press release** by
Loma Linda University
Medical Center describes
how one Paralympic
hopeful was fitted for
prosthetic legs for both
walking and running.

Loma Linda University Medical Center's Orthotics and Prosthetics Team Gives Brazilian Athlete Ability to Walk

A process that usually take six to eight weeks was expedited, giving athlete running and walking leg in less than three days.

Loma Linda, CA (PRWEB) July 11, 2013

Loma Linda University Medical Center's orthotics and prosthetics team gave Brazilian athlete and 2016 Paralympic hopeful, Marinalva de Almeida, the ability to walk for the first time in over 15 years. The team, led by Michael Davidson and Murray Brandstater, MD, had Marinalva walking just three days after she arrived in Loma Linda.

"We were definitely in uncharted territory when Marinalva came to us," said Davidson, who serves as the clinical manager for orthotics and prosthetics at LLUMC. "The evolution of the prosthetic from the design of the leg, to fitting it, to actually using it is a very thorough, detailed process that typically takes six to eight weeks. We made two legs, one for running and one for walking, in less than three days."

Dr. Brandstater, who is the chair of physical medicine and rehabilitation at LLUMC, was the first specialist at the hospital to see Marinalva. He evaluated her and outlined her specific needs. "I recognized a young, athletic individual who was a good candidate for a prosthesis," he said. "Upon her arrival, no one had anticipated anything more than just fitting her for a prosthetic. Although a challenge, Marinalva was able to return home with two new legs."

Dr. Brandstater admits, however, everything came together because "Michael and his staff are talented and experienced; we had the support of his students and not only was Marinalva young and fit, but her

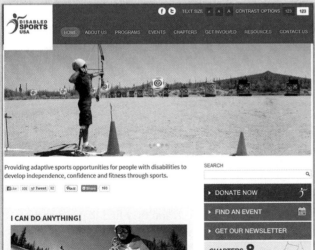

Providing adaptive sports opportunities for people with disabilities to develop independence, confidence and fitness through sports.

I CAN DO ANYTHING!

SEARCH

▶ DONATE NOW
▶ FIND AN EVENT
▶ GET OUR NEWSLETTER

CHAPTERS
Find a chapter near you

"I like changing the way people think when they see a disabled athlete."
ALEX TOMASZEWSKI
Youth athlete

◀ Web Site

This **Web site** for
Disabled Sports USA
provides categorized
information as well
as links to other
resources for those
interested in
participating in,
volunteering with, or
coaching adaptive
sports.

What Is Writing to Inform?

Many of the documents you encounter on a regular basis are informative: newspaper and magazine articles, manuals, brochures, and books (including this textbook) are among the genres — or types of documents — that allow writers to add information to conversations about a wide range of subjects. In writing and writing-intensive courses, typical informative-writing assignments include essays, reports, and Web sites. You might also be asked to create pamphlets, multimedia presentations, memos, or posters.

The Writer's Role: Reporter

PURPOSE
- To share information
- To answer questions

READERS
- Want to be informed
- Expect a fair and reasonable presentation of information, ideas, and arguments
- Need clear explanations of important ideas and concepts

SOURCES
- Information can be drawn from published studies and reports, news media, and personal experience.
- Information can be obtained firsthand, through interviews, observation, surveys, correspondence, and attendance at public events.

- Reporters check that their sources are credible and accurate.

CONTEXT
- The level of detail is adjusted to anticipate what readers are likely to know already and to make new information easier to follow.
- Informative documents often use illustrations — such as charts, tables, graphs, and images — to help readers understand concepts and ideas.

Writing to inform involves adopting the role of reporter. Reporters make others aware of the facts central to a written conversation. They might provide background information for people just starting to learn about a subject or might present new information to those with a long-standing interest in it. One reporter, for example, might describe the events leading to elections in a new democracy, while another might explain the United Nations' role in monitoring those elections.

Reporters typically refrain from interpreting or analyzing the information they provide, and they seldom ask their readers to respond in a particular way. Instead, reporters allow readers to draw their own conclusions and to decide whether — and how — to act on what they've learned.

Readers of informative documents might be interested in a subject for personal or intellectual reasons, but they are usually looking for an answer to a question — whether it's a simple quest for a fact or a more general desire to understand an issue. They look for a focused treatment of a subject, and they find that visual elements — such as photos, images, charts, graphs, and tables — can help them understand key points. Readers want writers to be fair and reasonable, they appreciate clarity, and they expect that sources will be documented.

In most cases, reporters spend time learning about a subject to ensure that they have enough information to share. Whether they interview experts, collect information from published materials, or use data to create graphs and tables, reporters ensure that their sources are reliable and check that the evidence they provide is accurate.

Writers of informative documents often connect the information they provide to the social, cultural, and historical contexts they share with their readers. For example, they might refer to events or people who have recently been featured in the news media, and they might mention important sources that address the subject. At the same time, reporters take into consideration what their readers might already know, leaving out details and explanations that are unnecessary for their purposes and focusing instead on what they want readers to understand about their subject.

Writers of informative documents are concerned primarily with helping readers and other writers advance their understanding of a subject. They do this in a variety of ways. They might report original research or provide a broad summary of existing knowledge, or offer a detailed discussion of a narrow area of interest. Regardless of their focus on the subject or the originality of their research, their contributions to a written conversation are essential to moving the conversation forward.

What Kinds of Documents Are Used to Inform?

Whether you are writing for a course, for publication, or in the workplace, you'll find yourself turning to — and creating — informative documents on a regular basis. If you are new to a conversation, informative documents can help you learn about a subject. As you prepare to contribute to the conversation, they can help you understand what is generally agreed upon about the subject and what remains unknown or open to debate. And as you draft your contribution, you can use information and ideas from informative documents to introduce your subject, to support your points, or to illustrate alternative perspectives.

View the e-Pages for informative writing at **bedfordstmartins.com /conversation/epages.**

Good writers select a genre that allows them to best address their purpose, their readers, and the context of the conversation they want to join. In the following sections, you'll find examples and discussions of some of the most common types of documents used to inform readers: informative essays, infographics, and profiles. In the e-Pages for this chapter, you'll find discussions and examples of Web sites, brochures, and maps.

Informative Essays

Informative essays share information about a subject in a well-organized, well-supported, readable form. Although instructors are usually the primary readers of academic essays, students are often asked to address a different audience, such as other students, parents, politicians, or members of a particular profession. For example, in courses that use service learning, the primary audience for informative essays might be the director of an organization, employees of a government agency, or the members of a community group. In some cases, the choice of audience is left to the writer.

In academic settings, such as writing and writing-intensive classes as well as scholarly publishing, informative essays draw on sources (articles, books, Web sites, interviews, and so on) to provide evidence for the information the writer presents. Those sources should always be cited using a documentation system, such as MLA or APA (see Chapters 21 and 22). Writers of informative essays typically attempt to present a subject fairly, although their experiences with and attitudes toward the subject are likely to influence their approach to the subject and their selection and presentation of information from sources.

George Chauncey
The Legacy of Antigay Discrimination

George Chauncey is a professor of history at Yale University and a gay rights activist. His books include *Gay New York: Gender, Urban Culture, and the Making of the Gay Male World, 1890–1940* (1995) and *Why Marriage? The History Shaping Today's Debate over Gay Equality* (2004), where "The Legacy of Antigay Discrimination" first appeared. In it, Chauncey recounts the history of laws and regulations aimed at American gays and lesbians during the first half of the twentieth century and shows how such practices existed in almost every aspect of social, legal, political, and private life. (Like most historians, he uses the *Chicago Manual of Style*, or CMS, documentation system to cite his sources.) The author suggests that we must recover and understand the past because it affects current debates around controversial issues such as same-sex marriage.

The Legacy of Antigay Discrimination

The place of lesbians and gay men in American society has dramatically changed in the last half century. The change has been so profound that the harsh discrimination once faced by gay people has virtually disappeared from popular memory. That history bears repeating, since its legacy shapes today's debate over marriage.

Although most people recognize that gay life was difficult before the growth of the gay movement in the 1970s, they often have only the vaguest sense of why: that gay people were scorned and ridiculed, made to feel ashamed, afraid, and alone. But antigay discrimination was much more systematic and powerful than this.

Fifty years ago, there was no *Will & Grace* or *Ellen*, no *Queer Eye for the Straight Guy*, no *Philadelphia* or *The Hours*, no annual Lesbian, Gay, Bisexual, and Transgender (LGBT) film festival. In fact, Hollywood films were *prohibited* from including lesbian or gay characters, discussing gay themes, or even inferring the existence of homosexuality. The Hollywood studios established these rules (popularly known as the Hays Code) in the 1930s under pressure from a censorship movement led by Catholic and other religious leaders, who threatened them with mass boycotts and restrictive federal legislation. The absolute ban on gay representation, vigorously enforced by Hollywood's own censorship board, remained in effect for some thirty years and effectively prohibited the discussion of homosexuality in the most important medium of the mid-twentieth century, even though some filmmakers found subtle ways to subvert it.[1]

Censorship extended to the stage as well. In 1927, after a serious lesbian drama opened on Broadway to critical acclaim—and after Mae West announced that she planned to open a play called *The Drag*—New York state passed a "padlock law" that threatened to shut down for a year any theater that dared to stage a play with lesbian or gay characters. Given Broadway's national importance as a staging ground for new plays, this law had dramatic effects on American theater for a generation.[2]

Fifty years ago, no openly gay people worked for the federal government. In fact, shortly after he became president in 1953, Dwight Eisenhower issued an executive order that banned homosexuals from government employment, civilian as well as military, and required companies with government contracts to ferret out and fire their gay employees. At the height of the McCarthy witch-hunt, the U.S. State Department fired more homosexuals than communists. In the 1950s and 1960s literally thousands of men and women were discharged or forced to resign from civilian positions in the federal government because they were suspected of being gay or lesbian.[3] It was only in 1975 that the ban on gay federal employees was lifted, and it took until the late 1990s before such discrimination in federal hiring was prohibited.

Fifty years ago, countless teachers, hospital workers, and other state and municipal employees also lost their jobs as a result of official policy. Beginning in 1958, for instance, the Florida Legislative Investigation Committee, which had been established by the legislature in 1956 to investigate and discredit civil rights activists, turned its attention to homosexuals working in the state's universities and public schools. Its initial investigation of the University of Florida resulted in the dismissal of fourteen faculty and staff members, and in the next five years it interrogated some 320 suspected gay men and lesbians. Under pressure from the committee, numerous teachers gave up their jobs and countless students were forced to drop out of college.[4]

Fifty years ago, there were no gay business associations or gay bars advertising in newspapers. In fact, many gay-oriented businesses were illegal, and gay people had no right to public assembly. In many states, following the repeal of prohibition in 1933, it even became illegal for restaurants and bars to serve lesbians or gay men. The New York State Liquor Authority, for instance, issued regulations prohibiting bars, restaurants, cabarets, and other establishments with liquor licenses from employing or serving homosexuals or allowing homosexuals to congregate on their premises.[5] The Authority's rationale was that the mere presence of homosexuals made an establishment "disorderly," and when the courts rejected that argument, the Authority began using evidence gathered by plainclothes investigators of one man trying to pick up another or of patrons' unconventional gender behavior to provide proof of a bar's disorderly character.[6] One bar in Times Square was closed in 1939, for instance, because the Liquor Authority alleged it "permitted the premises to become disorderly in permitting homosexuals, degenerates and other undesirable people to congregate on the premises." A Brooklyn bar was closed in 1960 because it became "a gathering place for homosexuals and degenerates who conducted themselves in an offensive and indecent manner" by, among other things, "wearing tight fitting trousers," walking "with a sway to their hips," and "gesturing with limp wrists." A bar in upstate New York was closed in 1963 after an investigator observed "two females, one mannish in appearance, [who was] holding the hands of the other female."[7]

Any restaurant or bar that gained a gay reputation faced constant harassment and police raids until the police shut it down for good. Some bars in New York and Los Angeles posted signs telling potential gay customers: *If You Are Gay, Please Stay Away*, or, more directly, *We Do Not Serve Homosexuals*. In the thirty-odd years between the enactment of such regulations by New York state in 1933 and their rejection by the New York state courts in the mid-1960s, the police closed *hundreds* of bars that had tolerated gay customers in New York City alone.[8]

Fifty years ago, elected officials did not court the gay vote and the nation's mayors did not proclaim LGBT Pride Week. Instead, many mayors periodically declared war on homosexuals — or sex deviates, as they were usually called. In many cities, gay residents knew that if the mayor needed to show he was tough on crime and vice just before an election, he would order a crackdown on gay bars. Hundreds of people would be arrested. Their names put in the paper. Their meeting places closed. This did not just happen once or twice, or just in smaller cities. Rather, it happened regularly in every major city, from New York and Miami to Chicago, San Francisco, and LA. After his administration's commitment to suppressing gay life became an issue in his 1959 re-election campaign, San Francisco's mayor launched a two-year-long crackdown on the city's gay bars and other meeting places. Forty to sixty men and women were arrested every week in bar sweeps, and within two years almost a third of the city's gay bars had been closed.[9] Miami's gay scene was relentlessly attacked by the police and press in 1954. New York launched major crackdowns on gay bars as part of its campaign to "clean up the city" before the 1939 and 1964 World's Fairs. During the course of a 1955 investigation of the gay scene in Boise, Idaho, 1,400 people were interrogated and coerced into identifying the names of other gay residents.[10] Across America, homosexuals were an easy target, with few allies.

Fifty years ago, there was no mass LGBT movement. In fact, the handful of early gay activists risked everything to speak up for their rights. When the police learned of the country's earliest known gay political group, which had been established by a postal worker in Chicago in 1924, they raided his home and seized his group's files and membership list. A quarter century later, when the first national gay rights group, the Mattachine Society, was founded, it repeatedly had to reassure its anxious members that the police would not seize its membership list. The U.S. Post Office banned its newspaper from the mails in 1954, and in some cities the police shut down newsstands that dared to carry it. In 1959, a few weeks after Mattachine held its first press conference during a national convention in Denver, the police raided the homes of three of its Denver organizers; one lost his job and spent sixty days in jail. Such harassment and censorship of free speech made it difficult for people to organize or speak on their own behalf and for all Americans to debate and learn about gay issues.[11]

Fifty years ago, no state had a gay rights law. Rather, every state had a sodomy law and other laws penalizing homosexual conduct. Beginning in the late nineteenth century, municipal police forces began using misdemeanor charges such as disorderly conduct, vagrancy, lewdness, and loitering to harass gay men.[12] In 1923, the New York state legislature tailored its statutes to specify for the first time that a man's "frequent[ing] or loiter[ing] about any public place soliciting men for the purpose of committing a crime against nature or other lewdness" was punishable as a form of disorderly conduct.[13] Many more men were arrested and prosecuted under this misdemeanor charge than for the felony charge of sodomy, since misdemeanor laws carried fewer procedural protections for defendants. Between 1923 and 1966, when Mayor John Lindsay ordered the police to stop using entrapment by plainclothes officers to secure arrests of gay men, more than 50,000 men had been arrested on this charge in New York City alone.[14] The number of arrests escalated dramatically after the Second World War. More than 3,000 New Yorkers were arrested every year on this charge in the late 1940s. By 1950, Philadelphia's six-man "morals squad" was arresting more gay men than the courts knew how to handle, some 200 a month. In the District of Columbia, there were more than a thousand arrests every year.[15]

Fifty years ago, more than half of the nation's states, including New York, Michigan, and California, enacted laws authorizing the police to force persons who were convicted of certain sexual offenses, including sodomy—or, in some states, merely suspected of being "sexual deviants"—to undergo psychiatric examinations. Many of these laws authorized the indefinite confinement of homosexuals in mental institutions, from which they were to be released only if they were cured of their homosexuality, something prison doctors soon began to complain was impossible. The medical director of a state hospital in California argued that "Whenever a doubt arises in the judge's mind" that a suspect "might be a sexual deviate, maybe by his mannerisms or his dress, something to attract the attention, I think he should immediately call for a psychiatric examination." Detroit's prosecuting attorney demanded the authority to arrest, examine, and possibly confine indefinitely "anyone who exhibited abnormal sexual behavior, whether or not dangerous."[16]

Fifty years ago, in other words, homosexuals were not just ridiculed and scorned. They were systematically denied their civil rights: their right to free assembly, to patronize public accommodations, to free speech, to a free press, to a form of intimacy of their own choosing. And they confronted a degree of policing and harassment that is almost unimaginable to us today.

NOTES

1. This chapter is more extensively footnoted than others, but it seemed important to provide documentation of the discriminatory measures it describes. The chapter draws heavily on sections I drafted for the Historians' Amicus

Brief submitted in *Lawrence v. Texas*, and following it, I cite the recent work of historians on these issues. There is also a large and useful literature produced by lawyers and legal scholars. On the history of film censorship, see Gregory Black, *Hollywood Censored: Morality Codes, Catholics, and the Movies* (Cambridge: Cambridge University Press, 1994); Vito Russo, *The Celluloid Closet: Homosexuality in the Movies* (New York: Harper and Row, 1981); and George Chauncey, *Gay New York: Gender, Urban Culture, and the Making of the Gay Male World, 1890–1940* (New York: Basic Books, 1994), 353 and n.57.

2. Kaier Curtin, *"We Can Always Call Them Bulgarians": The Emergence of Lesbians and Gay Men on the American Stage* (Boston: Alyson, 1987). Chauncey, *Gay New York*, 311–313.

3. David K. Johnson, *The Lavender Scare: The Cold War Persecution of Gays and Lesbians in the Federal Government* (Chicago: University of Chicago Press, 2004), 166 and passim; Robert D. Dean, *Imperial Brotherhood: Gender and the Making of Cold War Foreign Policy* (Amherst: University of Massachusetts Press, 2001).

4. Stacy Braukman, "'Nothing Else Matters But Sex': Cold War Narratives of Deviance and the Search for Lesbian Teachers in Florida, 1959–1963," *Feminist Studies* 27 (2001): 553, 555; see also 553–557, 573, and n.3.

5. Chauncey, *Gay New York*, 173, 337.

6. Ibid., 337.

7. See Chauncey, *Gay New York*, chapter 12, quotes on pp. 338, 344. Similar restrictions were imposed by the California Liquor Authority in the 1950s; see Nan Alamilla Boyd, *Wide Open Town: A History of Queer San Francisco* (Berkeley: University of California Press, 2003), 108–147. For similar policing in Buffalo, New York, see Elizabeth Lapovsky Kennedy and Madeline D. Davis, *Boots of Leather, Slippers of Gold: The History of a Lesbian Community* (New York: Routledge, 1993), 145–146.

8. Chauncey, *Gay New York*, 339.

9. John D'Emilio, *Sexual Politics, Sexual Communities: The Making of a Homosexual Minority, 1940–1970* (Chicago: University of Chicago Press, 1981), 182–184.

10. D'Emilio, *Sexual Politics*, 51; Chauncey, *Gay New York*, 340; Chauncey, *The Strange Career of the Closet: Gay Culture, Consciousness, and Politics from the Second World War to the Gay Liberation Era* (New York: Basic Books, forthcoming); John Gerassi, *The Boys of Boise: Furor, Vice, and Folly in an American City* (New York: Macmillan, 1966); Fred Fejes, "Murder, Perversion, and Moral Panic: The 1954 Media Campaign Against Miami's Homosexuals and the Discourse of Civic Betterment," *Journal of the History of Sexuality* 9 (2000): 305–347.

11. On the Chicago Group, see Jonathan Ned Katz, *Gay American History: Lesbians and Gay Men in the U.S.A.* (New York: Crowell, 1976), 385–389; Katz, *The Gay/Lesbian Almanac* (New York: Morrow, 1983), 554–561; on Mattachine, see D'Emilio, *Sexual Politics*, 115, 120–121.

12. See John D'Emilio and Estelle B. Freedman, *Intimate Matters: A History of Sexuality in America* (San Francisco/New York: Harper and Row, 1988), 150–156, 202–215; Chauncey, *Gay New York*, 137–141, 183–186, 197–198, 249–250; Paul Boyer, *Urban Masses and Moral Order in America, 1820–1920* (Cambridge: Harvard University Press, 1978), 191–219.

13. Chauncey, *Gay New York*, 172.

14. Chauncey, "A Gay World, Vibrant and Forgotten," *New York Times*, 26 June 1994, E17.

15. John D'Emilio, "The Homosexual Menace: The Politics of Sexuality in Cold War America," in *Passion and Power: Sexuality in History*, ed. Kathy Peiss and Christina Simmons, with Robert A. Padgug (Philadelphia: Temple University Press, 1989), 231; Chauncey, "The Postwar Sex Crime Panic," in *True Stories from the American Past*, ed. William Graebner (New York: McGraw-Hill, 1993), 160–178.

16. Estelle B. Freedman, "'Uncontrolled Desires': The Response to the Sexual Psychopath, 1920–1960," *Journal of American History* 74 (1987): 83–106; Chauncey, "Postwar Sex Crime Panic."

Starting a Conversation: Respond to "The Legacy of Antigay Discrimination"

In your writer's notebook, consider how Chauncey responds to his writing situation by answering the following questions:

1. Informative essays often begin with a question that readers might have about a subject. What question(s) does "The Legacy of Antigay Discrimination" attempt to answer?

2. Writing to inform involves adopting the role of reporter — a position that often requires a writer to refrain from interpreting, analyzing, or drawing specific responses from readers. How well does Chauncey adopt that role? In what ways does he seem impartial or partial in this essay?

3. Issues such as same-sex marriage and gay rights are contentious and controversial. What assumptions does Chauncey seem to make

about his readers throughout the essay? Do you think he anticipates resistance to his points, or agreement? Why?

4. Chauncey's essay is dense with historical information, all carefully documented, and the writer mentions that "it seemed important to provide documentation of the discriminatory measures" outlined in his essay (note 1). Besides a general obligation to cite sources in an academic essay, why would Chauncey feel a particular need to document his evidence in this essay? How do the extensive source notes fit with his overall purpose?

5. "The Legacy of Antigay Discrimination" focuses on intolerance of homosexuality half a century ago. How does this historical information connect to — and affect — contemporary debates about gay and lesbian rights, particularly same-sex marriage?

Infographics

An infographic is a visual representation of a set of facts or data. As informative documents, infographics typically present information in a seemingly unbiased way, and they sometimes include a list of sources for the facts and data presented. Time-lines are among the most common infographics, but in recent years innovative designers have taken advantage of easy-to-use graphic tools to create a slew of info-graphics that present information in unusual and unexpected ways. Because of their versatility and ability to present complex data in a format that is easy for readers to parse, infographics are useful in magazines and newspapers, on Web sites and blogs, in journal articles, and in a variety of other contexts. An infographic's design contributes in large part to its effectiveness, and a clear, cohesive design is key to its success.

AVG.com
History of the Internet

Created by the security software company AVG, the infographic shown here provides an overview of key events in the history of the Internet's growth. Incorporating text, illustrations, logos, and statistics, *History of the Internet* is set up as a timeline that marks certain events and milestones, such as the number of users on the Internet. The infographic also notes key dates in the creation and propagation of computer viruses over the Internet, the launches of popular Web sites and services, and advances in personal computing that contributed to the Internet's rising popularity.

HISTORY —of the— INTERNET

1969 - 2012

A connection is made between The University of California Los Angeles and The Stanford Research Institute – Arpanet is born; created by the US Department of Defense Advanced Research Projects Agency (Darpa).

Apple founded.

US National Science Foundation creates a non-military network for American universities

2,308

Arpanet and all networks users

:-)

Scott Fahlman, computer scientist at Carnegie Mellon University - adds a colon to the first online emoticon : -)

Microsoft IPO - market cap $770m

"Archie" the first search engine created by a student

Arpanet decomissioned

Tim Lee at CERN introduces the World Wide Web.

The first virus - Creeper- created.

Arpanet users 35

400 Arpanet users receive the first ever spam email inviting them to a product demo

Arpanet user Kevin Mackenzie uses the emoticon -)

Apple IPO - market cap £1.7bn

IBM

IBM launches the personal computer

The Elk cloner virus created

the US National Science Foundation created a network to link existing university supercomputer networks.

Stoned virus created

The first worm - "Morris"- created

Michelangelo virus created

Mosaic web browser launched

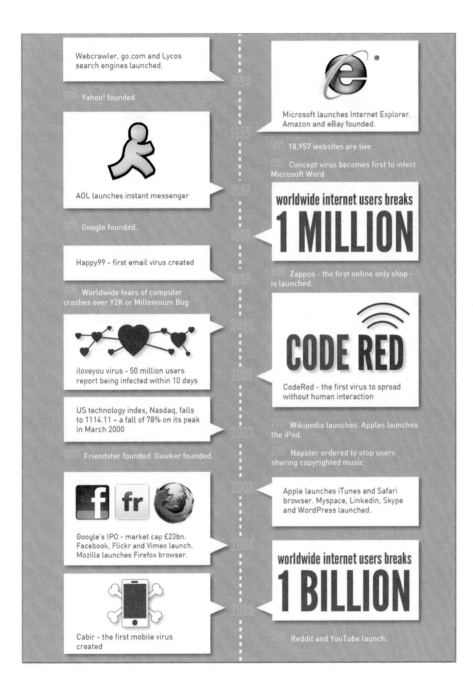

Webcrawler, go.com and Lycos search engines launched.

Yahoo! founded

AOL launches instant messenger

Google founded.

Happy99 - first email virus created

Worldwide fears of computer crashes over Y2K or Millennium Bug

iloveyou virus - 50 million users report being infected within 10 days

US technology index, Nasdaq, falls to 1114.11 – a fall of 78% on its peak in March 2000

Friendster founded. Gawker founded.

Google's IPO - market cap £23bn. Facebook, Flickr and Vimeo launch. Mozilla launches Firefox browser.

Cabir - the first mobile virus created

Microsoft launches Internet Explorer. Amazon and eBay founded.

18,957 websites are live

Concept virus becomes first to infect Microsoft Word

worldwide internet users breaks
1 MILLION

Zappos - the first online only shop - is launched.

CODE RED

CodeRed - the first virus to spread without human interaction

Wikipedia launches. Apples launches the iPod.

Napster ordered to stop users sharing copyrighted music

Apple launches iTunes and Safari browser. Myspace, Linkedin, Skype and WordPress launched.

worldwide internet users breaks
1 BILLION

Reddit and YouTube launch.

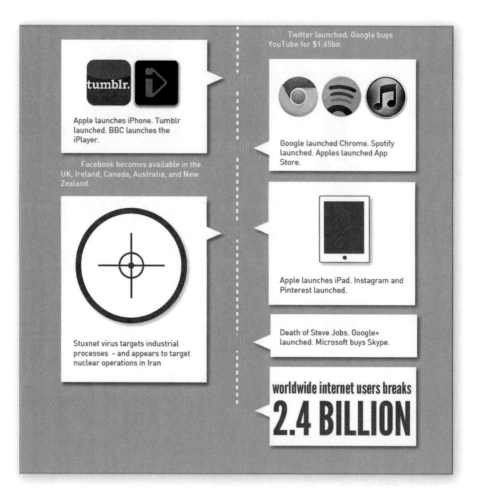

Apple launches iPhone. Tumblr launched. BBC launches the iPlayer.

Facebook becomes available in the UK, Ireland, Canada, Australia, and New Zealand.

Stuxnet virus targets industrial processes - and appears to target nuclear operations in Iran

Twitter launched. Google buys YouTube for $1.65bn

Google launched Chrome. Spotify launched. Apples launched App Store.

Apple launches iPad. Instagram and Pinterest launched.

Death of Steve Jobs. Google+ launched. Microsoft buys Skype.

worldwide internet users breaks
2.4 BILLION

Starting a Conversation: Respond to "History of the Internet" Infographic

1. This infographic was created by AVG, a software company that provides products to protect consumers against computer viruses and malware. What elements of the infographic reflect AVG's mission? What motives might the company have had for including those elements?

2. Look at the design of the infographic. Which events stand out the most, and what makes them stand out? Why do you think the infographic's designer chose to emphasize some events over others? What different choices would you have made if you were the designer?

3. The infographic is structured as a timeline, which is a logical choice for showing a series of events that happen over time. What other structures might have been useful here? How would you restructure the infographic — by type of event, by company, by decade, or by some other criterion?

4. Many infographics provide a list of sources for their information. Why do you think AVG might have chosen not to cite their sources here? Of the information contained in this infographic, what might be considered "common knowledge" (see p. 487)?

Profiles

Profiles use information to describe a place, a group, or a person, often someone who has been in the news or who represents a number of people affected by an issue. Following the widespread damage caused by Hurricane Sandy in 2012, for example, New Jersey governor Chris Christie was the subject of several profiles; at the same time, a number of New Jersey residents with no claim to fame were the subjects of profiles that conveyed the experiences of people who had lost family, friends, homes, and businesses to the disaster.

Because they appear so often in popular periodicals, most profiles are relatively brief. They also tend to focus on a particular moment in time, rather than on a lifetime. Profiles typically draw on interviews and observations, and sometimes on published sources such as biographies or news reports, to give readers a thorough understanding of the subject. Photographs of the subject of a profile are another common feature of this genre — although such images are not always strictly factual.

Colorado State Programs and People
Animal Welfare and Autism Champion

Written by the staff at Colorado State University, this profile of animal sciences professor Temple Grandin appears on the university's Web site. While this profile doesn't focus on a single event or moment in time, it does establish a timeline and a set of themes in discussing Grandin's path to her current profession. As you read it, notice the structure of the profile and how it organizes the wealth of information it provides about Grandin's life and career.

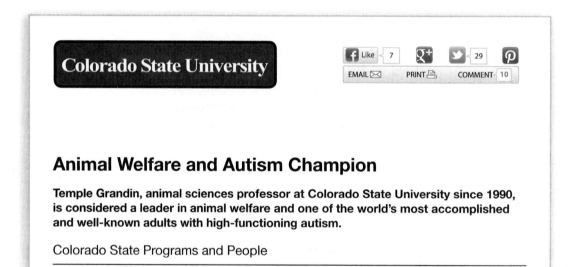

Colorado State University

Like 7   Q+   29   📌

EMAIL ✉   PRINT 🖶   COMMENT 10

Animal Welfare and Autism Champion

Temple Grandin, animal sciences professor at Colorado State University since 1990, is considered a leader in animal welfare and one of the world's most accomplished and well-known adults with high-functioning autism.

Colorado State Programs and People

A passionate and influential animal advocate, Temple Grandin is known for explaining how animals think. Her book, *Animals in Translation: Using the Mysteries of Autism to Decode Animal Behavior* (2005, Scribner), spent weeks on *The New York Times* national nonfiction best sellers list.

Celebrity with Adoring Fans

A popular guest speaker with a travel schedule rivaling any celebrity, Grandin has been featured on major television programs such as ABC's *Primetime Live* and *20/20*, CBS's *48 Hours*, CNN's *Larry King Live*, NBC's *Today Show*, and has been featured in *People* magazine, *The New York Times*, *Forbes*, *U.S. News and World Report*, and *Time* magazine. Bravo cable television network did a half-hour show on her life. Interviews with her have also been broadcast on National Public Radio.

▲ Temple Grandin, associate professor of animal sciences at Colorado State University.

A professional livestock facility designer and consultant for large corporations, including McDonald's, Wendy's, Burger King, and Swift, Grandin teaches popular courses on livestock behavior, handling, and animal welfare. She mentors and advocates for students who might otherwise lack the inspiration and motivation to succeed.

Renowned Animal Welfare Expert

Today, at least half of all cattle in the United States and Canada, as well as many in other countries, are handled in humane slaughter systems designed by Grandin. Her animal welfare guidelines have become the gold standard in the $80 billion meat-packing industry.

However, Grandin is considered autistic. She thinks in pictures rather than words, lacks complex emotion, and is hypersensitive to noise and other sensory stimuli. She was called names like "retard" as a child and was kicked out of high school for fighting.

In 1950, Grandin was labeled autistic and her parents were told she should be institutionalized. Good thing they didn't follow that advice.

Little Known about Autism in 1950s

Little was known about autism when Grandin was a child in Boston. Despite exhibiting autistic traits such as emotional distance, rocking, and fixation, professionals did not recognize her condition as autism for several years. She didn't talk until she was almost 4 years old, communicating her frustration instead by screaming, peeping, and humming.

She was placed in a structured nursery school and considers herself lucky to have had determined parents, good teachers, and supporting mentors throughout her schooling. Grandin is particularly grateful to Bill Carlock, her high school science teacher and mentor. She credits Carlock with helping her develop unique strengths through science experiments. Carlock opened his home to Grandin on the weekends and took the time to successfully develop her problem-solving skills and provide the necessary motivation for her to study.

She eventually attended a special boarding school with dairy cows and a stable with horses for the students to ride — and that experience eventually led to Grandin's career in animal behavior. "Animals saved me," Grandin says.

Surpassing all expectations, Grandin received her bachelor's in psychology in 1970 from Franklin Pierce College, a small liberal arts school in southwestern New Hampshire. She went on to receive her master's in animal science from Arizona State University in 1975 and her Ph.D. in animal science from the University of Illinois in 1989.

Sensory Overload a Big Challenge

Today, Grandin, 60, is comfortable in mainstream society, but her autism has been a constant challenge. On a daily basis, sensory overload is one of her biggest struggles. She describes hypersensitivity to loud noise and other sensory stimuli such as scratchy clothing, sudden movements, or extreme changes in lighting.

Grandin became well known after being profiled by neurologist Dr. Oliver Sacks in his book, *An Anthropologist on Mars*. The title of the book comes from Grandin's self-description of how she feels being unable to interpret social signals and of feeling mystified by cultural assumptions that allow most people to function with ease.

She thinks in terms of specific pictures — words are like a second language. She describes her thinking as having full-color movies playing in her head. Words are instantly translated into pictures. She has likened her mind to "Google for images" — if you put in a key word, it pulls up pictures.

"I was nearly paralyzed with anxiety as a child," Grandin recalls. At age 18, she invented an anxiety relieving squeeze or hug machine. While on vacation at her aunt's ranch in Arizona, Grandin noticed cattle being placed inside a contraption shaped like a "V" to keep them still during vaccinations. She noticed the cattle appeared almost serene when they were in the machine, so she got in the squeeze chute herself and found that the pressure helped calm her down.

With the help of a teacher, she eventually built her own squeeze machine, which she still uses. For Grandin and other children whose nervous systems seem to operate in hyper-drive, the simple pressure provides a calming release. The same kinds of devices are now being used at many schools specializing in autistic children.

Animal Behavior Expert and Livestock Facility Designer

Grandin's acute visual thinking has allowed her to create entire livestock handling facilities in her imagination. She has successfully designed equipment ranging from her own personal squeeze machine to corrals for handling cattle on ranches to systems for handling cattle and hogs during veterinary procedures and slaughter.

She figured out that cattle would move more easily through a livestock handling facility with curved lanes because it makes use of cattle's natural circling behavior. One of her first designs was for a curved lane leading into a dip vat at John Wayne's Red River feed yard in Arizona.

She later began successfully applying the curved lane design to systems for meat-packing plants. Though she had little experience with drawing in perspective, she was able to create elaborate blueprints. Drawing skills often appear in young autistic children, perhaps as a compensation for their lack of verbal skills.

Grandin advises people having a problem with an animal to try to see what the animal is seeing and experience what the animal is experiencing. Anything in the sensory realm can upset an animal. Things like smells, exposure to new experiences, and change in routine can upset an animal.

Admired Teacher

Students in Grandin's undergraduate livestock handling class cite the practical application of her lectures and insights. Jamie Cohn, a CSU junior majoring in animal and equine sciences, said that Grandin's first lecture of the semester immediately helped her understand her horse better. "I now realize my horse isn't stupid at times, just reacting to something in the environment."

Grandin is now focusing her life's work on transferring knowledge to future generations. She is also committed to helping develop the talents of other autistic individuals. While CSU classes remain a priority, much of her time is currently spent traveling to share her animal behavior and autism expertise.

The leading publisher on autism and Asperger's syndrome, Future Horizons, awards funds annually through the "Temple Grandin Award" to recognize the accomplishments of those who have been diagnosed with autism or Asperger's syndrome.

Starting a Conversation: Respond to "Animal Welfare and Autism Champion"

1. Aside from sharing the accomplishments of one of its faculty members, what reasons might Colorado State University have for profiling Temple Grandin? In what ways does the profile illustrate broader issues?

2. What do you think of the structure of the profile? Did you find it informative? Why or why not?

3. In what ways does the profile create a narrative of Grandin's life? How does that narrative contribute to your understanding of Grandin's roles in academic and industrial contexts today?

4. Where does the profile seem to find most of its evidence? What kind of evidence do you think is most compelling and most reliable in an informative profile? Why?

How Can I Write an Informative Essay?

The first step in writing a successful informative essay is recognizing that you don't have to be an expert on something to write about it — you simply have to know how to learn enough about it to share your findings with your readers. The second step is understanding how to collect and work with information. This doesn't mean that an informative essay needs to look like a research paper. As you've seen throughout this chapter, the amount and type of information used in informative documents can vary widely. What it does mean, however, is that you should understand where you can find information — for example, through interviews, published documents, the Web, direct observation, or personal experience — and how to work with it once you've collected it.

This section helps you tune in to the conversations around you and take on the role of reporter as you choose a subject, gather information, prepare your draft, and review and improve your draft. As you work on your essay, you'll follow the work of Ellen Page, a first-year student who wrote an informative essay about the use of DDT in the prevention of malaria.

Find a Conversation and Listen In

Informative essays offer a good opportunity to learn more about something that intrigues you and to report what you've learned to readers who share your interest in the subject. To get started on your informative essay, prepare yourself to take on the role of reporter, and spend some time thinking about your purpose, your readers, and the context in which your writing will be read (see p. 162). Look around for a topic of conversation that will interest both you and your readers — and that you can investigate in the time available to you.

EXPLORE YOUR INTERESTS

Nobody knows everything, but most of us know a little (or a lot) about a few things — especially if they involve us personally. As you search for ideas for an informative essay, examine your daily life for inspiration.

- **Personal interests and hobbies.** What do you like to do in your spare time? What magazines do you read? What television shows do you like to watch? What are your favorite Web sites? What makes you happy? Curious? Angry? What frightens you? Amuses you?

- **Academics.** Your major and your favorite classes are rich sources for essay ideas. Think about recent class discussions that interested you, questions that puzzled you, or information that surprised you when you first learned it.

- **Work.** Any past or current job, volunteer activity, or career you hope to enter involves specialized knowledge of some sort, from learning how to fill a soda machine to getting to know the U.S. tax code. Ask yourself whether you would be interested in informing others about this specialized knowledge.

- **Reading.** What have you read recently that interested or surprised you? What annoyed you or made you angry? What have you read that made you think?

Any of these areas can serve as a jumping-off point for generating ideas for an informative essay. Spend some time brainstorming or freewriting about these aspects of your life (see p. 32), and then review your notes to identify the areas that seem most promising. (For additional suggestions, see the writing project ideas at the end of this chapter.) As you think about your ideas, remember that the best subjects are usually out of the ordinary. Instead of writing about the broad issue of capital punishment, for example, you would do better to consider a little-known but potentially

In Process

An Informative Essay about the Use of DDT to Prevent Malaria

Ellen Page wrote an informative essay for her first-year seminar course in medical geography. To learn about her topic, Ellen read articles about malaria prevention and the effects of DDT. She also searched the Web for information from agencies such as the World Health Organization and the Centers for Disease Control and Prevention. Follow Ellen's efforts to inform her readers in the In Process boxes throughout this chapter.

important aspect of the subject, such as how inmates on death row spend their last day before execution or the role of DNA testing in overturning convictions. Once you've identified a few possible subjects, select one or two that interest you most, and jot down your thoughts about what you already know and what you need to learn before you start writing.

USE YOUR LIBRARY

Learn more about promising subjects by using your library. You can gain a preliminary understanding of a subject by searching the library catalog, browsing library shelves, searching library databases, and consulting librarians. Begin by generating a few keywords and phrases related to the subject, and then search the catalog with them. Your search results will give you an overview of the subject. The titles of books and journals on the subject will give you insights into what other writers think is important about it. You'll also be able to learn whether the subject is too broad to tackle on its own — or whether it's so specialized that you'll need to expand your focus.

If you are still interested in the subject after this preliminary research, spend a few minutes browsing the shelves in your library. Jot down or print out the call numbers for books and journals that appear promising, and locate them on the shelves. Skim these publications, and then look for nearby books and journals on the same subject. Spending as little as ten or fifteen minutes browsing the shelves can either confirm that a subject is worth pursuing or help you decide to look at others.

Working Together: Try It Out Loud

Before you start writing to inform, start a conversation with your classmates about something that interests you. Form small groups and choose a familiar subject (such as sports, family, your hometown, or the work of a favorite artist or musician). Take turns speaking while the other members of the group listen, respond, and ask questions. Your purpose is to inform the rest of the group, so try to present a fair and accurate view of your subject.

When you are finished, take a few minutes to reflect on the exercise. What did you learn about your audience? Did you have to adapt what you said based on their interest level and what they already knew? What kind of questions did they ask? What seemed to interest them the most about the subject?

Some subjects are so recent that few books or journals focus on them. If so, try to gain an overview of your subject by searching news and article databases such as LexisNexis Academic or Academic Search Premier using the keywords and phrases you generated for your catalog search. Examine the titles and descriptions of the sources you find. In some cases, you might find links to full-text articles. If so, skim them to learn about the subject.

You can read more about searching libraries and databases in Chapter 12.

In Process

Using the Library Catalog

To learn more about the issue of DDT use in the prevention of malaria, Ellen Page searched her library's catalog for sources that addressed her subject.

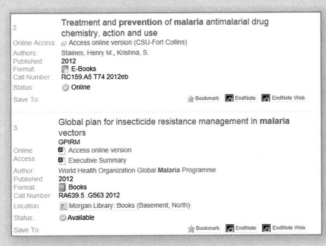

▲ Ellen's search of the library catalog

> Ellen searched for the phrase *malaria prevention*. She placed quotation marks around the phrase.

Ellen's searches produced several promising sources, including the following.

> Clicking on the title will show the complete record for the source.

2. Treatment and **prevention** of **malaria** antimalarial drug chemistry, action and use
Online Access: Access online version (CSU-Fort Collins)
Authors: Staines, Henry M., Krishna, S.
Published: 2012
Format: E-Books
Call Number: RC159.A5 T74 2012eb
Status: Online
Save To: Bookmark EndNote EndNote Web

3. Global plan for insecticide resistance management in **malaria** vectors
GPIRM
Online Access: Access online version
Executive Summary
Author: World Health Organization Global **Malaria** Programme
Published: 2012
Format: Books
Call Number: RA639.5 .G563 2012
Location: Morgan Library: Books (Basement, North)
Status: Available
Save To: Bookmark EndNote EndNote Web

> The results show whether the source is available, its location, and (if available) a link to its Web site.

▲ **Results of Ellen's library catalog search**

Finally, consider talking with a librarian about the subjects you've identified. Reference librarians or subject-area specialists can direct you to relevant sources, suggest related subjects, or help you narrow your focus.

ASK QUESTIONS ABOUT PROMISING SUBJECTS

Writers who adopt the role of reporter often find themselves confronted with a seemingly endless amount of information on their subject. Before you begin examining sources closely, narrow your focus by determining which subjects interest you the most and which conversation you want to join. Each of the following questions focuses your attention on a general subject in a different way, and each provides a useful starting point for an informative essay. Depending on the subject, you'll find that some questions are more relevant than others.

- **Importance.** Why is this an important subject? Who believes that it is important? Why do they believe it is important?

- **Process.** How does _____ work? What steps are involved?

- **History.** What is the origin of _____ ? What recent events are related to it? What are the implications of those events?

- **Limitations.** What is limiting the use of _____ ? What has kept _____ from succeeding? What must happen before _____ is accepted?

- **Benefits.** Who benefits from _____ ? How do they benefit? Why do they benefit?

- **Advantages and disadvantages.** What are the advantages of _____ ? What are the disadvantages?

Gather Information

No matter how much you already know about a subject, you'll want to learn more about it before you begin planning and drafting your essay. Informative essays tend to draw extensively on information from other sources and, to a lesser extent, on personal knowledge and experience. To learn more about your subject, create a search plan, collect sources, evaluate those sources, take notes, and consider conducting interviews.

CREATE A SEARCH PLAN

Depending on your subject and the kinds of information you are seeking, you might search library catalogs, databases, or the Web (see Chapter 12); browse library shelves and visit periodicals rooms (see p. 474); or conduct interviews (see p. 189), observations (see p. 135), or surveys (see p. 349). Creating a search plan before you begin will save time and keep you focused.

In Process

Asking Questions

After Ellen Page chose the general subject of "malaria prevention" and searched her library catalog to get a feel for the kinds of information available on her subject, she considered which conversations she might join by clustering (see p. 35). She placed the words *malaria prevention* at the center of her cluster and then wrote questions about her subject. She used the questions to explore strategies that had been used in the past century to prevent malaria, the advantages and disadvantages of those strategies, and approaches that are now in use. She represented her answers to these questions as words or phrases linked to each question.

After considering her assignment and writing situation, Ellen decided to focus on the advantages and disadvantages of using DDT to prevent malaria. She felt that this focus would allow her to accomplish her purpose of informing her readers about an important issue and believed that it would interest both her and her readers. She knew that the effects of DDT in agriculture had led to a ban on its use in most of the developed world, but she had also found articles that showed how it was being used to prevent malaria in developing countries. She decided that it would be possible to present a balanced, informed assessment of the use of DDT.

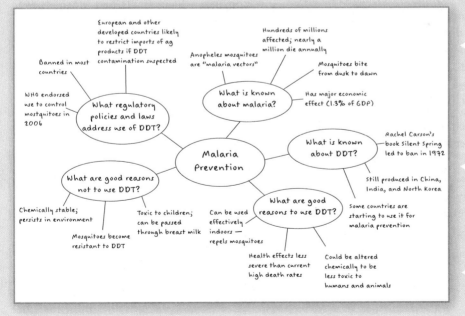

Ellen placed her general topic — malaria prevention — at the center of her cluster.

Ellen asked questions about her topic. Her questions focused on past and current strategies for malaria prevention, their benefits, their drawbacks, factors affecting their use, and so on.

Ellen wrote brief answers to her questions.

▲ Ellen's cluster

To develop a search plan, think about what you need to know and how you plan to use what you find. Then try to identify the types of sources most likely to provide the information you are looking for. If you are writing about recent developments in consumer robotics, for example, you want the most up-to-date information you can find. As a result, you should look in library databases focusing on the subject and search the Web. You might also want to interview an expert on the subject, such as a professor of engineering or computer science. In contrast, if you are writing about the influence of Greek culture on the Roman Empire, you would probably focus on books and scholarly journals that you find by searching your library catalog, browsing the shelves, and visiting periodicals rooms.

Working Together: Plan Your Search for Sources

Before you visit the library, search a database, or browse the Web, sit down with a group of classmates to generate ideas for a search. To carry out this activity, follow these steps:

1. Explain your subject and discuss your purpose for informing readers. If your readers go beyond the instructor and your classmates, describe your readers and their needs, interests, knowledge, and backgrounds. Talk briefly about specific ideas you have for gathering information on your subject.

2. Once you've explained your subject, the other members of your group should brainstorm ideas about useful resources for locating sources, such as the library catalog, specific databases, useful Web sites and directories, and relevant field research methods.

3. For each resource that has been identified, the group should brainstorm suggestions for using it effectively. For example, the group might generate a list of specific keywords and phrases to use in your search, create a list of good candidates for an interview and useful interview questions, and make suggestions about what to look for in an observation.

4. At the end of the discussion, ask any questions you have about the resources and search strategies your classmates have suggested.

If you are working face-to-face, take notes on the discussion. If you are using a chat or instant-messaging program, record a transcript of the session. The goal of the session should be to generate as many useful search resources and strategies as possible. Don't rule out any ideas, no matter how trivial or ridiculous they might seem at first. When the exchange is completed, turn to the next writer and repeat the process.

If you're not sure where to start, a reference librarian can suggest search strategies and relevant resources. You can learn more about creating a research plan and locating and using sources in Part Three.

COLLECT SOURCES

To collect sources, search for them in library catalogs, in databases, and on the Web. Visit your library to check out books and government reports, browse the shelves, and use the periodicals room. You can learn more about these activities in Part Three.

EVALUATE YOUR SOURCES

Depending on your subject, you might find yourself confronted with a dizzying array of promising sources, or you might find yourself gritting your teeth as one search after another comes up empty. In most cases, you'll collect at least a few useful sources, from books and scholarly articles to Web sites and blogs to video clips and news articles. Be aware, however, that not all information is created equal, and that some sources will be more appropriate for an academic essay than others. Before you decide to use a source, assess its credibility and usefulness for your purposes. To evaluate print and electronic sources for an informative essay, focus in particular on the following:

- **Relevance.** Be sure the information in a source will help you accomplish your purposes as a writer. It should address your subject directly, and it should help you learn more about aspects of the subject that are important to you. Your readers will also want to find information that meets their needs. If they know little about your subject, you'll need to provide them with information that will help them understand it. If they are already familiar with the subject, you'll want to locate information that will allow them to learn more about it.

- **Evidence.** Reliable sources provide details and supporting information to back up a writer's statements and assertions. Be wary of any source that makes sweeping generalizations without providing evidence.

- **Authority.** Look for sources written by experts on your subject. Scholarly sources (such as peer-reviewed journal articles) are usually more reliable than popular ones (such as general-interest magazines) because they go through an extensive peer-review process before being published. On the Web, information found on government (.gov), educational (.edu), and nonprofit (.org) domains is likely to be more reliable than information provided on business (.com) sites and personal pages.

- **Timeliness.** In most cases, the more recently a source was published or updated, the more pertinent the information will be for your purpose.

Need a refresher on evaluating sources? See Chapter 3.

TAKE NOTES

Once you've located enough reliable and credible sources to inform your essay, spend time taking notes on them. Because note taking often involves putting information about a subject into your own words, it can help you learn more about your subject and the writers who have been contributing to the conversation you want to join. Taking notes can also help you identify the most important information in your sources.

By studying a source and noting important information, ideas, and arguments, you'll gain a clearer understanding of the source and your subject. Careful note taking also helps you avoid plagiarism and lays the foundation for drafting your document. You can learn more about taking notes in Chapter 3.

In Process

Evaluating Sources

To learn more about the challenges associated with the use of DDT to prevent malaria, Ellen Page read several articles she found through her library's periodical databases to get a thorough understanding of the issue. She also searched the Web for up-to-date news and information. Not surprisingly, her searches of the Web pulled up several unreliable sources, such as this one.

Clip art and template design suggest an amateur Web author.

Web page provides no indication of authorship or authority to write on the subject.

Assertions are not backed up with evidence.

Site has not been updated in several years.

Malaria Facts

Fact # 3: Malaria is responsible for far too many deaths each year. The disease is spread by a certain type of mosquito that carries one of four known malaria parasites. Currently, insecticide-treated mosquito netting is by far the best prevention strategy, but new inventions and new medications are also increasing the odds of survival every year.

NEXT | BACK

UPDATED 2003-07-03

▲ **An unreliable source**

CONDUCT AN INTERVIEW

Interviews — in which one person seeks information from another — can provide firsthand accounts of an event, authoritative interpretations of an issue, and thoughts on a subject from the people who have been affected by it. You can conduct interviews face-to-face, over the telephone, via e-mail, and even through a chat program. Effective interviews usually involve the following activities.

Decide whether to conduct an interview. Before committing yourself to designing and conducting an interview, ask yourself what kind of results you expect and what role those results will play in your essay. Ask as well whether an interview is the best technique for gaining that information, or whether you might gain it more effectively and efficiently in another way.

Ellen's searches of the Web also brought her to the home page of the World Health Organization. On the site, she found an extensive collection of information about malaria, including a report about malaria control.

Ellen bookmarked the Web pages, saved copies of the pages on her laptop, and printed them.

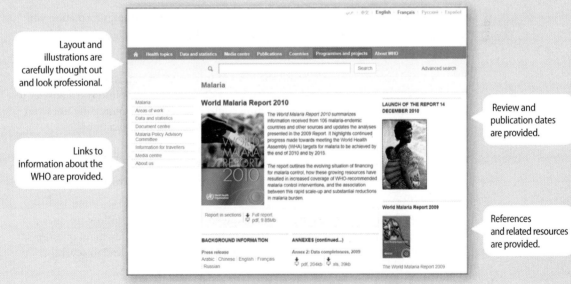

Layout and illustrations are carefully thought out and look professional.

Links to information about the WHO are provided.

Review and publication dates are provided.

References and related resources are provided.

▲ **A reliable source**

Sometimes the decision to interview is a natural extension of the kind of work you're doing. A writer exploring the effects of caffeine on athletic performance, for example, might decide to interview an athlete, a coach, or an exercise physiologist. Sometimes the decision to conduct an interview isn't so much the result of careful planning as it is the recognition of an available opportunity, such as knowing someone who has direct experience with your subject.

Decide whom to interview. Base your decisions about whom to interview on the kind of information you need for your essay.

- If you're trying to better understand a specific aspect of your subject, interview an expert in the field.

- If you want to learn what people in general think about your subject, interview a number of people who are affected by it.

- If you're hoping to collect quotations from authorities, interview someone who will be recognized as knowledgeable and credible.

When you contact someone to request an interview, be ready with a list of dates and times, as well as potential meeting locations, that are mutually convenient. Most people will be happy to answer questions for you, but be careful to respect their time. Provide an estimate of how long you expect the interview to take — and don't let it drag on longer than promised. Leave your phone number or e-mail address so that your interview candidate can contact you if a conflict arises.

Decide what to ask. Your questions should focus on the kinds of information you want to collect for your essay. Write them down ahead of time, keeping the following principles in mind:

- **Consider your purpose and the kind of information you want to collect.** Are you seeking background information, or do you want an opinion? An answer to the question "How did this situation come about?" will be quite different from an answer to the question "What do you think about this situation?"

- **Ask questions that require more than a yes/no answer.** You'll learn much more from an answer to a question such as "What factors will affect your vote on referendum X?" than from an answer to "Will you vote for referendum X?"

- **Prepare a limited number of main questions and several follow-up questions.** Good interviews seldom involve more than eight to ten main questions, but experienced interviewers know that each question can lead to several follow-up questions.

- **Be flexible.** Be ready for the interview to go in a different direction than you planned. Often the best information comes from questions and answers you didn't anticipate.

Carry out the interview. To increase the chances of a successful interview and leave the door open for additional questions following the interview, follow these guidelines:

1. Arrive early and review your questions.

2. Introduce yourself and ask for permission to record the interview.

3. Set up and test your recording equipment.

4. Ask your questions clearly, and be ready to respond with follow-up questions.

5. Take notes, even if you are using a video or audio recorder.

6. Be alert for related sources mentioned in the interview, and ask where you might find them.

7. Leave your contact information when the interview is over so that the interviewee can contact you in case new information comes up or clarifications need to be made.

8. Send a thank-you note.

Prepare a Draft

Writers of informative essays focus on reporting information to their readers. As you prepare a draft of your informative essay, you'll decide which information, ideas, and arguments to present and how you will share them with your readers.

Your decisions about what to focus on, which points to make, and what evidence to use will influence what your readers learn about your subject and how they are likely to understand it. Although reporters strive for objectivity in their writing, experienced writers recognize the difficulty of presenting information in a completely unbiased manner. They understand that their choices can (and will) lead readers to think about a subject in a particular way. Consider a writer selecting details for an informative essay about the impact of a recent ban on smoking in bars and restaurants. Statistical information about cash register receipts would focus readers' attention on financial implications of the ban for small business owners; a photograph of an asthmatic bartender might encourage readers to consider the positive public health effects of such a ban; and an interview with a smokers' rights advocate could emphasize concerns about eroding personal freedoms. No matter how objectively the writer presents the information, the final mix of statistics, images, and quotations will affect the conclusions readers draw from the document.

It's best to begin by choosing a main point and expressing it as a thesis statement. Then you can decide what supporting points and evidence will most effectively support your main point. During the drafting process, you should also decide whether to include visual information, how to organize your ideas, and how to frame your introduction and conclusion.

PRESENT YOUR MAIN POINT

In an informative essay, the main point is usually presented in the form of a thesis statement. A thesis statement, typically no more than a single sentence, directs readers' attention to what you want them to learn about a subject. Consider how the following thesis statements about voter turnout among younger Americans direct readers' attention in a particular way:

> The high turnout among younger voters in the last presidential election underscores the growing importance of young Americans on the political scene.

> The growing political commitment of voters under the age of twenty-five has led to higher voter turnout, which, in turn, has reduced the historic imbalance in the relative political influence of younger and older Americans.

> Regardless of the causes, the overall pattern of increasing voter turnout among younger voters should be cause for celebration among voters — young and old alike.

Although each of these thesis statements would provide a sound foundation for an informative essay, the essays would have little in common. By focusing on distinctly different aspects of the subject, they require the writer to provide different supporting points and evidence.

Is your thesis focused enough for your purpose? See Chapter 14 for more info.

Your thesis statement will be shaped by what you've learned about your subject; your purpose; your readers' purposes, needs, and interests; your readers' knowledge and backgrounds; and the requirements and limitations of your writing project.

DEVELOP SUPPORTING POINTS AND EVIDENCE

Most readers want more than a thesis statement — they want to know why they should accept it. If readers who are thinking about purchasing a car come across a thesis statement such as "For many drivers, renting a car on an occasional basis is a cost-effective alternative to owning one," they'll want to know why renting could be a better choice. If readers interested in financing a college education read a thesis statement such as "Today's college students have a wide range of options for reducing the overall cost of a college education," they'll want to know what those options are. To convince readers to accept your thesis statement, you'll need to provide supporting points and offer evidence for each point.

Choose your supporting points. Supporting points are the reasons you give readers to accept your main point. They are usually expressed as topic sentences in the form of general statements, such as "Renting a car means you can pay less in car insurance" or "If your family qualifies, Pell Grants can significantly reduce the cost of a college education." Consider, for instance, the way George Chauncey presents the supporting points for his essay about discrimination against gay and lesbian Americans (p. 164). Each paragraph opens with a clearly stated topic sentence ("Fifty years ago . . .") that identifies a form of discrimination from the past. As you choose your supporting points, keep in mind that not only should they serve as reasons to accept your main point but they should also be consistent with how you've presented your thesis statement. In short, you should resist the urge to include every idea you've come across. You can find more advice on developing support for a thesis statement in Chapter 14.

Identify evidence for each supporting point. Without evidence to support them, even the most clearly expressed supporting points will not be enough to inform your readers fully. You need evidence to help them understand why they should accept the reasons you've used to support your thesis statement. In a profile of Temple Grandin (p. 176), for instance, the author used evidence to illustrate a point about Grandin's contribution to animal welfare in the livestock industry:

> Today, at least half of all cattle in the United States and Canada, as well as many in other countries, are handled in humane slaughter systems designed by Grandin. Her animal welfare guidelines have become the gold standard in the $80 billion meat-packing industry.

Writers of informative essays also use information from sources to present ideas and clarify statements. You might define a concept by quoting from an interview, paraphrasing an article, or summarizing a report. You might amplify a statement by providing examples from sources. Or you might qualify a statement by noting that it applies only to specific situations and then use a quotation or paraphrase from a source to back that up, as George Chauncey does in his essay about discrimination against gay and lesbian Americans (p. 164):

The absolute ban on gay representation, vigorously enforced by Hollywood's own censorship board, remained in effect for some thirty years and effectively prohibited the discussion of homosexuality in the most important medium of the mid-twentieth century, even though some filmmakers found subtle ways to subvert it.

As you select information from sources for your essay, consider your writing situation (see p. 11). Be sure that the evidence you choose will help you accomplish your purpose; that you provide enough detail and explanation to help readers understand the information, ideas, or arguments you present to them; and that you can present the evidence in a way that won't conflict with your readers' values and beliefs.

In Process

Developing Support

For her informative essay on the use of DDT to prevent malaria, Ellen Page identified the following supporting points:

1. The history of DDT use in preventing malaria
2. The effects of DDT on humans and the environment
3. The relative risks of using — and not using — DDT
4. Alternatives to DDT

For her first draft, she expressed the third point as a general statement and offered evidence from a source to support it.

Ellen drew on information from a scholarly journal article. She used MLA in-text citation style to acknowledge her sources.

In the face of uncertainty about the effects of DDT on human health, the fundamental issue of "the right of people to a safe environment" demands that research continue on its effects (Bouwmann 746). Simply put, we must weigh the question of whether people should be exposed to a chemical that, although it prevents malaria, might cause physical harm later on. Here lies the main ethical argument in which the health risks and benefits must be weighed. To do this, we must understand not only the risks but also the benefits of using DDT.

Ellen's third supporting point

To identify evidence to support your points, follow these guidelines:

1. List your supporting points.

2. Review your notes to identify evidence for each point.

3. If necessary, review your sources (or find new ones) for additional information.

4. Avoid relying too heavily on one type of information.

5. Avoid relying too heavily on information from a single source.

6. Consider how the evidence fits your writing situation.

CONSIDER GENRE AND DESIGN

As is the case with other academic essays, the basic design of your informative essay will reflect the formatting requirements of your assignment and the expectations of your readers, particularly your instructor. Typically, those requirements specify the use of wide (one-inch) margins, double-spaced lines, page numbers, and a readable font. These design features make it easier for instructors and classmates to read and comment on the essay.

Working Together: Brainstorm Supporting Points and Evidence

You can use group brainstorming sessions to help generate supporting points and evidence. You can work in person or online (using chat, instant messaging, or a threaded discussion forum). To carry out the activity, follow these steps:

1. The writer should describe his or her writing project, main point, and ideas for supporting points.

2. Each member of the group should make suggestions about the supporting points the writer mentions.

3. Each member of the group should suggest additional supporting points.

4. Each member of the group should make suggestions about potential sources of evidence to support each point.

If you are working face-to-face, ask one member of the group to take notes on the discussion. If you are using a chat or instant-messaging program, be sure to record a transcript of the session. The goal of the session is to generate as many potential supporting points as possible. Take care not to rule out any ideas, no matter how trivial or ridiculous they might seem at first. When the exchange is completed, turn to the next writer and repeat the process.

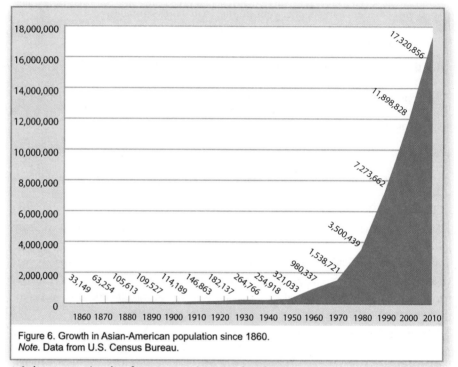

Figure 6. Growth in Asian-American population since 1860.
Note. Data from U.S. Census Bureau.

▲ A chart converting data from a source into visual evidence

Other design elements can help you clarify information for your readers and add visual interest to your essay. As you think about how you will present information to your readers, consider the benefits of using visual evidence to support your points.

- **Illustrations** such as photographs and drawings allow you to clarify abstract concepts and demonstrate processes that might be difficult to follow were they presented in the main text of your essay.
- **Charts, graphs, and tables** let you convert dense numerical information or statistical data into more easily understood visual summaries.

You can draw on your sources for visual evidence in two ways. You might borrow an illustration from a print or online source to help readers understand a complex concept or process, such as the steps involved in cellular respiration. Or you might use data from one or more sources to create an original chart, graph, or table to clarify a point, such as the growth of the Asian American population.

As you draft your informative essay, carefully consider the use and placement of illustrations. You must acknowledge the source of any images or numerical information (see Chapter 13). Images, graphs, and tables should appear as close as possible to the point where they are mentioned in the text, and a title or caption should identify or explain the illustration.

You can read more about document design in Chapters 16, 17, and 18.

FRAME YOUR INFORMATION

After you've settled on the supporting points you want to make and the evidence you'll use to develop your ideas, spend some time thinking about how you will put everything together for your readers.

Introduction. Your introduction sets the tone for your essay and influences how your readers understand and interpret the information that you give them. Most informative essays present the thesis statement in the introduction so that readers will grasp the writer's main idea from the start. Beyond stating your thesis, you can use a range of strategies to introduce your ideas. Two effective options are providing a historical account and asking a question. Historical accounts, such as the one George Chauncey offers at the beginning of "The Legacy of Antigay Discrimination" (p. 164), can help your readers understand the origins of a subject and how the situation has changed over time. Asking a question invites your readers to become participants in the conversation.

Organization. The organization of your essay also affects how readers respond to your points. Your organizing strategy should take into account your purposes and your readers' needs and interests, as well as the nature and amount of evidence you've assembled to support your points. To organize your essay, choose an organizing pattern and create an outline or a map. You can use a wide range of organizing patterns in an informative essay, but some are better suited to the genre than others. If you are informing your readers about an event or a series of events, for instance, you might want to use chronological order to structure your essay. If you are providing an overview of competing ideas about an issue, you might choose comparison and contrast. And if you are explaining the defining characteristics of a subject, such as the typical attitudes of college-age voters, description might be a useful pattern to follow.

Conclusion. You've probably read conclusions that simply summarize a document. These summaries can be effective, especially if your essay has presented complex concepts. A conclusion can do more, however, than simply restate your points. If you asked a question in your introduction, for instance, consider answering it in your conclusion. And if you want your readers to continue thinking about your subject after they've finished reading your essay, you might conclude by offering additional insights about what the information you've provided might mean for readers, as featured writer Ellen Page does in her finished essay (p. 201).

Chapter 16 provides additional strategies for writing introductions and conclusions. Chapter 15 provides information about organizing patterns, outlines, and maps.

Review and Improve Your Draft

Writing an informative essay involves juggling information, identifying main and supporting points, providing evidence for those points, and framing your ideas to accomplish your purposes. Any one of these activities can pose a significant challenge to a writer. Add them together and you've created a complex task that is sure to require additional work beyond a first draft. As you review your draft, pay particular attention to how well you've focused your discussion of the main point, the clarity of your discussion, your use of information from sources, and the effectiveness of your introduction and conclusion.

FOCUS YOUR DISCUSSION

Maintaining a clear focus is one of the most difficult challenges faced by writers of informative essays. Even when dealing with the most obscure subjects, the amount of information available to writers is still likely to be so large that it can be difficult to decide what to use and what to set aside. As you review your essay, make sure that your draft focuses on a single main point, that your thesis statement clearly conveys that point, and that every supporting point is relevant and well defined.

ENSURE CLARITY

Readers invest time reading an informative document because they want to learn about a subject. If the document is unclear or difficult to follow, they'll look elsewhere. Review your essay to ensure that you've discussed your subject as clearly as possible. To ensure clarity, make certain that you use information from sources accurately and that you refer to concepts and ideas consistently. Make your prose as economical as possible, and choose the right words for your purpose, readers, and subject. In addition, vary the structure of your sentences and paragraphs without making them overly complex. You can read more about strategies for ensuring a clear discussion in Chapters 16 and 20.

REVIEW YOUR USE OF SOURCES

The effectiveness of your informative essay depends heavily on your selection and use of sources. As you revise, ask yourself these questions: Have you chosen the right sources to support your points? Have you used enough sources to make your points effectively? Have you used the right amount of evidence from your sources? Have you clearly differentiated your own ideas from those of your sources? Have you clearly identified the sources from which you've drawn information? Have you provided appropriate citations in both the text and the works cited list? Have you paraphrased accurately and fairly? Have you quoted properly?

You can learn more about using information from sources in Chapter 19. For a fuller discussion of why you should document sources, see Chapter 13. For guidelines on the MLA and APA documentation systems, see Chapters 21 and 22.

ASSESS YOUR INTRODUCTION AND CONCLUSION

Your introduction and conclusion serve not only as the beginning and end of your essay but also as a means of framing your discussion. Your introduction calls your readers' attention to specific aspects of your subject — while turning their attention away from others — and your conclusion reinforces their understanding of the points you've made in the essay. If your introduction, conclusion, supporting points, and evidence are inconsistent with one another, your essay will be ineffective. To avoid inconsistencies, review your introduction and conclusion, keeping in mind your main point, supporting points, and use of evidence from sources. You can read more about framing your introduction and conclusion in Chapter 16.

Once you've revised your essay, ask yourself how you might polish and edit it so that your readers will find it easy to read — and ask a friend, relative, or classmate to proofread your final draft to make sure that it is free of distracting errors. For a discussion of editing and proofreading strategies, see Chapter 20.

Peer Review: Improve Your Informative Essay

One of the biggest challenges writers face is reading a draft of their own work as a reader rather than as the writer. Because you know what you're trying to say, you find it easy to understand your draft. To determine how you should revise your draft, ask a friend or classmate to read your essay and to consider how well you've adopted the role of reporter (see p. 162).

Purpose	1. Did you find the essay informative? Did you learn anything new? 2. What questions does the essay answer? Do I need to address any other questions?
Readers	3. Did you find the essay interesting? Why or why not? 4. Does the information I've included in my essay address my readers' needs, interests, knowledge, and backgrounds? 5. Does the essay seem fair? Did you detect any bias or agenda in the way I presented information?
Sources	6. Does the information make sense? Can I add, clarify, or rearrange anything to help you understand the subject better? Do you think any of the details are unnecessary? 7. Do my sources strike you as reliable and appropriate? Does any of the information seem questionable?
Context	8. Is my subject sufficiently narrow and focused? Is my thesis statement clear? 9. Would any of the information be better presented in visual form? 10. Is the physical appearance of my essay appropriate? Did you find the font easy to read? Did you have enough room to write down comments?

For each of the points listed above, ask your reviewers to provide concrete advice about what you should do to improve your draft. It can help if you ask them to adopt the role of an editor — someone who is working with you to improve your draft. You can read more about peer review in Chapter 4.

Student Essay

Ellen Page, "To Spray or Not to Spray: The Issue of DDT Use for Indoor Residual Spraying"

The following informative essay was written by featured writer Ellen Page.

To Spray or Not to Spray:

The Issue of DDT Use in Indoor Residual Spraying

APA notes that requirements for title pages on student essays vary. Check with your instructor first.

Ellen Page

Medical Geography

Professor Pratt

December 5, 2012

Information about the writer, course, and submission date is provided on the cover page.

The essay's title is repeated and centered.

To Spray or Not To Spray: The Issue of DDT Use in Indoor Residual Spraying

In many parts of the world, mosquitoes are far more than just a nuisance. When mosquitoes infected with the *Plasmodium* parasite bite humans, they transmit the often fatal disease malaria. Vector control—killing the mosquitoes that spread the disease—is the primary strategy in reducing malaria deaths worldwide. Currently, the most frequently implemented methods for malaria vector-control include insecticide-treated bed-nets (ITNs) and indoor residual spraying (IRS) with pesticides (World Health Organization [WHO] 2010, p. xiii). But such pesticides carry risks of their own. One insecticide in particular, DDT,

Ellen's thesis statement

has offered both the most success and the greatest risk in malaria vector control. Scientists and governments devising approaches to eradicating malaria consider three main factors in determining whether DDT should be used in IRS: health consequences, environmental consequences, and degree of resistance.

The writer frames the subject with an overview of the history of using DDT to treat malaria.

Since the discovery of the insecticide dichlorodiphenyltrichloroethane (DDT) in 1939, a long and controversial battle has waged over its use in the prevention of malaria (Centers for Disease Control [CDC], 2010). DDT was first used in World War II, and in 1955, the World Health Organization (WHO)

For sources with three, four, or five authors, APA style uses an ampersand before the last author's name.

proposed a global malaria eradication program in which DDT would be a key player (CDC, 2010). According to Sadasivaiah, Tozan, & Breman (2007), following the 1962 release of Rachel Carson's book *Silent Spring*, which questioned DDT's safety and environmental consequences, public support for DDT declined dramatically (p. 250). This lack of support, combined with other pitfalls encountered by the World Health Organization's eradication plan (such as "weak healthcare systems [and] insufficient administrati[on]"), brought DDT use to a

In APA style, subsequent references to the source use "et al." in place of all but the first author's name.

halt in 1969 (Sadasivaiah et al., 2007, p. 249).

Although DDT's use in agricultural applications largely diminished after the 1970s, it continues to be used in other malaria control strategies (Sadasivaiah et al., 2007, p.250). For instance, DDT is found in the insecticide-treated bed-nets that are frequently used worldwide (WHO, 2010, p. xiii). Given the growing health and economic impact of malaria as a "disease of poverty,"

TO SPRAY OR NOT TO SPRAY   2

renewed global efforts and support for control and eradication of the disease

have caused divisions among many countries, researchers, and organizations over

the appropriate use of DDT in IRS (2011, b). According to many sources, DDT is

the most economically sustainable and effective pesticide currently available for

IRS, so much so that the chemical was granted an exemption for malaria control

in the 2001 Stockholm Convention on Persistent Organic Pollutants, a global

treaty aimed at eliminating the use of toxic chemicals ("Stockholm Convention,"

2009).

> A source that does not have an author is identified by a shortened title and publication year.

> The main reason supporting the use of DDT for malaria control.

Currently, DDT is used in IRS for malaria control in 16 countries (WHO, 2010,

p. 23). IRS is applied on the surfaces inside of a dwelling and "keeps mosquitoes

out of and away from sprayed houses and reduces feeding rates and shortens

resting periods" of malaria-carrying mosquitoes (Sadasivaiah et al., 2007,

p. 249). A major benefit of IRS is its "applica[bility] in many epidemiological

settings" (WHO, 2010, p. 6); IRS works regardless of factors such as geographic

location, climate, and housing structure.

> Brackets are used to modify a quotation.

As with all pesticide use, one major threat to malaria vector control is

the development of resistance to the chemical. The more pesticide used and

the larger the area it is used to treat, the more likely resistance is to occur

(Sadasivaiah et al., 2007, pp. 252-253). Mosquitoes have already demonstrated

resistance in the form of genetic changes in areas of western and southern

Africa (Beerbohm, 2007, p. 14). If the pesticides used to kill mosquitoes are

rendered useless, the number of malaria cases worldwide would almost certainly

escalate. During the World Health Organization's global eradication program,

the development of mosquito resistance to pesticides caused many countries to

stop supporting and funding the eradication campaign (Sadasivaiah et al., 2007,

p. 249). To prevent the development of resistance, the World Health Organization

recommends not "using the same insecticide for multiple successive IRS cycles"

and instead implementing "a system of rotation with a different insecticide class

being used each year" (WHO, 2010, p. 6). It is unlikely that pesticide use will

ever be discontinued, but the enforcement of pesticide regulation and limiting

TO SPRAY OR NOT TO SPRAY   3

its use can reduce the possibility of resistance and increase the efficacy of the
pesticide in protecting human health.

    Another factor that scientists must critically examine is the environmental
consequences of DDT. DDT is chemically very stable; it doesn't break down in the
environment but persists for long periods of time and can bio-accumulate in a
food chain (WHO, 2011c, p. 6). The toxicity of DDT in the environment is clear;
the pesticide's negative effects have been documented by a host of researchers
since the 1960s, with the majority of concern involving the contamination
of agricultural crops. It is unclear, however, whether IRS with DDT causes the
same effects as agricultural use of DDT, especially since the amount of DDT
used to control the spread of malaria does not come close to the amount used
for agriculture in the mid-to-late 1900s (Sadasivaiah et al., 2007, p. 250).
Figure 1 shows the gradual decline of DDT use worldwide from 6,800,000 kg to
900,000 kg between 1995 and 2005 (Sadasivaiah et al., 2007, p. 252). The strict
management of IRS virtually eliminates overuse of the pesticide to a degree that
would cause harm (WHO, 2010, p. 23). Given the low levels of DDT used in IRS
and the strict enforcement of global policies concerning DDT, there is little risk
that IRS could contaminate agricultural crops to the point of causing negative
human health effects and substantial economic harm.

    Finally, there are still unanswered questions as to how DDT use in IRS
affects human health. The health outcomes of DDT exposure from spraying in
the home are less well understood than the well-documented environmental
outcomes. The World Health Organization's report, *DDT in Indoor Residual
Spraying: Human Health Aspects* (2011a), stated that "in terms of potential risks
at levels of exposure of the general population in countries using [indoor residual
spraying], research is needed on reproductive effects in females and certain child
developmental effects to better evaluate risks that were suggested in the studies
that were reviewed" (p. 16). Many studies have suggested that DDT causes "early
pregnancy loss, fertility loss, leukemia, pancreatic cancer, neurodevelopmental
deficits, diabetes, and breast cancer," yet conflicting outcomes in experiments

A transition moves the essay forward.

Since the title and publication year of the source are given in the sentence, the citation includes only the page number.

TO SPRAY OR NOT TO SPRAY   4

Figure 1. Quantities of commonly used insecticides for malaria vector control

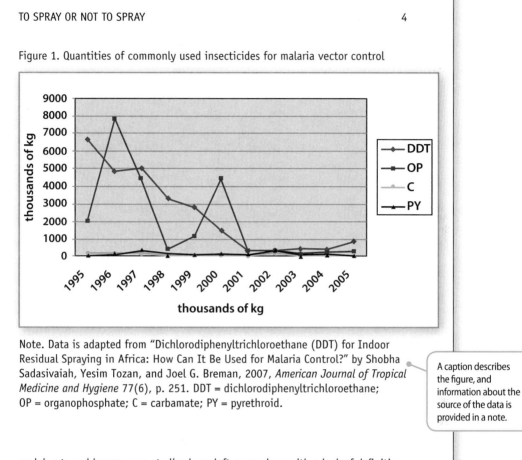

Note. Data is adapted from "Dichlorodiphenyltrichloroethane (DDT) for Indoor Residual Spraying in Africa: How Can It Be Used for Malaria Control?" by Shobha Sadasivaiah, Yesim Tozan, and Joel G. Breman, 2007, *American Journal of Tropical Medicine and Hygiene* 77(6), p. 251. DDT = dichlorodiphenyltrichloroethane; OP = organophosphate; C = carbamate; PY = pyrethroid.

A caption describes the figure, and information about the source of the data is provided in a note.

on lab rats and human case studies have left researchers with a lack of definitive evidence regarding human health risks associated with DDT exposure (van den B.H., 2009, p. 1658). Collectively, these studies point to a need for further research into many of the human health concerns related to DDT and a more critical review of claims about DDT's harmful effects. .

To understand the controversy over DDT in IRS, we must understand not only its risks but also its benefits. Cost is an extremely important aspect of malaria control. When compared with other pesticides available for use in IRS, the cost of DDT is significantly lower. As shown in Table 1, the pesticide Deltamethrin ranks similarly to DDT as far as cost is concerned, but it is slightly more expensive to

Table 1. WHO Insecticide Cost Comparison in U.S. Dollars

A table provides statistical information in a readable format. A note indicates the source of the data.

Insecticide	Approximate duration of residual effect on mud surfaces (months)	Number of spraying rounds per 6 months	Approximate amount of formulated product required per house per 6 months (kg)	Approximate cost of formulated product (US$ per kg)	Cost per house per 6 months (US$)	Cost ratio (DDT = 1)
DDT	6	1	0.5	3.0	1.6	1.0
Deltamethrin	3	2	0.4	4.0	1.6	1.0
Malathion	2	3	2.4	3.4	8.2	5.1
Lambda-cyhalothrin	3	2	0.1	72.0	8.6	5.4
Bendiocarb	2	3	0.3	46.0	13.8	8.6
Fenitrothion	3	2	2.0	7.4	14.8	9.3
Propoxur	3	2	1.0	18.8	18.8	11.8

Note. Data is adapted from "Dichlorodiphenyltrichloroethane (DDT) for Indoor Residual Spraying in Africa: How Can It Be Used for Malaria Control?" by Shobha Sadasivaiah, Yesim Tozan, and Joel G. Breman, 2007, *American Journal of Tropical Medicine and Hygiene 77*(6), p. 254.

produce and does not last as long as DDT. Other pesticides cost as much as six times more than DDT and are not yet as effective (Sadasivaiah et al., 2007, p. 254). Furthermore, DDT does not have to be reapplied for at least six months whereas other pesticides used in IRS have to be reapplied every three to six months (Sadasivaiah et al., 2007, p, 251). When these considerations are coupled with the health costs of malaria, DDT appears to be the most cost-effective pesticide choice at this time.

The stigma around DDT has caused many countries to forgo using it for vector control, but switching to a different pesticide can have its own drawbacks. In 1996, Kwa-zulu Natal, a province in South Africa, abandoned DDT because of health concerns and switched to pyrethrenoid pesticides (Sadasivaiah et al., 2007, p. 256). Unfortunately, this measure which was taken to improve health ended up doing more harm than good. Mosquitoes became resistant to the

TO SPRAY OR NOT TO SPRAY   6

new pesticides and malaria cases increased; when DDT was re-introduced, cases decreased by a drastic 90% (Sadasivaiah et al., 2007, p. 256). Because of such dramatic cases, in 2006, the World Health Organization "formally endors[ed] the use of" DDT in South Africa (Beerbohm, 2007, p. 3).

Given "the right of people to a safe environment," researchers and governments consider whether people should be exposed to a chemical that, although it prevents malaria, might cause physical harm down the road (Bouwman, 2011, p. 746). Do the health risks of malaria outweigh the health risks of using DDT? Unfortunately, it is a difficult question to answer. The continued evolution of resistance in malaria-carrying mosquito species, the substantial environmental consequences of DDT, and the uncertain effects on human health are all serious concerns. However, the health risks malaria posed by malaria cannot be ignored. In the 2010 *World Malaria Report 2010*, the World Health Organization estimated that 225 million cases of malaria occurred in 2009 and that 781,000 of these cases resulted in death (WHO, 2010, p. xii). Compounded by poor healthcare systems in many of the countries faced with malaria, the overall health effects of the disease can be severe. For countries with high rates of malaria and little funding available for expensive control strategies, IRS with DDT may continue to be the answer.

> In her conclusion, the writer emphasizes the main question posed by the essay.

TO SPRAY OR NOT TO SPRAY 7

References

Beerbohm, E. (2007). *A Pilot Expert Elicitation to Assess the Risks of Malaria Vector Control Strategies in East Africa*. (Master's thesis). Duke University. Retrieved from http://dukespace.lib.duke.edu/dspace/handle/10161/370

Bouwman, H., van den Berg, H., & Kylin, H. (2011). DDT and malaria prevention: Addressing the paradox. *Environmental Health Perspectives, 119(6)*, 744-747.

Centers for Disease Control and Prevention. (2008). *About malaria*. Retrieved from http://www.cdc.gov/malaria/about/history/

Sadasivaiah, S., Tozan, Y., & Breman, J.G. (2007, December). Dichlorodiphenyltrichloroethane (DDT) for indoor residual spraying in Africa: How can it be used for malaria control? *The American Journal of Tropical Medicine and Hygiene, 77*(6), 249-63. Retrieved from http://www.ncbi.nlm.nih.gov/books/NBK1724/#pg249.r73

Stockholm Convention. (2009, May). *Governments unite to step-up reduction on global DDT reliance and add nine new chemicals under international treaty*. Retrieved from http://chm.pops.int/Convention/Media/Press%20releases/COP4%20%20Geneva,%209%20May%202009/tabid/542/Default.aspx

Van den Berg, H. (2009). Global status of DDT and its alternatives for use in vector control to prevent disease. *Environmental Health Perspectives, 117*(11), 1656-1663.

World Health Organization. (2010). *World malaria report 2010*. Retrieved from http://www.who.int/malaria/world_malaria_report_2010/en/index.html

World Health Organization. (2011). *DDT in indoor residual spraying: Human health aspects*. Retrieved from http://www.who.int/ipcs/publications/ehc/ehc241.pdf

World Health Organization. (2011, May). *The use of DDT in malaria vector control: WHO position statement* World Health Organization. Retrieved from http://www.who.int/malaria/publications/atoz/who_htm_gmp_2011/en/index.html

World Health Organization. (2011, October). *Malaria factsheet*. Retrieved from http://www.who.int/mediacentre/factsheets/fs094/en/index.html

In APA style, the references are listed on a separate page, with a centered heading.

Sources are alphabetized by the author's last name and are formatted with hanging indents.

A Web source

An article from a scholarly journal

In APA style, multiple works by the same author are listed chronologically.

✱ Project Ideas

The following suggestions offer ideas for writing an informative essay or another type of informative document.

Suggestions for Essays

1. DESCRIBE A SITUATION TO YOUR CLASSMATES

Inform your classmates about a situation that is likely to affect them. For example, you might report on changes to your school's course registration system, or you might let them know about a proposed student fee increase. In your essay, describe the situation clearly, drawing on personal observation, an interview with someone who is familiar with the situation, or written sources.

2. EXPLAIN HOW SOMETHING WORKS

Explain how something works to an audience of your choice, such as your class-mates, other college students, your instructor, your parents, or members of the com-munity. For example, you might explain how a new technology improves the performance of a digital music player, or how a new diet supplement affects the health of those who use it. In your essay, identify the key features or processes that allow the subject of your essay to accomplish its purpose.

3. CHRONICLE A SEQUENCE OF EVENTS

Write an informative essay that describes a series of events. You might choose a historical event, such as the first Gulf War or the decision to send manned missions to the moon, or a more recent event, such as the decision to fire the coach of a local professional sports team, a major layoff at a national high-technology firm, or a recently passed law that has caused some controversy. In your essay, identify the event you will chronicle and lay out the sequence of events that led up to it.

4. DEFINE A PROBLEM

Write an essay that clearly defines a problem. Address your essay to your instructor, to people affected by the problem, or to those in a position to solve the problem. In your essay, describe the situation that you view as problematic. For example, you might call attention to a potential funding shortfall for your college or university or for a local school system. Or you might identify the lack of natural resources needed for a particular purpose, such as farming, manufacturing, power generation, or trans-portation. Then describe the potential consequences of the situation, indicate who or what will be affected by those consequences, and describe the severity of the effects.

5. REPORT THE NEWS

Share news of a recent event, discovery, or disaster with an audience of your choice. You might direct your essay to your instructor, your classmates, other college students, your friends, or people from your hometown. Choose a subject that would interest your readers but that they are unlikely to know about. For example, if you are writing to people from your hometown, you might choose to write about something that has occurred at your college or university. If you are writing to your instructor or classmates, you might choose something that recently occurred in your hometown.

Suggestions for Other Genres

6. CREATE AN INFORMATIVE BROCHURE

Begin working on your brochure by considering your purpose and your readers. Identify the single most important message you want to convey to your readers, and determine how you would like them to react to your message. Then brainstorm the organizing patterns and design strategies you might use to convey that message. Once you've decided on the content, organization, and design of your brochure, create a mockup and ask for feedback from a friend, a classmate, a relative, or an instructor. Keep their feedback in mind as you revise and edit your brochure.

7. DEVELOP AN INFORMATIVE WEB SITE

Begin working on your Web site by considering your purpose and your readers. Once you've identified the information you want to provide, consider how best to present it. Give some thought to the overall structure of your site — that is, the number of and relations among the pages on your site. Then determine which information you will present on each page, and choose the type of navigation tools you'll provide so that your readers can easily move from page to page.

Once you've worked out the overall structure of the site, spend time developing a consistent look and feel for your pages. Your pages should have a similar design (such as a standard color scheme, consistent placement of navigation tools, consistent fonts for headers and body text, and so on). Finally, decide on the type of illustrations and the nature of communication tools, if any, that you'll use on the site. (For guidance on designing Web sites, see Chapter 17.)

8. DRAFT AND DESIGN AN INFORMATIVE ARTICLE FOR A PRINT PUBLICATION

First, decide whether you want to write about a particular subject or to publish in a particular magazine, journal, or newspaper. If you want to write about a particular subject, search your library's databases and the Web for relevant articles. This search can also help you identify publications that might be interested in your article. If you want to publish your article in a particular publication, read it carefully to determine the kinds of subjects it normally addresses. Once you've selected a target publication, analyze it to determine its writing conventions (such as level of formality and the manner in which sources are acknowledged) and design conventions.

As you learn about your subject and plan, organize, and design your article, keep in mind what you've learned about the articles you've read. Your article should reflect those writing and design conventions.

9. WRITE A PROFILE OF A FRIEND OR FAMILY MEMBER

Select a friend or family member and write a profile for a newspaper, magazine, journal, blog, or Web site. Interview the person you plan to profile and, if possible, interview friends or family members who are well acquainted with the subject of your profile. Your profile should offer insights into the person's character and contributions to your life. Support your reflections about him or her with personal experience, information from interviews, and your own reasoning.

10. WRITE A PROFILE OF A PUBLIC FIGURE

Select a public figure who interests you on a personal, professional, or academic level, and write a profile for a newspaper, magazine, journal, blog, or Web site. If you can, interview the person. If you cannot conduct an interview, locate sources that offer information about the person. Your profile should offer insights into his or her accomplishments, interests, and plans. You should reflect on the person's impact on society and the implications of his or her work for the future. Support your reflections with personal experience, information from a published source or an interview with someone who is aware of or acquainted with the person, and your own reasoning.

In Summary: Writing an Informative Essay

✳ **Find a conversation and listen in.**
- Explore your interests (p. 181).
- Use your library (p. 182).
- Ask questions about promising subjects (p. 184).

✳ **Gather information.**
- Create a search plan (p. 184).
- Collect sources (p. 187).
- Evaluate your sources (p. 187).
- Take notes (p. 188).
- Conduct an interview (p. 189).

✳ **Prepare a draft.**
- Present your main point (p. 192).
- Develop supporting points and evidence (p. 192).
- Consider genre and design (p. 195).
- Frame your information (p. 197).

✳ **Review and improve your draft.**
- Focus your discussion (p. 198).
- Ensure clarity (p. 198).
- Review your use of sources (p. 199).
- Assess your introduction and conclusion (p. 199).

Writing to Analyze

When I analyze
a topic, I take
on the role of
interpreter.

GENRES IN CONVERSATION

Reflective Writing | Informative Writing | **Analytical Writing** | Evaluative Writing | Problem-Solving Writing | Argumentative Writing

e-Pages

You can view the full documents shown here and respond to questions about analytical genres at **bedforstmartins.com /conversation/epages.**

Despite recent trends toward eliminating recess in elementary schools, scientists have long suspected play is crucial in children's cognitive development. Imagine you are a member of a school board trying to decide whether or not to eliminate recess from local public schools. In the process of researching evidence of the connection between children's play and learning, you discover a **magazine article**, a **webcast**, and a **professional report**. Each document focuses on children's need to explore their world through play but uses a distinct genre to do so.

Magazine Article ▶

This **magazine article** about children's innate ability to develop theories about the world around them came from an ongoing university study and cites particular studies, even though it is intended for a general audience.

GROWTH

"The first and simplest emotion which we discover in the human mind is, Curiosity." Edmund Burke

A leading researcher in the field of cognitive development says when children pretend, they're not just being silly—they're doing science

WHY PLAY IS SERIES

Walk into any preschool and you'll find toddling superheroes battling imaginary monsters. We take it for granted that young children play and, especially, pretend. Why do they spend so much time in fantasy worlds?

People have suspected that play helps children learn, but until recently there was little research that showed this or explained why it might be true. In my lab at the University of California at Berkeley, we've been trying to explain how very young children can learn so much so quickly, and we've developed a new scientific approach to children's learning.

Where does pretending come in? It relates to what philosophers call "counter-factual" thinking, like Einstein wondering what would happen if a train went at the speed of light.

In one study, my student Daphna Buchsbaum introduced 3-and-4-year-olds to a stuffed monkey and a musical toy and told them, "It's Monkey's birthday, and this is a birthday machine we can use to sing to Monkey. It plays 'Happy Birthday' when you put a zando (a funny-looking object) "on it like this." Then she held up a different object and explained that it wasn't a zando and therefore wouldn't make the music play. Then she asked some tricky counterfactual questions: "If this zando wasn't a zando, would the machine play

music or not?" What if the non-zando was a zando? About half the 3-year-olds answered correctly.

Then a confederate took away the toys and Daphna said, "We could just pretend that this box is the machine and that this block is a zando and this other one isn't. Let's put the blocks on the machine. What will happen next?" About half said the pretend zando made pretend music, while the pretend non-zando did nothing (well, pretend nothing, which is quite a concept even if you're older than 3).

We found children who were better at pretending could reason better about counterfactuals—they were better at thinking about different possibilities. And thinking about possibilities plays a crucial role in the latest understanding about how children learn. The idea is that children at play are like pint-sized scientists testing theories. They imagine ways the world could work and predict the pattern of data that would follow if their theories were true, and then compare that pattern with the pattern they actually see. Even toddlers turn out to be smarter than we would have thought if we ask them the right questions in the right way.

Play is under pressure right now, as parents and policymakers try to make preschools more like schools. But pretend play is not only important for kids; it's a crucial part of what makes all humans so smart.

What keeps Alison Gopnik up at night? Watch a conversation at Smithsonian.com/gopnik

BY ALISON GOPNIK

JULY | AUGUST 2012 · SMITHSONIAN.COM 15

Map | CalMail | bConnected | Directory | Search | Google™ Custom Sea

Latest News   Categories ▸   Events   Sports   Multimedia ▸   Media Relations ▸

Scientists tap the genius of babies and youngsters to make computers smarter

By Yasmin Anwar, Media Relations | March 12, 2012

BERKELEY — People often wonder if computers make children smarter. Scientists at the University of California, Berkeley, are asking the reverse question: Can children make computers smarter? And the answer appears to be 'yes.'

UC Berkeley researchers are tapping the cognitive smarts of babies, toddlers and preschoolers to program computers to think more like humans.

(Video produced by Roxanne Makasdjian, Media Relations)

If replicated in machines, the computational models based on baby brainpower could give a major boost to artificial intelligence, which historically has had difficulty handling nuances and uncertainty, researchers said

"Children are the greatest learning machines in the universe. Imagine if computers could learn as much and as quickly as they do," said Alison Gopnik a developmental psychologist at UC Berkeley and author of "The Scientist in the Crib" and "The Philosophical Baby."

In a wide range of experiments involving lollipops, flashing and spinning toys, and music makers, among other props, UC Berkeley researchers are finding that children – at younger and younger ages – are testing hypotheses, detecting statistical patterns and drawing conclusions while constantly adapting to changes.

"Young children are capable of solving problems that still pose a challenge for computers, such as learning languages and figuring out causal relationships," said Tom Griffiths, director of UC Berkeley's Computational Cognitive Science Lab. "We are hoping to make computers smarter by making them a little more like children."

For example, researchers said, computers programmed with kids' cognitive smarts could interact more intelligently and responsively with humans in applications such as computer tutoring programs and phone-answering robots.

And that's not all.

"Your computer could be able to discover causal relationships, ranging from simple cases such as recognizing that you work more slowly when you haven't had coffee, to complex ones such as identifying which genes cause greater susceptibility to diseases," said Griffiths. He is applying a statistical method known as Bayesian probability theory to translate the calculations that children make during learning tasks into computational models.

Share this story
Email

Latest News

Robert Hass, poet and professor, up for PEN essay award

Dirks takes to the air on KQED's 'Forum' ◀))

Napolitano selected as new UC president

Dirks makes the case for higher education

What transit-oriented development means for original communities

Popular Stories

Read | Mailed

Napolitano selected as new UC president

An illusion floats on Mining Circle pool

Big boost for multicultural student programs

Design students look upward in global competition

Robert Hass, poet and professor, up for PEN essay award

Tags

admin
astron
awar
Berkeley
Chanc
chemis
divers

◀ **Webcast**

This **webcast** released to the public by UC Berkeley provides experts' commentary on behind-the-scenes footage of children in action.

Professional Report ▸

A **professional report** by a coalition of educators and health professionals places "play" in a historical and international context in order to analyze focused, playful classrooms in a test-driven society.

Summary and Recommendations of

CRISIS IN THE KINDERGARTEN

Why Children Need to Play in School

A report from the Alliance for Childhood by **Edward Miller** *and* **Joan Almon**

THE IMPORTANCE OF PLAY to young children's healthy development and learning has been documented beyond question by research. Yet play is rapidly disappearing from kindergarten and early education as a whole. We believe that the stifling of play has dire consequences—not only for children but for the future of our nation. This report is meant to bring broad public attention to the crisis in our kindergartens and to spur collective action to reverse the damage now being done.

Kindergarten has changed radically in the last two decades. Children now spend far more time being taught and tested on literacy and math skills than they do learning through play and exploration, exercising their bodies, and using their imaginations. Many kindergartens use highly prescriptive curricula geared to new state standards and linked to standardized tests. In an increasing number of kindergartens, teachers must follow scripts from which they may not deviate. These practices, which are not well grounded in research, violate long-established principles of child development and good teaching. It is increasingly clear that they are compromising both children's health and their long-term prospects for success in school.

The argument of this report, that child-initiated play must be restored to kindergarten, will be dismissed and even ridiculed in some quarters. In spite of the fact that the vital importance of play has been shown in study after study, many people believe that play is a waste of time in school. School, they say, should be a place for learning. There's plenty of time for play at home.

Skepticism about the value of play is compounded by the widespread assumption that the earlier children begin to master the basic elements of reading, such as phonics and letter recognition, the more likely they are to succeed in school. And so kindergarten education has become heavily focused on teaching literacy and other academic skills, and preschool is rapidly following suit.

The common misconceptions about young children's play fall apart when we look closely at what is really going on. We see the difference between superficial play and the complex make-believe play that can engage five-year-olds for an hour or more, fueled by their own original ideas and rich use of language. We start to distinguish between the sound of a chaotic classroom and the hum of energy when children are deeply engaged in the flow of play.

We also see the difference between didactic teaching of discrete skills in phonics, decoding, and word recognition, which may yield short-term gains in test scores in the early grades, and the deeper experiential learning whose benefits last into fourth grade and

☀ Alliance for Childhood

What Is Writing to Analyze?

Analytical writing begins with a question: To what extent does government surveillance of suspected terrorists affect the civil liberties of ordinary citizens? How will new environmental regulations affect plans to drill for oil near a state park? Why do animated films from Pixar Studios appeal to so many adults? The types of documents — or genres (see p. 255) — writers create to share their answers are as varied as the questions they ask. And each document, in turn, reflects aspects of the writing situations in which writers find themselves: their purposes for analyzing a subject, the interests and expectations of their intended readers, the sources used to support the analysis, and the context in which the document will be read.

Analysis involves adopting the role of *interpreter*. Writers who adopt this role help readers understand the origins, qualities, significance, or potential impact of a subject. An interpreter might address the causes of a recent economic downturn, for example, while another might explore the cultural implications of a new album by Kanye West. Another writer might present a historical analysis of U.S. involvement in foreign wars, while yet another might try to help college students understand the impact of proposed legislation on the cost of attending college.

In many cases, interpreters are already knowledgeable about their subjects. More often, however, they spend time learning about a subject to ensure that they can offer a well-grounded interpretation. Whether they draw on the subject itself, interview experts, collect information from published sources, or use statistical evidence, effective interpreters provide even knowledgeable readers with enough information about a subject to explain the focus of their analyses and to ensure that their interpretations will make sense in the context in which they're read.

Readers of analytical documents usually share the writer's interest in the subject and want to understand it in greater depth, either because it affects them in

The Writer's Role: Interpreter

PURPOSE

- To find patterns of meaning
- To trace causes and effects
- To determine significance

READERS

- Want to understand the subject
- Expect a careful and appropriate use of analytical techniques
- Expect coherent, focused reasons and evidence for the writer's interpretation

SOURCES

- Especially in the case of textual analysis, the subject itself is often the main source.
- Data, background information, and other writers' interpretations are often obtained from published material.
- Field research (interviews, observation, surveys, correspondence) and personal experience can add details and support.

CONTEXT

- Analytical questions, interpretive frameworks, and genres are shaped by reader expectations and disciplinary standards and expectations.
- Interpreters usually need to frame a subject for readers before analyzing it.

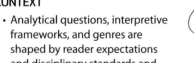

some way or because they are curious about it. They expect a clear introduction to the subject, focused interpretation, thorough explanations of how the writer arrived at his or her conclusions, and reasonable support for those conclusions. Readers also tend to expect that an analytical document will use an interpretive framework that is appropriate to the subject and similar to those typically used by other writers in the field. For example, readers with a literary background would be surprised if an analysis of a major novel was based on the book's sales history, rather than on some form of textual interpretation. Similarly, readers with a background in political science might find an article that focused on the aesthetic qualities of a speech by a presidential candidate less interesting than one that analyzed the political implications of the candidate's arguments.

Interpreters' choices about interpretive framework, sources, and perspective can and do lead to different — sometimes extremely different — conclusions about a subject. As a result, analytical documents not only serve as significant contributions to a conversation but also provide a foundation for further contributions to the conversation.

What Kinds of Documents Are Used to Present an Analysis?

Writers share their interpretations of subjects through a strikingly large array of genres. Soldiers and aid workers in Iraq and Afghanistan, for example, have interpreted the events in which they are involved through books, blogs, and social-networking sites. Commentators analyze the political landscape through columns, editorials, and data analyses. Scholars examine subjects as diverse as Shakespeare's sonnets, the possibility of life on Mars, and the potential for electoral college reform through journal articles and conference presentations. And students are frequently asked to share their interpretations through essays, reports, and presentations.

Regardless of the genre a writer decides to use, most analytical writing begins with an attempt to understand how other writers have approached the challenges of analyzing a particular subject. Examining analytical documents can spark ideas about how to focus an analysis, offer insights into the kinds of interpretive frameworks that have been used to direct past analyses, and provide an understanding of the conclusions other writers have drawn. In the following sections, you'll find examples and discussions of magazine articles, rhetorical analyses, and analytical blog posts. In the e-Pages for this chapter, you'll find discussions and examples of news analyses, documentary films, and analytical essays.

View the e-Pages for analytical writing at bedfordstmartins.com /conversation/epages.

Magazine Articles

Magazine and newspaper articles often provide analyses of issues, events, or problems. Because most articles are written for a specific publication, writers typically have a clear picture of their readers (in terms of age, income, education, hobbies, and so forth) and can target their analysis to the needs and interests of a narrowly defined group. An article about an election, for example, might analyze turnout among younger voters, analyze the campaign of a recently elected senator from the Midwest, or analyze the impact of organizations such as the Teamsters or the National Rifle Association.

Analytical articles rely heavily on information obtained by the author from sources such as books, Web sites, government reports, interviews, surveys, and observation. Writers often use illustrations to highlight key points in their analysis, to present information or data, or to explain complicated concepts; most also draw on quotations from interviews to present or expand on important points.

 ### Sito Negron
Baghdad, Mexico

"Baghdad, Mexico," an analysis of U.S. attitudes and policies toward the border city of Juárez, Mexico, relies primarily on the direct observation and research of its author, El Paso native Sito Negron. The article originally appeared in *Texas Monthly*, a magazine that covers current events, culture, and leisure in Texas. But as you read, notice how Negron's analysis — particularly in his sustained comparison between Juárez and Iraq — is designed to appeal to an American audience beyond his state's borders. Negron is a former reporter for the *El Paso Times* and editor of The Newspaper Tree, a news, politics, and culture Web site.

Baghdad, Mexico

**It's time we saw El Paso's sister
city for what it is — a war zone.**

by Sito Negron

January 2009

A story about Juárez made the rounds in El Paso last summer. Surrounded by guards, a well-dressed, impeccably polite man enters a restaurant. He apologizes as the guards round up cell phones and cameras. No one is allowed to get up as the man sits and eats. When he leaves, he apologizes again and pays the tab for everyone. The man is said to be Joaquín "El Chapo" Guzmán, head of the Sinaloa cartel.

This is an urban legend. No one who tells it was there. I've heard it several times from people who said a friend of a friend heard it from a first-hand source. Also, the story has likely been told elsewhere about other outlaws. Versions of this story were probably told in Al Capone's Chicago.

Here's something that is true: Last year in Juárez, more than 1,300 people were murdered. That number includes at least 8 people killed during a prayer meeting at a rehabilitation center in August, where the machine gun fire lasted fifteen minutes and eyewitnesses reported that soldiers parked nearby did nothing; 4 men gunned down in October at an amusement park filled with civilians; and in November, a headless body hung from an overpass, a burned, headless, handless body dumped on the sidewalk in front of a police station, and 16 people killed in a single day, including 7 executed beside a school's soccer field. Yet only a handful of people have been brought before a judge for any of these crimes.

The legend and the truth combine to explain something fundamental about what is happening in Juárez, a city with an international reputation for cheap labor, murdered women, and drug cartels. There is a total breakdown in civil order. To put the death toll in context, in 2007, the bloodiest year of the Iraq war, 904 U.S. servicemen and -women were killed. As in Baghdad or Ramadi or Fallujah, the violence in Juárez has spared no one. Almost everybody I know who lives or does business across the river has a story about a crime he or she experienced, a relative who was kidnapped or a friend who was carjacked. A friend of the family told my uncle that one of her relatives was killed but that, to prevent reprisals, police advised her not to report it as a murder.

No one is sure what to believe or who is in charge. Well, that's not entirely true. Whoever has a gun trained on you is in charge. In a city where the law holds no sway, this raw exercise of power provides at least an illusion of order. For example, other than the cartels, the military has the firepower. When Mexican president Felipe Calderón sent 2,500 troops into northern Mexico to help keep order and clean up the corrupt police forces, the public reaction could be summed up in two ways. One was fear of yet another group of armed men acting with impunity. The other was a shrug. Many people have the understanding that the military, or at least elements of the military, is involved in the violence. According to one theory, the troops are in Juárez to help Guzmán's Sinaloa cartel finish off the Juárez cartel.

That might be the only way order can be restored. Not to stop the drug trade, a ridiculous idea, but to at least get the business back to where most of the killing takes place among those involved in the trafficking.

Juárez has always been a rough town, and bodies rolled in blankets in the desert or stuffed in car trunks are part of the local business. So is an occasional outburst of public violence, as in the rash of killings following the 1997 death of Amado Carrillo Fuentes, the man who took the Juárez cartel to the peak of its power and perished in a Mexico City operating room while undergoing plastic surgery to alter his facial appearance.

But nothing like these new killings in my 25 years in El Paso. Perhaps nothing like this since the Mexican Revolution.

Those on the inside saw it coming. In May, when the explosion of violence was still relatively fresh, an e-mail circulated among some Department of Homeland Security officials citing a bleak Drug Enforcement Administration report that predicted that "the situation in Juárez will be very bad for at least 6–8 months." The e-mail was part of a string that also included information about a Mexican police officer seeking asylum because "the Cartel/Narcos have announced to everyone that this coming Saturday, May 24, 2008, there will be a lot of dead police officers and it's going to get very bloody in Cd. [Ciudad] Juárez."

I used to have a talk radio show here in El Paso, and when the violence began, I said that it was nothing for civilians to get worked up about. It was just a battle among violent businessmen that would sort itself out, as it had before. One day, a caller berated me for putting my head in the sand, arguing that the violence would spill over to El Paso. It has not, although dozens of victims have been treated at El Paso's Thomason Hospital, and there were reports in August that the cartels had sanctioned killings in the United States. But from the relative safety of El Paso, I can see that less than a mile as the crow flies from where I live, something terrible has happened to Juárez.

Juárez and El Paso are twins, bound by a river. The Rio Grande does more than define a boundary here. In fact, this crease in the rocks where the water turns from south to southeast is not so much a boundary as an axis, a point where roads come together and deals are made. Goods naturally move through such transfer points — counterfeit toys, cigarettes, meat, avocados, toilet paper, purses, auto parts, furniture, coupons, medicines. Not to mention cheap pot, cocaine, even meth.

> This drug war crossed the border years ago. We can measure its impact on our country in many ways — jail sentences, seized property, lives ruined, the growth of law enforcement.

The passage of men and products through this axis goes back as far as El Camino Real de Tierra Adentro, the Royal Road to the Interior, which connected Mexico City to Santa Fe, but it was not until the railroad arrived, in the 1880s, that El Paso and Juárez really took off. Here the raw materials of northern Mexico, primarily from the region's mines, were converted into wealth. During the Mexican Revolution, guns flowed south; during Prohibition, liquor flowed north. By 1960 the population of both cities was roughly a quarter million each; since then Juárez has surpassed El Paso and now has about 1.3 million residents to El Paso County's 750,000.

A part of El Paso's population has always consisted of people who live on both sides of the border. But that number has spiked as Juárez in particular and Mexico in general descend into chaos and the wealthy and middle class flee. In May, George Friedman, the founder and CEO of Stratfor, a private intelligence service based in Austin, wrote that Mexico—with the second-largest economy in Latin America and the eleventh-largest population in the world—was at risk of becoming a "failed state," similar to countries in the Middle East where government has become paralyzed and has little or no control over its territory. Chillingly, Friedman also recognized a parallel to the recent history of Colombia.

"Mexico now faces a classic problem," he wrote. "Multiple, well-armed organized groups have emerged. They are fighting among themselves while simultaneously fighting the government. The groups are fueled by vast amounts of money earned via drug smuggling to the United States. The amount of money involved—estimated at some $40 billion a year—is sufficient to increase tension between these criminal groups and give them the resources to conduct wars against each other. It also provides them with resources to bribe and intimidate government officials. The resources they deploy in some ways are superior to the resources the government employs."

Money also links the cartels directly to the highest levels of government. In late October, the *Wall Street Journal* reported that the Sinaloa cartel may have had a mole in the U.S. embassy in Mexico City who gave the drug lords information from the U.S. DEA.

In Colombia, where U.S. forces still operate in the jungles, overt cartel violence has stabilized, but the war continues. U.S. forces are a key part of Plan Colombia, which was initiated in 2000 and has provided more than $2 billion, the bulk for military aid. Mexico has its own Plan Colombia. It's called the Mérida Initiative, and under this proposal the Bush administration has requested $1.1 billion in aid over the next two fiscal budgets to be used for equipment and training (this number includes a small amount for Central America).

But who will be the beneficiary of this infusion? The cynical observer might take note of the private jet that crashed near Mérida in September 2007, filled with more than three tons of Guzmán's cocaine. The same aircraft has been linked to CIA rendition flights to Guantánamo Bay. The cynical observer might wonder if this extralegal mixture of drugs and national security could be the real Mérida Initiative. Iran-Contra, anyone?

Like the tribal militias in Iraq, the people who control the streets of Juárez act with impunity. In October, the *El Paso Times* reported that cartels were shaking down merchants to raise money for their operations. Who can protect the innocent? The soldiers? Allegations against the military have included torture, robbery, and kidnapping. In September, Gustavo de la Rosa Hickerson, of the Chihuahua State Human Rights Commission, told Newspaper Tree, the El Paso politics and culture Web site that I edit, that human rights violations by the military in Juárez had risen from 20 instances in 2007 to more than 250 in 2008. The number has increased since then.

The police? They're either on the run for their lives or working for the cartels or both. One of the subgroups involved in the war in Juárez is known as La Linea ("the Line"), a collection of corrupt police officials that might be considered subcontractors to the cartels. Alfredo Corchado, the Mexico bureau chief for the *Dallas Morning News* (and a former El Pasoan), described La Linea in 2004 as "a group of drug traffickers and Juárez and Chihuahua state police officers who authorities say protect cartel leaders and smuggle drugs across the border." (Speaking of impunity, Corchado reported that La Linea was being investigated for the infamous killings of women in Juárez.)

I imagine La Linea to be similar to corrupt police in Baghdad who have terrorist or criminal affiliates. Let's say there is a commander who reports to a cartel lieutenant, and he has several groups of lower-ranking officers who perform various tasks. Say a couple of those guys have a relative with a load of drugs. They figure they'll freelance. The commander finds out, and they're dead. Or they're guarding a sanctioned load of dope, and they decide to make a deal with the Sinaloa cartel. Or maybe they don't make a deal, and the Sinaloa cartel wants the dope and wants to send a message, so there's some torture involved. Then they go after the family. You've heard this story before, involving different motives and countries, but what is always the same is the control of the ground versus the power of an outside army—and always bodies, too often of the innocent.

I opened this piece with an anecdote. As the bloody days have turned into weeks and months, the anecdotes pile up, blurring and changing shape and form until they might no longer resemble what happened but still capture the awful, bewildering truth.

More than 1,300 people were killed in Juárez in 2008. Let that sink in. It's not just hit men and drug smugglers and corrupt policemen; it's children, teenagers, innocent family members. They have been shot, burned, tortured, beheaded. Go to YouTube, search for "Juárez Sinaloa cartel," and see for yourself how similar the violence is to what has transpired in Baghdad.

The similarities go a long way. Like Iraq, which is rich in oil, Mexico is rich in drugs (either as producer or transporter), and the biggest market for these commodities is in the United States. Both oil and illegal drugs are imported from countries that struggle with unstable political systems. And now, because of a battle for control of the market—either to own the biggest percentage of the flow or to shut it down—we are in a drug war, just as we have found ourselves in a war for oil.

We could learn from history, but how likely is that?

Friedman, the Stratfor analyst, draws a comparison between Mexico as a potentially failed state and Al Capone's Chicago: "Smuggling alcohol created huge pools of money . . . [and] gave these criminals huge amounts of power, which they used to intimidate and effectively absorb the city government."

Ending Prohibition destroyed the crime rings. Would legalizing drugs do the same thing to the cartels? That's a subject for another article and for a more rational public discourse, one that's not likely anytime soon.

Meanwhile in Mexico, drug war violence and corruption threaten the government (as this article was being written, an airplane carrying Interior Minister Juan Camilo Mouriño and other top government officials crashed in a Mexico City neighborhood in what some suspect was an assassination). In Juárez people do not trust the police, and they fear the military. The civil order has collapsed.

This drug war crossed the border years ago. We can measure its impact on our country in many ways—jail sentences, seized property, lives ruined, the growth of law enforcement. In some inner-city neighborhoods of the United States, the impact is measured in bodies.

So it is now on the border, where some days I stand in my yard and stare across the river at Juárez, looking at a Baghdad that is largely of our creation and wondering when the chickens will come home to roost.

Starting a Conversation: Respond to "Baghdad, Mexico"

In your writer's notebook, reflect on Negron's analysis by responding to the following questions:

1. "Baghdad, Mexico" sets up a parallel between the city of Juárez, Mexico, and Iraq. Do you agree that the "similarities go a long way" (para. 23)? What criteria is Negron using to make his case? How does the evidence establish the significance of his subject and suggest why readers outside of Texas should care about violence in Juárez?

2. How does Negron establish his credibility on this subject? Point to specific parts of the essay where he demonstrates his knowledge or authority.

3. Negron writes, "The legend and the truth combine to explain something fundamental about what is happening in Juárez" (para. 4). How does he demonstrate the validity of this assertion about "legend" and "truth" in his opening paragraphs — and later in the essay? Why does he include a story that is not true?

4. In paragraph 17, the writer switches to the third person, using the term "cynical observer" to speculate about a plane crash in Mérida, Mexico. Why do you think he does this? How does it suggest a problem with U.S. policies toward Mexico? What assumptions does he seem to be making about his readers?

5. How would you characterize Negron's attitude and tone in "Baghdad, Mexico"? Does he propose a solution to the problem he identifies or see any way that "civil order" in Juárez could be reestablished? How might "Baghdad, Mexico" contribute to a larger conversation about relations between the United States and Mexico?

Rhetorical Analyses

Rhetorical analyses take numerous forms, from articles and essays to blogs, Web pages, and — as in the case of Brooke Gladstone's graphic analysis — comics. Rhetorical analyses typically address factors such as the writer's purpose and background, the nature of the audience involved in a particular communication situation, the context in which a particular communication act took place, or the source of the information used in a particular exchange. Writers of rhetorical analyses often draw on sources of information that reflect the knowledge and interests of their intended readers. A rhetorical analysis written for a scholarly journal in political science, for example, might rely more heavily on scholarly articles and books than would an analysis directed to a general audience, which might rely more heavily on observation, interviews, and references to news articles or broadcasts.

Brooke Gladstone
The Goldilocks Number

"The Goldilocks Number" first appeared in Brooke Gladstone's book *The Influencing Machine: Brooke Gladstone on the Media*, illustrated by Josh Neufeld, and it was adapted from a radio segment Gladstone produced for NPR in 2010. Gladstone, a journalist and media analyst, calls *The Influencing Machine* a "media manifesto" in which she challenges readers' common assumptions about media. As you read, pay attention to how the illustrations enhance Gladstone's analysis and help distinguish her own ideas from those of her sources.

Starting a Conversation: Respond to "The Goldilocks Number"

In your writer's notebook, reflect on Gladstone's analysis on pp. 225–227 by responding to the following questions:

1. "The Goldilocks Number" begins by inquiring into the story behind a seemingly improbable statistic. What leads Gladstone to question the numbers she keeps hearing? Why do you think she chooses the sources she does to find answers?

2. Gladstone traces her evidence back through several layers in order to find out the truth behind the statistic, and in the last panel of the first page, Neufeld depicts Gladstone in a detective's outfit with a magnifying glass. In what ways does Gladstone's research resemble that of a detective? What questions does she return to as she tracks down each new source? How do those questions — and the answers she finds — shape her analysis?

3. Rhetorical analysis is a specific type of analysis (see p. 223 for more information). In what ways is Gladstone's analysis of the Goldilocks number a rhetorical analysis? How does she take into consideration the context and audience around her questions?

4. Many of the experts Gladstone cites in her analysis were also cited in a 2006 *National Law Journal* article by Jason McClure that addresses the very same misuse of the number 50,000. How might Gladstone have better acknowledged this article in her work?

5. Gladstone concludes with the comment, "Sometimes the simplest reasons are the scariest." What does she mean, exactly? In what ways are the "simplest reasons" the most frightening in this situation, and to whom?

Analytical Blog Posts

Blogs — short for Weblogs — are online forums that allow writers to present their opinions, observations, and reflections to a broad readership. They can consist of the contributions of a single writer, or they can draw on contributions from multiple writers. Blogs can be published and maintained by individuals, in a manner similar to putting material on a personal Web site. They can also be sponsored by news organizations, public interest groups, government agencies, corporations, and other organizations. When a blog is sponsored by an organization or a publication, the writer takes into account the purpose of the organization or publication and the interests, needs, and backgrounds of readers who visit the blog.

Blogs are frequently used in analytical and informative writing. Entries typically are brief and often present a personal perspective on an issue. However, because blogs have fewer length limitations than a newspaper, magazine, or journal article might have, blog entries are more likely to rely on evidence from other sources than are opinion columns and letters to the editor. Because of their electronic format, they can also use multimedia illustrations, such as video and audio clips or interactive polls, and link to other sources. And because readers can reply publicly to a blog entry by posting responses and analyses of their own, conversations can be extended over time and can involve readers and writers more actively.

Nick Bilton
Disruptions: Digital Era Redefining Etiquette

The *New York Times'* Bits Blog offers analysis of the technology industry, using posts from multiple authors and experts to comment on wide-ranging topics in technology news. Nick Bilton is a British American technology and business journalist for the *New York Times*. His book *I Live in the Future: And Here's How It Works* (2010) looks at the effects of the new digital culture on our brains, and his forthcoming book *The Twitter Story* addresses the history of Twitter and its impact on society. As you read, consider the context of Bilton's analysis and its likely audience, along with his purpose and reasons for choosing this topic.

Disruptions

Digital Era Redefining Etiquette

By Nick Bilton

Some people are so rude. Really, who sends an e-mail or text message that just says "Thank you"? Who leaves a voice mail message when you don't answer, rather than texting you? Who asks for a fact easily found on Google?

Don't these people realize that they're wasting your time?

Of course, some people might think me the rude one for not appreciating life's little courtesies. But many social norms just don't make sense to people drowning in digital communication.

Take the "thank you" message. Daniel Post Senning, a great-great-grandson of Emily Post and a co-author of the 18th edition of *Emily Post's Etiquette*, asked: "At what point does appreciation and showing appreciation outweigh the cost?"

That said, he added, "it gives the impression that digital natives can't be bothered to nurture relationships, and there's balance to be found."

Then there is voice mail, another impolite way of trying to connect with someone. Think of how long it takes to access your voice mail and listen to one of those long-winded messages. "Hi, this is so-and-so. . ." In text messages, you don't have to declare who you are, or even say hello. E-mail, too, leaves something to be desired, with subject lines and "hi" and "bye," because the communication could happen faster by text. And then there are the worst offenders of all: those who leave a voice mail message and then e-mail to tell you they left a voice mail message.

My father learned this lesson last year after leaving me a dozen voice mail messages, none of which I listened to. Exasperated, he called my sister to complain that I never returned his calls. "Why are you leaving him voice mails?" my sister asked. "No one listens to voice mail anymore. Just text him."

My mother realized this long ago. Now we communicate mostly through Twitter.

Tom Boellstorff, a professor of digital anthropology at the University of California, Irvine, said part of the problem is that offline and online communications borrow from each other. For example, the e-mail term CC stands for carbon copy, as in the carbon paper used to copy a letter. But some gestures, like opening an e-mail with "hello" or signing off with "sincerely," are disappearing from the medium.

This is by no means the first conundrum with a new communication technology. In the late 1870s, when the telephone was invented, people didn't know how to greet a caller. Often, there was just silence. Alexander Graham Bell, the inventor, suggested that people say "Ahoy!" Others proposed, "What is wanted?" Eventually "Hello" won out, and it hastened its use in face-to-face communications.

Now, with Google and online maps at our fingertips, what was once normal can be seen as uncivilized — like asking someone for directions to a house, restaurant, or office, when they can easily be found on Google Maps.

I once asked a friend something easily discovered on the Internet, and he responded with a link to lmgtfy.com, which stands for Let Me Google That For You.

In the age of the smartphone, there is no reason to ask once-acceptable questions: the weather forecast, a business phone number, a store's hours. But some people still do. And when you answer them, they respond with a thank-you e-mail.

"I have decreasing amounts of tolerance for unnecessary communication because it is a burden and a cost," said Baratunde Thurston, co-founder of Cultivated Wit, a comedic creative company. "It's almost too easy to not think before we express ourselves because expression is so cheap, yet it often costs the receiver more."

Mr. Thurston said he encountered another kind of irksome communication when a friend asked, by text message, about his schedule for the South by Southwest festival. "I don't even know how to respond to that," he said. "The answer would be so long. There's no way I'm going to type out my schedule in a text."

He said people often asked him on social media where to buy his book, rather than simply Googling the question. You're already on a computer, he exclaimed. "You're on the thing that has the answer to the thing you want to know!"

How to handle these differing standards? Easy: think of your audience. Some people, especially older ones, appreciate a thank-you message. Others, like me, want no reply. "It is important to think about who the relationship is with," Mr. Senning said.

The anthropologist Margaret Mead once said that in traditional societies, the young learn from the old. But in modern societies, the old can also learn from the young. Here's hoping that politeness never goes out of fashion, but that time-wasting forms of communication do.

In your writer's notebook, reflect on Bilton's analytical blog post by responding to the following questions:

1. Consider the tone that Bilton takes in his introduction. Why do you think he feigns outrage at what would normally be considered polite gestures? What point is he making by taking this tone? How is his audience likely to react?

2. The question "At what point does appreciation and showing appreciation outweigh the cost?" lies at the heart of Bilton's analysis of digital communication. How would you answer that question? To what extent does your answer depend on your context, the technology in use, and the audience for your communication?

3. In paragraph 9, Tom Boellstorff notes that "part of the problem is that offline and online communications borrow from each other," and Bilton mentions a few of the conventions that blur the lines between our online and offline lives. How does this observation support his main point? How does he extend this observation to strengthen his analysis?

4. What kinds of examples — and what sources — does Bilton use to support his analysis? To what extent do these examples and sources come from his own purpose and background as a writer and a person? If you were writing a blog entry on the same topic, what sources and examples would you be likely to draw on from your own experience and knowledge?

5. Bilton concludes his blog entry by offering advice for navigating the seemingly contradictory rules that govern digital communication: "How to handle these differing standards? Easy: think of your audience." Is the advice he offers as "easy" as he claims it to be? In what situations might it be difficult or impossible to determine an appropriate way to communicate based on audience alone? What other factors might you consider in those cases?

How Can I Write an Analytical Essay?

Got questions? Got an inquiring mind? Got the discipline to follow up on a question carefully and thoroughly? If you answered "yes" to these questions, you've got what it takes to start writing an analytical essay.

That's not all it takes, of course. Writing an analytical essay also involves refining your question, gaining a fuller understanding of your subject, applying an appropriate interpretive framework, and drafting your response to your analytical question. But the foundation of an analytical essay — and of all analytical documents, for that matter — is developing and responding to a question about a subject.

In Process

An Analytical Essay about Football & Health

Ali Bizzul wrote an analytical essay for her introductory composition course. Ali learned about her topic by reading articles about the short-term and long-term health risks football players face when they put on extra weight. Follow Ali's efforts to write her analytical essay by reading the In Process boxes throughout this chapter.

As you work on your analytical essay, you'll follow the work of Ali Bizzul, a first-year student who wrote an analytical essay about the health risks football players face when they put on extra weight.

Find a Conversation and Listen In

Analytical essays allow you to share your interpretation of a subject with your readers. Your analysis will reflect not only your analytical question and interpretive framework but also what other writers involved in the conversation about your subject have written and the types of analyses they've conducted. It will also reflect the demands of your writing assignment. To get started on your analytical essay, review your assignment and spend some time thinking about your writing situation: your purposes for writing; your readers' needs, interests, knowledge, and background; potential sources of evidence; and the contexts that might affect your analysis (see p. 14). Then start generating ideas about the kinds of questions you could ask, find a conversation worth joining, and learn more about it.

EXPLORE YOUR SURROUNDINGS

Analysis is largely a search for patterns — and searching for patterns is something we do on a daily basis. As we learn to drive, for example, we start noticing the typical behaviors of other drivers as they approach an intersection. It doesn't take long to learn that we can reliably predict whether other drivers are planning to go through the intersection, stop, turn left, or turn right — even when they fail to use turn signals. When we see behaviors that are unusual or unexpected, we go on alert, making sure that we aren't hit by a driver who isn't paying attention. Similarly, we look for patterns in everything from playing tennis (noticing, for instance, how a player grips the racket before returning a shot) to reading the newspaper (learning where we can find stories that interest us or how to distinguish news from advertisements).

Humans are quite good at identifying and responding to patterns. But it takes time to notice them and even more time to figure out how they work. Before choosing a specific focus for your analytical essay, identify general topics that might interest you enough to explore in depth. One good way to begin is to brainstorm (see p. 32), freewrite (see p. 33), or loop (see p. 34) about the objects and events that surround you.

- **Your shelves.** Scan your collection of music, books, and movies, and think about anything you've listened to, read, or watched that grabbed your attention. You might be rewarded by looking beneath the surface for meaning or themes, or you might find yourself intrigued by a plot line or a style that appears to be part of a larger trend.

- **The daily news.** Whether you follow current events in newspapers, on television, or on the Web, recent and ongoing news stories offer rich opportunities for analysis: Why were some groups offended by a magazine cover? Is third-party health insurance to blame for the high cost of medical care? How do "bad girl" celebrities influence children's behavior? Be alert to the questions that occur to you as you read, to reactions (other people's and your own) that surprise you, and to themes that seem to pop up from one day to the next. You're likely to notice something you want to investigate further.

- **Your leisure activities.** No matter what you do for fun — participate in a sport, play video games, take photographs — you can probably find some aspects of your lifestyle that raise questions or suggest a trend. For instance, perhaps you've wondered whether the X Games will become more popular than the Olympics, or noticed that massively multiplayer online games have become more popular than first-person shooters.

- **Your physical environment.** Take a look around you. A favorite poster in your bedroom, for instance, might be a good candidate for interpretation. A new bank in town might inspire questions about interest rates, community service, or architectural style. An overflowing trash bin might suggest an analytical essay on recycling or municipal waste management.

As you consider possible topics for your writing project, look for new or surprising ideas that interest you and your readers and lend themselves to analysis. If you come across a subject or a question that makes a good candidate for your essay, add it to your writer's notebook.

You'll find additional writing project ideas at the end of this chapter (p. 268).

ASK INTERPRETIVE QUESTIONS

The foundation for analysis is a question that is open to interpretation. For example, asking whether you have enough money to purchase a ticket to the latest Robert Downey Jr. movie would not require an interpretive response. Either you have enough money or you don't. Asking whether Downey's performance breaks new ground, however, would require an analysis of his work in the film. Similarly, while a driver wouldn't need to conduct an analysis to determine whether a car has a full tank of fuel, a city planner might find it necessary to carry out an analysis to anticipate how high the cost of fuel must rise before commuters leave their cars at home and take public transportation.

You can generate potential interpretive questions about promising topics by brainstorming, freewriting, or clustering in response to the following prompts. Each prompt focuses your attention on a general topic in a different way, and each provides a useful starting point for an analytical essay. Depending on your topic, you'll find that some prompts are more productive than others.

- **Elements.** Think about the subject in terms of its parts. How does it break down into smaller pieces, or how can it be divided in different ways? Which parts are most important, and which are less significant?

- **Categories.** What groups does the subject belong to? How is it similar to or different from other subjects in a particular group? How can comparing the subject to related subjects help you and your readers understand it in a new way?

- **History.** Look into the origins of the subject. What recent events are related to the subject, and what are the implications of those events? Does your subject build on previous events? Will it continue to have influences in the future, and if so, how will it do so?

- **Causes and effects.** What caused the subject, and why is it the way it is? What are the subject's influences on people, events, and objects? Who or what affects the subject? What effects is the subject likely (or unlikely) to cause in the future?

- **Relationships.** How is the subject connected to other ideas, events, or objects? For example, are changes in the subject related to changes in related ideas, events, or objects?

- **Meaning.** What is the subject's significance and implications? Can different people find different meanings in the subject, and if so, why? Does a close examination of the subject reveal a new way of looking at it?

As you ponder ways to turn a general topic area into the subject of your analytical essay, spend time learning about other people's answers to the most promising questions you've generated. You can discuss the subject with people you know, skim sources published on the subject, or even observe the subject firsthand. You can learn more about gathering information in Chapter 2 and in Part Three.

SEARCH DATABASES

Once you've identified a promising question, learn whether — and how — other writers have attempted to answer it. Analytical essays tend to draw on information and analyses from other sources in addition to the writer's personal knowledge and interpretation, so even if you already know a great deal about a subject, be sure to review other writers' contributions to the conversation and to look for sources you can use to support your analysis.

Databases can give you an in-depth understanding of your subject, as well as a sense of useful interpretive frameworks, existing interpretations, and unanswered questions. They allow you to search for analyses that have been published on a particular subject or in a particular discipline. Although some databases, such as ERIC (eric.ed.gov), can be accessed publicly through the Web, most are available only through a library's computers or Web site.

Working Together: Try It Out Loud

Working in a small group, choose a popular song that everyone in your group likes, or choose one of the top songs of the week on Billboard or the iTunes store. Then use one set of the interpretive question prompts in the previous section to analyze the song. If you are doing this activity during class, the class might choose a single song, and each group might choose a different set of prompts. Take turns asking questions about the song while the other members of the group try to answer them. Record your answers, noting both agreements and disagreements. Your purpose is to interpret, so don't get distracted by whether the song is good or bad; instead, focus on its significance and implications. If you are doing this activity during class, each group should report its results to the class.

When you are finished, take a few minutes to reflect on the activity. What did you learn about different ways of approaching an analysis? Did some interpretive question prompts produce more useful or interesting results than the others? How did examining the song from multiple perspectives affect your interpretation of it?

To identify databases that might be relevant to the subject you are analyzing, review your library's list of databases or consult a reference librarian. The following questions can get you started.

- **Has the subject been addressed in recent news coverage?** If so, consider searching databases that focus on newspapers and weekly magazines, such as LexisNexis Academic, ProQuest Newspapers, or Alternative Press Index.

- **Is the subject related to a broad area of interest, such as business, education, or government?** If so, search databases that focus on general publications, such as Academic Search Premier, Articles First, or Catalog of U.S. Government Publications.

- **Is the subject related to a particular profession or academic discipline?** If so, consult databases that focus on that area. Many libraries provide guidance on which databases are relevant to a particular profession or discipline.

- **Have I already identified any promising sources?** By searching citation indexes (databases that identify sources that cite a particular source), you can identify additional sources that refer to the sources you already have. Depending

In Process

Searching Databases

Ali Bizzul used her interpretive question — *Why do so many football players risk their health by adding extra weight?* — to develop search terms for searches of her library's databases. She knew from exploring her subject that it had been addressed in newspapers and magazines, so she searched databases such as LexisNexis Academic and Newspaper Source. Because she also wondered whether scientific studies had been conducted on the subject, she also searched the MedLine and PubMed databases.

Ali used the search terms *football*, *health*, and *weight*. She searched all fields in the database and used the Boolean operator AND to require that all three words be present (see Chapter 12).

Search	Ovid MEDLINE(R) and Ovid OLDMEDLINE(R) 1948 to Present with Daily Update

| Basic Search | Find Citation | Search Tools | Search Fields | Advanced Ovid Search | **Multi-Field Search** |

Enter a search term, select a specific field to search in, and click "Search". Click "Add New Row" to add more terms.

	football	All Fields	▼
AND ▼	health	All Fields	▼
AND ▼	weight	All Fields	▼

Search ≫   Add New Row

▶ Limits (Click to expand)

▲ **Ali's search of the MedLine database**

on your subject, you might search the Science Citation Index, Social Sciences Citation Index, or Arts & Humanities Citation Index.

- **Is the full text of the source available?** Full-text databases offer the complete source for viewing or downloading. They cut out the middle step of searching for the physical periodical that published the article. If you don't know whether your library owns the sources provided by a database, or if you would simply like to locate them more quickly, consider using full-text databases. Databases such as Academic Search Premier, ERIC, and LexisNexis Academic offer some or all of their sources in full text.

Generate keywords and phrases that are related to your interpretive question, and search a few different databases for potential resources. Using the citation information provided by the database, check your library's online catalog for the title of the publication in which the article appears. Your library might own many of the sources you'll identify through a database search, but if it doesn't, you can usually request promising materials through interlibrary loan.

The search produced 54 results. The database allowed her to view abstracts (summaries of the source) and complete reference information.

The database allowed Ali to narrow her search.

▲ **Ali's search results**

Ali's database searches produced sources in newspapers, magazines, and academic journals. She located one of the articles, about the rate of metabolic syndrome among retired NFL players, and printed it.

You can read more about searching databases as well as interlibrary loan in Chapter 12.

Conduct Your Analysis

An analytical essay helps readers understand the origins, qualities, significance, or potential effects of a subject. A successful essay builds on a carefully crafted analytical question, a thorough understanding of the subject, and a rigorous and fair application of an appropriate interpretive framework. It also builds on a clear understanding of your writing situation.

REFINE YOUR QUESTION

Begin your analysis by reviewing the interpretive questions you generated about your subject (see p. 234). Choose one that interests you and will allow you to carry out your assignment. Then review and refine your question. Ask yourself:

- How might I respond to this question? Will my response be complex enough to justify writing an essay about it? Will it be too complex for my assignment?
- Is the question appropriate for the conversation that I'm planning to join?
- Will the question help me accomplish my purposes?
- Will my response interest my readers or address their needs?

A good analytical question is open to interpretation. Questions that focus on factual or yes/no answers seldom provide a strong foundation for an analytical essay. In contrast, questions that lead you to investigate the origins or potential impacts of a subject, to consider its qualities, to weigh its significance, or to explore its meaning are more likely to lead to success. Consider the differences between the following sets of questions.

Questions Leading to Factual or Yes/No Answers	Questions Open to Interpretation
When did the Iraq War begin?	What caused the Iraq War?
Has NASA's annual budget kept pace with inflation?	How can NASA pursue its mission on a reduced annual budget?
Who were the villains in the first Indiana Jones movie?	In what ways do the key themes of the first Indiana Jones movie reflect changes in American foreign relations?
Who won the last World Series?	What contributed to the success of the last World Series champions?

You should also consider how a question will direct your thinking about your subject. For example, you might want to understand the potential effects of a proposal to reduce the cost of attending your state's public colleges and universities by increasing class size and laying off faculty and staff. Asking a question about the plan's impact on education might direct your attention toward students and the trade-offs between lower costs and the quality of instruction. In contrast, asking a question about the plan's impact on the state budget might lead you to view the subject through the lens of business concerns and economic forecasts. Although the questions are related, they would lead to significantly different analyses.

SEEK A FULLER UNDERSTANDING OF YOUR SUBJECT

If you've ever talked with people who don't know what they're talking about but nonetheless are certain of their opinions, you'll recognize the dangers of applying an interpretive framework before you thoroughly understand your subject. To enhance your understanding of your subject, use division and classification. Division allows you to identify the elements that make up a subject. Classification allows you to explore a subject in relation to other subjects and to consider the similarities, differences, and relationships among its elements.

Division. Division breaks a subject into its parts and considers what each contributes to the whole. A financial analyst, for example, might examine the various groups within a company to understand what each group does and how it contributes to the overall value of the company. Similarly, a literary critic might consider how each scene in a play relates to other scenes and how it contributes to the play's major theme.

As you use division to examine a subject, keep in mind the following guidelines:

- **Pick a focus.** Division can take place on many levels. Just as you can divide numbers in different ways (100, for example, can be seen as ten 10s, five 20s, four 25s, and so on), you can divide subjects differently. A government agency, for instance, might be considered in terms of its responsibilities, its departments, or its employees. Trying to understand all of these aspects at once, however, would be difficult and unproductive. Use your analytical question as a guide to determine how best to divide your subject.

- **Examine the parts.** Most subjects can be thought of as a system of interrelated parts. As you divide your subject, determine what role each part plays, individually and in relation to other parts.

- **Assess contributions to the whole.** As you divide a subject, be sure to consider the contributions that each part makes to the larger whole. In some cases, you'll find that a part is essential. In other cases, you'll find that it makes little or no contribution to the whole.

Even though you can divide and reassemble a subject in a variety of ways, always take into account your purpose and your readers' needs, interests, and expectations. It might be easier to focus on a government agency's departments than on its functions, but if your question focuses on how the agency works or what it does, you'll be more successful if you examine its functions.

Classification. Classification places your subject — or each part of your subject — into a category. By categorizing a subject or its parts, you can discover how and to what extent your subject or a part of your subject is similar to others in the same category and how it differs from those in other categories. Identifying those similarities and differences, in turn, allows you to consider the subject, or its parts, in relation to the other items in your categories. As you use classification to gain a better understanding of your subject, consider the following guidelines:

- **Choose a classification scheme.** The categories you work with might be established already, or you might create them specifically to support your analysis. For example, if you are analyzing state representatives, you might place them into standard categories: Democrat, Republican, Libertarian, Green, and so on. Or you might create categories especially for your analysis, such as who voted for and against particular types of legislation.

- **Look at both similarities and differences.** When you place an item in a category, you decide that it is more similar to the other items in the category than to those in other categories. However, even though the items in a broad category will share many similarities, they will also differ in important ways. Botanists, for example, have developed a complex system of categories and subcategories to help them understand general types of plants (such as algae, roses, and corn) as well as to consider subtle differences among similar plants (such as corn bred for animal feed, for human consumption, and for biofuels).

- **Justify your choices.** Your decisions about what to place in a given category will be based on your definition of the category, if you've created it yourself, or your understanding of categories that have been established by someone else. In most cases, you'll need to explain why a particular category is the best fit for your subject. If you wanted readers to accept your classification of Walmart as a mom-and-pop retailer, for instance, you would have to explain that your category is defined by origin (not current size) and then inform readers that the chain started as a single discount store in Arkansas.

Classification and division are often used in combination, particularly when you want to consider similarities and differences among different parts of your subject. For example, if you are examining a complex organization, you might use division to analyze each department; in addition, you might use classification so that you can analyze groups of departments that have similar functions, such as customer service and technical support, and contrast those departments with departments in other categories, such as sales, marketing, and research and development.

APPLY AN INTERPRETIVE FRAMEWORK

An interpretive framework is a set of strategies for identifying patterns that has been used successfully and refined over time by writers interested in a given subject area or working in a particular field. Writers can choose from hundreds (perhaps thousands) of specialized frameworks used in disciplines across the arts, sciences, social sciences, humanities, engineering, and business. A historian, for example, might apply a feminist, social, political, or cultural analysis to interpret diaries written by women who worked in defense plants during World War II, while a sociologist might conduct correlational tests to interpret the results of a survey. In a writing course, you'll most likely use one of the broad interpretive frameworks discussed here: trend analysis, causal analysis, data analysis, text analysis, and rhetorical analysis.

By definition, analysis is subjective. Your interpretation will be shaped by the question you ask, the sources you consult, and your personal experience and perspective. But analysis is also conducted within the context of a written conversation. As you consider your choice of interpretive framework, reflect on the interpretive frameworks you encounter in your sources and those you've used in the past. Keep in mind that different interpretive frameworks will lead to different ways of seeing and understanding a subject. The key to success is choosing one that can guide you as you try to answer your question.

Need help with context? See Chapter 1 for more information.

Trend analysis. Trends are patterns that hold up over time. Trend analysis, as a result, focuses on sequences of events and the relationships among them. It is based on the assumption that understanding what has happened in the past allows us to make sense of what is happening in the present and to draw inferences about what is likely to happen in the future.

Trends can be identified and analyzed in nearly every field, from politics to consumer affairs to the arts. For example, many economists have analyzed historical accounts of fuel crises in the 1970s to understand the recent surge in fuel prices. Sports and entertainment analysts also use trend analysis — to forecast the next NBA champion, for instance, or to explain the reemergence of superheroes in popular culture during the last decade.

To conduct a trend analysis, follow these guidelines:

- **Gather information.** Trend analysis is most useful when it relies on an extensive set of long-term observations. News reports about NASA since the mid-1960s, for example, can tell you whether the coverage of the U.S. space program has changed over time. By examining these changes, you can decide whether a trend exists. You might find, for instance, that the press has become progressively less positive in its treatment of the U.S. space program. However, if you don't gather enough information to thoroughly establish the trend, your readers might lack confidence in your conclusions.

- **Establish that a trend exists.** Some analysts seem willing to declare a trend on the flimsiest set of observations: when a team wins an NFL championship for the second year in a row, for instance, fans are quick to announce the start of a dynasty. As you look for trends, cast a wide net. Learn as much as you can about the history of your subject, and carefully assess it to determine how often events related to your subject have moved in one direction or another. By understanding the variations that have occurred over time, you can better judge whether you've actually found a trend.

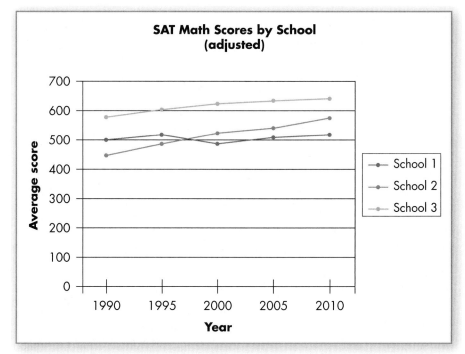

▲ Trend analysis looks for patterns that hold up over time.

- **Draw conclusions.** Trend analysis allows you to understand the historical context that shapes a subject and, in some cases, to make predictions about the subject. The conclusions you draw should be grounded strongly in the evidence you've collected. They should also reflect your writing situation — your purposes, readers, and context. As you draw your conclusions, exercise caution. Ask whether you have enough information to support your conclusions. Search for evidence that contradicts your conclusions. Most important, on the basis of the information you've collected so far, ask whether your conclusions make sense.

Causal analysis. Causal analysis focuses on the factors that bring about a particular situation. It can be applied to a wide range of subjects, such as the dot-com collapse in the late 1990s, the rise of terrorist groups, or the impact of calorie restriction on longevity. Writers carry out causal analysis when they believe that understanding the underlying reasons for a situation will help people address the situation, increase the likelihood of its happening again, or appreciate its potential consequences.

In many ways, causal analysis is a form of detective work. It involves tracing a sequence of events and exploring the connections among them. Because the connections are almost always more complex than they appear, it pays to be thorough. If you choose to conduct a causal analysis, keep in mind the following guidelines:

- **Uncover as many causes as you can.** Effects rarely emerge from a single cause. Most effects are the results of a complex web of causes, some of which are related to one another and some of which are not. Although it might be tempting, for example, to say that a murder victim died (the effect) from a gunshot wound (the cause), that would tell only part of the story. You would need to work backward from the murderer's decision to pull the trigger to the factors that led to that decision, and then further back to the causes underlying those factors.

  Effects can also become causes. While investigating the murder, for instance, you might find that the murderer had long been envious of the victim's success, that he was jumpy from the steroids he'd been taking in an ill-advised attempt to qualify for the Olympic trials in weight lifting, and that he had just found his girlfriend in the victim's arms. Exploring how these factors might be related — and determining when they are not — will help you understand the web of causes leading to the effect.

- **Determine which causes are significant.** Not all causes contribute equally to an effect. Perhaps our murderer was cut off on the freeway on his way to meet his girlfriend. Lingering anger at the other driver might have been enough to push him over the edge, but it probably wouldn't have caused the shooting by itself.

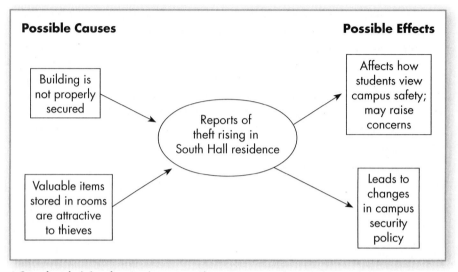

▲ Causal analysis involves tracing connections among events.

- **Distinguish between correlation and cause.** Too often, we assume that because one event occurred just before another, the first event caused the second. We might conclude that finding his girlfriend with another man drove the murderer to shoot in a fit of passion — only to discover that he had begun planning the murder months before, when the victim threatened to reveal his use of steroids to the press just prior to the Olympic trials.

- **Look beyond the obvious.** A thorough causal analysis considers not only the primary causes and effects but also those that might appear only slightly related to the subject. For example, you might consider the immediate effects of the murder not only on the victim and perpetrator but also on their families and friends, on the wider community, on the lawyers and judges involved in the case, on an overburdened judicial system, even on attitudes toward Olympic athletes. By looking beyond the obvious causes and effects, you can deepen your understanding of the subject and begin to explore a much wider set of implications than you might have initially expected.

Data analysis. Data is any type of information, such as facts and observations, and is often expressed numerically. Most of us analyze data in an informal way on a daily basis. For example, if you've looked at the percentage of people who favor a particular political candidate over another, you've engaged in data analysis. Similarly, if you've checked your bank account to determine whether you have enough money for a planned purchase, you've carried out a form of data analysis. As a writer, you can analyze numerical information related to your subject to better understand the subject as a whole, to look for differences among the subject's parts, and to explore relationships among the parts.

To begin a data analysis, gather your data and enter the numbers into a spreadsheet or statistics program. You can use the program's tools to sort the data and conduct tests. If your set of data is small, you can use a piece of paper and a calculator. As you carry out your analysis, keep the following guidelines in mind:

- **Do the math.** Let's say you conducted a survey of student and faculty attitudes about a proposed change to the graduation requirements at your school. Tabulating the results might reveal that 52 percent of your respondents were female, 83 percent were between the ages of eighteen and twenty-two, 38 percent were juniors or seniors, and 76 percent were majoring in the biological sciences. You might also find that, of the faculty who responded, 75 percent were tenured. Based on these numbers, you could draw conclusions about whether the responses are representative of your school's overall population. If they are not, you might decide to ask more people to take your survey. Once you're certain

Use of Social-networking Sites		
	# surveyed	% who use social networking regularly
Gender		
Male	48	56%
Female	42	65%
Age		
16–20	20	85%
21–30	31	71%
31–45	28	46%
45+	11	27%
Education		
Some high school	12	35%
High school graduate	25	56%
Some college	34	65%
College graduate	16	64%
Graduate school	7	62%

▲ **Data analysis can involve assessing information from a variety of sources.**

In Process

Applying Interpretive Frameworks

Ali Bizzul used a combination of trend analysis and causal analysis in her essay about the health risks football players face as they put on weight. After reading several reports of a rise in heat-related injuries among larger players (the effects), she tried to identify the factors contributing to this trend (the causes). Drawing on information from an article about obesity among players in the National Football League, she used freewriting to explore her ideas.

> Ali doesn't worry about writing in complete sentences. She gets her ideas and reactions down as quickly as possible.

The study shows that football players, especially the guards, are becoming increasingly larger. 97% overweight and many of those class 2 and 3 obese. This is crazy. It causes health problems, such as high blood pressure and heart failure. It was also shown that it didn't really help rankings, so why would they do it? It is all in the minds of people. It is common sense that a bigger guy running into you is going to stop you better than a smaller guy. Even though it doesn't help scores, it can help in the defensive area. These men, the guards, are meant to be a sort of battering ram and are not hired for their speed and agility. The high school kids are seeing this on TV and thinking that they have to be just as large as the guys in the NFL. So they think that all they need to do is bulk up, but find that they can't carry the weight as well and it hurts more than it helps. Coaches are doing their part to help these guys stay healthy, but they don't really seem to try to educate their students about the implications of being overweight. They are just telling them to lose some weight, and that is just on a case-to-case basis. It really is just in these kids' minds. They think that the only way they will be noticed by recruiters is to be big and able to throw their weight around. Don't present a solution, just explain why it is happening. . . . Everyone believes that bigger is better. But it isn't. It is going to kill these guys, and it is setting a bad example for the younger generation.

> Ali reminds herself about the purpose of her analytical essay.

that you've collected enough data, you can draw conclusions about the overall results and determine, for example, the percentage of respondents who favored, opposed, or were undecided about the proposed change.

- **Categorize your data.** Difference tests can help you make distinctions among groups. To classify the results of your survey, for example, you might compare male and female student responses. Similarly, you might examine differences in the responses between other groups — such as faculty and students; tenured and untenured faculty; and freshmen, sophomores, juniors, and seniors. To carry out your analysis, you might look at each group's average level of agreement with the proposed changes. Or you might use statistical techniques such as T-Tests, which offer more sensitive assessments of difference than comparisons of averages. You can conduct these kinds of tests using spreadsheet programs, such as Microsoft Excel, or statistical programs, such as SAS and SPSS.

- **Explore relationships.** Correlation tests allow you to draw conclusions about your subject. For example, you might want to know whether support for proposed changes to graduation requirements increases or decreases according to GPA. A correlation test might indicate that a positive relationship exists — that support goes up as GPA increases. Be cautious, however, as you examine relationships. In particular, be wary of confusing causation with correlation. Tests will show, for example, that as shoe size increases, so do scores on reading tests. Does this mean that large feet improve reading? Not really. The cause of higher reading scores appears to be attending school longer. High school students tend to score better on reading tests than do students in elementary school — and, on average, high school students tend to have much larger feet. As is the case with difference tests, you can use many spreadsheet and statistical programs to explore relationships. If your set of data is small enough, you can also use a piece of paper to examine it.

- **Be thorough.** Take great care to ensure the integrity of your analysis. You will run into problems if you collect too little data, if the data is not representative, or if the data is collected sloppily. Similarly, you should base your conclusions on a thoughtful and careful examination of the results of your tests. Picking and choosing evidence that supports your conclusion might be tempting, but you'll do a disservice to yourself and your readers if you fail to consider all the results of your analysis.

Text analysis. Today, the word *text* can refer to a wide range of printed or digital works — and even some forms of artistic expression that we might not think of as documents. Texts open to interpretation include novels, poems, plays, essays, articles, movies, speeches, blogs, songs, paintings, photographs, sculptures, performances, Web pages, videos, television shows, and computer games.

Students enrolled in writing classes often use the elements of literary analysis to analyze texts. In this form of analysis, interpreters focus on theme, plot, setting, characterization, imagery, style, and structure, as well as the contexts — social, cultural, political, and historical — that shape a work. Writers who use this form of analysis focus both on what is actually presented in the text and on what is implied or conveyed "between the lines." They rely heavily on close reading of the text to discern meaning, critique an author's technique, and search for patterns that help them understand the text as fully as possible. They also tend to consider other elements of the wider writing situation in which the text was produced — in particular, the author's purpose, intended audience, use of sources, and choice of genre.

If you carry out a text analysis, keep the following guidelines in mind:

- **Focus on the text itself.** In any form of text analysis, the text should take center stage. Although you will typically reflect on the issues raised by your interpretation, maintain a clear focus on the text in front of you, and keep your analysis grounded firmly in what you can locate within it. Background information and related sources, such as scholarly articles and essays, can support and enhance your analysis, but they can't do the work of interpretation for you.

- **Consider the text in its entirety.** Particularly in the early stages of learning about a text, it is easy to be distracted by a startling idea or an intriguing concept. Try not to focus on a particular aspect of the text, however, until you've fully reviewed all of it. You might well decide to narrow your analysis to a particular aspect of the text, but lay the foundation for a fair, well-informed interpretation by first considering the text as a whole.

In the song "What Is New Orleans, Part 2," recorded by Kermit Ruffins and the Rebirth Brass Band, a call-and-response pattern structures both the lyrics ("What is New Orleans? New Orleans is . . .") and also the interaction between Ruffins and the musicians. Frequently, after Ruffins sings a pattern of syllables, the musicians echo or answer him, as though the music itself is to be considered a sufficient response. Meanwhile, the song's lyrics highlight the importance of food in the city's culture by beginning with a list of meals. Each meal is associated with a specific time and day of the week, giving the impression that the rest of the week's events are scheduled around these meals. Ruffins then lists musicians and locations, moving from the specific to the general, from individual lounges to entire neighborhoods.

▲ **Text analysis can focus on a wide range of artistic expression.**

- **Avoid "cherry-picking."** Cherry-picking refers to the process of using only those materials from a text that support your overall interpretation and ignoring aspects that might weaken or contradict your interpretation. As you carry out your analysis, factor in *all* the evidence. If the text doesn't support your interpretation, rethink your conclusions.

Rhetorical analysis. In much the same way that you can assess the writing situation that shapes your work on a particular assignment, you can analyze the rhetorical situation (see p. 12) that shaped the creation of and response to a particular document. A rhetorical analysis, for example, might focus on how a particular document (written, visual, or some other form) achieved its purpose or on why readers reacted to it in a specific way.

Rhetorical analysis focuses on one or more aspects of the rhetorical situation.

- **Writer and purpose.** What did the writer hope to accomplish? Was it accomplished and, if so, how well? If not, why not? What strategies did the writer use to pursue the purpose? Did the writer choose the best genre for the purpose? Why did the writer choose this purpose over others? Are there any clear connections between the purpose and the writer's background, values, and beliefs?

- **Readers/audience.** Was the document addressed to the right audience? Did readers react to the document as the writer hoped? Why or why not? What aspects of the needs, interests, backgrounds, values, and beliefs of the audience might have led them to react to the document as they did?

- **Sources.** What sources were used? Which information, ideas, and arguments from the sources were used in the document? How effectively were they used? How credible were the sources? Were enough sources used? Were the sources appropriate?

- **Context.** How did the context in which the document was composed shape its effectiveness? How did the context in which it was read shape the reaction of the audience? What physical, social, cultural, disciplinary, and historical contexts shaped the document's development? What contexts shaped how readers reacted to it?

Rhetorical analysis can also involve an assessment of the argument used in a document. You might examine the structure of an argument, focusing on the writer's use of appeals — such as appeals to logic, emotion, character, and so on (see p. 415) — and the quality of the evidence that was provided. Or you might ask whether the argument contains any logical fallacies (see p. 410). In general, when argument is a key part of a rhetorical analysis, the writer will typically connect the analysis to one or more of the major elements of the rhetorical situation. For example, the writer might explore readers' reactions to the evidence used to support an argument. Or, as Brooke Gladstone does in her analysis of the Goldilocks number (p. 225), you might focus on how evidence migrates from one document to another.

Carrying out a rhetorical analysis almost always involves a close reading (or viewing) of the document (see p. 24 for a discussion of text analysis). It can also involve research into the origins of the document and its effects on its audience. For example, a rhetorical analysis of the Declaration of Independence might focus not only on its content but also on the political, economic, and historical contexts that brought it into existence; reactions to it by American colonists and English citizens; and its eventual impact on the development of the U.S. Constitution.

As you carry out a rhetorical analysis, consider the following guidelines:

- **Remember that the elements of a rhetorical situation are interrelated.** Writers' purposes do not emerge from a vacuum. They are shaped by their experiences, values, and beliefs — each of which is influenced by the physical, social, cultural, disciplinary, and historical contexts out of which a particular document emerges. In turn, writers usually shape their arguments to reflect their understanding of their readers' needs, interests, knowledge, values, beliefs, and backgrounds. Writers also choose their sources and select genres that reflect their purpose, their knowledge of their readers, and the context in which a document will be written and read.

- **If you analyze the argument in a document, focus on its structure and quality.** Rhetorical analysis focuses on the document as a means of communication. It might be tempting to praise an argument you agree with or to criticize one that offends your values or beliefs. If you do so, however, you won't be carrying out a rhetorical analysis. This form of analysis is intended to help your readers understand your conclusions about the origins, structure, quality, and potential impact of the document.

- **Don't underestimate the complexity of analyzing rhetorical context.** Understanding context is one of the most challenging aspects of a rhetorical analysis. Context is multifaceted. You can consider the physical context in which a document is written and read. You can examine its social context. And you can explore the cultural, disciplinary, and historical contexts that shaped a document. Each of these contexts will affect a document in important ways. Taken together, the interactions among these various aspects of context can be difficult to trace. In fact, a full analysis of context is likely to take far more space and time than most academic documents allow. As you carry out your analysis, focus on the aspects of context that you determine are most relevant to your own writing situation.

Prepare a Draft

As you prepare to draft your analytical essay, you'll decide how to present the results of your analysis to your readers. Your draft will reflect not only your conclusions and your interpretive framework but also what others involved in the conversation have written about your subject and the types of analyses they've conducted. As you write, you'll focus on making an interpretive claim, explaining your interpretation, designing your essay, and framing your analysis.

MAKE AN INTERPRETIVE CLAIM

Your interpretive claim is a brief statement — usually in the form of a thesis statement (see Chapter 14) — that helps readers understand the overall results of your analysis. Essentially, it's a one- or two-sentence answer to your interpretive question. Just as your question should be open to interpretation, your claim should be open to debate. If it simply repeats the obvious — either because it is factually true or because it has long been agreed to by those involved in your written conversation — it will do little to advance the conversation.

Your claim will frame your readers' understanding of your subject in a particular way. It will also reflect the interpretive framework you've decided to use. Consider the differences among the following claims about distance running:

> Evidence collected since the mid-1990s suggests that distance running can enhance self-image among college students.

> Although a carefully monitored exercise program built around distance running appears to have positive effects for most cardiac patients, heart attack survivors who engage in at least two hours of running each week have a 30 percent higher survival rate than coronary artery bypass surgery patients who engage in the same amount of distance running.

> Since 2000, distance running has undergone a resurgence in the United States, allowing the country to regain its standing as a leader in the international running community.

> Distance running, when it is addressed at all in contemporary novels, is usually used to represent a desire to escape from the pressures of modern life.

Each of these interpretive claims would lead a writer to focus on different aspects of the subject, and each would reflect a different interpretive framework. The first calls readers' attention to a causal relationship between distance running and mental health. The second explores differences in the effect of distance running on two groups of cardiac patients. The third directs attention to a trend analysis of increasing competitiveness among elite distance runners. And the fourth makes a claim about how distance running is treated in literature.

EXPLAIN YOUR INTERPRETATION

People who read analyses are intelligent, curious people. They want to know more than just what you think of a subject; they want to know how you arrived at your interpretation and why your analysis is reasonable. Your readers won't always agree with your interpretation, and that's fine — but even if you can't persuade them to accept your analysis, you do want to convince readers that your take on the subject is insightful and well considered.

Provide relevant reasons for your interpretation. Build on your interpretive claim by presenting reasons for your readers to accept your analysis. The overall results of your analysis form your main point, and the reasons to accept your analysis become your supporting points.

Look over the results of your analysis, and ask yourself why readers should agree with your interpretation. You might come up with more reasons than you can possibly use — or you might find yourself struggling to find enough reasons to support your claim. Either way, try to generate as many potential reasons as possible, taking care not to rule out any at first, no matter how trivial or ridiculous they might seem.

Working Together: Generate Reasons for Your Interpretation

The goal of this collaborative activity is to generate potential reasons supporting your interpretation of your subject. You can work in person or online (using chat, instant messaging, or a threaded discussion forum). If you are working face-to-face, one member of the group should take notes on the discussion. If you are using a chat or instant-messaging program, be sure to record a transcript of the session.

To carry out the activity, follow these steps:

1. One writer should describe his or her writing project, the overall results of the analysis, and the reasons that will be offered to support the analysis.

2. Each member of the group should help evaluate the reasons identified by the writer. Are the reasons sound, appropriate, and credible?

3. Each member of the group should also suggest additional reasons the writer might consider.

When the exchange is completed, turn to the next writer and repeat the process.

Once you have generated a substantial list of potential reasons, select the ones that seem most likely to convince your readers that your analysis is sound. Some reasons will be more relevant than others. Rather than list every possible reason to accept your analysis, identify those reasons that are most directly related to your interpretive claim. The reasons you choose should also be consistent with the interpretive framework you've decided to follow. For example, you might find several reasons to support your analysis of a new novel's significance, among them comments published in literary journals such as *Proceedings of the Modern Language Association* and endorsements by celebrities such as Oprah Winfrey and Gwyneth Paltrow. If you are using text analysis as your interpretive framework, you might find commentary offered by authorities in the field of literary studies more useful than celebrity endorsements.

Support your reasons with evidence. No matter which reasons you choose, each of them must be supported by evidence. Analytical essays tend to rely on a mix of evidence from the subject itself (particularly in the case of text analyses and rhetorical analyses), from the writer's reflections and personal experience, and from published or field sources. Evidence can include the following:

- language or images from a text that is being analyzed
- quotations, paraphrases, and summaries from published sources such as reports and journal articles
- illustrations in the form of images, charts, graphs, and tables
- statements from personal interviews
- notes from an observation
- numerical information

You can use evidence to provide examples and illustrations, to define ideas and concepts, to illustrate processes, and to associate particular ideas and concepts with authorities, such as political leaders, subject-matter experts, or people who have been affected by the subject.

To organize your evidence, list all the reasons you will use to support your overall analysis, review your notes to find evidence that supports each reason, and then list the evidence below each reason. You might need to review your sources to locate additional evidence, or even obtain additional sources. If you are conducting a text analysis, be careful to avoid cherry-picking your evidence (see p. 249). If you are conducting another type of analysis, make sure that you haven't relied too heavily on a single source of evidence.

You can read more about how to use evidence to support your analysis in Chapter 14.

Establish the context. It's quite possible — even likely — that others involved in a conversation will have conducted their own analyses of your subject. Be sure to check for those analyses so that you can place your analysis in a larger context. Ideally, you'll be able to present your interpretation as a contribution to a growing understanding of the subject, rather than simply as an isolated set of observations.

As you draft your analytical essay, keep in mind the other interpretations you've encountered. Review the sources you consulted as you learned about your subject and conducted your analysis. If you find reasonable interpretations that support — or contradict — yours, consider how to address them in your essay. You might offer similar interpretations to back up one or more of your reasons, or you might explain why another writer's analysis is less adequate than your own. In either case, you should briefly define significant existing analyses for your readers and explain how your interpretation complicates or improves upon what's been said before. You might also need to draw on evidence from other sources or from the subject itself.

In Process

Supporting Reasons with Evidence

Ali Bizzul identified three major reasons to support her interpretive claim that gaining weight hurts football players more than it helps:

> Reason 1: Heat-related injuries associated with the use of diet supplements
>
> Reason 2: Long-term health problems associated with obesity
>
> Reason 3: Decrease in athletic performance

Ali used each of these reasons as the basis for a general statement in her draft. Here is her preliminary list of evidence to support her second reason, the long-term health problems associated with obesity:

> The extra weight gained for football can complicate the health of ex-athletes:
> — metabolic syndrome (Miller et al.)
> — joint damage/arthritis (Groeschen)
> — heart disease (Longman)
> — diabetes (Longman)

As she drafted her essay, Ali used her lists of evidence to remind herself of sources she might turn to while making her points.

CONSIDER GENRE AND DESIGN

A well-written analytical essay uses design for three primary reasons: to improve readability, to simplify the presentation of complex concepts and information, and to enhance the writer's ability to achieve his or her goals.

As you contemplate design options for your essay, make note of any formatting requirements specified in your assignment (such as margins, spacing, font, and the like). Consider as well the expectations of your readers, particularly your instructor. You might also think about including visual evidence such as figures and images.

- **Figures**, such as charts and graphs, can help readers better understand complex concepts or see trends that would be difficult to discern through textual descriptions alone. A chart, for example, can clearly show comparative cost figures for a state plan to subsidize public transportation. A graph could show changes over time in ridership of those who use trains, buses, subways, or private automobiles.

- **Images**, particularly when you are analyzing a visual text such as a photograph, video, or painting, can help readers better understand the subject and increase the likelihood that they'll accept your interpretation as valid and well founded.

- **Captions** are a necessary complement to figures and images. Be sure to include a caption for each figure or image in your essay. At a minimum, a caption should provide a figure number cross-referenced in the text, a descriptive label, and source information. You can also use the caption to briefly describe what is shown and to explain what it contributes to your analysis.

If you use figures and images in your essay, place them near their first mention in the text. You can learn more about figures, illustrations, captions, and other aspects of document design in Chapters 16 and 17.

FRAME YOUR ANALYSIS

The results of your analysis will be strongly influenced by your interpretive question, interpretive framework, and sources of evidence. You can increase the odds that your readers will accept your conclusions if you help them understand your choices.

Introduction. Rather than launching immediately into your interpretation, begin by introducing readers to your subject and explaining its significance. Provide enough information about your subject — in the form of a summary or description of a text, an overview of a trend, or a report of a recent event — to help readers understand your focus and follow your line of thinking. Another useful strategy is to start by

In Process

Using a Figure to Support a Point

Ali Bizzul found a chart in a research study published by the *American Journal of Cardiology*. She included it her essay as evidence to support a point in her analysis of the health risks associated with weight gain among football players.

Heatstroke is not the only danger associated with increased size. Excess weight can cause serious health problems, even if some of the pounds are due to high muscle mass. And many of those problems aren't clear until years later. Added weight can be difficult to lose, and later in life it can complicate the health of ex-athletes.

Researchers at the Mount Sinai Medical Center in New York studied more than 500 retired NFL players and found that 85% of former linemen were obese, compared with 50% of non-linemen (see Fig. 1) (Miller et al., 2008). Moreover, they found that linemen were almost twice as likely as non-linemen to have metabolic syndrome — the set of factors that can increase the risk of heart disease, stroke, and diabetes (Miller et al., 2008).

Text is "wrapped" around the figure.

The illustration has a caption. The source of the illustration is identified in a note below the caption.

Ali refers to the figure in parentheses. She places the figure close to where she mentions it.

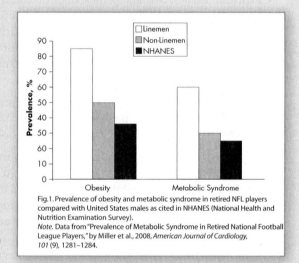

Fig. 1. Prevalence of obesity and metabolic syndrome in retired NFL players compared with United States males as cited in NHANES (National Health and Nutrition Examination Survey).
Note. Data from "Prevalence of Metabolic Syndrome in Retired National Football League Players," by Miller et al., 2008, *American Journal of Cardiology, 101* (9), 1281–1284.

▲ A chart used as evidence

offering some context about the conversation you've decided to join. Consider, for example, how Sito Negron begins his analysis of recent events in Juárez.

> A story about Juárez made the rounds in El Paso last summer. Surrounded by guards, a well-dressed, impeccably polite man enters a restaurant. He apologizes as the guards round up cell phones and cameras. No one is allowed to get up as the man sits and eats. When he leaves, he apologizes again and pays the tab for everyone. The man is said to be Joaquín "El Chapo" Guzmán, head of the Sinaloa cartel.
>
> This is an urban legend. No one who tells it was there. I've heard it several times from people who said a friend of a friend heard it from a firsthand source. Also, the story has likely been told elsewhere about other outlaws. Versions of this story were probably told in Al Capone's Chicago.
>
> Here's something that is true: Last year in Juárez, more than 1,300 people were murdered. . . .

Conclusion. Because analytical essays so often begin with a question, interpreters frequently withhold the thesis statement (the answer) until the end — after they've given readers sufficient reasons to accept their conclusions as reasonable. You might also wrap up your analysis by contemplating the implications of your interpretation, raising a related question for readers to ponder (as Ali Bizzul does in her final draft; see p. 49), or speculating about the future, as Nick Bilton does in his blog post.

> The anthropologist Margaret Mead once said that in traditional societies, the young learn from the old. But in modern societies, the old can also learn from the young. Here's hoping that politeness never goes out of fashion, but that time-wasting forms of communication do.

You can learn more about using your introduction and conclusion to frame the results of your analysis in Chapter 16.

Organization. The organization of your essay can also help frame your analysis, because it will affect the order in which you present your reasons and evidence. Your choice of organizing pattern should take into account your purposes and your readers' needs and interests. For instance, if you are reporting the results of a trend analysis, you might want to use chronological order as your organizing pattern. If, by contrast, you are conducting a causal analysis, you might use the cause-and-effect organizing pattern. Creating an outline or a map (see p. 512) can also help you organize your thoughts, especially if your assignment calls for a relatively long essay, if you are combining interpretive frameworks, or if you expect to present a lot of reasons or evidence to support your interpretive claim. You can read more about organizing patterns and outlines in Chapter 15.

Review and Improve Your Draft

Creating the first draft of an analytical essay is a complex and rewarding process. In the course of learning about a subject, you've developed an interpretive question, chosen an interpretive framework, and conducted an analysis; you've made and supported an interpretive claim; and you've organized your reasons and evidence and framed your essay. Once you complete your first draft, you should step back and assess its strengths and weaknesses. A careful review — done individually and with the help of others — can help you pinpoint where you should invest time in improving your essay.

ENSURE THAT YOUR CLAIM IS DEBATABLE

If your interpretive claim is not debatable (see p. 251), it will do little to advance the conversation about your subject. As you review your essay, focus on your interpretive claim, and ask how your readers will react to it. For example, will your interpretive claim lead readers to disagree with you, or will it surprise or shock them? Will it make them think about the subject in a new way? Will it force them to reconsider their assumptions? If you think that your readers might respond by asking "so what?" you should take another look at your claim.

CHALLENGE YOUR CONCLUSIONS

As you review your essay, challenge your findings by considering alternative explanations and asking your own "so what?" questions. Your initial impressions of a subject will often benefit from additional reflection. Those impressions might be refined, or perhaps even changed substantially, through additional analysis. Or they might be reinforced, typically by locating additional evidence.

EXAMINE THE APPLICATION OF YOUR INTERPRETIVE FRAMEWORK

Ask whether you've applied your interpretive framework fairly and rigorously to your subject. If you are carrying out a causal analysis, for example, ask whether you've ruled out the possibility that the causal relationships you are exploring are simply correlations. If you're conducting a text analysis, ask whether you've fully and fairly represented the text and whether you have considered alternative interpretations. Review how you've used your interpretive framework to make sure that you've applied it carefully and evenhandedly to your subject.

Peer Review: Improve Your Analytical Essay

One of the biggest challenges writers face is reading a draft of their own work as a reader rather than as the writer. Because you know what you're trying to say, you find it easy to understand your draft. To determine how you should revise your draft, ask a friend or classmate to read your essay and consider how well you've adopted the role of interpreter (see p. 216).

Purpose	1.	Is my interpretive claim clear and easy to understand? Is it debatable?
	2.	Have I offered a careful and thorough analysis to support my claim?
Readers	3.	Did the essay help you understand my subject in a new way? Why or why not?
	4.	Does the analysis seem fair to you? Did you notice any cherry-picking? Can you think of any aspects of my subject that I neglected to consider?
Sources	5.	Are the reasons I've offered for my interpretation coherent? Have I provided enough evidence to support each reason? Should I add or drop anything?
	6.	Do my sources strike you as reliable and appropriate? Does any of the evidence I've used seem questionable?
Context	7.	Did I provide enough (or too much) information about my subject to ground the analysis?
	8.	Does the interpretive framework I've chosen seem like an appropriate choice for analyzing my subject? Would a different framework have been more effective?

For each of the points listed above, ask your reviewers to provide concrete advice about what you could do to improve your draft. It can help if you ask them to adopt the role of an editor — someone who is working with you to improve your draft. You can read more about peer review in Chapter 4.

ASSESS YOUR ORGANIZATION

When readers can anticipate the sequence of reasoning and evidence that appears in your analytical essay, they'll conclude that the essay is well organized. If an essay is confusing or difficult to follow, however, they'll conclude that it is poorly written or, worse, that the analysis is flawed. As you review your essay, ask whether your reasons and evidence seem easy to follow. If you find yourself growing puzzled as you try to read your essay, take another look at your choice of organizing pattern. Check, as well, whether your reasons are presented in an order that allows them to build on one another. If you have difficulty figuring out how you've organized your essay, consider creating a backward outline, an outline based on an already written draft. You can read more about organizing your essay and outlining in Chapter 15.

Once you've revised your essay, ask yourself how you might polish and edit your writing so that your readers will find your analysis easy to read. For an overview of editing strategies, see Chapter 20.

★ Student Essay

Ali Bizzul, "Living (and Dying) Large"

The following analytical essay was written by featured writer Ali Bizzul. Ali's essay follows the requirements of the sixth edition of the *APA Publication Manual*. However, this edition does not include specific instructions for formatting student essays, so Ali's essay has been formatted to fit typical requirements for undergraduate student writing.

LIVING (AND DYING) LARGE   1

Living (and Dying) Large

Ali Bizzul

COCC150 College Composition

Professor Palmquist

September 20, 2013

Information about the writer, class, and submission date is provided on the cover page.

The title is centered.

Living (and Dying) Large

Bigger is better—or so says the adage that seems to drive much of
American culture. From fast food to television sets to the "average" house, everything seems to be getting bigger. This is especially true for the athletes who play
America's favorite fall sport—football. Twelve- and thirteen-year-olds are bulking
up so they can make their junior-high football teams. High school players are
adding weight to earn college scholarships. And the best college players are
pulling out all the stops in hopes of making an NFL team. All of this is occurring
despite the belief of many football coaches that extra weight does little to
enhance a football player's performance—and might even derail it. Even worse,
the drive to put on the pounds carries significant health risks for football players,
both now and later in life. Despite what they believe, overweight players are less
effective than their lighter peers—and at far greater risk of devastating harm.

While football requires both strength and speed, the media image of pro
football players focuses mostly on their weight. Recent data corroborates the
attention paid to football players' size. In less than 70 years, the average weight of
offensive linemen has risen by almost 100 pounds, topping out at over 273 pounds
in 2008, compared with 178 pounds in 1940 (Meyer, 2012). NFL offensive linemen
who weigh less than 300 pounds are often described as "undersized," so it's no
surprise that young football players are getting the message that bigger is
better—and bulking up. A study of high school linemen in Iowa showed that 45%
were overweight and 9% were severely obese by adult standards; in comparison,
only 18% of other young males were overweight. Even more troubling, a study in
Michigan revealed that among football players from ages 9 to 14, 45% could be
considered overweight or obese (as cited in Popke, 2008). Even those players who
recognize that their size is unhealthy are reluctant to trim down. Consider
Jeffery Espadron, a high school player who weighs 332 pounds: He is willing to
lose some weight, but he refuses to go below 300 pounds because he sees NFL
linemen weighing in at 290 to 300 pounds and believes he must do the same

The writer frames the subject by calling attention to a common saying and then arguing that it does not apply to this case.

The essay's main point

First reason supporting the analysis: a connection between the behavior of NFL players and players as young as 9 years of age

Following APA style, information cited in a source is identified using the phrase "as cited in."

LIVING (AND DYING) LARGE   3

(Longman, 2007). As younger players like Espadron follow the footsteps of ever-bigger college and professional linemen, they appear to believe that simply packing on the pounds will get them recognized by colleges and maybe even the NFL.

In order to add weight and muscle mass quickly, however, some football players go to dangerous extremes. Many have even turned to legal but unproven dietary supplements as a way of increasing muscle mass, and in some cases, the consequences have been fatal. Minnesota Viking Korey Stringer, a 335-pound offensive lineman who was believed to be taking a dietary supplement, died of heatstroke during a July 2001 training camp. Four years later, San Francisco offensive tackle Thomas Herrion died of heart disease after a preseason game, and in 2010, 37-year-old former New York Giants defensive lineman Norman Hand, who weighed more than 300 pounds, died of cardiovascular disease (Longman, 2011). Although such fatalities are unusual, a growing number of doctors believe that use of dietary supplements increases the risk of heatstroke among football players. In an editorial in the medical journal *Neurosurgery*, three sports-medicine specialists noted that after a 1994 federal law exempted dietary supplements from regulation by the Food and Drug Administration, heat-related injuries among football players began to rise (Bailes, Cantu, & Day, 2002). They further argued that the increase appears to be related to the use of supplements such as ephedrine and creatine monohydrate (Bailes et al., 2002). Marketed as an energy booster and body builder, ephedrine has an effect similar to amphetamine: It can increase core body temperatures and decrease the body's ability to cool itself. Creatine monohydrate, which is marketed as a muscle builder, can shift body water from the bloodstream into muscle cells, increasing the likelihood of heatstroke. Bailes et al. (2002) noted that, despite such health risks, "the use of nutritional supplements [among football players] seems to be the rule rather than the exception" (p. 287). Many young football players today seem willing to overlook the potential harm in these supplements in the hope of gaining a small advantage on the field.

Second reason supporting the analysis: impact of dietary supplements on health

APA style uses author names and publication dates to identify sources.

Brackets are used in a quotation to provide missing information.

The page number for the quotation is provided.

LIVING (AND DYING) LARGE   4

Third reason
supporting the
analysis: effect of
excess weight on
health

Summary of a relevant
study

Reference to a figure
is provided in the text.

The figure is wrapped
by text and located
near its reference in
the text. A caption
describes the figure,
and information
about the source of
the data for the figure
is provided in a note.

The credentials of an
expert cited in a
source are provided.

A block quotation is
used to present a
longer quotation.

Heatstroke is not the only danger associated with increased size. Excess weight can cause serious health problems, even if some of the pounds are due to high muscle mass. And many of those problems aren't clear until years later. Added weight can be difficult to lose, and later in life it can complicate the health of ex-athletes. Researchers at the Mount Sinai Medical Center in New York studied more than 500 retired NFL players and found that 85% of former linemen were obese, compared with 50% of non-linemen (see Fig. 1) (Miller et al., 2008). Moreover, they found that linemen were almost twice as likely as non-linemen to have metabolic syndrome — the set of factors that can increase the risk of heart disease, stroke, and diabetes (Miller et al., 2008). Sports reporters Groeschen (2008) and Longman (2011) have described studies establishing that diabetes, high blood pressure, heart disease, high cholesterol, joint damage, and sleep apnea are common among those who are overweight, even current or former athletes. As Dr. Tim Kremchek, a team physician for several high schools in the Cincinnati area, has warned, for overweight players,

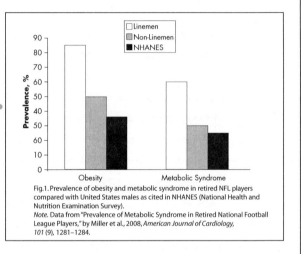

Fig. 1. Prevalence of obesity and metabolic syndrome in retired NFL players compared with United States males as cited in NHANES (National Health and Nutrition Examination Survey).
Note. Data from "Prevalence of Metabolic Syndrome in Retired National Football League Players," by Miller et al., 2008, *American Journal of Cardiology, 101* (9), 1281–1284.

> the issue is [that] they're not only hurting themselves for the short term, but [that] the long term effects are horrible. They're going to have arthritic problems in their joints. They'll need operations for their cartilage. They'll have herniated discs in their lower backs, they'll have

LIVING (AND DYING) LARGE   5

> more knee injuries, ankle injuries, hamstrings. . . . (as cited in
>
> Groeschen, 2008, para. 8)

As dire as Kremchek's warnings sound, such effects are already evident in recently retired NFL players. Barry Pettyjohn, a high school coach and former NFL offensive lineman, increased his weight from 250 pounds to 280 for college, and again to 300 at the beginning of his NFL career; after he stopped playing, his weight ballooned to 375 pounds, and he has had 14 operations on his shoulders, knees, and elbows (Groeschen, 2008). While injuries on the field are often unavoidable, these kinds of self-inflicted injuries are not. It's up to the players themselves to make sure they don't cause their bodies any unnecessary, lasting harm by packing on weight.

When professional football players believe that bigger is better despite evidence to the contrary, it is not surprising that athletes as young as 12 and 13 are trying to become as big as they can as quickly as they can. Most coaches agree that it is skill, not weight, that impresses the scouts, but their message is ignored. Their advice to slim down and focus on technique doesn't seem to change the minds of young players, nor do reports of the deaths of college and professional athletes. Instead, the desire to outweigh opponents overshadows everything else. Professor Dawn Comstock of the Ohio State University's Center for Injury Research and Policy agrees, saying that parents need to become more aware of the risks: "One mother looked up at her very large son with pride and told me, 'Oh, you'll really want to survey him. He's been working hard to get ready for football next fall and has been having creatine every single day'" (as cited in Popke, 2008). In some sense, comments like these may be an example of players or their families thinking that they are invincible. However, for many young players dreaming of a pro football career, this kind of thinking is both harmful and counterproductive.

Health issues aside, many football players might be surprised to learn that bigger players aren't necessarily better. The widespread assumption is that larger

> Fourth reason supporting the analysis: bigger isn't better when it comes to performance on the field.

LIVING (AND DYING) LARGE   6

football players — particularly those playing the line — are more effective than smaller players. Jeffery Espadron, for example, has noticed that college recruiters value bigger players, and he believes that "they're going to notice me because of my size" (as cited in Longman, 2007). Most coaches, however, disagree with that assumption and insist that bulk is a liability. As high school football coach Mickey Joseph commented, "The bigger they are, the worse they are. They can't move. They can't get out of their stance. They're out of breath" (as cited in Longman, 2007). Perhaps this observation should be shared with more professional players as well. Players who deliberately bulk up may sacrifice speed and agility for sheer size, a strategy that does not always pay off when they're on the field.

A partial quotation is used to support a point.

Given the potential dangers to their health and the fact that being large does little to make them effective players, why do athletes work so hard to get bigger? Perhaps they think that the statistics won't apply to them personally — that adding pounds will improve their individual performance. Athletes also know that gaining weight is much easier than gaining muscle, and if weight gives players the slightest advantage, they may think the risks are worth it. Do these players love their sport so much that they will continue to sacrifice their health — or even their lives — for it? They may, if they remain unaware of the consequences, and if they push themselves to their limits without fully understanding the risks.

In the conclusion, the writer speculates about why athletes are willing to endanger their health.

LIVING (AND DYING) LARGE   7

References

Bailes, J. E., Cantu, R. C., & Day, A. L. (2002). The neurosurgeon in sport: Awareness of the risks of heatstroke and dietary supplements. *Neurosurgery, 51,* 283-288. doi:10.1097/00006123-200208000-00002

Groeschen, T. (2008, October 17). Growing concern: Supersize me. *Cincinnati Enquirer.* Retrieved from http://news.cincinnati.com

Longman, J. (2007, November 30). Putting on weight for football glory. *New York Times.* Retrieved from http://www.nytimes.com

Longman, J. (2011, January 28). N.F.L. linemen tip the scales. *New York Times.* Retrieved from http://www.nytimes.com

Meyer, C. (2012, November 9). Varsity xtra: Players' size continues to increase with passage of time. *Pittsburgh Post-Gazette.* Retrieved from http://www.post-gazette.com

Miller, M. A., Croft, L. B., Belanger, A. R., Romero-Corral, A., Somers, V. K., Roberts, A. J., & Goldman, M. E. (2008). Prevalence of metabolic syndrome in retired National Football League players. *American Journal of Cardiology, 101*(9), 1281-1284. doi:10.1016/j.amjcard.2007.12.029

Popke, M. (2008, December). High school coaches and administrators should discourage unhealthy weight gains. Retrieved from http://www.athleticbusiness.com

The References heading is centered type.

Two works by the same author, the earlier one listed first

A newspaper article obtained through the Web

The citation for a journal article includes the digital object identifier (DOI) number. APA recommends the use of DOI numbers in place of URLs.

✳ Project Ideas

The following suggestions can help you focus your work on an analytical essay or another type of analytical document.

Suggestions for Essays

1. ANALYZE AN ACADEMIC TREND

Identify a trend in a field of study that interests you. For instance, you might have noticed the increasing use of statistical methods and advanced mathematics in biology courses, a decreasing emphasis on politics and great leaders in history courses, or a new focus on ethics in business courses. Confirm that the trend exists, and then analyze its implications for students in the discipline. To support your analysis, consult scholarly journals, survey instructors in the field, or interview students who are majoring in the field.

2. SPECULATE ABOUT A POPULAR TREND

Write an essay that explores a popular trend, such as the rise in popularity of a particular kind of music or growing interest in a particular area of study. Address your essay to your instructor. In your essay, describe the trend and provide evidence that shows how it has developed over time. To support your analysis, draw on written sources, or conduct field research using interviews, observations, or surveys.

3. TRACE THE CAUSES OF A RECENT EVENT

Interpret a recent event for an audience of your choice, such as your classmates, other college students, your instructor, your parents, or members of the community. The event might be a local ballot initiative, a natural disaster affecting your region, an incident involving law enforcement officers and college students, or anything you've read about in the news that intrigues or worries you. In your essay, describe the event and provide an analysis of its possible causes. Draw on written sources, interviews, or observations to support your analysis.

4. ASSESS THE EFFECTS OF A HISTORICAL EVENT

Analyze the long-term consequences of a historical event for an audience of your choice. You might direct your essay to your instructor, your classmates, other college students, your friends, or people working in a particular profession. Choose a historical event that has implications for your audience. For example, if you are writing for people from your hometown, you might choose to write about something that occurred when the town was founded. If you are writing for your instructor or classmates, you might choose something related to education, such as the passage of Title IX, which banned discrimination on the basis of sex in educational programs that receive federal funding, or the Morrill Act, which established public land-grant universities. In your essay, describe the event clearly, identify the sources you used to learn about it, and discuss the implications of the event for your readers.

5. ANALYZE AN ADVERTISEMENT

Write an essay that uses rhetorical analysis to interpret an advertisement. Address your essay to your instructor. Choose an ad that interests you, and develop an interpretive question to guide your analysis. For example, you might ask how ads for a credit card company use appeals to character or logic to elicit a positive response from readers, or you might ask how an ad for a popular brand of beer uses emotional appeals to distinguish the beer from its competitors. If possible, include part or all of the ad as an illustration in your essay. To support your analysis, draw on written sources, or conduct field research using interviews, observations, or surveys.

Suggestions for Other Genres

6. DRAFT AND DESIGN A COLUMN FOR A MAGAZINE

First decide whether you want to write about a particular subject or submit your column to a particular magazine. If you have a specific subject in mind, search your library's databases and the Web for articles that address it. This can help you identify magazines that might be interested in your column. If you want to publish your column in a particular magazine, read two or three issues cover-to-cover to determine the kinds of subjects it normally addresses. Once you've selected a target magazine, analyze it to determine its writing conventions (such as the level of formality and the manner in which sources are acknowledged) and design conventions. As you learn about your subject and plan, organize, and design your column, keep in mind what you've learned about the columns you've read. Your column should reflect those writing and design conventions.

7. CREATE A NEWS ANALYSIS

Begin working on your news analysis by identifying an event to analyze. Consider whether analyzing this event will help you accomplish your purposes as a writer. Then reflect on whether your readers will want or need to know about the event.

Finally, identify the newspaper, magazine, or Web site where you'd like to publish your news analysis. Once you've made these preliminary decisions, learn more about the event by consulting your library's databases. Use what you learn about the event to plan, organize, and design your news analysis. Be sure to seek feedback on your drafts from other writers (friends, classmates, relatives) and from your instructor.

8. DEVELOP A MULTIMEDIA PRESENTATION

Begin working on your presentation by considering your purpose and your audience. After you've chosen a subject and conducted your analysis, identify the overall point you want to convey; choose the reasons you'll use to convince your readers to accept your analysis; and identify the evidence you'll use to support your reasons. Then consider the setting in which your audience will view your presentation, choose an organization for your points, and select an appealing and consistent design for your slides. Remember that an effective slide usually focuses on a single point and provides a limited amount of information to support that point. As you develop your presentation, ask for feedback from friends, classmates, instructors, or relatives.

9. ANALYZE A POEM, SHORT STORY, OR NOVEL

Analyze a poem, short story, or novel that you've read recently. Address your analysis to your instructor and other readers who share your interest in this work of literature. Focus on a clearly stated interpretive question, and use text analysis as your interpretive framework. Support your analysis by drawing on the work of literature and published reviews or journal articles. In your essay, identify and briefly describe the work you're analyzing. Then offer your interpretation of the work.

10. POST A BLOG ENTRY

Identify a subject that is suitable for analysis and likely to interest a general group of readers. Then create a blog entry that analyzes the subject. As you write your entry, consider the possibilities and limitations associated with writing for the Web, and in particular for a blog. In your blog entry, provide enough background information on your subject to ground your analysis, introduce your interpretive question, and present your analysis. You should support your analysis by drawing on the subject and linking to other documents on the Web.

In Summary: Writing an Analytical Essay

* **Find a conversation and listen in.**
    - Explore your surroundings (p. 232).
    - Ask interpretive questions (p. 234).
    - Search databases (p. 235).

* **Conduct your analysis.**
    - Refine your question (p. 238).
    - Seek a fuller understanding of your subject (p. 239).
    - Apply an interpretive framework (p. 241).

* **Prepare a draft.**
    - Make an interpretive claim (p. 251).
    - Explain your interpretation (p. 252).
    - Consider genre and design (p. 255).
    - Frame your analysis (p. 255).

* **Review and improve your draft.**
    - Ensure that your claim is debatable (p. 258).
    - Challenge your conclusions (p. 258).
    - Examine the application of your interpretive framework (p. 258).
    - Assess your organization (p. 260).

08 Writing to Evaluate

As an evaluator, I write with certain criteria in mind.

GENRES IN CONVERSATION

Reflective Writing | Informative Writing | Analytical Writing | **Evaluative Writing** | Problem-Solving Writing | Argumentative Writing

Rising rates of obesity and greater access to technology have sparked interest in fitness apps for weight loss. As a student, you are likely juggling classes, a job, volunteer work, your social life, and maybe even a family, all while trying to stay healthy. While researching the best gadgets to keep you on track, you come across an **online article**, a **government blog**, and a **video review**. These three examples illustrate how different genres can be used to accomplish the same purpose.

 e-Pages

You can view the full documents shown here and respond to questions about reflective genres at **bedfordstmartins.com/conversation/epages.**

Online Article ▶

This **online article** from the *Popular Mechanics* Web site, the author compares the effectiveness of fitness trackers and games vs. exercising with a professional personal trainer.

15 Fitness Gadgets vs. One Personal Trainer

How many gadgets does it take to get one man into shape? PM Senior Editor Glenn Derene sought the answer, working out with a barrage of fitness gizmos and comparing the digital experience to a human one—exercising with a real-live personal trainer.

BY GLENN DERENE

GET THE LATEST ON TECHNOLOGY & INNOVATIONS | SUBSCRIBE & SAVE »

Submit   4   Share   Like 14   Pinit   Tweet 8   +1   1 of 4 ▶

Phillip Friedman

View Thumbnails

As yet, there is still no technological substitute for human willpower. But in the quest to get in shape, we flabby citizens have a long history of leaning on gadgets to get us up and active. The first pedometer design is attributed to Leonardo da Vinci, while Thomas Jefferson built his own such device to measure his walks. Since then vibrating belts, electric shocks, and sweaty sauna suits have been touted as high-tech routes to fitness. And in the 1980s, a former Viet Cong sympathizer leveraged the popularity of the VHS to turn herself into a domestic exercise icon with a series of workout tapes.

Believe it or not, Jane Fonda is still at it, finally upgrading to the DVD format in 2010. But her discs are lost in a sea of video games with motion-capture avatars that track your body movements and encourage/hector you in real time. And those games are just the tip of the high-tech-fitness iceberg, with a wide variety of gadgets that promise to inspire you to become a leaner, stronger, healthier you.

The gold standard for fitness coaching is the personal trainer—a real person certified as a professional exercise instructor. But hiring one can be extremely expensive—upwards of $60 per session, which could cause many clients to go broke before they get fit.

Can a bunch of high-tech doodads provide instruction and inspiration comparable to what you'd get from a trained professional? I donned my tracksuit and covered myself in sensors to find out.

1 of 4 ▶

Government Blog ▶

This **government blog** post by the Georgia Department of Public Health quotes health experts and cites recent studies evaluating mobile health apps.

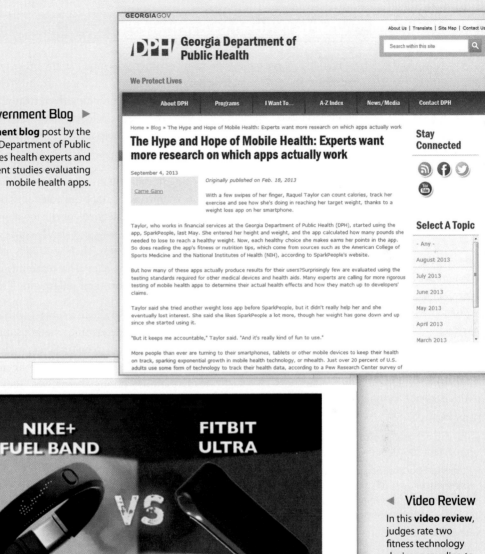

DPH Georgia Department of Public Health

Search within this site

We Protect Lives

About DPH | Programs | I Want To... | A-Z Index | News/Media | Contact DPH

Home » Blog » The Hype and Hope of Mobile Health: Experts want more research on which apps actually work

The Hype and Hope of Mobile Health: Experts want more research on which apps actually work

September 4, 2013

Carrie Gann

Originally published on Feb. 18, 2013

With a few swipes of her finger, Raquel Taylor can count calories, track her exercise and see how she's doing in reaching her target weight, thanks to a weight loss app on her smartphone.

Taylor, who works in financial services at the Georgia Department of Public Health (DPH), started using the app, SparkPeople, last May. She entered her height and weight, and the app calculated how many pounds she needed to lose to reach a healthy weight. Now, each healthy choice she makes earns her points in the app. So does reading the app's fitness or nutrition tips, which come from sources such as the American College of Sports Medicine and the National Institutes of Health (NIH), according to SparkPeople's website.

But how many of these apps actually produce results for their users?Surprisingly few are evaluated using the testing standards required for other medical devices and health aids. Many experts are calling for more rigorous testing of mobile health apps to determine their actual health effects and how they match up to developers' claims.

Taylor said she tried another weight loss app before SparkPeople, but it didn't really help her and she eventually lost interest. She said she likes SparkPeople a lot more, though her weight has gone down and up since she started using it.

"But it keeps me accountable," Taylor said. "And it's really kind of fun to use."

More people than ever are turning to their smartphones, tablets or other mobile devices to keep their health on track, sparking exponential growth in mobile health technology, or mhealth. Just over 20 percent of U.S. adults use some form of technology to track their health data, according to a Pew Research Center survey of

Stay Connected

Select A Topic

- Any -
August 2013
July 2013
June 2013
May 2013
April 2013
March 2013

You Tube

Nike+ Fuelband vs. FitBit Ultra - Prizefight

NIKE+ FUEL BAND VS FITBIT ULTRA

c|net

0:17 / 4:46

CNETTV 4,787 videos

Subscribe 391,304

49,052

👍 290 👎 23

👍 Like

About | Share | Add to

◀ Video Review

In this **video review**, judges rate two fitness technology devices according to five unique criteria, capturing the interest of a general audience by framing their evaluation as a prizefight boxing match.

What Is Writing to Evaluate?

As readers, we seek out evaluative documents as much as any other type of writing. We search for reviews of new movies and restaurants; we surf the Web to learn about the strengths and weaknesses of products ranging from treadmills to smartphones to insect repellents; and we read editorials, letters to the editor, and columns in online magazines in the hope that they will help us develop an informed opinion about recent issues and events.

The Writer's Role: Evaluator

PURPOSE

- To determine whether something has succeeded or failed
- To improve or refine something
- To provide a basis for choosing among alternatives

READERS

- Want another person's opinion
- Expect judgments to be based on appropriate criteria and supported with evidence and analysis

SOURCES

- The subject itself is often an important source of evidence.
- Published documents, personal experiences, and, in some cases, interviews and observations provide additional support.
- Reviewing other sources alerts evaluators to alternative opinions and perspectives.

CONTEXT

- Decisions about criteria and evidence reflect a writer's knowledge of readers, of the subject, and of its background and setting.
- Effective evaluations balance positive and negative assessments and acknowledge alternative perspectives.

Writing to evaluate involves adopting the role of *evaluator*. Writers who adopt this role focus on reaching an informed, well-reasoned conclusion about a subject's worth or effectiveness and clearly conveying their judgments to readers. Their writing is usually balanced, and they generally offer clear reasoning and ample evidence to support their judgments.

Writers typically evaluate a subject with one of three general goals: to determine whether something has succeeded or failed, to help readers understand how something might be improved or refined, or to help readers choose among alternatives. They form their conclusions by learning about their subject and considering how well it meets a given set of *criteria* — the standards or principles on which judgments are based.

Readers of evaluations typically share the writer's interest in a subject and hope to learn more about it. They often share the writer's assumptions about which criteria are appropriate — few readers, for example, expect movie reviewers to justify their choice of criteria. Readers expect the writer to provide evidence and reasoning to support his or her judgments, and readers usually want the writer to acknowledge and address alternative opinions about the subject. In fact, not only are readers likely to know that alternative opinions exist (usually through reading other evaluations) but they might also hold those opinions themselves. As a result, readers are likely to dismiss an evaluation that seems unfair or unaware of different points of view.

Writers' decisions about criteria and evidence are shaped by the contexts in which they find themselves. Writers who address a general audience, for example, might need to define their criteria carefully, while those who write to professionals in a particular field might reasonably expect their readers to be familiar with the criteria they've selected. Similarly, a writer's choice of evidence reflects the nature of the subject and readers' knowledge, expertise, and social and cultural backgrounds. For instance, an evaluation of a creative production such as a movie or a television documentary will usually draw most heavily on the subject itself for evidence, citing examples from the work and referring to expectations about the genre to support the writer's judgments. An evaluation of a building restoration project, on the other hand, is likely to bring in evidence from outside sources — such as budget reports, building codes, and interviews with community members and architects — to support the writer's assessment of the project's relative success or failure and recommendations for improving it.

Evaluative documents make important contributions not only to our personal lives but also to written conversations. On an individual level, evaluations help us make decisions that can affect everything from the brand of car we drive to how we vote in the next election to where we attend college. Within a written conversation, evaluations provide the basis for making collective judgments about how to move the conversation forward.

What Kinds of Documents Are Used to Share Evaluations?

Writers can draw on a wide range of documents to share their judgments. Their evaluations might appear in print, as is often the case with articles and editorials, or on the Web, which is increasingly home to reviews, many of them posted to discussion boards and electronic mailing lists. In writing and writing-intensive courses, the most frequently assigned evaluative projects include essays, reports, blog entries, and source evaluations.

Evaluative documents make important contributions to conversations that focus on the relative merits of products, media, policies, proposals, and artistic works, and they often stand on their own as assessments, opinions, or advice that readers seek out as they try to form their own judgments. Evaluations can also contribute to broader conversations that focus less on judgment alone and more on problem solving or argument. For example, an evaluative report on a U.S. government program might help a writer support a proposal to change foreign policy. The following sections offer

View the e-Pages for evaluative writing at bedfordstmartins.com /conversation.

discussions and examples of three of the most common evaluative genres: evaluative essays, product reviews, and food reviews. In the e-Pages for this chapter, you'll find discussions and examples of progress reports, ratings Web sites, and comparison tools.

Evaluative Essays

Evaluative essays convey a writer's judgments to readers who share an interest in a subject. The criteria that direct the writer's evaluation are usually identified early and are influenced by several factors, including the subject itself, the writer's purpose and perspective, prevailing opinions, and readers' knowledge of the subject. Unlike reviews, which usually focus on a single place or thing, or reports, which typically assess a particular project or initiative for a narrowly defined audience, evaluative essays often examine broader questions or issues for a more general group of readers.

In most cases, evidence from sources (such as published articles, personal interviews, direct observation, Web sites, and government documents) provides the basis for determining whether the subject of an evaluative essay measures up to the criteria. For example, details about the cost of an inner-city summer jobs program might be obtained from an interview with the program director or from published government reports.

Readers of evaluative essays — whether instructors, other students, politicians, or members of a particular profession — expect the writer's ideas to be well organized, well supported, and easy to read. Readers also expect the evaluation to be presented fairly and honestly, although they usually realize that writers will be influenced by their purposes, personal beliefs, and experiences.

Christina Hoff Sommers and Sally Satel, MD
Emotional Correctness

In this essay, drawn from the book *One Nation under Therapy: How the Helping Culture Is Eroding Self-Reliance* (2005), Christina Hoff Sommers and Sally Satel evaluate the effectiveness of talk therapy for psychological health. The authors question the conventional wisdom that the most "well-adjusted" people are those who "focus attention on and talk about their feelings." Drawing on a wide range of sources, Sommers and Satel suggest that this dominant view comes up short and lacks empirical support. Christina Hoff Sommers is a philosopher and critic whose books include *Who Stole Feminism?* (1995) and *The War against Boys* (2001). Sally Satel is a psychiatrist and author whose work has appeared in the *New Republic*, the *Wall Street Journal*, and the *New York Times*.

Emotional Correctness

When the columnist Molly Ivins learned in 1999 that she had stage III inflammatory breast cancer, friends urged her to confront her feelings. Ivins tried it and found the experience "awful." As she wrote in *Time* magazine: "I am one of those people who are out of touch with their emotions. I tend to treat my emotions like unpleasant relatives—a long-distance call once or twice a year is more than enough. If I got in touch with them, they might come to stay."[1]

In an age when talking about one's feelings has become a mark of personal authenticity, Ivins's spirited refusal to open up is a breath of fresh air. Over the past thirty years or so, emotive outpouring has become routine on television and radio and in our leading news magazines. So powerful is this trend that Ivins's reluctance to dwell on her feelings about her cancer seems almost an affront. Merely suggesting to someone that she is talking too much about herself can be taken as "a form of abuse," observed Wendy Kaminer in her 1992 bestseller *I'm Dysfunctional, You're Dysfunctional.*[2] "What might have once been called whining is now exalted as a process of exerting selfhood," Kaminer continued, and "self-absorption is regarded as a form of self-expression."[3]

More than a decade after Kaminer's incisive exposé of confessional culture, the *New York Times Magazine* carried an article with the improbable title "Repress Yourself."[4] The author, psychologist Lauren Slater, sought to show that science was bearing out the value of self-restraint. "New research," she wrote, "shows that some traumatized people may be better off repressing the experience."[5] Slater cited recent studies showing that heart attack victims and bereaved spouses who "minimize, distract, and deny" felt far less anxious about their illness or loss months later.

Slater wasn't talking about everyone, of course. But she wanted to show that recounting one's anxieties (again and again) or pondering them (over and over) is not required for psychological health. It soon became clear that Slater had tapped a rich vein of rebellion against the still-pervasive idea that the well adjusted are those who focus attention on and talk about their feelings. Wrote one appreciative reader, "Maybe the talking cure would be helpful if you talked once, but most shrinks want the patient to go on and on, reducing you to only your horror story."[6] Another recalled Don Imus's remark "that in at least one of the early 'sessions' at the New Mexico ranch [for children with cancer], the children said, 'Send those psychologists home.'"[7]

By some definitions of "emotional intelligence" Slater and these readers are to be pitied. They are emotionally obtuse. Their reticence is supposed to put them at a disadvantage. But is this true?

About thirty years ago, a psychiatrist at the University of Wisconsin named John R. Marshall sought to confirm the already dominant view that openness was critical to mental health. In his essay "The Expression of Feelings," published in the *Archives of General Psychiatry*, Marshall noted that most mental health experts as well as the general public held the belief "that if a person can be convinced, allowed, or helped to express his feelings, he will in some way benefit from it."[8]

"Surely," Marshall postulated, "a concept so ubiquitous should be relatively easy to validate." But when he reviewed the literature for evidence of the benefits of sharing one's feelings, he found a confusing muddle of "ambiguous and contradictory studies."[9] The intervening years have produced a sizable and compelling body of research demonstrating that the expression of feelings is not a sure pathway to fulfillment. On the contrary, it often leads to unhappiness.

Consider anger. Charles Darwin was one of the first to observe that the verbal and physical expression of anger often begets anger. In *The Expression of the Emotions in Man and Animals*, published in 1872, he wrote that "the free expression by outward signs of an emotion intensifies it" and that "he who gives way to violent gestures will increase his rage."[10] A century later, experimental studies were confirming Darwin's observations.[11] By 1973 the president of the American Psychological Association, Albert Bandura, was calling for a moratorium on the use of "venting" in therapy.[12] That same year the psychologist Leonard Berkowitz, renowned for his work on aggression, wrote an article in *Psychology Today* called "The Case for Bottling Up Rage" in which he criticized "ventilationist" therapists.[13]

Following these pronouncements, data have continued to spill out of journals confirming, with few exceptions, that physical and verbal expression of anger is usually self-reinforcing.[14] Nor does talking about negative experiences necessarily ameliorate the anxiety accompanying them. Despite the claims of Jon G. Allen, a psychologist and author of *Treatment Approaches to Coping with Trauma*, who states that "the universal prescription for trauma [is to] talk about it with any trusted person who will listen," a number of studies show that talking per se has little effect on emotional recovery.[15] For example, Yale psychiatrists found no relationship between the degree to which Gulf War veterans talked with family about their experiences and their ratings of residual war-related anxiety.[16] After the 1989 Loma Prieta earthquake in Northern California, a Stanford University psychologist found no difference in distress between college students who talked about their experiences and those who did not.[17] Other researchers found a similar lack of protective effect of so-called social sharing on symptoms of distress.[18]

What about self-absorption? Intense contemplation of one's inner landscape, especially during times of distress, has long been considered necessary for deeper self-knowledge and, ultimately, for mental well-being. But this, too, turns out to be psychological lore. An incident from the life of John Stuart Mill, the nineteenth-century philosopher and one of the founders of utilitarianism, is exemplary.

Happiness was a state that Mill deemed the greatest good and believed it came from the pleasurable fulfillment of human desire. Now one might think this philosophy favors therapism since it seems to demand that we all pay a great deal of attention to our feelings and desires. But Mill found otherwise. A section in his autobiography called "A Crisis In My Mental History" describes his painful discovery that self-preoccupation can be disastrous.

In the fall of 1826, at age twenty, Mill suffered a debilitating, long-lasting depression. Antidepressants were not available to him. Nor was talk therapy; it was thirty years before Freud was even born. Mill's depression persisted and deepened. Relief came only by accident. Mill happened to read a very moving story that caused him to forget about his own psyche for a brief spell—and the depression lifted. This experience had a profound effect on him, leading the philosopher to adopt what he called an "anti-self-consciousness" theory. Here is how Mill describes the lesson he learned:

> The experience of this period had [a] very marked effect on my opinions and character. . . . Those only are happy who have their minds fixed on some object other than their own happiness; on the happiness of others, on the improvement of mankind, even on some art or pursuit. . . . Aiming thus at something else, they find happiness by the way. . . . The only chance is to treat, not happiness, but some end external to it, as the purpose of life. Let your self-consciousness, your scrutiny, your self-interrogation, exhaust themselves on [some external end].[19]

It is possible that Mill's depression was starting to fade before he found relief through literary distraction. In fact, an improvement in mood may be what gave him the capacity to be distracted in the first place; after all, a prominent symptom of major depression is the inability to focus on a task. In Mill's case, even if his depression were starting to melt as part of the natural cycle of remission, his ability to distract himself surely accelerated his recovery.[20] Ample research demonstrates that purposeful distraction can lift one's mood when depressed, just as ruminating about problems and the meaning of negative feelings can amplify them.

Now, two centuries after Mill and three decades after Marshall, despite a large body of research challenging the virtue of dwelling on and expressing one's emotions, those bedrock principles of therapism remain alive and well. We do not suggest that naturally passionate or voluble people should suppress their emotions or their desire to talk. But we caution against pressing, shaming, or subtly coercing anyone into trying to feel more deeply or be more expressive than befits his natural style.

NOTES

1. Molly Ivins, "Who Needs Breasts, Anyway?" *Time*, February 18, 2002, p. 58.
2. Wendy Kaminer, *I'm Dysfunctional, You're Dysfunctional: The Recovery Movement and Other Self-Help Fashions* (New York: Vintage Books, 1993), p. 30.
3. Ibid., p. 31.
4. Lauren Slater, "Repress Yourself," *New York Times Magazine*, February 23, 2003.
5. Slater uses the term "repression" to refer to the conscious tamping down of particular thoughts and feelings rather than to a defensive process that operates outside of awareness. Freud used the term interchangeably. Slater might have used the word "suppression" (which refers to a conscious process only), but the article made her meaning clear.
6. *New York Times Magazine* discussion forum, entry 38 of 135, dated February 23, 2003.
7. Ibid., entry 30 of 135.
8. J. R. Marshall, "The Expression of Feelings," *Archives of General Psychiatry* 27, no. 6 (1972), pp. 786–90.
9. Ibid., p. 786.
10. Charles Darwin, *The Expression of the Emotions in Man and Animals*, 3rd ed. (New York: Oxford University Press, 1998), pp. 359–60.
11. Almost fifty years ago psychologist Seymour Feshbach encouraged a group of normal little boys to kick furniture and play with toy guns and generally run wild. Subsequently, they behaved much more aggressively during their free play times than they did before permission to run amok; see S. Feshbach, "The Catharsis Hypothesis and Some Consequences of Interaction with Aggression and Neutral Play Objects," *Journal of Personality and Social Psychology* 24 (1956), pp. 449–62; Shahbaz Khan Mallick and Boyd R. McCandless, "A Study of Catharsis Aggression," *Journal of Personality and Social Psychology* 4

(1966), pp. 591–96. A few years later psychologist R. Hornberger examined anger in adults. His subjects were insulted by a designated provoker and half of them instructed to pound nails into an object for about ten minutes. The other subjects did nothing. Next, all participants were given a chance to criticize the person who taunted them. Unexpectedly, the pounders, presumably having "released" their anger, were more hostile toward the person who insulted them than the nonpounders; see R. Hornberger, "The Differential Reduction of Aggressive Responses as a Function of Interpolated Activities," *American Psychology* 14 (1959), p. 354, abstract.

12. Albert Bandura in B. J. Bushman, "Does Venting Anger Feed or Extinguish the Flame? Catharsis, Rumination, Distraction, Anger, and Aggressive Responding," *Personality and Social Psychology Bulletin* 28 (2002), pp. 724–31.

13. Leonard Berkowitz, "The Case for Bottling Up Rage," *Psychology Today*, July 1973, p. 31; Leonard Berkowitz, "Experimental Investigations of Hostility Catharsis," *Journal of Consulting and Clinical Psychology* 35 (1970), pp. 1–7.

14. Carol Tavris, *Anger: The Misunderstood Emotion* (New York: Touchstone Books, 1989).

15. Jon G. Allen, *Coping with Trauma: A Guide to Self-Understanding* (Washington, D.C.: American Psychiatric Press, 1995), p. 237.

16. S. M. Southwick, C. A. Morgan III, and R. Rosenberg, "Social Sharing of Gulf War Experiences. Association with Trauma-Related Psychological Symptoms," *Journal of Nervous and Mental Disease* 188 (2000), pp. 695–700.

17. S. Nolen-Hoeksema and J. Morrow, "A Prospective Study of Depression and Posttraumatic Stress Symptoms After a Natural Disaster: The 1989 Loma Prieta Earthquake," *Journal of Personality and Social Psychology* 61, no. 1 (1991), pp. 115–21.

18. T. D. Borkovec and E. Costello, "Efficacy of Applied Relaxation and Cognitive Behavioral Therapy in the Treatment of Generalized Anxiety Disorder," *Journal of Consulting and Clinical Psychology* 61 (1993), pp. 611–19; Bernard Rime, "Mental Rumination, Social Sharing, and the Recovery From Emotional Exposure," in *Emotion, Disclosure, and Health*, ed. James W. Pennebaker (Washington, D.C.: American Psychological Association, 1995), pp. 271–92; P. P. Schnurr, J. D. Ford, M. J. Friedman, et al., "PTSD in World War II Mustard Gas Test Participants: A Preliminary Report," *Annals of the New York Academy of Science* 821 (1997), pp. 425–29; R. Tait and R. C. Silver, "Coming to Terms with Major Negative Life Events," in *Unintended Thought*, ed. John A. Bargh and James S. Uleman (New York: Guilford Press, 1989), pp. 351–82.

19. John Stuart Mill, *Autobiography* (New York: Penguin, 1989), pp. 117–18.
20. Notably, Mill biographers believe that his encounter with depression created a need to reconcile the intellectual, rational self with the feeling self and thus led to a broader definition of liberalism. See Bruce Mazlish, *James and John Stuart Mill* (New York: Basic Books, 1975); J. Geller, "A Crisis in My Mental History," *Psychiatric Services* 54, no. 10 (2003), pp. 1347–49.

In your writer's notebook, consider how Sommers and Satel respond to their writing situation by answering the following questions:

Starting a Conversation: Respond to "Emotional Correctness"

1. Sommers and Satel question a "still-pervasive idea" (para. 4) that is broadly accepted throughout American culture. What is this idea, and how do they characterize it? What does their characterization reveal about their own attitude toward the subject?

2. The authors use the phrase "emotional intelligence" (para. 5) but do not define it explicitly. What do you think the term means? Why is it relevant to their evaluation?

3. What criteria do Sommers and Satel rely on to evaluate the effectiveness of emotional openness and the "talking cure"? What is their overall judgment, and how do they translate that judgment into a recommendation for their readers?

4. Sommers and Satel draw on several different kinds of sources to support their evaluation. Locate examples of anecdotal evidence, psychological studies, self-help literature, and historical perspective. To what end do the authors use each type of evidence? How does the mix of sources contribute to their overall purpose?

5. In paragraph 9, Sommers and Satel quote an author with whom they disagree. Why do they do this? How does it support their point?

Media Reviews

Media reviews present an evaluation of a work of art, a song or music album, a television program, a book, a movie or play, a computer game, a DVD, a Web site, or any of a number of other cultural productions. The subject of the review reflects the shared interests of the group of writers and readers involved in a written conversation. For example, a group of horror fans might be interested in a new film based on one of Dean Koontz's novels, while people who play a particular video game will probably be interested in the latest version of the game.

Because media reviewers expect their readers to understand what's necessary for success in a particular medium, they often do not define their criteria. For example, a movie critic will assume that readers are familiar with the importance of acting, plot, and cinematography. The evidence used to determine whether the subject of a review has met the criteria for success is most often drawn from the subject itself and from the reviewer's personal interpretation, although writers sometimes include evidence from interviews, surveys, or published sources to support their evaluations.

 Lindsay Zoladz
Review of Thao & the Get Down Stay Down, **We the Common**

This review of Thao & the Get Down Stay Down's 2013 album *We the Common* was published by *Pitchfork*, a daily Internet site featuring music reviews, music news, and artist interviews. *Pitchfork*'s readers tend to be more curious about discovering new music than those who read reviews in general-interest publications. But most still want the answer to a simple question: Should I buy this band's music? After reading the following review, would you buy Thao & the Get Down Stay Down's album? Lindsay Zoladz, a Brooklyn-based journalist, is a staff writer for *Pitchfork* and has published her work in *The Believer, Slate, Salon,* and *Washington City Paper.*

Review of Thao & the Get Down Stay Down, *We the Common*

(Ribbon Music, 2013)

By Lindsay Zoladz

Feb. 4, 2013 | Creative people have long been in pursuit of that ephemeral quality they call "life experience"; this is why we have things like gap years, the Peace Corps, and hallucinogenic mushrooms. It's also the fuel driving *We the Common*, the fourth album from spirited folk-popper Thao Nguyen. Including her three records with the Get Down Stay Down and a 2011 collaboration with Mirah, the prolific Nguyen has been involved in so many projects that she's spent most of her 20s on the road. Last year, when the rootlessness of the touring life was starting to get her down, she went out in conscious search of that elusive life experience — or, in her words, "I wanted to try to be a real live person, rather than just singing songs about them." So she settled in San Francisco. She didn't write much, and instead did some deep thinking about her life's direction. She made an effort to be a part of her community, spending time working with an organization that advocates for prisoners' rights. Then, she did what most creative people in self-conscious pursuit of "life experience" end up doing: she used it to write some new songs. For a record she'll inevitably tour. The cycle of rootlessness continues.

But on *We the Common*, her most sharply written record to date, she's well aware of that irony. Its 12 songs are smart, sometimes piercingly self-aware meditations on the creative life, teasing out the tension between life and art, the individual and the community — and perhaps most of all — security and restlessness. "We love some strangers every night," she sings with mock-flippancy on "We Don't Call," which is as much about the emotional stamina required to regularly pour your heart out on stage as it is the havoc that lifestyle can wreak on long-term relationships. Like most of the songs on *We the Common*, the arrangement is nimble and the instrumentation is varied but never overcrowded — a vibraphone tiptoes around the vocal melody and horns accent but don't overpower the emotional nuances of her lyrics. "Bye bye baby, I'm going to work/ Chase myself all over the earth," she sings later, with a subtle tinge of weariness. *We the Common*'s best songs are its most dynamic. "City" is driving, percussive, and dotted with distorted guitar riffs that touch down unexpectedly, like lightning bolts. The chaotic and kinetic "Move" seems to pick up a few tricks from Nguyen's pal Merrill Garbus of tUnE-yArDs — lurching at a midtempo stagger that suddenly explodes into one of the record's most satisfying moments, when Nguyen shakes off her composure and screams, "Oh, to be free!" From a distance, it would be too easy for those with the oft-diagnosed allergy to uptempo banjos and vibraphone solos to dismiss Nguyen as "quirky," but closer listens even to her earliest records show that her lyrics and sound have always packed an unexpectedly blunt punch. John Congleton's excellent production emphasizes the jagged edges and negative space, making each sound pop as vividly as he did on St. Vincent's *Strange Mercy*.

And speaking of indie marquee names, the song on *We the Common* liable to generate the most chatter is probably "Kindness Be Conceived," a sprightly and predictably pastoral duet with Joanna Newsom. (According to Thao, the two met somewhere that I assure you is not a soundstage for a "Portlandia sketch" but an actual place in the world: "a Virginia Woolf-style farm paradise where women writers get their own cabins and write all day and meet in the evening for dinner.") Pleasant as it is, it's not one of the album's most memorable songs, and the irrepressible quirk in Newsom's voice only highlights the biggest issue with *We the Common*: Nguyen doesn't always have the personality to sell these songs. Her voice has a tendency to go a little monochrome, and this causes some of the slower numbers, like "Clouds for Brains" and "The Day Long," to fade into indistinct and unmemorable hues. On "Kindness," both vocalists sing the same melody over the top of each other, but it's the magnetic charisma of Newsom's that draws you in.

Still, Nguyen's most quietly affecting vocal comes in the last song, "Age of Ice," another track that seems to address the emotional life of the wanderer. It's a song about survival — the necessity of acting tough and building up defenses ("What of all the stone I invented/ To coat my hands and my face"), but it also contains the possibility of a thaw. "I remember you with a feeling or two," she sings with a hint of self-deprecation, as though she's wishing to feel and experience more. But ultimately *We the Common* shows that "life experience" can happen anywhere — even in a cramped tour bus or on a brightly lit stage. Nguyen may have spent her youth unconventionally, but that doesn't mean she's not "a real live person." Her songs are stuffed with the wisdom and strengths she gained from her years on the road — resilience, hopefulness, and self-reliance. "Rest and be strong, wash and be clean," she sings in the powerful last seconds of "City." "Start a new year whenever you need."

Starting a Conversation: Respond to "Review of Thao & the Get Down Stay Down, *We the Common*"

In your writer's notebook, record your thoughts on the music review by responding to the following questions:

1. In this generally positive review, Zoladz goes into great detail about both the band's music and the context of Thao Nguyen's personal life. Where in the essay do you find the clearest statement of her main thesis? How would you express it in your own words?

2. Zoladz approvingly describes Nguyen as a "spirited folk-popper" (para. 1) whose "songs are stuffed with the wisdom and strengths she gained from her years on the road" (para. 4). What does the statement reveal about Zoladz's taste preferences and criteria for evaluating music? Do you share them?

3. The writer includes a broad range of cultural references, from "gap years" to the television show *Portlandia*. Does her writing seem inaccessible? What kind of assumptions does Zoladz make about her readers? How are those assumptions related to her larger points about the band, its fans, and its detractors?

4. Zoladz relies on comparison and contrast to describe and evoke the sounds of Thao Nguyen and guest singer Joanna Newsom. Point to places in the review where she does this. How do the examples support Zoladz's larger evaluation of the album?

Food Reviews

Questions about what we eat and how it's prepared have long been an important part of American culture, but until relatively recently most Americans were more likely to bite into a hot dog than to engage in spirited discussions about the finer details of food and its preparation. That's no longer the case. Over the past decade, food and its preparation have become something of a national obsession. From restaurant reviews to discussions of the latest developments on the Food Network to articles in magazines such as *Saveur*, *Bon Appétit*, and *Vegetarian Times*, it's hard to get through a week without encountering a review of something related to food.

In response to this interest, the "food review" has emerged as a popular form of evaluation. Like restaurant reviews, the writers of food reviews seldom define their evaluative criteria. They assume that readers share their values, such as taste and the use of healthy ingredients. Unlike restaurant reviews, which tend to focus on the context in which the food is prepared and served, food reviews tend to focus more on the food itself, often calling attention to the distinctive qualities of particular foods and the experience of preparing or eating the food.

In most cases, this focus reflects a desire to help readers understand the growing range of options — healthy and otherwise — that they can explore. Sometimes, as in the review that follows, food reviews are closely tied to location and culture. Travelers who are visiting a city for the first time, for example, will frequently want to learn about the cuisines associated with the area and their origins. Food reviews provide a response to their needs and interests.

 Steve Garbarino
The Crescent City's Greatest Po'Boys

"The Crescent City's Greatest Po'Boys" is a food review from the *Wall Street Journal*'s Food & Drink section. In it, journalist and editor Steve Garbarino evaluates the merits of traditional and unconventional variations on the po'boy sandwich, one of New Orleans' most famous culinary creations. Garbarino first offers some context and history about the sandwich, and he outlines the debates that have sprung up over the criteria for a good po'boy and the rivalries that have developed between passionate shop owners. He ends his review with an evaluation of the city's eight best sandwiches, describing each in enough detail to appeal to audiences far beyond the Crescent City.

The Crescent City's Greatest Po'Boys

Food & Drink | March 5, 2011

By Steve Garbarino

Just how passionate New Orleans is about its most famous sandwich is evident in a battle that's been brewing for months, between two po'boy shops situated a mere block from each other in the city's Irish Channel neighborhood.

On one corner, there's Parasol's, a hallowed po'boy pit stop that dates to 1952, recently purchased by a transplant from St. Petersburg, Florida. On the other corner, there's Tracey's, a sprawling po'boy shop and barroom opened last September by Parasol's former proprietor, a local ousted when his digs were sold to the highest bidder: the Floridian.

The food-fighting rivalry is high drama in the Crescent City, celebrating Mardi Gras this Tuesday, and everybody has something to say about the situation, little of it good. Under its new ownership, Parasol's is an impostor and the real deal is now a block away, so intoned some of the city's foodie blogs, fueling the flame. Now the local newspaper, weeklies, and TV newscasts are keeping a steady vigil.

"New Orleans just doesn't like change. And it's steeped in po'boy tradition," Parasol's new owner, John Hogan, 54, says. Since taking it over with his wife, a New Orleans native, he's left the rickety look intact, continued to allow smoking, and he's concocted his own roast-beef po'boy recipe, using an oven-roasted inside round and a gravy made from beef broth, drippings, flour, and spices. Despite that, "they've been calling me all kinds of things," Mr. Hogan says—even spreading rumors that he plans to turn Parasol's into a Big Easy–themed chain. He won't say who "they" are—it's that delicate.

It's also affecting business. On a late February afternoon, at the height of the city's carnival season, there were a number of empty bar stools at Parasol's. "We're just going to focus on the food, earn the neighborhood's trust over time, while respecting the provenance of the Parasol's name," Mr. Hogan says.

Counters Jeff Carreras, the owner of Tracey's, "I'm not bad-mouthing him. It is what it is. I've heard mixed reviews, good and bad, of the place." Mr. Carreras, 40, carried over his award-winning roast-beef po'boy recipes to the new space, which is 8,000 square feet compared with the old 2,000, and he is taking out ads in local weeklies, even renting a billboard, to announce the new location and fill the (also sparsely occupied) seats.

So much commotion over so humble a dish. A po'boy (also "po-boy") is a sandwich made

▲ At GW Fins battered chunks of lobster are served on an airy French loaf with remoulade and Creole mustard dippers, homemade slaw, and BBQ chips.

▲ Roll Call: Mahony's shrimp-and-fried-green-tomato po'boy

with locally baked French bread loaves—crusty on the outside, cotton candy–fluffy on the inside. The loaf is sliced open and filled, traditionally, with batter-fried shrimp or oysters. Other popular versions are stuffed with andouille and spicy Italian sausage, soft-shell crab, and catfish. In recent years, the popularity of roast-beef po'boys (with Swiss cheese and beef gravy) has given shrimp and oyster a run.

The po'boy was named in 1929 by brothers Bennie and Clovis Martin, New Orleans bakers and former trolley conductors who fed drivers immersed in a historic streetcar strike free sandwiches filled with scraps. (These days, 6- to 8-inch-long "shorties" cost from $5 to $11, depending on fillings.) As a new worker approached the food line outside their French Market bakery and restaurant, the brothers, according to authenticated family letters, would shout to each other, "Here comes another poor boy."

A food icon was born. It was perfected by the Martins and a baker named John Gendusa, whose family still sells the all-important loaves to many po'boy shops. "All about da bread," you hear all over town. To most po'boy enthusiasts and shops (including, incidentally, Parasol's and Tracey's), the best loaves are made by the circa-1896 Leidenheimer Baking Co., which produces one million pounds of bread annually. Its delivery trucks, marked with its slogan, "Sink ya teeth into a piece of New Orleans cultcha," are part of the city's fabric.

In recent years, there have been mutterings that some of the po'boy temples have been resting on their laurels, using pre-sliced beef, powdered gravy mixes, and frozen shrimp. While New Orleans may not embrace change, that's given some newcomers—self-described po'boy purists—an opening.

The city's white-tablecloth chefs are dreaming up inventive takes on the sandwich, too, inspired largely by the New Orleans Po-Boy Preservation Festival—a four-year-old event that awards best-of accolades to po'boys at its annual bake-off on Oak Street. Fried green tomatoes are an accepted new stuffing. And gaining favor (and earning awards) are po'boys made with fried chicken livers and bacon (Mahony's), roasted duck and cochon (Crabby Jack's), and even fried lobster.

"It's a 'rich-boy,' not a po'boy," concedes Tenney Flynn, chef of the French Quarter seafood restaurant GW Fins, whose fried-

Maine-lobster po'boy took "Best of Show" at last November's festival.

Even New Orleans communities that own no share of the po'boy tradition have realized the dish's versatility. Tony Tocco, owner of Uptown's bayou-inspired Café Atchafalaya, says his favorite po'boy is actually Vietnamese, concocted at Tan Dinh in New Orleans's Gretna suburb. "It's made with baked pistolette bread," says Mr. Tocco, "stuffed with charred pork, jalapeños, and Asian pickled vegetables, smeared with house-made pâté."

▲ Crabby Jack's slow-roasted duck po'boy with gravy and jalapeños

Says Brett Anderson, the restaurant critic for New Orleans's daily newspaper, the *Times-Picayune*: "I'm not a purist about them, save for the bread. But if you want to invent a delicious po'boy that doesn't involve something ridiculous, I'll try it. If it's good enough, I'll love it, without apology."

We sampled versions at a dozen New Orleans–area po'boy shops, both iconic and new. None were bad and most were sloppy-delicious. But the eight spotlighted here rose to levels of savory greatness. Oh, and both Parasol's and Tracey's made the cut.

The Classic: Domilise's Po-Boys

Devoted locals and savvy tourists vie for a four-top or bar stool in this wood-paneled Uptown corner legend, open for at least 100 years. We're pleased to report it's decidedly not laurel-resting. And at 88, nor is Dot Domilise, still helming the narrow kitchen. Take a ticket, get in line (there's no table service), and ask for the sublime fried shrimp po'boy with Swiss cheese and beef gravy: a dark, resonant roux, as tasty on the shrimp as on the sausage. *5240 Annunciation St., 504-899-9126*

The Game Keeper: Crabby Jack's

When locals get "character" overload, they drive to an industrial section of Jefferson Parish to this yum-fest run by kitchen dervish Jacques Leonardi. It's all about the cochon (pig), rabbit, and duck he brings with gusto to the po'boy plate. "Over-stuffed" is an understatement. The slow-roasted duck po'boy with gravy and jalapeños is love-me tender, sophisticatedly rich. A classic born. *428 Jefferson Highway, crabby-jacks.com*

The Quarter Master: Johnny's Po-Boys

This tiny cafeteria with checked tablecloths is, oddly, one of the few authentic po'boy haunts in the French Quarter. Variety rules: you can order the po'boys on a French loaf or a large bun, or as a triple-decker. Go for the surf-and-turf po'boy: hot roast beef and gravy topped with fried shrimp, lettuce, tomato, and mayonnaise. *511 St. Louis St., johnnyspoboy.com*

▲ Casamento's Restaurant's fried oyster loaf

The Roadside Attraction: Sammy's Food Service & Deli

Located in the Gentilly neighborhood, off the tour-bus maps, this local luncheon favorite is loved for its consistent blue-plate specials like fried pork chops and stuffed shrimp. Last year, the garlic-stuffed roast-beef po'boy — airy and juicy, with clove-crunching aroma, built on Leidenheimer bread (one of its trucks) — won the "Best Roast Beef" award at the Po-Boy Festival. Not bad for a family pit stop. *3000 Elysian Fields Ave., sammysfood.com*

The Shining Pearl: Casamento's Restaurant

Unconventional hours haven't kept this 89-year-old oyster mecca from drawing lines outside its tiled quarters. Accolades and food shows have followed, mainly for its blissful po'boy hybrid: the fried oyster loaf. Made with thick-cut white Bunny Bread, it is packed four inches high with lightly cornfloured oysters simmered in lard in cast iron pots. *4330 Magazine St., casamentosrestaurant.com*

The Claw Breaker: *GW Fins*

Budget-leaning po'boy purists will say this upscale seafood restaurant in the French Quarter has no place on the list. But last year, chef Tenney Flynn and his sous chef nabbed top honors at the New Orleans Po-Boy Preservation Festival with their fried-Maine-lobster po'boy. The buttery, battered chunks of lobster are served on an airy French loaf with remoulade and Creole mustard dippers, homemade slaw, and BBQ chips. *808 Bienville St., gwfins.com*

The New-old Guard: Mahony's Po-Boy Shop

The *Times-Picayune* restaurant critic Brett Anderson says it takes "more than five years, and maybe as long as 80," for a po'boy shop to be "established." Not anymore. This three-year-old po'boy outfit has been snatching laurels with its fresh ingredients and recipes (root beer–glazed ham and cheese, anyone?). Hope that chef-owner Ben Wick's 86-year-old grandma, Judy Sekinger, serves your grilled-shrimp-and-fried-green-tomato po'boy. *3454 Magazine St., mahonyspoboys.com*

The Torch Bearer: Parkway Bakery & Tavern

Owner Jay Nix managed to avoid the "newcomer" stigma when he re-opened this '20s po'boy shop and bar in 2003. The building has since quadrupled in size — as have the lines. Parkway tops "best po'boy" lists annually and earned a visit last year from the Obamas. It wins our love with its fried shrimp po'boy and super-sloppy, "classic" roast beef, dressed to the nines. *538 Hagan Ave., parkwaybakeryandtavernnola.com*

Starting a Conversation: Respond to "The Crescent City's Greatest Po'Boys"

In your writer's notebook, analyze the ideas presented in Garbarino's evaluation by responding to the following questions:

1. Rather than providing a numerical rating or a number of stars, as is common in food reviews, Garbarino chooses the best eight out of twelve po'boy shops and assigns each a title ("The Torch Bearer," "The Classic") before providing a more detailed assessment. Why do you think he might have chosen this method of evaluation? What does it offer that a more standard rating system does not? How do you think his readers are likely to respond?

2. Examine the evidence Garbarino provides early in his review before evaluating each restaurant. From what sources does he gather evidence? What criteria does he establish based on this evidence? Why do you think he chooses the sources he does?

3. Garbarino devotes much of the review to describing the rivalries between po'boy shops and apparent controversy around less traditional versions of the sandwich. What do these details about the rivalries contribute to his evaluation? Why might he have chosen to include them? What kind of reader is he trying to reach or appeal to by including such information?

4. Garbarino is not a native resident of New Orleans, but he is familiar with the city through his work for the *Times-Picayune* newspaper, based in New Orleans. How do you think his evaluation of the city's po'boy shops might differ if he were a New Orleans native? What other aspects of the city's food culture would his review have been likely to highlight?

5. How would you characterize the language (formal, informal, friendly, etc.) Garbarino uses to describe each po'boy sandwich and its ingredients? How does he describe the shops, the owners, and the chefs? What does his writing style contribute to the review? How are the descriptions likely to affect his readers?

How Can I Write an Evaluative Essay?

If you regularly make purchases online, you've almost certainly run into reviews on sites such as Amazon or NexTag. Chances are also good that you've turned to your local newspaper or searched the Web for help deciding which movie to watch or which new restaurant to try. It turns out that product and media reviews are both plentiful and easy to locate. That's not the case, however, for other types of evaluations. For instance, if you're hoping to learn whether it would be better to work an extra ten hours per week or to take out a college loan, or if you're trying to determine whether your community should invest in renewable energy credits or start its own wind farm, you're likely to find that the best place to look for answers is in the mirror.

Evaluative essays allow you to address subjects — some as complex as genetic engineering in agriculture and others as seemingly straightforward as deciding how to travel between home and school — that connect to your personal, academic, or professional life. Like other academic essays, they also present some intriguing challenges for writers. In addition to choosing an appropriate subject for evaluation, you must identify criteria on which to base your judgment, learn enough about your subject to make an informed judgment about how well it measures up to your criteria, and convey your judgments in a well-written, well-organized, readable manner.

This section helps you tune in to the conversations around you and take on the role of evaluator as you choose a subject, conduct your evaluation, prepare your draft, and review and improve your draft. As you work on your essay, you'll follow Dwight Haynes, a first-year student who wrote an evaluative essay about approaches to reducing alcohol consumption by college students.

Find a Conversation and Listen In

Evaluative essays allow you to share your judgments with readers who will consider your conclusions seriously and, in many cases, act on your recommendations. Your decision about which conversation to join should reflect your interests and your writing assignment. For example, were you surprised by a government plan to regulate the

In Process

An Evaluative Essay about Programs to Reduce College Drinking

Dwight Haynes wrote an evaluative essay for his introductory composition course. Dwight learned about his topic by reading articles about approaches to reducing alcohol consumption by college students. Follow Dwight's efforts to write his evaluative essay by reading the In Process boxes throughout this chapter.

banking industry? Are you wondering whether a promising new television show has a future? Are you skeptical about claims that a new battery technology will finally usher in the age of the electric car? If so, ask yourself what interests you most about the subject, and then start listening to what others have had to say about it.

EXPLORE YOUR NEEDS, INTERESTS, AND CONCERNS

Evaluative documents are most successful when their subject matches up with readers' needs, interests, or concerns. Readers of *Skiing* magazine, for instance, typically view the sport as an important part of their lives and are interested in new developments in equipment and techniques. An evaluation of the latest skis from Rossignol is likely to address the needs and interests of these readers, many of whom might be in the market for new equipment. Similarly, readers of the magazine might be interested in an evaluation of the effectiveness of conditioning techniques or energy bars.

Readers are also likely to read evaluative documents that address their concerns. Subscribers to *Skiing*, for example, might be concerned about the impact of climate change on skiing or about plans to allow oil shale excavation in areas near ski resorts.

Engaging and effective evaluative essays deal with subjects that address not only your readers' needs, interests, and concerns but also your own. As you consider potential subjects for your essay, ask yourself what has caught your attention lately — or better yet, what has long been a matter of interest or concern to you. And be sure to consider your current needs. If you can write about a subject that will help you address your needs, you'll be more invested in conducting the evaluation. To explore your needs, interests, and concerns, cast a wide net. Use idea-generating strategies such as brainstorming, freewriting, or clustering (see pp. 32–35) to respond to questions like these:

- **Products.** Take an inventory of your personal interests, such as hobbies, outdoor activities, or sports. What new products have been introduced lately? Are you thinking of buying (or have you bought) any of them? Are they truly useful, or has the manufacturer overhyped them? Would you recommend them to others?

- **Media.** What's new and interesting in books, movies, television, music, video games, or the Web? What have you read, watched, or listened to that made you think? Have you noticed any developments that trouble you? Have you heard or read criticisms that you think are unfair?

- **Campus life.** Are you thinking about joining a club, team, or group but can't decide if it's worth your time? Do your peers engage in any behaviors that seem dangerous or unhealthy to you? Have you attended a guest lecture or student performance that you felt was overrated or underappreciated? Has a new building or work of public art sparked controversy?

- **Ideas.** Have you been worried or intrigued by a new development you read about in a professional or trade journal? Have you heard an unusual proposal for a new public policy or business incentive? How have you responded to the different teaching methods you've encountered in your high school and college classes? What do you make of conflicting arguments in your course readings?

You'll find additional ideas for evaluative writing projects at the end of this chapter (p. 320).

SEARCH THE WEB

The World Wide Web is a rich source of information and ideas for writers conducting evaluations. Product and media reviews are among the most popular items on the Web, and online editions of newspapers and magazines offer a seemingly endless collection of commentary and critique on everything from the latest diets to pending legislation to new techniques for studying and taking exams. If you're interested in whether professional soccer has a future in the United States, for example,

Working Together: Try It Out Loud

Before you start conducting an evaluation, start a conversation with your classmates about the advantages and disadvantages of majoring in a particular subject. Form small groups and choose a subject area to evaluate, such as English, history, business, psychology, chemistry, math, art, or sociology. As a group, identify the kinds of criteria you will use to evaluate each major, such as personal rewards, academic challenges, skill development, or future employment opportunities. Then take turns applying the criteria to your major (or the major that currently interests you most) while the other members of

the group listen, respond, and ask questions. After everyone has had a chance to speak, revisit your criteria. Were they useful in helping you evaluate the majors? Would you consider changing these criteria?

If you are doing this activity during class, share your conclusions about your criteria with other groups. Then, as a class, take a few minutes to reflect on the exercise. Did every group use the same criteria? If not, what might account for the differences?

you could find data and opinions on Web sites such as SoccerTimes.com and USSoccer.com, check out developments reported in the sports sections of newspapers that have a Web presence, and read the online versions of magazines such as *SoccerAmerica* and *90:00*. To search for information and evaluations for just about any subject that intrigues you, consult the following Web search resources.

General web search. The easiest way to learn about a subject through the Web is to visit an established search site, such as Google (google.com), Ask (ask.com), Bing (Bing.com), or Yahoo! (yahoo.com). In response to your keywords and phrases, these sites present ranked lists of sites they judge relevant to your search terms. These sites also provide advanced search forms that allow you to specify which keywords and phrases must, might, or should not appear on a page; to limit search results to particular domains such as .gov or .org; and to limit your search to Web sites updated within a specific time period, such as the last week or month.

Web directories. You can also search the Web using Web directories, such as Open Directory Project (dmoz.org) and WWW Virtual Library (http://vlib.org). Directories allow you to browse lists of prescreened sites by clicking on general topics, such as Arts or Business, and then successively narrow your search by clicking on subtopics. The lists are created and maintained by people — rather than by computer programs — so they provide more selective results than a broad search can; however, these lists also reflect the biases and assumptions of their creators, so you might miss out on other sites that are relevant to your topic.

Meta search. Meta search sites, such as Dogpile (dogpile.com) and Metacrawler (metacrawler.com), allow you to conduct a single search and return results from several Web search engines or Web directories at the same time. These sites typically search leading general search sites and directories and then present a limited number of results on a single page.

News search. To conduct focused searches for current and archived news reports, try sites such as Google News (http://news.google.com) and Digg (digg.com).

Reference search. Sites such as Encyclopedia.com (encyclopedia.com) and Information Please (infoplease.com) allow you to search for information that has been collected in encyclopedias, almanacs, atlases, dictionaries, and other reference resources.

Media search. The Web is home not only to textual information but also to a growing collection of other types of media, such as photographs, podcasts, and streaming video. You can locate useful information about your subject by searching for recordings of radio broadcasts, television shows, documentaries, podcasts, and other media using established search sites, such as Ask, Google, and Yahoo!, as well as specialized sites such as YouTube (www.youtube.com) for video, Picsearch (www.picsearch.com) for images, and Find Sounds (www.findsounds.com) for audio.

You can learn more about searching the Web in Chapter 12.

In Process

Searching the Web

Dwight Haynes learned about promising subjects by searching for information on the Web.

Dwight used the search terms *alcohol* and *college*. He found several journal articles on the Harvard School of Public Health's College Alcohol Study Web site.

Dwight used a search engine to look for Web sites with keywords such as *alcohol, higher education, drinking, college, students,* and *awareness*. His searches allowed him to identify and locate enough sources that he was able to get a good initial understanding of the subject. Because he was particularly interested in how colleges respond to student drinking, he decided to download a study written by E. R. Weitzman and her colleagues at the Harvard School of Public Health, who had found correlations between a particular type of alcohol prevention campaign — the environmental approach — and reduced alcohol consumption among students.

NARROW YOUR FOCUS BY ASKING QUESTIONS

As you learn about possible subjects for your evaluation, use the following questions to identify which ones capture your interest and best meet the needs of your assignment. Each question focuses your attention on a subject in a different way, and each provides a useful starting point for an evaluative essay. Depending on the subject, you'll find that some questions are more relevant than others.

- **Importance.** Do you think this is an important subject? If so, why? Who else believes that it's important? Why do they believe that it's important? What would readers do with an evaluation of this subject?

- **Appropriateness.** What aspects of this topic lend themselves to evaluation? Do you have the resources and the time to learn about it and examine it closely?

- **Effectiveness.** Is _____ an effective response to _____? Is it designed well? Is it likely to produce the intended results?

- **Costs/benefits.** What are the benefits of _____? What are the costs? Are the benefits worth the costs?

In Process

Focusing on a Subject

Dwight Haynes brainstormed in response to the questions above about a subject he was considering for his evaluative essay: binge drinking among college students. As he asked and answered questions, two promising focuses emerged: the costs and benefits that college students associate with drinking and the effectiveness of different approaches to reducing drinking on college campuses.

> Dwight used two sets of questions to guide his brainstorming. He generated lists of ideas in response to each approach.

Costs: delayed graduation, failure to graduate, health problems, social problems (losing friends), poorer academic performance/lower GPA, less learning (just getting by)

Benefits: fun, relaxation, less difficult to talk with people, being part of the group, looking cool

Effectiveness of approaches for stopping or reducing drinking:
— education (might work)
— punishment/prevention (hasn't worked very well)
— alternative activities (might work for some)

After reviewing the results of his brainstorming, Dwight decided that it would be difficult to evaluate the costs and benefits of drinking. Instead, he chose to focus on the effectiveness of approaches to reducing drinking on campus.

- **Prevailing opinion.** How have others responded to this subject? How did they reach their conclusions? What have they neglected to consider?

Conduct Your Evaluation

Far too many evaluators tell readers little more than "this is good (or bad or ineffective or the best choice) because I say so." It's as if these writers believe that readers will accept their conclusions without question or doubt.

As a reader, when was the last time you did that?

If you're like most readers, you probably expect evaluators to provide sound reasoning and appropriate evidence to back up their judgments. As a writer, you should strive to offer the same things to your readers. The judgments you reach in your evaluation should move beyond knee-jerk reactions or general pronouncements. For example, rather than saying a baseball manager should be fired merely because the team failed to win the division, you should also consider the quality of players available throughout the season, the strength of the competition, and the decisions made during key games.

An effective evaluative essay is based on a clear understanding of your subject, a carefully chosen set of criteria, and well-supported judgments — first, about how well the subject of your evaluation meets each criterion and, second, about the overall results of your evaluation. As you conduct your evaluation, start by choosing a set of criteria that is relevant and clearly defined. Then review what you've learned about your subject, and consider whether you've collected enough evidence to make an informed judgment. Finally, use your criteria and evidence to make your judgments, making an effort to ensure that your evaluation is balanced and fair.

DEFINE YOUR CRITERIA

Criteria are the factors on which your judgments about a subject are based. In many written conversations, criteria are well established. Movie reviewers, for example, typically base their judgments on plot, characterization, cinematography, editing, and directing, while restaurant reviewers tend to use criteria such as the taste and presentation of the food, the attentiveness and courteousness of the waitstaff, the cleanliness and attractiveness of the restaurant, and the cost of a meal. Similarly, writers of progress reports tend to focus on a fairly consistent set of criteria, most often results, responses to unexpected challenges, and cost-effectiveness.

Even when evaluating well-established subjects, however, writers often depart from the norm. A movie reviewer might focus on the use of product placement in a film, while a music reviewer might draw criteria from poetry or drama to evaluate a new rap album.

Often, you will have the option of choosing among a wide range of evaluative criteria. Consider, for example, the criteria you might use to evaluate competing health plans for employees at a small company:

- overall cost to the company
- cost per employee to participate in the plan
- deductibles
- coverage
- choice of health care providers
- ease of access to plan information
- access to plan administrators
- required paperwork
- speed of reimbursement to employees

If you chose all these criteria, your evaluation would be quite lengthy. To keep the evaluation brief and to the point — and, of course, useful for readers — you would focus on fewer criteria. If you were creating a brief overview of competing health care plans for managers, you might focus on overall cost to the company, employee costs, coverage, required paperwork, and access to plan administrators. If you were creating a report for employees, on the other hand, criteria might include employee costs, deductibles, coverage, choice of health care providers, ease of access to plan information, and speed of reimbursement. The key is to choose those criteria most relevant to your subject, your purpose, and the needs, interests, and backgrounds of your readers.

IDENTIFY EVIDENCE

Evidence provides evaluators with a basis for making their judgments. Evaluative essays tend to rely on a mix of evidence from published sources, observations, and personal experience.

Some evidence is quantitative — that is, it can be measured. For instance, the rate of inflation over the past decade or the number of people participating in a noontime activity program can be found through sources such as public documents or direct observation. Other evidence is qualitative — that is, it is based on the writer's experiences with and reactions to the subject. Music reviewers, for example, usually base their evaluations on the originality of the music, the quality of the performance, and the quality of the recording and production. Some criteria, such as cost, can be judged on both quantitative and qualitative evidence. For instance, you can calculate the amount of money that would be required to pay for a particular program or solution, but you can also view cost in terms of its impact on quality of life or on the environment.

To identify evidence for your evaluation, list the criteria you'll use to conduct your evaluation. Determine whether each criterion will rely on quantitative or qualitative evidence. Then pinpoint potential sources of evidence for your evaluation by reviewing your initial research and any notes you've taken. Next to each criterion, list the evidence on which you'll base your judgments. If you find that you don't have enough evidence to support a thorough evaluation, look for more information.

MAKE YOUR JUDGMENTS

Once you've identified and organized your evidence, you're ready to determine how well your subject measures up to the criteria you've selected. The quality of your judgments depends not only on the number and kinds of criteria you've defined and the amount and types of evidence you've collected but also on your commitment to being fair and reasonable. If you are applying quantitative evidence to a small number of criteria, making your judgments might be a fairly straightforward process. However, if you are making multiple judgments on the basis of qualitative evidence, it might take significantly more time and effort to complete your evaluation. The challenge you face in making your judgments will also depend on how much impact your decision has on your life or the lives of others. For example, weighing which of three job offers to accept is of far greater consequence than comparing the features and costs of two video game systems.

To make judgments about your subject, list your criteria and examine the evidence you've assembled. Write down your judgments in as much detail as possible so that you can draw on them as you draft your essay.

Prepare a Draft

Writers of evaluative essays focus on conveying the results of their evaluation processes to their readers. As you prepare your draft, you'll decide how to convey the overall result of your evaluation, present and define your criteria, share the evidence on which you've based your judgments, design your essay, and frame your evaluation for your readers.

Making Judgments

For his evaluation of approaches to reducing college drinking, Dwight Haynes selected two criteria: the overall effectiveness of programs that used a particular approach and the effort required to create programs based on an approach. To sort through his notes and decide what information would best support his evaluation, he created a table that identified possible evidence for his criteria as they applied to two competing approaches and then made preliminary judgments about each approach.

Approach	Criterion	Evidence	Judgment
Social norms	Effort	Relatively low effort. Turner says it focuses on marketing and education, using ads on Facebook, campus posters, etc.	Easy to start and maintain without tons of work.
	Effectiveness	Some research raises concerns about effectiveness (Wechsler et al.), but DeJong et al. found it associated with lower perceptions of student drinking levels and lower alcohol consumption.	Effective. Good choice for smaller schools or those without the resources for another approach.
Environmental	Effort	Larger and more ambitious than social norms programs. Includes collaborations with local law enforcement agencies, the local business community, and local health care providers (Weitzman et al.).	Complex, but justified by effectiveness.
	Effectiveness	Effective because it addresses more of the factors involved in student drinking (Weitzman et al. and Dowdall interview).	Most effective.

Your draft will be strongly influenced by the purpose of your evaluation. If your intention is to help readers understand whether something has succeeded or failed, for example, consider how your readers will react to your judgments. If you are arguing that a project has failed, you might want to discuss whether the project should be carried out with specific changes or whether it should be abandoned altogether. If you are offering your judgments about which of several options is best, you might want to discuss the trade-offs associated with accepting your judgment. And if you are trying to help readers understand how your subject might be improved or refined, you might want to include guidance about how to put those improvements or refinements into practice.

STATE YOUR OVERALL JUDGMENT

The goal of an evaluative essay is to share your judgment about a subject, often with the intention of helping readers make a decision. It's usually a good idea, then, to give readers a summary of your overall judgment — your verdict — in the form of a thesis statement. In some cases, you'll want to mention the criteria on which your judgment is based so that readers understand the thinking behind your evaluation. Your thesis statement can also frame your subject in a way that helps achieve your purpose and address the needs and interests of your readers. Consider, for example, how the following thesis statements about locally grown produce set up different expectations among readers.

> **Thesis statement 1:** Buying your fruits and vegetables at a farmer's market might be a little less convenient and a little more expensive than going to the supermarket, but you'll be rewarded with healthier, tastier food.

> **Thesis statement 2:** Importing fruits and vegetables carries hidden environmental costs that outweigh the benefits of having year-round access to seasonable produce.

> **Thesis statement 3:** By insisting on produce that has been grown nearby, consumers can support family farms and have a positive impact on their local economies.

Each of these thesis statements focuses on different aspects of the same subject. The first one emphasizes consumer concerns about price, convenience, and quality. The second thesis statement directs attention to the environmental consequences of shipping food long distances. The third one points to the economic benefits of supporting local businesses. These thesis statements would lead to quite different evaluative essays.

Where you place your thesis statement depends largely on your understanding of your readers' needs and interests. Sharing your overall judgment at the beginning of

Is your thesis
statement
focused enough?
See Chapter 14
for help.

the essay allows readers to follow the logic of your evaluation process and better understand how the criteria and evidence relate to the evaluation's overall result. However, if your overall judgment is likely to be seen as unusual or controversial, it might be best to share it later in the essay, after allowing evidence to unfold in a way that helps readers understand the reasons underlying your conclusions.

PRESENT YOUR EVALUATION

To be effective, your evaluative essay must do more than present a straightforward report of criteria, evidence, and judgments. It should help readers understand your subject in a particular way and show them that you've chosen appropriate criteria and evidence. Equally important, your essay should prove to your readers that you've based your judgments on sound and thorough reasoning and that you've conducted a balanced evaluation.

Explain your criteria. Criteria are an essential part of any evaluation (see p. 301). Your readers should understand not only what your criteria are but also why you've selected them. In some cases, you can rely on general knowledge to supply the rationale for your choice of one or more of your criteria. If you were evaluating an advertising campaign for a new soft drink, for example, you could probably rely on a widespread understanding that sales figures are an important factor in the evaluation. Similarly, you wouldn't need to justify your use of nutrition and weight loss in an evaluation of diet programs.

In most cases, however, you should define your criteria explicitly. For example, if you were evaluating a new state program that encourages high school students to take additional driver education courses after receiving their licenses, you might use criteria such as teenagers' willingness to sign up for the courses and the effectiveness of the program. But how would you define a criterion such as effectiveness? In the context of continuing education courses for newly licensed drivers, it might mean lowering the number of accidents attributable to inexperience, or preventing injuries or deaths associated with teenage drivers, or increasing drivers' awareness of the problems caused by distraction or impatience, or some combination of these factors. Your readers should understand how you've defined your criteria so that they can follow — and, ideally, accept — your evaluation.

Support your judgments with evidence. Providing evidence to explain the reasoning behind your judgments helps readers accept your evaluation as valid and carefully thought out. Evidence can also help deepen your discussion of the overall results of your evaluation. In general, you'll want to apply evidence to each of your criteria to show readers how your subject measures up. You can also use evidence to

- introduce your subject
- define your criteria
- provide examples and illustrations
- associate particular ideas and concepts with authorities, such as political leaders, subject-matter experts, or people who have been affected by your subject

In Process

Using Evidence to Support Judgments

Dwight Haynes drew on information and opinions from his sources to support his judgment that the social norms marketing approach to reducing alcohol consumption among college students is not as effective as it might seem.

The environmental approach involves a mix of strategies designed to reduce or eliminate alcohol consumption, using the resources of both the campus community and the surrounding town or city. According to Weitzman et al. (2004), "Drinking-related norms and behaviors result from interactions over time and space between individuals and their environments" (p. 188). By changing the "contextual forces," like availability of alcohol, that encourage students to drink, this approach more strongly emphasizes policies that directly put a stop to excessive drinking — unlike the social norms marketing approach, which relies on influencing individual behavior (p. 187). As George W. Dowdall, author of *College Drinking: Reframing a Social Problem*, has argued, "Informational approaches used alone simply don't work. Trying to deal with college drinking as only an individual's choice doesn't work either. Instead, colleges should try to shape the entire environment that shapes college drinking" (as cited in Jaschik, 2009). By cracking down on when and how alcohol is available on campus, and by taking steps to keep underage students from accessing alcohol off campus, colleges that adopt the environmental approach tend to be more successful in decreasing the overall rate of student drinking and the negative consequences that can come from excessive alcohol use.

Dwight cites information from a journal article, identified by the authors' names. He includes the page on which the quotation can be found.

An expert is identified in an attribution.

Using APA style, Dwight notes that one source is cited in another.

Whether you draw your evidence from print, broadcast, or electronic sources or from field research, be sure to identify your sources. Evaluative essays typically rely on citation systems such as those provided by the Modern Language Association and the American Psychological Association to identify sources. If you are unsure about which citation system to use, consult your instructor. (You can read more about how to use evidence to support your evaluation in Chapter 14.)

Be fair. To be effective, your evaluation must be fair. The notion of fairness is sometimes confused with objectivity. In fact, being truly objective is difficult — and perhaps impossible. Each writer approaches an evaluation with a particular set of experiences, values, and beliefs that lead to a particular outlook on a subject. These differences among writers — even the most disciplined and rigorous — lead to minor and sometimes major differences in their judgments, even when they work with the same criteria and evidence. Being fair and reasonable, as a result, does not necessarily mean coming to the same conclusion as another writer. Instead, it means taking the time to consider different points of view, weighing evidence carefully, and being as consistent in your judgments as possible.

One way to ensure fairness is to provide a context for your evaluation. By making it clear to your readers what you've evaluated, what you've considered during the evaluation process, and how you've approached the evaluation process, you can help them understand how and why you've come to your conclusions. If a reviewer has concerns about the size of a new phone, for example, she might point out that she has small hands or that she prefers to send texts using one hand. By providing context, you'll increase the likelihood that your readers will view your evaluation as sound and well supported.

Working Together: Ask Whether Your Judgments Are Fair

Use feedback from other writers to assess the fairness of your judgments. Describe your subject, briefly define your criteria, present your evidence, and discuss your judgments. The other members of the group should pose reasonable questions about your choice of criteria, selection of evidence, and judgments, paying particular attention to the reasonableness of your judgments. Whenever possible, they should also suggest alternative judgments. Take notes on the doubts expressed by other members of the group so that you can consider them during revision.

CONSIDER GENRE AND DESIGN

Like other academic essays, evaluative essays can benefit from thoughtful consideration of design. Bear in mind your readers' expectations about design elements such as wide margins, double-spaced lines, page numbers, and a readable body font. In addition, consider the benefits of using headings and subheadings and bulleted and numbered lists.

- **Headings and subheadings** can help readers understand the organization of the essay, serve as transitional devices between sections and subsections, and add visual interest to what would otherwise be pages of unbroken text.

- **Numbered and bulleted lists** display brief passages of related information using numbers or symbols (usually round "bullets"). The surrounding white space draws the eye to the list, highlighting the information for your readers, while the brief content in each entry can make concepts or processes easier to understand.

These design elements can make significant contributions to the readability and overall effectiveness of your essay. Headings and subheadings identify and briefly summarize the sections of your essay, helping readers to compare the judgments you've made in different sections of your essay. Numbered and bulleted lists allow you to present evidence or a series of judgments about a subject in a compact form. If you use similar lists — for example, of strengths and weaknesses or of costs and benefits — in different sections of your essay, readers will find it easier to locate and compare the lists.

You can find discussions of document design in Chapters 16, 17, and 18.

FRAME YOUR EVALUATION

The choices you make as you structure your essay will affect how your readers understand and interpret your evaluation. Your strategies for organizing, introducing, and concluding your essay should take into account your purposes — for example, whether you are assessing success and failure or making a recommendation, and what you hope readers will do after they've read your essay — as well as your readers' needs and interests. They should also take into account your criteria and the nature and amount of evidence you've assembled to support your judgments.

Organization. To decide how to organize your criteria, evidence, and judgments, create an outline or a map (see p. 512). Most evaluative essays are organized either according to the items that are being evaluated or by the criteria used to evaluate them. If you are evaluating a single item, such as a proposed change to class registration procedures or the performance of a musical group on a recently released album, you are likely to present your evaluation as a series of judgments, applying one criterion after another to your subject. If you are evaluating more than one item, you can use your criteria to organize your discussion, or, as Steve Garbarino does in his review of New Orleans sandwich shops (p. 290), you can discuss each item in turn. Evaluative essays can also employ several of the organizing patterns discussed in Chapter 15, such as comparison and contrast, costs and benefits, or strengths and weaknesses.

Introduction. Most evaluative essays begin with some explanation of the context and a description of the subject. In some cases, your readers will be unfamiliar with particular aspects of the subject — or even with the subject as a whole. For example, if you are evaluating a new technology for distributing movies online, your readers will probably appreciate a brief discussion of how it works. Similarly, if you are reviewing a movie, it can help to provide some details about its plot, characters, and setting — although not, of course, its ending or surprising plot twists. Once you've established the parameters of your evaluation and decided how to frame your introduction, you can use a range of strategies to put it into words, including asking questions, leading with a quotation, or telling a story. You can read more about strategies for introducing your essay in Chapter 16.

Conclusion. Your conclusion offers an opportunity to highlight or even to present the overall results of your evaluation. If you've already presented your overall results in the form of a thesis statement earlier in the essay, you might use your conclusion to reiterate your main judgment or to make a recommendation for your readers. You can also turn to other strategies to conclude your essay, such as linking to your introduction, asking a question, or speculating about the future. Chapter 16 provides more strategies for using your conclusion to frame the results of your evaluation.

Review and Improve Your Draft

Writing a successful evaluative essay depends on choosing an appropriate subject, considering your writing situation, selecting appropriate criteria and evidence, making fair judgments, and deciding how to frame and organize your evaluation. Don't be surprised if your first draft doesn't successfully address all of these challenges: few first drafts do. Instead, take advantage of the opportunity to revise. As you review your draft, pay particular attention to your choice of criteria, your selection of evidence, and the fairness of your judgments.

REVIEW YOUR CRITERIA

Once you've written a first draft, read it carefully. Then step back and ask questions about your criteria. Ask whether you've used enough — or too many — criteria (generally, evaluative essays include between two and five). Most important, ask whether you've considered the most significant criteria. For example, an evaluation of competing approaches to funding intercollegiate athletic programs that doesn't consider the impact of those approaches on tuition and fees is missing an important criterion.

RECONSIDER YOUR EVIDENCE

Good criteria and reasonable judgments are the heart of an effective evaluative essay, but they are seldom sufficient to convince readers to accept your point of view. Presenting an evaluation — even a careful one — that lacks well-chosen evidence is like telling your readers, "Look. I'm really smart, and I'm making good judgments. Trust me." Few readers, of course, give their trust so easily. As you review your essay, ask whether you've provided enough evidence to support your judgments. Then ask whether you've chosen the right evidence. As you conduct your review, make sure that you haven't relied so heavily on a single source of evidence that it appears as though you're simply borrowing someone else's evaluation. Try to draw evidence from multiple sources, such as published documents and personal experience.

ENSURE THAT YOUR JUDGMENTS ARE FAIR AND REASONABLE

The most important question you can ask about your evaluative essay is whether your judgments are well grounded and convincing. Individual judgments should reflect the criteria and evidence you've presented to your readers. And your overall conclusion should reflect your judgments as a whole. If your judgments do not line up with your criteria and evidence, your readers will question your conclusions. Similarly, if your judgments are based on poorly chosen criteria or inadequate evidence, your readers will also question your conclusions. On the other hand, if your readers see your criteria as appropriate and your judgments as reasonable and well supported, they'll be far more likely to act on your evaluation.

Peer Review: Improve Your Evaluative Essay

One of the biggest challenges writers face is reading a draft of their own work as a reader rather than as the writer. Because you know what you're trying to say, you find it easy to understand your draft. To determine how you should revise your draft, ask a friend or classmate to read your essay and consider how well you've adopted the role of evaluator (see p. 276).

Purpose	1. What subject does the essay address? Is it a subject that readers will need or want to know about?
	2. Does the thesis statement clearly convey an overall judgment?
	3. What role does this essay take on? Is it recommending improvements or making a final judgment?
Readers	4. Did you find the essay interesting? Why or why not?
	5. Does the evaluation address my readers' needs, interests, and backgrounds?
	6. Do the criteria seem appropriate for the subject? Did I use too many criteria? Too few? Should I add or remove any criteria?
Sources	7. Have I provided enough evidence to support my judgments? Too much?
	8. Have I relied on a particular source — or a particular type of source — too heavily?
	9. Do my sources strike you as reliable and appropriate? Does any of the evidence I've used seem questionable?
Context	10. Have I provided enough information about the subject? About my reasons for evaluating it?
	11. Do the judgments made in the essay seem fair? Did you detect any bias or agenda in the way I presented my evaluation? Do you know of any alternative points of view that I should take into consideration?
	12. Is the physical appearance of my essay appropriate? Should I consider adding headings or lists?

For each of the points listed above, ask your reviewers to provide concrete advice about what you should do to improve your draft. It can help if you ask them to adopt the role of an editor — someone who is working with you to improve your draft. You can read more about peer review in Chapter 4.

✳ Student Essay

Dwight Haynes, "Making Better Choices: Two Approaches to Reducing College Drinking"

The following evaluative essay was written by featured writer Dwight Haynes. Dwight's essay follows the requirements of the sixth edition of the *APA Publication Manual*. However, this edition does not include specific instructions or formatting student essays, so Dwight's essay has been formatted to fit typical requirements for undergraduate student writing.

MAKING BETTER CHOICES   1

Making Better Choices: Two Approaches to Reducing College Drinking

Dwight Haynes

CO150 College Composition

Professor Palmquist

March 20, 2013

> A cover page provides the essay title and information about the writer, class, and submission date.

MAKING BETTER CHOICES   2

Making Better Choices: Two Approaches to Reducing College Drinking

Over the past few decades, alcohol consumption among college students has received a great deal of attention. Despite humorous portrayals of college parties and the drunken antics depicted in movies and on television, serious concerns have been raised about health, safety, and academic issues associated with heavy drinking on campus. Most alarming, excessive levels of drinking are thought to cause between 1,400 and 1,700 student deaths each year (Jaschik, 2009). Also significant are the physical harm and violent behavior that tend to arise from heavy drinking: 500,000 students each year sustain injuries as a result of alcohol use, and another 600,000 per year report being victims of alcohol-fueled assaults, including rape (Wechsler et al., 2003). Heavy drinking has been blamed for a host of other problems as well, including vandalism, alcohol poisoning, and academic failure. Rather than waiting until after students suffer the consequences of alcohol abuse to intervene, colleges have found that preventative programs can teach better habits and help students avoid the problems caused by underage or irresponsible drinking. What kinds of approaches are colleges using to reduce student drinking, and how well do they work?

Two current strategies being tried on college campuses are the social norms marketing approach and the environmental approach. The *social norms marketing* approach assumes that college students drink heavily because they think everyone else does it. Supporters of this approach argue that telling students about normal drinking behaviors, typically through mass marketing campaigns, will lead them to drink less (Turner, Perkins, & Bauerle, 2008). The *environmental* approach focuses on changing the factors within the campus and community — like discount drink specials at local bars and inconsistent enforcement of underage drinking laws — that may encourage college students to drink (Weitzman, Nelson, Lee, & Wechsler, 2004). Supporters of the environmental approach believe that students are unlikely to change their behavior in an environment that supports harmful levels of drinking. This essay will look at each of these approaches in turn, examining their effectiveness by

---

The writer contrasts humorous depictions of college drinking with sobering statistics about drinking-related deaths, injuries, and crimes.

Following APA style, source information is cited in parentheses.

The writer identifies and defines the two leading approaches that he will evaluate.

An overview of the essay is provided.

MAKING BETTER CHOICES   3

comparing the reported rates of student drinking and harmful consequences after

each approach is used, and by considering how easily their strategies can be

implemented.

The Social Norms Marketing Approach

The social norms marketing approach is based on the theory that correcting

a person's misperceptions will lead to a change in behavior (Turner et al., 2008).

This approach is popular and relatively easy to implement, since it focuses

largely on standard education and marketing techniques — something colleges

and universities are well equipped to provide (Turner et al., 2008). DeJong

et al. (2006) found that, when done with pervasive and consistent marketing

messages, social norms campaigns were associated not only with lower

perceptions of student drinking levels but also with lower alcohol consumption.

Turner et al. (2008) used posters, Facebook ads, student newspaper articles, and

e-mails over the course of six years to inform students at one college how often

their fellow students consumed alcohol (and how much), as well as how often

they showed "protective behaviors" like helping friends avoid driving while

drunk (p. 86). Between 2001 and 2005, the percentage of students who reported

experiencing negative consequences of drinking, like performing poorly in class

or being the victim of assault, dropped significantly (Turner et al., 2008).

Likewise, DeJong et al. (2006) found that social norms marketing campaigns at

18 colleges and universities across the country provided a "meaningful . . .

effect," with students consuming fewer drinks per week and at parties than

before the campaign (p. 878). These results indicate that students absorbed the

social norms messages put forth by their schools, and although they didn't stop

drinking entirely, they did change their behavior to match their perceptions of

other students' drinking habits.

However, Wechsler et al. (2003) analyzed trends at schools using social

norms marketing and revealed that the campaigns did not necessarily decrease

student drinking; in some cases, schools even reported higher alcohol

consumption, according to seven criteria that measured whether students drank,

---

Annotations:

The evaluation criteria — effectiveness and ease of implementation — are introduced and defined.

A heading is set off from body text using bold formatting.

A source is cited using APA style.

A partial quotation indicates that the phrase is taken from the source named in the attribution. The page number of the quotation is provided.

An evaluation of the effectiveness of the approach is provided.

A summary of contrasting evidence is provided, indicating that the approach might not be effective at all schools.

MAKING BETTER CHOICES   4

how much, and how often. The team, of the Harvard School of Public Health's College Alcohol Study, suggested that because social norms marketing was first developed at a small school that wasn't very diverse, it might not be as suitable for schools with many different kinds of people. As the researchers explained, "Individual students' drinking behaviors align more closely to the drinking behaviors of their immediate social group rather than to the overall student population at a given school" (p. 492). Students at larger schools, then, might not be as receptive to the social norms marketing approach as other studies indicated, especially if their personal experience contradicts the messages distributed in a campaign.

> A quotation conveys conclusions offered by the researchers who conducted the study. The page number is provided.

> The writer offers his interpretation of the results of the study.

Unexpected factors may also complicate the perceived success of social norms marketing campaigns. One study noted that campaigns at several schools resulted in only "relatively small changes in [heavy] drinking behavior, from a 1.1% decrease to a 10.6% increase" over three years, while a control group of schools not using any kind of alcohol prevention experienced surprising increases in heavy drinking — between 17.5% and 24.7% (DeJong et al., 2006, p. 877). Although social norms marketing in this case did not appear to reduce consumption, the fact that alcohol use increased so much in the control group indicates that the social norms marketing may have served to keep drinking levels steady at schools that might have otherwise experienced a similar jump in alcohol use.

> Additional information is offered regarding the potential positive effects of the approach.

Given this evidence, it seems clear that social norms marketing is not a one-size-fits-all solution. Students might ignore statistics and facts in social norms advertisements because they don't believe the ads represent the peers whose opinions they care about most. But for smaller schools looking to curb heavy drinking and its consequences, social norms marketing might be a good strategy, especially where colleges want to change student behavior without making significant changes to school or community alcohol policies.

> An overall judgment on the approach is provided.

MAKING BETTER CHOICES   5

The Environmental Approach

The environmental approach involves a mix of strategies designed to reduce or eliminate alcohol consumption, using the resources of both the campus community and the surrounding town or city. According to Weitzman et al. (2004), "Drinking-related norms and behaviors result from interactions over time and space between individuals and their environments" (p. 188). By changing the "contextual forces," like availability of alcohol, that encourage students to drink, this approach more strongly emphasizes policies that directly put a stop to excessive drinking — unlike the social norms marketing approach, which relies on influencing individual behavior (p. 187). As George W. Dowdall, author of *College Drinking: Reframing a Social Problem*, has argued, "Informational approaches used alone simply don't work. Trying to deal with college drinking as only an individual's choice doesn't work either. Instead, colleges should try to shape the entire environment that shapes college drinking" (as cited in Jaschik, 2009). By cracking down on when and how alcohol is available on campus, and by taking steps to keep underage students from accessing alcohol off campus, colleges that adopt the environmental approach tend to be more successful in decreasing the overall rate of student drinking and the negative consequences that can come from excessive alcohol use.

One drawback of the environmental approach is that it can be more time-consuming and difficult to implement than social norms marketing, as it relies on the cooperation of campus administrators, faculty, community members, law enforcement, and business owners in enforcing sometimes unpopular changes in alcohol policies. However, Dowdall pointed out that harmful levels of drinking among students already result in arrests and disciplinary actions, which involve community and campus resources after the fact (as cited in Jaschik, 2009). Instead of using these resources in reaction to drinking-related problems, schools and towns that adopt an environmental approach can use them pro-actively to prevent problems from happening in the first place.

A detailed definition of the second approach is provided.

Following APA style, information cited in a source is identified using the phrase "as cited in."

A weakness of the approach is considered in light of the implementation criterion.

A summary of a source provides evidence about the effectiveness of the approach.

MAKING BETTER CHOICES   6

In fact, research suggests that environmental changes are needed for consistent and lasting change in student drinking levels. Weitzman et al. (2004) looked at an environmental approach program that decreased the availability and appeal of alcohol at several colleges through many different, simultaneous methods like police enforcement of party regulations, substance-free residence halls, and parental notification for alcohol-related violations. The team found that significantly fewer students experienced drinking-related problems, like missed classes and alcohol-fueled fights, after the program was implemented. Just as important, and in contrast with the results of some social norms marketing programs, students across the sample also reported lower amounts of drinking overall. The study looked at public and private colleges of different sizes across the nation, showing that the environmental approach works for a range of different student populations (Weitzman et al., 2004). Environmental changes reach beyond the individual student to shape the community as a whole, making sure that the campus and its surroundings are not contributing to the problem of student drinking but helping to solve it.

Conclusions

While social norms marketing appears to offer a strong combination of positive outcomes and ease of implementation, the environmental approach is more effective overall. Despite being more complicated and demanding more school and community resources, it delivers stronger results by involving students' entire college community. The environmental approach has a much greater scope than that of the social norms marketing approach and is suitable for schools of all sizes and types. Therefore, it has the potential to affect not only students who drink heavily because they think that's the normal thing to do but also students who either are unaware of the dangers of using alcohol or will moderate their drinking only in the face of severe consequences for not doing so. Given appropriate resources, a program based on the environmental approach to curb heavy drinking is likely to be the best choice.

> The conclusion focuses on the higher level of overall effectiveness of the environmental approach, despite the complexities involved with its implementation.

MAKING BETTER CHOICES7

References

DeJong, W., Schneider, S. K., Towvim, L. G., Murphy, M. J., Doerr, E. E., Simonsen, . . . Scribner, R. A. (2006). A multisite randomized trial of social norms marketing campaigns to reduce college student drinking. *Journal of Studies on Alcohol, 67*(6), 868-879.

Jaschik, S. (2009, February 26). College drinking: Reframing a social problem. *Inside Higher Ed*. Retrieved from http://www.insidehighered.com/

Turner, J., Perkins, H. W., & Bauerle, J. (2008). Declining negative consequences related to alcohol misuse among students exposed to a social norms marketing intervention on a college campus. *Journal of American College Health, 57*(1), 85-93. doi:10.3200/JACH.57.1.85-94

Wechsler, H., Nelson, T. F., Lee, J. E., Seibring, M., Lewis, C., & Keeling, R. P. (2003). Perception and reality: A national evaluation of social norms marketing interventions to reduce college students' heavy alcohol use. *Journal of Studies on Alcohol, 64*(4), 484-494.

Weitzman, E. R., Nelson, T. F., Lee, H., and Wechsler, H. (2004). Reducing drinking and related harms in college: Evaluation of the "A Matter of Degree" program. *American Journal of Preventive Medicine, 27*(3), 187-196. doi:10.1016 /j.amepre.2004.06.008

Following APA style, the list of works cited is titled "References."

Entries in the list are formatted with hanging indents.

A news article retrieved from the Web

Journal article

A journal article retrieved from the Web

⁂ Project Ideas

The following suggestions provide means of focusing your work on an evaluative essay or another type of evaluative document.

Suggestions for Essays

1. EVALUATE A PROPOSED SOLUTION TO A PROBLEM

Evaluate a proposed solution to a problem. You might focus on proposed legislation for addressing problems with public schools in your state, or on a proposal for addressing a foreign policy problem. Or you might evaluate a new means of dealing with copyright on digital media such as music or videos. You should define the problem, outline the proposed solution, identify and define a set of criteria on which to base your evaluation, and collect information about the problem and its proposed solution by gathering sources or interviewing an expert.

2. EVALUATE THE EFFECTIVENESS OF A PUBLIC OFFICIAL OR GROUP

Write an essay that evaluates the effectiveness of an elected official or group, such as a mayor, a state legislator, or a city council. Your evaluation might focus on overall performance, or on performance related to a specific issue, such as addressing urban growth. Identify and define the criteria you'll use to conduct your evaluation. Collect information from published sources. If you can, interview or correspond with the official or a representative of the group.

3. EVALUATE A PERFORMANCE

Review a public performance, such as a concert, a play, or a poetry reading, for your classmates. To prepare, read reviews that have appeared in print and online publications, and familiarize yourself with the criteria that other reviewers have used. In your review, describe the performance and evaluate it, keeping in mind the characteristics of your readers. Take notes and, if possible, interview others who attended the performance. If you can, interview one of the performers. Your review should focus primarily on your personal assessment of the performance. You should draw on your notes and interviews to introduce ideas, illustrate a point, or support your conclusions.

4. EVALUATE A PRODUCT

Select a product you are thinking about purchasing, such as a kitchen gadget, television, laser printer, cosmetic, or piece of athletic equipment. Evaluate it using the criteria of effectiveness, cost, and quality. Provide clear definitions of each criterion in terms of the product you've chosen to evaluate. Your evaluation should draw on written sources, interviews with people who have used the product, and, if possible, your own use of the product.

5. EVALUATE AN ATHLETE OR A COACH

Evaluate the performance of a professional athlete, such as a basketball or baseball player, or evaluate the effectiveness of a coach. Select criteria such as the contributions made to the team's success, leadership qualities, entertainment provided to fans, contributions to the community, and so on. In your essay, identify the athlete or coach, explain the contributions that person has made to his or her team or sport, identify and define the criteria you are using to evaluate his or her performance, and present your evaluation to your readers. To support your evaluation, draw on your observations of the athlete or coach, interviews or surveys of other sports fans familiar with the athlete or coach, and published sources that discuss the athlete or coach. If possible, you might also interview the athlete or coach.

Suggestions for Other Genres

6. POST A MOVIE REVIEW

Review a recently released movie for the readers of a specific blog or Web site. To prepare, read movie reviews that have appeared on the site you have selected, and familiarize yourself with its conventions. In your review, describe the movie and evaluate it, keeping in mind the interests of your readers. Take notes and, if possible, interview others who have seen the movie. Visit the movie's Web site to learn about the movie, its director, and its cast. Your review should focus primarily on your personal assessment of the movie. Draw on your notes, interviews, and materials from the movie's Web site to introduce ideas, illustrate a point, or support your conclusions.

7. POST A RESTAURANT REVIEW

Review a restaurant for the readers of a specific blog or Web site. To prepare, read restaurant reviews that have appeared in the blog or on the Web site you have selected, and familiarize yourself with its conventions. To conduct the review, have a meal at the restaurant with one or more friends. Order a variety of items, examine the decor, and keep track of the quality of the service provided by the waitstaff. After you leave the restaurant, take notes to remind yourself of your impressions of the food, decor, and service. Ask your friends for their reactions, and take note of them as well. In your review, describe the restaurant and evaluate it, keeping in mind the interests of readers who read the blog or visit the site. Your review should focus primarily on your personal assessment of the restaurant. Draw on your notes to introduce ideas, illustrate a point, or support your conclusions.

8. EVALUATE A SOURCE

Choose a source that you might use in another assignment (if possible, a group assignment) for your writing class. Evaluate the source for your instructor and your classmates. Select criteria such as the source's relevance to the project, use of evidence, clarity and organization, timeliness, comprehensiveness, author, and publisher. Using these criteria, evaluate the contribution the source might make to your writing project. To support your evaluation, draw on the requirements of the assignment and your reading of the source.

9. EVALUATE AN ASSIGNMENT

Choose an assignment you've been given in one of your classes, and evaluate it for your instructor and your classmates. Select criteria such as the assignment's contribution to your understanding of the subject, the amount of work required to obtain an educational benefit from the assignment, the clarity of the assignment, its relevance to the course, and so on. Describe the course and the assignment, identify and define the criteria you are using to evaluate the assignment, and present your evaluation to your readers. To support your evaluation, draw on your experiences with the assignment, interviews or surveys of other students who have completed the assignment, and related course materials. You can also interview the instructor who gave the assignment.

10. WRITE A PROGRESS REPORT

Write a report that evaluates the progress that a group or organization you belong to has made during a particular period of time, such as the last six months or the last year. To develop the criteria for your progress report, interview key members of the group or organization, or locate any written documents that define its goals. Draw on your personal experience with the group, interviews, and documents (such as funding proposals or a Web site) as sources of evidence for your evaluation. Your report should define the group's or organization's goals and assess its progress in meeting them. The report might also include recommendations about strategies for enhancing the group's or organization's efforts to meet its goals.

In Summary: Writing an Evaluative Essay

* **Find a conversation and listen in.**

  - Explore your needs, interests, and concerns (p. 296).
  - Search the Web (p. 297).
  - Narrow your focus by asking questions (p. 300).

* **Conduct your evaluation.**

  - Define your criteria (p. 301).
  - Identify evidence (p. 302).
  - Make your judgments (p. 303).

* **Prepare a draft.**

  - State your overall judgment (p. 305).
  - Present your evaluation (p. 306).
  - Consider genre and design (p. 309).
  - Frame your evaluation (p. 309).

* **Review and improve your draft.**

  - Review your criteria (p. 311).
  - Reconsider your evidence (p. 311).
  - Ensure that your judgments are fair and reasonable (p. 311).

09

Writing to Solve Problems

Problem Solvers like me define a problem and offer possible solutions.

GENRES IN CONVERSATION

Reflective Writing | Informative Writing | Analytical Writing | Evaluative Writing | **Problem-Solving Writing** | Argumentative Writing

The growing problem of identity theft has sparked a large number of conversations devoted to understanding it and finding solutions. Some of these conversations focus on penalties for people who steal identities. Others focus on technological solutions. Still others focus on the impact of identity theft on victims and communities. The documents shown here—a **magazine article**, an **online news article**, and a **government Web site**—share a common purpose of helping people avoid identity theft. Notice how each genre accomplishes that purpose through the careful use of visual design.

e-Pages

You can view the full documents shown here and respond to questions about problem-solving genres at **bedforstmartins .com/conversation /epages.**

Magazine Article ▶

This **article** in *PC Magazine*, formatted in a typical magazine layout using columns and graphics, is aimed at computer-literate readers and draws on interviews with industry leaders, published reports, and the writer's personal experience and expertise.

SECURITY **WATCH**

Defending Your Identity

Hardly a week goes by without companies and universities losing digital identities. What can be done?

BY ROBERT LEMOS

IDENTITY THEFT IS A BOOMING business, and not just for the criminals. We frequently hear news of companies and universities losing digital information for large numbers of consumers. In April, for example, the University of Texas at Austin warned that a hacker had breached a system at the UT business school, downloading personal data—in many cases including Social Security numbers—on 197,000 students, alumni, and employees. And the state of Ohio recalled CDs containing information on 7.7 million voters from more than 20 political campaign offices after it discovered that the discs included the voters' Social Security numbers, the key to consumers' financial accounts.

When such institutions are so careless with personal information, it's no wonder that identity theft is a relatively common occurrence. By far the greatest share—about 37 percent—of the fraud complaints that the Federal Trade Commission received in 2005 was due to identity theft. A 2005 study from Javelin Research pegged the total loss to U.S. businesses and consumers at $52.6 billion. Not all indicators are bad, however. Between 2004 and 2005, the estimated number of victims of identity theft in the U.S. decreased from 10.1 million to 9.3 million. The average time to resolve identity theft also dropped 15 percent, to 28 hours.

Despite threats of phishing, stolen databases, and other online fraud, most people become victims via off-line methods. According to the Javelin study, only 11.6 percent of identity theft occurred online. Users who monitored their accounts online suffered an average of $451 in losses, far less than the average of $4,543 for cases detected by paper statements.

Unfortunately, the law does not give consumers much control. Correcting mistakes in a credit report can take days, if not weeks or months. And though in 2003 Congress passed the Fair and Accurate Credit Transactions Act (FACTA), which allows consumers annual access to their credit reports, the law bars states from adopting stronger consumer protections and requires a police report before a long-term fraud alert may be placed on a credit account.

Credit-card companies and credit bureaus have created a variety of Internet solutions to help con-

SCORING YOUR CREDIT *Identity-protection sites generally show a credit score, its factors, and data on open accounts.*

sumers. But some of these companies are responsible for the poor security of people's financial records in the first place.

Other services have popped up to add security to the credit-approval process. LifeLock puts fraud alerts on accounts to block credit offers and unsolicited access to credit information. And a startup, Debix, is testing a service that attempts to lock access to a person's account, requiring a one-time key for any company or person to open a new credit account in the owner's name.

For you, one of these services may be overkill. So a good place to start is to get a free credit report and check it over carefully. From there you can decide whether you need one of the monitoring or credit-security services in the sidebar on this page.

Since the majority of identity theft still takes place outside cyberspace, don't just toss old bills, bank statements, and financial records. Invest in a paper shredder and use it. Don't carry your Social Security card in your wallet, and when registering for Web sites don't enter personal information that can be traced to financial records. And you should never give any information to telemarketers or respond to phishing e-mails that spoof sites such as PayPal asking you to update your account information. Consumers and businesses must work in tandem to prevent identity theft.

Robert Lemos is a freelance technology journalist and the editor-at-large for SecurityFocus.

SECURITY BLANKETS

AnnualCreditReport.com
www.annualcredit report.com
Industry-created site that helps consumers get annual credit reports from the three major credit bureaus. Free.

IdentityGuard
identityguard.com
Quarterly access to reports; daily notification of changes by e-mail monitoring credit card accounts; $20,000 in insurance. $12.99 per month.

LifeLock
www.lifelock.com
Annual access to four different credit reports; removes consumers from junk-mail lists and preapproved credit-card lists; monitors checking accounts; $1 million in insurance. $10 per month, $110 per year.

MyFICO Identity Theft Security (Fair Isaac)
www.myfico.com/ Products/IDF/ Description.aspx
Quarterly credit reports from TransUnion; weekly notifications of changes; $25,000 in insurance. $4.95 per month, $49.95 per year.

▶▶ KEEP YOURSELF SAFE!
Subscribe to our Security Watch newsletter and get up-to-date info on the latest threats delivered to your inbox automatically: go.pcmag.com/ securitywatchletter

► **Online News Article**

Along with ten tips for avoiding identity theft, this **online news article** from CBSnews.com includes links to other Web resources on the topic.

ⓒCBS money watch

Markets Investing Tech Leadership **Small Business** Saving Spending

DOW 15126.84   S&P 500 1680.49   NASDAQ 3767.67   WILSHIRE

Full episodes Get the ⓒCBS app. ⓒ for iPad

By **DAVE JOHNSON** / **MONEYWATCH** / *March 8, 2013, 6:45 AM*

How to prevent identity theft

1 Comment / f Shares / 🐦 Tweets / ⓒ Stumble / @ Email   More +

(MoneyWatch) It's a dangerous world we live in. There was a time when the worst thing that could happen if you got your wallet stolen was to lose the cash you had on hand. These days, your wallet is a gateway to identity theft, which can quite literally ruin your entire life for months or even years afterwards. It pays to take all the reasonable precautions you can against identity theft.

Recently, Gizmodo ran a great article with five recommendations for avoiding identity theft. I heartily agree with Lifehacker, and have a few more to add to the list, for a total of 10 tips:

Don't keep your Social Security card on your person. There was a time when it made sense to carry your social security card in your wallet or purse, but those days ended in the 70s. Memorize your SSAN and lock the card up at home. Don't make it that easy for thieves who lift your wallet.

→ The most insecure passwords on the Internet
→ Keep yourself safe on your next business trip with a decoy wallet
→ Stop identity theft at work

Don't use your Social Security number unless you have to. There are still businesses that identify you by your Social security number. This is a really dangerous practice, since it spreads your number around in places where it is easier to steal. If you find that a bank is using your social -- even just the last four digits -- to identify your account, ask them to stop. If they don't (or can't), close the account and take your business elsewhere.

Don't share personal information with anyone on the phone. Especially "cold calls." If someone claiming to be from your bank calls and says they need details like your Social Security number, address or mother's maiden name, you might be getting scammed. There are few -- very few -- scenarios in which you'd ever have to give that info up over the phone.

FEDERAL TRADE COMMISSION

CONSUMER INFORMATIO

Vea esta página en español

| MONEY & CREDIT |
| HOMES & MORTGAGES |
| HEALTH & FITNESS |
| JOBS & MAKING MONEY |
| PRIVACY & IDENTITY |
| BLOG |
| VIDEO & MEDIA |
| SCAM ALERTS ⚠ |

IDENTITY THEFT

Identity theft happens when someone steals your personal information and uses it without your permission. It's a serious crime that can wreak havoc with your finances, credit history, and reputation — and can take time, money, and patience to resolve.

What to Do Right Away
Immediate Steps to Repair Identity Theft
Here's how to begin to limit the harm from identity theft.

What to Do Next
Extended Fraud Alerts and Credit Freezes
Placing both extended fraud alerts and credit freezes on your credit reports can make it more difficult for an identity thief to open new accounts in your name.

Repairing Your Credit After Identity Theft
Here are step-by-step instructions for disputing fraudulent charges and accounts related to identity theft.

Lost or Stolen Credit, ATM, and Debit Cards
Federal law limits your liability if your credit, ATM, or debit card is lost or stolen, but your liability may depend on how quickly you report the loss or theft.

Related Items

What is Identity Theft?

● ● ●

IDENTITY THEFT RESOURCES

GUIDE TO ASSISTING IDENTITY THEFT VICTIMS

◄ **Government Web Site**

A **government Web site** offers resources for addressing identity theft and links to instructional videos, an online guide for victims, related blog posts, and published sources.

What Is Writing to Solve Problems?

The word *problem* is slippery. When a problem affects us directly, it might take on the dimensions of a crisis: we want to know how to solve it — and the sooner the better. When a problem affects someone else, it might seem, to us, more like an interesting challenge than an imminent disaster. And sometimes a problem is nothing of the sort. It's simply a label for lack of knowledge. For example, when a research scientist says that she's working on an interesting problem, she usually means that she's investigating an intriguing puzzle, which, when solved, will advance our knowledge in a specific area.

The Writer's Role: Problem Solver

PURPOSE

- To identify or define a problem
- To explain the significance of a problem
- To propose solutions

READERS

- Expect information, ideas, and insights to be presented fairly
- Expect a clear explanation of a proposed solution

SOURCES

- Published information (such as studies, reports, blogs, the Web, and news media), personal experience, and field research (including interviews, observation, surveys, and correspondence) help writers define and learn about previous attempts to solve problems.

CONTEXT

- Writers consider what readers are likely to know, assume, and value, and they focus on what readers want or need to understand about the problem.

- Illustrations — such as charts, tables, graphs, and images — can improve readers' understanding.

Writers who adopt the role of *problem solver* carry out activities such as calling readers' attention to problems, discussing the nature and extent of those problems, or proposing solutions. Whether a writer focuses on defining, discussing, or proposing a solution to a problem depends on how much is known about it. Consider, for example, the evolution of our understanding of the HIV/AIDS epidemic. In the early 1980s, when little was known about HIV — the virus that causes AIDS — it wasn't clear that the growing number of illnesses caused by HIV were related to one another. As a result, the first writers who addressed the problem focused largely on defining the symptoms and arguing that a problem existed. Later, as more information became available about the origin and effects of the disease, medical researchers began writing reports and scholarly articles that discussed its potential impact on people who carried the virus and on society. As researchers began to understand how the disease was spread and what might be done to prevent infection, writers proposed solutions to reduce the spread of HIV. Eventually, as the nature of HIV became better understood, writers began proposing programs of medical research that might be carried out to develop a way of preventing, and perhaps even eradicating, the spread of the virus.

A writer's decisions about how to address a problem depend largely on context. Until the nature and significance of a problem are understood, it does little good to propose a solution. Because of the critical role played by writers who help define and understand problems, they are actively involved in solving these problems — even when they don't propose a fully developed solution.

No matter how aware readers are of a problem, however, more often than not they are seeking a solution. Readers expect a clear definition of the problem and a thorough discussion of options for addressing it. And although readers might not be surprised when a writer uses emotionally charged language, they usually prefer that problem-solving documents discuss the problem in a straightforward, balanced manner.

Most readers also expect writers not only to explain and discuss the benefits of their proposed solution but also to address its advantages over other solutions. They expect a fair and reasonable presentation of a subject, clear explanations of important ideas and concepts, and thorough documentation of sources. Readers usually react favorably to the use of visual elements — such as photos, images, charts, graphs, and tables — that help them understand the problem and its solution.

Writers of problem-solving documents are concerned primarily with helping readers understand the nature of and potential solutions to a problem. Sometimes they define and discuss the origins or impact of a problem. Sometimes they reflect on the strengths and weaknesses of potential solutions to a problem. In most cases, however, they analyze a problem and offer readers a thoroughly considered, well-supported solution. In doing so, they play a critical role in advancing our understanding of and response to problems.

What Kinds of Documents Are Used to Solve Problems?

It's rare to spend a day without running across documents that promise to solve a problem: advertisements alert us to solutions for problems (with our health, our love lives, our breath) that we might not know we have; e-mail messages ask us for our help with problems ranging from hunger to funding for the arts; and entire Web sites, such as Project Vote Smart and FightGlobalWarming.com, promote solutions to problems. Unfortunately, the number of unsolved problems far exceeds those with solutions. As a result, writing to solve problems is a common occurrence.

View the e-Pages for problem-solving writing at **bedfordstmartins.com /conversation/epages**.

In your work writing a problem-solving essay, you might turn to sources as varied as books, reports, pamphlets, posters, memos, opinion columns, and blog entries — any of which might define a problem or advance solutions to a problem. The following examples illustrate three of the problem-solving documents you're likely to encounter: problem-solving essays, proposals, and news features. In the e-Pages for this chapter, you'll find discussions and examples of guest editorials, advice, and audio reports.

Problem-Solving Essays

Like other types of problem-solving documents, essays define problems and offer solutions for readers who share a writer's interest in an issue. What distinguishes essays from other problem-solving genres, however, is their tendency to offer a more reflective and comprehensive treatment of a problem. In addition to explaining a problem and offering a concrete solution, they are also likely to offer the writer's personal insights into the problem, the situation out of which it emerges, and the reasons why the proposed solution is preferable to competing solutions. While writers of problem-solving essays typically do their best to define a problem and propose a solution as fairly as possible, they frequently allow their experiences with and attitudes toward the problem to influence both their presentation of the problem and their selection and presentation of information from sources, such as articles, Web sites, and interviews.

Readers of problem-solving essays might be part of a broad audience, such as subscribers to a general-interest magazine such as *Time* or *Atlantic Monthly*, or they might be part of a more narrowly defined group, such as community college administrators, parents of autistic children, small-town mayors, or members of a particular church. In academic settings, instructors are usually the primary readers, although students are often asked to address a different audience, such as fellow students, politicians, or the members of a particular community.

Richard H. Thaler and Cass R. Sunstein
How to Make Lazy People Do the Right Thing

The following problem-solving essay first appeared in the *New Republic*, a magazine that covers American politics and culture. In "How to Make Lazy People Do the Right Thing," economist Richard H. Thaler and legal scholar Cass R. Sunstein suggest that business and government should use "choice architecture" to "nudge" people into making better decisions, while at the same time preserving individual freedom. Thaler teaches at the University of Chicago; Sunstein is a professor at Harvard School of Law and was picked by the Obama administration to lead the Federal Office of Information and Regulatory Affairs. They collaborated on the book *Nudge: Improving Decisions about Wealth, Health, and Happiness* (2008).

How to Make Lazy People Do the Right Thing

by Richard H. Thaler and Cass R. Sunstein

As everyone knows, many guys are slobs. And, yes, we plead guilty to being guys. It is not that we set out to be sloppy. We have a lot of important stuff on our minds. Whom can we find for a tennis game tomorrow? How is our team going to defend against their three excellent wide receivers? You can see the problem. With these burdens distracting us, how can we be expected to keep a neat desk?

As all women who have ever shared a toilet with a man can attest, men can be especially spacey when it comes to their, er, aim. In the privacy of a home, that may be a mere annoyance. But, in a busy airport restroom used by throngs of travelers each day, the unpleasant effects of bad aim can add up rather quickly. Enter an ingenious economist who worked for Schiphol International Airport in Amsterdam. His idea was to etch an image of a black house fly onto the bowls of the airport's urinals, just to the left of the drain. The result: Spillage declined 80 percent. It turns out that, if you give men a target, they can't help but aim at it.

In the grand sweep of global affairs, dirty bathrooms may be a relatively minor problem. But, on its urinals, the Amsterdam airport was using a technique with broad applications in the world of business and even politics. We call that technique "choice architecture." A choice architect is anyone who influences the context in which people choose—say, by deciding what order to put menu items in, or what path to encourage shoppers to take through a supermarket, or what information to give investors about their retirement savings options, or what to tell patients deciding how to deal with a medical problem. Because seemingly tiny changes in the environment can influence behavior, choice architects wield immense power. Theirs is a gentle power, since they merely nudge rather than coerce. But their nudges can have major effects.

To see why choice architects wield so much power, consider several aspects of human nature. For one thing, there are limits on the number of items to which we can pay attention at one time. We are surrounded by stimuli, and, to survive, we have to direct our attention to what seems most important (such as the road in front of us while we are driving). As a result, we may miss things that are also significant but not currently in focus. When men use an airport urinal, chances are they have things on their mind other than making sure their aim is precise. Placing a fly image in a urinal upends this state of affairs: It causes men to focus on something they would normally ignore — nudging them toward behavior that produces a socially desirable outcome.

Choice architecture derives additional power from two other human fallibilities: inertia and limited self-control. When in doubt, humans tend to do nothing, even when the costs of making a change are trivial and the benefits are significant. We can even be too lazy to pick up the remote and change the channel, which is why networks spend so much time thinking about which show should follow another. We also often have trouble managing ourselves. To take an obvious example, an alarming percentage of Americans are overweight. Most of them would like to be thinner but can't get themselves to diet or exercise. Ever since Adam took a bite of that apple, human beings have tended to show a weakness of will.

> Because seemingly tiny changes in the environment can influence behavior, choice architects wield immense power.

In light of these human traits, one important tool at the choice architect's disposal is the designation of a default option. The default option determines what happens if the decision-maker takes no action. Because of limited attention, inertia, and lack of will, the selection of the default can have pronounced effects. Defaults are ubiquitous and powerful. They are also unavoidable, because, for any system of choice architecture, there must be a rule that determines what happens if you do nothing. Of course, the usual answer is that, if you do nothing, nothing changes; whatever is happening continues to happen. But not always. Some dangerous machines, such as chain saws and lawn mowers, are designed with "dead man's switches," so that, once you are no longer gripping the machine, it stops. When you leave your computer alone to answer a phone

call, nothing will happen — for a time. But, if you talk long enough, the screen saver will come on; and, if you neglect the computer for longer still, it may lock itself. Of course, you can choose how long it takes before your screen saver appears, but that, in and of itself, takes some action. Your computer probably came with a default time lag for the screen saver. Chances are, that is the one you still have.

Many businesses have discovered the power of default options. When people subscribe to a magazine or website these days, they are typically enrolled in an automatic renewal program. When their subscription runs out, it is automatically renewed unless the subscriber takes some action; and, in many cases, the action requires quite a bit of patience and persistence. One of us (not to mention names, but the lawyer) still has subscriptions to several magazines that he never reads and actually hates, because he has not gotten around to canceling them.

Businesses can manipulate default options toward good ends too, not just selfish ones. Take the issue of employee savings. Economists have long argued that Americans do not save enough for retirement. How might they be nudged to do so? Are tax incentives necessary? New government programs? Actually, there is a much easier way.

Traditionally, when employees first become eligible to join their company's 401(k) plan, they receive a notification from the human resources department along with a bunch of forms. Essentially they are told, if you want to join the plan, fill in these forms, choose a savings rate, decide how you want your money invested, and send the forms back. When it comes to filling in forms, many of us have a tendency to procrastinate, especially if those forms seem to require making important decisions. The tendency is to think, "Oh, I better do some research on which funds to pick before I sign up." The problem is that, once put off, signing up for the plan gets in line with everything else on the "to do" list, right after cleaning the garage.

To solve this problem, some companies have adopted what has come to be called automatic enrollment. Under this regime, when employees become eligible, they get the same package in the mail but are told that, unless they fill out some forms, they will be automatically enrolled with a prespecified savings rate and investment plan. Studies have shown that automatic enrollment greatly increases participation in 401(k) plans. (Workers are more likely to join, and they join sooner.) Since joining the plan is almost always an excellent idea, especially when the firm is making some matching contributions, automatic enrollment successfully nudges workers toward better choices.

Companies have also nudged employees to save more by giving them a chance to commit to gradually increasing their savings rates. One system, devised by one of us (Thaler) and collaborator Shlomo Benartzi, is called "Save More Tomorrow." The idea is that workers are offered the opportunity to sign up for a plan under which their savings rates automatically increase every time they get a pay raise, until they reach some savings cap. In the first firm that adopted this plan, those who joined more than tripled their savings rates. Of course, workers can switch out of this plan at any time. The point is to have a default option going forward that calls for their savings rates to increase along with their wages. Research is now underway on an extension of this idea known as "Give More Tomorrow," by which

workers commit themselves to donating part of their future wage increases to charity. It seems possible that Give More Tomorrow, if offered widely, could produce dramatic increases in charitable contributions.

The government is inevitably involved in choice architecture and nudging as well. Some of these nudges involve default options, while others — much like placing fly images in urinals — simply create an incentive where none had previously existed. The 2006 Pension Protection Act, for instance, gently nudges firms to adopt automatic enrollment and a primitive form of Save More Tomorrow. If firms adopt those features and match employee contributions at a specified rate, then they are exempted from the somewhat onerous process of showing they were in compliance with certain federal regulations. No firm is required to adopt these policies — just given a small incentive to do so.

Of course, some government nudging makes people nervous, and rightly so. We would not want public officials to nudge people toward certain religious convictions. We would not want the government (meaning incumbents) manipulating the order in which candidates are displayed on ballots, since the candidate listed first gets a 2 to 5 percent bump in votes. In this domain, the proper thing for government to do is to insist that ballot order be settled randomly — or, better yet, varied across voting places, so the benefit of being listed first is shared by all candidates.

But, sometimes, government can do much better than pick things at random. An infuriating example of inept government choice architecture is the Medicare Part D prescription drug program. Although this program is heavily subsidized and mostly a good deal for seniors, it is much reviled, not only by seniors but by their grown children who get roped into helping them deal with the intricacies of the plan. Those who designed the plan thought that the most important thing to offer seniors was choices; so, in most states, seniors are asked to choose from about 50 different insurance plans. "The more choices you have, the more likely it is you'll be able to find a program that suits your specific needs," President Bush told a clubhouse of Florida seniors in 2006. "In other words, one-size-fits-all is not a consumer-friendly program. And I believe in consumers. I believe in trusting people."

It is great to believe in trusting people, but, sometimes, it is also a good idea to offer them a helping hand. We wanted to see what exactly seniors face in making this decision, so we asked a friend of ours to give us a list of the drugs that her mother takes. Then we went to the Medicare Part D website and tried to figure out which insurance plan would work best for her. The first step is to type in a list of all the drugs you take. What a nightmare! The site does not have a spell checker; if you type "Zanax" instead of Xanax, you don't get one of those helpful "Did you mean" Google suggestions. This is a problem because drug names often resemble strings of random letters, so typing errors are to be expected. Other difficulties related to using the site — such as needing to select the correct dosages for all your medications — probably couldn't have been avoided. But the fact is, most senior citizens are bound to find the process arduous. After a couple of hours on the Part D website, we felt that we would soon need some Xanax ourselves.

Given how difficult this process is, you might think that the government would offer a default option for those who did not want to choose for themselves. The Bush administration decided not to do this — that trust thing again. But there was one group of participants for whom the government did have to create a default option:

Medicare users who had previously been covered by Medicaid. Non-Medicaid users who didn't sign up for Medicare Part D simply would not be enrolled. But Medicaid users were required to switch to Medicare for their prescription drug coverage. Of course, some did not get around to choosing a plan, so the government had to make a choice for them. What do you think that choice was? We will let you pause to consider how you would do it.

Amazingly, the method the government picked was to choose a plan at random! This makes no sense. For many people, and especially for the elderly, it is actually pretty easy to predict what drugs you will take next year — namely, the same drugs you are taking this year. A fact of life is that, the longer you live, the more drugs you take routinely. And, for many of these drugs, once you start, you take them as long as you live. Since the government knows what drugs a patient is taking (from last year's claims) and knows what prices the insurance companies are charging, it is a straightforward matter to make a decent guess about which plan would be best. In fact, the state of Maine, alert to the importance of good choice architecture, has adopted such a plan. It is called "Intelligent Assignment." But the Bush administration has not encouraged other states to adopt the idea. Perhaps, if Maine had called its plan "Intelligent Design," it would have gone further.

Private and public institutions have unlimited opportunities to use good choice architecture to improve people's lives — in domains as varied as protecting the environment, increasing organ donations, and promoting fair divorces. If we want to cut greenhouse gas emissions, for example, we can nudge people simply by giving them vivid information about their current energy uses. Southern California Edison has encouraged consumers to conserve energy by giving them an Ambient Orb, a little ball that glows red when they are using lots of energy but green when their use is modest. Users of the Orb reduced their energy consumption in peak periods by 40 percent. If we want to increase the supply of organs to people whose lives depend on them, we can presume that people want their organs, at the time of death, to be available for use by others. The general American practice is to treat non-donation as the default, but many European countries have adopted the opposite system, called "presumed consent." A study by Eric Johnson and Dan Goldstein showed that changing the default could save thousands of lives annually. And, if we want to protect women, who are especially vulnerable during divorce, we can rely on suitable default rules, which would ensure, as many states do not, that women's income does not fall dramatically in the period after divorce. In all kinds of situations, governments and employers can nudge people toward making better decisions simply by making the better choice easier to adopt.

During the second half of the twentieth century, there was a lot of talk about the possibility of developing some kind of Third Way between capitalism and socialism. Now that socialism is dead, many Americans have come to think that the real decision is between two visions of capitalism — laissez-faire capitalism, which relies on unrestricted free markets, and progressive capitalism, which relies on government mandates and bans to ensure good outcomes. But this is frequently a false dichotomy. In countless domains, good choice architecture can allow governments to preserve freedom while encouraging people to make wise decisions. Sometimes, of course, governments do need to rely on mandates and bans to advance legitimate goals. But often a freedom-preserving nudge is the simplest and most effective tool of all.

In your writer's notebook, reflect on the problems and solutions presented in Thaler and Sunstein's essay by answering the following questions:

Starting a Conversation: Respond to "How to Make Lazy People Do the Right Thing"

1. Thaler and Sunstein touch on a broad range of subjects in this essay, from dirty public restrooms to the difficulties seniors have with Medicare Part D. What do these problems have in common? To what extent are the authors more interested in promoting a particular solution than in addressing individual problems? How can you tell?

2. What, exactly, is choice architecture? According to the authors, why do choice architects wield so much power?

3. In paragraph 13, Thaler and Sunstein acknowledge that "some government nudging makes people nervous, and rightly so." Why

do they admit that this objection is reasonable? How do they respond to it?

4. At several points in the essay, the authors use generalizations and stereotypes. Identify at least three instances of this. How do these examples support — or undermine — their claims?

5. Although their focus is not explicitly political, Thaler and Sunstein do refer to former president George W. Bush and policies associated with his administration. What can you tell about their political views from these references? What can you tell about the views of their presumed readers?

Proposals

Proposals offer a plan for solving a specific problem. They are usually presented to groups or individuals who have resources that might be used to address the problem, or who can grant permission for putting a plan into effect. For example, a nonprofit organization might propose that a charitable foundation fund an after-school tutoring program for children of one-parent families. Or a research center at a university might request approval from a city council for a pilot program to improve wheelchair access in local parks.

Proposals typically define a problem, describe a plan for addressing the problem, and argue that the person or group making the proposal has the capacity to carry out the plan. They might also include budgets, plans for evaluating outcomes, and information about the person or group making the proposal.

The structure and general appearance of proposals vary widely and tend to reflect the interests of the intended audience; often, proposals must follow strict guidelines outlined in grant application instructions or a call for proposals. Some proposals resemble academic essays, with wide margins, double-spaced lines, headings and subheadings, and limited use of color and illustrations. Others more closely resemble magazine articles or brochures, with heavy use of color, illustrations, columns, and other design elements.

 Dan Hughes
Proposal for Skateparks under Bridges

Skateboarding enthusiast Dan Hughes submitted the following proposal to the city of Seattle. The proposal offers background on the benefits of skateboarding for young people and identifies a problem in the lack of appropriate venues for young skateboarders in the city. The proposal then offers a detailed plan for solving the problem by creating skateparks under bridges and highway overpasses. In structure, style, and tone, the proposal anticipates potential objections from city officials and offers persuasive details to support the plan as a viable solution.

PROPOSAL FOR SKATEPARKS UNDER BRIDGES

BACKGROUND

Skateboarding is a high-energy activity that builds both physical and mental strength, as it requires an individual to be self-reliant while sharing space with other individuals.

Part of what makes skateboarding a positive activity is that it allows people to focus on their personal abilities and skills. As a sport, skateboarding has no pre-scribed rules, no governing body, and no restrictions that require a team effort. Kids who are not served by team sports are attracted to skateboarding because it doesn't require them to join a team and compete until a winner and a loser are declared. It is an activity in which there are no losers, only winners. Anyone can simply grab a board and skate anytime to improve his or her skills.

Skateboarding has other positive attributes, as older skaters can attest. It builds confidence, and often it's this confidence in oneself that allows one to make the right choices in life. It also teaches kids that they can do things they never thought possible. For parents and kids alike, skating also provides opportunities for learning and acting as positive role models. One only has to look at champion skater Tony Hawk to see how skateboarding has become a way for him to connect with his kids.

It is well known that social problems occur in cities when adequate facilities and challenging activities for young people are not available. Skateboarding offers one solution, but skateboarding cannot occur in the rain, or when it's excessively hot, or in the dark winter months. Ultimately, a well-designed and well-built skate-park is necessary to provide a challenging and safe environment for young skaters. Older skaters would also use and enjoy such a park, and this mix of age groups would give younger skaters the opportunity to learn and grow, not only as skaters but also as people.

PROPOSAL

This proposal puts forth a plan for building skateparks in underutilized spaces under bridges and overpasses in Seattle. Skateparks can take organic, asymmetrical forms; they need not be bound in squares like other sports fields. This key feature allows for more efficient use of space that otherwise may be rendered useless (such as land under bridges or freeways).

Using land under a bridge has two main advantages compared to other skate-park locations. First, it largely eliminates the "N.I.M.B.Y." (Not In My Back Yard) problem, which happens when local residents do not want loud or disruptive activities near their houses. Because these areas already accommodate a freeway or a noisy bridge, skatepark-generated noise is no longer an issue. Second, skateparks discourage illegal activities that often occur under bridges of this sort. A good example is the area under the Burnside Bridge in Portland. This location was home to all kinds of criminal activity (drug deals, prostitution, abandoned cars, and so on) before Mark Scott and other skaters started building a skatepark there in 1990. The skaters cleaned up the area and kept the criminals out, to the point that the surrounding businesses took notice and volunteered their time and money toward expanding the skatepark. Even the local police chief donated money towards the effort. (This information was taken from a personal interview with Joanne Ferrero, who is owner and operator of Ferrero Equity Inc., a company right next to the Burnside Skatepark.)

In addition to these advantages for cities, using land under bridges and over-passes also provides an advantage for skaters. The bridge provides protection from rain in the winter and excessive heat in the summer. With the addition of lights, the skatepark can be used after dark as well.

OBJECTIVES

1. Give skaters a good, covered place to skate that can be used rain or shine, day or night, throughout the year.
2. Effectively use space that most wouldn't think to use as park land. Effective use of this space fulfills the goals of the City by providing a designated area for skateboarders and serves the community by freeing up more land to be used for other types of parks.
3. Provide kids with a healthy and intense activity. At skateparks, kids learn how to skateboard and are given a positive kinesthetic and creative outlet for their energy.

PROJECT DETAILS

Suggested Locations

1. <u>Under I-90 along Royal Brougham.</u> This area is centrally located with access to public transportation. It features a large covered space that is largely unused.

2. <u>Under I-5 between NE 40th Street and NE 42nd St.</u> This area is close to the University District, where there are lots of students who skateboard. It, too, features access to public transportation and a very large covered area that is largely unused.

Clientele

Two different groups would be likely to use skateparks in the suggested locations. The first and most important group is made up of young people who live nearby and who frequently skate in the area already. The second group is made up of skaters of all ages who live in various parts of the city and who would travel to this park (either by car or bus) because it is usable even in the rain, unlike most other outdoor skate parks.

Both clientele groups are essential components of this project, and it is expected that both would make significant use of the skatepark. Skateboarding is currently one of the fastest growing sports, and facilities such as these are used more heavily than basketball courts or baseball fields in similar locations.

Methods

The primary methods for achieving these objectives:

- The design and construction of a skatepark using concrete as its surface material.
- The use of experienced design and contracting companies comprised of skateboarders.
- The development of the area under a bridge as a full-fledged city park, complete with restrooms, trash cans, and lights.

Potential Objections and Responses

Skateparks under bridges are hidden, allowing for illegal activities. As the Burnside skatepark has proven, skateparks under bridges actually discourage crime in these areas. Skateboarders concentrate on their skateboarding, not on illegal activities. Lights, restrooms, picnic tables, a play area for toddlers, and vending machines will attract parents of the kids who are skateboarding. In Newberg, Oregon, this adult-friendly approach has been very successful at promoting self-policing of the skatepark.

Seismic safety. Traffic safety engineers design such bridges specifically to withstand the weight and stress of consistent car travel. If the bridge is safe for auto travel, one can reasonably assume it is safe for skateboarders beneath the bridge.

The land is not the property of the city. Currently there is a skatepark under I-90 in Spokane, Washington, which sets a precedent that Seattle can follow.

A park that attracts people from surrounding cities doesn't serve Seattle. In fact, it does. A good example is the skate bowl in Ballard Commons Park. Skaters come from all around to skate there, and the surrounding businesses, such as the QFC and Texaco, benefit—as does the city. The bottom line is that skaters spend money when they travel, and if they travel to Seattle, they will spend money in Seattle.

Lights are expensive. Darkness arrives early during Seattle's winter, just after the school day ends. This causes skaters to look for lighted places to skate, such as the streets or parking garages, both of which are illegal. It's far better to have the kids in one place like a skatepark, where their parents and the authorities can keep track of them. If lights can be used at a tennis court, then they can be used in the same way for a skatepark. Lights need not stay on all night. They can shut off automatically at a designated time or have a coin-operated switch to turn them on (to help offset the cost).

Needed Resources

- **Site Acquisition/Lease from Washington State Department of Transportation or the City of Seattle**
- **Personnel**: No personnel will be needed to staff the park.
- **Facilities Maintenance**: Emptying trash, cleaning restrooms, changing lights, and so on.
- **Design and Construction Costs**: Central Contractors Association estimates approx. $15/sq ft.
- **Infrastructure Maintenance Costs:**
    - Skate-only and concrete with steel coping: $0
    - Skate-only with pool coping: about $3000 the first year and $2000 a year thereafter
    - BMX: about $5000 a year

Additional Possibilities for Sites in Seattle

1. Under the Ballard Bridge
2. Under Interstate 5 in Seattle along Airport Way
3. Under the 12th Street Bridge and Dearborn Ave.
4. Under 45th St. next to University Village
5. Under Highway 509 at the intersection of Highway 99 and 509 and W. Marginal Way
6. Under Highway 99 at South Hanford St.
7. Under Hwy 99 at South Atlantic St.
8. Under I-5 and Spokane St.
9. Under I-5 at Shelby St.
10. I-90 next to Rainer Ave. and Goodwill
11. Under West Seattle Bridge at Duwammish St.

Dan Hughes
NorthwestSkater.com

Starting a Conversation: Respond to "Proposal for Skateparks under Bridges"

In your writer's notebook, evaluate Hughes's proposal by responding to the following questions:

1. What elements of Hughes's proposal demonstrate his sensitivity to the concerns of skateboarders? What elements demonstrate his awareness of the concerns of city officials?

2. How would you characterize the structure of this proposal? In what ways does the form — background, problem definition, proposed solution, and so on — help the writer achieve his purpose?

3. Hughes addresses possible objections to his proposed solution in the section "Potential Objections and Responses." Where else in the proposal does he address potential objections, and how does he refute them? Can you think of additional possible objections? What questions might remain in readers' minds?

4. At several points in his proposal, Hughes refers to examples such as the Ballard Skatepark and the Burnside Skatepark. How do these sources support his claims? What important details, if any, are missing?

5. Do you think Hughes's proposal is likely to be accepted or rejected? Why?

News Features

News features depart from the standard reporting found in newspapers, magazines, and Web news sites. They offer insights into key issues facing readers and their communities. Depending on their audience, news features might also focus on state, national, and international issues, as CNN frequently does in the Politics, Tech, and Money sections on its Web site. When news features offer solutions to problems, they tend to follow the relatively standard format of problem definition/problem solution, introducing the problem and leading readers or viewers toward a recommended solution.

The design of news features varies widely, in both format and medium. Magazines, newspapers, and many Web sites offer news features in formats nearly identical to that of standard articles or opinion columns. These news features make use of design elements typically associated with those genres, such as text formatting, the use of columns and sidebars, and the use of illustrations such as images, charts, and tables. News features can also appear in video or audio, however, either with or without accompanying text. When news features are presented on a news Web site such as

CNN, NPR, or Fox, for example, they are frequently accompanied by a related article or a transcript.

Readers and viewers of news features expect a clear definition of the problem and a well-defined solution or, if a solution is not offered, some discussion of options that might be considered by people who hope to address the problem. They expect evidence to be provided, in the form of either analysis, direct observation, reports from people who have been affected by the problem, or commentary from experts or authorities. Readers and viewers generally do not expect the sources of evidence to be documented beyond the use of names and titles or descriptions of locations where observations were made.

Jody Greenstone Miller
How to Get More Working Women to the Top

Jody Greenstone Miller is the cofounder and CEO of the consulting firm Business Talent Group, and she has held executive positions in several companies and also served in the White House as a staff member in two administrations. Her news feature, published in the *Wall Street Journal*, focuses on the problems women face in securing and keeping top positions in their fields. While Greenstone Miller's article begins in response to Sheryl Sandberg's recommendation that women invest more time and energy in their careers, she goes on to reframe the problem and provide some proven solutions from her own experience as a CEO in a demanding industry.

How to Get More Working Women to the Top

By Jody Greenstone Miller | March 11, 2013

Why aren't more women running things in America? It isn't for lack of ambition or life skills or credentials. The real barrier to getting more women to the top is the unsexy but immensely difficult issue of time commitment: Today's top jobs in major organizations demand 60-plus hours of work a week.

In her much-discussed new book, Facebook Chief Operating Officer Sheryl Sandberg tells women with high aspirations that they need to "lean in" at work—that is, assert themselves more. It's fine advice, but it misdiagnoses the problem. It isn't any shortage of drive that leads those phalanxes of female Harvard Business School grads to opt out. It's the assumption that senior roles have to consume their every waking moment. More great women don't "lean in" because they don't like the world they're being asked to lean into.

It doesn't have to be this way. A little organizational imagination bolstered by a commitment from the C-suite can point the path to a saner, more satisfying blend of the things that ambitious women want from work and life. It's time that we put the clock at the heart of this debate.

I know this is doable because I run a growing startup company in which more than half the professionals work fewer than 40 hours a week by choice. They are alumnae of top schools and firms like General Electric and McKinsey, and they are mostly women. The key is that we design jobs to enable people to contribute at varying levels of time commitment while still meeting our overall goals for the company.

This isn't advanced physics, but it does mean thinking through the math of how work in a company adds up. It's also an iterative process; we hardly get it right every time. But for businesses and reformers serious about cracking the real glass ceiling for women—and making their firms magnets for the huge swath of American talent now sitting on the sidelines—here are four ways to start going about it.

Rethink time

Break away from the arbitrary notion that high-level work can be done only by people who work 10 or more hours a day, five or more days a week, 12 months a year. Why not just three days a week, or six hours a day, or 10 months a year?

It sounds simple, but the only thing that matters is quantifying the work that needs to get done and having the right set of resources in place to do it. Senior roles should actually be easier to reimagine in this way because highly paid people have the ability and, often, the desire to give up some income in order to work less. Flexibility and working from home can soften the blow, of course, but they don't solve the overall time problem.

Break work into projects

Once work is quantified, it must be broken up into discrete parts to allow for varying time commitments. Instead of thinking in terms of broad functions like the head of marketing, finance, corporate development, or sales, a firm needs to define key roles in terms of specific, measurable tasks.

Once you think of work as a series of projects, it's easy to see how people can tailor how much to take on. The growth of consulting and outsourcing came precisely when firms realized they could carve work into projects that could be done more effectively outside. The next step is to design internal roles in smaller bites, too. An experienced marketer for a pharma company could lead one major drug launch, for example, without having to oversee all drug launches. Instead of managing a portfolio with 10 products, a senior person could manage five. If a client-service executive working five days a week has a quota of 10 deals a month, then one who chooses to work three days a week has a quota of only six. Lower the quota but not the quality of the work or the executive's seniority.

One reason this doesn't happen more is managerial laziness: It's easier to find a "superwoman" to lead marketing (someone who will work as long as humanly possible) than it is to design work around discrete projects. But even superwoman has a limit, and when she hits it, organizations adjust by breaking up jobs and adding staff. Why not do this before people hit the wall?

Availability matters

It's important to differentiate between availability and absolute time commitments. Many professional women would happily agree to check email even seven days a week and jump in, if necessary, for intense project stints—so long as over the course of a year, the time devoted to work is more limited. Managers need to be clear about what's needed: 24/7 availability is not the same thing as a 24/7 workload.

Quality is the goal, not quantity

Leaders need to create a culture in which talented people are judged not by the quantity of their work, but by the quality of their contributions. This can't be hollow blather. Someone who works 20 hours a week and who delivers exceptional results on a pro rata basis should be eligible for promotions and viewed as a top performer. American corporations need to get rid of the notion that wanting to work less makes someone a "B player."

Promoting this kind of innovation, where companies start to look more like puzzles than pyramids, has to become part of feminism's new agenda. It's the only way to give millions of capable women the ability to recalibrate the time that they devote to work at different stages of their lives.

We have been putting smart women on the couch for 40 years, since psychologist Matina Horner published her famous studies on "fear of success." But the portion of top jobs that go to women is still shockingly low. That's the irony of Ms. Sandberg's cheerleading for women to stay ambitious: She fails to see that her own agenda isn't nearly ambitious enough.

"Leaning in" may help the relative handful of talented women who can live with the way that top jobs are structured today—and if that's their choice, more power to them. But only a small percentage of women will choose this route. Until the rest of us get serious about altering the way work gets done in American corporations, we're destined to howl at the moon over the injustice of it all while changing almost nothing.

Ms. Greenstone Miller is co-founder and chief executive officer of Business Talent Group.

A version of this article appeared March 9, 2013, on page C3 in the U.S. edition of The Wall Street Journal, *with the headline: The Real Women's Issue: Time.*

Starting a Conversation: Respond to "How to Get More Working Women to the Top"

In your writer's notebook, record your analysis of Greenstone Miller's news feature by responding to the following questions:

1. Greenstone Miller begins her news feature by critiquing one proposed solution to a problem and then redefining the problem itself. Why do you think she does so? What would she stand to gain or lose by keeping to the original definition of the problem?

2. What kind of reader is Greenstone Miller addressing? What aspects of her news feature might appeal to readers beyond her intended audience? Why?

3. Greenstone Miller writes, "More great women don't 'lean in' because they don't like the world they're being asked to lean into" (para. 2). What assumptions does this statement reveal about the author's beliefs? Who does the author mean when she says "great women," for instance?

4. From what kinds of sources does Greenstone Miller gather evidence to support her four solutions? How well do her examples allow her to meet the needs and interests of her readers and help them to understand the solutions she proposes?

5. Greenstone Miller notes that balancing a company's needs with a worker's time commitment is "an iterative process" (para. 5). What does *iterative* mean? How well does the author help you understand how her proposed solutions contribute to that process?

In Process

How Can I Write a Problem-Solving Essay?

A Problem-Solving Essay about College Tuition

Jennie Tillson wrote a problem-solving essay for her introductory composition course. Jennie learned about her topic by reading articles about the cost of higher education. Follow her efforts to write her problem-solving essay in the In Progress boxes throughout this chapter.

We all have problems. Some of us have more than others. You've probably heard someone say, "I've got a problem. My taxes are due." Or "I'm about to be evicted from my apartment." Or "My hard drive crashed." When people make statements like these, they are assuming that you share their understanding of the problem. Unfortunately, that's not always the case. You might assume that the person who has a problem paying taxes lacks the money to do so and that the best solution is to get a loan or pick up a part-time job. In fact, the problem might be based on a moral objection to how the government uses funds raised through taxes.

Until people share an understanding of a problem, it can be difficult to develop a solution and put it into effect. A successful problem-solving essay begins with the recognition that explaining a problem to others involves far more than saying, "I've got a problem with that. You know what I mean?" In this chapter, we'll work from the assumption that a problem is best understood as a situation that has negative consequences for an individual or a group. To address such a situation in writing, you need to carefully define your problem, consider its significance for readers, review past efforts to address it, and either develop your own solution or argue for the adoption of one that's been proposed by someone else.

As you work on your own problem-solving essay, you'll follow the work of Jennie Tillson, a first-year student who wrote a problem-solving essay about the high cost of college tuition.

Find a Conversation and Listen In

Taking on the role of problem solver requires you to understand the nature of problems — an understanding that a surprisingly large number of writers appear to lack. By learning about problems, you can begin to identify and understand them, and even to address them in meaningful ways. Once you gain an understanding of what constitutes a problem, you can begin to look for and learn about problems that intrigue you. In the process, you'll position yourself to choose a problem to address in your essay.

EXPLORE DIFFICULTIES

A good problem-solving essay begins with what educational philosopher John Dewey called a "felt difficulty" — the recognition that something isn't right. As you learn about an issue, you might find yourself wondering why something is the way it is, or perhaps you'll say to yourself, "That's not right." Treasure these early moments of recognizing a problem. If you feel that something isn't right, there's a good chance that a problem is near at hand.

As you search for felt difficulties in the world around you, keep in mind the idea that a problem is a situation with negative consequences for an individual or a group. Your responses to the following sets of questions can help you identify subjects that might serve as the focus for a problem-solving essay. (For additional suggestions, see the writing project ideas on p. 373.)

- **Community.** What kind of difficulties have you encountered or noticed in your neighborhood? Have you been stuck in long lines at a bank or post office? Have you volunteered at a food pantry that has been overwhelmed by an influx of new clients? Run across a pothole so deep that it ruined one of your tires? Been bothered by the recent actions of local politicians or law enforcement officials?

- **Economy.** Are any of your friends or relatives having financial difficulties? Have you worried about what the future holds for you? For your parents? For your children?

- **Work.** Do any issues at your workplace need to be addressed? Is the industry in which you work facing any challenges? Have you grown aware, through your course work or general reading, of difficulties facing people in your field of study?

- **News.** What have you read recently that surprised or worried you? What annoyed you or made you angry? What have you read that made you think? What controversies have you noticed on the evening news or on the Web sites you visit?

To begin turning a felt difficulty into a defined problem, jot down what doesn't feel right and then brainstorm or freewrite about it (see pp. 32–33). As you list ideas or write about your felt difficulty, the problem will begin to come into focus.

It can take time to sketch the outlines of a problem. You might find it helpful to think about the problem over a period of a few days or a week. During that time, you might read more about the problem or talk with others about it. As you reflect on the problem, keep track of your ideas by recording them in your writer's notebook or in a word-processing file.

ASK QUESTIONS ABOUT PROMISING SUBJECTS

Even if you think you know a great deal about each of the problems you've identified as potential subjects for your essay, check them out thoroughly before you begin trying to solve one. To learn more about a promising problem, reflect on your own experiences with it, discuss it with others, and find and review relevant published

Working Together: Ask Whether Your Judgments Are Fair

Before you start working on your problem-solving essay, start a conversation with a small group of your classmates about a minor problem that affects you. Explain the problem as clearly as you can, and tell the members of your group about how you think you might solve it. Ask them whether your preliminary solution seems likely to work and why. Then ask them to suggest additional solutions you should consider trying. Take turns speaking while the members of the group listen, respond, and ask questions.

When you are finished, take a few minutes to reflect on the exercise. What did you learn about your audience? Did they understand the problem right away, or did you have to adapt your initial explanation to overcome their assumptions? How much detail did you have to give them before your solution made sense? Did they think your solution was reasonable? What kinds of solutions did they suggest as alternatives? Did their questions and suggestions help you develop a better understanding of your problem or give you new ideas about how to solve it?

sources through your library or the Web. (You can learn more about locating, collecting, and managing information in Part Three.)

Once you've learned about the most promising problems, select those that continue to hold your interest, and then spend a few minutes responding to the following questions. Each set of questions focuses your attention on a problem in a different way, allowing you to think not only about the problem but also about its potential as the focus of your problem-solving essay. Depending on the problem you work with, you'll find that some questions are more useful than others.

- **Relevance.** Is this problem widespread, or does it involve only a small group of people? Who is affected by it, and how are they affected? Will my readers think it's important? Can I address it within the limits of my assignment?

- **Definition.** What, exactly, is the problem? How can I explain it? What kinds of information will readers need to understand it?

- **Context.** When and where did this problem begin? How much is known about it? What solutions have been tried? Why haven't they worked?

- **Causes and effects.** What caused this problem? What must happen before it can be solved? What is likely to happen if it isn't solved?

As you think about your ideas, remember that the best problems to tackle in an essay are usually highly specific. For example, instead of writing about the general problem of encouraging college students to become teachers, you might focus on how to encourage students in a particular discipline, such as math or biology, to become high school teachers in rural school districts.

CONDUCT A SURVEY

A survey can help you learn about the beliefs, attitudes, or behaviors of people associated with a problem. For example, you might use a survey to discover whether the attitudes and beliefs about education differ among students who stay in school and those who drop out. Or you might use a survey to explore whether students who put a high value on community involvement are highly engaged in volunteer activities.

Typically, surveys help you answer *what*, *who*, or *how* questions — such as "What kinds of exercise do you engage in at least once a week?," "Who will you vote for in the next election?," or "How likely are you to use public transportation?" Surveys are less useful in obtaining the answers to *why* questions. In an interview, for instance, you can ask, "Why did you vote the way you did in the last election?" and expect to get a reasonably well-thought-out response (see p. 190 to learn about interviews). In contrast, survey respondents seldom write lengthy answers to questions.

Conducting an effective survey usually involves the following activities.

Decide whether to conduct a survey. Your decision about whether to conduct a survey should be based on the role it will play in your essay, the amount of work required to do a good job, and the kind of information you are seeking. Surveys are useful if you want to collect evidence to support your assertion that a problem exists, or if you want to learn about the attitudes and behaviors of a large group of people (more than five or ten). If you simply want opinions from a handful of people, you can gain that information more efficiently by interviewing or corresponding with them.

Decide whom to survey. Most surveys collect information from selected members of a particular group to estimate the beliefs, attitudes, or behaviors of the group as a whole. For example, surveys completed by a hundred students might be used as evidence about the beliefs, attitudes, and behaviors of all students at a school. Similarly, "national" polls seldom survey more than a thousand people, yet they are used to provide an indication of the opinions of everyone in the country.

To select participants, you can choose people from your target group at random. For example, if you are interested in surveying students at your college or university, you could open your school's telephone directory and pick every twentieth name. Or you can stratify your sample. For example, you could randomly select a specific number of first-year, second-year, third-year, and fourth-year students — and then make sure that the number of men and women in each group is proportional to enrollment.

Decide what to ask and how to ask it. Designing effective surveys can be challenging. A survey item, such as a multiple-choice question or a true/false statement, that seems perfectly clear to you might confuse someone else. To identify confusing items, ask a few classmates, friends, or family members to try out your survey. Ask them what they think about each survey item. Then rewrite any items that caused confusion, and test the survey again. Doing so will help you improve the clarity of your survey.

Understanding the strengths and weaknesses of the kinds of items that are frequently used in surveys is a good way to get started.

- **Yes/no items** divide respondents into two groups.

    Example: Do you check your Facebook news feed more than once a day?   ☐ Yes   ☐ No

- **True/false items** deal more often with attitudes or beliefs than with behaviors or events.

Example: People who have a Facebook account are in better touch with their closest friends than are people who don't have Facebook accounts.   □ True   □ False

- **Ranking items** forces respondents to place items along a continuum.

  Example: Rank the following social-networking sites from best to worst using the numbers 1 (best) through 4 (worst):

  ___ Facebook

  ___ Google+

  ___ Twitter

  ___ Tumblr

- **Likert-scale items** measure respondents' levels of agreement with a statement, their assessments of the importance of something, or how frequently they engage in a behavior.

  Example: If you have a Facebook account, how often do you check it?

Never	Once a month	Once a week	Every day	Several times each day
□	□	□	□	□

- **Multiple-choice items** indicate whether a respondent knows something or engages in specific behaviors. Because they seldom include every possible answer, be careful when including them.

  Example: I use the following tools on social-networking sites:

  ___ Blogs

  ___ Messaging

  ___ Friends

  ___ "Walls"

  ___ Organization pages

  ___ Applications

- **Short-answer items** allow greater freedom of response, but they can be difficult to tabulate.

  Example: What do you like best about social-networking sites?

Conduct your survey. The large number of surveys people are asked to complete has reduced the public's willingness to respond to them. In fact, a "good" response rate for a survey is 60 percent. The following guidelines can help increase your response rate:

In Process

Developing a Survey

Jennie Tillson created a brief survey to learn what students at her university had considered when they were applying for college. She kept it brief so that more students would respond. She collected eighty-seven responses to the survey.

1. Which do you personally consider the most important factor when choosing a college? (Please check one.)

    ____ Academic ranking

    ____ Athletic programs

    ____ Tuition cost

    ____ Geographic location

    Comment:

> A multiple-choice question asks respondents to pick one answer.

> Room is provided for brief comments.

2. When you applied to college, which kinds of schools did you consider attending? (Check all that apply.)

    ____ Four-year private university

    ____ Four-year public university

    ____ Community college

    ____ Trade school

    ____ Other: _____

    Comment:

> A multiple-choice question asks respondents to pick multiple answers.

3. If you knew that a sibling or friend was concerned about being able to afford college, how likely would you be to recommend that they think about community college? (Please check one.)

    ____ Very likely

    ____ Somewhat likely

    ____ Neither likely nor unlikely

    ____ Somewhat unlikely

    ____ Not at all likely

    Comment:

> A Likert-scale question asks students to indicate the likelihood that they would recommend community college.

- Keep your survey short, preferably no longer than a single page.

- Make sure your survey is easy to read. Don't crowd the questions onto the page or jam questions into an e-mail message.

- Explain the purpose of your survey in a brief statement. If you are handing out your survey in person or during a class, provide a brief statement on the first page. If you are distributing the survey via e-mail or the Web, include a brief statement in the message or at the top of the Web page. A clear explanation can increase a respondent's willingness to complete the survey.

- Treat survey respondents with respect. If you are mailing your survey, address the envelopes by hand and use a cover letter to explain the survey.

- Make the survey easy to return. If you mail the survey, include a stamped, self-addressed envelope. If you are conducting your survey on the Web or via e-mail, provide directions for returning completed surveys.

Analyze your results. It's usually best to tabulate survey responses using a spreadsheet or statistics program. These kinds of programs provide flexibility when you want to analyze your results. For example, they offer statistical tests that allow you to look for differences between groups of respondents in the average rating given to a survey item. (You can learn about these tests through the program's online help.) If you prefer, you can also organize the results in a table in a word-processing program.

If you conduct a survey and use its results in your essay, include a copy of your survey questions in an appendix.

Develop a Solution

Once you've identified a promising problem and learned about it, you can begin to develop a solution to the problem. If your problem has already attracted the attention of other writers, the solution you choose might be one that another writer has already advanced, or it might be an improved version of someone else's proposed solution. If the problem has remained unresolved for some time, however, you might find it best to develop a new solution. If your problem is relatively new or is one that has not yet attracted the attention of other writers, you might develop your own solution to the problem, or you might look at how similar problems have been addressed and then adapt one of those solutions.

Whatever approach you take, remember that a clear problem definition is the single most important element in a problem-solving essay. Without it, even the most elegant solution won't be convincing. A problem definition enables you to take a problem apart, examine its causes and effects, and understand whom or what it affects. It also influences how your readers understand the problem and how they are likely to react to your solution.

In addition, remember that a solution must be practical. Few readers will be impressed by a solution that costs too much or takes too long to put into effect or that causes even more problems than it solves. As you consider potential solutions to your problem, carefully assess their feasibility and potential consequences.

DEFINE THE PROBLEM

Some people define a problem with a particular solution in mind. As a result, their solution usually looks good in theory. But a solution based on a weak problem definition seldom works well in practice, and it is unlikely to convince your readers. For this and other reasons, you should define your problem as clearly and accurately as possible.

You can define your problem by exploring situation and effects, focusing on actions, examining severity and duration, and considering goals and barriers.

Situation/effects. Explore the effects a problematic situation has on people or things. Ask yourself:

- What is the situation?

- What are its effects?

- Who or what is affected?

Agent/goals/actions/results. Focus on actions that have unwanted results. Ask yourself:

- Who or what is the *agent* (the person, group, or thing that acts in a manner that causes a problem)?

- What are the agent's *goals*?

- What *actions* does the agent carry out to accomplish the goals?

- What are the *results* of the agent's actions?

Severity and duration. Analyze the severity and duration of the effects of a problematic situation. Ask yourself:

- What is the situation?

- What effects are associated with the situation?

- How severe are the effects?

- What is the duration of the effects?

Goals and barriers. Identify goals, and ask what obstacles stand in the way of accomplishing them. Ask yourself:

- What are the goals?
- What barriers stand in the way of accomplishing the goals?

In Process

Defining a Problem

Jennie Tillson used the situation/effects questions (p. 354) to develop her problem definition by identifying the problematic situation and examining its effects on specific groups of people.

> **What is the situation?** Over the last ten years, tuition at two-year colleges has risen by 53% and at four-year colleges by 85% (see Quinn). This increase has been paralleled by a comparable increase in family earning for middle- and upper-income Americans, but the cost has risen sharply for poor families (Quinn). Although the availability of financial aid has increased (College Board, cited in Quinn), more aid is coming as loans rather than as grants. And more aid is being given for merit rather than for financial need (College Board, cited in Quinn).
>
> **What are the effects?** Some students have delayed or given up on a college education. Some have not been able to enroll at their first- or second-choice college or university, a problem that can affect the quality of education they receive. Some are working full-time as they take classes. Some students are graduating with a higher level of debt than classmates from wealthier families. Some colleges and universities have kept tuition lower by increasing class size, offering fewer classes, and hiring adjunct faculty rather than full-time faculty.
>
> **Who is affected?** Poorer students and their families are affected directly. Indirectly, all Americans are affected because, as it gets harder to attend college, the gap between rich and poor will grow, and higher education will become segregated by income class (see Nyhan).

Because Jennie was trying to approach the problem of increasing tuition as a situation that affected all Americans, the situation/effects questions worked well for her. If she had been trying to identify the causes of the problem, she might have used the agent/goals/actions/results questions. If she had been interested in assessing how serious the problem is and its long-term impact, she might have used the questions that address severity and duration.

Most of these methods of defining a problem focus on cause/effect relationships, and many involve unintended consequences. However, each one allows you to view a problem from a different perspective. Because your problem definition has powerful effects on the development of a solution to your problem, it can be useful to experiment with different ways of defining the problem.

CONSIDER POTENTIAL SOLUTIONS

Use your problem definition to weigh potential solutions. If your problem definition focuses on the causes of the problem or barriers to achieving a goal, for example, consider solutions that address those causes or barriers. If your problem definition focuses on actions that have had unexpected or undesired effects, explore solutions that might address those effects. If your problem definition focuses on the duration and severity of a problem, ask yourself how the duration and severity of the problem might be reduced, or perhaps even eliminated.

As you generate ideas for possible solutions, keep in mind what you've learned about your problem. If you're dealing with a problem that other writers have addressed, pay attention to the solutions they've proposed. Even if those solutions have failed to solve the problem — which is likely, given the continuing existence of the problem — they might have helped address at least some of its effects. Consider the impact of these earlier solutions, weigh their negative consequences, and ask whether you might adapt them — or parts of them — for your own use.

In your writer's notebook, create a list of potential solutions — both your own and those of other writers — and briefly describe them. Evaluate each solution by answering the following questions:

- How well does this solution address the causes of the problem?
- How well does this solution address the effects of the problem?
- To what extent does this solution address the needs of the people or things affected by the problem?
- What costs would be associated with this solution?
- What advantages does this solution have over other solutions?
- What disadvantages does this solution have?

Review your responses to the questions, and identify your most promising solutions. If you've identified more than one solution, ask whether the best features of each might be combined into a single solution. As you consider each solution, you'll gain a better understanding of the problem itself. Your problem-solving essay will be most effective if you clearly connect your solution to your problem definition, so you might find it useful to revise your definition to reflect the additional thinking you've put into the problem. Remember that your problem definition isn't set in stone. It can be revised and improved throughout the process of writing your essay.

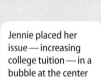

In Process

Developing a Solution

To begin solving the problem she had defined, Jennie Tillson created a cluster map. Jennie used the situation/effects questions on page 354 to explore causes, effects, and potential solutions to the problem of rising college tuition.

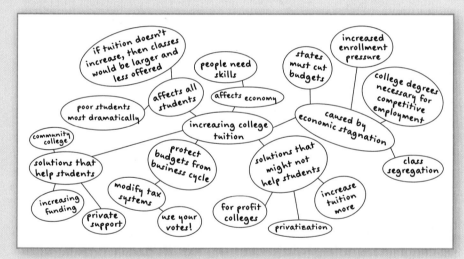

Jennie placed her issue — increasing college tuition — in a bubble at the center of her cluster.

Each cause, effect, and solution generated more specific ideas.

Jennie's cluster map helped her lay out potential solutions for students from poor and working-class families. With that in mind, she used freewriting to generate ideas that might solve that aspect of the problem.

> The most viable option might be voting. People can vote for tax reform to make it easier for kids from poor families to attend college. People can vote to increase funding for higher ed. They can vote to set up rainy-day funds for colleges. They can make colleges set aside money for hard times. These things can help lower the real cost of college tuition, even if tuition still continues to rise.

ASSESS THE PRACTICALITY OF YOUR SOLUTION

Most problems can be solved given unlimited time, vast sums of money, revisions to the laws of physics, or changes in human nature. If your solution requires any or all of these, however, your readers are likely to question its practicality. Before you start drafting your essay, ensure that your solution is feasible by asking whether your solution can be implemented

- in a reasonable amount of time
- with available funding
- with available resources
- given current knowledge and technology
- without causing additional problems

Consider as well how your readers' needs, interests, and backgrounds will affect their responses to your solution. For example, if your readers have strong religious beliefs about the use of birth control, they probably won't react favorably to a proposal to reduce teenage pregnancies by requiring public schools to dispense contraceptives.

Finally, consider potential objections to your solution. If your solution requires funding or resources that might be used for other purposes, for example, ask whether readers will object to reducing funding for those purposes. If you think that your readers will not accept the trade-offs associated with your solution, take another look at it. You might be able to modify your solution to account for likely objections, or you might want to prepare an argument about why the trade-offs are better than just leaving things as they are.

Prepare a Draft

As you get ready to draft your essay, review your problem definition, the solutions you've examined, and your notes on your proposed solution. You'll need to decide how to explain the problem, present your solution, and convince readers that your solution is worth pursuing. You'll also want to consider the role of document design in your essay, how you'll organize your ideas, and how you'll frame your introduction and conclusion.

EXPLAIN THE PROBLEM

Your problem definition is the single most important element of your problem-solving essay. It sets up your solution and shapes your thesis statement. It also affects your choice of sources and evidence to support the points you make in your essay. As is the case with so many aspects of writing, however, you should pay attention not only to the content of your problem definition but also to how you present it to readers.

For example, consider how a reader might react to the statement "Teachers are the reason education is in trouble." Which of the following thoughts flashed through your mind?

- Teachers are lazy.

- Teachers are poorly prepared.

- Teachers are spreading left-wing propaganda and infecting the minds of our youth.

- Teachers are extraordinarily boring.

- Good teachers are quitting to become stockbrokers or advertising executives.

All of the above? None of the above? Now substitute "students" or "parents" or "politicians" or "television" or "video games" in the same statement. What flashes through your mind?

Statements like these are unclear because they don't define the problem. They don't explain, for example, what it is about teachers that causes education to be in trouble.

Consider the differences between "Teachers are the reason education is in trouble" and the following problem definitions.

Problem definition 1: The lack of certified science teachers in public schools has limited the development of a general understanding of key scientific concepts among Americans. Without that understanding, it will be difficult to carry out informed debates about policies that rely on an understanding of scientific concepts, such as the development of a hydrogen economy or decisions about how we deal with the causes of global climate change.

Problem definition 2: The relatively low salaries offered to beginning teachers, combined with the growing cost of higher education and the high debt burden incurred by many college graduates, have reduced the attractiveness of pursuing a career as an educator. The result is a growing shortage of qualified teachers in key areas, such as the sciences, mathematics, and the arts. Because of this shortage, students are not receiving the education they deserve.

Each of these problem definitions calls attention to the effects of a particular situation on specific groups or individuals. In the first example, the situation — a lack of certified science teachers — affects Americans' ability to understand and participate in debates about scientific issues. In the second example, the economic situation faced by beginning teachers affects college students' willingness to pursue careers as teachers, which in turn affects the education of students. Through their clarity and detail, both of these problem definitions offer significant advantages over "Teachers are the reason education is in trouble."

As you consider how best to explain your problem definition to your readers, reflect on what they already know about it. If they are already familiar with the problem, you might be able to convey your problem definition in one or two sentences that frame the solution that will follow. If they are unfamiliar with the problem, however, you might need to devote a significant portion of your essay to establishing the existence of the problem and explaining its consequences.

PROPOSE YOUR SOLUTION

Most problem-solving essays frame the problem in a way that prepares readers to accept the proposed solution. The problem of skyrocketing fuel prices, for example, might be framed so that the best solution would seem to involve the development of new technologies, while the problem of a growing national debt might be framed so that the best solution would appear to rely on changes in tax laws.

After you introduce a problem to your readers, you can present a thesis statement that summarizes your proposed solution. Your thesis statement should be closely tied to your problem definition, and it should suggest a logical and reasonable means of addressing the problem. Because your thesis statement will frame readers' understanding of your solution in a certain way, it serves as a powerful tool for influencing your readers. Consider the differences among the following thesis statements addressing the problem of low salaries for teachers who leave college with high levels of debt:

> **Thesis statement 1:** If we are to ensure an adequate supply of qualified teachers, we must increase their starting salaries.
>
> **Thesis statement 2:** The most promising approach to ensuring an adequate supply of qualified teachers is paying the tuition and fees for college students who promise to spend at least five years teaching in our public schools.
>
> **Thesis statement 3:** A public-private partnership designed to identify and support promising new teachers is the key to ensuring an adequate supply of qualified teachers in our public schools.

Each of these thesis statements calls attention to a different solution to the problem. The first focuses on salaries, suggesting that the promise of higher salaries will lead more students to consider a career in teaching and perhaps will encourage those who do become teachers to stay in the profession. The second thesis statement focuses on the cost of attending college, borrowing an approach used successfully to attract new doctors to rural parts of the country. The third focuses on recruiting students into the teaching profession. Each thesis statement offers a reasonable solution to the problem as it has been defined, yet each would also lead the writer to produce a significantly different essay.

Is your thesis statement focused enough? See Chapter 14 for help.

EXPLAIN YOUR SOLUTION

Your solution is what most readers will remember about your essay. Once you've defined the problem and proposed your solution, explain your solution by going into detail, offering support for your ideas, and considering your solution in light of promising alternatives.

Go into detail. A surprising number of problem-solving essays spend several pages defining and discussing the consequences of a problem, only to offer a skimpy discussion of a proposed solution. However, readers are rarely satisfied by such an approach, so be sure to spend some time identifying the key aspects of your solution. Help your readers understand, in detail, how you would implement the solution, how much it would cost to put into effect, what kinds of effects the solution would have on the problem, and how you would judge its effectiveness in addressing the problem.

Provide support for your points. Most problem-solving essays rely heavily on evidence to establish the existence of a problem, support a proposed solution, and dismiss alternative solutions. Your solution should offer a reasonable and thoughtful response to the problem, and it should be clear that your proposed solution is superior to alternatives.

You can use evidence to

- identify and frame your solution
- provide examples and illustrations
- illustrate processes that might be required to put the solution into place
- associate particular ideas and concepts with authorities, such as political leaders, subject-matter experts, or people who have been affected by the problem

To develop support, list the key points you are making about your proposed solution. For each point, review your sources and notes to identify relevant evidence, and then list the evidence below each point. If your sources support your solution, draw on evidence from them to show your readers why your solution is likely to be effective. If your sources do not directly address your solution, consider using personal experience. You can read more about how to use evidence to support your points in Chapter 14.

Address promising alternative solutions. As you draft your problem-solving essay, be sure to consider alternative solutions that are likely to occur to your readers. In proposing a solution to a problem, you are essentially making an argument that your solution is preferable to others. If your readers can think of alternatives, especially alternatives that might be less expensive or more effective than yours, they might wonder why you haven't mentioned them.

To address (and dismiss) alternative solutions, you can do the following:

- Identify the strongest alternative solution, explain why it's the best of several alternatives, and then explain why your solution is better.

In Process

Providing Support for Key Points

Jennie Tillson identified support for her key points by listing each point, reviewing her notes to locate sources that would support her points, and listing the relevant sources next to each point.

Key Points	Support
College tuition is increasing.	Quinn
Tuition costs are hitting low-income students and families hardest, discouraging talented students from attending college.	Quinn, Lewin
We're all affected by this. It will cause a greater gap between rich and poor.	Nyhan
Change must begin with colleges and universities.	Clark, Lewin
Government must also play a role.	Quinn, Clark, Lewin
Students and their families must also play a role.	Young, my survey

- Identify a group of alternative solutions that share the same weakness, such as high cost or impracticality, and explain why this group of solutions is weaker than your solution.

- Identify a group of promising alternatives, and dismiss each solution, one after the other.

You can gain insights into effective strategies for organizing your response to alternative solutions by reading about organizing patterns in Chapter 15.

CONSIDER GENRE AND DESIGN

Depending on the complexity of the problem you're addressing and the nature of the solution you propose, design can contribute greatly to the overall effectiveness of your essay. As is the case with other academic essays, you'll need to consider the expectations of your readers about design elements such as wide margins, double-spaced lines, page numbers, and a readable body font. But you can also use page layout elements as well as color, shading, borders, and rules to enhance the effectiveness of your essay.

- **Page layout elements**, such as marginal glosses, pull quotes, and headings and subheadings, can draw readers' attention to key points in your essay. For example, a pull quote — a passage of text set off from the body of your essay using borders or white space — can highlight an important idea. Similarly, headings and subheadings can help readers understand at a glance the main idea of a section in your essay.

- **Color, shading, borders, and rules** can be used to call attention to key information and ideas in your essay. For instance, you might use a shaded box to present a dramatic example or related information that doesn't fit well within the body of your essay, or you might use a contrasting color to draw the reader's eye to an important passage.

Other design elements — such as illustrations and captions, tables and figures, and bulleted and numbered lists — can also contribute to the effectiveness of your essay. As you consider how best to connect with your readers, reflect on which design strategies will help you accomplish your purpose. Chapters 16, 17, and 18 provide a detailed discussion of document design principles and elements.

FRAME YOUR ESSAY

Once you've worked out how to define the problem and present your proposed solution, decide how you'll organize, introduce, and conclude your essay.

Organization. Most problem-solving essays start with an introduction, then define the problem and explain the proposed solution, and finish with a conclusion. Longer problem-solving essays often make use of the organizing patterns discussed in Chapter 15. For instance, process explanation can offer a helpful outline for explaining the steps involved in implementing a solution. The costs/benefits and strengths/weaknesses patterns provide a practical structure for both analyzing a problem and examining a solution's potential. And problem-solving essays that address several alternative solutions often take advantage of the comparison/contrast pattern.

Introduction. Your introduction creates a framework within which you can present your thesis statement and prepare your readers to understand how you've defined your problem. You can draw on a number of strategies to draw your readers in:

- Use an anecdote (a brief story) to personalize the problem.

- Use dramatic statistics, as Jennie Tillson does in her essay, to illustrate the scope of the problem.

- Use quotations from experts, or from people who have been affected by a problem, to make the problem hit home with your readers.

- Draw comparisons between this problem and other, more widely understood problems.

You can read more about strategies for introducing your essay in Chapter 16.

Conclusion. In much the same way that you can use your introduction to direct readers toward a particular understanding of a problem, you can use your conclusion to encourage them to accept your ideas for solving it. Most problem-solving essays end with a call to action, in which the writer urges readers to do something specific to help put the solution into effect. Other strategies you can employ to conclude your essay include summarizing your problem definition and proposed solution, circling back to the introduction, and speculating about the future. You can learn more about framing your conclusion in Chapter 16.

Review and Improve Your Draft

The success of your problem-solving essay rests heavily on how well you can define your problem, present your solution, convince readers that your solution is feasible, and consider alternatives and potential objections to your solution. Few writers can manage all these tasks in a first draft, so keep them in mind as you assess your draft and revise your essay.

REASSESS YOUR PROBLEM DEFINITION

Now that your essay is in draft form, consider how well you present your problem definition and how effectively it leads to your proposed solution. Your problem definition should direct your readers' attention to the problem in a particular way. If not, they'll find it difficult to understand how your definition of the problem is related to your proposed solution. As you draft your essay — and spend additional time thinking about the problem — you will almost certainly deepen your understanding of the problem. Take a few moments now to ask whether your problem definition fully reflects that understanding.

Then ask some harder questions: Have you defined your problem in the best way (with *best* defined in light of the solution you've proposed and the needs, interests, and backgrounds of your readers)? Will your readers accept the problem definition you've developed? If you suspect that they'll object to it or find it inadequate, how can you change it to address their likely concerns?

REVIEW THE PRESENTATION OF YOUR SOLUTION

When you're in the midst of drafting, it's normal to spend more time on some aspects of your solution than others or to overlook key steps that will be required to put the solution into effect. As you review your draft, take a careful look at how you've presented your solution. Have you explained it logically and clearly? Have you provided your readers with a sufficiently detailed understanding of what the solution involves and how it could work? Have you presented sufficient evidence to support your points?

CHECK THE FEASIBILITY OF YOUR SOLUTION

When you're caught up in the details of presenting a solution, it's easy to lose sight of whether the solution will actually work. During your review, ask whether the solution you've proposed can be put into practice given the time, funding, and resources that are available. If you suspect that you've proposed a solution that might not be cost-effective — such as solving the problem of rising tuition costs by giving everyone who wants to attend college a $100,000 scholarship, a solution that would cost taxpayers roughly $1.8 trillion — reconsider your solution. Similarly, if the time and resources necessary to achieve a solution are simply not available, take another look at your options.

CONSIDER OBJECTIONS AND ALTERNATIVE SOLUTIONS

Put yourself in the position of your readers, and ask some hard questions. Why is this solution better than another? What are the major drawbacks of your proposed solution? Under what conditions would your solution be likely to fail? Identify the

Peer Review: Improve Your Problem-Solving Essay

One of the biggest challenges writers face is reading a draft of their own work as a reader rather than as the writer. Because you know what you're trying to say, you find it easy to understand your draft. To determine what you should do to revise your draft, ask a friend or classmate to read your essay and to assess how well you have adopted the role of problem solver (see p. 328) by answering the following questions.

Purpose	1. Is my problem definition sufficiently narrow and focused? Is it clear and easy to understand?
	2. Do you believe the problem is significant? Why or why not?
	3. Is my solution clearly presented? Does it seem like a reasonable response to the problem I've defined?
Readers	4. Were you aware of the problem before you read the essay? Are other readers likely to be familiar with it? Do I need to say more about it to help readers understand?
	5. Are you convinced that my solution can work? Does it seem feasible? Why or why not?
	6. Have I presented ideas fairly? Are you aware of any potential objections or alternative solutions that I should have addressed?
Sources	7. Does the evidence I've offered to define the problem and support my proposed solution make sense? Can I add or clarify anything to help you understand the problem and solution better? Do you think any of the evidence is unnecessary?
	8. Do my sources strike you as reliable and appropriate? Does any of the evidence I've used seem questionable?
Context	9. Have I taken my readers' knowledge, assumptions, and values into consideration?
	10. Would any of the information I've drawn on in this essay be better presented in visual form? Could I make changes in page layout, color, shading, or rules to improve the essay's appearance?

For each of the points listed above, ask your reviewers to provide concrete advice about what you should do to improve your draft. It can help if you ask them to adopt the role of an editor—someone who is working with you to improve your draft. You can read more about peer review in Chapter 4.

objections your readers might have to your solution, and address them in your essay. Look as well for challenges to your solution that your readers might not consider but that you've become aware of in the course of your reading. Then address each challenge, explaining clearly why your solution is preferable to the alternatives you've identified.

★ Student Essay

Jennie Tillson, "Death, Taxes, and College Tuition"

The following problem-solving essay was written by featured writer Jennie Tillson. Follow Jennie's efforts to write her essay by visiting **bedfordstmartins.com/conversation**. You can read excerpts of interviews in which she discusses her work on her essay, read the assignment, and read drafts of her essay.

TILLSON 1

Jennie Tillson

Professor Palmquist

March 3, 2013

COCC150 College Composition

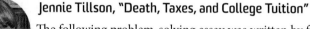

Death, Taxes, and College Tuition

"In this world nothing can be said to be certain, except death and taxes."

— *Benjamin Franklin, in a letter to Jean-Baptiste Leroy,*

November 13, 1789

Please add one more item to that list, Mr. Franklin: higher college tuition. Each year, college tuition increases as surely as winter follows fall and spring follows winter. According to noted economic adviser Jane Bryant Quinn, over the past decade, tuition at two-year colleges has increased by 53% and at four-year colleges by 85%, more than double the rate of inflation. For the millions of

> Information about the writer, class, and submission date is formatted according to MLA guidelines.

> Following MLA guidelines, the title is centered.

> The writer provides a quotation to frame the issue.

> The writer plays off the opening quotation, explaining its relevance to readers.

TILLSON   2

Americans attempting to survive in an intensely competitive job market, a college

degree can be a necessity. However, few students can ignore rising college tuition,

and fewer still can afford to pay for college without draining family income or

taking on enormous debt. Especially for students from low-income families,

attending college may become an unreachable goal—not for academic reasons,

but for financial ones. College administrations, government agencies, and

students and their families all need to take action to address the rising costs of

college tuition. No one group can solve this problem alone; the crisis has grown

to the point where all involved must contribute and sacrifice in order to make

college more accessible for tomorrow's students.

> The writer uses a situation/effects problem definition to help readers understand the issue.

> The writer provides an overview of the solution she'll present in detail later in the essay.

During today's recession, many families are dealing with tight budgets and lost

jobs, which can make paying for college difficult—if not impossible. This crisis

affects students from lower-income families the most. While the cost of college as a

percentage of family income remained fairly stable for students from upper-income

and middle-income families over the course of a decade, the cost has risen sharply

for lower-income families (Quinn). In 1999, the cost of sending a child to a public

university was about 39% of a poor family's income. By 2008, that cost had

increased to 55% (Lewin). While more and more middle-class college applicants are

turning to loans to finance their education, going into debt is not always an option

for low-income families (Lewin). More important, those students who receive

federally funded Pell grants (which cover roughly 39% of a public four-year

education for low-income students) are facing lower admission rates when compared

to more well-off and out-of-state students who pay higher tuition (Quinn). Added

together, these factors can discourage or even prevent many talented students

from attending college just because they and their families can't afford it.

> The writer makes a key point about the impact of a difficult financial situation on families.

> An online source without page or paragraph numbers is cited by author only.

> The writer offers an overall assessment of the situation, based on information drawn from sources.

This situation affects all of us. As it becomes increasingly difficult for poor

and working-class Americans to attend college, the gap between rich and poor

will continue to grow, and American higher education will once again become

segregated—this time by income class (Armario). As Education Secretary Arne

Duncan explains, "If the costs of [college tuition] keep on rising, especially at a

> The writer makes a second key point.

> The source of a quotation is named in an attribution.

TILLSON 3

time when family incomes are hurting, college will become increasingly unaffordable for the middle class" (qtd. in Armario). A college education offers the clearest path out of poverty, adding tremendously to graduates' expected income. As a smaller and smaller proportion of students from low-income families enroll in colleges and universities, however, fewer will be able to take that path. For the nation as a whole, this means that fewer bright and capable citizens will reach their full potential, and the contributions they would otherwise have made to society will be lost.

The writer indicates that the quotation appeared in another source.

Information from a source is paraphrased.

Change must begin with the colleges and universities. A recent report by the College Board concluded that financial aid budgets did not increase with tuition, leaving students to make up the difference (Clark). Some of the biggest increases in college spending are surprisingly not in the area of classroom education, but instead in administration, support services, and maintenance. Vennie Gore, an assistant vice president at Michigan State University, says that facilities updates are necessary to remain attractive to students. Schools like his "have to raise dorm costs to fund repairs, update older dorms, and build new residence halls that meet today's student's expectations for technology, privacy, and space" (Clark). While this is true, colleges must find ways to fund these new programs without affecting the quality of classroom education that students receive, or enrollment may suffer. In order to keep quality education in place, colleges will need to spend money strategically in ways that are most effective for the success of all students, regardless of family income.

The solution is introduced. The writer focuses first on the role that will be played by colleges and universities.

One way colleges should use tuition money to benefit students is by redesigning their financial aid systems. Although colleges have reportedly increased their need-based financial aid, most of these precious funds go to boost tuition aid for middle-class students. Tamar Lewin from the *New York Times* writes, "Student borrowing has more than doubled in the last decade, and students from lower-income families, on average, get smaller grants from the colleges they attend than students from more affluent families." Basing more award decisions on financial need instead of merit would allow more students from lower-income families to attend college. As hard economic times continue to affect family finances, some

The writer argues that financial aid systems must be revamped.

TILLSON   4

colleges are even offering emergency aid and loans, particularly in cases where

parents have lost jobs. More colleges must take similar steps to ensure that students

from all economic backgrounds have a fighting chance at affording an education.

However, many state colleges and universities cannot begin to make significant

changes to help the student population without support and funding from the

government. State and federal governments must play a large role in ensuring

college affordability, especially during the economic downturn. Solutions to the

problem of increasing tuition costs are likely to be effective only if they address its

root economic causes. Quinn, among others, has recognized that tuition is rising at

public institutions, which educate roughly 80% of all American college students. This

is in large part because state and federal funding for higher education has not kept

pace with costs (Quinn). In the last ten years, a majority of states have actually cut

funding for higher education, while most of the remaining states have either held

funding steady (which amounts to a cut, given inflation) or raised funding only by

modest amounts (Quinn). Over the past year alone, after accounting for inflation

and financial aid, students faced a 4.6% increase in costs to attend a public

university (Clark). And in the coming year, many worry that state budgets will

require further tuition increases. Unless this trend changes, which appears unlikely

in the current economic climate, public higher education institutions will continue

to cover their costs by raising tuition and fees.

Instead of cutting education funding, states should provide more money for

schools, especially now when jobs are scarce and even trained workers are eager

to return to school. Patrick Callan, president of the National Center for Public

Policy and Higher Education, said:

> When the economy is good, and state universities are somewhat better
>
> funded, we raise tuition as little as possible. When the economy is bad, we
>
> raise tuition and sock it to families, when people can least afford it. That's
>
> exactly the opposite of what we need. (qtd. in Lewin)

Only by investing in educating their citizens during hard economic times will

states see the benefits of having educated workers and business owners — and

Marginal annotations:

The writer argues that government must also play a role in the solution.

The writer speculates about what will happen if the government does not get involved in solving the problem.

The writer argues that states should add to their higher education funding.

A block quotation is used for a longer quotation.

TILLSON   5

higher-earning taxpayers—in the state during better times. For this reason, higher education should be a top priority in even trimmed-down state budgets so that students and their families won't face drastic increases in tuition.

At the same time, students still ultimately bear the responsibility for finding the best path to an affordable college education. Students and their families are a necessary part of the solution. They should be willing to apply to a variety of schools, including those they can afford more easily without financial aid. Many students and their families are now considering less expensive routes to a college degree, such as enrolling in public universities or community colleges in their home states (Saleh). Out of eighty-seven college freshmen surveyed at Colorado State University, 80% were likely to recommend community college to a sibling or friend concerned about tuition costs (Tillson). When asked about the benefits of attending community college, students responded that they saw it as "easier to afford" and appreciated that it "makes it easier to work and attend school at the same time" (see fig. 1). The survey shows that students today are giving community colleges serious thought as an alternative to a four-year university.

Although community colleges are in no way immune to the funding problems that four-year public institutions face, they are still much less expensive. While

■ Easier to afford	33%
■ Easier to work & attend school	32%
☐ Smaller class sizes	21%
■ Career-oriented courses	14%

Fig. 1: The perceived benefits of choosing a community college.
Based on survey data from Tillson.

The writer presents the third part of the solution: the role of students and their families.

The writer presents findings from a survey that she conducted on her campus.

Statistics and partial quotations are drawn from the survey.

A pie chart provides an effective visual presentation of information. The chart is captioned, and the source is identified.

TILLSON 6

private universities averaged $33,000 per year in tuition and fees for 2010-2011, community colleges averaged around $3,200 (Clark). Students can pay for just the classes they take, rather than paying a lump sum for a semester, making it much less expensive to earn a college degree. In many cases, students can also transfer credits to a four-year college and continue on the path to a bachelor's degree—for much less money and less debt. Students hoping to minimize college expenses can also take advantage of Advanced Placement courses during high school and summer courses during college, cutting down on the number of semesters they pay full tuition. Using a combination of strategies will help students get the college education they want without the expense and debt they can't handle.

The rising price of higher education affects not only students and their families but the larger American society and economy as well. If we do not address the lack of access to higher education for the least affluent members of our society, we run the risk of creating a permanent gap between the poor and the wealthy, where even the best and brightest from poor and working-class families can't pursue the American dream. Our colleges, our students, and our government all must commit themselves to solving the problem of college tuition so that we protect the opportunities of all students to earn a college degree and a more financially secure life. Our future depends on it.

> The writer speculates about the future if steps are not taken to address the problem and argues that colleges, students, and government must all contribute to the solution she has proposed.

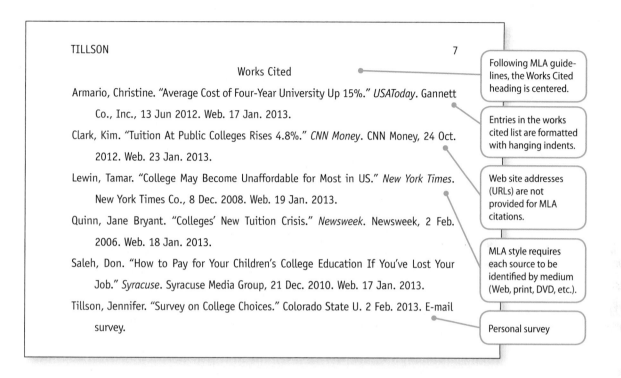

TILLSON   7

Works Cited

Armario, Christine. "Average Cost of Four-Year University Up 15%." *USAToday*. Gannett
    Co., Inc., 13 Jun 2012. Web. 17 Jan. 2013.

Clark, Kim. "Tuition At Public Colleges Rises 4.8%." *CNN Money*. CNN Money, 24 Oct.
    2012. Web. 23 Jan. 2013.

Lewin, Tamar. "College May Become Unaffordable for Most in US." *New York Times*.
    New York Times Co., 8 Dec. 2008. Web. 19 Jan. 2013.

Quinn, Jane Bryant. "Colleges' New Tuition Crisis." *Newsweek*. Newsweek, 2 Feb.
    2006. Web. 18 Jan. 2013.

Saleh, Don. "How to Pay for Your Children's College Education If You've Lost Your
    Job." *Syracuse*. Syracuse Media Group, 21 Dec. 2010. Web. 17 Jan. 2013.

Tillson, Jennifer. "Survey on College Choices." Colorado State U. 2 Feb. 2013. E-mail
    survey.

Following MLA guide-lines, the Works Cited heading is centered.

Entries in the works cited list are formatted with hanging indents.

Web site addresses (URLs) are not provided for MLA citations.

MLA style requires each source to be identified by medium (Web, print, DVD, etc.).

Personal survey

To see Jennie Tillson's survey questions, see page 352.

✳ Project Ideas

The following suggestions provide a means of focusing your work on a problem-solving essay or another type of problem-solving document.

Suggestions for Essays

1. DEFINE A PROBLEM AT YOUR SCHOOL

In a brief essay, define a problem at your college or university. Using one of the sets of problem-definition questions provided on page 354, describe the problem in as much detail as possible, and define its consequences if left unaddressed. Use a survey of affected students to collect information about the problem.

2. PROPOSE A SOLUTION TO A LOCAL PROBLEM

Identify and define a problem at your school or in your community, and then propose a solution. Collect information about the problem from published sources, such as a community newspaper, an alumni magazine, or local-area Web sites. Conduct research to locate other communities with a similar problem and find out how they've addressed it. If possible, interview or correspond with someone who knows about or has been affected by the problem. In your essay, discuss the potential consequences of the problem if left unaddressed, identify potential solutions to the problem, and argue for a particular solution.

3. IDENTIFY A CRITICAL PROBLEM IN YOUR MAJOR AREA OF STUDY

Define and discuss the potential consequences of a problem within your major area of study. Use one of the problem-definition question sets provided on pages 354–355 to define the problem. To support your discussion of the potential consequences of the problem, locate sources in scholarly journals and on Web sites sponsored by one or more of the discipline's professional organizations. If time permits, conduct a survey of professors who teach in the field. You can find lists of names through scholarly associations; ask your instructor or a librarian for help identifying them.

4. TRACE THE DEVELOPMENT OF A PROBLEM

Identify a problem that has not yet been solved, and trace its development. Discuss its causes, factors that contribute to its ongoing status as a problem, and factors that have worked against the creation of a successful solution. To support your discussion, locate published sources that have considered the problem. If you can, collect evidence firsthand through observation, surveys, or interviews. Although you are not required to offer a solution, consider using your conclusion to suggest directions that might be pursued to solve the problem.

5. EVALUATE PROPOSED SOLUTIONS TO A PROBLEM

Evaluate solutions that have been proposed to solve a problem. In your essay, briefly define the problem, and discuss the long-term consequences of the problem if left unsolved. Then identify general approaches that have been proposed to solve the problem. Choose at least two and no more than four proposed solutions to evaluate. Define your evaluation criteria (see p. 303), and discuss how well each of the proposed solutions measures up. In your conclusion, offer your assessment of whether the solution you've judged to be most likely to succeed will actually be implemented. To support your discussion, locate published sources that have addressed the problem.

Suggestions for Other Genres

6. DRAFT AND DESIGN A PROBLEM-SOLVING ARTICLE FOR A NEWSPAPER OR MAGAZINE

Begin working on your article by deciding whether you want to write about a particular problem or publish in a particular newspaper or magazine. If you want to write about a particular problem, search your library's databases for articles about the problem. This can help you identify newspapers and magazines that have published articles dealing with the problem. If you want to publish your article in a particular newspaper or magazine, read a few issues of the publication carefully to determine the kinds of problems it normally addresses. Once you've selected a target publication, analyze it to determine its writing conventions (such as level of formality and the manner in which sources are acknowledged) and design conventions.

As you learn about your problem and plan, organize, and design your article, keep in mind what you've learned about the articles you've read. Your article should reflect those writing and design conventions. In your article, define the problem you are addressing, argue for the importance of solving the problem, propose your solution, and consider and dismiss alternative solutions. You should support your argument with evidence from other sources, such as journal and magazine articles, newspaper articles, blogs, and Web sites. You can also interview an expert, such as a professor, or correspond with someone who has been affected by the problem.

7. WRITE A PROPOSAL TO SOLVE A PROBLEM

Locate a call for proposals (sometimes called a request for proposals) on an issue of interest to you, and write a proposal to solve a problem related to that issue. Your proposal should conform as much as possible to the formatting and content guidelines provided in the call for proposals. In your proposal, identify, define, and propose a solution for a specific problem. You should draw on published sources and interviews with experts to support your proposal. You should also provide a budget and an assessment plan. If you have questions about how best to complete the proposal, discuss them with your instructor.

8. PROPOSE A SOLUTION BY MAIL

Write a letter, a memo, or an e-mail message that proposes a solution to a problem. Your correspondence should be addressed to a person, a group, or an agency that has the capacity to solve the problem. To prepare your proposal, conduct research on the problem and on the person, group, or agency. Your letter, memo, or e-mail message should be no longer than 750 words. It should briefly define the problem, propose a solution, and explain why the person, group, or agency should take action to put the proposal into effect. If you have questions about how best to compose the letter, memo, or e-mail message, discuss them with your instructor.

9. WRITE A LETTER OF COMPLAINT

Write a letter that identifies and complains about a problem you've experienced with a product or service. Your letter should be addressed to a person, a group, or an agency that has the capacity to address the problem. To prepare your letter of complaint, conduct research on the problem and on the person, group, or agency. Your letter should be no longer than 1,000 words. It should clearly define the problem, explain why the recipient of the letter is in a position to address the problem, and explain how the complaint should be addressed. If you have questions about how best to compose the letter, discuss them with your instructor.

10. POST A PROBLEM-SOLVING ENTRY ON A BLOG

Identify a blog that is relevant to the problem you want to address and that allows contributions from readers, in the form of either a new entry or a response to an existing entry. Write an entry or a response that proposes a solution to the problem. To prepare your entry or response, conduct research on the problem and on the authors and readers of the blog. Your post should be no longer than 1,250 words. If you have questions about how best to compose your entry or response, discuss them with your instructor.

In Summary: Writing a Problem-Solving Essay

* **Find a conversation and listen in.**
  - Explore difficulties (p. 347).
  - Ask questions about promising subjects (p. 348).
  - Conduct a survey (p. 349).

* **Develop a solution.**
  - Define the problem (p. 354).
  - Consider potential solutions (p. 356).
  - Assess the practicality of your solution (p. 358).

* **Prepare a draft.**
  - Explain the problem (p. 358).
  - Propose your solution (p. 360).

  - Explain your solution (p. 361).
  - Consider genre and design (p. 363).
  - Frame your essay (p. 363).

* **Review and improve your draft.**
  - Reassess your problem definition (p. 365).
  - Review the presentation of your solution (p. 365).
  - Check the feasibility of your solution (p. 365).
  - Consider objections and alternative solutions (p. 365).

10

Writing to Convince or Persuade

> As an **advocate**, I write to convince or persuade my readers to see my perspective on a subject.

GENRES IN CONVERSATION

| Reflective Writing | Informative Writing | Analytical Writing | Evaluative Writing | Problem-Solving Writing | **Argumentative Writing** |

Faced with shrinking budgets, administrators in many school districts feel they must sacrifice the arts to ensure adequate funding for core educational programs. However, four high school juniors decided to push back after their school announced cuts to its music program. They hoped to persuade the school board that removing music from the curriculum would do more harm than good. With the assistance of their school librarian, the students found a wide range of argumentative documents to help build their case, including those shown here—a **professional article**, a **case history**, and a **brochure**. Notice how each genre makes a valuable contribution to this conversation.

e-Pages

You can view the full documents shown here and respond to questions about problem-solving genres at **bedforstmartins .com/conversation /epages.**

Professional Article ▶

This **professional article** from *American School Board Journal* aims to convince educators that the arts can—and should—be integrated into the core curriculum.

ASBJ SPECIAL REPORT: A RICH PICTURE

Arts at the Core

How six school districts integrate arts education into the curriculum

RUTH E. STERNBERG

The performing and visual arts challenge students to use reasoning skills—both concrete and abstract—to draw conclusions and formulate ideas. They encourage creativity and imagination, from concept to process to completion. And in districts both large and small across the United States, they enhance learning for students and adults alike, as these six programs demonstrate.

BEAUFORT COUNTY SCHOOL DISTRICT
WWW.BEAUFORT.K12.SC.US

Students at South Carolina's Beaufort Middle School are learning about cell structure from an artist who draws for scientific journals. The artist, Melba Cooper, is also their classroom teacher.

"She takes the lab notebooks and coaches [students] to employ artistic principles to make their drawings more accurate," says Kristy Smith, arts coordinator for the Beaufort County School District. "A cell or a riverbed or the texture of a flower—the kids love it. Some kids get the science concepts, but they are not excited about doing a lab. Yet they love drawing the lab."

Another class prepares for a complicated project by taking a drumming break, guided by Dianne Hemmings, a teacher who learned the art form in Nigeria. "It's not written; it's observation and responding," Smith says of Hemmings' project. "It's important to note eye contact and body lan-

guage, so you know when to come in and pull out. It teaches students how to follow directions."

Approaching subjects from various viewpoints is the mission of the district, which serves the fastest growing county in South Carolina. This affluent coastal community spends $5 million annually to support more than 100 specialists in art, music, dance, drama, band, and voice and in such high school specialties as ceramics, photography, painting, and welding.

Some activities are supported through partnerships with the South Carolina Arts Commission, state and National Endowments for the Humanities, and the federal Title V program, but the rest are paid for with local tax dollars. Visiting artists from the local community also donate their time, bringing with them expertise and real-world perspectives.

By integrating the arts throughout the curriculum, teachers have found new ways to assess student gains and losses beyond

the state's traditional testing system. Visiting artist/educators train teachers to use the arts as a measure of success in all core subjects. Each teacher has a "statistical studio"—also known as a data wall—that displays student progress along with visual art, writing, photographs, or videos.

"Teachers might give a pre- and posttest, and since they used the arts to teach the unit, the evidence might be the arts interaction activities on display," says Smith. "It could be about Shakespeare. Do they know the story lines and what Elizabethan language is? What do they know before I go too far?"

Beaufort County's success, Smith says, proves that the arts can be a valuable tool for all school districts.

"You're preparing them for the world," she says. "The core subjects are a given. We shouldn't even be having that conversation anymore. We should be talking about the next couple of centuries and how our students are going to be creative problem solvers. It's no longer about one set of skills."

CLEVELAND MUNICIPAL SCHOOL DISTRICT
WWW.CMSDNET.NET

Gloria Doering might have been embarrassed. Her fourth-graders entered the galleries at the Cleveland Museum of Art and headed straight for a Vincent Van Gogh

Case History ▶

This **case history** from the American Music Conference cites numerical data and real-world examples to counter claims that cutting music education saves money.

This table illustrates the relative value of a music performance teacher to a regular classroom teacher. In this case, the average student load of a 1.0 FTE teacher is 150 students, and the average student load of a music performance teacher is 200 – a common comparison. Numbers will, of course vary greatly from district to district. It is also important to realize that only part of a music performance teacher's load may be in band, choir and/or orchestra; and therefore, they may not actually be a 1.0 FTE in their area. Each teacher load must be carefully calculated or your figures will be inaccurate, potentially undermining the credibility of your analysis. (See the Music Participation Survey on the CD-ROM, file name: MuPartSurvey).

A Case History

The significance of this disparity is seen in this chart of a real-world case in FTE miscalculation.

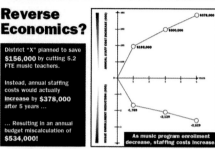

Reverse Economics?

District "X" planned to save **$156,000** by cutting 5.2 FTE music teachers.

Instead, annual staffing costs would actually increase by **$378,000** after 5 years ...

... Resulting in an annual budget miscalculation of **$534,000!**

As music program enrollment decrease, staffing costs increase.

In this district case study, the administration proposed the elimination of 5.2 FTE band and orchestra instructors to "save" $156,000.

There were 2529 students (grades 4-12) involved in those two programs. Cuts would have necessitated the elimination of nearly 1800 students the first year, requiring the addition of 6.4 FTE classroom teachers to replace the 5.2 FTE music performance teachers proposed for elimination.

In other words, instead of saving $156,000, they would have been required to spend $192,000 the first year on replacement teachers with lesser FTE value.

The problem gets worse.

Extensive national case studies indicate that the elimination of an elementary feeder system will cause a minimum 65% loss in student participation at the secondary level within two to four years. This is in part because no new elementary students will be started (in this case) until year three, and a similar amount of students will have been graduated. So by year five, the annual budget miscalculation would exceed $500,000.

Short-sighted thinking on the part of administrators and boards, as well as a failure to realize the high FTE value of music teachers, have led many districts into an unpleasant budget shock.

Music study is valuable and essential in educating well-rounded citizens, both for its intrinsic value and as a building-block of intelligence. It is also a financially efficient way to provide for our children's education. When a music program is threatened, the entire community is in danger of suffering a loss. Music advocates are our first line of defense.

WANT MORE INFO?

Dr. John L. Benham has been involved in school district crisis intervention since 1981. His diverse background includes roles as parent, music teacher, administrator, businessman and two-term member of a local school board. He, and those under his mentorship, have saved and restored over $72,000,000 in music programs that were targeted for cuts.

He is the author of *Music Advocacy: Moving From Survival to Vision*, co-published by the National Association for Music Education and Rowman & Littlefield (2011)

He is co-author of *The Georgia Project: A Status Profile on Arts Education in the State of Georgia*, available in electronic form directly from the author.

Dr. John L. Benham
John Benham & Associates LLC
Office: 763-767-1466
Mobile: 763-232-6018
Email: jbenham@save-music.org
Web: http://www.save-music.org

(13)

▲ Brochure

A **brochure** intended for parents uses large, appealing photographs, a colorful design, and a quotation from a student to highlight the academic benefits of music lessons.

What Is Writing to Convince or Persuade?

Some people love a good argument. Others go out of their way to avoid conflict. Regardless of where you stand, it's hard to deny the important role that debate and discussion play in our daily lives. Unfortunately, few of the arguments we encounter on a daily basis are well grounded and fully thought out. Whether you're listening to a talk show, reading the lunatic ravings of a misinformed blogger, or streaming a clever clip on YouTube about the issue of the day, it can be almost comically easy to pick out the flaws in a weak argument.

An effective argument, on the other hand, makes a well-supported, well-considered point about an issue in an attempt to convince or persuade readers. *Convincing* involves gaining readers' agreement that a position on an issue is reasonable and well founded. *Persuading* involves getting them to take action. One writer, for example, might seek to convince readers that the drinking age should be lowered to eighteen, while another might attempt to persuade teenagers to take a vow of sobriety.

Whether they attempt to convince or persuade, writers who make arguments adopt the role of *advocate*. An effective advocate considers not only the argument he or she will advance but also how best to formulate and express that argument for a particular audience. Although readers of arguments typically share the writer's assumption that an issue is important and are willing to consider new ideas, they bring their own values, beliefs, and experiences to the conversation. A writer who wants to change readers' minds or persuade them to act must give careful thought to who readers are and where they come from, what they value, how resistant or receptive they might be to an argument, and what kinds of argumentative strategies — such as appeals to logic, emotion, or authority — are most likely to sway them.

Sources of evidence used in argumentative documents include numerical data, reports of a writer's direct

The Writer's Role: Advocate

PURPOSE

- To stake a position on an issue
- To convince others to agree with the position
- To persuade readers to take action

READERS

- Want thoughtful consideration of an issue that is important to them
- Look for a clearly stated claim supported by ample reasons and reliable evidence
- Expect a fair and reasonable presentation of information, ideas, and competing arguments

SOURCES

- Advocates appeal to readers' reason, emotion, and trust as they present arguments.
- Evidence can come from personal observation, print and electronic documents, or field research.
- Supporting information is often presented in visual form.

CONTEXT

- Effective writers consider opposing points of view and choose argumentative strategies that establish common ground with readers.
- Advocates might use color and images to set a mood and often present supporting information in visual forms — such as charts, tables, and graphs — to help readers understand an issue.

observation, and statements by experts, to name just a few. Advocates sometimes use charged language, but more often than not they adopt a straightforward, reasonable tone. They typically offer evidence and reasoning to align their arguments with authorities and with other writers, provide background information, support their claims and reasoning, and refute opposing arguments. Advocates might also offer evidence in the form of illustrations, such as images, video and audio clips, or tables and charts, to set a mood or call attention to specific points. Their decisions about the type of evidence they use are shaped by both the type of document they choose to write and the context in which they find themselves.

Argumentative documents are the means through which many written conversations make progress on an issue. By stating a claim and providing evidence to support it, advocates help readers understand options for addressing an issue. By pointing out the drawbacks of competing arguments, they help participants in the conversation weigh alternatives. More than any other type of document, written arguments help us decide — individually and as a group — what we should believe and how we should act. In doing so, they have a profound effect on how we live our lives.

What Kinds of Documents Are Used to Convince or Persuade?

Argumentation involves making a claim, supporting it with reasons and evidence, addressing reasonable alternatives, and urging readers to accept or act on the writer's main point. Virtually any type of writing, then, can contain an argument — and even documents that serve primarily to reflect, inform, analyze, evaluate, or solve problems often contain some elements of argumentation.

Understanding the genres that can be used to convince or persuade can help you prepare to write your own argument. In this section, you'll find three examples of common argumentative documents: argumentative essays, advertisements, and point/counterpoint editorials. In the e-Pages for this chapter, you'll find discussions and examples of speeches, opinion columns, and letters. As you read these documents, reflect on the contexts in which the writers found themselves. Ask, for example, what readers need to know about an issue to be convinced or persuaded. Ask about the kinds of evidence that readers interested in a particular issue might accept — or reject. And ask about the design elements that might influence readers — positively or negatively — as they consider an argument.

View the e-Pages for argumentative writing at **bedfordstmartins.com /conversation/epages**.

Argumentative Essays

To some extent, argumentative essays resemble written debates. Writers typically advance a thoroughly considered and well-supported argument that addresses competing positions on the issue and explains why the writer's position is preferable to the others. Argumentative essays almost always draw on information from other sources (articles, books, Web sites, statistics, interviews, and so on) to provide evidence that supports the effort to convince readers of the merits of a particular stance on an issue or to persuade them to take action. Argumentative essays can also draw extensively on a writer's personal experience with an issue.

Writers of argumentative essays must carefully consider readers' needs, interests, backgrounds, and knowledge of an issue. A thorough understanding of readers' familiarity with the issue, their purposes for reading the essay, and the values, beliefs, and assumptions they bring to a reading of the essay can help a writer make thoughtful, strategic choices about how to present and support an argument. It can also help a writer determine how best to acknowledge and argue for the comparative inadequacy of competing positions on the issue.

Anu Partanen
What Americans Keep Ignoring about Finland's School Success

In comparing and contrasting Finland's education policies with America's, Anu Partanen sets up evidence for compelling claims about equity in education. This argumentative essay originally appeared in the *Atlantic*, a monthly magazine devoted to political, cultural, and literary topics. Partanen, a journalist born in Finland and currently based in New York, has written for several American and Scandinavian publications and is writing a book about lessons from Nordic society that can help Americans.

What Americans Keep Ignoring about Finland's School Success

by Anu Partanen

Everyone agrees the United States needs to improve its education system dramatically, but how? One of the hottest trends in education reform lately is looking at the stunning success of the West's reigning education superpower, Finland. Trouble is, when it comes to the lessons that Finnish schools have to offer, most of the discussion seems to be missing the point.

The small Nordic country of Finland used to be known—if it was known for anything at all—as the home of Nokia, the mobile phone giant. But lately Finland has been attracting attention on global surveys of quality of life—*Newsweek* ranked it number one last year—and Finland's national education system has been receiving particular praise, because in recent years Finnish students have been turning in some of the highest test scores in the world.

Finland's schools owe their newfound fame primarily to one study: the PISA survey, conducted every three years by the Organization for Economic Co-operation and Development (OECD). The survey compares 15-year-olds in different countries in reading, math, and science. Finland has ranked at or near the top in all three competencies on every survey since 2000, neck and neck with superachievers such as South Korea and Singapore. In the most recent survey in 2009 Finland slipped slightly, with students in Shanghai, China, taking the best scores, but the Finns are still near the very top. Throughout the same period, the PISA performance of the United States has been middling, at best.

Compared with the stereotype of the East Asian model—long hours of exhaustive cramming and rote memorization—Finland's success is especially intriguing because Finnish schools assign less homework and engage children in more creative play. All this has led to a continuous stream of foreign delegations making the pilgrimage to Finland to visit schools and talk with the nation's education experts, and constant coverage in the worldwide media marveling at the Finnish miracle.

So there was considerable interest in a recent visit to the U.S. by one of the leading Finnish authorities on education reform, Pasi Sahlberg, director of the Finnish Ministry of Education's Center for International Mobility and author of the new book *Finnish Lessons: What Can the World Learn from Educational Change in Finland?* Earlier this month, Sahlberg stopped by the Dwight School in New York City to speak with educators and students, and his visit received national media attention and generated much discussion.

And yet it wasn't clear that Sahlberg's message was actually getting through. As Sahlberg put it to me later, there are certain things nobody in America really wants to talk about.

During the afternoon that Sahlberg spent at the Dwight School, a photographer from the *New York Times* jockeyed for position with Dan Rather's TV crew as Sahlberg participated in a round-table chat with students. The subsequent article in the *Times* about the event would focus on Finland as an "intriguing school-reform model."

Yet one of the most significant things Sahlberg said passed practically unnoticed. "Oh," he mentioned at one point, "and there are no private schools in Finland."

This notion may seem difficult for an American to digest, but it's true. Only a small number of independent schools exist in Finland, and even they are all publicly financed. None is allowed to charge tuition fees. There are no private universities, either. This means that practically every person in Finland attends public school, whether for pre-K or a Ph.D.

The irony of Sahlberg's making this comment during a talk at the Dwight School seemed obvious. Like many of America's best schools, Dwight is a private institution that costs high-school students upward of $35,000 a year to attend—not to mention that Dwight, in particular, is run for profit, an increasing trend in the U.S. Yet no one in the room commented on Sahlberg's statement. I found this surprising. Sahlberg himself did not.

Sahlberg knows what Americans like to talk about when it comes to education, because he's become their go-to guy in Finland. The son of two teachers, he grew up in a Finnish school. He taught mathematics and physics in a junior high school in Helsinki, worked his way through a variety of positions in the Finnish Ministry of Education, and spent years as an education expert at the OECD, the World Bank, and other international organizations.

Now, in addition to his other duties, Sahlberg hosts about a hundred visits a year by foreign educators, including many Americans, who want to know the secret of Finland's success. Sahlberg's new book is partly an attempt to help answer the questions he always gets asked.

From his point of view, Americans are consistently obsessed with certain questions: How can you keep track of students' performance if you don't test them constantly? How can you improve teaching if you have no accountability for bad teachers or merit pay for good teachers? How do you foster competition and engage the private sector? How do you provide school choice?

The answers Finland provides seem to run counter to just about everything America's school reformers are trying to do.

For starters, Finland has no standardized tests. The only exception is what's called the National Matriculation Exam, which everyone takes at the end of a voluntary upper-secondary school, roughly the equivalent of American high school.

> Finland's experience shows that it is possible to achieve excellence by focusing not on competition, but on cooperation, and not on choice, but on equity.

Instead, the public school system's teachers are trained to assess children in classrooms using independent tests they create themselves. All children receive a report card at the end of each semester, but these reports are based on individualized grading by each teacher. Periodically, the Ministry of Education tracks national progress by testing a few sample groups across a range of different schools.

As for accountability of teachers and administrators, Sahlberg shrugs. "There's no word for accountability in Finnish," he later told an audience at the Teachers College of Columbia University. "Accountability is something that is left when responsibility has been subtracted."

For Sahlberg what matters is that in Finland all teachers and administrators are given prestige, decent pay, and a lot of responsibility. A master's degree is required to enter the profession, and teacher training programs are among the most selective professional schools in the country. If a teacher is bad, it is the principal's responsibility to notice and deal with it.

And while Americans love to talk about competition, Sahlberg points out that nothing makes Finns more uncomfortable. In his book Sahlberg quotes a line from Finnish writer Samuli Paronen: "Real winners do not compete." It's hard to think of a more un-American idea, but when it comes to education, Finland's success shows that the Finnish attitude might have merits. There are no lists of best schools or teachers in Finland. The main driver of education policy is not competition between teachers and between schools, but cooperation.

Finally, in Finland, school choice is noticeably not a priority, nor is engaging the private sector at all. Which brings us back to the silence after Sahlberg's comment at the Dwight School that schools like Dwight don't exist in Finland.

"Here in America," Sahlberg said at the Teachers College, "parents can choose to take their kids to private schools. It's the same idea of a marketplace that applies to, say, shops. Schools are a shop and parents can buy whatever they want. In Finland parents can also choose. But the options are all the same."

Herein lay the real shocker. As Sahlberg continued, his core message emerged, whether or not anyone in his American audience heard it.

Decades ago, when the Finnish school system was badly in need of reform, the goal of the program that Finland instituted, resulting in so much success today, was never excellence. It was equity.

Since the 1980s, the main driver of Finnish education policy has been the idea that every child should have exactly the same opportunity to learn, regardless of family background, income, or geographic location. Education has been seen first and foremost not as a way to produce star performers, but as an instrument to even out social inequality.

In the Finnish view, as Sahlberg describes it, this means that schools should be healthy, safe environments for children. This starts with the basics. Finland offers all pupils free school meals, easy access to health care, psychological counseling, and individualized student guidance.

In fact, since academic excellence wasn't a particular priority on the Finnish to-do list, when Finland's students scored so high on the first PISA survey in 2001, many Finns thought the results must be a mistake. But subsequent PISA tests confirmed that Finland — unlike, say, very similar countries such as Norway — was producing academic excellence through its particular policy focus on equity.

That this point is almost always ignored or brushed aside in the U.S. seems especially poignant at the moment, after the financial crisis and Occupy Wall Street movement have brought the problems of inequality in America into such sharp focus. The chasm between those who can afford $35,000 in tuition per child per year — or even just the price of a house in a good public school district — and the other "99 percent" is painfully plain to see.

Pasi Sahlberg goes out of his way to emphasize that his book *Finnish Lessons* is not meant as a how-to guide for fixing the education systems of other countries. All countries are different, and as many Americans point out, Finland is a small nation with a much more homogeneous population than the United States.

Yet Sahlberg doesn't think that questions of size or homogeneity should give Americans reason to dismiss the Finnish example. Finland *is* a relatively homogeneous country — as of 2010, just 4.6 percent of Finnish residents had been born in another country, compared with 12.7 percent in the United States. But the number of foreign-born residents in Finland doubled during the decade leading up to 2010, and the country didn't lose its edge in education. Immigrants tended to concentrate in certain areas, causing some schools to become much more mixed than others, yet there has not been much change in the remarkable lack of variation between Finnish schools in the PISA surveys across the same period.

Samuel Abrams, a visiting scholar at Columbia University's Teachers College, has addressed the effects of size and homogeneity on a nation's education performance by comparing Finland with another Nordic country: Norway. Like Finland, Norway is small and not especially diverse overall, but unlike Finland it has taken an approach to education that is more American than Finnish. The result? Mediocre performance in the PISA survey. Educational policy, Abrams suggests, is probably more important to the success of a country's school system than the nation's size or ethnic makeup.

Indeed, Finland's population of 5.4 million can be compared to many an American state — after all, most American education is managed at the state level. According to the Migration Policy Institute, a research organization in Washington, there were 18 states in the U.S. in 2010 with an identical or significantly smaller percentage of foreign-born residents than Finland.

What's more, despite their many differences, Finland and the U.S. have an educational goal in common. When Finnish policymakers decided to reform the country's education system in the 1970s, they did so because they realized that to be competitive, Finland couldn't rely on manufacturing or its scant natural resources and instead had to invest in a knowledge-based economy.

With America's manufacturing industries now in decline, the goal of educational policy in the U.S. — as articulated by most everyone from President Obama on down — is to preserve American competitiveness by doing the same thing. Finland's experience suggests that to win at that game, a country has to prepare not just some of its population well, but all of its population well, for the new economy. To possess some of the best schools in the world might still not be good enough if there are children being left behind.

Is that an impossible goal? Sahlberg says that while his book isn't meant to be a how-to manual, it is meant to be a "pamphlet of hope."

"When President Kennedy was making his appeal for advancing American science and technology by putting a man on the moon by the end of the 1960's, many said it couldn't be done," Sahlberg said during his visit to New York. "But he had a dream. Just like Martin Luther King a few years later had a dream. Those dreams came true. Finland's dream was that we want to have a good public education for every child regardless of where they go to school or what kind of families they come from, and many even in Finland said it couldn't be done."

Clearly, many were wrong. It is possible to create equality. And perhaps even more important — as a challenge to the American way of thinking about education reform — Finland's experience shows that it is possible to achieve excellence by focusing not on competition, but on cooperation, and not on choice, but on equity.

The problem facing education in America isn't the ethnic diversity of the population but the economic inequality of society, and this is precisely the problem that Finnish education reform addressed. More equity at home might just be what America needs to be more competitive abroad.

Starting a Conversation: Respond to "What Americans Keep Ignoring about Finland's School Success"

In your writer's notebook, record your analysis of Partanen's essay by responding to the following questions:

1. Partanen begins her argument with a question: "Everyone agrees the United States needs to improve its education system dramatically, but how?" What assumptions is Partanen making about her readers? How do you think readers are likely to respond to these assumptions?

2. Partanen notes that when it comes to education, "there are certain things nobody in America really wants to talk about" (para. 6). To what things, specifically, does she refer? Why do you think she says Americans don't want to talk about them?

3. Aside from advocate, what roles does Partanen take on as she presents her argument? How does she signal to her readers when she is changing roles?

4. What counterarguments does Partanen raise in her essay? How does she respond to ideas and information that don't seem to support her argument? How effective would you say her responses are, and why?

5. Partanen quotes one Finnish school expert as saying that his book isn't intended as a "how-to manual" for reforming American education; rather, "it is meant to be a 'pamphlet of hope'" (para. 34). What do you think this statement means? How might a "pamphlet of hope" be a better approach than a "how-to manual"?

Advertisements

Advertisements seek to persuade the people who see or hear them to take a specific action — whether it's purchasing a product, supporting a cause, applying for a job, donating to a nonprofit organization, or voting for a political candidate. The argument usually takes the form of a simple claim, which might be conveyed through a brief slogan, such as "The Best Food in Texas"; through an image, such as a photo of people having a good time while they use a particular product (an adult beverage, for example, or a new sports car); or through an endorsement in which a celebrity extols the virtues of a particular product. The argument might even take the form of a detailed list of features and benefits, such as you might see in a brochure for a smartphone or a new prescription drug. In some cases, such as political campaigns or the battle between cable and satellite television providers, advertisements can also make negative claims.

Few readers seek out advertisements. They usually encounter them as they flip through a magazine, browse the Web, watch television, listen to the radio, or drive along a highway studded with billboards. Because most readers don't devote a great deal of time to considering an advertisement, most ads are designed to capture the reader's or viewer's attention and convey their claim as quickly as possible. As a result, they typically rely on images and limit the amount of written text. For example, the long-running advertising campaign originated by the California Milk Processors Board asks the simple question "Got Milk?" Another, developed by the U.S. Marines, urges enlistment with the slogan "The few. The proud. The Marines." Yet another ad, used so heavily in the 1980s and 1990s that it has become part of our cultural landscape, urges youth to "Just say no to drugs."

 ### Men Can Stop Rape
Where Do You Stand?

The following advertisements, developed by the nonprofit organization Men Can Stop Rape for its "Where Do You Stand?" campaign, challenge men to help prevent rape with a mix of imagery and brief passages of text. Representing an effort to model effective intervention strategies, the ads are designed to appear as banners, postcards, and posters. They target young adults on college campuses.

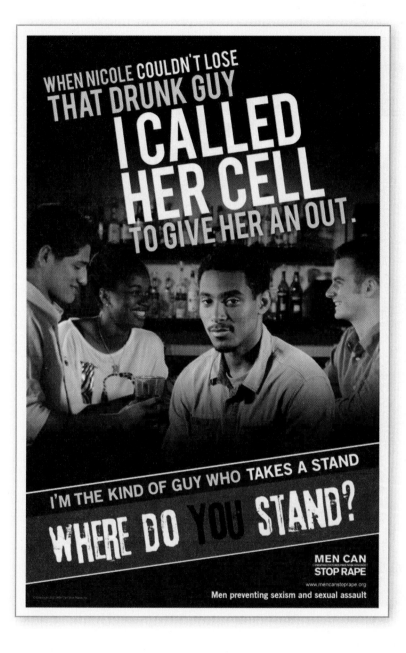

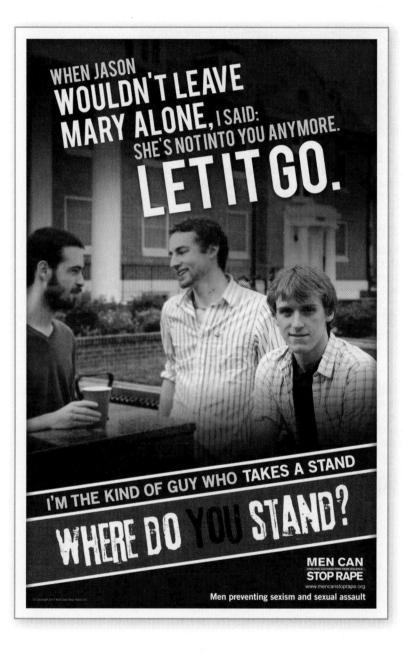

4 THINGS **YOU** CAN DO TO TAKE A STAND

1 Distraction

Call your friend's cell to ask her a question or suggest it's time to go. You can also distract the guy harassing her: "Hey man, didn't I see you at [fill in the blank]?"

2 Group Intervention

Ask your/her friends to help out with distraction or separation. They can pull her aside to check in. Or they can say to him: "We see what you're doing and it's not okay."

3 Get an authority

Ask the bartender, bouncer, or any other authority figure to help support the intervention.

4 Prepare Yourself

Be aware of the pressures men face not to take a stand and choose what kind of man you want to be.

WHERE DO YOU STAND?

Starting a Conversation: Respond to "Where Do You Stand?" Advertisements

In your writer's notebook, record your analysis of the "Where Do You Stand?" advertisements by responding to the following questions:

1. Although the four advertisements are part of the same campaign, their specific messages are different. What particular actions does each advocate? What characteristics do they share?

2. How would you describe the relationship between text and image in these advertisements? What effect does the design of the ads and the images used in them have on their overall message?

3. This campaign was aimed at college students and young adults between the ages of eighteen and twenty-five. How are these ads meant to appeal to that audience? In what ways do the ads reflect the culture and values of their presumed readers?

4. The "Where Do You Stand?" campaign represents one of many Men Can Stop Rape initiatives that have sought to encourage awareness and prevention of sexual assault among men. What assumptions do these particular ads make with regard to harassment, assault, college-age men, and college-age women?

Point/Counterpoint Editorials

Point/counterpoint editorials are used by newspapers, magazines, and other news media to illustrate opposing views about an issue. If disagreement exists about a proposed amendment to a state constitution, for example, a newspaper might invite proponents and opponents of the amendment to contribute to a point/counterpoint editorial. The two editorials might be placed side by side on a single page, or, depending on the size of the page and the amount of space given to their writers, they might be placed on facing pages.

Like other editorials and opinion columns, point/counterpoint editorials are typically brief, usually containing fewer than a thousand words. Because they tend to address issues of larger public interest, however, point/counterpoint editorials are more likely than are opinion columns to include evidence such as quotations or paraphrases from published sources, quotations from interviews, or statistical data drawn from published studies. In this sense, point/counterpoint editorials are more similar to reports and essays than they are to opinion columns and letters to the editor.

In general, point/counterpoint editorials are designed simply. In some cases, they might include charts, tables, photographs, and other illustrations — should the editors of the newspaper, magazine, or Web site wish to call attention to the relative importance of the issue being addressed. Most often, however, they do not include illustrations or headings.

Alexandra Le Tellier
Judge Stops NYC Soda Ban, but Don't Celebrate

Alexandra Le Tellier, a journalist and Web producer for the *Los Angeles Times* opinion pages, wrote the following editorial in response to the reversal of a ban on the sale of large sodas in New York City. In her editorial, Le Tellier points to the larger issues of health and nutrition behind the political controversy over the ban. Her argument draws on authoritative sources to help convince her readers to support a ban on large, sugary drinks.

Judge Stops NYC Soda Ban, but Don't Celebrate

by Alexandra Le Tellier | March 11, 2013

Sugar addicts and libertarians rejoice! A judge put the kibosh on New York City's ban of super-sized sugary drinks sold in restaurants, which was to go into effect Tuesday.

But don't go too wild on the 16-ounce sodas. Most sugary drinks contain absolutely no nutritional value. Worse, drinking these sugar bombs can go a long way toward destroying your health.

Writing about the backlash against the pending ban last year, the *New York Times*' Mark Bittman reminded opponents that "sugar-sweetened beverages are nothing more than sugar delivery systems, and sugar is probably the most dangerous part of our current diet. People will argue forever about whether sugar-sweetened beverages lead directly to obesity, but [Mayor] Bloomberg's ban should be framed first and foremost as an effort to reduce sugar consumption."

Bittman also pointed out the obvious, although sadly not so obvious to everyone: Soda isn't food.

After laying out the definitions of "nutritious" and "food," he wrote:

"Sugar-sweetened beverages don't meet this description any more than do beer and tobacco and, for that matter, heroin, and they have more in common with these things than they do with carrots."

Of course, people will push back and argue that it's their right to destroy their bodies and risk their lives in whatever way they choose. Some people go to tanning salons, others ride bikes without helmets. When it comes to hazards to our health and safety, what makes soda any worse?

Well, according to psychologist and human behavior expert Wendy Walsh, most people are powerless against sugar. "We have an unfettered desire and craving for [sugar, salt, and fat] that many of us actually can't control," she said on CNN during a weekend debate over the soda ban, arguing rather convincingly that big corporations are playing into human biology to exploit consumers.

"Modern capitalist America has capitalized on that and made sure that they put large doses of that in everything they give us. So, how can we be making free choice when we're addicted?" Walsh argued.

It's hard to argue with that. You'd think those who're especially dedicated to the cause of personal freedom would agree with Walsh that we don't want big corporations controlling us in any way, much less profiting while consumers deteriorate.

Then again, Walsh's opponent on the CNN segment said a good Saturday night would include steak, cigarettes, and gambling. So maybe Mr. Personal Freedom wants to be controlled?

I'm siding with Walsh. And with Bittman. We need to make it harder for people to get hooked on substances that will render them powerless—and might kill them too.

Karin Klein
Soda's a Problem, but Bloomberg Doesn't Have the Solution

Although Karin Klein, an editorial writer for the *Los Angeles Times,* agrees with Alexandra Le Tellier about the unhealthy consequences of soda consumption, she argues in her editorial that "it's wrong for one man . . . to dictate to people how big a cup of sugary soda they're allowed." Klein refutes many of Le Tellier's points, arguing for the importance of an informed public and raising new questions about how effective government intervention in people's food consumption habits really is.

Soda's a Problem, but Bloomberg Doesn't Have the Solution

by **Karin Klein** | **March 11, 2013**

The intentions of New York Mayor Michael R. Bloomberg may be laudable, but it's wrong for one man, even an elected official and even a well-meaning one at that, to dictate to people how big a cup of sugary soda they're allowed.

Not that I have tremendous regard for soda. It's bad for you, especially in large quantities. The evidence against it mounts on a semi-regular basis. But the mayor's initiative goes further than something like a soda tax, which might aim to discourage people from purchasing something by making it cost a bit more but leaves the decision in their hands. Bloomberg is playing nanny in the worst sort of way by interfering in a basic, private transaction involving a perfectly legal substance. In restaurants and other establishments overseen by the city's health inspectors, it would have been illegal to sell a serving of most sugary drinks (except fruit juice; I always wonder about that exemption, considering the sugar calories in apple juice) that's more than 16 ounces.

Convenience stores such as 7-Eleven are overseen by the state and would be exempt, but a Burger King across the street would be restricted. A pizza restaurant would not be able to sell a 2-liter bottle of soda that would be shared out among the children at a birthday party. But they could all have a 16-ounce cup.

The inherent contradictions that make it easy to sneer at such rules have been well-reported and were a good part of why earlier this week a judge stopped the new rules from being implemented. But he also pointed out a deeper problem: Bloomberg essentially made this decision himself. It was approved by the Board of Health, but that's a board of the administration, appointed by the mayor. That was an overreach that thwarted the system of checks and balances, according to the judge: The separately elected City Council would have to approve the law.

That still leaves the question of whether governments or their leaders can begin dictating the look of an individual's meal, the portion sizes for each aspect. There are times when government has to step in on obviously dangerous situations—especially those, such as smoking, that affect people other than the person whose behavior would be curbed—but it's my belief that we want to scrutinize them carefully and keep them to a minimum. For that matter, it's not as though the mayor is moving to limit sales of tobacco to two cigarettes per transaction.

Not that government has to aid and abet the situation. Schools don't have to sell junk foods, and, thankfully, after years of sacrificing their students' health to their desire to raise more money, most of them have stopped allowing vending machines stocked with sodas. Governments are under no obligation to sell such stuff in park or pool vending machines or in their offices. In such cases, government is simply the vendor making a decision about what it wants to sell.

I don't buy the argument that people are helpless in the face of sugar and that it's better to have the government rather than the corporations dictate their behaviors. If people are so helpless against soda, the mayor's edict would be even more meaningless because people would simply buy two 16-ounce cups. But people are not helpless, and it's worrisome to promote a philosophy that infantilizes the individual. The public is simply ill-informed. It takes a while for people to become aware, but they do and they react. Soda consumption already is slipping nationwide.

Let's not forget that scientists and even governments have at times pushed people—with better intentions than food corporations, certainly—into eating high levels of refined carbohydrates and sugars by sending out word that the only thing that really matters when it comes to obesity is to eat a very low-fat diet.

Starting a Conversation: Respond to Point/ Counterpoint Editorials

In your writer's notebook, record your analysis of Le Tellier's and Klein's editorials by responding to the following questions:

1. What would you say is each writer's overall claim? How well do you think each writer supports her claim with appropriate reasons and evidence?

2. What stake does each of these writers have in this issue? What stake do their readers have? Why might readers in Los Angeles be interested in a ban on large, sugary drinks in New York?

3. How would you characterize the tone of each writer's editorial? How do their tones differ, and how are they similar? How do their tones affect the persuasiveness of the editorial?

4. Klein responds to Le Tellier's argument, in part, by attacking her primary assumptions, such as the claim that "most people are powerless against sugar." On what grounds does Klein refute Le Tellier's points? How does Klein support her own claims?

How Can I Write an Argumentative Essay?

Many people believe that an argument is effective only if it's won, that unless they convince or persuade someone, they've failed in their mission to change the world — or their community or the minds of people they hang out with, or the people who read their Facebook pages. In fact, most written arguments aren't so much about winning or losing as about sharing the writer's perspective with others who are interested in an issue. Think of it as exploring alternative ways of thinking, acting, and believing — as advancing a conversation about an issue. If you follow this line of thinking, you'll recognize that the effectiveness of your essay isn't based on whether you win the argument. It is based on your ability to affect the community of readers and writers to whom you direct your argument.

In Process

An Argumentative Essay about Online Gaming

Vince Reid wrote an argumentative essay for his introductory composition course. Vince learned about his topic through personal experience, by reading articles and blogs about gaming, and by interviewing friends. Follow his efforts to write his argumentative essay in the In Progress boxes throughout this chapter.

Then again, sometimes winning is all that matters. Application essays for medical or business school, no matter how well written, are seldom considered successful if the writer isn't accepted. The same is true of letters requesting scholarships. And if you're a teenage driver, either you get to borrow the car or you don't.

In this section, you'll learn about the processes and strategies involved in writing an argumentative essay. As you work on your essay, you'll follow the work of Vince Reid, a first-year student who wrote an argumentative essay about the advantages of the competitive League approach to game design.

Find a Conversation and Listen In

Argumentative essays grow out of a belief that a choice must be made, a situation should be changed, or a mistake should be corrected. In general, people don't argue when they're happy with a situation, nor do they argue when they agree with one another. They argue because they believe that someone or something — a person, a group, a movement, a government — is wrong. As you consider possible subjects for your argumentative essay, take stock of the conversations taking place around you. Ask what bothers you. Ask what conflicts affect you, individually or as a member of a community. Look for an issue that matters not only to you but also to the people who might read your essay. Then take on the role of advocate, and reflect on your writing situation — your purpose, your readers, and the contexts in which your writing will be read (see p. 10).

EXPLORE DISAGREEMENTS

Unless they're deeply conflicted, few people carry on extended arguments with themselves. The kinds of arguments that are worth addressing in academic essays revolve around issues that affect a larger community. To identify issues that might interest you and your readers, explore popular, professional, and academic conversations. In almost every case, you'll find points of disagreement and debate that bring people together in discussions — sometimes polite and sometimes anything but — about the challenges that confront us.

- **Popular conversations.** What's new in the media and the popular press? What's new on the Web? You can visit the opinion sections on Web sites such as CNN.com and National Public Radio (www.npr.org) to learn about issues that have sparked discussion. On sites such as these, you can read commentary

In Process

Generating Ideas about Conversations

Vince Reid's interests in gaming led him to explore conversations related to approaches to game design.

I've never played an MMO for more than a few months, but I've played League for almost two years now. I've somehow avoided the moment when I realize that the game I'm playing has grown stale and repetitive. Why is this? I'm not the only one. I know that since I've started playing, League's playerbase has grown at a tremendous rate. So what about League makes us want to play yet another match? I don't believe that it's the players or at least not just the players. I've played WoW and Aion with some of the same people I now play League with, and their presence only delayed my departure from those snooze fests. Maybe I like League because it's free. I always disliked when I had to pay $50 just to get the game and then had to pay $15 for a monthly subscription. But League isn't entirely free either. League has an in-game store, and I've definitely spent more than $50 in it. Maybe, instead of looking at just one thing, I should look at League from several angles. What do I like most about the game? The regular updates, the professional tournaments, or the simple fact that I can win?

Vince used the results of his freewriting to direct his attention to discussions about how the game he had been playing, League of Legends, had succeeded in keeping players' interest. The discussions he found in blogs and on Web sites led him to learn more about the decisions made by the designers of the game and why they kept the game interesting.

from other visitors to the site, read blogs and opinion columns, and view the latest news reports on issues that have spurred popular debate.

- **Professional conversations.** If you are involved or are planning to become involved in a particular profession, tune in to the conversations taking place in your field of interest. If you're working as an intern or at a part-time job, for example, listen to what your coworkers are talking about. Skim some trade and professional journals to find points of disagreement. Read some blogs that focus on your profession, and notice what people are arguing about.

- **Academic conversations.** Just as you will find disagreements in public and professional life, you will find them in academic disciplines. Look for disagreements in course readings, and pay attention to controversies addressed during class discussions and lectures. Ask professors and graduate students what's "hot" in their fields. Scan the tables of contents of recent issues of academic journals. Visit Web sites that focus on your discipline.

Recognizing ongoing conversations can give you insights into debatable issues that might serve as the basis for your argumentative essay. Try listing issues from one or more of these areas — or from the writing project ideas at the end of this chapter — and then explore your thoughts about them (see pp. 32–38 for an overview of strategies for generating ideas). When you've finished, review what you've written to identify the areas that seem most promising, and then select one or two that interest you most. Jot down your thoughts about what you already know and what you would need to learn before you can develop your argument.

Working Together: Try It Out Loud

Before you start developing your argument, hold an informal debate with your classmates about an issue that affects all of you. Form small groups, and choose an issue you're familiar with and that lends itself to argument, such as a disagreement affecting your hometown, school, or state. You might scan the school paper or a local publication for current issues worth discussing. Explain your perspective on the issue, and then state your position. Offer reasons and, if possible, evidence from personal experience or readings to support your argument. Ask the other members of your group to identify counterarguments,

giving their own reasons and evidence. Take turns speaking while the other members of the group listen, respond, and ask questions.

When you are finished, take a few minutes to reflect on the exercise. What did you learn about presenting an argument? Did you have to adapt what you said based on your classmates' values, beliefs, and concerns? What kind of questions did they ask? What seemed to interest them the most about the issue? How did they react to your argument? What reasoning and evidence did they find most convincing? Least convincing?

TRACK ONLINE CONVERSATIONS

Issues worth arguing about almost always become a topic of conversation. Increasingly, that conversation takes place online, through blogs and social media sites. These resources are designed specifically to support exchanges among writers and readers. By following these online conversations, you can not only learn more about your subject but also discover what other writers and readers think about it.

Blogs consist of chronologically ordered entries on a Web site and most closely resemble entries in a diary or journal. Blog entries usually include a title and a text message and can also incorporate images, audio, video, and other types of media. Many entries provide links to other pages on the Web. Blogs allow readers to post their responses to entries, so a single blog entry might be accompanied by several — sometimes hundreds — of responses.

You can find blogs that address your subject by turning to sites such as Technorati (technorati.com) and Google blogs (google.com/blogsearch). Read more about blogs in Chapter 12.

Social media sites such as Facebook, Google+, Tumblr, Twitter, and LinkedIn provide opportunities to identify people who share your interest in an issue. By searching these sites, you can identify individuals who might be knowledgeable about an issue or have been affected by it. If you have an account with a social media site such as Facebook, you can use its search tools to locate individuals and groups that share your interest. Facebook's Graph Search, for example, allows you to create complex searches of Facebook members and events.

Even though these resources can be helpful as you explore potential issues for your essay, take the time to learn more about the conversations you find online. You can locate print and electronic sources through your library's catalog and through Web search sites and directories. If the sources you collect leave you with unanswered questions, you can conduct additional searches, talk to a librarian, or collect information through observations or interviews. Depending on your issue, you might also want to search for government documents.

Do you know how to locate online sources? See Chapter 12 for help.

ASK QUESTIONS ABOUT PROMISING ISSUES

Before you begin constructing an argument, determine which aspect of an issue interests you most. The best written arguments are usually focused and narrow. Be wary of writing about something as broadly defined as climate change or ethics in politics. Instead, try to find a subtopic that you can manage in the space and time available to you. For example, if you're interested in climate change, take a look at issues such as the carbon emissions that result from producing the batteries used in hybrid cars and trucks. Each of the following questions focuses your attention on a general issue in a different way, and each provides a useful starting point for an argumentative essay. Depending on the subject, you'll find that some questions are more relevant than others.

- **Values.** Why is this important to me? What about it will matter to readers? Can I make an argument without letting my emotions run away with me?

- **Definition.** Why do people disagree about this issue? What, exactly, is at stake?

- **Possibilities.** What could be accomplished if this issue is addressed? What might happen if it is not addressed?

- **Positions.** What positions have been taken on this issue? What intrigues me about those positions?

- **Strengths and weaknesses.** What are the strengths of other writers' arguments? What are the weaknesses?

As you narrow your focus, ask yourself one last question: Is your goal to convince your readers to agree with you, or to persuade them to act? Be aware that getting people to act can be a far greater challenge than getting them to agree with you. For example, it's easy to convince someone that it's a good idea to spend more time studying. It can be far more difficult to persuade that person to set aside two more hours each day to do so. As you consider how you'll focus your argument, remember that it will take a strong argument to persuade your readers to act.

Build Your Argument

Putting together an effective argumentative essay starts with knowing what you want others to believe or how you want them to act. But that's just the beginning. To build your argument, you must develop a strategy for achieving your goal. Your strategy should reflect not only your overall goal but also a thorough understanding of your readers — their purposes in reading your essay, their knowledge of the issue, and their needs, interests, and backgrounds.

In short, you'll need to figure out how to get your readers to accept your argument. To do so, start by defining your overall claim, and then identify the reasons and supporting evidence that will be most convincing or persuasive to your readers. In addition, consider how opposing positions affect your argument, and make sure that your reasoning is sound.

In Process

Locating Sources

Vince Reid was interested in learning why one of the games he played on a regular basis had become so successful. He also wanted to find out whether other game designers were starting to adopt a similar approach. His Web searches led him to an online article that discussed the issue of game design in depth and that had a series of comments from readers.

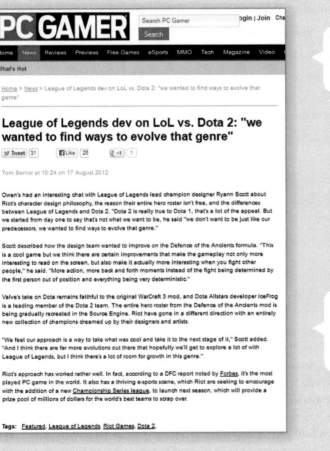

Vince located an article by Tom Senior on the PCGamer Web site.

Several readers had replied to the article, in some cases extending and refining the argument.

Vince saved a copy of this article. Then he followed the links in it to related materials and saved those as well. Later, he printed a copy and highlighted key passages.

DEFINE YOUR OVERALL CLAIM

It's important that you understand precisely what you want your readers to believe or do before you begin drafting. Your overall claim — the heart of the argument you want to make — will serve as a touchstone as you juggle the complexities of crafting an argument. Your claim should take into account your purpose as a writer, the conversation you've decided to join, and the readers you hope to convince or persuade.

You can begin to define your overall claim by brainstorming or freewriting (see pp. 32–33) in response to the following questions:

- What is my position on this issue?

- Which aspects of this issue interest me most?

- Which aspects of this issue do I feel most strongly about?

- What do I want my readers to believe or do as a result of reading my essay?

- What are my readers likely to think about this issue? What will it take to change their minds or get them to act?

- How does my position differ from those advanced by other writers? How is it similar?

Review what you've written. Then try to express, in one or two sentences, your over-all claim. Later, your claim can serve as the basis for a thesis statement (see Chapter 14). For now, use it to direct your thinking about the argument you want to formulate.

DEVELOP REASONS TO ACCEPT YOUR OVERALL CLAIM

Few readers will accept "because I'm right" as a good reason to accept your position on an issue. They expect you to explain why you're right. Developing an explanation begins with identifying reasons that are consistent with your own perspective on the issue. At this stage of your writing process, don't worry about whether your readers will be convinced or persuaded by your reasoning. Instead, treat your efforts to develop reasons to accept your overall claim as you would any other form of brain-storming. As you generate a list of potential reasons, you can certainly begin to ask whether the reasons you've identified are well grounded, logical, and consistent with the values and beliefs held by you and your readers. And later, as you draft your essay, you can decide how to present your reasons to your readers. For now, though, your primary goal is to generate as many potential reasons as possible to support your overall claim.

Generate ideas about potential reasons. Your understanding of an issue and the conversations surrounding it will provide a framework within which you can develop a set of reasons to support your overall claim. To guide your efforts, ask questions such as the following, and respond to them by brainstorming, freewriting, blindwriting, looping, clustering, or mapping:

- **Costs.** What costs are associated with not accepting and acting on your overall claim? Are there monetary costs? Will time and effort be lost or wasted? Will valuable resources be wasted? Will people be unable to lead fulfilling lives? Will human potential be wasted? Will lives be lost?

- **Benefits.** What will be gained by accepting and acting on your overall claim? Who or what will benefit if the claim is accepted and acted on? What form will these benefits take?

- **Alternatives, choices, and trade-offs.** What is gained by accepting and acting on your overall claim? What is lost by not doing so? In what ways are the potential costs or benefits associated with your overall claim preferable to those associated with rejecting it?

- **Parallels.** Can you find similarities between the overall claim you are making about this issue and claims made about other issues? Can you argue that, if your claim is accepted and acted on, the outcomes will be similar to those found for other issues? What consensus, if any, exists among experts on this issue about what similar situations have led to in the past?

- **Personal experience.** What does your personal experience tell you is likely to happen if your claim is accepted and acted on? What does it tell you might happen if it is rejected?

- **Historical context.** What does history tell you is likely to happen — or not happen — if your claim is accepted and acted on? What does it tell you might happen if it is rejected? What consensus, if any, exists among experts on this issue about what similar situations have led to in the past?

- **Values and beliefs.** In what ways is your overall claim consistent with your values and beliefs? With those of your readers? In what ways is it consistent with larger societal and cultural values and beliefs? How might it further those values and beliefs?

Examine the list of reasons you've generated to determine which ones fit best with your overall claim, your purpose, and what you know about your readers. Select the reasons that, individually and as a group, best support your overall claim.

Decide how your reasons support your overall claim. Effective arguments make connections (sometimes called **warrants**) between the overall claim and the reasons offered to support it. Sometimes readers accept a connection because they share the writer's values and beliefs or have similar experiences with and knowledge of an issue. In other cases, readers accept a connection because the writer explains it effectively. This explanation (sometimes called backing) provides readers with information and analysis that help them understand and accept the connection.

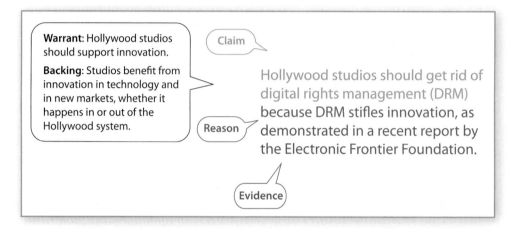

The reasons you choose to support your overall claim should reflect your understanding of the conversation you've decided to join. Your reasons should emerge from careful thought about the information, ideas, and arguments you've encountered in your reading. Your reasons should reflect your purpose and goals. And they should take into account your readers' needs, interests, backgrounds, and knowledge of the issue.

As you consider your reasons, ask how clearly they connect to your overall claim. Ask whether you should explain each connection or leave it unstated. Your answers will depend in part on the extent to which your readers share your values, beliefs, experience, and knowledge of the issue. If your readers' backgrounds and knowledge differ from yours, connections that make sense to you might not be clear to them.

CHOOSE EVIDENCE TO SUPPORT YOUR REASONS

Your argument will be effective only if you back up each of your reasons with evidence. Most readers will expect you to provide some sort of justification for accepting your reasons, and their assessment of your evidence will affect their willingness to accept your argument. The form your evidence takes will depend on your overall claim, the reasons themselves, and your readers' values and assumptions. In general, however, consider drawing on the following types of evidence to support your reasons:

- textual evidence, in the form of quotations, paraphrases, and summaries
- numerical and statistical data
- images, including photographs, drawings, animations, and video
- tables, charts, and graphs
- information and ideas from interviews, observations, and surveys
- personal experience
- expert opinion

Take the following steps to identify evidence to support your reasons:

1. List the reasons you are using to support your overall claim.

2. For each reason, review your notes to identify relevant evidence.

3. List your evidence below each point.

4. Identify reasons that need more support, and locate additional evidence as necessary.

5. Consider dismissing or revising reasons for which you don't have sufficient evidence.

Effective arguments typically provide evidence that is both plentiful and varied in type. A writer arguing about the need to improve the U.S. health care system, for example, might draw on personal experience, interviews with friends and relatives, policy briefs from the American Medical Association, commentary by bloggers, reports issued by government agencies, and articles in popular and scholarly journals.

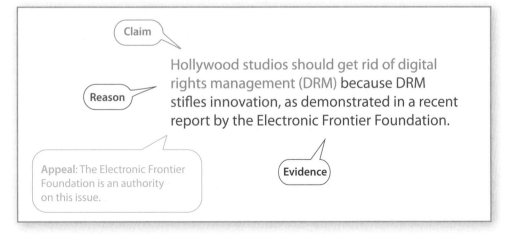

As you choose evidence to support your reasons, think about whether — and, if so, how — you will show the connections between reasons and evidence. These connections, often called appeals, help readers understand why a reason is appropriate and valid. Common appeals include citing authorities on an issue; using emotion to sway readers; calling attention to shared principles, values, and beliefs; asking readers to trust the writer; and using logic.

In Process

Choosing Evidence

Vince Reid chose the evidence he would use in his essay by creating a list of reasons to support his overall claim that League of Legends offered a superior approach to online gaming. He reviewed his notes and sources, listing sources next to each reason, and decided whether he needed more or better evidence for each reason. He created a table in a word-processing file to keep track of his evidence.

Reason	Evidence/Source	Notes
League has adopted a business model that is the best of both worlds.	League of Legends Community Forum: http://na.leagueoflegends.com/board/showthread.php?t=2830551	World of Warcraft is "the" subscription model. Selling power is a serious problem that a lot of games face. Approaches: Subscription vs. Microtransaction vs. FTP
Frequent updates keep players excited and coming back for more.	LOL Patch Notes: http://lol-patch.com/ Top 10 Reasons to Play: http://www.urbantitan.com/top-10-reasons-to-play-league-of-legends/	Having one champion every few weeks instead of a month of content every half year keeps players coming back regularly.
League of Legends is a sport.	ESPN: http://espn.go.com/blog/ playbook/tech/post/_/id/3979/league-of-legends-mimics-regular-sports	It is harder to stop playing a sport than it is to stop playing a game. Key elements: sports atmosphere, community, pros, "minor leagues"

You can read more about using appeals on page 414. You can read about how to identify evidence to support your reasons in Chapter 14.

IDENTIFY AND CONSIDER OPPOSING CLAIMS

A critical part of developing and supporting your argument is identifying opposing claims, or counterarguments. You might assume that calling attention to competing positions in your essay will weaken your argument. Nothing is further from the truth. Identifying opposing claims provides opportunities to test and strengthen your reasons and evidence by comparing them with those put forth by other writers. Considering counterarguments also allows you to anticipate questions and concerns your readers are likely to bring to your essay. And later, as you are writing your draft, your responses to these opposing claims provide a basis for clearly explaining to your readers why your argument is superior to others.

Remember that you're making an argument about your issue because people disagree about how to address it. If reasonable alternatives to your argument didn't exist, there would be no need for an argument in the first place. As a writer contributing to an ongoing conversation, you have a responsibility to indicate that you're aware of what has been said and who has said it. More important, you have a responsibility to consider carefully how your argument improves on the arguments made by other members of the conversation.

To identify opposing claims, review the sources you encountered as you learned about your issue. Identify the most compelling arguments you found, and ask how the reasons and evidence offered to support them compare to yours. Then ask whether you can think of reasonable alternative positions that haven't been

Working Together: Identify and Consider Opposing Claims

Working with a group of two or more classmates, carry out a "devil's advocate" exercise to identify and consider opposing claims. First, briefly describe your issue, overall claim, and reasons. Other members of the group should offer reasonable alternative arguments. One member of the group should serve as a recorder, taking careful notes on the exchange and listing opposing claims, reasons supporting those claims, and your response to the claims. Once the exchange (which might last between three and ten minutes) is completed, switch roles and repeat the activity for every other member of the group.

This activity can be carried out face-to-face or electronically. If you are working on the activity using a chat program or a threaded discussion forum, you can record your exchange for later review. Most chat programs allow you to create a transcript of a session, and threaded discussion forums will automatically record your exchange.

addressed in the sources you've consulted. Finally, talk with others about your issue, and ask them what they think about it.

For each reason you expect to use in support of your overall claim, create a list of opposing points of view, briefly describing each one and noting where you found it. To determine whether you're making the best possible argument, consider each of these opposing claims in turn. Take notes on your response to each one, considering both its merits and its faults. Use what you've learned to reflect on and refine your overall claim and the reasons and evidence you've identified to support it. Later, you can use what you've learned to address counterarguments in your essay (see p. 417).

ENSURE THE INTEGRITY OF YOUR ARGUMENT

If you're familiar with the "buy this car and get a date with this girl (or guy)" school of advertising, you know that arguments often lack integrity. Although weak arguments might be easier to develop, they usually backfire (setting aside the enduring success of automobile ads filled with attractive young men and women). Readers who recognize errors in reasoning or the use of inappropriate evidence are likely to reject an argument out of hand.

Acquainting yourself with common logical fallacies can help you not only ensure the integrity of your argument but also identify and address counterarguments based on fallacious reasoning and weak or inappropriate forms of evidence.

Some of the most common logical fallacies are described below.

Fallacies based on distraction

- **A red herring** is an irrelevant or distracting point. The term originated with the practice of sweeping a red herring (a particularly fragrant type of fish) across the trail being followed by a pack of hunting dogs to throw them off the scent of their prey. For example, the question *Why worry about the rising cost of tuition when the government is tapping our phones?* is a red herring (government surveillance has nothing to do with increases in college tuition).

- **Ad hominem attacks** attempt to discredit an idea or argument by suggesting that a person or group associated with it should not be trusted. These kinds of attacks might be subtle or vicious. If you hear someone say that a proposed wind farm should be rejected because its main supporter cheated on her taxes, or that school vouchers are bad because a principal who swindled a school district supports them, you're listening to an ad hominem attack.

- **Irrelevant history** is another form of distraction. For example, arguing that a proposal is bad because someone came up with the idea while they were using cocaine suggests that the state of mind of the person who originates an idea has something to do with its merits. It might well be the case that the idea is flawed, but you should base your assessment on an analysis of its strengths and weaknesses. Otherwise, you might as well say that an idea is undoubtedly sound because someone thought of it while he or she was sober.

Fallacies based on questionable assumptions

- **Sweeping generalizations**, sometimes known as *hasty generalizations*, are based on stereotypes. Asserting that the rich are conservative voters, for example, assumes that everyone who is rich is just like everyone else who is rich. These kinds of arguments don't account for variation within a group, nor do they consider exceptions to the rule.

- **Straw-man attacks** oversimplify or distort another person's argument so it can be dismissed more easily. Just as a boxer can easily knock down a scarecrow, a writer who commits this fallacy might characterize an opposing position as more extreme than it actually is, or might refute obviously flawed counter-arguments while ignoring valid objections.

- **Citing inappropriate authorities** can take several forms: citing as an authority someone who is not an expert on a subject, citing a source with a strong bias on an issue, suggesting that an individual voice represents consensus when that person's ideas are far from the mainstream, or treating paid celebrity endorsements as expert opinion.

- **Jumping on a bandwagon**, also known as *argument from consensus*, implies that if enough people believe something, it must be true. This type of argument substitutes group thinking for careful analysis. The idea of jumping on a bandwagon refers to the practice, in early American politics, of parading a candidate through town on a bandwagon. To show support for the candidate, people would climb onto the wagon.

Fallacies based on misrepresentation

- **Stacking the deck** refers to the practice of presenting evidence for only one side of an argument. Most readers will assume that a writer has done this deliberately and will wonder what he or she is trying to hide.

- **Base-rate fallacies** are commonly found in arguments based on statistics. If you read that drinking coffee will triple your risk of developing cancer, you might be alarmed. However, if you knew that the risk rose from one in a billion to three in a billion, you might pour another cup.

- **Questionable analogies**, also known as *false analogies*, make inappropriate comparisons. They are based on the assumption that if two things are similar in one way, they must be similar in others. For example, a writer might argue that global warming is like a fever, and that just as a fever usually runs its course on its own, so too will the climate recover without intervention.

Fallacies based on careless reasoning

- **Post hoc fallacies**, formally known as *post hoc, ergo propter hoc* fallacies ("after this, therefore because of this"), argue that because one event happened before a second event, the first event must have caused the second event. For example, a student might conclude that she received a low grade on an essay exam because she argued with an instructor during class. In fact, the real cause might be the poor quality of her exam responses.

- **Slippery-slope arguments** warn that a single step will inevitably lead to a bad situation. For instance, one of the most common arguments against decriminalizing marijuana is that it leads to the use of stronger narcotics. Indeed, some heroin or cocaine addicts might have first tried marijuana, but there is no evidence that *all* marijuana users inevitably move on to harder drugs.

- **Either/or arguments** present two choices, one of which is usually characterized as extremely undesirable. In fact, there might be a third choice, or a fourth, or a fifth.

- **Non sequiturs** are statements that do not follow logically from what has been said. For example, arguing that buying a particular type of car will lead to a successful love life is a non sequitur.

- **Circular reasoning**, also known as *begging the question*, restates a point that has just been made as evidence for itself. Arguing that a decline in voter turnout is a result of fewer people voting is an example of circular reasoning.

As you build your argument — and in particular, as you consider counterarguments and check your reasoning for fallacies — you might find that you need to refine your overall claim. In fact, most writers refine their arguments as they learn more about an issue and consider how best to contribute to a conversation. As you prepare to write a first draft of your argumentative essay, take another look at your overall claim, reasons, and evidence. Do they still make sense? Do they stack up well against competing arguments? Do you have enough evidence to convince or persuade your intended readers? If you answer "no" to any of these questions, continue to develop and refine your argument.

Prepare a Draft

Building your argument prepares you to draft your essay. It allows you to decide how to frame your thesis statement, appeal to your readers, address counter-arguments, take advantage of design opportunities, and organize your reasons and evidence.

MAKE AN ARGUMENTATIVE CLAIM

The overall claim you developed as you built your argument (p. 404) provides the foundation for your thesis statement — a brief statement that conveys the main point you want to make about your issue. In an argumentative essay, a thesis statement should be debatable, plausible, and clear.

- **A debatable thesis statement is one with which readers can disagree.** Saying that we should take good care of our children, for example, isn't particularly debatable. Saying that we need to invest more public funding in mandatory immunization programs, however, would almost certainly lead some readers to disagree. Even though your goal in writing an argumentative essay is to convince readers to accept or act on your argument, there's little to be gained in arguing for something with which everyone will agree. An argumentative essay is useful only if it makes people think and, ideally, change their attitudes, beliefs, or behaviors.

- **A plausible thesis statement appears at the very least to be reasonable, and in fact the claim it makes might appear to be convincing or persuasive on its own.** That is, although your claim should be debatable, don't make it so extreme that it comes across as ridiculous or absurd. For example, it's one thing to argue that the news media should pay more attention to political candidates' platforms and leadership qualities than to their personal failings; it's quite another to argue that a candidate's criminal record should be ignored.

- **A clear thesis statement advances a claim that is easy to follow.** It explains what readers should believe or how they should act. Typically, this involves using words such as *should*, *must*, or *ought*. It's important to remember that you are attempting to convince or persuade your readers. Unless you tell them what to believe or how to act, they won't be sure of your position.

An effective thesis statement will shape your readers' understanding of the issue, directing their attention to particular aspects of the issue and away from others. Consider, for example, the following thesis statements about athletes' use of performance-enhancing drugs.

Thesis statement 1: If for no other reason, athletes should avoid the use of performance-enhancing drugs to safeguard their personal health.

Thesis statement 2: To eliminate the use of performance-enhancing drugs, athletes themselves must take the lead in policing their sports.

Thesis statement 3: National and international governing bodies for sports should engage in a coordinated effort to educate aspiring athletes about ethics and sportsmanship.

Is your
thesis statement
focused enough?
See Chapter 14
for help.

These thesis statements would lead to significantly different argumentative essays. The first thesis statement directs readers' attention to the health consequences for athletes who use performance-enhancing drugs. The second suggests that athletes themselves should take charge of efforts to eradicate this form of cheating. The third thesis statement focuses attention on the contributions that might be made by what are essentially large corporate and government agencies. Each thesis statement is plausible and debatable, and each one tells readers what they should believe or act on. Yet each leads the reader to view the issue in a significantly different way.

APPEAL TO YOUR READERS

As you work on your draft, consider the strategies you'll use to convince or persuade your readers to accept your argument. These strategies are essentially a means of appealing to — or asking — your readers to consider the reasons you are offering to support your overall claim and, if they accept them as appropriate and valid, to believe or act in a certain way.

Fortunately, you won't have to invent strategies on your own. For thousands of years, writers and speakers have used a wide range of appeals to ask readers to accept their reasons as appropriate and valid. Much of the work of ancient Greek and Roman thinkers such as Aristotle and Cicero revolved around strategies for presenting an argument to an audience. Their work still serves as a foundation for how we think about argumentation.

You can ask readers to accept your reasons by appealing to authority; emotion; principles, values, and beliefs; character; or logic. Most arguments are built on a combination of these appeals. The combination you choose will reflect your issue, purpose, readers, sources, and context.

Appeals to authority. When you present a reason by making an appeal to authority, you ask readers to accept it because someone in a position of authority endorses it. The evidence used to support this kind of appeal typically takes the form of quotations, paraphrases, or summaries of the ideas of experts in a given subject area, of political leaders, or of people who have been affected by an issue. As you consider whether this kind of appeal might be appropriate for your argumentative essay, reflect on the notes you've taken on your sources. Have you identified experts, leaders, or people who have been affected by an issue? If so, can you use them to convince your readers that your argument has merit?

Appeals to emotion attempt to elicit an emotional response to an issue. The famous "win one for the Gipper" speech delivered by Pat O'Brien, who portrayed Notre Dame coach Knute Rockne in the 1940 film *Knute Rockne: All American*, is an example of an appeal to emotion. At halftime during a game with Army, with Notre Dame trailing, he said:

> Well, boys . . . I haven't a thing to say. Played a great game . . . all of you. Great game. I guess we just can't expect to win 'em all.

> I'm going to tell you something I've kept to myself for years. None of you ever knew George Gipp. It was long before your time. But you know what a tradition he is at Notre Dame. . . . And the last thing he said to me — "Rock," he said, "sometime, when the team is up against it — and the breaks are beating the boys — tell them to go out there with all they got and win just one for the Gipper. . . . I don't know where I'll be then, Rock," he said — "but I'll know about it — and I'll be happy."

Using emotional appeals to frame an argument — that is, to help readers view an issue in a particular way — is a tried-and-true strategy. But use it carefully, if you use it at all. In some types of documents, such as scholarly articles and essays, emotional appeals are used infrequently, and readers of such documents are likely to ask why you would play on their emotions instead of making an appeal to logic (see p. 416) or an appeal to authority.

Appeals to principles, values, and beliefs rely on the assumption that your readers value a given set of principles. Religious and ethical arguments are often based on appeals to principles, such as the need to respect God, to love one another, to trust in the innate goodness of people, to believe that all of us are created equal, or to believe that security should never be purchased at the price of individual liberty. If you make an appeal to principles, values, or beliefs, be sure your readers share the particular principle, value, or belief you are using. If they don't, you might need to state and justify your underlying assumptions at the outset — or you might want to try a different kind of appeal.

Appeals to character. Writers frequently use appeals to character. When politicians refer to their military experience, for example, they are saying, "Look at me. I'm a patriotic person who has served our country." When celebrities endorse a product, they are saying, "You know and like me, so please believe me when I say that this product is worth purchasing." Appeals to character can also reflect a person's professional accomplishment. When scientists or philosophers present an argument, for example, they sometimes refer to their background and experience, or perhaps to their previous publications. In doing so, they are implicitly telling their readers that they have been accurate and truthful in the past and that readers can continue to trust them. Essentially, you can think of an appeal to character as the "trust me" strategy. As you consider this kind of appeal, reflect on your character, accomplishments, and experiences, and ask how they might lead your readers to trust you.

Appeals to logic. A logical appeal refers to the concept of reasoning through a set of propositions to reach a considered conclusion. For example, you might argue that a suspect is guilty of murder because police found her fingerprints on the murder weapon, her blood under the murder victim's fingernails, scratches on the suspect's face, and video of the murder from a surveillance camera. Your argument would rely on the logical presentation of evidence to convince jurors that the suspect was the murderer and to persuade them to return a verdict of guilty. As you develop reasons to support your claim, consider using logical appeals such as deduction and induction.

- **Deduction** is a form of logical reasoning that moves from general principles to a conclusion. It usually involves two propositions and a conclusion.

   Proposition 1 (usually a general principle): Stealing is wrong.

   Proposition 2 (usually an observation): John stole a candy bar from the store.

   Conclusion (results of deductive analysis): John's theft of the candy bar was wrong.

   Deduction is often used to present arguments that have ethical and moral dimensions, such as birth control, welfare reform, and immigration policy.

- **Induction** is a form of logical reasoning that moves from specific observations to general conclusions, often drawing on numerical data to reveal patterns. Medical researchers, for example, typically collect a large number of observations about the effectiveness and side effects of new medications and then analyze their observations to draw conclusions about the effectiveness of the medications. Induction is based on probability — that is, whether something seems likely to occur in the future based on what has been observed. Three commonly used forms of induction are trend analysis (see p. 241), causal analysis (see p. 243), and data analysis (see p. 244).

You can use different types of appeals to support your claim. Emotional appeals can be mixed with appeals to character. A coach's address to a team before an important athletic competition often relies not only on appeals to emotion but also on appeals to character, asking the players to trust what the coach has to say and to trust in themselves and their own abilities. Similarly, appeals to principle can be combined with appeals to emotion and logic.

To choose your appeals, reflect on your purpose, readers, sources, context, and overall claim. In your writer's notebook, record your responses to the following:

1. Put your overall claim in the form of a thesis statement.
2. List the reasons you will offer to accept your overall claim.
3. Identify the evidence you will use to accept each reason.
4. Ask what sort of appeals will help you connect each reason to the evidence you have chosen.
5. Sketch out promising appeals. Ask, for example, how you would appeal to authority, or how you would appeal to logic.
6. Ask how your readers are likely to respond to a given appeal.
7. Ask whether each appeal is appropriate in light of your overall argument. An emotional appeal might seem effective by itself, for example, but if the argument you've developed relies largely on appeals to logic and authority, an emotional appeal might surprise your readers.

ADDRESS COUNTERARGUMENTS

Your readers will expect you to consider and address reasonable alternatives to your overall claim. They'll do so not only because it is appropriate to acknowledge the contributions of other authors who have written about an issue, but also because they want to understand why your argument is superior to the alternatives. If your readers are aware of opposing claims but notice that you haven't addressed them, they'll question your credibility. They might conclude that you haven't thought carefully about the issue, or they might wonder whether you haven't addressed opposing claims in your essay because you think the other claims are stronger than yours.

To address counterarguments, review the work you did to identify and consider opposing claims as you built your argument (see p. 407). Consider the strengths and weaknesses of each claim in relation to your argument and in relation to the other opposing claims you identified. Then decide whether to concede, refute, or ignore each claim.

Concede valid claims. Show your readers that you are being fair — and establish common ground with readers who might otherwise be inclined to disagree with you — by acknowledging opposing points of view and accepting reasonable aspects of counterarguments. For example, if you are arguing that your state government should spend more to repair roads and bridges, acknowledge that this will probably mean reducing funding for other state programs or increasing state taxes.

You can qualify your concession by explaining that although part of a counterargument is sound, readers should consider the argument's weaknesses. You might note, for example, that reducing funding for some state programs could be offset by instituting fees for those who use those programs most.

Refute widely held claims. A counterargument might be widely advocated or generally accepted yet still have significant weaknesses. If you identify widely held claims that have weaknesses such as cost, undesirable outcomes, or logical flaws, describe the counterargument, point out its flaws, and explain why your claim or reason is superior. For example, you might note that although it is costly to maintain roads and bridges, allowing them to fall into disrepair will cost far more in the long run — in terms of both funding and loss of life.

Ignore competing claims. Don't assume that addressing counterarguments means giving every competing claim equal time. Some counterarguments will be much stronger than others, and some will be so closely related to one another that you can dismiss them as a group. Once you've addressed valid and widely held competing claims, you can safely ignore the rest. Even though your sense of fairness might suggest that you should address every counterargument, doing so will result in a less effective (and potentially much longer) essay.

As you present your discussion of counterarguments, maintain a reasonable and polite tone. You gain little, if anything, by insulting or belittling writers with whom you disagree, particularly when it's possible that some of your readers think a certain counterargument has merit. It is preferable — and generally more effective in terms of winning your argument — to carefully and politely point out the limitations of a particular counterargument.

CONSIDER GENRE AND DESIGN

A well-written argumentative essay uses design to help readers understand your argument more clearly, usually by simplifying the presentation of reasons and evidence or by setting a mood through the use of carefully selected illustrations. The design of your essay should reflect the formatting requirements of your assignment and the expectations of your readers, particularly your instructor.

In many cases, the appeals you choose to make to your readers will suggest design elements that can enhance your argument.

- **Photographs** can strengthen (or serve as) an emotional appeal. For instance, an argument in favor of tightening lending restrictions might show a family in front of the home they've lost to foreclosure.

- **Headings and subheadings** can help readers follow your reasoning about an issue.

- **Color** and **pull quotes** can underscore appeals to values, beliefs, and principles by calling a reader's attention to shared assumptions and important ideas.

- **Sidebars** can highlight an appeal to character by giving related information about a writer or a source without interfering with the flow of the argument.

- Appeals to authority often present statistical data in the form of **tables**, **charts**, and **graphs**.

Consider the placement of visual evidence carefully. In general, place illustrations as close as possible to the point where they are mentioned in the text, provide a title or caption that identifies or explains the illustration, and cite the source of the information.

You can find discussions of document design in Chapters 16, 17, and 18.

FRAME YOUR ARGUMENT

Most written arguments rely on a well-established set of elements: a clearly expressed thesis statement, a thorough discussion of the reasons and evidence supporting the overall claim, careful consideration of counterarguments, and an introduction and a conclusion. The presentation of these elements, however, is as varied as the issues addressed in argumentative essays and the writers who tackle them.

Organization. As you organize your argumentative essay, give some thought to the sequence in which you present your reasons and evidence and discuss counterarguments. If you are drawing heavily on emotional appeals, for example, you might lead with a particularly striking appeal, one designed to outrage or excite your readers — or at least to get them to continue reading your essay. Similarly, you might end with a reason that would leave your readers feeling that they must do something about the issue you've raised. If you are crafting an argument that relies heavily on logical analysis, you should ask whether any of your appeals build on (or logically follow) other appeals. You should also ask whether some appeals are easier to understand and accept than others. If so, be sure to present them before you advance more complex or objectionable appeals. Counterarguments might all be addressed early on, discussed in turn, or withheld until you've established the reasons in support of your overall claim. Refer to Chapter 15 for additional guidelines on organizing and outlining an essay.

Introduction and Conclusion.   Pay particular attention to your introduction and conclusion. These important elements not only provide the framework within which your readers will understand the issue you are addressing but also influence their willingness to accept your argument. Once you've decided how to frame your introduction and conclusion, you can use a range of strategies to put them into words. In their introductions, writers of argumentative essays frequently rely on strategies such as asking a question, leading with a quotation, and telling a story. In their conclusions, they often use strategies such as speculating about the future, asking a question, and closing with a quotation. You can read more about strategies for introducing and concluding your essay in Chapter 16.

Review and Improve Your Draft

An effective argumentative essay makes its claim in such a manner that readers will understand an issue in a particular way, provides plausible and well-supported appeals to accept that claim, addresses likely counterarguments, and avoids the traps posed by logical fallacies and other forms of argument that lack integrity. Few writers can fully address all these elements in a first draft, so don't expect to produce a finished essay in one sitting. Set aside enough time to review your draft and to revise it at least once. Allowing at least a day or two between completing your draft and reviewing it makes it easier to recognize opportunities for improvement and to clarify your thinking.

CONSIDER YOUR OVERALL CLAIM

Before you review any other part of your draft, spend some time reassessing your overall claim. Is it presented in such a manner that your readers will understand the issue in a specific way? Have you stated it clearly? Is it possible that your readers might reasonably misinterpret your claim, or might think of the issue differently than you do? Finally, is the claim stated in a way that is consistent with how you've framed your introduction and conclusion?

REVIEW YOUR REASONS, EVIDENCE, AND APPEALS

The presentation of your overall claim will set up expectations among your readers about how you're likely to support it. For example, if you've said that the city council needs to increase funding for a flood mitigation program, your readers are likely to expect that at least some of your reasons for making the claim will touch on the consequences of failing to fund the program at a reasonable level. As you review your draft, ask whether your reasons make sense individually, and then ask whether they work well together. Most important, ask how your readers are likely to react to each reason and whether you've provided enough evidence to support it.

Peer Review: Improve Your Argumentative Essay

One of the biggest challenges writers face is reading their own work as a reader rather than as the writer. Because you know what you're trying to say, you'll find it easy to understand your draft. To determine what you should do to revise your draft, ask a friend or classmate to read your essay and to answer the following questions.

Purpose	1. How do you interpret my purpose for writing? Does my goal seem to be to convince or to persuade?
	2. Is my overall claim plausible and debatable? Do you agree with what I am saying? If not, what should I do to convince you?
	3. Do the reasons I've offered to support my claim seem sufficient and appropriate?
Readers	4. Do you accept the connections I've made (or have assumed to exist) between my reasons and my overall claim?
	5. Do you find the issue significant? Why or why not?
	6. Does my reasoning seem sound? Did you catch any fallacies?
	7. Have I used argumentative appeals appropriately and effectively? Should I consider making any other kinds of appeals?
Sources	8. Does the evidence I've offered to support my appeals make sense? Can I add or clarify anything to help you understand the argument better? Do you think any of the evidence is unnecessary?
	9. Do my sources strike you as reliable and appropriate? Does any of the evidence I've used seem questionable? Have I relied on any sources too heavily?
	10. Is it clear which ideas and information are my own and which came from my sources?
Context	11. Have I clearly introduced and effectively handled counterarguments? Did I present them fairly?
	12. How familiar were you with this issue before reading my essay? Do I need to provide more (or less) background information or context? Did I fail to include any reasons or evidence that you expected?
	13. Could I strengthen any of my appeals by bringing in design elements, such as photographs or tables?

For each of the points listed above, ask your reviewers to provide concrete advice about what you should do to improve your draft. It can help if you ask them to adopt the role of an editor — someone who is working with you to improve your draft. You can read more about peer review in Chapter 4.

In addition, ask whether your readers are likely to accept the kinds of appeals you've used to present your reasons and evidence. Always consider your readers' needs, interests, backgrounds, and knowledge of the issue. You might conclude, for instance, that an emotional appeal will backfire, or that your readers will expect more evidence from authorities, or that you could strengthen an appeal to values by explaining an underlying assumption.

EXAMINE YOUR TREATMENT OF COUNTERARGUMENTS

As you review how you've addressed counterarguments, put yourself in your readers' place. Doing so allows you to pose reasonable arguments that contradict your overall claim about the issue. If you believe a counterargument is plausible and likely to be raised by your readers, make sure you've responded to it. Your response need not be lengthy, but it should let readers know that you've considered the counterargument and found it less effective than the argument you're making.

ENSURE THE INTEGRITY OF YOUR ARGUMENT

Carefully review the reasons and evidence you've offered to support your overall claim. Then review the list of common logical fallacies starting on page 410. Make sure that your argument is free of these fallacies. Even an otherwise strong argument can fail to convince or persuade readers if it relies in part on questionable argumentative strategies.

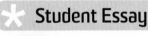

Student Essay

Vince Reid, "The Changing Face of Online Gaming"

Reid 1

Vince Reid

Prof. Dunlap

CTW H1

November 30, 2013

The Changing Face of Online Gaming

In 2009, the most popular massively multiplayer online game, or MMOG, in the world was *World of Warcraft*, a role-playing game produced by one of the largest videogame developers in the USA, Blizzard. Like its fellow MMOGs, *World of Warcraft* establishes a persistent online environment in which thousands, even millions of players around the world can interact at the same time. *World of Warcraft* dominated the MMOG market for years, with 12 million subscribers at its peak (qtd. in Fahey). Three years later, however, the world's most popular online game had become *League of Legends*, a type of game known as a multiplayer online battle arena (MOBA), in which small teams of players compete in a match. In 2012, *League* boasted an astounding 32 million players each month (Riot Games). *League*'s rapid rise is a lesson for game developers everywhere. *League of Legends* became popular by positioning itself as closer to a sport than a mere game, allowing an even playing field for competitors that isn't based solely on the amount of money they spend. To establish a community of loyal players, game developers should prioritize the user experience and embrace the sports-like qualities of the game.

The first aspect game developers need to consider is their business model. Almost every online game relies on one of two business models, the subscription model or the micro-transaction model. *World of Warcraft* and other MMOGs from major developers operate on the subscription model. *WoW* costs roughly fifty dollars for the game and an additional fifteen dollars a month for server access. This might not sound like a huge amount of money, but the percentage of gamers who are willing to pay full price for a game is dropping (Cox, "Subscription").

Information about the writer, class, and submission date is formatted according to MLA guidelines.

Following MLA guidelines, the title is centered.

The writer begins with a brief overview of the most successful online games.

Following MLA guidelines, information cited in a source is identified using the abbreviation "qtd. in".

The writer presents his main argument.

A brief title distinguishes two sources by the same author.

Reid 2

Unlike single-player games which do not require Internet connections, you cannot pirate an online game because you need an account with an active subscription to play, and online games like *World of Warcraft* are notorious for almost never going on sale. If you want to play, you usually have to pay full price. Enough gamers are willing to pay for the subscription and keep the major game developers in business, while everyone else turns to games that use the microtransaction business model.

Microtransaction games are free to play but have built-in stores which sell things like game equipment and weapons, access to additional play areas, in-game money, and additional characters. The costs of these items vary. Weapons might be purchased for as little as two dollars, while new characters can cost as much as ten dollars each. The problem with microtransaction games, however, is that they sell items that bestow power, such as stronger weapons or rare abilities. The sale of power for real money rapidly creates a core group of players who are much more powerful than most of the other players. As a result, only players willing to pay for power can compete at the top level. Selling power keeps companies in business by providing a steady stream of money, but it also pushes away players who aren't willing to or can't afford to pay at the highest levels and just want to play a game.

League of Legends modifies the microtransaction model in an important way: it does not sell power. *League*'s built-in store only allows players to buy items that alter character appearance. These new "skins" have no direct impact on gameplay, they provide no power to the player, and they cost around ten dollars each. And they're not required to play, either. Each week, *League* provides ten champions, as the characters are known, who are free to play, so players who don't want to spend a dime don't have to. Writing about another free to play online game, *Guild Wars 2*, Matt Miller of Gameinformer.com explains the appeal of such micro-transactions:

> Not only is [*Guild Wars 2*] a full-featured game without a subscription fee, but its in-game store doesn't feel exploitative. Additional cosmetic

The writer makes a transition from one paragraph to the next.

Supporting evidence is provided in the form of a block quotation.

Reid 3

items let players express themselves above and beyond an already excellent array of free clothing and color options. The game offers ample inventory space, but gives you the option of buying additional slots. In short, *Guild Wars 2* and games like it establish a functional and fun game in their own right, but give users the option to pay for individual features that are important to them. Players purchase additional items because they already love what they're playing, and they want to customize or expand the experience into something they'll enjoy even more.

Interestingly, the microtransaction model has led *League* to be kept in business by a smaller percentage of paying players. Fewer people are willing to buy an item that only makes you look different. But, because *League* offers equal opportunity to all players, more players choose to play *League* overall than other microtransaction games. The weekly free champions offer a range of playing levels to suit novice and experienced players alike. League players advance based on skill and experience rather than on monetary investment in the game, much as athletes gain recognition in their chosen sports through practice and competition.

A good business model, however, is not enough to make a game successful. Companies also have to plan their development cycles carefully, and this is where an aspect unique to online games comes into play. Because most videogames are played offline and sold in a disk format, they are never updated after their release. In contrast, because online games require an Internet connection, it's easy for developers to continue adding content to their games or fix bugs in the programming by streaming the updates whenever a player connects to their servers (much as a smartphone app can be updated periodically to fix bugs or add features). Most online games tend to withhold new content until enough new content has been developed to justify releasing a major update to the game. Typically, this takes six months to two years, depending on the game. When they are released, expansion packs, as these updates are called, are always met with excitement. Expansion packs may add new special

Reid 4

abilities for characters, extend the online universe, or create new quests or opponents. However, it's almost guaranteed that most players will finish the new content quickly and have nothing to do while they wait. For gamers, this creates a situation where eleven months out of the year they feel like they're starving, saving their money for one glorious month when they can eat as much as they want. The binge is enjoyable, but it doesn't last.

League's developer, Riot Games, does not release expansion packs for the game. Instead, twice a month, they release a new champion for play. These releases don't create as much sustained excitement among players as the release of an expansion pack does in other games. Most players who were interested in the newest character will decide about a week after the update was released whether they prefer the character they were already playing. As soon as it fades, the excitement will be building again as players discuss how the next new character will impact the game and begin preparing items and strategies to take advantage of the new abilities the character will bring. In this way, *League*'s developers position the game as something more like a sport; each new character is greeted as eagerly and with as much speculation as a talented rookie might be welcomed to a hockey team (Robinson). These frequent character releases keep League's player base interested in its content, and the game enjoys a comparatively high retention rate. *World of Warcraft*, for example, averaged a little under twelve million players a month at its height (qtd. in Fahey). *League*, in comparison, has twelve million players each day, with over seventy million registered accounts (Riot Games).

> **Numerical information supports the reasons behind the author's argument.**

As important as the business model and development cycle may be, game developers must also invest in making the game more like a sport. League's battle arena format mimics a sports game in that players team up and compete, and each battle has a clear winner at the end. Moreover, in 2010, Riot Games released a content update that added a ranking system to *League*. Players were able to see who the best players were, and the best players began to create teams and compete with one another. This might seem like a small thing, but before the ranking system was added, *League* worked like other online games.

> **The author develops his point about a game vs. a sport.**

Reid 5

When players signed up for a match, they couldn't know the skill levels of the other players they were paired with and against. They were playing blind. When the ranking system was introduced, it became possible for players to compete on an even footing and experience measurable improvement. In addition, as the top players emerged and achieved higher and higher rank, they began streaming videos of their games live with commentary and collecting player stats. Professional teams emerged, complete with team names and logos, each champion playing a different position (Robinson). In 2011 Riot began organizing world tournament, played live in arenas and with cash prizes for the winning team. These championships have attracted huge crowds, both in person and online. The second annual world championship games drew more than 8,000 live spectators and more than 8 million online spectators (qtd. in Cox, "Championships"). In fact, this past summer the U.S. Immigration and Citizenship Service actually recognized *League* as a professional sport, granting sports visas to *League* players just as they would to soccer or baseball players from other countries (Robertson).

Why, you might ask, does it matter that *League* is a sport instead of a game? It matters because a game is something people play, but a sport is something people are a part of. A sport is a game with a community built around it. Professional athletes have millions of fans, and professional teams are built from a tiny fraction of a vast group of athletes who all strive to make it to the top. Friendships are formed around a shared enjoyment of a sport. It is much harder to stop being a part of a sport than it is to stop playing a game. Indeed, most videogames are played for two to three years at most before something better comes out, and as *League* has become more and more successful other games have copied it and attempted to take its place. Giving up *League* means more than just giving up a game, it means giving up a community that you are a part of. Game developers seeking to make their mark should focus on the player experience. By bringing players together into true sports communities, game companies can develop loyal followings, expand their player base, and likely turn a profit, too.

> The author concludes by explaining why the sports-like approach makes a difference.

Reid 5

Works Cited

Cox, Kate. "The Subscription MMO Is Dead." *Kotaku*. Gawker Media, 24 Aug. 2010.

    Web. 15 Nov. 2013.

----- . "League of Legends World Championship Draws Over 8 Million Viewers."

    Kotaku. Gawker Media, 22 Oct. 2012. Web. 20 Nov. 2013.

Fahey, Mike. "World of Warcraft: No Growth Since 2008." *Kotaku*. Gawker Media, 10

    Feb. 2010. Web. 13 Nov. 2013.

Miller, Matt. "How Microtransactions Are Bad for Gaming." *Game Informer*. Game-

    Stop Network, 12 Sep. 2012. Web. 15 Nov. 2013.

Riot Games. "The Major League (of Legends): League of Legend's Global Reach."

    Riot Games. Riot Games, n.d. Web. 20 Nov. 2013.

Robertson, Adi. "U.S. Visa Bureau Says 'League of Legends' Is a Professional Sport."

    The Verge. Vox Media, Inc., 13 July 2013. Web. 20 Nov. 2013.

Robinson, Jon. "'League of Legends' Mimics Regular Sports." *ESPN*. ESPN Internet

    Ventures, 30 Jan. 2013. Web. 15 Nov. 2013.

Annotations:

Following MLA guidelines, the Works Cited heading is centered.

Entries in the list are formatted with hanging indents.

Two sources by the same author

Because Web sites may change, MLA does not require URLs in Web citations.

"n.d." indicates that the Web source did not list a date.

✳ Project Ideas

The following suggestions provide means of focusing your work on an argumentative essay or another type of argumentative document.

Suggestions for Essays

1. ARGUE ABOUT A SOCIAL TREND

Identify and discuss the relevance of a social trend, such as text-messaging, joining social-networking Web sites, or dressing in a particular manner. Then make an argument about (a) the advisability of following the trend, (b) the likely effects — short- or long-term — of the trend on society, or (c) the likelihood that the trend will have a lasting impact on society. Use evidence from online conversations and your personal observations to support your argument.

2. ARGUE AGAINST A COMMONLY HELD BELIEF

Urge your readers to reject a commonly held belief. For example, you might argue that the widespread belief that writing ability is a gift rather than an acquired skill causes students to give up too easily on efforts to improve their writing. Or you might argue that a particular belief about the innate character of men or women is inaccurate and condescending. In your essay, define the belief and make an overall claim about the effects of accepting it. Offer reasons and evidence to support your claim. Base your appeals on logic and on principles, values, and beliefs.

3. URGE READERS TO PATRONIZE THE ARTS

Make an argument about the value of attending a play or concert, viewing a movie or watching a television show, attending a poetry reading or an art exhibition, or purchasing a new music album or video game. Your argument should be based on the benefits of patronizing the arts for personal or professional growth. To support your argument, draw on your observations and interpretations of the artistic event or object. You might also use evidence from interviews or surveys.

4. ARGUE ABOUT A DEFINITION

Make an argument about a definition, such as how a problem or an issue has been defined or how a particular standard has been developed and applied. For example, you might argue that characterizations of state support for public education as a financial issue are inappropriate, and that it would be better to understand the issue as one of ensuring that citizens are well prepared to participate in a democracy. Or you might argue that your state's definition of intoxication (for example, .08 percent blood alcohol content) is inappropriate, and that it ought to be higher or lower. Use evidence from published sources to support your argument.

5. ARGUE ABOUT AN ISSUE IN YOUR AREA OF STUDY

Write an argumentative essay about an issue in a discipline or profession in which you have an interest. For example, if you are interested in human resources, you might argue about the implications of allowing employers to access employees' genetic profiles. The issue you choose should be under debate in the discipline or profession, so be sure to search professional or academic journals and online conversations among members of the discipline or profession for prevailing arguments.

Suggestions for Other Genres

6. WRITE AN OPINION COLUMN ABOUT A NEW LAW OR REGULATION

In an opinion column, identify a recently passed law or a new regulation (federal, state, or local), and discuss its potential impact. Offer a brief summary evaluation of its appropriateness or likely effects, and make recommendations to your readers about how to respond to the law. For example, you might argue that a new law is so flawed that it should be repealed. Or you might argue that only by providing adequate funding to a local or state agency can a regulation be enforced effectively. Use evidence from government documents to support your argument.

7. WRITE A LETTER TO THE EDITOR ABOUT SUPPORTING A LOCAL INITIATIVE

In a brief letter to the editor (no longer than 300 words), argue that readers should support a local initiative, such as a food drive or a get-out-the-vote effort. Your letter should clearly state your overall claim and offer reasons to accept it. Because of the brevity of the letter, you should limit your use of evidence and rely primarily on reasoning.

8. WRITE A LETTER TO THE EDITOR ABOUT A PUBLISHED ARTICLE, EDITORIAL, OR OPINION COLUMN

Write a letter to the editor that responds to an article, editorial, or opinion column. In your letter, briefly summarize the argument made in the published piece, and then offer a counterargument that is well supported by reasoning and evidence. Use evidence from the published piece as well as from other published sources and your personal experience.

9. WRITE A BLOG ENTRY ABOUT AN ISSUE RAISED IN ANOTHER BLOG

In a blog, argue about an issue addressed by the author of another blog. For example, you might take issue with an argument about the economic and political trade-offs of government rescues of failed financial institutions. Or you might argue about the advisability of joining social-networking Web sites such as Facebook or LinkedIn. Your blog entry should link to the blog entry that raised the issue, as well as to other relevant blogs. Use evidence from blogs and other published sources to support your argument. You should refer to your sources by using phrases such as "in an article published in *Time* on July 23, 2013, Ann Smith argues" or by linking directly to the source.

10. CREATE A PUBLIC SERVICE ADVERTISEMENT

Create a full-page ad suitable for a magazine or Web site that urges readers to take action on a social issue, such as adoption or hunger. Your ad should use visual images and only enough text to clearly identify the issue and convey your argument to your readers. For inspiration, examine the ads shown on pages 389–392.

In Summary: Writing an Argumentative Essay

* **Find a conversation and listen in.**
  - Explore disagreements (p. 399).
  - Track online conversations (p. 401).
  - Ask questions about promising issues (p. 401).

* **Build your argument.**
  - Define your overall claim (p. 404).
  - Develop reasons to accept your overall claim (p. 404).
  - Choose evidence to support your reasons (p. 406).
  - Identify and consider opposing claims (p. 407).
  - Ensure the integrity of your argument (p. 410).

* **Prepare a draft.**
  - Make an argumentative claim (p. 413).
  - Appeal to your readers (p. 414).
  - Address counterarguments (p. 417).
  - Consider genre and design (p. 418).
  - Frame your argument (p. 419).

* **Review and improve your draft.**
  - Consider your overall claim (p. 420).
  - Review your reasons, evidence, and appeals (p. 420).
  - Examine your treatment of counterarguments (p. 422).
  - Ensure the integrity of your argument (p. 422).

PART THREE

Working with Sources

11

Beginning Your Search

▶▶ Given the amount of information available through library collections, databases, and the Web, writers have become less worried about finding enough sources and far more concerned about finding the right sources. This chapter explores strategies for collecting information for a writing project and then looks at how you can keep track of that information.

How Should I Focus My Search for Sources?

As you prepare to search for sources, it's best to have an idea of what you're looking for. Focus your efforts to collect, read, evaluate, and take notes on sources by developing a research question — a brief question that asks about a specific aspect of your subject, reflects your writing situation, and is narrow enough to allow you to collect information in time to meet your deadlines.

To develop your research question, generate ideas for potential questions and assess them in light of your interests, role, and writing situation.

Generate Potential Research Questions

Most research questions begin with the words *what*, *why*, *when*, *where*, *who*, or *how*. Some research questions use the words *would* or *could* to ask whether something is possible. Still others use the word *should* to analyze the appropriateness of a particular action, policy, procedure, or decision. Questions can focus on the following:

- **Information**: what is known — and not known — about a subject
- **History**: what has occurred in the past that is relevant to a subject
- **Assumptions**: what conclusions — merited or not — writers and readers have already made about a subject
- **Goals**: what the writers and readers involved in this conversation want to see happen (or not happen)
- **Outcomes**: what has happened so far, or what is likely to happen
- **Policies**: what the best procedures are for carrying out actions or for making decisions

Questions can also lead you to engage in the following kinds of thinking processes. These processes will be shaped, in turn, by your purpose and role as an author (see Part Two).

- **Reflecting**: considering the significance of a subject
- **Reporting**: seeking information; conveying what is known about a subject
- **Analyzing**: looking for similarities and differences among subjects or aspects of a subject; asking what leads to a specific result; asking about a series of events
- **Evaluating**: asking about strengths and weaknesses, advantages and disadvantages, or appropriateness

- **Problem solving**: defining problems, considering the outcomes of a problem, assessing potential solutions, and/or offering solutions
- **Advocating**: advancing arguments about a subject

By combining a specific focus, such as assumptions or goals, with a specific type of thinking process, such as problem solving, you can create carefully tailored research questions, such as the ones that featured writer Jennie Tillson considered for her essay about the cost of college.

What assumptions have shaped debates about rising tuitions?

What assumptions have worked against a resolution of this problem?

Why have college administrators been unable (or unwilling) to control tuition hikes?

Why do so many families take out loans to pay for a college education?

What can the government do to help reduce tuition costs?

What can students do to manage tuition costs?

Use specific question words to start generating potential research questions. If you are interested in conducting an analysis, for example, ask questions using the words *what, why, when, where, who,* and *how.* If you want to explore goals and outcomes, use the words *would* or *could.* If the conversation focuses on determining an appropriate course of action, generate questions using the word *should.* Consider the differences among these questions:

What are the benefits of a college education?

Would it be feasible to require colleges and universities to commit 5 percent of their endowments to financial aid?

Should the U.S. Congress pass legislation to control tuition costs?

Each question would lead to differences in how to search for and select sources of information, what role to adopt as a writer, and how to organize and design the document.

Select and Refine Your Question

Once you have a list of potential research questions, select a question that interests you, is consistent with the role you have adopted, and is appropriate for your writing situation. Then refine your question by referring to shared assumptions and existing conditions, narrowing its scope, and conducting preliminary searches.

REFLECT ON YOUR WRITING SITUATION

As you consider potential research questions, pay attention to your purpose and role. Your efforts to collect information should help you accomplish your purpose and address your readers' needs, interests, values, and beliefs. Keep in mind, however, that as you learn more about your subject, you might refine your purpose. In turn, that might lead to changes in your research question. If you think of your research question as a flexible guide — as a question subject to revision — you can increase the effectiveness of your document.

REFER TO SHARED ASSUMPTIONS AND EXISTING CONDITIONS

You can refine your research question by calling attention to assumptions that have been made by the community of writers and readers who are addressing your subject, or by referring to existing conditions relevant to your subject. Note the difference among these three versions of featured writer Ali Bizzul's research question about the health risks associated with weight gain among football players.

Original Question:
Why would football players risk their health — and even their lives — by putting on extra weight?

Alternative 1:
Given the widespread belief among coaches that extra bulk might reduce performance on the field, why would football players risk their health — and even their lives — by putting on extra weight?

Alternative 2:
In the face of recent high-profile deaths among college and professional football players, why would football players risk their health — and even their lives — by putting on extra weight?

As you refine your research question, experiment with using qualifying words and phrases such as the following:

Mix . . .	and Match
Although	we know that . . .
Because	it is uncertain . . .
Even though	it is clear that . . .
Given that	studies indicate . . .
If	recent events . . .

Now that	it has been shown . . .
Since	the lack of . . .
While	we cannot . . .

NARROW YOUR SCOPE

Early research questions typically lack focus. You can narrow the scope of your question by looking for vague words and phrases and replacing them with more specific words or phrases. The process of moving from a broad research question to one that might be addressed effectively in an academic essay might produce the following sequence:

Original Question:

What is behind the increased popularity of women's sports?

Refined:

What has led to the increased popularity of women's sports in colleges and universities?

Further Refined:

How has Title IX increased opportunities for women athletes in American colleges and universities?

In this example, the writer has narrowed the scope of the research question in two ways. First, the writer has shifted the focus from women's sports in general to women's sports in American colleges and universities. Second, the writer has moved from a general focus on the increased popularity of women's sports to a more specific focus on the opportunities brought about by Title IX, the federal legislation that mandated equal opportunities for women athletes.

✈ TECH TIP: CONDUCT PRELIMINARY SEARCHES

One of the best ways to test your research question is to conduct some preliminary searches in an online library catalog or database or on the Web. If you locate a vast amount of information in your searches, you might need to revise your question so that it focuses on a more manageable aspect of the subject. In contrast, if you find almost nothing, you might need to expand the scope of your question.

How Can I Develop a Search Plan?

Once you've created your research question, you'll need to decide how to search for and collect information. Your search plan — a brief, informal plan that records your ideas about how to locate and collect information — will be shaped by your research question and your writing situation.

Identify Relevant Types of Sources

Writers use information found in a variety of sources — electronic, print, and field — to support the points they make in their documents. To identify relevant sources for your writing project, consider the scope of the conversation you are joining, the timeliness of your subject, the information you'll need to develop your ideas, and the evidence you'll need to support your points.

CONSIDER THE SCOPE OF YOUR CONVERSATION

If the conversation focuses on a highly specialized issue within a scholarly discipline, such as a discussion of gene splicing in biology, the best sources usually are scholarly books and journal articles. If it addresses a subject that has broad appeal, such as transportation problems in your state or region, you can draw on a much wider range of sources, including newspaper and magazine articles, editorials and opinion columns, blogs, and Web sites.

CONSIDER THE TIMELINESS OF YOUR SUBJECT

Some subjects, such as funding for higher education or reducing alcohol consumption by college students, tend to be discussed over an extended period of time in a wide range of sources. If your subject focuses on a recent event, however, it might be best to turn to magazine and newspaper articles, the Web, blogs, observation, surveys, or interviews.

CONSIDER WHAT YOU NEED TO LEARN

If your subject is unfamiliar to you, look for sources that offer general overviews or discuss important aspects of the subject. You can also look for overviews of a subject in magazine articles, in professional journal articles, and on the Web.

CONSIDER THE EVIDENCE YOU'LL NEED

Think about the kind of evidence other writers have used to make their points. Have they used numerical data from scholarly research reports? Have they referred to expert opinion? If so, search for sources that can provide these kinds of evidence.

Identify Appropriate Search Tools and Research Methods

In general, you can use three sets of resources to locate information.

- **Electronic search tools**, such as library catalogs, databases, and Web search sites, allow you to search and browse for sources using a computer. Electronic search tools provide access to publication information about — and in some cases to the complete text of — print and digital sources.

- **Print resources**, such as bibliographies, indexes, encyclopedias, dictionaries, handbooks, almanacs, and atlases, can be found in library reference and periodical rooms. Unlike electronic search tools, which typically cover recent publications, many print resources provide information about publications over several decades — and in some cases over more than a century.

- **Field research methods** allow you to collect information firsthand. These methods include conducting observations, interviews, and surveys; corresponding with experts; attending public events and performances; and viewing or listening to television and radio programs.

Featured writer Ellen Page, who wrote an informative essay about the use of DDT in the prevention of malaria (see p. 155), knew that her topic would require recent sources. As she put together her search plan, she decided to search databases for recent scholarly articles and to look for Web sites that reported recent research. To obtain the most up-to-date information, she also scheduled an interview with a professor at her university who had expertise in the area.

Review and Refine Your Plan

Your search plan might be an informal set of notes or a list of step-by-step instructions complete with details such as keywords to search, interview questions to ask, and observation forms to fill out. No matter how informal it is, you should write it down. A written plan will help you remember the decisions you've made as you've prepared to collect your sources.

Use your plan to schedule time to search for and collect information. Next to each activity — such as searching a database or conducting an interview — identify start dates and projected completion dates. Creating a schedule will help you budget and manage your time.

Share your plan with your instructor, your supervisor, your classmates, or a librarian. Each might suggest additional search tools, research methods, shortcuts, and alternative research strategies for your project. Take notes on the feedback you receive, and, if necessary, revise your plan.

How Can I Keep Track of My Sources?

If you've ever forgotten a phone number or misplaced tickets to a concert, you know how frustrating it can be to lose something. It can be just as frustrating to lose your interview notes or forget where you found a quotation or fact. Your writer's notebook is a good place to keep track of the information you collect during a writing project. You can also organize and save your sources, create a working bibliography, and create an annotated bibliography.

Manage Print Materials

Depending on the scope of your writing project, you might accumulate a great deal of print information, such as

- your written notes (in a notebook, on loose pieces of paper, on sticky notes, and so on)
- printouts from Web pages and databases
- articles sent through a library's fax-on-demand or interlibrary loan service
- printed word-processing documents, such as your outline and rough drafts
- books, magazines, newspapers, brochures, pamphlets, and government documents
- photocopies of articles, book chapters, and other documents
- letters, printed e-mail messages, and survey results

Rather than letting all this material build up in messy piles on your desk, create a filing system to keep track of your print documents. Filing systems can range from well-organized piles of paper labeled with sticky notes, to three-ring binders, to file cabinets filled with neatly labeled file folders.

Regardless of the approach you take, keep the following principles in mind:

- **Make it easy to locate your print materials.** Decide whether you want to group materials by topic, by date, by argument, by type of material (Web pages, photocopies, original documents, field sources, and so on), or by author.
- **Stick with your organizing scheme.** You'll find it difficult to locate materials if you use different approaches at different points in your writing project.
- **Always include complete publication information.** If a source doesn't contain publication information, write it on the document. You'll need it later. Publication information includes author, title, publisher, place and date of publication, and — for a Web source — sponsoring organization and URL.
- **Write a brief note on each of your print materials.** Indicate how it might contribute to your project.

- **Record the date.** Indicating the date when you found a source can help you reconstruct what you might have been doing at the time. Dates are also essential for documenting Web sources and other online sources (see Chapters 21 and 22).

Manage Digital Materials

The single most important strategy for managing digital information is keeping it organized. Save your sources in a folder and use descriptive file names. Rather than naming a file "Notes 1.doc," for instance, name it "Interview Notes from John Garcia, April 22.doc." If you find that you are storing a large amount of information, use subfolders to group your sources.

DOWNLOADING

Downloading electronic sources to a hard drive, a flash drive, or a network-based service such as DropBox or iCloud allows you to open them later in a Web browser or word-processing program. Downloading sources can save you time toward the end of your writing project, particularly when you are drafting or revising your document.

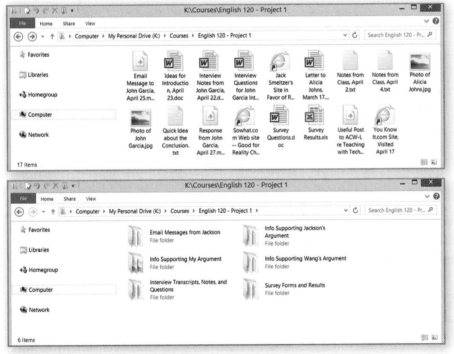

▲ Saving work in folders and subfolders

In the File menu, select Save Page As . . . to save a Web page.

▲ **Downloading a source**

To download entire Web pages, right-click (for Windows), Command-click (for Macs), or press and hold a finger (on phones and tablets) on the page, and choose the Save command. To download images and other media materials from the Web, click or press and hold on the item you want, and select the appropriate command.

Remember that saving a source does not automatically record the URL or the date on which you viewed the source for the first time. Be sure to record that information in your writing log, in your working bibliography (see p. 446), or in a document in the folder where you've saved your files.

COPYING AND PASTING

You can save text from relevant sources as notes in a word-processing document. Be sure to keep track of source information, such as the URL and the date you viewed a source, so that you can return to it if necessary and cite it appropriately.

New Search | Publications | Subject Terms | Cited References | More ▾   Sign In to My EBSCOhost   🖶 Folder

EBSCO   **E-mail Manager**
            ◀ Back

Articles

Number of items to be e-mailed: 4

E-mail from:	ephost@epnet.com	**Include when sending:**
E-mail to:	ali.bizzul@students.colostate.edu	☑ **HTML Full Text (when available)**
	Separate each e-mail address with a semicolon.	
Subject:	Sources for Football Essay	◯ **Standard Field Format**
		Detailed Citation and Abstract ▾
Comments:	Sources from Academic Search Premier, searched on football and health.	◉ **Citation Format**
		MLA (Modern Language Assoc.) ▾
		◯ **Customized Field Format**

Format: ◉ **Rich Text**   ◯ **Plain Text**

☑ **Remove these items from folder after e-mailing**
For information on e-mailing Linked Full Text, see online help. For information on using Citation Formats, see online citation help

Send

▲ **Sending e-mail from a database**

You can also use Web clipping tools, which work with your browser as toolbars or "add-ons" (a term used for programs that work within browsers) to copy all or part of a Web page. Leading, no-fee Web capture tools include ClipMarks (http://clipmarks.com), Diigo (www.diigo.com), and Zotero (www.zotero.org).

USING E-MAIL

You can e-mail yourself messages containing electronic documents you've found in your research. Some databases, such as EBSCO and OCLC/FirstSearch, allow you to e-mail the text of selected records directly from the database.

✈ TECH TIP: TAKING PHOTOS, MAKING RECORDINGS, AND SAVING NOTES

If you have a smartphone or a tablet, you can record conversations with others, record voice memos that contain ideas about your project, save video, take photos of sources you find in the periodical room (see p. 474), and surf the Web to locate sources. Most smartphone and tablet operating systems provide access to "apps"

Subject:

Books:
Bacigalupi
Banks - Hydro-
gen Sonata
Cobley - Seeds
Mullen - Revisions
Simmons - Olympos
Robert J. Sawyer

A note lists relevant authors

A photo records a location

Voice recording apps can be used to conduct interviews or record ideas

(or applications), often at no or low cost, that allow you to collect and organize information in the same way you would on a laptop or desktop computer.

As you save information with these tools, keep your work well organized. Use descriptive names, save work in folders or albums, and include notes about where and when you found the information. Talk with other writers about the apps they've found useful, and if they're free, try them out yourself.

SAVING BOOKMARKS AND FAVORITES IN YOUR BROWSER

You can use a Bookmarks or Favorites list in a Web browser on your computer, tablet, or smartphone to keep track of online sources. Keep these lists organized by putting related items into folders and giving the items on your list descriptive names. If you use this strategy, however, remember that pages on the Web can and do change — perhaps before you finish your writing project. Be aware as well that some Web pages are generated by database programs, which can result in unwieldy URLs such as

http://firstsearch.oclc.org/FUNC/QUERY:%7Fnext=NEXTCMD%7F%22/FUNC
/SRCH_RESULTS%22%7FentityListType=0%7Fentitycntr=1%7FentityItemCount
=0%7F%3Asessionid=1265726%7F4%7F/fsres4.txt

Although this long string of characters starts out looking like a normal URL, the majority of the characters are used by the database program to determine which records to display on a page. In many cases, the URL works only while you are conducting your search. If you add such a URL to your Bookmarks or Favorites list, there's a good chance it won't work later.

BACKING UP YOUR FILES

Whatever strategies you use to save and organize digital materials, replacing lost information takes time and effort. Avoid the risk of lost information by taking the time to make copies of your electronic files, saved Web pages, e-mail messages, and Bookmarks or Favorites lists.

How Can I Create a Bibliography?

A bibliography is a list of sources with complete publication information, usually formatted according to the rules of a documentation system such as the Modern Language Association system (see Chapter 21) or the American Psychological Association system (see Chapter 22). As you start collecting information, create a working bibliography or an annotated bibliography to keep track of the sources you are using.

List Sources in a Working Bibliography

A working bibliography is a running list of the sources you've explored and plan to use in your writing project — with publication information for each source. The organization of your working bibliography can vary according to your needs and preferences. You can organize your sources in any of the following ways:

- in the order in which you collected your sources
- in categories
- by author
- by publication title
- according to an outline of your project document

Information You Should List in a Bibliography

Type of Source	Information You Should List
All Sources	• Author(s) • Title • Publication year • Brief note — or annotation — describing or commenting on the source, indicating how you might use it in your document, or showing how it is related to other sources (for annotated bibliographies only)
Book	• Editor(s) of book (if applicable) • Publication city • Publisher • Series and series editor (if applicable) • Translator (if applicable) • Volume (if applicable) • Edition (if applicable)
Chapter in an Edited Book	• Chapter title • Publication city • Publisher • Editor(s) of book • Book title • Page numbers
Journal, Magazine, and Newspaper Article	• Journal title • Volume number or date • Issue number or date • Page numbers
Web Page, Blog Entry or Reply, Discussion Forum or Newsgroup Post, E-mail Message, and Chat Transcript	• URL • Access date (the date you read the source) • Sponsoring organization, if listed
Field Research	• Title (usually a description of the source, such as "Personal Interview with Ellen Page" or "Observation of Reid Vincent's Class at Dunn Elementary School") • Date (usually the date on which the field research was conducted)

The entries in a working bibliography should include as much publication information about a source as you can gather.

Your working bibliography will change significantly over the course of your writing project. As you explore and narrow your topic and, later, as you collect and work with your sources, you will add potentially useful sources and delete sources that are no longer relevant. Eventually, your working bibliography will become one of the following:

- **a works cited or reference list** — a formal list of the sources you have referred to in a document

- **a bibliography or works consulted list** — a formal list of the sources that contributed to your thinking about a subject, even if those sources are not referred to explicitly in the text of the document

You can read more about works cited and reference lists in Part Five.

Keeping your working bibliography up-to-date is a critical part of your writing process. It helps you keep track of your sources and increases the likelihood that you will cite all the sources you use in your document — an important contribution to your efforts to avoid plagiarism.

The first five sources from featured writer Ali Bizzul's working bibliography are shown in the illustration below.

Bailes, J. E., Cantu, R. C., & Day, A. L. (2002). The neurosurgeon in sport: Awareness
  of the risks of heatstroke and dietary supplements. *Neurosurgery, 51,* 283-288.
  doi:10.1097/00006123-200208000-00002

Groeschen, T. (2008, October 17). Growing concern: Supersize me. *Cincinnati Enquirer.*
  Retrieved from http://news.cincinnati.com

Longman, J. (2007, November 30). Putting on weight for football glory. *New York
  Times.* Retrieved from http://www.nytimes.com

Longman, J. (2011, January 28). N.F.L. linemen tip the scales. *New York Times.*
  Retrieved from http://www.nytimes.com

Meyer, C. (2012, November 9). Varsity xtra: Players' size continues to increase
  with passage of time. *Pittsburgh Post-Gazette.* Retrieved from http://www.
  post-gazette.com

Entries follow APA style (see Chapter 22).

▲ **Part of Ali Bizzul's working bibliography**

Summarize Sources in an Annotated Bibliography

In addition to complete citation information, an **annotated bibliography** provides a brief note — two or three sentences long — about each of your sources. Consider your purposes for creating an annotated bibliography, and tailor the content, focus, and length of your annotations accordingly.

- In some writing projects, you will submit an annotated bibliography to your instructor for review and comment. In this situation, your instructor will most likely expect a clear description of the content of each source and some indication of how you might use the source.

- In other writing projects, the annotated bibliography serves simply as a planning tool — a more detailed version of a working bibliography. As a result, your annotations might highlight key passages or information in a source, suggest how you can use information or ideas from the source, or emphasize relationships between sources.

- In still other projects, the annotated bibliography will be the final result of your efforts. In such cases, you would write your annotations for your readers, keeping their purposes, needs, interests, and backgrounds in mind.

An annotated bibliography is a useful tool even if you aren't required to submit it for a grade. By turning your working bibliography into an annotated bibliography, you can remind yourself of each source's information, ideas, and arguments and how the source might be used in your document.

The annotated bibliography on page 451 provides information that an instructor could use to assess a student's progress on a writing project.

Bailes, J. E., Cantu, R. C., & Day, A. L. (2002). The neurosurgeon in sport: Awareness of the risks of heatstroke and dietary supplements. *Neurosurgery, 51*, 283-288. doi:10.1097/00006123-200208000-00002

Bailes, Cantu, and Day discuss the rising numbers of heatstroke injuries and deaths among football players in the United States, and their study links some of these incidents to the use of dietary supplements. This source may help explain some of the extreme measures football players will take to gain or maintain weight, and the possibly fatal consequences of their decisions.

> Annotations provide brief summaries of the purpose and content of the sources.

Groeschen, T. (2008, October 17). Growing concern: Supersize me. *Cincinnati Enquirer.* **Retrieved from http://news.cincinnati.com**

Groeschen interviews local experts in the Cincinnati area, including former NFL players, coaches, and team physicians, about the problem of weight gain among football players. He also cites alarming statistics from studies about obesity in young players. This article will help explain the perspectives of players and coaches themselves, showing that they regret focusing so much on their weight and that they're trying to help today's players stay healthy.

> Annotations are intended for the writer and the instructor. They indicate how and where the writer will use the source in the document.

Meyer, C. (2012, November 9). Varsity xtra: Players' size continues to increase with passage of time. *Pittsburgh Post-Gazette.* **Retrieved from http://www.post-gazette.com**

Meyer notes that, in general, modern high school players are larger than at any time in the past 50 years. The steady growth in weight among offensive and defensive lineman, in particular, raises health concerns. Citing sources, Meyer reports that the rate of obesity among high school football players is higher than that of Americans as a whole. Meyer also points out, however, that some players are simply "big, strong kids" who spend a lot of time lifting weights. Meyer explores the role of nutritional supplements in the increase in size, the impact of added weight on athletic performance, and the outlook for continued growth in football player weight (which appears, he says, to be slowing).

▲ **Part of Ali Bizzul's annotated bibliography**

In Summary: Beginning Your Search

* Develop and refine a research question (p. 436).

* Plan your search for sources (p. 439).

* Review and refine your plan (p. 441).

* Save and organize print and digital sources (p. 442).

* Create a working bibliography (p. 446).

* Consider creating an annotated bibliography (p. 448).

Locating Sources

▶▶ Your search plan prepares you to start collecting sources. In this chapter, you'll find discussions of how to generate search terms; how to use library catalogs, databases, the Web, and media search sites; how to take advantage of the print resources in a library; and how to use field research methods. As you start to locate sources, keep in mind your writing situation and the conversation you've decided to join. Focusing on your purpose, readers, and context can help you decide which resources and search techniques to use.

How Can I Locate Sources Using Electronic Resources?

Writers can turn to four general sets of electronic resources to locate information about their subjects: library catalogs, databases, the Web, and media search sites. You can search these resources using techniques ranging from basic to advanced searches.

Generate Search Terms and Strategies

Regardless of which electronic resource you use, the results of your searches will be only as good as your search terms. Even the best search tools can produce poor results — and all too often that's exactly what happens. To increase your chances of obtaining good results, spend time identifying search terms related to your subject and learning about the types of searches you might conduct.

IDENTIFY KEYWORDS AND PHRASES

You can identify useful search terms by building on your research question (see p. 436) or thesis statement (see Chapter 14) or by using a range of idea-generating techniques, such as brainstorming, freewriting, looping, and clustering (see p. 32). Dwight Haynes, for example, used freewriting to generate ideas for his searches. Then he highlighted promising keywords and phrases.

> I'm most interested in finding sources that can help me understand why some approaches to reducing college drinking — and binge drinking in particular, although it's not the only problem (date rape, drunk driving, and falling out of windows or trees, for example, are related to too much drinking) — work better than others. What's been done by schools with successful programs? How much do those programs cost? And why haven't schools made more progress on this problem? Is it just something that college students have to go through? But if that's the case, why do so many students swear off drinking altogether — or maybe it's just a case of extremes all around, with some people drinking too much and some people swearing off it even though they wouldn't mind having a beer now and then?

You can also generate search terms by using your research question or thesis statement as a starting point. One student, for example, typed her research question in a word-processing program, formatted the most important words and phrases in color, and then brainstormed a list of related words and phrases.

What barriers **stand in the way of** widespread use **of** hydrogen fuel **in the** United States?

limits	adoption	"fuel cells"	U.S.
limitations	utilization	"clean energy"	America
obstacles	usage	"hydrogen power"	American
hurdles		"clean power"	
difficulties			
impediment			
expense			

PLAN BASIC SEARCHES

A basic search allows you to look for documents that contain a single word or phrase in the subject, title, or text or, in the case of databases, in other parts of a database record (see p. 461 for more information about databases). Basic searches can return large sets of results. To increase the odds that your results will be relevant to your subject, consider adding keywords, using exact phrases, and using wildcards.

Add keywords. In most cases, using several keywords together will limit the number of results returned by your search. This strategy is especially helpful when searching the Web, which tends to produce thousands (sometimes millions) of hits for individual words or phrases.

Adding *college* to a search for the keywords *binge* and *drinking* on Google reduces the number of results by roughly 25 percent.

Adding *students* reduces the number by an additional 80 percent.

To find out how a search tool treats multiple keywords, consult its help page, or conduct some test searches and review your results.

▲ **Planning simple searches**

Search for exact phrases. Sometimes the best way to locate information is to search for an exact phrase. To further refine your search, you might use *binge drinking* and *college students* as phrases. This would eliminate sources in which the words *binge* and *drinking* appear but are separated by other words. The simple search format in many catalogs, databases, and Web search sites permits you to specify phrases using quotation marks.

> In many catalogs, databases, and Web search sites, you can specify phrases using quotation marks.

Google   "binge drinking" "college students"

Search   About 404,000 results (0.21 seconds)

▲ A simple search with exact phrases

Use Wildcards. Sometimes you might not be sure what form of a word is most likely to occur. Rather than conducting several searches for *drink, drinking, drinkers, drunk,* and *drunken,* for example, you can combine keywords into a single wildcard search. Wildcards are symbols that take the place of letters or strings of letters. By standing in for multiple letters, they allow you to expand the scope of your search.

The following are the most commonly used wildcard symbols:

    * usually takes the place of one or more characters, such as *drink**

    ? usually takes the place of a single character, such as *dr?nk*

Other wildcard symbols include !, +, #, and $. To find out whether wildcard symbols are supported, consult the help section in a catalog or database or the advanced search page of a Web search engine.

✦ TECH TIP: PLAN ADVANCED SEARCHES

You are probably fairly comfortable doing basic searches already, but they can take your research only so far. To make bigger strides on your research and find more targeted results, try out some advanced searches. Most library catalogs, databases, and Web search sites provide an advanced search page. These pages allow you to focus your searches in powerful ways using Boolean operators (which are used to search for all, some, or none of the words or phrases in a search box) and search limits (such as publication date and document characteristics).

Focus searches with Boolean operators. Boolean operators let you focus a search by specifying whether keywords or phrases *can, must,* or *must not* appear in the results. Some Boolean operators also allow you to search for keywords or phrases that appear next to, before or after, or within a certain distance from one another in a document. Here is a list of commonly used Boolean operators and their functions.

Boolean Operator	Function	Example
AND/+ (plus)	Finds sources that include both search terms (either keywords or phrases)	hydrogen AND economy
OR	Finds sources that include either search term	energy OR power
NOT/–	Finds sources that include one search term but not the other	gasoline NOT oil
ADJ (adjacent)	Finds sources in which the search terms appear next to each other	fuel ADJ cells
NEAR	Finds sources in which the search terms appear within a specified number of words from each other	alternative NEAR energy
BEFORE	Finds sources in which search terms appear in a particular order	clean BEFORE power
Parentheses ( )	Parentheses are used to group search terms and Boolean operators	hydrogen AND (fuel OR energy) AND (economy NOT economics)

Limit searches. Search limits allow you to limit your searches to documents that have particular characteristics, such as publication date and document type. Although the specific limits that are available in an advanced search form vary across databases, library catalogs, and Web search sites, common limits include publication date (or, in the case of Web pages, the date on which a page was last updated), type of document, and the availability of full text (for databases).

Search Library Catalogs

Library catalogs provide information about the materials in a library's collection. Online catalogs provide information about the author(s), title, publication date, subject heading, and call number for each source in the library's collection. Typically, they also indicate the location of the source in the library and whether the source is available for checkout.

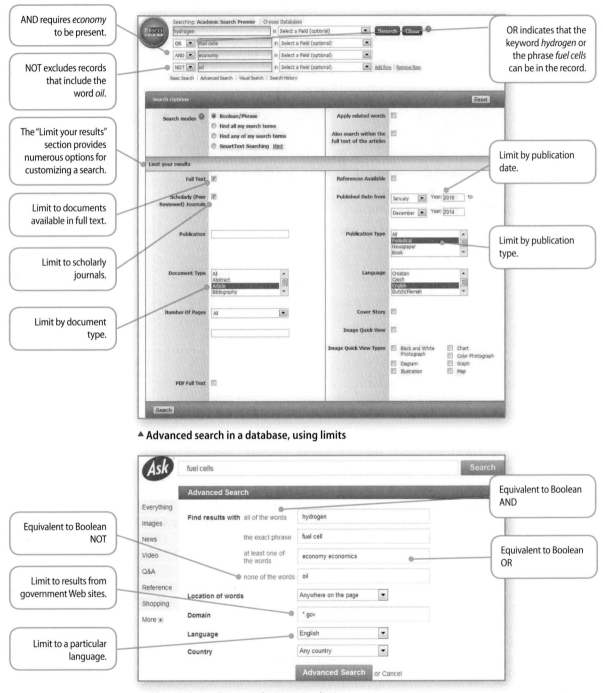

AND requires *economy* to be present.

NOT excludes records that include the word *oil*.

The "Limit your results" section provides numerous options for customizing a search.

Limit to documents available in full text.

Limit to scholarly journals.

Limit by document type.

OR indicates that the keyword *hydrogen* or the phrase *fuel cells* can be in the record.

Limit by publication date.

Limit by publication type.

▲ Advanced search in a database, using limits

Equivalent to Boolean NOT

Limit to results from government Web sites.

Limit to a particular language.

Equivalent to Boolean AND

Equivalent to Boolean OR

▲ Advanced search on a web site, using limits

Library catalogs typically help you locate

- books
- journals owned by the library (although not individual articles)
- newspapers and magazines owned by the library (although not individual articles)
- documents stored on microfilm or microfiche
- videotapes, audiotapes, and other multimedia items owned by the library
- maps
- theses and dissertations completed by college or university graduate students

In addition to searching the library catalog at your college or university, you can also benefit from searching other catalogs available on the Web. The Library of Congress online catalog (catalog.loc.gov), for example, presents a comprehensive list of publications on a particular subject or by a particular author. Some sites, such as World-Cat (www.worldcat.org), allow you to locate or search multiple libraries. If you find a promising source that your library doesn't own, you can request it through interlibrary loan.

Most library catalogs allow you to search or browse for sources by keywords and phrases, author(s), title, subject, and call number. The following examples illustrate common types of searches.

Search by keyword. You can search for a specific keyword or phrase.

▲ **Searching by keyword**

Search by author. If you search by author, you can find sources written by a particular person or organization.

Most library catalogs assume that you will enter the last name of the author first, followed by a first name or initial.

Some catalogs allow you to search for sources by entering all or part of a last name. You might be able to use wildcard symbols, such as * or ? (see p. 456).

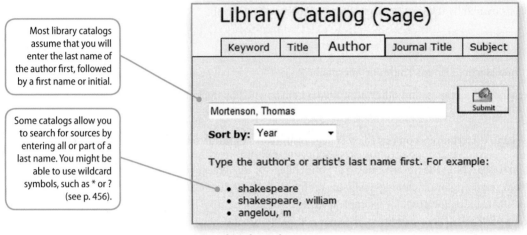

Library Catalog (Sage)

| Keyword | Title | Author | Journal Title | Subject |

Mortenson, Thomas   [Submit]

Sort by: Year ▾

Type the author's or artist's last name first. For example:

- shakespeare
- shakespeare, william
- angelou, m

▲ Searching by author

Search by title. If you know either the exact title of a source or some of the words in the title, you can search by title to find sources.

You can search for a complete or a partial title. Searching for partial titles produces a list of sources whose titles begin with the phrase or word you enter.

Library Catalog (Sage)

| Keyword | Title | Author | Journal Title | Subject |

College Tuition   [Submit]

Sort by: Title ▾

Search here for exact titles of materials. Begin with the first w
Initial articles in English (A, An, The) are not necessary. T
initial articles (La, El, Das, etc.) to retrieve all possible items.

- merchant of venice
- el nino and health
- streetcar named d

▲ Searching by title

Browse by call number or subject heading. To locate sources related to a promising result, search by either call number or subject heading.

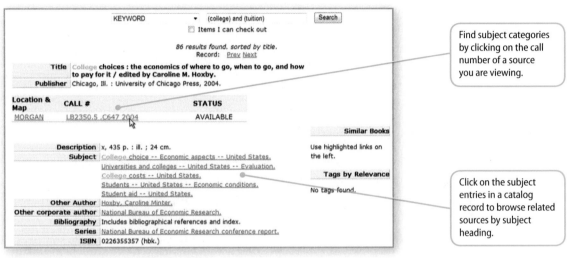

KEYWORD ▾ (college) and (tuition) [Search]
☐ Items I can check out

86 results found, sorted by title.
Record: Prev Next

Title | College **choices : the economics of where to go, when to go, and how to pay for it / edited by Caroline M. Hoxby.**
Publisher | Chicago, Ill. : University of Chicago Press, 2004.

Location & Map	CALL #	STATUS
MORGAN	LB2350.5 .C647 2004	AVAILABLE

Similar Books

Description | x, 435 p. : ill. ; 24 cm.
Subject | College choice -- Economic aspects -- United States.
Universities and colleges -- United States -- Evaluation.
College costs -- United States.
Students -- United States -- Economic conditions.
Student aid -- United States.
Other Author | Hoxby, Caroline Minter.
Other corporate author | National Bureau of Economic Research.
Bibliography | Includes bibliographical references and index.
Series | National Bureau of Economic Research conference report.
ISBN | 0226355357 (hbk.)

Use highlighted links on the left.

Tags by Relevance

No tags found.

Find subject categories by clicking on the call number of a source you are viewing.

Click on the subject entries in a catalog record to browse related sources by subject heading.

▲ Searching call number or subject heading

Search Databases

Databases operate much like library catalogs, although they focus on a different collection of sources. While a library catalog allows you to search for publications owned by the library, a database allows you to search for sources that have been published on a particular topic or in a particular discipline regardless of whether the library owns the sources. Although some databases, such as ERIC, MedLine, and Science Direct, are available publicly via the Web (see p. 463), most are available only through library computers or a library Web site.

Databases supply publication information and brief descriptions of the information in a source; some — but not all — provide electronic copies of the source. Using the citation information provided by the database, you can check your library's catalog for the title of the publication in which the source appears. If your library does not own the publication, you can request it through interlibrary loan.

IDENTIFY RELEVANT DATABASES
Databases tend to specialize in particular subject areas and types of sources. To focus your search, try to identify the databases that will be most relevant to your

subject. Your decisions about which databases to search will be affected by your library's holdings. Large research libraries often subscribe to hundreds of databases, while smaller libraries might subscribe to only a handful. Most libraries provide a list of available databases. You can also consult a librarian about which databases might be appropriate for your search.

Databases generally fall into one of the following categories:

- **News and information databases**, which focus on recently published articles in newspapers and popular magazines.
- **Subject databases**, which focus on a broad subject area, such as education, business, or government.
- **Bibliographies**, which focus on publications in a specific discipline or profession, such as literary studies, computational linguistics, or the social sciences.
- **Citation indexes**, which identify sources that have referenced a specific publication, such as an article in a journal or a conference proceeding.
- **Media databases**, which provide access to images, video, and audio sources.

To identify databases that might be relevant to your issue, review your library's list of databases or consult a reference librarian. Ask yourself the following questions.

Am I focusing on an issue that is likely to have been addressed in recent news coverage? If so, search databases that focus on newspapers and weekly news magazines, such as

- LexisNexis Academic
- ProQuest Newspapers
- Alternative Press Index
- Newspaper Source

Am I focusing on a broad area of interest, such as business, education, or government? If so, search databases that focus on more general issues, such as

- Academic Search Premier
- Article First
- Catalog of U.S. Government Publications
- WorldCat

Am I focusing on an issue that is related to a particular profession or academic discipline? If so, consult bibliographies that focus on that area. Many library Web sites categorize databases by profession or discipline. For example, if you are interested in an issue related to sociology, you might consult the following databases:

- Family and Society Studies Worldwide
- Social Science Abstracts
- Sociological Abstracts

Have I already identified sources about my issue? If you have already located promising sources, search citation indexes to identify sources that refer to your sources. Depending on your area, you might search the following databases:

- Science Citation Index
- Social Sciences Citation Index
- Arts & Humanities Citation Index

Is the full text of the source available? Full-text databases offer the complete source for viewing or download. These databases cut out the middle step of locating the specific periodical that published the article. Databases that offer some of or all their sources in full text include

- Academic Search Premier
- ERIC
- IEEE Xplore
- LexisNexis Academic
- ScienceDirect

Am I searching for images, video, or audio? If you are seeking nontextual sources, turn to media databases such as the following:

- ARTstor
- AccessScience
- Mountain West Digital Library

SEARCH WITHIN DATABASE FIELDS

To search for sources using a database, type keywords and phrases in the database's search fields. If you are conducting a basic search, the process will be similar to a search on a Web search site (see p. 455). The following illustrations show an advanced search that featured writer Dwight Haynes conducted in ProQuest and the results that were returned.

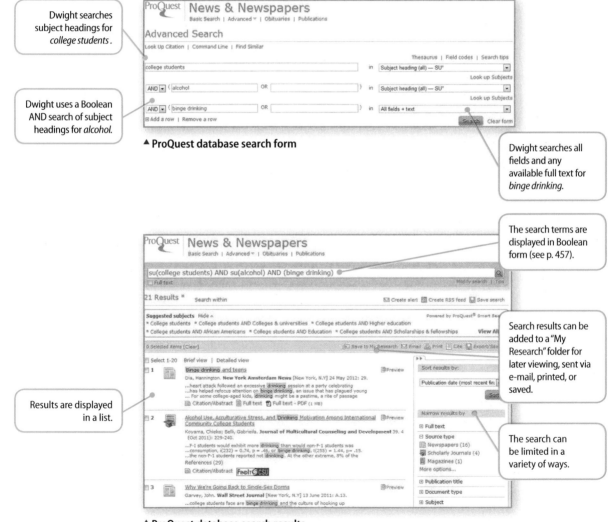

Dwight searches subject headings for *college students*.

Dwight uses a Boolean AND search of subject headings for *alcohol*.

▲ **ProQuest database search form**

Dwight searches all fields and any available full text for *binge drinking*.

The search terms are displayed in Boolean form (see p. 457).

Search results can be added to a "My Research" folder for later viewing, sent via e-mail, printed, or saved.

Results are displayed in a list.

The search can be limited in a variety of ways.

▲ **ProQuest database search results**

Search the Web

The Web has become the largest and most accessible "library" in the world. Its "collection" includes Web pages, blogs, reviews, social-networking sites, magazine and journal articles, books, music, photos, and video, among many other items. To search this collection of sources, you can use a wide range of Web search sites.

Like library catalogs and databases, Web search sites help you locate information quickly and easily. Keep in mind, however, that the sources found through Web search sites have not been carefully selected by librarians and editors, as is typically the case with the sources found through library catalogs and databases. Instead, sources found on the Web can be uneven in quality, ranging from peer-reviewed articles in scholarly journals to home pages created by eighth graders.

USE WEB SEARCH ENGINES

Web search engines keep track of Web pages and other forms of information on the Internet — including PDF files, PowerPoint files, Word files, blogs (see p. 469), and newsgroup posts — by locating documents on Web sites and entering them in a searchable database.

Leading Web search engines include

- AltaVista: altavista.com
- Ask: ask.com
- Bing: bing.com
- Blekko: blekko.com
- Duck Duck Go: duckduckgo.com
- Excite: excite.com
- Gigablast: gigablast.com
- Google: google.com
- Lycos: lycos.com
- Yahoo!: search.yahoo.com

Keep two cautions in mind as you use Web search engines. First, the sheer size and rapid growth of the Web make it difficult for search engines to create a complete index (recent estimates suggest that at least one trillion pages have been created). As a result, you should use more than one search engine. Even if you don't find what you're looking for in your first choice, you might find it in another. Second, Web

Google offers search suggestions as you type in the search box.

▲ Google search

pages can be moved, deleted, or revised. This means that a search engine's results can be inaccurate.

BROWSE WEB DIRECTORIES

Unlike search engines, Web directories employ human editors to organize information about Web pages into categories and subcategories. Directories allow you to browse lists of Web sites by clicking on general topics, such as health or education, and then to successively narrow your search by clicking on subtopics. Many directories also permit you to conduct keyword searches within specific categories. Leading Web directories include

- About.com: about.com
- Best of the Web: botw.org
- Internet Public Library: ipl.org
- Open Directory Project: dmoz.org
- WWW Virtual Library: vlib.org
- Yahoo! Directory: dir.yahoo.com

USE META SEARCH SITES

On a meta search site, you can conduct a search on several Web search engines or Web directories at the same time. These sites typically search the major search engines and directories and then present a limited number of results on a single page. Leading meta search sites include:

- Dogpile: dogpile.com
- Mamma: mamma.com

- Metacrawler: metacrawler.com

- Search.com: search.com

- Zuula: zuula.com

USE NEWS SEARCH SITES

You can search for news on most major Web search sites and directories, such as Bing, Google, and Yahoo!, as well as the sites for news providers such as BBC, CNN, and Reuters. In addition, specialized news search sites allow you to conduct focused searches for current and archived news reports, while social news sites such as Digg and Stumbleupon allow you to view news stories and videos that have been recommended by other readers. Leading news search sites include

- AltaVista News: altavista.com/news

- Ask News: news.ask.com

- Bing News: bing.com/news

- Digg: digg.com

- Google News: news.google.com

- Stumbleupon: stumbleupon.com

- Yahoo! News: news.yahoo.com

USE REFERENCE SITES

A reference site allows you to search for information that has been collected in encyclopedias, almanacs, atlases, dictionaries, and other reference resources. Some reference sites, such as Encyclopedia Britannica Online, offer limited access to information from their encyclopedias at no charge and complete access for a fee. Other sites, such as Information Please and Bartleby.com, allow unrestricted access to recently published reference works, including the *Columbia Encyclopedia*, *The Encyclopedia of World History*, and *The World Factbook*.

One widely used reference site is Wikipedia, whose articles are collaboratively written by its readers. Because of its comprehensiveness, Wikipedia can serve as a useful starting point for research on a topic. However, because any reader can make changes to most of the pages on the site, it's best to double-check any information you find there.

Leading reference search sites include the following:

- Bartleby.com Reference: bartleby.com/reference

- Encyclopedia.com: encyclopedia.com

- Encyclopedia Britannica Online: britannica.com
- Information Please: infoplease.com
- Wikipedia: en.wikipedia.org

USE GOVERNMENT SEARCH SITES AND DIRECTORIES

Many government agencies and institutions have turned to the Web as the primary means of distributing their publications. FirstGov, sponsored by the U.S. government, allows you to search the federal government's network of online resources. Government Printing Office Access provides publication information about print documents and links to those publications that are available online. Sites such as FedStats and FedWorld give access to a wide range of government-related materials. In addition to these specialized sites, you can locate government publications through many Web directories, such as Yahoo!. Leading government document sites include the following:

- About.com's U.S. Government Information Directory: usgovinfo.about.com
- Canadian Government Search Engines: recherche-search.gc.ca
- FedStats: fedstats.org
- FedWorld: fedworld.gov
- Google U.S. Government Search: google.com/unclesam
- Government Printing Office Access: gpoaccess.gov
- GovSpot.com: govspot.com
- SearchGov.com: searchgov.com
- State and Local Government Directory: statelocalgov.net
- USA.gov: usa.gov

TECH TIP: USE E-BOOK SITES

E-book sites make it easy to locate books — and in many cases read reviews and view books on the same or related topics. You have probably purchased or previewed pages from books on commercial sites, such as Amazon, Apple, Barnes & Noble, and Sony, but you may not be as familiar with open-access sites. These sites, such as Project Gutenberg and the Internet Archive Community Text collection, provide free access to historical texts that are no longer under copyright, as well as to books released under various open-access licenses. You can also locate books through Google Books, which offers books from leading publishers and university libraries, including Harvard, Stanford, and the University of Michigan. Skimming the interior of a book (its table of contents or its introduction, for instance) on your computer, tablet, or smartphone can be an incredible time-saver in the long run. E-book sites include

- Amazon: amazon.com
- Barnes & Noble: barnesandnoble.com/ebooks
- Google Books: books.google.com
- Internet Archive Community Books: archive.org/details/texts
- Online Books Page: onlinebooks.library.upenn.edu
- Project Gutenberg: gutenberg.org
- Sony: ebookstore.sony.com
- Wikibooks: wikibooks.org

SEARCH BLOGS

Blogs — short for Weblogs — consist of chronologically ordered entries on a Web site and most closely resemble entries in a diary or journal. Blog entries usually include a title and a text message and can also incorporate images, audio, video, and other types of media. Many entries provide links to other pages on the Web. Blogs have a number of purposes:

- Some blogs report on events and issues. The bloggers who provided daily — sometimes hourly — reports on the 2012 political conventions offered valuable, firsthand insights into aspects of the conventions that were not addressed through the mainstream media. Similarly, the bloggers who reported on the wars in Iraq and Afghanistan offered a perspective on events that would not have been available otherwise.

- Some blogs alert readers to information elsewhere on the Web. These blogs cite recently published news reports and articles, the latest developments in a particular discipline, and new contributions to an ongoing debate — and provide commentary on that information.

- Some blogs serve as public relations spaces for institutions and organizations, such as corporations, government agencies, and colleges. These blogs typically focus on services or activities associated with the institution or organization.

- Some blogs serve largely as a space for personal reflection and expression. A blogger might share his or her thoughts about daily life, current events, or other issues with friends and family.

Writers can use blogs as sources of information and commentary on an issue and as sources of firsthand accounts by people affected by an issue. If you find blogs by experts in the field, you can begin a discussion with people involved in or knowledgeable about your topic. To locate blogs that are relevant to your research question, use the following sites:

- Alltop: alltop.com
- Best of the Web Blogs: search.botw.org
- BlogCatalog: blogcatalog.com
- Blogdigger: blogdigger.com
- Google Blogsearch: google.com/blogsearch
- IceRocket: icerocket.com
- Technorati: technorati.com

SEARCH SOCIAL MEDIA SITES

Sites such as Facebook, Google+, Tumblr, Twitter, and LinkedIn provide opportunities to identify people who share your interest in an issue. By searching these sites, you can identify individuals who might be knowledgeable about an issue or have been affected by it. You can search social networks using the following sites:

Facebook Search: facebook.com/search

Google+ Search: plus.google.com

LinkedIn Search: linkedin.com

MySpace Search: http://myspace.com/browse/people

Social Network Search: socialnetworksearch.com

Social Mention: socialmention.com

Twitter Search: twitter.com/search

Tumblr Search: tumblr.com/tagged/tumblr+search

Search Media Sites

The Web is home not only to textual information, such as articles and books, but also to a growing collection of other types of media, such as photographs, podcasts, and streaming videos. You can search for media using established search sites, such as Ask, Google, and Yahoo!, as well as newer search sites that focus on specific media.

USE IMAGE SEARCH SITES AND DIRECTORIES

Image searches have long been among the search tools available to writers. Using Google's image search, for example, you can search for images using keywords and phrases, and you can conduct advanced searches by specifying the size and kind of image you desire. The following search sites and directories allow you to locate images:

- Ask Image Search: ask.com/?tool=img
- Bing Image Search: bing.com/images
- Flickr: flickr.com
- Google Image Search: images.google.com
- PicFindr: picfindr.com
- Picsearch: picsearch.com
- Yahoo! Image Search: images.search.yahoo.com

USE AUDIO SEARCH SITES

Thinking of the Web as the first place to visit for new music has become second nature for many of us. But the audio content available through the Web includes more than just music. You can also find radio broadcasts, recordings of speeches, recordings of natural phenomena, and other forms of sound. Sites such as FindSounds allow you to search for sounds and listen to them before down-loading. Leading audio search sites include the following:

- FindSounds: findsounds.com
- Historical Voices: historicalvoices.org
- Internet Archive: archive.org/details/audio
- Library of Congress American Memory: memory.loc.gov/ammem
- Podscope: podscope.com
- Wav Central: wavcentral.com

USE VIDEO SEARCH SITES

Through sites such as YouTube and Yahoo! Video, Web-based video has become one of the fastest-growing parts of the Web. You can view everything from news reports on CNN.com, to a video about the effects of a recent earthquake, to documentaries about the Iraq War. Of course, much of the material will be of little use in a writing project. With careful selection and evaluation, however, you might find video that will help you better understand and contribute to the discussion of your subject. The following are some leading video search sites:

- AOL Video: video.aol.com
- Ask Video Search: ask.com/?tool=vid
- Bing Video Search: bing.com/videos
- Blinkx: blinkx.com
- Google Video: video.google.com
- Hulu: hulu.com
- Yahoo! Video Search: video.search.yahoo.com
- YouTube: youtube.com

Keep Track of Your Searches

One of the most important strategies you can use as you collect information is keeping track of your searches. Note the keywords or phrases and the search strategies you used with them (wildcards, Boolean search, author search, and so on), as well as how many sources the search turned up and whether those sources were relevant to your writing project. Keeping track of your searches will help you identify promising approaches; it will also ensure that you don't repeat your efforts.

In your writer's notebook, record the following information for each source you search:

Checklist for Recording Search Terms

✔ Resource that was searched

✔ Search terms used (keywords, phrases, names)

✔ Search strategies used (basic search, exact-phrase search, wildcard search, Boolean search)

✔ Date the search was conducted

✔ Number of results produced by the search

✔ Relevance of the results

How Can I Locate Sources Using Print Resources?

Contrary to recent claims, there is life (and information) beyond the World Wide Web. The print resources available in a library can help you locate a wealth of relevant material that you won't find online. If you are working on a writing project that has a historical component, for example, you'll find that bibliographies and indexes can point you toward sources that cannot be located using a database or a Web search site. By relying on the careful selections librarians make when adding to a collection, you will be able to find useful, credible sources that reflect your purpose and address your subject.

To locate information using print resources, discuss your search plan with a librarian, visit the library stacks, browse periodicals, and check reference works.

Discuss Your Search Plan with a Librarian

As you begin collecting information about your subject, use your search plan to capitalize on your library's print resources. If you are uncertain about how you might use these resources, discuss your project with a reference librarian. Given the wide range of specialized print resources that are available, a few minutes of discussion with a knowledgeable librarian could save you a great deal of time or point you to key resources you might have overlooked.

Visit the Library Stacks

The library stacks — or shelves — house the library's collection of bound publications. By browsing the stacks and checking publications' works cited pages, you can locate related sources. Once you've decided that a source is relevant to your project, you can check it out or request it through interlibrary loan.

BROWSE THE STACKS

One of the advantages of the classification systems used by most libraries — typically the Library of Congress or Dewey decimal classification system — is that they are subject-based. Because books on similar subjects are shelved together, you can browse the stacks to look for sources on a topic. For example, if your research takes you to the stacks for books about alcohol abuse, you're likely to find books about drug abuse, treatment programs, and codependency nearby. When you find a publication that seems useful, check the works cited list for related works. The combination of browsing the stacks for sources and checking those sources' works cited lists can lead you to publications relevant to your subject.

CHECK OUT RELEVANT ITEMS

You can usually take library books — and some periodicals and media items — home with you to read or view at your own pace. In some cases, a publication you want might not be available because it has been checked out, reserved for a course, or placed in off-site storage. If a publication has been checked out, you might be able to recall it — that is, ask that it be returned to the library and held for you. If it has been placed on reserve, ask whether you can photocopy or take notes on it. If it has been placed in off-site storage, you can usually request it at the circulation desk.

✦ TECH TIP: USE INTERLIBRARY LOAN

If you can't obtain a particular book, periodical, or media item from your library, use interlibrary loan to borrow it from another library. You can fill out a request form in person, but most libraries allow you to request materials through the library catalog, too. You may even be able to check the status of your request or renew interlibrary loan materials in the same way. To learn how to use interlibrary loan, consult your library's Web site or ask a librarian.

Browse Periodicals

Periodicals include newspapers, magazines, and academic and professional journals. A periodicals room — or journals room — contains recent issues that library visitors may browse. Many libraries also have a separate room for newspapers published in the last few weeks or months. To ensure everyone's access to recently published issues, most libraries don't allow you to check out periodicals published within the last year, and they usually don't allow newspapers to be checked out at all.

Older periodicals are sometimes placed in bound volumes in the stacks. Few libraries, however, keep back issues of newspapers in paper form. Instead, you can often find back issues of leading newspapers in full-text databases or in microform. *Microform* is a generic name for both microfilm, a strip of film containing greatly reduced images of printed pages, and microfiche, film roughly the size of an index card containing the same kinds of miniaturized images. You view these images using a microform reader, a projection unit that looks something like a large computer monitor. Many microform readers allow you to print copies of the pages.

Electronic databases of periodicals can help you locate specific articles on your subject, since these databases are more likely than print indexes and bibliographies to contain listings of recent publications. Once you've identified an article you want to review, you'll need to find the periodical in which it appears. Conduct a title search for the periodical in the same way you conduct a title search for a book. The library catalog will tell you the call number of the periodical and usually will give information about its location in the library. In addition, some libraries provide a printed list that identifies where periodicals are located. If you have difficulty finding a periodical or judging which publications are likely to be useful for your writing project, ask a librarian for assistance.

Check Reference Works

Reference rooms contain reliable print resources on a range of topics, from government to finance to philosophy to science. Although many of these reference books serve the same purposes as electronic databases, others offer information not available in databases. Using reference books to locate print resources has several advantages over using databases.

- **Most databases have short memories.** Databases typically index sources only as far back as the mid-1980s and seldom index anything published before 1970. Depending on your subject, a database might not include some important sources. If you use a reference book, however, you might be able to locate print resources dating back a century or more.

- **Most databases focus on short works.** In contrast, many of the print resources in library reference rooms will refer you to books and longer publications as well as to articles in periodicals.

- **Many library reference resources are unavailable in electronic form.** For instance, the *Encyclopedia of Creativity*, which offers more than two hundred articles, is available only in print form.

- **Entries in print indexes are easier to browse.** Despite efforts to aid browsing, databases support searching far better than they do browsing.

Some of the most important print resources you can consult in a reference room include bibliographies, indexes, biographies, general and specialized encyclopedias, handbooks, almanacs, and atlases.

BIBLIOGRAPHIES

Bibliographies list books, articles, and other publications that have been judged relevant to a topic. Some bibliographies provide only citations, while others include abstracts — brief descriptions — of listed sources. Complete bibliographies attempt to list all the sources published about a topic, while selective bibliographies attempt to list only the best sources on a topic. Some bibliographies limit their inclusion of sources by time period, often focusing on sources published during a given year.

You're likely to find several types of bibliographies in your library's reference room or stacks.

- **Trade bibliographies** allow you to locate books published about a particular topic. Leading trade bibliographies include *The Subject Guide to Books in Print*, *Books in Print*, and *Cumulative Book Index*.

- **General bibliographies** cover a wide range of topics, usually in selective lists. For sources on humanities topics, consult *The Humanities: A Selective Guide to Information Sources*. For sources on social science topics, see *Social Science Reference Sources: A Practical Guide*. For sources on science topics, go to bibliographies such as *Information Sources in Science and Technology*, *Guide to Information Sources in the Botanical Sciences*, and *Guide to Information Sources in the Physical Sciences*.

- **Specialized bibliographies** typically provide lists of sources — often annotated — about a specific topic. For example, *Bibliography of Modern American Philosophers* focuses on sources about important American philosophers.

Although most general and trade bibliographies can be found in the library reference room, specialized bibliographies are usually shelved in the library's stacks. To locate them, start by consulting a cumulative bibliography, such as *The Bibliographic Index: A Cumulative Bibliography of Bibliographies*, which identifies bibliographies on a wide range of topics and is updated annually. You might also search your library's catalog using keywords related to your subject plus the keyword *bibliography*. If you need help finding bibliographies that are relevant to your subject, ask a reference librarian.

INDEXES

Indexes provide citation information for sources found in a particular set of publications. Many indexes also include abstracts — brief descriptions — that can help you determine whether a source is worth locating and reviewing. The following types of indexes can be found in libraries:

- **Periodical indexes** list sources published in magazines, trade journals, scholarly journals, and newspapers. Some periodical indexes, such as *The Reader's Guide to Periodical Literature*, cover a wide range of general-interest publications. Others, such as *Art Index*, focus on periodicals that address a single subject. Still others focus on a small set or even an individual periodical; *The New York Times Index*, for example, lists articles published only in that newspaper and organizes entries by subject, geography, organization, and references to individuals.

- **Indexes of materials in books** can help you locate articles in edited books. Turn to resources such as the *Essay and General Literature Index*, which indexes nearly five thousand book-length collections of articles and essays in the arts, humanities, and social sciences. You might also find subject-specific indexes. *The Cumulative Bibliography of Asian Studies*, for example, covers articles in edited books.

- **Pamphlet indexes** list the pamphlets that libraries frequently collect. If your subject is likely to be addressed in pamphlets, ask a reference librarian whether your library has a pamphlet index. You can also consult the *Vertical File Index*, which lists roughly three thousand brief sources on ten to fifteen newsworthy topics each month.

- **Government documents indexes** list publications from federal, state, and local governments. The most useful indexes include *Monthly Catalog of United States Government Publications*, *CIS Index to Publications of the United States Congress*, *Congressional Record* (for daily proceedings of the House of Representatives and the Senate), *United States Reports* (for Supreme Court documents), and *Statistical Abstract of the United States* (for census data and other statistical records). These types of indexes might be found in either the reference room or a separate government documents collection in your library. Ask a reference librarian for help.

- **Citation indexes** allow you to determine which sources make reference to other publications, a useful strategy for finding sources that are engaged in the same conversation. For example, to learn which sources refer to an article published in a scientific journal, consult the *Science Citation Index*.

BIOGRAPHIES

Biographies cover key figures in a field, time period, or geographic region. *Who's Who in America*, for instance, provides brief biographies of important figures in the United States during a given year, while *Great Lives from History* takes a broader view, offering biographies of key figures in world history.

ENCYCLOPEDIAS

General encyclopedias attempt to provide a little knowledge about a lot of subjects. The purpose of a general encyclopedia, such as the *New Encyclopaedia Britannica*, is to present enough information about a subject to get you started on a more detailed search. Specialized encyclopedias, such as *The MIT Encyclopedia of the Cognitive Sciences*, take a narrower focus, usually covering a field of study or a historical period. Articles in specialized encyclopedias are typically longer than articles in general encyclopedias and offer more detailed coverage of subjects.

HANDBOOKS

Like encyclopedias, handbooks provide useful background information about a subject in a compact form. Unlike encyclopedias, most handbooks, such as *The Engineering Handbook* and the *International Handbook of Psychology*, cover a specific topic area. The entries in handbooks are also much shorter than the articles found in encyclopedias.

ALMANACS

Almanacs contain lists, charts, and tables of information of various types. You might be familiar with *The Old Farmer's Almanac*, which is known for its accuracy in predicting weather over the course of a year. Information in almanacs can range from the average rainfall in Australia to the batting averages of the 1927 Yankees to the average income of Germans and Poles before World War II.

ATLASES

Atlases provide maps and related information about a region or country. Some atlases take a historical perspective, while others take a topical perspective.

How Can I Gather Information Using Field Research?

Published documents aren't the only source of information for a writing project. Nor are they always the best. Publications — such as books, articles, Web sites, or television reports — offer someone else's interpretation of an event or an issue. By relying on such sources, you are looking through that person's eyes rather than through your own.

You don't have to use published reports to find out how an event or issue has affected people — you can ask them yourself. You don't have to watch television coverage of an event — you can go to the event yourself. You don't have to rely on someone else's survey of public opinion — you can conduct your own. And you don't have to do field research by yourself — you can form a team and share the work.

Choose Your Methods

Field research is research you conduct on your own, without consulting the Web or a library. Rather than relying on what someone has written, you can collect the information yourself. By conducting field research, you can draw your own conclusions.

Common forms of field research include interviews, observations, and surveys. You can also correspond with people who know about or have been affected by an issue or event, attend public events, and refer to informational radio and television programs.

INTERVIEWS

Interviews allow you to gather information about your subject from people who can provide firsthand accounts of events, authoritative interpretations of an issue, and reflections about their personal experiences. Interviews can be conducted in a face-to-face setting, on the telephone, or online — via e-mail, instant messaging, or Web cam. Interviews that are not conducted online are usually recorded and later transcribed for analysis. You can learn more about conducting interviews on page 190.

OBSERVATIONS

Observation allows you to learn about your subject by immersing yourself in it. For example, you might visit a mall to observe shopping habits in the last few days of the holiday season. Or you might study how activists approach students walking to the student center at midday. To keep track of your observations, you can take field notes, fill out an observation checklist, or record your observations in a voice recorder. Observing a subject firsthand allows you to understand it differently than you can through secondhand reports. Observation can also increase your credibility as a writer, in much the same way that a reporter on the scene has a degree of authority that a news anchor in a television studio cannot provide. You can read more about conducting an observation on page 135.

SURVEYS

Surveys allow you to obtain information from large groups of people. They can be conducted via paper forms, electronic forms, and even telephone calls. To learn about student and faculty attitudes and behaviors associated with academic integrity, for example, you might distribute a questionnaire at your college or university. The survey could help you answer *what, who,* or *how* questions such as the following: "What kinds of behaviors do you consider violations of academic integrity?" "Whom would you contact if you wanted to learn more about academic integrity issues?" "How likely are you to include sources you haven't actually read in a research essay's works cited list?" Surveys are less useful in obtaining the answers to *why* questions. In an interview, for instance, you can ask, "Why do you think students cheat or plagiarize?" and expect to get a reasonably well-thought-out response. In a survey, however, respondents seldom write lengthy responses to questions. You can learn more about surveys on page 349.

CORRESPONDENCE

Correspondence includes any textual communication — such as letters, faxes, and e-mail — as well as real-time communication using chat or text messaging. If you use chat or text messaging, be sure to save a transcript of the exchange. You can correspond with experts in a particular area; people who have been affected by or involved with an issue or event; staff at corporations, organizations, and government agencies; or even journalists who have written about a subject. In general, it's helpful to explain who you are, what you are writing about, and why you want to correspond.

ATTENDING PUBLIC EVENTS

Public events, such as lectures, conferences, and public meetings and hearings, often provide writers with useful information. You can record public events by taking notes or using a smartphone or digital recorder to capture (if permitted). If you attend a public event in person or on the Web, find out whether a transcript of the proceedings will be available.

VIEWING OR LISTENING TO BROADCAST MEDIA

Writers frequently overlook radio and television as sources of information. News and information programs on television, such as *48 Hours*, might help you learn about the conversation you plan to join. To examine the programs in detail, you might want to record them. In addition, check the Web for radio programs and transcripts. National Public Radio's news information program *All Things Considered*, for instance, has audio archives going back to January 1996 that you can listen to online (visit www.npr.org and search the program's archives).

Enlist Help

Conducting field research can be time intensive. If you and your classmates are working on an assignment that involves fieldwork, consider forming collaborative teams to collect information. You can use one or more of the following strategies:

- If you are conducting an observation or attending a public event, you'll find that a single perspective might limit your ability to see what's happening. If another classmate is also conducting observations, you can help each other out. You might observe at the same time as your classmate so that together you can see more of what's happening. Or you and your classmate might observe the same setting at different times, effectively doubling the amount of information you can obtain. The additional information will help you better understand the contexts being observed. If you decide to work with a classmate, consider creating an observation checklist so that each observer will know what to look for.

- If you are conducting an interview, share your interview questions with a class-mate before conducting the interview. Have your classmate role-play the inter-viewee. Then ask him or her how you might improve your questions.

- If you are gathering information through correspondence, ask a classmate to review your letter or message before you send it and to offer suggestions for improving it. Your classmate can follow the guidelines for conducting an effec-tive peer review (see p. 89).

- If you are conducting a survey, share drafts of your survey with a few class-mates. Ask them to note any questions that seem unclear, irrelevant, or ineffec-tive. If they identify any questions that could be improved, ask them why they found the questions problematic and whether they have any suggestions for revision.

ASSESS YOUR INFORMATION

Field research methods don't always produce the results a writer needs. Before you use information collected through interviews, observation, or surveys, evaluate its accuracy and relevance by using the following checklist:

✔ Is the information you collected in an observation still relevant? Are your observation notes as complete as you had hoped they would be?	Checklist for Assessing Field Sources
✔ Are the questions you asked in an interview or through correspondence still relevant to your writing project?	
✔ Are the people you interviewed or corresponded with as qualified and knowledgeable as you expected?	
✔ Were the questions you asked in an interview or through correspondence answered fully and honestly?	
✔ Did survey respondents have adequate time to complete the survey? Did they appear to believe that their privacy would be respected?	

In Summary: Locating Sources

* Generate search terms and choose search strategies (p. 454).

* Search your library's catalog (p. 457).

* Search relevant databases (p. 461).

* Use appropriate Web search sites (p. 465) and social media search sites (p. 470).

* Browse the library stacks (p. 473).

* Examine periodicals (p. 474).

* Check reference works (p. 475).

* Conduct field research (p. 478).

Avoiding Plagiarism

Few writers intentionally try to pass off the work of others as their own. However, deadlines and other pressures can lead writers to take notes poorly and to cite sources improperly. In addition, access to documents through the Web and full-text databases has made it all too easy to copy and paste work from other writers without acknowledging its source.

Failing to cite your sources can lead to serious problems. Your readers will not be able to determine which information, ideas, and arguments are your own and which are drawn from your sources. If they suspect you are failing to acknowledge your sources, they might doubt your credibility and even stop reading your document. More seriously, submitting academic work that does not properly identify sources might result in a failing grade or other disciplinary action.

What Is Plagiarism?

Plagiarism is a form of intellectual dishonesty. It involves either unintentionally using someone else's work without properly acknowledging where the ideas or information came from (the most common form of plagiarism) or intentionally passing off someone else's work as your own (the most serious form of plagiarism).

Plagiarism is based on the notion of copyright, or ownership of a document or an idea. Like a patent, which protects an invention, a copyright protects an author's investment of time and energy in the creation of a document. Essentially, it assures authors that someone else won't be able to steal ideas from their work and profit from that theft without penalty.

In this sense, plagiarism in academic writing differs in important ways from the kind of mixing and remixing that can take place in popular culture. The expectations of readers and writers differ in important ways from those of composers and listeners. Musicians, for example, often use other songs as springboards or inspiration for their own work, sometimes sampling other songs or creating mixes. Writers of books, magazine articles, or academic journal articles, in contrast, don't have that freedom. Readers would be surprised to find an unattributed passage that they recognize as the work of another writer, while writers would be alarmed if they came across an unattributed passage of their own in someone else's document. In general, writers are pleased when someone else quotes their work. But they are quick to take offense — and have good reason to do so — when another writer uses their work without giving proper credit. Context matters, and in this case the context of academic writing differs significantly from that of popular culture.

Unintentional Plagiarism

In most cases, plagiarism is unintentional, and most cases of unintentional plagiarism result from taking poor notes or failing to use notes properly. You are plagiarizing if you

- quote a passage in a note but neglect to include quotation marks and then later insert the quotation into your document without remembering that it is a direct quotation
- include a paraphrase that differs so slightly from the original passage that it might as well be a direct quotation

- don't clearly distinguish between your ideas and those that come from your sources

- neglect to list the source of a paraphrase, quotation, or summary in your text or in your works cited list

Although unintentional plagiarism is, by definition, something that the writer hasn't planned to do, it is nonetheless a serious issue and, when detected, is likely to have consequences. Some instructors might require that an assignment be rewritten; others might impose a penalty, such as a lowered or failing grade.

Intentional Plagiarism

Intentional plagiarism, although less common than unintentional plagiarism, can lead to serious academic penalties, ranging from a reduced grade on an assignment, to failure of a course, to expulsion. Intentional plagiarism includes

- engaging in "patchwork writing," or piecing together passages from multiple sources without acknowledging the sources of the passages and without properly quoting or paraphrasing

- creating fake citations to mislead a reader about the sources of information used in a document

- copying or closely paraphrasing extended passages from another document and passing them off as the writer's original work

- copying an entire document and passing it off as the writer's original work

- purchasing a document and passing it off as the writer's original work

Plagiarism in Group Projects

Peer review and other collaborative activities raise important, and potentially confusing, questions.

- If another writer suggests changes to your document and you subsequently incorporate them into your document, are you plagiarizing?

- What if those suggestions significantly change your document?

- If you work with a group of writers on a project, do you need to identify which parts each of you wrote?

- Is it acceptable to list yourself as a coauthor if another writer does most of the work on a collaborative writing project?

The answers to these questions will vary from situation to situation. In general, it's appropriate to use comments from reviewers in your document without citing them. If a reviewer's comments are particularly helpful, you might acknowledge his or her contributions in your document; writers often thank reviewers in a footnote or an endnote or in an acknowledgments section. It is usually appropriate to list coauthors on a collaboratively written document without identifying the text that each coauthor wrote, although some instructors ask that individual contributions be noted in the document or on a cover page. If you are uncertain about what is appropriate, ask your instructor.

What Are Research Ethics?

Research ethics are based on the notion that writing is an honest exchange of information, ideas, and arguments among writers and readers who share an interest in a subject. As a writer, you'll want to behave honestly and ethically. In general, you should do the following:

- Acknowledge the sources of the information, ideas, and arguments you use in your document. By doing so, you show respect for the work that others have done before you.

- Accurately and fairly represent the information, ideas, and arguments from your sources to ensure that you do not misrepresent other writers' work to your readers.

- Provide citation information for your sources. These citations help your readers understand how you have drawn your conclusions and where they can locate those sources should they want to consult them.

These three rules are the essence of research ethics. Ultimately, failing to act ethically — even when the failure is unintentional — can reflect poorly on you and your document. If your readers suspect that you have acted unethically, they will question the accuracy and credibility of the information, ideas, and arguments in your document. If they suspect that you have sacrificed research ethics altogether, they'll probably stop reading your document.

By adhering to research ethics — acknowledging your sources, representing them fairly, and citing them accurately — you can earn the trust of your readers and increase the chances that they'll pay attention to your argument. The illustration on the next page, from Jennie Tillson's essay about the high costs of college tuition, demonstrates a writer's adherence to research ethics.

One way colleges should use tuition money to benefit students is by redesigning their financial aid systems. Although colleges have reportedly increased their need-based financial aid, most of these precious funds go to boost tuition aid for middle-class students. Tamar Lewin from the *New York Times* wrote, "Student borrowing has more than doubled in the last decade, and students from lower-income families, on average, get smaller grants from the colleges they attend than students from more affluent families." Basing more award decisions on financial need instead of merit would allow more students from lower-income families to attend college. As hard economic times continue to affect family finances, some colleges are even offering emergency aid and loans, particularly in cases where parents have lost jobs (Saleh). More colleges must take similar steps to ensure that students from all economic backgrounds have a fighting chance at affording an education.

> An attribution identifies the source of a quotation.

> Quotation marks indicate a partial quotation. Since this Web source has no page or paragraph number, no parenthetical citation is included.

> A parenthetical source citation indicates a paraphrase.

Clark, Kim. "Tuition At Public Colleges Rises 4.8%." *CNN Money*. CNN Money, 24 Oct. 2012. Web. 23 Jan. 2013.

Lewin, Tamar. "College May Become Unaffordable for Most in US." *New York Times*. New York Times Co., 8 Dec. 2008. Web. 19 Jan. 2013.

Quinn, Jane Bryant. "Colleges' New Tuition Crisis." *Newsweek*. Newsweek, 2 Feb. 2006. Web. 18 Jan. 2013.

Saleh, Don. "How to Pay for Your Children's College Education If You've Lost Your Job." *Syracuse*. Syracuse Media Group, 21 Dec. 2010. Web. 17 Jan. 2013.

Tillson, Jennifer. "Survey on College Choices." Colorado State U. 2 Feb. 2013. E-mail survey.

> Complete source information is included in the works cited list.

> Sources are cited in MLA style.

▲ Adhering to research ethics

Understand Common Knowledge

Although crediting other authors for their work is important, you don't need to document every fact and idea used in your document because some of that information falls under the category of common knowledge. Common knowledge is information that is widely known, such as the fact that the Declaration of Independence was signed in 1776. Or it might be the kind of knowledge that people working in a particular field, such as petroleum engineering, use on a regular basis.

If you're relatively new to your topic, it can be difficult to determine whether information in a source is common knowledge. As you explore your topic, however, you will begin to identify what is generally known. For instance, if three or more sources use the same information without citing its source, you can assume that the information is common knowledge. However, if those sources cite the source of that information, make sure you cite it as well.

Ask Permission to Use a Source

The concept of fair use deals with how much of a source you can borrow or quote. According to Section 107 of the Copyright Act of 1976 — the fair use provision (available at www.copyright.gov/title17/) — writers can use copyrighted materials for purposes of "criticism, comment, news reporting, teaching (including multiple copies for classroom use), scholarship, or research." In other words, writers generally don't need to seek permission to make brief quotations from a source or to summarize or paraphrase a source.

If you are working on an assignment for a course — and do not plan to publish the assignment on the Web or in print — you generally can use material from another source without seeking permission. Remember, however, that in all cases you must still cite the source of the material you use.

Writers who plan to publish their work — in a newspaper or magazine, in a blog, or on a public Web site, for example — should seek permission to use material from a source if they want to quote a lengthy passage or, in the case of shorter works such as poems and song lyrics, if they want to quote a significant percentage of the source. Writers who wish to use multimedia sources, such as images, audio, or video, should consider either seeking permission to use the source or linking directly to it. Be cautious, however, about linking directly to multimedia sources, since some Web sites specifically ask that you not link to content on their site (typically because doing so increases the demand on Web servers).

If you seek permission to use a source, explain why and how you want to use it. Many authors and publishers allow academic use of their work but frown on commercial uses. When you contact an author or a publisher, include your name and contact information, the source you wish to use, the purpose for which you will use the source, and the time during which it will be used.

If you contact an author or a publisher by mail, include a self-addressed, stamped envelope. It will save the recipient the cost of responding by mail, indicates that you are serious, and, perhaps most important, shows good manners.

Dear Ms. Jackson:

I am a student and am writing an essay for my writing class, English Composition 200, at Colorado State University. The essay will be used only for educational purposes and will be distributed on our class Web site, which is available only to my instructor and members of my class, for a period of three weeks during April and May of this year.

> Or ". . . on the Web at www.myschool.edu"

I would like to include in my essay the following image, which is displayed on your site at www.westernliving.org/images/2302a.jpg, and would greatly appreciate your permission to do so:

> Insert or describe the passage or image. For example: "paragraphs 3 to 5 of the article," a thumbnail of the image, or the URL of a document or an image on the Web.

If you are able to grant me the requested permission, please respond to this e-mail message. My deadline for completing my project is April 22. I appreciate your quick response.

> Or ". . . sign the enclosed copy of this letter and return it to me."

If you are not the copyright holder or do not have authority to grant this request, I would appreciate any information you can provide concerning the current copyright holder.

Thank you for considering this request.

Sincerely,

Sara Petrovich
Sara.Petrovich@students.colostate.edu
(970) 555-1515

> Provide contact information, such as name, address, e-mail address, phone number, fax number.

▲ **Sample permission request**

How Can I Avoid Plagiarism?

In most cases, writers who plagiarize do so unintentionally. You can avoid unintentional plagiarism by learning how to

- conduct a knowledge inventory
- take notes accurately
- distinguish between your ideas and those drawn from your sources
- cite sources in the text and in a works cited or references list (see Chapters 21 and 22)
- recognize misconceptions about intentional plagiarism

Conduct a Knowledge Inventory

You can avoid unintentional plagiarism by having a clear understanding of your subject. When you are just beginning to learn about a conversation, you might find it difficult not only to express your own ideas clearly but also to restate or reframe the information, ideas, and arguments you've encountered in your sources. The result might be a document composed of passages that have been copied without attribution or paraphrased too closely. To prevent these difficulties, conduct a knowledge inventory by answering three questions:

1. What do you already know about the subject?
2. What don't you know?
3. What do you want to know?

Your answers can serve as a starting point for brainstorming, collecting and working with sources, and planning. They can also serve as a guide for discussing the subject with others. Once you've completed your knowledge inventory, meet with your instructor, consult a librarian, or talk with people who are knowledgeable about the subject. Ideally, these discussions will help you determine the most productive way to learn more about your subject.

Take Notes Carefully

Unintentional plagiarism often results from sloppy note taking. Notes might contain direct quotations that are not surrounded with quotation marks, paraphrases that differ in only minor ways from the original passage, and summaries that contain original passages from a source. Quoting, paraphrasing, and summarizing accurately and appropriately as you take notes is the first — and arguably the most important — step in avoiding unintentional plagiarism.

For guidance on quoting, paraphrasing, and summarizing, see Chapter 3. To learn more about integrating quotations, paraphrases, summaries, numerical information, and illustrations into your document, see Chapter 19.

Attribute Ideas Appropriately

To distinguish between your ideas and those obtained from your sources, use attributions — words and phrases that alert your readers to the source of the ideas or information you are using. As you draft your document, use the author's name or the title of the source whenever you introduce ideas from that source. Phrases such as "According to Tom Siller . . ." or "As Heather Landers indicates . . ." let your readers know that information from a source will follow.

You can learn more about using attributions to identify the origin of quotations, paraphrases, and summaries in Chapter 19.

Identify Your Sources

Include a complete citation for each source you refer to in your document. The citation should appear both in the text of the document and in a works cited or references list.

In the following examples, the writer includes MLA-style parenthetical citations that refer readers to a works cited list at the end of the document. Both MLA style and APA style use a combination of attributions and parenthetical information to refer to sources.

> Jessica Richards argues, "We need to develop an efficient, cost-effective means of distributing hydrogen fuels before we can move to a hydrogen economy. If we don't, we'll be operating in crisis mode when the next serious oil shortage arrives" (322).

> "We need to develop an efficient, cost-effective means of distributing hydrogen fuels before we can move to a hydrogen economy" (Richards 322).

Be sure to cite the page or paragraph numbers for paraphrased and summarized information as well as for direct quotations. The following paraphrase of Jessica Richards's comments about energy needs includes the page number of the original passage in parentheses.

Jessica Richards argues that we need to create an "efficient, cost-effective" system for delivering hydrogen fuels now, instead of while we are facing a critical oil shortage (322).

To learn how to document sources using the MLA and APA documentation systems, see Chapters 21 and 22.

Understand Why Writers Plagiarize

Although most plagiarism is unintentional, some students do plagiarize deliberately. The causes of intentional plagiarism range from running out of time to seeing little value in a course. The most common reasons offered to explain intentional plagiarism — and the steps you can take to avoid falling victim to the temptation to engage in it — are listed below.

- **"It's easier to plagiarize."** Some people believe that it takes less work to cheat than to create an original document. That's probably true — but only in the short term. If you are pursuing a college degree, you will probably work in a profession that requires writing ability and an understanding of how to work with information. When you're assigned to write a report or a proposal down the road, you might regret not taking the time to hone your writing and research skills.

- **"I ran out of time."** Most writers occasionally find themselves wondering where all the time has gone and how they can possibly complete an assignment on schedule. If you find yourself in this situation, contact your instructor about a revised deadline. You might face a penalty for turning in work late, but it will almost certainly be less severe than the penalty for intentional plagiarism.

- **"I couldn't care less about this assignment."** It's not unusual to put off assignments that don't interest you. Rather than avoiding the work, try to approach the assignment in a way that interests you (see p. 32). If that fails, ask your instructor if you can customize the assignment so that it better aligns with your interests.

- **"I'm no good at writing."** A lot of people have doubts about their ability to earn a good grade in a writing course. Occasionally, however, some students convince themselves that plagiarizing is a reasonable alternative to writing their own document. If you lack confidence, seek assistance from your instructor, a campus writing center, a tutoring center, one of the many writing centers on the Web (such as the Writing@CSU Web site at writing.colostate.edu), or a friend or family member. Even with only modest support, you'll probably do much better than you think you can.

- **"I didn't think I'd get caught."** Some students believe — and might even have experiences to support their belief — that they won't get caught plagiarizing. Most writing instructors, however, become familiar with their students' writing styles. If they notice a sudden change in style, or encounter varying styles in the same document, they might become suspicious. The availability of plagiarism detection software also increases the likelihood that plagiarism will be detected.

- **"Everybody cheats."** Some students plagiarize because they believe that many of their classmates are doing so. They fear that if they don't plagiarize, they'll be at a competitive disadvantage. In fact, however, the number of students who plagiarize is quite low. Don't be persuaded by dramatic statistics showing that cheating is the norm. The reality is that few students plagiarize intentionally, and those who do still tend to earn lower grades than their peers.

- **"This course is a waste of my time."** If you view a course as little more than a box that needs to be checked, you might be tempted to put in as little effort as possible. However, turning in work that isn't your own can backfire. If you are caught plagiarizing, you'll probably receive a reduced — or failing — grade for the assignment or the course. Instead of plagiarizing, talk with your instructor or an academic adviser about your lack of interest. You might find that the course actually has some relevance to your interests and career plans.

What Should I Do If I'm Accused of Plagiarism?

If your instructor expresses concerns about the originality of your work or the manner in which you've documented information, ideas, and arguments from sources, ask for a meeting to discuss the situation. To prepare for the meeting, do the following:

- Review your document to identify passages that might have raised suspicions.

- Collect the materials you used in your writing project, such as copies of your sources, responses to surveys, interview transcripts, and so on.

- Collect materials you wrote during the project, such as the results of brainstorming and freewriting sessions; any outlines, clusters, or maps; and drafts of your document.

- Reflect on your writing process.

During the meeting, listen to your instructor's concerns before responding. It's natural to feel defensive, but you'll probably be more comfortable if you take notes and try to understand why your instructor has questions about your document. Once your instructor is finished expressing his or her concerns, think carefully about what has been said and respond as clearly as possible. Your instructor might ask follow-up questions, most likely about the sources you've used, your writing process, and the document you've written.

If you find that you have engaged in unintentional plagiarism, ask your instructor for guidance about how to avoid it in the future, and ask what sort of penalty you will face. If your instructor determines that you have plagiarized intentionally, ask what consequences you will face.

If you and your instructor are unable to resolve the situation, you might face a disciplinary process. To prepare for that process, learn as much as you can about the academic integrity policies at your institution.

In Summary: Avoiding Plagiarism

* **Understand the definition of plagiarism and the concept of copyright (p. 484).**

* **Understand and follow research ethics (p. 486).**

* **Understand what is meant by common knowledge (p. 487).**

* **Seek permission to use sources when necessary (p. 488).**

* **Conduct a knowledge inventory (p. 490).**

* **Cite and document your sources (p. 491).**

* **Resist temptations to plagiarize intentionally (p. 492).**

* **Know what to do if you are accused of plagiarism (p. 493).**

PART FOUR

Crafting and Polishing
Your Contribution

14

Developing a Thesis Statement

 As you shift your attention toward crafting your contribution to a conversation, you'll start to plan your document. That process begins with choosing a main point and drafting a thesis statement. It also includes choosing the points and evidence you will use to support your thesis statement.

How Can I Choose a Main Point?

Your main point is the most important argument or idea you want to convey to your readers. Your choice of a main point will be influenced by what you've learned about your subject and by your writing situation.

Review Your Notes

Begin choosing your main point by reading quickly through your notes. As you review your notes, do the following:

- List important information, ideas, and arguments that you've come across in your reading.
- Consider what interests you about the information, ideas, and arguments you've identified in your notes.
- Review and elaborate on the ideas and arguments that you've come up with as a result of your own thinking about the subject.

When you complete your review, identify the ideas you would most like to address in your document.

Consider Your Writing Situation

Reviewing your notes will help you deepen your understanding of your subject. That understanding, in turn, will affect how you view your purpose and role as a writer and, by extension, the main point you want to make in your document. Use the following questions about your writing situation to help you choose your main point:

- How have the sources you've consulted changed your thinking about the subject?
- Have your purposes — the reasons you are working on this project — changed since you started the project? If so, how do you view your purpose now?
- Has your role as a writer — for example, to inform or to solve a problem — changed since you started your project? If so, how do you view your role now?
- Will focusing on a particular idea help you address your readers' purposes, needs, interests, and backgrounds?
- Can you address this idea given the requirements and limitations of your writing project?

After you've answered these questions, choose a main point that is both interesting to you and consistent with the demands of your writing situation. Jot it down in a sentence or two.

How Can I Draft My Thesis Statement?

Your thesis statement provides a clear, focused expression of your main point. To develop your thesis statement, think about how your main point relates to the type of document you will write and to the information, ideas, and arguments you want to include. Then try out different ways of phrasing your thesis statement. As you develop each new version, try to predict how your readers will react to it.

Consider the Type of Document You Will Write

An effective thesis statement will reflect the type of document — or genre — you plan to write (see p. 18). Depending on the genre, your readers will have different expectations about how you present your thesis statement. Readers of an academic essay will expect a calm, clearly written statement of what you want them to learn, believe, or do. Readers of an informative newspaper article will expect you to identify, in a balanced and seemingly unbiased manner, what you want them to learn. Readers of an opinion column will expect you to be more assertive, and perhaps even more entertaining, about your main point. Consider how the following thesis statements, all addressing problems with the recruitment of athletes at a university, reflect the type of document the writer plans to draft.

Argumentative Academic Essay

The university should ensure that its recruiting practices are in full compliance with NCAA regulations.

> A strong but formal assertion

Informative Newspaper Article

The university is taking steps to bring its recruiting practices in line with NCAA regulations.

> A seemingly unbiased statement of fact

Opinion Column

The university's coaches need to get their act together before the NCAA slaps them with sanctions.

> An informal tone

Identify Important Information, Ideas, and Arguments Related to Your Main Point

Begin developing your thesis statement by identifying important information, ideas, and arguments related to your main point. When you first explored a conversation (see Chapter 2), you asked questions to learn about your subject. Review those questions and examine them for key words and phrases. Then look through your notes to see how your sources address those questions or use those key words and phrases. Consider the following example, which shows a list of initial questions and important information, ideas, and arguments found in sources that address the challenge of finding jobs for returning veterans.

> Mia circled key words and phrases in her initial questions about her subject and then identified which sources address those key words and phrases.

Questions about jobs for returning veterans:

Do veterans face higher unemployment rates than nonveterans?

Who should be involved in finding jobs for veterans?

What kinds of jobs are best for veterans?

What skills do veterans have that would be useful in civilian work?

How good are veterans at new green jobs?

What my sources say:

Veterans are more likely to be unemployed than nonveterans (Doe and Marks para. 1).

Employers, employees, and local and state governments all bear responsibility for seeking out and hiring veterans in need of employment (Doe and Marks para. 7).

Many green jobs put veterans in familiar situations and make use of their physical and mental skills (Barringer para. 8).

Veterans employed by conservation groups often work in the wilderness on risky, large-scale operations, much as they did in the military (Barringer para. 18).

You can use the key words and phrases you've identified in your questions and notes in the various versions of thesis statements that you try out.

Draft Alternatives

An effective thesis statement can invite your readers to learn something new, suggest that they change their attitudes or beliefs, or argue that they should take action of some kind. Consider how the following thesis statements reflect these three ways of focusing a main point.

Main Point

Government, business, and nonprofit organizations should address the problem of unemployment among veterans by creating programs that prepare returning veterans for green jobs.

Thesis Statement: Asking Readers to Learn Something New

Veterans currently face higher unemployment rates than do nonveterans, and programs that prepare veterans for green jobs can help address that problem, especially when supported by government, business, and nonprofit organizations.

Thesis Statement: Asking Readers to Change Their Attitudes or Beliefs

We should view high unemployment rates among veterans not as a military problem or a veterans' problem but as a problem that businesses, nonprofits, and government organizations can help solve by preparing veterans for green jobs.

Thesis Statement: Asking Readers to Take Action

People should support organizations and businesses that help prepare veterans for suitable jobs, particularly green jobs that benefit the environment, in order to address the problem of unemployment among veterans.

Experiment with different approaches to determine which one works best for your writing situation. The thesis statement you choose should convey your main point in a way that addresses your purpose and your readers' needs, interests, backgrounds, and knowledge of a subject. For example, if you're focusing on the causes of a problem, your thesis statement should identify those causes. If you're advocating a particular solution to a problem, your thesis statement should identify that solution.

Focus Your Thesis Statement

A broad thesis statement does not encourage your readers to learn anything new, change their attitudes or beliefs, or take action. The following thesis statement is too broad.

Broad Thesis Statement

The high rate of unemployment among veterans is a problem that will take effort to solve.

There's no conversation to be had about this topic because few people would argue with such a statement. A more focused thesis statement would define what should be done and who should do it.

Focused Thesis Statement

> Government, business, and nonprofit organizations should address the problem of unemployment among veterans by creating programs that prepare returning veterans for green jobs that benefit both our country and those who have served in its name.

To focus your thesis statement, ask what your readers would want to know about your subject, what attitudes should be changed, or what action should be taken. Consider their likely responses to your thesis statement, and attempt to head off potential counterarguments or questions.

How Can I Support My Thesis Statement?

Presenting your thesis statement effectively involves far more than knowing what you want others to understand or believe or how you want them to act. You must develop a strategy to accomplish your goal. Developing your strategy involves reflecting on your purposes, your readers, and the conventions typically used in the type of document you plan to write.

Choose Reasons to Accept Your Thesis Statement

In longer documents, such as essays, reports, and Web sites, writers usually present readers with several reasons to accept their thesis statement. The kinds of reasons writers present will vary according to the types of documents they are writing. In informative documents, for example, writers might focus on the three or four most important aspects of the subject they want readers to understand. In analytical documents, they might choose points that help readers understand the results of the analysis. In argumentative documents, writers usually offer a series of claims that will lead readers to accept the arguments they are advancing.

To choose the reasons you'll offer to support your thesis statement, consider brainstorming, freewriting, looping, or clustering (see p. 33). As you generate ideas, reflect on your purpose, your role as a writer, the type of document you intend to write, and your readers.

- **Writing to reflect.** Which of your observations are most significant? What kind of impression do you want to create? (See Chapter 5.)

- **Writing to inform.** What do you want to convey to your readers? What are they most likely to want to know about the subject? (See Chapter 6.)

- **Writing to analyze.** How will you present the results of your analysis? What questions might your readers have about each part of your analysis? (See Chapter 7.)

- **Writing to evaluate.** What is the best way to present your criteria and the results of your evaluation? (See Chapter 8.)

- **Writing to solve problems.** How will you define the problem, and how will you present your solution? What questions do you think your readers will have about your problem definition, proposed solution, and alternative solutions? (See Chapter 9.)

- **Writing to convince or persuade.** How can you convince your readers to accept your thesis statement? How do you think they might respond to your argument? What sort of counterarguments might they propose? (See Chapter 10.)

Select Evidence to Support Your Reasons

For each reason you offer to support your thesis statement, you'll need evidence — such as details, facts, personal observations, and expert opinions — to back up your assertions and help your readers understand your ideas. The evidence you choose plays a central role in gaining your readers' acceptance of your thesis statement.

You can draw evidence from your sources in the form of quotations, paraphrases, summaries, numerical data, and visual images. You can also gather evidence first-hand by conducting interviews, observations, and surveys, or by reflecting on your personal experience. Chapters 5 through 10 offer detailed suggestions for locating and choosing evidence for specific purposes.

Use the following prompts to identify evidence to support your reasons:

1. List the reasons you are using to support your thesis statement.

2. Identify relevant evidence from your sources, personal experience, or your own field research, and then list that evidence below each reason. You might need to review your sources to locate additional evidence, or even obtain additional sources.

3. Determine whether you are relying too heavily on information from a single source, or on one type of evidence.

As you select supporting evidence, consider the genre of your document. Genre conventions (see p. 558) often determine how and how much evidence is used in a document. Articles in magazines, newspapers, and Web sites, for example, are more likely to rely on interviews, observation, and illustrations as primary sources of evidence than are academic essays, whose writers tend to draw information from published sources found in a library or database. Multimodal essays, in contrast, are likely to use not only textual information and images but also audio, video, and animation.

In Summary: Developing a Thesis Statement

* Choose a main point (p. 498).

* Review your notes (p. 498).

* Consider your writing situation (p. 498).

* Draft your thesis statement (p. 499).

* Choose reasons to accept your thesis statement (p. 502).

* Select evidence to support your reasons (p. 503).

Organizing

A well-organized document allows a reader to predict what will come next. Choose an appropriate organizing pattern by reflecting on your writing situation, thesis statement, reasons, and evidence. With that pattern in mind, use labeling, grouping, clustering, and mapping to arrange your argument and formal and informal outlining strategies to organize your document.

How Can I Choose an Organizing Pattern?

Organizing patterns provide an overall principle for arranging your argument and document. The pattern you choose should help you organize your document in a manner that your readers can follow easily. It should also help you achieve your purpose and adapt to your readers and context.

Understand the Types of Organizing Patterns

Common organizing patterns include the following.

Chronology reflects the order in which events occur over time. For example, you might focus on a sequence of events in a recent election or during someone's life. Biographies and memoirs, for example, are often organized chronologically, portraying early events first and moving forward in time.

Description provides a point-by-point account of the physical attributes of a subject. For example, you might focus on what you see as you walk the streets of a city. Description is best for documents that address physical spaces, objects, or people — things that we can see and observe — rather than theories or processes that are not visible.

Definition lays out the distinguishing characteristics of a subject and then provides examples and reasoning to explain what differentiates it from other subjects. For instance, an essay defining *pride* might begin by stating that it is an emotion and then move on to explain why that particular emotion is not as harmful as many people believe.

Cause/effect patterns focus on the factors that lead to (cause) an outcome (effect). For example, you might identify the reasons behind a recent strike by grocery store employees or the health risks that contribute to heart disease.

Process explanations outline the steps involved in doing something or explain how something happens. For example, you might help readers understand the stages of nuclear fission or teach them what to do to prepare for a hurricane.

Pro/con organizing patterns present arguments made for (pro) and against (con) a particular position. For example, you might consider the arguments for and against increased reliance on wind power.

Multiple perspectives organizing patterns arrange information, ideas, and arguments according to a range of perspectives about a subject. Writers who use this pattern frequently provide an analysis supporting one perspective. For example, a writer addressing the use of tidal power as an alternative energy source might present the perspectives of utility companies, environmentalists, oceanographers, legislators, and waterfront residents and ultimately favor one group over the others.

Comparison/contrast patterns can help you explore similarities and differences among the information, ideas, and arguments relevant to a subject. A writer analyzing a policy initiative to decriminalize marijuana possession, for example, might consider how current drug laws are like or unlike alcohol prohibition. Another writer might compare and contrast medical and recreational uses of marijuana.

Strengths/weaknesses patterns can help you examine positive and negative aspects of a subject, such as increasing federal funding for health care by instituting a national lottery, or the overall quality of life in a particular city. Writers who choose this organizing principle typically work toward a conclusion where one or two considerations outweigh the others.

Costs/benefits organizing patterns present the trade-offs associated with a subject, usually a choice or proposal of some sort. For example, the writer of an evaluative essay might discuss why the expenses associated with implementing a particular educational initiative are justified (or not) by the potential for higher test scores.

Problem/solution organizing patterns involve defining a problem and discussing the appropriateness of one or more solutions. If multiple solutions are proposed, the writer usually argues for the superiority of one over the others. For instance, an informative article might explain the problem of "brain drain," in which highly educated and skilled workers move out of state, and then argue in support of a proposal to retain and attract more skilled workers.

Reflect on Your Writing Situation

Your choice of organizing pattern will reflect your purpose and the role or roles you adopt as a writer (see Chapters 5 through 10). Consider which pattern will help you achieve your goals as a writer, meet the needs and interests of your readers, adapt to your context, and be consistent with the genre (or type of document) you've chosen. Your choice of organizing pattern should also reflect the reasons and evidence you offer to convince readers to accept your thesis statement.

Keep in mind that a writer may use more than one organizing pattern in a document. For instance, a process explanation often works in tandem with chronology, since both present steps in a sequence. Similarly, a document presenting multiple perspectives might use the strengths/weaknesses pattern to evaluate the merits of each perspective.

How Can I Arrange My Argument?

Once you have selected an organizing pattern, you can use strategies such as labeling, grouping, clustering, and mapping to determine how to present your argument. These strategies will also help you later as you develop an outline for your document.

Labeling

Labeling can help you understand at a glance how and where you will use your evidence. For example, you might label notes or sources containing the evidence you want to use in your introduction with "Introduction," those that you plan to use to define a concept with the name of that concept, and so on. Digital notes and sources can be labeled by changing a file name or editing the document text. Print notes and sources can be labeled with pen or pencil or with sticky notes.

Once you've labeled your notes and sources, you can organize them into groups and put them in order.

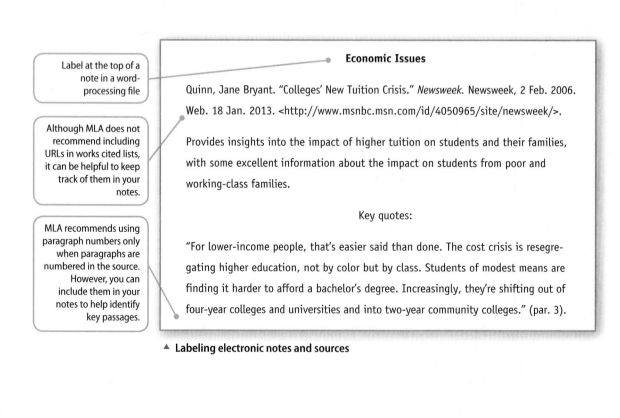

Label at the top of a note in a word-processing file

Although MLA does not recommend including URLs in works cited lists, it can be helpful to keep track of them in your notes.

MLA recommends using paragraph numbers only when paragraphs are numbered in the source. However, you can include them in your notes to help identify key passages.

Economic Issues

Quinn, Jane Bryant. "Colleges' New Tuition Crisis." *Newsweek*. Newsweek, 2 Feb. 2006. Web. 18 Jan. 2013. <http://www.msnbc.msn.com/id/4050965/site/newsweek/>.

Provides insights into the impact of higher tuition on students and their families, with some excellent information about the impact on students from poor and working-class families.

Key quotes:

"For lower-income people, that's easier said than done. The cost crisis is resegre-gating higher education, not by color but by class. Students of modest means are finding it harder to afford a bachelor's degree. Increasingly, they're shifting out of four-year colleges and universities and into two-year community colleges." (par. 3).

▲ **Labeling electronic notes and sources**

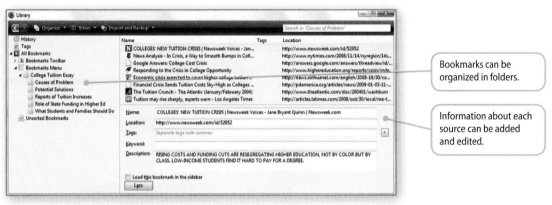

▲ Grouping electronic notes and sources

Grouping

Grouping involves categorizing the evidence you've obtained from your sources. Paper-based notes and copies of sources can be placed in related piles or file folders; sources and notes in word-processing files or on a smartphone can be saved in larger files or placed in folders; items in Bookmarks or Favorites lists can be sorted by category. Placing things that are similar in groups allows you to locate the evidence you've collected more easily and helps you understand the range of evidence you might use to support a particular point.

Clustering

You can use clustering to explore the relationships among your thesis statement, reasons, and evidence. Clustering involves arranging these elements visually on a sheet of paper or on a computer, phone, or tablet screen (using a word-processing program or an app such as iThoughtsHD).

Mapping

Mapping allows you to explore sequences of reasons and evidence. For example, you might use mapping to create a timeline or to show how an argument builds on one reason after another. Mapping can be particularly effective as you begin to think about organizing your document, and it often relies on the organizing patterns discussed earlier in this chapter, such as chronology, cause/effect, comparison/contrast, costs/benefits, and problem/solution.

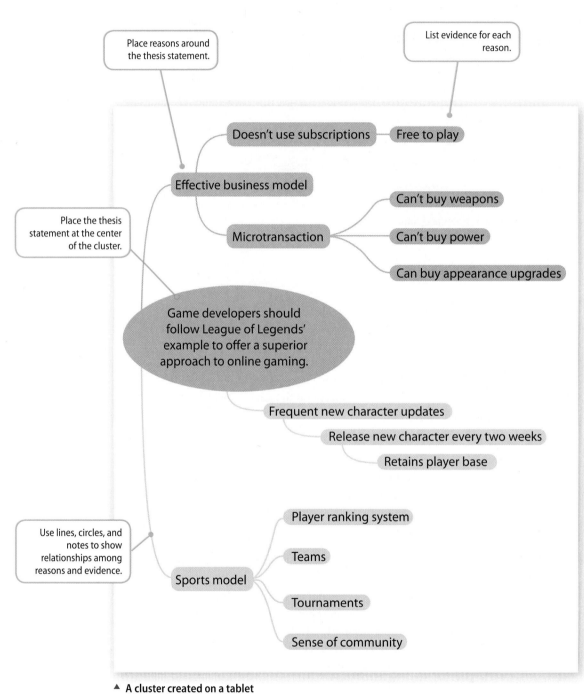

Place reasons around the thesis statement.

List evidence for each reason.

Doesn't use subscriptions — Free to play

Effective business model

Place the thesis statement at the center of the cluster.

Can't buy weapons

Microtransaction — Can't buy power

Can buy appearance upgrades

Game developers should follow League of Legends' example to offer a superior approach to online gaming.

Frequent new character updates

Release new character every two weeks

Retains player base

Player ranking system

Teams

Use lines, circles, and notes to show relationships among reasons and evidence.

Sports model

Tournaments

Sense of community

▲ **A cluster created on a tablet**

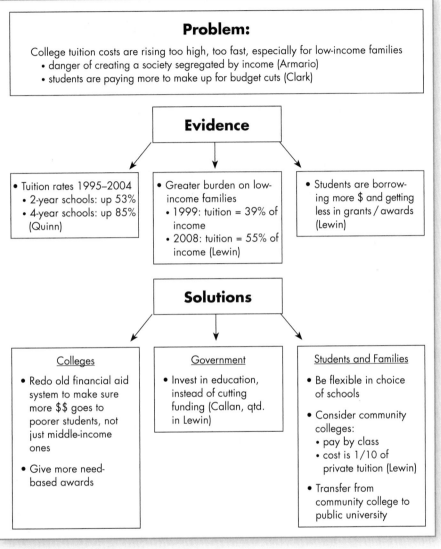

Problem:

College tuition costs are rising too high, too fast, especially for low-income families
- danger of creating a society segregated by income (Armario)
- students are paying more to make up for budget cuts (Clark)

Evidence

- Tuition rates 1995–2004
  - 2-year schools: up 53%
  - 4-year schools: up 85% (Quinn)

- Greater burden on low-income families
  - 1999: tuition = 39% of income
  - 2008: tuition = 55% of income (Lewin)

- Students are borrowing more $ and getting less in grants / awards (Lewin)

Solutions

Colleges

- Redo old financial aid system to make sure more $$ goes to poorer students, not just middle-income ones

- Give more need-based awards

Government

- Invest in education, instead of cutting funding (Callan, qtd. in Lewin)

Students and Families

- Be flexible in choice of schools

- Consider community colleges:
  - pay by class
  - cost is 1/10 of private tuition (Lewin)

- Transfer from community college to public university

▲ Mapping

How Can I Create an Outline?

Not all documents require an outline, but creating one will usually help you put your thoughts in order. As you develop an outline, you'll make decisions about the sequence in which you'll present your reasons and the evidence you'll use to back them up.

Create an Informal Outline

Informal outlines can take many forms: a brief list of words, a series of short phrases, or even a series of sentences. You can use informal outlines to remind yourself of key points to address in your document or of notes you should refer to as you draft. Featured writer Dwight Haynes, who wrote an evaluative essay about anti-drinking campaigns on college campuses, created the following informal outline. Each item in his outline represents a section he planned to include in his essay.

> 1. Introduction
> 2. Establish two approaches to addressing binge drinking on campus
> 3. Evaluate each approach
>   - Social norms (Turner, Wechsler, DeJong)
>   - Environmental (Weitzman, Jaschik)
> 4. Conclusion

Dwight identified sources he could use in each subsection.

▲ **Dwight Haynes's informal outline**

You can also create a "thumbnail outline," a type of informal outline that helps you group your ideas into major sections. Featured writer Vince Reid wrote the thumbnail outline on the following page as he worked on his argumentative essay about online gaming. Vince identified the major sections he wanted to include in his essay and noted which sources he could use to provide background information and to support his argument.

Create a Formal Outline

A formal outline provides a complete and accurate list of the points you want to address in your document. Formal outlines use Roman numerals, letters, and Arabic numerals to indicate the hierarchy of information. An alternative approach, common in business and the sciences, uses numbering with decimal points.

Introduction

In 2009, the most popular massively multiplayer online game, or MMOG, in the world was World of Warcraft, a role-playing game produced by one of the largest videogame developers in the USA, Blizzard. World of Warcraft had dominated the MMOG market for the previous five years and tens of million people played it worldwide each month. Now, three years later, the world's most popular online game is League of Legends, which was released in October 2009 and is currently played by thirty million gamers each month. How did League become this success-ful? (Use Fahey and Riot Games inographic for number of players.)

Thesis Statement

Game developers should follow League of Legends' example to offer a superior approach to online gaming.

League has adopted a business model that is the best of both worlds.

Most online games rely on subscriptions or microtransactions. (Use Cox to discuss the subscription model.) The problem is that subscriptions are expensive and microtransactions, although costing less, usually allow players to buy weapons or power (especially powerful weapons or rare abilities), creating an uneven playing field. This drives other players away. League of Legends uses a microtransaction model (free to play) but doesn't sell weapons or power—only alterations in character appearance. This makes the game fair for all players.

Frequent updates keep players excited and coming back for more.

Most online games have a slow release schedule—releasing only major updates (usually every six months to two years). Because League releases updates (new characters) twice each month, it is able to keep a larger percentage of its player base.

League of Legends is a sport.

In 2010, League of Legends gained a ranking system for players. Players began creating teams, and tournaments were organized. (Use Cox and Robertson.) Eventually, a professional circuit of high-ranking players was created. Why did this work? Because a game is something people play while a sport is something people are part of. It introduces the idea of community among players.

Conclusion

League has been successful because it had a different vision, giving players a chance to compete on an even basis and the opportunity to belong to a community.

▲ Vince Reid's thumbnail outline

Thesis Statement: Scientists and governments devising approaches to eradicating malaria consider three main factors in determining whether DDT should be used in indoor residual spraying: health consequences, environmental consequences, and degree of resistance.

I. Introduction
   a. DDT, discovered in 1939, was first used for malaria vector control in World War II (CDC, 2010).
   b. WHO proposed global malaria eradication program in 1995, with DDT as a key player (CDC).
   c. Publication of Rachel Carson's *Silent Spring* leads to banning of DDT in agriculture in 1969 (Sadasivaiah, Tozan, and Breman, 250).
   d. Despite ban, DDT continues to be used, particularly in poorer countries (Sadasivaiah, Tozan, and Breman).
      i. Approved at the 2009 Conference of the Parties Stockholm Convention (WHO).
      ii. Among most economical options for malaria prevention.
   e. A key question is whether indoor use of DDT has the same impact on health as agricultural uses (WHO, *DDT in Indoor Residual Spraying*, 16; WHO, *World Malaria Report*, 23).
      i. Lower amounts used
      ii. Use strictly enforced
      iii. Mitigation strategies can be used to protect health.
II. Human health effects of DDT
   a. DDT is highly toxic to children (Sadasivaiah, Tozan, and Breman).
III. Environmental consequences
   a. DDT is chemically stable and harmful to crops (WHO, *The Use of DDT in Malaria Vector Control*, 6).
IV. Resistance to DDT
   a. Resistance to the chemical is a major obstacle to all pesticide use.
   b. Parts of Africa already seeing genetic changes in disease-carrying mosquitoes (Beerbohm, 14).
V. Risks versus benefits
   a. Research on DDT use must continue (Bouwmann, 746).
   b. Currently used in 16 countries (WHO, *World Malaria Report*, 23).
      i. Effective
      ii. Low cost
   c. Resistance to alternative pesticides (Sadasivaiah, Tozan, and Breman, 256).
VI. Conclusion
   a. Evaluation of benefits and risks is complex and difficult.
   b. Malaria's health risks must be weighed against those associated with DDT.
   c. We should use all tools available, including funding for health care and infrastructure.

▲ Ellen Page's topical outline

Writers use formal outlines to identify the hierarchy of arguments, ideas, and information. You can create a formal outline to identify

- your thesis statement
- the reasons you offer to support your thesis statement
- the sequence in which your reasons should be presented
- evidence to support your reasons
- the notes and sources you should refer to as you work on your draft

The most common types of formal outlines are topical outlines and sentence outlines.

Topical outlines present the topics and subtopics you plan to include in your document as a series of words and phrases. Items at the same level of importance should be phrased in parallel grammatical form. In her topical outline for her informative essay about DDT use in the prevention of malaria, featured writer Ellen Page identified her main point, listed her reasons, mapped out the supporting evidence for her reasons, and used a conventional system of Roman numerals and letters.

Sentence outlines use complete sentences to identify the points you want to cover. Sentence outlines begin the process of converting an outline into a draft of your document. They can also help you assess the structure of a document that you have already written.

Using her topical outline as a starting point, Ellen Page wrote a sentence outline to test her ideas. Part of her sentence outline is shown below.

Thesis Statement: Scientists and governments devising approaches to eradicating malaria consider three main factors in determining whether DDT should be used in indoor residual spraying: health consequences, environmental consequences, and degree of resistance.

II. Human health effects of DDT
   a. The major concerns surrounding human health and the use of DDT are consumption of the pesticide by children (this has been deemed toxic) and exposure of the pesticide to pregnant women (Sadasivaiah, Tozan, and Breman, 251; WHO, *DDT in Indoor Residual Spraying*, 9).
   b. Many studies have suggested that DDT causes pregnancy loss, fertility loss, leukemia, cancer, diabetes, and other health problems (Van Den Berg, 1658).

▲ **Part of Ellen Page's sentence outline**

In Summary: Organizing

❋ Choose an appropriate organizing pattern (p. 506).

❋ Use labeling, grouping, clustering, and/ or mapping to organize your argument (p. 508).

❋ Create a formal or an informal outline (p. 512).

Drafting and Designing

⏩ As you've learned about and considered your subject, you've encountered new information, ideas, and arguments. In response, you've considered how to craft your own contribution to the conversation you've decided to join. How you frame your contribution — that is, how you organize your

(Continued)

argument, construct your paragraphs, introduce and conclude your document, and design your document — can have a profound effect on readers' understanding of your subject and on their willingness to accept your main idea. This chapter offers guidance on how to use what you've learned to create an effective, readable document.

How Can I Use My Outline to Begin Drafting?

Your outline provides a framework you can use to draft your document. Your outline likely includes your plans for

- the points you will include in your document
- the order in which you will make your points
- the amount of space you plan to devote to each point

As you review your purpose and your outline, check that you have organized your document in a way that will allow you to achieve your purpose and address the needs and interests of your readers.

If you have listed information about the sources you will use to support your points, you can check whether you are

- providing enough evidence to support your points
- relying too heavily on a limited number of sources
- relying too heavily on support from sources that favor just one side of the conversation

If you created an informal outline, you can begin to flesh it out by translating key points in your outline into sentences or paragraphs. If you created a formal outline, you can turn major headings in the outline into headings or subheadings in your draft and then use the points under each heading as the basis for topic sentences for paragraphs. If your outline is highly detailed, you can use minor points as the basis for supporting sentences within each paragraph.

If your outline contains references to specific notes or sources, make sure that you use those notes or sources in your draft. Take advantage of the time you spent thinking about which sources are most appropriate for a particular section of your document.

As you work on your draft, you might find it necessary to reorganize your ideas. Think of your outline as a flexible guide rather than a rigid blueprint.

How Can I Draft an Effective Document?

Effective documents contribute to the conversation in a way that reflects and adapts to your writing situation. Your document should help you accomplish your purpose, address your readers effectively, and help you take advantage of — or work within — the contexts in which it will be read.

Create Paragraphs That Focus on a Central Idea

Writers use paragraphs to present and develop a central idea. Depending on the complexity of your thesis statement and the type of document you are writing, a single paragraph might be all you need to present a supporting point and its associated reasoning and evidence — or it might play only a small role in conveying your thinking about your subject. You can enhance the effectiveness of your document by creating paragraphs that are focused, organized, and well developed and by using transitions that clearly convey the relationships among paragraphs.

Each of your paragraphs should focus on a single idea. Paragraphs often have a topic sentence in which the writer makes an assertion, offers an observation, or asks a question. The rest of the sentences in the paragraph elaborate on the topic. Consider the following paragraph, drawn from Richard H. Thaler and Cass R. Sunstein's problem-solving essay (p. 330).

The central idea of the paragraph is provided in the first sentence.

The second sentence offers evidence by way of an example.

The third and fourth sentences describe the example in more detail and support it with a humorous admission.

> Many businesses have discovered the power of default options. When people subscribe to a magazine or website these days, they are typically enrolled in an automatic renewal program. When their subscription runs out, it is automatically renewed unless the subscriber takes some action; and, in many cases, the action requires a bit of patience and persistence. One of us (not to mention names, but the lawyer) still has subscriptions to several magazines that he never reads and actually hates, because he has not gotten around to canceling them.

Create Paragraphs That Use Appropriate Organizing Patterns

Effective documents follow an organizing pattern, often the same one that the document as a whole follows, such as chronology, description, or costs/benefits (see p. 506). These common patterns help readers anticipate what you'll say. Readers who recognize a pattern, such as process explanation, will find it easier to focus on your ideas and argument if they understand how you are organizing your paragraph. Note how the following paragraph uses the problem/solution organizing pattern.

> What can we do to help adolescent female athletes avoid illicit drug use? How can we help them avoid the pitfalls of competitive athletics? Parents, coaches, and the athletes themselves all play a crucial role in averting bad choices. First, parents and coaches need to be aware that performance-enhancing drugs are a problem. Some adults believe that steroid use is either minimal or nonexistent among teenagers, but one study concluded that "over half the teens who use steroids start before age 16, sometimes with the encouragement of their parents. . . . Seven percent said they first took 'juice' by age ten" (Dudley, 2010, p. 235).

The paragraph uses a problem/solution organizing pattern.

The central idea of the paragraph is provided in the third sentence.

One part of the solution to the larger problem is provided.

The fifth sentence provides evidence from a source to illustrate the nature of the problem.

Integrate Information from Sources Effectively

Information from sources can be used to introduce an important concept, establish the strength of your argument, and elaborate on the central ideas in your document. Writers frequently state a point, offer a reason to accept it, and support their reasoning with evidence from a source, typically in the form of quotations, paraphrases, and summaries. In the following example, a quotation and a paraphrase are used to support a point introduced in the first sentence of the paragraph:

> In fact, pollution from power plants may worsen as the demand for electric power continues to increase. The U.S. Department of Energy (2012b) notes that "it is likely that the nation's reliance on fossil fuels to power an expanding economy will actually increase over at least the next two decades even with aggressive development and deployment of new renewable and nuclear technologies" (para. 1). Moreover, demand in developing nations is expected to increase even more dramatically. Of the nearly 1,200 conventional, coal-fired power plants now on the drawing board world wide, most are in developing countries (Plumer, 2012). The addition of so many new plants will almost certainly lead to more global air pollution in the near term.

Quoting an authority on the issue, the U.S. Department of Energy, lends strength to the argument. The quotation, along with a subsequent paraphrase of a passage from another source, serves as evidence to support the point. The writer follows the quotation and paraphrase with a sentence that restates the point. (See Chapter 19 for more about integrating information from sources.)

Write Clearly and Concisely

Readers don't want to work any harder than necessary to understand and engage with the information, ideas, and arguments in a document. They get unhappy if they have to put in extra effort to read a document — so unhappy, in fact, that they'll often give up.

To keep your readers engaged with your document, write clearly and concisely. Consider the following passages.

> Please join me, Dr. Watson. I have concluded that I am in a situation in which I require your assistance.

> Come here, Dr. Watson. I need you.

> Help!

The second example, reputed to be the first words ever spoken on a telephone, was spoken by Alexander Graham Bell after he'd spilled acid on his pants. Had he spoken the first sentence instead, he might have wasted crucial time while he waited a few extra seconds for his assistant to figure out what he was being asked to do. The simple exclamation of "Help!" might have been even more effective and would certainly have taken less time to utter. Then again, it might have been too vague for his assistant to figure out just how he needed to act and what sort of help was required.

In general, if two sentences provide the same information, the briefer sentence is usually easier to understand. In some cases, however, writing too little will leave your readers wondering what you are trying to get across.

The following three techniques can help you write with economy:

- **Avoid unnecessary modifiers.** Unnecessary modifiers are words that provide little or no additional information to a reader, such as *fine, many, somewhat, great, quite, sort of, lots, really,* and *very*.

Example Sentence with Unnecessary Modifiers

> The Volvo S80 serves as a really excellent example of a very fine performance sedan.

Revised Example

> The Volvo S80 serves as an excellent example of a performance sedan.

- **Avoid unnecessary introductory phrases.** Avoid phrases such as *there are, there is, these have, these are, here are, here is, it has been reported that, it has been said* *that, it is evident that, it is obvious that*, and so on. Sentences beginning with *It goes without saying*, for example, allow you to emphasize a point, but you can often recast such sentences more concisely by simply stating the point.

Example Sentence with Unnecessary Introductory Phrase

It goes without saying that drinking water should be clean.

Revised Example

Drinking water should be clean.

- **Avoid stock phrases.** Search your document for phrases that you can replace with fewer words, such as the following.

Stock Phrase	Alternative
as a matter of fact	in fact
at all times	always
at that point in time	then
at this point in time	now, currently
at the present time	now, currently
because of the fact that	because
by means of	by
due to the fact that	because
in order to	to
in spite of the fact that	although, though
in the event that	if

Example Sentence with Stock Phrase

Call the security desk in the event that the alarm sounds.

Revised Example

Call the security desk if the alarm sounds.

Engage Your Readers

As you draft your document, consider how you'll keep your readers' attention — and be aware of how your sentences can affect their willingness to keep reading. One of the easiest things you can do is to write your sentences in *active voice*. A sentence written in active voice specifies an actor — a person or thing — who carries out an action.

Active Voice

> Juan took an exam.
>
> The tornado leveled the town.
>
> Carmelo Anthony scored the game-winning basket with 0.2 seconds remaining in overtime.

In contrast, a sentence written in passive voice indicates that something was done, but it does not necessarily specify who or what did it.

Passive Voice

> The exam was taken by Juan.
>
> The town was leveled.
>
> The game-winning basket was scored with 0.2 seconds remaining in overtime.

In general, you'll want to emphasize the actor, because sentences written in active voice are easier to understand and provide more information.

Passive voice, however, can be effective when active voice would require the inclusion of unnecessary information. For example, many scientific experiments are conducted by large teams of researchers. Few readers would want to know which members of the team carried out every task discussed in an article about the experiment. Rather than using active voice (for example, "Heather Landers, assisted by Sandy Chapman and Shaun Beaty, anesthetized the mice, and then Greta Steber and Justin Switzer examined their eyes for lesions"), you can use passive voice ("The mice were anesthetized, and their eyes were examined for lesions"). In this case, the sentence written in passive voice is clearer, easier to understand, and free of unnecessary information.

Passive voice is also useful if you wish to emphasize the recipient of the action, rather than the person or thing carrying out the action. Police reports, for example, often use passive voice ("The suspect was apprehended at the corner of Oak and Main Streets").

Use Details to Capture Your Readers' Attention

An effective document does more than simply convey information — it provides details that bring a subject to life. Consider the differences between the following passages from featured writer Caitlin Guariglia's essay on her family trip to Italy.

Example 1: Minimal Details

The next morning we met our tour guide. He was full of life. He took us to the main historical sites that day. They were spectacular, but I enjoyed listening to Marco more than anything we saw.

Example 2: Extensive, Concrete Details

The next morning we met our tour guide Marco. A large, sturdy man who looked like my grandmother cooked for him, he was confident and full of life. He took us to the main historical sites that day: the Vatican, the Colosseum, the Pantheon, the Roman Forum. While all that was spectacular, I enjoyed listening to Marco more than anything we saw. He was a true Roman, big, proud, and loud. The Italian accent made it seem like he was singing everything he said, making it all seem that much more beautiful.

Both examples convey the same main idea. The first example, however, does little more than state the facts. The second example, by providing details about the tour guide's physical appearance, personality, and voice, gives readers a more concrete and more intimate understanding of the subject. (For advice about integrating details from your sources effectively, see Chapter 19.)

Create Transitions within and between Paragraphs

Transitions help readers understand the relationships among sentences, paragraphs, and even sections of a document. Essentially, they smooth the way for readers, helping them understand how information, ideas, and arguments are related to one another. Transitions are most effective when they don't call attention to themselves, but instead move the reader's eye along to the next sentence, paragraph, or section. Consider the following examples of the steps involved in preparing fish.

No Transitions

Catch the fish. Clean the fish. Filet the fish. Cook the fish. Eat the fish. Catch another fish.

Inconsistent Transitions

First, catch the fish. Secondly, clean the fish. When you've done that, filet the fish. Next, cook the fish. Fifth, eat the fish. After all is said and done, catch another fish.

Consistent Transitions

First, catch the fish. Second, clean the fish. Third, filet the fish. Fourth, cook the fish. Fifth, eat the fish. Finally, catch another fish.

Transitions frequently appear as words and phrases, such as those used in the previous example. They can also take the form of sentences and paragraphs. Transitional sentences, such as the following, often appear at the end or the beginning of paragraphs and serve to link two paragraphs.

> The results of the tests revealed a surprising trend.

> Incredibly, the outcome was far better than we could have hoped.

Transitional paragraphs, such as the following example, call attention to a major shift in focus within a document.

> In the next section, we explore the reasons behind this surprising development. We focus first on the event itself. Then we consider the reasons underlying the event. Our goal is to call attention to the unique set of relationships that made this development possible.

Headings and subheadings can also act as transitions. Section headings serve as transitions by signaling to the reader, through formatting that differs from body text, that a new section is beginning. You can read more about formatting headings and subheadings later in this chapter.

As you create transitions, pay attention to the order in which you introduce new information and ideas in your document. In general, it is best to begin a sentence with a reference to information and ideas that have already been presented and to introduce new information and ideas at the end of the sentence.

Common transitions and their functions are presented below.

To Help Readers Follow a Sequence
furthermore
in addition
moreover
next
first/second/third

To Elaborate or Provide Examples
for example
for instance
such as
in fact
indeed
to illustrate

To Compare
similarly
in the same manner
like
as in

To Contrast
however
on the other hand
nevertheless
nonetheless
despite
although/though

To Signal a Concession
I admit that
of course
granted

To Introduce a Conclusion
as a result
as a consequence
because of
therefore
thus
for this reason

How Can I Draft My Introduction?

All readers expect documents to include some sort of introduction. Whether they are reading a home page on a Web site or an opening paragraph in a research report, readers want to learn quickly what a document is about. As you begin to draft, consider strategies you might use to frame and introduce your main point. Keep track of those strategies so that you can revise your introduction later on. Many writers find that crafting an effective introduction is the most challenging part of drafting. If you run into difficulties, put your introduction aside and come back to it after you've made more progress on the rest of the document. There's no law that says you have to write the introduction first.

Frame Your Introduction

Your introduction provides a framework within which your readers can understand and interpret your main point. By calling attention to a specific situation, by asking a particular question, or by conveying a carefully chosen set of details, you can help your readers view your subject in a particular way. Consider, for example, the differences between two introductions to an essay about buying habits among younger Americans.

Introduction 1

In the face of a downturn in the economy, frugality is undergoing a revival in America. Young people are cutting up their credit cards, clipping coupons, and sticking to detailed budgets. In effect, they are adopting the very habits they mocked during the heady days of easy credit and weekend shopping sprees. Secondhand stores and thrift stores like Goodwill and the Salvation Army are drawing record numbers of customers, while once stable retail giants like Circuit City and Sharper Image have gone out of business (*Wall Street Journal*). In fact, retail sales during the Christmas season were down 2.8% last year, the lowest since 1995 (CNNMoney.com). The causes of this sea change in the spending habits of young Americans are complex and varied: high rates of unemployment, fewer jobs for recent graduates, difficulty securing credit, and that elusive factor economists call "consumer confidence."

Introduction 2

The new frugal spending habits of American consumers between the ages of 18 and 34 are endangering the very people who are trying to save money. Plagued with rising unemployment, widespread hiring freezes, and difficulty securing credit, young Americans are naturally turning to their spending habits as one area they can control. They are cutting down on how much money they spend in restaurants, bars, retail stores, and entertainment. As a result, usually robust Christmas sales were down an alarming 2.8% last year, the lowest since 1995 (CNNMoney.com). Even once stable retail giants like Circuit City and Sharper Image have gone out of business *(Wall Street Journal)*. Although the desire to hold on to their money is logical, all this coupon clipping, budgeting, and thrift-store shopping threatens the key to economic recovery, what economists call "consumer confidence." If we don't loosen our grip on our wallets and inject some much-needed cash into the system, we will face far more dire economic consequences in the years to come.

The first introduction frames the subject as an explanation of the causes of changing habits of consumption. The second introduction frames the subject as a warning that these changing habits might be causing more harm than good. Even though each introduction draws on the same basic information about current rates of spending, and even though both do a good job of introducing the essay, they ask readers to focus their attention on different aspects of the subject.

You can frame your discussion by calling attention to specific aspects of a topic, including

- the agent: a person, an organization, or a thing that is acting in a particular way
- the action: what is being done by the actor
- the goal: what the actor wants to achieve by carrying out the action
- the result: the outcome of the action

Agent

Action

Goal

Result

Introduction 2

The new frugal spending habits of American consumers between the ages of 18 and 34 are endangering the very people who are trying to save money. Plagued with rising unemployment, widespread hiring freezes, and difficulty securing credit, young Americans are naturally turning to their spending habits as one area they can control.

They are cutting down on how much money they spend in restaurants, bars, retail stores, and entertainment. As a result, usually robust Christmas sales were down an alarming 2.8% last year, the lowest since 1995 (CNNMoney.com). Even once stable retail giants like Circuit City and Sharper Image have gone out of business (*Wall Street Journal*). Although the desire to hold on to their money is logical, all this coupon clipping, budgeting, and thrift-store shopping threatens the key to economic recovery, what economists call "consumer confidence." If we don't loosen our grip on our wallets and inject some much-needed cash into the system, we will face far more dire economic consequences in the years to come.

Select an Introductory Strategy

The ability to frame your readers' understanding of a subject is a powerful tool. By directing their attention to one aspect of a subject, rather than to others, you can influence their beliefs and, potentially, their willingness to take action.

Your introduction offers probably the best opportunity to grab your readers' attention and shape their response to your ideas. You can introduce your document using one of several strategies.

STATE THE TOPIC

Tell your readers what your subject is, what conversation you are focusing on, and what your document will tell them about it. In the following example, George Chauncey begins by announcing his topic in a straightforward manner (see p. 118).

> The place of lesbians and gay men in American society has dramatically changed in the last half century. The change has been so profound that the harsh discrimination once faced by gay people has virtually disappeared from popular memory. That history bears repeating, since its legacy shapes today's debate over marriage.

ESTABLISH THE CONTEXT

In some cases, you'll want to give your readers background information about your subject or an overview of the conversation that has been taking place about it. Notice, for example, how Anu Partanen sets up her argumentative essay (see p. 382).

> Everyone agrees the United States needs to improve its education system dramatically, but how? One of the hottest trends in education reform lately is looking at the stunning success of the West's reigning education superpower, Finland. Trouble is, when it comes to the lessons that Finnish schools have to offer, most of the discussion seems to be missing the point.

The small Nordic country of Finland used to be known — if it was known for anything at all — as the home of Nokia, the mobile phone giant. But lately Finland has been attracting attention on global surveys of quality of life — *Newsweek* ranked it number one last year — and Finland's national education system has been receiving particular praise, because in recent years Finnish students have been turning in some of the highest test scores in the world.

STATE YOUR THESIS

If your essay urges readers to accept an argument, an evaluation, a solution, or an interpretation, use your introduction to get right to your main point. In her analytical essay, featured writer Ali Bizzul describes the situation many younger football players find themselves in (see p. 262).

Bigger is better — or so says the adage that seems to drive much of American culture. From fast food to television sets to the "average" house, everything seems to be getting bigger. This is especially true for the athletes who play America's favorite fall sport — football. Twelve- and thirteen-year-olds are bulking up so they can make their junior-high football teams. High school players are adding weight to earn college scholarships. And the best college players are pulling out all the stops in hopes of making an NFL team. All of this is occurring despite the belief of many football coaches that extra weight does little to enhance a football player's performance — and might even derail it. Even worse, the drive to put on the pounds carries significant health risks for football players, both now and later in life. Despite what they believe, overweight players are less effective than their lighter peers — and at far greater risk of devastating harm.

DEFINE A PROBLEM

If your purpose is to propose a solution to a problem, you might begin your document by defining the problem. Jody Greenstone Miller uses this strategy to introduce her news feature about the difficulty of keeping women in top jobs (see p. 343).

Why aren't more women running things in America? It isn't for lack of ambition or life skills or credentials. The real barrier to getting more women to the top is the unsexy but immensely difficult issue of time commitment: Today's top jobs in major organizations demand 60-plus hours of work a week.

In her much-discussed new book, Facebook Chief Operating Officer Sheryl Sandberg tells women with high aspirations that they need to "lean in" at work — that is, assert themselves more. It's fine advice, but it misdiagnoses the problem. It isn't any shortage of drive that leads those phalanxes of female Harvard Business School grads to opt out. It's the assumption that senior roles have to consume their every waking moment. More great women don't "lean in" because they don't like the world they're being asked to lean into.

MAKE A SURPRISING STATEMENT

Grab your readers' attention by telling them something they don't already know. It's even better if the information is shocking, unusual, or strange. Consider, for example, how Salvatore Scibona opens his literacy narrative (see the e-Pages for Chapter 5).

> I did my best to flunk out of high school. I failed English literature, American literature, Spanish, precalculus, chemistry, physics. Once, in a fit of melancholic vanity, I burned my report card in the sink of the KFC where I worked scraping carbonized grease from the pressure cookers. I loved that job the way a dog loves a carcass in a ditch. I came home stinking of it. It was a prudent first career in that I wanted with certainty only one thing, to get out of Ohio, and the Colonel might hire me anywhere in the world. The starting wage was $3.85 an hour. I was saving for the future.

ASK A QUESTION

Asking a question invites your readers to become participants in the conversation. At the end of his introduction, featured writer Dwight Haynes asks a question and invites his readers to take an interest in his evaluation of programs that aim to prevent binge drinking (see p. 314).

> Over the past few decades, alcohol consumption among college students has received a great deal of attention. Despite humorous portrayals of college parties and the drunken antics depicted in movies and on television, serious concerns have been raised about health, safety, and academic issues associated with heavy drinking on campus. Most alarming, excessive levels of drinking are thought to cause between 1,400 and 1,700 student deaths each year (Jaschik, 2009). Also significant are the physical harm and violent behavior that tend to arise from heavy drinking: 500,000 students each year sustain injuries as a result of alcohol use, and another 600,000 per year report being victims of alcohol-fueled assaults, including rape (Wechsler et al., 2003). Heavy drinking has been blamed for a host of other problems as well, including vandalism, alcohol poisoning, and academic failure. Rather than waiting until after students suffer the consequences of alcohol abuse to intervene, colleges have found that preventative programs can teach better habits and help students avoid the problems caused by

underage or irresponsible drinking. What kinds of approaches are colleges using to reduce student drinking, and how well do they work?

TELL A STORY

Everyone loves a story, assuming that it's told well and has a point. You can use a story to introduce a subject to your readers, as featured writer Caitlin Guariglia does for her reflective essay about a trip to Italy (see p. 150).

> Crash! The sound of metal hitting a concrete wall is my first vivid memory of Rome. Our tour bus could not get any farther down the tiny road because cars were parked along both sides. This, our bus driver told us, was illegal. He did not tell us, exactly; he grumbled it as he stepped out of the bus. He stood there with his hands on his hips, pondering the situation. Soon, people in the cars behind us started wandering up to stand next to the bus driver and ponder along with him. That, or they honked a great deal.

PROVIDE A HISTORICAL ACCOUNT

Historical accounts can help your readers understand the origins of a situation and how the situation has changed over time. One writer compares the days of Henry Ford with the drivers of today to introduce her informative essay about moving toward a hydrogen economy.

> In the early twentieth century, the products of Henry Ford's assembly lines introduced Americans to the joys of the open road. Large, powerful automobiles quickly became a symbol of wealth and success. With gas prices sky-high, Americans today are being forced to take a good, long look at their choices. The SUVs, trucks, and minivans popular until recently are largely viewed as symbols of excess and environmental irresponsibility, and many consumers now prefer fuel-efficient or hybrid vehicles, like the successful Toyota Prius. In fact, some drivers have become so determined to escape their pricey dependence on fossil fuels that they've begun to seek out alternative energy sources.

LEAD WITH A QUOTATION

A quotation allows your readers to learn about the subject from someone who knows it well or has been affected by it. Featured writer Jennie Tillson prefaces her problem-solving essay with a quotation from Benjamin Franklin (see p. 367).

> "In this world nothing can be said to be certain, except death and taxes."
> — Benjamin Franklin, in a letter to Jean-Baptiste Leroy,
> November 13, 1789

Please add one more item to that list, Mr. Franklin: higher college tuition. Each year, college tuition increases as surely as winter follows fall and spring follows winter.

DRAW A CONTRAST

Drawing a contrast asks your readers to make a comparison. Cyrus Habib, for example, begins his opinion column "Show Us the Money" by contrasting the everyday experiences of the blind with those of sighted Americans (see the e-Pages for Chapter 10).

Blind Americans may soon find themselves able to use money just like anyone else. That is unless the Treasury Department is successful this month in its appeal of a recent federal court order that paper currency be made recognizable to the blind, who are currently unable to distinguish one denomination from another.

PROVIDE A MAP

The most direct way of signaling the organization of your document is to provide a map, or preview, of your supporting points in your introduction.

This report will cover three approaches to treating cancer of the bladder: chemotherapy, a combination of chemotherapy and radiation, and surgical removal of the organ.

How Can I Draft My Conclusion?

Your conclusion provides an opportunity to reinforce your message. It offers one last chance to achieve your purposes as a writer and to share your final thoughts about the subject with your readers.

Reinforce Your Points

At a minimum, your conclusion should sum up the major reasons you've offered to support your thesis statement. You might also want to restate your thesis statement (in different words) to reinforce your main point. If you didn't include a thesis statement in your introduction, consider stating your main point in your conclusion. Ending with a clear indication of what you want someone to think, believe, understand, or do as a result of reading your document gives you one final opportunity to influence your readers.

In her problem-solving essay, Jennie Tillson summarizes her problem definition and argues for the need to address it (see p. 367).

> The rising price of higher education affects not only students and their families but the larger American society and economy as well. If we do not address the lack of access to higher education for the least affluent members of our society, we run the risk of creating a permanent gap between the poor and the wealthy, where even the best and brightest from poor and working-class families can't pursue the American dream. Our colleges, our students, and our government all must commit themselves to solving the problem of college tuition so that we protect the opportunities of all students to earn a college degree and a more financially secure life. Our future depends on it.

Select a Concluding Strategy

Conclusions that simply summarize a document, like Jennie's, are common — and sometimes effective, especially when the writer has presented complex concepts. But a conclusion can do much more than simply restate your points. It can also give your readers an incentive to continue thinking about what they've read, to take action about the subject, or to read more about it.

As you draft, think about what you want to accomplish. You can choose from a range of strategies to write an effective conclusion.

OFFER ADDITIONAL ANALYSIS

Extend your discussion of a subject by supplying additional insights. In his evaluative essay, featured writer Dwight Haynes summarizes and reflects on the results of his evaluation of programs to reduce binge drinking (see p. 314).

> While social norms marketing appears to offer a strong combination of positive outcomes and ease of implementation, the environmental approach is more effective overall. Despite being more complicated and demanding more school and community resources, it delivers stronger results by involving students' entire college community. The environmental approach has a much greater scope than that of the social norms marketing approach and is suitable for schools of all sizes and types. Therefore, it has the potential to affect not only students who drink heavily because they think that's the normal thing to do but also students who either are unaware of the dangers of using alcohol or will moderate their drinking only in the face of severe consequences for not doing so. Given appropriate resources, a

program based on the environmental approach to curb heavy drinking is likely to be the best choice.

SPECULATE ABOUT THE FUTURE

Reflect on what might happen next. One writer speculates about the future in her informative essay.

> It is certain, though, that at some point, the fossil fuels that have sustained our society's electricity and run our motor vehicles for over a century will run out — or become so expensive that they'll no longer provide an economically viable source of energy. Whether that day comes in five years or fifty, we need to shift to a new energy source — one that is practical, economical, and environmentally friendly. Hydrogen has demonstrated great promise as a new candidate for fuel. To realize that promise, however, we must work to remove the barriers that currently prevent hydrogen's emergence as a mainstay of our future economy.

CLOSE WITH A QUOTATION

Select a quotation or paraphrase that does one of the following:

- offers deeper insight into the points you've made in your document
- points to the future of the subject
- suggests a solution to a problem
- illustrates what you would like to see happen
- makes a further observation about the subject
- presents a personalized viewpoint from someone who has experienced the subject you are portraying

Nick Bilton concludes his analytical blog entry about digital etiquette (see p. 230) with a paraphrase of a Margaret Mead quotation. (See pp. 161–63 for more on the differences between a paraphrase and a quotation.)

> The anthropologist Margaret Mead once said that in traditional societies, the young learn from the old. But in modern societies, the old can also learn from the young. Here's hoping that politeness never goes out of fashion, but that time-wasting forms of communication do.

CLOSE WITH A STORY

Tell a story about the subject you've discussed in your document. The story might suggest a potential solution to the problem, offer hope about a desired outcome, or illustrate what might happen if a desired outcome isn't realized. For instance, Firoozeh Dumas concludes her memoir piece with a story that summarizes her swimming experiences later in life (see the e-Pages for Chapter 5).

> Years later, when we moved to Newport Beach, I discovered that one of the greatest joys in life is jumping from a boat into the deep, blue Pacific Ocean. That was before I discovered snorkeling in the crystal-clear waters of the Bahamas with sea turtles and manta rays swimming around me. Later still, my husband introduced me to the cerulean waters of the Greek islands, where I spent hours swimming with the hot Mediterranean sun burning on my back. But despite my dips in the many beautiful bodies of the water in the world, I have never forgotten that first gentle wave in the Caspian Sea, the one that lifted me and assured me that, yes, the pilot has had enough sleep.

CLOSE WITH A QUESTION

Questions provide an effective means of inviting readers to consider the implications of the ideas explored in an essay. After summarizing the information she provided in her analytical essay, featured writer Ali Bizzul closes with a compelling question (see p. 266).

> Given the potential dangers to their health and the fact that being large does little to make them effective players, why do athletes work so hard to get bigger? Perhaps they think the statistics won't apply to them personally — that adding pounds will improve their individual performance. Athletes also know that gaining weight is much easier than gaining muscle, and if weight gives players the slightest advantage, they may think the risks are worth it. Do these players love their sport so much that they will continue to sacrifice their health — or even their lives — for it? They may, if they remain unaware of the consequences, and if they push themselves to their limits without fully understanding the risks.

CALL YOUR READERS TO ACTION

Make a recommendation or urge your readers to do something specific. For example, you might ask them to participate in solving a problem by donating time, money, or effort to a project. Or you might ask them to write to someone, such as a politician or corporate executive, about an issue. Calls to action ask readers not just to accept what you've written but to do something about it, as Cyrus Habib does in his opinion column "Show Us the Money" (see the e-Pages for Chapter 10).

When it comes to accommodating disabilities such as blindness, let us continue to lead the world in practice as well as in principle. More important still, let us tell the world that we, too, believe that blindness should not be an obstacle to financial independence. In doing so, let us also take a significant step toward ameliorating the living conditions of blind Americans, now and for years to come.

The Treasury Department should obey Judge Robertson's order and show us the money.

LINK TO YOUR INTRODUCTION

This technique is sometimes called a "bookends" approach because it positions your introduction and conclusion as related ends of your document. The basic idea is to turn your conclusion into an extension of your introduction.

- If your introduction uses a quotation, end with a related quotation or respond to the quotation.
- If your introduction uses a story, extend that story or retell it with a different ending.
- If your introduction asks a question, answer the question, restate the question, or ask a new question.
- If your introduction defines a problem, provide a solution to the problem, restate the problem, or suggest that readers need to move on to a new problem.

How Can I Help Readers Follow My Argument?

As you draft your document, think about how you'll help your readers follow your line of argument. Surprises can be pleasant, but few readers will be able — or willing — to follow a complex argument without at least a general sense of where you plan to lead them. Clue your readers in right from the start and provide useful guidance throughout your document about its overall organization. A well-organized document will provide an introduction that states or suggests your purpose, gives enough organizational cues to help your readers follow your argument, makes them want to keep reading, and does so as concisely as possible.

Let Readers Know Where Your Document Is Taking Them

You can use several strategies to give your readers a sense of where your document is going to take them. The most direct strategy, and one that's common in most genres of academic writing, is to provide a "map" — a preview of your main point and supporting points. You can also take advantage of commonly used organizing patterns, such as pro/con or cause/effect, that readers will understand and be ready to follow.

GIVE READERS A MAP

Think of maps as promises to your readers that help establish their expectations and convey your purpose for writing. If you are working on an informative document, you might promise to explain the details of a complex issue to your readers. If you define a problem in your introduction, that definition serves as a promise to present a solution by the end of your document. If you begin with a surprising argument, you are promising to back it up with reasons and evidence that will intrigue your readers.

Making a promise in a written document differs pleasantly from making a promise in person, because in writing you haven't really promised it until you submit your final draft. As you draft and revise your document, keep your eyes open for unfulfilled promises. Depending on how your argument has developed as you've drafted your document, you might find that you no longer need to follow through on your promise. If so, take it out. If you still need it, be sure to include it.

BUILD ON READERS' EXPERIENCES

Like you, your readers probably have read a large number of documents and have become familiar with some of the more commonly used organizing patterns, such as pro/con, cause/effect, or comparison/contrast. Let their experiences work to your advantage. Try to provide what readers are likely to expect where they are most likely to expect it. However, your content doesn't need to be exactly what they expect. Instead, focus on their expectations about structure and organization. If you've presented the pro side of an argument, for instance, you can be fairly confident that your readers will expect to read the con side before long.

If you succeed at anticipating and meeting expectations, you'll increase readers' confidence in you. Moreover, you won't need to keep announcing what's coming next or circling around to explain why you said what you just said — they'll already know.

Keep Related Ideas Together

The best way to help readers follow where you're going is to structure your document logically, with related ideas presented in a sequence that readers will be able to follow. For example, if a particular idea needs to be explained so that readers can understand the rest of your argument, start with that idea. Presenting ideas in a logical order is critical, largely because readers find it challenging to rethink the order of entire sections and paragraphs so that they can follow your argument. Readers count on writers to organize clearly in the first place.

Presenting ideas in a logical order can be tricky because, while writing is linear, the relationships among ideas may not be. As you think about how to organize a complex set of ideas, think again about readers' expectations. Ask what idea your readers are likely to expect to learn about next. Or set their expectations with a map at the beginning of a section.

Your readers will also expect you to provide enough information about an idea for them to understand it. When you introduce a new idea, ask yourself how much your readers will know about it. If it's likely to be unfamiliar to them, you'll need to help them understand it. Unfortunately, providing enough information to help readers understand an idea can detract from your argument. Handled badly, explaining complicated background information just when your readers are expecting you to launch into your new idea can make your document seem unorganized. You can solve this problem by signaling to your readers why you're providing background information before moving on to your next major point.

Keep the Flow of Your Document Moving Forward

You're pursuing a particular purpose — for example, to inform your readers about an emerging style of music, to evaluate a travel destination, or to argue against new local regulations. So far, you've met expectations and even built them up, so that your readers are coming along with you gladly. Don't frustrate them now. Keep moving forward.

If you're relating something chronological, it's logical to use a chronological organizing pattern (see p. 506). If you've provided a map early in your document, you can simply refer back to it. When referring to a map, you don't have to say anything as obvious as "The third point to be made is . . ." Instead, you might simply connect one point to the next with transition words (see p. 525) or a connecting sentence. If you've kept readers clued in about what you're doing, you won't need to keep telling them. They're already expecting you to do as you said.

You can also use your readers' expectations to show them how you're moving forward. If, for instance, you're developing a pro/con argument, readers are expecting you to make a claim, present evidence to support the claim, present evidence against it, and so on. Simply by following this standard sequence, you'll maintain your readers' momentum.

Be wary of cramming material in somewhere just because you can't think of a better place to put it. This can stop your readers from moving forward. If you think you might be doing this, ask whether your readers will need to know the information to understand your main point. If the answer is "no," consider leaving it out. If it's necessary but seems to be slowing down your readers, study your outline to determine whether it might fit better somewhere else.

Say Things Just Once

Writers frustrate their readers when they repeat themselves. Sometimes writers do this because they think the idea or information is important and they want to emphasize it. Unfortunately, readers are more likely to view the repetition as a waste of their time than as a helpful reinforcement of a key idea.

As you write, watch out for ideas that seem a little too familiar. That feeling of familiarity probably means that you're repeating yourself. When you find a familiar passage, check your outline, decide on a logical place to make the point, and make it there definitively. Then either get rid of the repetitive passage or change it so that it refers to your definitive discussion of the point.

You can refer to another part of your composition with words and phrases such as the following:

Again,

As I will explain,

As previously noted,

As we'll see,

Here, too, it's worth keeping in mind . . .

You'll recall that . . .

Some of these phrases — such as *I will explain* and *As we'll see* — work best when you're in the middle of making a point and want to introduce the new point later in your document. Keep in mind, however, that readers prefer to get information near the first place it's relevant. They don't like to wait. It's best to refer to ideas and information that you've already addressed, using phrases such as *You'll recall that* or *As previously noted.*

How Can I Design My Document?

Many writers think of designing a document as something that comes at the end of the writing process, after drafting, revision, and editing are complete. In fact, design can be a powerful tool during the planning and drafting stages. By considering design as you plan and work on your draft, you can create a document whose appearance helps you achieve your purpose, address your readers effectively, and take advantage of the context in which it will be read.

Understand Design Principles

Before you begin formatting text or inserting illustrations, consider how the design principles of *balance*, *emphasis*, *placement*, *repetition*, and *consistency* can help you accomplish your goals as a writer.

Balance is the vertical and horizontal alignment of elements on your pages (see the example on p. 542). Symmetrical designs create a sense of rest and stability and lead readers' eyes to focus on a particular part of a document. In contrast, asym-metrical — or unbalanced — designs suggest movement and guide readers' eyes across the page.

Emphasis is the placement and formatting of elements, such as headings and sub-headings, so that they catch your readers' attention. You can emphasize an element in a document by using a color or font that distinguishes it from other elements; by placing a border around it and adding a shaded background; or by using an illus-tration, such as a photograph, drawing, or graph.

Placement is the location of elements on your pages. Placing elements next to or near each other suggests that they are related. An illustration, for example, is usually placed near the passage in which it is mentioned.

Repetition is the use of elements, such as headers and footers, navigation menus, and page numbers, throughout the pages in your document. As readers move from page to page, they tend to expect navigation elements, such as page numbers, to appear in the same place. In addition, repeated elements, such as a logo or Web navigation menu, help establish a sense of identity across the pages in your document.

Hydrogen Economy: The Role of Fuel Cells

The key to a hydrogen economy is the fuel cell, which uses hydrogen gas and oxygen to produce electricity. In a way, a fuel cell is like a battery, but it never requires charging and it produces only electricity, heat, and water vapor (see Fig. 1). The U.S. Department of Energy (DOE) explains that hydrogen fuel cells use electrode plates to separate hydrogen's protons and electrons, diverting the stream of electrons to create electricity. A "stack" of fuel cells is scalable, so the same basic structure has many different uses ("Hydrogen Fuel"). In theory, stacks of hydrogen fuel cells could be made to run cars and heat homes of any size, saving energy, money, and the environment.

> In theory, stacks of hydrogen fuel cells could be made to run cars and heat homes of any size.

Refining pure hydrogen gas in the first place, though, is currently too costly and environmentally inefficient to be effective. Although hydrogen is the most abundant element in the universe, it is usually bonded to other elements. For example, two hydrogen atoms and an oxygen atom form water (H_2O), and hydrogen and chloride form hydrochloric acid (HCl). Hydrogen is a fairly faithful substance, and once bonded, it does not like to let go. For hydrogen to be used as an independent fuel, however, those bonds must be broken. The separation process requires a lot of energy—and a lot of money. Strangely, research done by scientists at the DOE found that one of the most cost-effective means of obtaining hydrogen

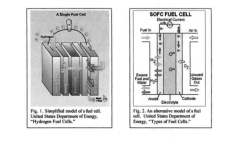

Fig. 1. Simplified model of a fuel cell. United States Department of Energy, "Hydrogen Fuel Cells."

Fig. 2. An alternative model of a fuel cell. United States Department of Energy, "Types of Fuel Cells."

Hydrogen Economy: The Role of Fuel Cells

The key to a hydrogen economy is the fuel cell, which uses hydrogen gas and oxygen to produce electricity. In a way, a fuel cell is like a battery, but it never requires charging and it produces only electricity, heat, and water vapor (see Fig. 1). The U.S. Department of Energy (DOE) explains that hydrogen fuel cells use electrode plates to separate hydrogen's protons and electrons, diverting the stream of electrons to create electricity. A "stack" of fuel cells is scalable, so the same basic structure has many different uses ("Hydrogen Fuel"). In theory, stacks of hydrogen fuel cells could be made to run cars and heat homes of any size, saving energy, money, and the environment.

Fig. 1. Simplified model of a fuel cell. United States Department of Energy, "Hydrogen Fuel Cells."

Refining pure hydrogen gas in the first place, though, is currently too costly and environmentally inefficient to be effective. Although hydrogen is the most abundant element in the universe, it is usually bonded to other elements. For example, two hydrogen atoms and an oxygen atom form water (H_2O), and hydrogen and chloride form hydrochloric acid (HCl). Hydrogen is a fairly faithful substance, and once bonded, it does not like to let go. For hydrogen to be used as an independent fuel, however, those bonds must be broken. The separation process requires a lot of energy—and a lot of money. Strangely, research done by scientists at the DOE found that one of the most cost-effective means of obtaining hydrogen is to separate it from natural gas, which explains why the vast majority of the U.S. hydrogen supply currently comes from reforming the methane in natural gas ("Production"). This approach is not environmentally

> In theory, stacks of hydrogen fuel cells could be made to run cars and heat homes of any size.

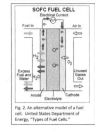

Fig. 2. An alternative model of a fuel cell. United States Department of Energy, "Types of Fuel Cells."

▲ Symmetrical (left) and asymmetrical (right) layouts

Consistency is the extent to which you format and place text and illustrations in the same way throughout your document. Treating each design element — such as illustrations, headings, and footnotes — consistently will help readers recognize the role it plays in your document and, by extension, will help them locate the information they seek. A consistent design can also convey a sense of competence and professionalism to your readers, increasing their confidence in the quality and credibility of your document.

You should also keep two other principles in mind: simplicity and moderation. An overly complex design can obscure important ideas and information. Using design elements moderately to create a simple yet effective design is the best approach.

▲ Using images to create an emotional impact

Design for a Purpose

A well-designed document presents your information, ideas, and arguments in a manner that helps you accomplish your purposes.

You might use design to achieve any of the following goals:

- **Setting a tone.** One of the most powerful tools writers have for accomplishing their purpose is establishing an emotional context for their readers. You can set a tone by using a particular color scheme, such as bright, cheerful hues, or by selecting photographs or drawings with a strong emotional impact.

- **Helping readers understand a point.** Design your document so that your main and supporting points are clear and easy to understand. Headings or pull quotes can call your readers' attention to important ideas and information. To introduce a main point, you might use a contrasting font or color to signal the importance of the information. To highlight a definition or an example, you might enclose it inside a border or place the passage in a pull quote. You can also help readers understand a point by using illustrations.

- **Convincing readers to accept a point.** The key to convincing readers is providing them with appropriate, relevant evidence. Drawing on the principles of emphasis and placement, you can use illustrations, marginal glosses, pull quotes, and bulleted lists to call attention to that evidence.

- **Clarifying complex concepts.** Sometimes a picture really is worth a thousand words. Rather than attempting to explain a complex concept using text alone, add an illustration. A well-chosen, well-placed photograph, flowchart, diagram, or table can define a complex concept such as photosynthesis in far less space, and in many cases far more effectively, than a long passage of text can. You can also clarify the key elements of a complex concept with bulleted and numbered lists.

Design for Your Readers

A well-designed document helps readers understand its organization, locate information and ideas, and recognize the function of its different parts. It is also easy on your readers' eyes: readers working with a well-designed document will not have to strain to read the text or discern illustrations. Use document design to do the following.

Help readers understand the organization of a document. You can use headings and subheadings to signal the content of each part of the document. If you do, keep in mind the design principles of emphasis and consistency: format your headings in a consistent manner that helps them stand out from other parts of the document.

Help readers locate information and ideas. Many longer print documents use tables of contents and indexes to help readers locate information and ideas. Web sites typically provide a mix of menus and navigation headers and footers to help readers move around the site. You can distinguish these navigation aids from the surrounding text by using bordered or shaded boxes or contrasting fonts.

Help readers recognize the function of parts of a document. If you include passages that differ from the main text of your document, such as sidebars and "For More Information" sections, help readers understand their function by designing them to stand out visually. Using emphasis, you might design a sidebar with a shaded or colored box or format a list of related readings or Web links in a contrasting font or color.

Jenna Alberter
Professor Garcia
AR414
27 April 2013

Images of Women in Seventeenth-Century Dutch Art and Literature

Artists and their artwork do not exist in a vacuum. The images artists create help shape and in turn are shaped by the society and culture in which they are created. The artists and artworks in the Dutch Baroque period are no exception. In this seventeenth-century society of merchants and workers, people of all classes purchased art to display in their homes. As a result, artists in the period catered to the wishes of the people, producing art that depicted the everyday world (Kleiner and Tansey 864). It is too simplistic, however, to assume that this relationship was unidirectional. Dutch Baroque genre paintings did not simply reflect the reality surrounding them; they also helped to shape that reality. For instance, members of seventeenth-century Dutch society had very specific ideas regarding the roles of women. These ideas, which permeated every level of society, are represented in the literature and visual art of the period (Franits, Paragons 17).

The Concept of Domesticity

During the seventeenth century, the concept of domesticity appears to have been very important in all levels of Dutch society; literally hundreds of surviving paintings reflect this theme. Such paintings depict members of every class and occupation, and according to Wayne Franits, a specialist in seventeenth-century Dutch art, they served the dual purpose of both entertaining and instructing the viewer. They invite the viewer to inspect and enjoy their vivid details, but also to contemplate the values and ideals they represent (Franits, "Domesticity" 13).

Images of domesticity in the visual arts grew immensely in popularity around the middle of the seventeenth century. Although there is no definitive explanation for this rise in popularity, there is a long history in Dutch art and literature of focusing on domestic themes. In the early sixteenth century, Protestant reformers and humanists wrote books and treatises on domestic issues. Their main focus was the roles and responsibilities of members of the family, especially the women.

Alberter 2

This type of literature continued to be produced, and flourished, in the first half of the seventeenth century (Franits, "Domesticity" 13). Perhaps the most well-known and influential work of literature of this type is Jacob Cats's book Houwelyck, or Marriage. Published in 1625, this was a comprehensive reference book for women of all ages, but especially young women, regarding matters of marriage and family. Although many other similar books were being published in the Netherlands and England during this period, Cats's work was perhaps the most extensive; it even contained an alphabetical index for quick reference (Franits, Paragons 5).

Cat's How to Guide: Houwelyck

Houwelyck, which by mid-century had sold over 50,000 copies, making it a best-seller for its time, contained instruction for women on the proper behavior for the six stages of life: Maiden, Sweetheart, Bride, Housewife, Mother, and Widow. It is particularly telling that these stages of life were defined in reference to the roles of men. Although Cats's book specifically addressed women, it had implications for men as well (Westermann 119). According to Cats, by laying out the roles and duties of the woman, his book "encompasses also the masculine counter-duties" (qtd. in Westermann 119).

The illustration on the title page of the first edition of Cats's work shows what was considered the ideal role for a woman at this time. Created by Adriaen van de Venne, Stages of Life (Fig. 1) depicts several figural groups arranged on a hill. It shows life as a large hill, with marriage as its pinnacle, and then heading down toward widowhood and death (Westermann 120). This depiction seems to reflect the expectations society held for its women—that a woman's goal in life should be to provide a man with a good, proper wife and, once that duty has been fulfilled, to wait dutifully for death.

Images of young women are numerous in the visual art of this period. Gerard Dou's Portrait of a Young Woman (Fig. 2) exemplifies this type of work. This painting demonstrates that portraiture was highly influenced by contemporary ideals of feminine virtue. The young woman's pose is passive, self-contained, and somewhat rigid, communicating her dignity, humility, and modesty, which were all considered very important in a young girl. She holds a songbook in her lap, which not only indicated her skill in the arts but was also considered a symbol of docility. Near her rest

Use of a contrasting font and color helps readers understand the document's organization.

▲ Headings and subheadings in an essay

Design to Address Genre Conventions

Understanding the design conventions of the type of document you plan to write will help you create a document that meets the expectations of your readers. Genres are characterized not only by distinctive writing styles, types of evidence, and organizing patterns but also by distinctive types of design. An article in a magazine such as *Time* or *Rolling Stone*, for example, is characterized by the use of columns, headings and subheadings, pull quotes, and illustrations, while an academic essay is characterized by wide margins, double-spaced lines, and comparatively restrained use of color and illustrations. Your readers will expect your document to be similar in design to other examples of that genre. This doesn't mean that you can't depart from those conventions should the need arise, but it does mean that you should take their expectations into account as you design your document.

Use Design Elements Effectively

Understanding the range of design elements at your disposal will enable you to decide which of these options to use as you design your document. These elements include fonts, line spacing, and alignment; page layout strategies; color, shading, borders, and rules; and illustrations.

USE FONTS, LINE SPACING, AND ALIGNMENT

Font, line spacing, and alignment choices are the most common design decisions that writers make. They are also among the most important, since poor choices can make a document difficult to read. The examples on pages 547–550 provide an overview of the key features of fonts as well as the uses of fonts, line spacing, and alignment.

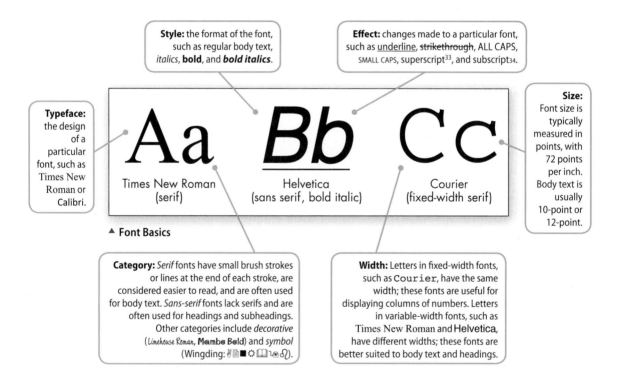

Style: the format of the font, such as regular body text, *italics*, **bold**, and ***bold italics***.

Effect: changes made to a particular font, such as underline, ~~strikethrough~~, ALL CAPS, SMALL CAPS, superscript[33], and subscript[34].

Typeface: the design of a particular font, such as Times New Roman or Calibri.

Size: Font size is typically measured in points, with 72 points per inch. Body text is usually 10-point or 12-point.

Times New Roman (serif)

Helvetica (sans serif, bold italic)

Courier (fixed-width serif)

▲ **Font Basics**

Category: *Serif* fonts have small brush strokes or lines at the end of each stroke, are considered easier to read, and are often used for body text. *Sans-serif* fonts lack serifs and are often used for headings and subheadings. Other categories include *decorative* (Limehouse Roman, **Mambo Bold**) and *symbol* (Wingding: ✌✉■✿📖🐾🦁).

Width: Letters in fixed-width fonts, such as Courier, have the same width; these fonts are useful for displaying columns of numbers. Letters in variable-width fonts, such as Times New Roman and Helvetica, have different widths; these fonts are better suited to body text and headings.

Line spacing refers to the amount of space between lines of text. Larger line spacing appears easier to read, so you'll often find increased line spacing in introductory paragraphs, executive summaries (which provide an overview of a longer document), and sidebars (see p. 548).

When text is crammed together vertically, it is difficult to read and to add comments. Keep this in mind if you are creating a document such as an essay on which someone else might write comments.

CLIMATE**COUNTDOWN**

Best-case
scenario for a
Copenhagen deal?
Twice the
warming the
planet can take.
**BY BILL
McKIBBEN**

Alignment refers to the horizontal arrangement of text and illustrations (such as photos and drawings). You can select four types of alignment.
- **Left alignment** has a straight left margin and a "ragged" right margin; it is typically the easiest to read.
- **Right alignment** has a straight right margin and a ragged left margin.
- **Centered alignment** is seldom used for body text but can make headings stand out.
- **Justified alignment** has straight alignment on both the left and right margins. It adds a polished look and can be effective in documents that use columns — but it also produces irregular word spacing and hyphenation, which can slow the reading process.

TOO HOT
TO HANDLE

wo decades ago, when I was writing what would be one of the first books on global warming, I interviewed a professor at Harvard's Kennedy School of Government, one of the few academics already thinking about the emerging problem. He hemmed and hawed for a little while, and then he said, "This is the public policy problem from hell. There are just too many conflicting interests. It won't be solved."

This December may be the last real chance to prove him wrong as the nations of the world meet in Copenhagen for a climate conference billed as make or break, do or die, perhaps quite literally sink or swim. In fact, you could make a fair argument that this will be the most important diplomatic gathering in the world's history. Versailles, sure. Yalta, yes—but their failures were measured in decades of pain and millions of lives. Failure to rein in climate change will reverberate for tens of thousands of years, across generations not even yet imagined.

Which is not to say the 12 days of final negotiations will be august or easy to follow or even coherent. I remember the last big talks of this sort, in Kyoto in 1997. The sessions took place, as they will in Copenhagen, in a conference center miles from town. It became its own insulated world, with reporters and delegates and oil company lobbyists and NGO representatives endlessly querying each other about what was going on. (There was even a daily paper, and sometimes a parody version.) The answer to the queries was always the same: We're waiting for the US and the Europeans to strike a deal. The official palaver was taking place in a big hall, with delegates making amendments and offering motions, but all the real action was behind closed doors.

ILLUSTRATION BY ANITA KUNZ

▲ Using fonts, line spacing, and alignment

Fonts are a complete set of type of a particular size and typeface. As you choose fonts, consider the following:
- **Select fonts that are easy to read.** For body text, avoid decorative fonts and italics.
- **Select fonts that complement each other.** A serif body font, such as Times New Roman or Garamond, works well with a sans-serif heading font, such as Arial, Helvetica, or Calibri.
- **Exercise restraint.** Generally, use no more than four different fonts in a document.

Pull quotes (not shown) highlight a passage of text — frequently a quotation — through the use of borders, white space, distinctive fonts, and contrasting colors.

Numbered and bulleted lists (not shown) display brief passages of related information using numbers or symbols (usually round "bullets"). The surrounding white space draws the eye to the list, highlighting the information for your readers, while the brief content in each entry can make concepts or processes easier to understand.

Sidebars (not shown) are brief discussions of information related to, but not a central part of, your document. Sidebars simplify the task of integrating related or supporting information into the body of the article by setting that information off in a clearly defined area.

Margins are the white space between the edge of the page or screen (top, bottom, right, and left) and the text or graphics in your document.

White space — literally, empty space — frames and separates elements on a page.

Columns generally appear in newspaper and magazine articles — and, to a growing extent, in articles published on the Web. Essays, on the other hand, are typically formatted in a single column. Columns can improve the readability of a document by limiting the eyes' physical movement across the page and by framing other elements.

Headings and subheadings identify sections and subsections, serve as transitions, and allow readers to locate information more easily.

Marginal glosses are brief notes in a margin that explain or expand on text in the body of the document.

▲ Using page layout elements

Headers, footers, and page numbers (not shown) appear at the top or bottom of the page, set apart from the main text. They help readers find their way through a document; they provide information, such as the title of the document, its publication date, and its author; and they frame a page visually.

Captions describe or explain an illustration, such as a photograph or chart.

USE PAGE LAYOUT ELEMENTS

Page layout is the placement of text, illustrations, and other objects on a page or screen. Successful page layout draws on a number of design elements, including white space, margins, columns, headers and footers, page numbers, headings, lists, captions, marginal glosses and pull quotes, and sidebars. The example on page 548 illustrates these design elements.

USE COLOR, SHADING, BORDERS, AND RULES

Color, shading, borders, and rules (lines running horizontally or vertically on a page) can increase the overall attractiveness of your document, call attention to important information, help readers understand the organization of your document, help readers recognize the function of specific passages of text, and signal transitions between sections. As you use these design elements, exercise restraint. Avoid using more than three colors on a page, unless you are using a photograph or work of art. Be cautious, as well, about using multiple styles of rules or borders in a document.

USE ILLUSTRATIONS

Illustrations — charts, graphs, tables, photographs and other images, animations, audio clips, and video clips — can expand on or demonstrate points made in the text of your document. They can also reduce the amount of text needed to make a point, help readers better understand your points, and increase the visual appeal of your document.

Photographs and other images. Photographs and other images, such as drawings, paintings, and sketches, are frequently used to set a mood, emphasize a point, or demonstrate a point more fully than is possible with text alone.

Charts and graphs. Charts and graphs represent information visually. They are used to make a point more succinctly than is possible with text alone or to present complex information in a compact and more accessible form. They frequently rely on numerical information.

Tables. Like charts and graphs, tables can present complex information, both textual and numerical, in a compact form.

Other digital illustrations. Digital publications allow you to include a wider range of illustrations, including audio, video, and animations, which bring sound and movement to your document.

Signal the organization of a document. In a longer print document, headers, footers, headings, and subheadings might be formatted with a particular color to help readers recognize which section they are reading. On a Web site, pages in each section could share the same background or heading color.

Be consistent. Use the same colors for top-level headings throughout your document, another color for lower-level headings, and so on. Use the same borders and shading for sidebars. Use rules consistently in pull quotes, headers, and footers. Don't mix and match.

Signal the function of text. A colored or shaded background, as well as colored type, can be used to differentiate captions and pull quotes from body text. Rules can also separate columns of text on a page or screen.

Call attention to important information. Color, borders, and shading can subtly yet clearly emphasize an illustration, such as a table or chart, or an important passage of text, by distinguishing it from the surrounding body text.

THE WELL-BEING BALANCING ACT

Pleasure and purpose work together

EVEN THE MOST ardent strivers will agree that a life of purpose that is devoid of pleasures is, frankly, no fun. Happy people know that allowing yourself to enjoy easy momentary indulgences that are personally rewarding—taking a long, leisurely bath, vegging out with your daughter's copy of *The Hunger Games*, or occasionally skipping your Saturday workout in favor of catching the soccer match on TV—is a crucial aspect of living a satisfying life. Still, if you're primarily focused on activities that feel good in the moment, you may miss out on the benefits of developing a clear purpose. Purpose is what drives us to take risks and make changes—even in the face of hardship and when sacrificing short-term happiness.

Working to uncover how happy people balance pleasure and purpose, Colorado State's Steger and his colleagues have shown that the act of trying to comprehend and navigate our world generally causes us to deviate from happiness. After all, this mission is fraught with tension, uncertainty, complexity, short bursts of intrigue and excitement, and conflicts between the desire to feel good and the desire to make progress toward what we care about most. Yet overall, people who are the happiest tend to be superior at sacrificing short-term pleasures when there is a good opportunity to make progress toward what they aspire to become in life.

If you want to envision a happy person's stance, imagine one foot rooted in the present with mindful appreciation of what one has—and the other foot reaching toward the future for yet-to-be-uncovered sources of meaning. Indeed,

research by neuroscientist Richard Davidson of the University of Wisconsin at Madison has revealed that making advances toward achievement of our goals not only causes us to feel more engaged, it actually helps us tolerate any negative feelings that arise during the journey.

Nobody would pretend that finding purpose is easy or that it can be done in a simple exercise, but thinking about which activities you found most rewarding and meaningful in the past week, what you're good at and often recognized for, what experiences you'd be unwilling to give up, and which ones you crave more time for can help. Also, notice whether your answers reflect something you feel that you ought to say as opposed to what you truly love. For example, being a parent doesn't necessarily mean that spending time with your children is the most energizing, meaningful part of your life—and it's important to accept that. Lying to yourself is one of the biggest barriers to creating purpose. The happiest people have a knack for being honest about what does and does not energize them—and in addition to building in time for sensory pleasures each day, they are able to integrate the activities they most care about into a life of purpose and satisfaction. **PT**

TODD B. KASHDAN is a psychologist at George Mason University and the author of *Mindfulness, Acceptance, and Positive Psychology*. **ROBERT BISWAS-DIENER** is the author of *The Courage Quotient*. Together they are coauthoring a book on a new approach to well-being in the business world.

HAPPINESS BY THE NUMBERS

.62
Distance from home, in miles, at which point people's tweets begin declining in expressed happiness (about the distance expected for a short work commute).

40
The percentage of our capacity for happiness that is within our power to change, according to University of California, Riverside researcher Sonja Lyubomirsky.

85
Number of residents out of every 100 who report feeling positive emotions in Panama and Paraguay, the most positive countries in the world.

20
The percentage of the U.S. population wealthy enough that their feelings of happiness are not affected by fluctuations in Americans' income equality.

Sources: The University of Vermont, *The How of Happiness*, Gallup, *Psychological Science*

THERAPISTS: *Interested in receiving Continuing Ed credit for reading this article? Visit* **NBCC.org**

July/August 2013 **Psychology Today** 59

▲ Using color, shading, borders, and rules

As you work with illustrations, keep the following guidelines in mind:

- **Use an illustration for a purpose.** Illustrations are best used when they serve a clear function in your document. Avoid including illustrations simply because you think they might make your document "look better."

- **Place illustrations near the text they illustrate.** In general, place illustrations as close as possible to the point where they are mentioned in the text. If they are not explicitly mentioned (as is often the case with photographs), place them at a point in the document where they are most relevant to the information and ideas being discussed.

- **Include a title or caption that identifies or explains the illustration.** The documentation system you are using, such as MLA or APA, will usually offer advice on the placement and format of titles and captions. In general, documentation systems suggest that you distinguish between tables and figures (which are all other illustrations), number tables and figures in the order in which they appear in the document, and use compound numbering of tables and figures in longer documents (for example, the second table in Chapter 5 would be labeled "Table 5.2"). Consult the documentation system you are using for specific guidelines on illustrations.

What Should I Consider as I Design an Academic Essay?

Some writers might be surprised to see the terms *design* and *academic essay* used in the same sentence. They're aware, of course, that they should use wide margins, readable fonts, and double-spaced lines, and they generally understand that they should do this to help readers — typically an instructor — read and respond to their work. Beyond these elements, however, they think of design as having little or no role in their essays.

They're wrong. Thoughtful design can help you achieve your goals, address your readers' expectations, and adapt to the context in which your essay will be written and read.

Consider How Design Elements Can Help You Achieve Your Writing Goals

Traditionally, essay assignments have focused on the written expression of ideas and arguments. As a result, writers have tended to use images sparingly, if at all, and to make limited use of design elements such as color, shading, borders, and rules in their academic essays. Writers have also tended to avoid the use of tables and charts, perhaps thinking that these kinds of design elements would be more appropriate for genres such as reports and professional articles.

Yet these design elements can help you present complex information and ideas more clearly, distinguish between items considered in an evaluation, illustrate the aspects of a particular problem, or frame your argument by calling readers' attention to particular information and ideas. As you draft your essay, consider how the wide range of design elements discussed on pages 541–551 might help you accomplish your goals as a writer. As you consider your options, keep in mind your instructor's preferences regarding the use of these elements. If you are uncertain about your instructor's preferences, ask for guidance.

Consider Reader Expectations

Readers approach an essay with a set of writing and design conventions in mind. They expect you to make a main point, to support your point with reasons and evidence, and to identify the sources you've drawn on in your essay. They also expect you to follow generally accepted design conventions, such as the guidelines provided by documentation systems such as MLA and APA (see Chapters 21 and 22). Your assignment will frequently provide guidance on how to format an academic essay. You can also consult your instructor if you have any questions.

As you design your essay, consider not only what your readers expect but also how you can build on those expectations to accomplish your goals as a writer. You can use design elements such as fonts, color, shading, borders, and rules to help readers anticipate and more easily follow the organization of your essay. You can use tables, charts, and figures to let your readers view, understand, and analyze the information you include in your essay. If you are distributing your essay in digital form, you can help readers access related information, such as video clips, audio clips, animations, and related data sets, via links — or you can embed these materials directly in your essay. You can read more about how these design elements can help you in these areas on pages 541–551.

Consider Your Context

The context in which your essay is written and read can affect your design decisions in important ways. Think carefully about the resources you can use to write and design your essay. Do you own a computer or tablet? Do you have access to computers at your college or university? Do you have access to color printers? What kind of software programs or Web-based resources can you use, and how well do you know them? If you are working on a deadline, you might have limited time to learn how to use a new software program or electronic portfolio tool. You might have to decide whether the time required to use these resources would be better spent on collecting additional sources or revising and editing your draft.

Think equally carefully about how you will submit your essay. Will you deliver your essay to an instructor in printed form, send it as an e-mail attachment, or submit it through a course management system? Will it be included in a print or digital portfolio along with your other work? Will it be available on a blog or Web page?

Finally, consider how and where your essay will be read. Will it be read in print in a quiet office or perhaps on a bus or train during a commute? Will it be "required reading" — that is, will it get the careful attention an instructor provides during grading? Or is it something that can be put aside in favor of something else, as might happen if it were being read by a visitor to a Web site or blog?

As you consider the contexts in which your essay will be written and read, think about how design can help you adapt to those contexts. You can read more about how you can use design elements to adapt to particular contexts on pages 557–582.

View an Essay

The following pages are from an essay written by college freshman Gaele Lopez for his composition class. They reflect his awareness of his instructor's expectations about line spacing, margins, documentation system, page numbers, and a title page.

For another sample essay formatted in MLA style, see page 150. For a sample essay formatted in APA style, see page 313.

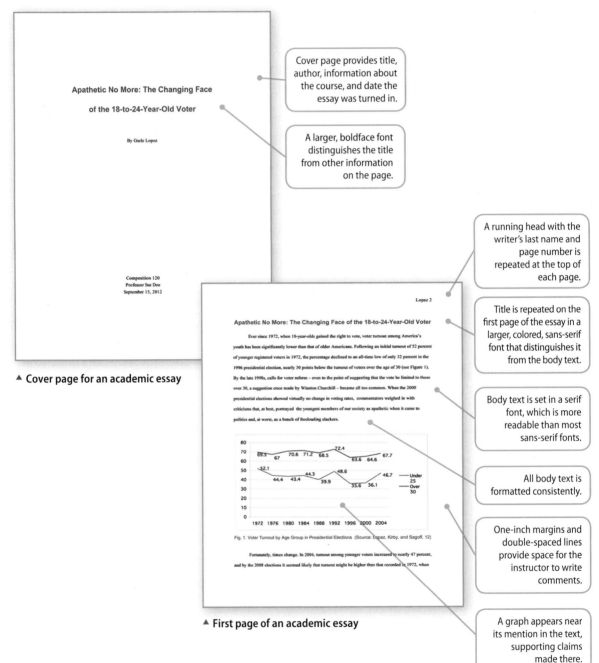

▲ Cover page for an academic essay

▲ First page of an academic essay

Cover page provides title, author, information about the course, and date the essay was turned in.

A larger, boldface font distinguishes the title from other information on the page.

A running head with the writer's last name and page number is repeated at the top of each page.

Title is repeated on the first page of the essay in a larger, colored, sans-serif font that distinguishes it from the body text.

Body text is set in a serif font, which is more readable than most sans-serif fonts.

All body text is formatted consistently.

One-inch margins and double-spaced lines provide space for the instructor to write comments.

A graph appears near its mention in the text, supporting claims made there.

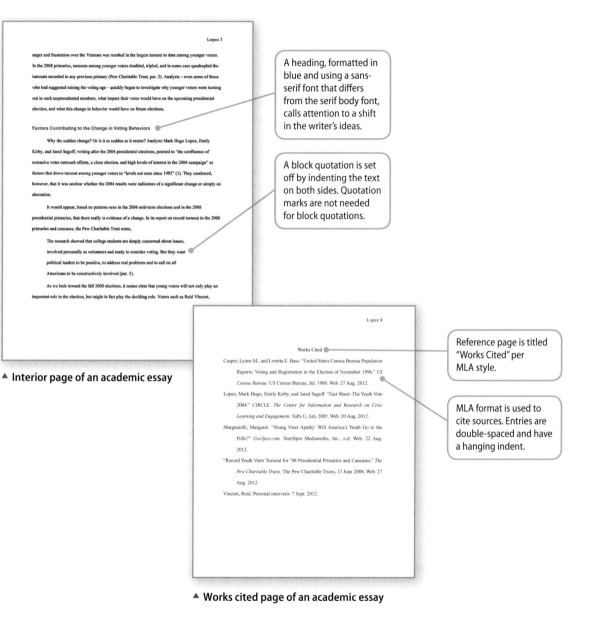

Lopez 3

anger and frustration over the Vietnam war resulted in the largest turnout to date among younger voters. In the 2008 primaries, turnouts among younger voters doubled, tripled, and in some case quadrupled the turnouts recorded in any previous primary (Pew Charitable Trust, par. 2). Analysts – even some of those who had suggested raising the voting age – quickly began to investigate why younger voters were turning out in such unprecedented numbers, what impact their votes would have on the upcoming presidential election, and what this change in behavior would have on future elections.

Factors Contributing to the Change in Voting Behaviors

Why the sudden change? Or is it as sudden as it seems? Analysts Mark Hugo Lopez, Emily Kirby, and Jared Sagoff, writing after the 2004 presidential elections, pointed to "the confluence of extensive voter outreach efforts, a close election, and high levels of interest in the 2004 campaign" as factors that drove turnout among younger voters to "levels not seen since 1992" (1). They cautioned, however, that it was unclear whether the 2004 results were indicators of a significant change or simply an aberration.

It would appear, based on patterns seen in the 2006 mid-term elections and in the 2008 presidential primaries, that there really is evidence of a change. In its report on record turnout in the 2008 primaries and caucuses, the Pew Charitable Trust notes,

> The research showed that college students are deeply concerned about issues, involved personally as volunteers and ready to consider voting. But they want political leaders to be positive, to address real problems and to call on all Americans to be constructively involved (par. 5).

As we look toward the fall 2008 elections, it seems clear that young voters will not only play an important role in the election, but might in fact play the deciding role. Voters such as Reid Vincent,

A heading, formatted in blue and using a sans-serif font that differs from the serif body font, calls attention to a shift in the writer's ideas.

A block quotation is set off by indenting the text on both sides. Quotation marks are not needed for block quotations.

▲ **Interior page of an academic essay**

Lopez 4

Works Cited

Casper, Lynne M., and Loretta E. Bass. "United States Census Bureau Population Reports: Voting and Registration in the Election of November 1996." *US Census Bureau.* US Census Bureau, Jul. 1988. Web. 27 Aug. 2012.

Lopez, Mark Hugo, Emily Kirby, and Jared Sagoff. "Fact Sheet: The Youth Vote 2004." *CIRCLE: The Center for Information and Research on Civic Learning and Engagement.* Tufts U, July 2005. Web. 20 Aug. 2012.

Margnarelli, Margaret. "Young Voter Apathy: Will America's Youth Go to the Polls?" *GovSpot.com.* StartSpot Mediaworks, Inc., n.d. Web. 22 Aug. 2012.

"Record Youth Voter Turnout for '08 Presidential Primaries and Caucuses." *The Pew Charitable Trusts.* The Pew Charitable Trusts, 13 June 2008. Web. 27 Aug. 2012.

Vincent, Reid. Personal interview. 7 Sept. 2012.

Reference page is titled "Works Cited" per MLA style.

MLA format is used to cite sources. Entries are double-spaced and have a hanging indent.

▲ **Works cited page of an academic essay**

Checklist for Designing Academic Essays

✔ Reflect on how design can help you accomplish your purpose and carry out your role as a writer.

✔ Consider how design can help you address reader expectations.

✔ Think about how the context in which you write your essay will affect your design decisions.

✔ Think about how the context in which your essay will be read will affect your design decisions.

✔ Be aware of the design conventions associated with academic essays, including the following:

- Cover page or essay header, depending on your instructor's preferences or the formatting requirements of the documentation style you are following

- Readable body font (example: 12-point Times New Roman)

- Double-spaced lines

- Wide margins, at least one inch

- Consistent use of the documentation system you are following

- Headers and footers in a readable font distinct from the body font

- If used, headings and subheadings formatted in fonts and colors that distinguish them from the body text and show the relative importance of heading levels

- If used, illustrations labeled and placed either within the text near relevant passages or in an appendix, according to your instructor's preferences

In Summary: Drafting and Designing

* Use your outline to begin drafting your document (p. 519).

* Write clearly and effectively (p. 520).

* Draft your introduction (p. 527).

* Draft your conclusion (p. 533).

* Help readers follow your line of argument (p. 537).

* Design your document (p. 541).

* Design an academic essay (p. 551).

17 Working with Genres

▶▶ At times, you might have the opportunity to decide which genre you'll use to make your contribution to a conversation. Or you might be asked to adapt the contents of an academic essay for presentation in another genre, such as a brochure or Web page. As you consider your choices, you'll find a wide array of documents that you can use to reach your readers. In this chapter, you'll find discussions of how to draft and design some of the most important print and digital genres.

How Can I Choose the Right Genre?

Experienced writers base their choice of genre on three primary factors: their purpose and role, the expectations of their readers, and the context in which their document will be written and read. In most cases, one of these factors will be more important than the others. For example, if your readers are unlikely to treat your document seriously unless it is presented in a particular genre, such as a scientific journal article, then you would be foolish to choose another genre. To choose an appropriate genre, analyze your assignment, reflect on your writing situation, and consider the resources you can draw on as you compose your document.

Analyze Your Assignment

If you are writing in response to an assignment for a class, determine whether your assignment restricts your choice of genre. If your assignment contains a statement such as *write an essay* or *create a Web page*, then you'll know that your instructor has a specific genre in mind.

If you find no mention of a particular genre, you should look for statements that can help you choose an appropriate genre.

- **Look for statements about your readers.** Your assignment might provide information about the characteristics of your readers, such as their ages, their educational backgrounds, and their interests. You might be asked, for example, to address the members of a particular academic discipline. If so, identify genres that are commonly used in that discipline.

- **Look for statements about your purpose and role.** Most assignments offer guidance on what you should attempt to accomplish. Words such as *inform* and *report*, for example, suggest that your purpose is to write an informative document. In contrast, words such as *convince* and *persuade* indicate that you should write an argumentative document. Although you'll find that some genres, such as essays, articles, and blog posts, can be used to accomplish both purposes, some are better suited to one purpose than to another. Opinion columns, for example, are typically used to advocate an argumentative position, while reports are used primarily to inform.

- **Look for statements about your context.** If your assignment indicates the format in which your document should be submitted, use that information to help determine which genres might be appropriate. If you are expected to submit a printed document, for example, you'll be more likely to choose an essay, a report, or an article than a Web page, a blog post, or a multimodal essay. Look as well for any statements that indicate where your document might be read, such as references to particular types of publications (newspapers, magazines, Web sites, and so on).

- **Look for statements about limitations.** Many assignments provide information about word limits or page length. You'll also find guidance about due dates, deadlines for rough drafts or activities such as the development of working bibliographies or outlines, and the type of documentation system you should use. Use this information to choose your genre. Length limitations are particularly useful, since many genres would simply be too long for an assignment that asked for a document of no more than 500 words. Similarly, some documents, such as a multimodal essay, would be difficult to complete in a short period of time.

You can read more about analyzing an assignment on page 28.

Reflect on Your Purpose, Readers, and Context

If you are not given a detailed assignment, use your understanding of your writing situation to choose your genre.

- Spend time thinking about your purpose and role, and then ask yourself which genres might best help you accomplish your goals.

- Reflect on the knowledge, interests, purposes, and backgrounds of your readers, and then ask what this might tell you about appropriate genres. Try to understand what your readers are likely to expect from you and what they might find familiar and easy to read. A well-written scientific report, for example, might be less effective than an informative essay or article simply because your readers might be unfamiliar with the scientific-report genre.

- Reflect on the context in which your document will be read. If you know that your readers have easy access to computers, tablets, or smartphones, you'll have more options than if you know that they can read documents only in print form.

Consider Your Writing Resources

In addition to your assignment and your writing situation, think about the tools you can use to write and design your document. In some cases, you might lack the tools necessary to create a particular genre. Lack of access to a particular type of software or a computer or tablet powerful enough to run that software might work against a decision to develop a multimodal essay or a Web page. Similarly, lack of access to a color printer might work against creating a colorful brochure or flyer.

Your choice of genre might also be influenced — in a more positive way — by what you know how to do. If you have experience using desktop publishing programs such as Microsoft Publisher or Adobe InDesign, you'll have far more options for creating a polished print or digital document. Similarly, you can create Web pages if you know how to use a Web editing program such as Adobe Dreamweaver or are familiar with online Web page creation tools such as Google Sites.

As you consider your writing resources, keep in mind the wide range of documents that can be created using widely available word-processing and presentation tools such as Word, Pages, Keynote, and PowerPoint. These programs include templates that you can use to create a variety of genres.

How Can I Write an Article?

Articles appear in a wide range of publications, including newspapers, magazines, scholarly and professional journals, and Web sites. Articles rely heavily on information obtained from sources such as books, Web sites, government reports, interviews, surveys, and observation. Writers of articles should consider several factors as they plan, draft, design, revise, and edit an article: the audience addressed by their target publication, the subjects typically written about in the publication, the style and tone used by other articles in the publication, and the overall design of the publication.

Consider Your Purpose and Role

The writers of articles adopt a variety of purposes and roles, from informing to evaluating to solving problems to advocating, and their writers often find themselves adopting different roles as they learn about, reflect on, and eventually offer their perspective on a particular issue. As you consider how to write an article, keep your purpose and role in mind. If you are writing about a complex problem, for example, you'll want to read widely about the problem's origins and effects. You'll also want to find out as much as you can about how the problem has been defined, what solutions have been offered, and which solutions have been tried so far. As you learn more about the problem, you're likely to become interested in a particular solution and to want to advocate for that solution in your article. Whether you move into the role of advocate will depend on the nature of the publication in which you publish your article. Some publications, such as *Time*, focus largely on informing their readers, while others, such as the *Nation*, routinely publish work that takes a strong position on problems and issues.

Analyze Your Target Publication

Analyzing a publication involves asking questions about its readers, the subjects its articles address, its writing conventions, and its design. To locate a print publication, visit your library's periodicals room (see p. 474), or consult a reference librarian. You can also search for information about the publication on the Web (see p. 465) or in databases (see p. 461). To locate information about a digital publication, such as *Slate*, visit its Web site, conduct database searches, or consult a reference librarian.

Readers. Examine the publication as a whole to learn what you can about its readers.

- Can you find a letters-to-the-editor section? If so, reading the letters and any responses from the editors might give you insights into who reads the publication and why they read it.

- If the publication contains advertisements, do they tell you anything about the readers? Who advertises in the publication? What products or services do they offer, or what issues or problems do they address?

- What can you learn about the readers from the range of subjects or issues addressed in articles and other parts of the publication?

- Can you find any information about the publisher? Can you tell whether it is a commercial enterprise, a government agency, a nonprofit organization, a scholarly or professional organization, or an individual? Does the publication have a mission statement? Does the publication describe its purpose or goals, the audience it hopes to reach, or its origins? If so, what does that information tell you about the target audience?

Subjects. Look at recently published articles in the publication. You can often find them in tables of contents, article indexes, and digital archives. Depending on the publication, you might also be able to search a full-text database (see p. 463) or search the Web for archived articles.

- What issues and subjects do the articles address?

- How long are the articles? Which are the shortest? Which are the longest? Where do they fall on average?

- What do you think is the purpose of the publication? Is its goal to inform, to advocate, to address problems? Or does it address a range of purposes?

Writing Conventions. Study the articles in the publication to learn about its writing conventions.

- How would you characterize the style and tone of the articles? Is the tone generally formal, informal, or somewhere in between? Are contractions (*can't, won't, isn't*) used? Are individuals identified by their full names and titles ("Dr. Shaun Beaty")?

- How are sources identified? Do the articles use an in-text citation system, such as MLA or APA (see Chapters 21 and 22)? Do they use footnotes or endnotes? Do the articles link directly to the source? Do they informally identify the source?

- What do the authors of articles seem to assume about their readers? Do they use specialized language (or jargon)? Do they expect you to know a great deal about the subject? Do you think the authors expect you to be an expert in the field to understand their articles?

Design. To gain an understanding of your readers' expectations about the design of your article, scan articles in the publication, read a few carefully, and take notes.

- Would you characterize the articles as heavy on text? Or are images, tables, charts, figures, and other illustrations used liberally? If the article is published in a digital format, does it include audio or video clips? Does it include other digital illustrations, such as animations or apps that a reader could work with?

- How is color used in the article, if at all? Does the article make use of borders, rules, and shading?

- Does the article use headings and subheadings? If so, how are they formatted? What kinds of fonts are used? Is there much variety in the fonts?

- How is the article laid out? Does it use columns? Sidebars? Block quotes?

Your answers to questions about readers, subjects, writing conventions, and design can help you gain an overall understanding of the publication that might publish your article. You're likely to find, of course, that articles in even the most narrowly focused publication display quite a bit of variety. But understanding your potential readers and the subjects they seem to care about can help you compose a better article. Similarly, applying what you've learned about the writing and design conventions of articles that have appeared in the publication will show its editors — the people who ultimately decide what is accepted for publication — that you have tailored your article to their needs.

Develop and Organize Your Argument

Your line of argument should reflect your understanding of the issues and subjects addressed in your target publication and the needs, interests, and knowledge of its readers. As in other types of documents, you should develop a main point, select reasons to accept it, and choose evidence to support your reasons (see Chapter 14). Then you should choose an organizing pattern that is consistent with your purpose and role and create a map or an outline of your argument (see Chapter 15).

Your choice of organizing pattern will vary according to your role and purpose as well as the expectations of your readers. In general, you'll find that the chronology and description patterns are often used in informative articles, while the strengths/weaknesses and costs/benefits patterns are well suited to articles that focus on analysis, evaluation, and argument. You can read more about organizing patterns on pages 506–507.

Collect and Work with Sources

The sources you choose to provide evidence in your article should reflect your understanding of the types of sources typically found in other articles in the publication. Some publications, particularly those focused on news and current events, depend heavily on field research — primarily interviews, observation, and correspondence (see p. 479) — and personal experience. Others, such as professional and scholarly journals, rely primarily on published work and, in some cases, original research. To increase the likelihood that your article will be successful, make sure that your sources are consistent with those published in the articles you've studied during your publication analysis.

Draft, Design, and Review Your Article

The process of writing, designing, revising, and editing an article is similar to that used for academic essays (see Chapter 16). You'll find some differences in the areas of word choice, design, and source documentation. Your choice of words should be consistent with that of the other published articles you've reviewed in the publication. In particular, you should pay attention to the level of formality (including the use of contractions and slang), the use of specialized terminology (jargon), and references to the work of other authors. Review your publication analysis to determine how you should address these issues.

The design of your article should also build on what you learned through your publication analysis. It is generally not necessary to design your article so that it mimics the layout used in the publication. It can be helpful, however, to draft your article with particular design elements in mind. By placing images, tables, charts, and figures in your draft, you can gain a sense of how the article will appear to readers. By creating sidebars (see p. 548) or setting up pull quotes (see p. 548), you can determine which points will be highlighted for your readers. Similarly, you can format your headings and subheadings in ways that mirror how they are formatted in the publication and use colors to set a particular mood or to highlight key information. Using design as a composing element can help you view your draft as your readers will, allowing you to anticipate how they are likely to view and understand your article.

As you revise and edit your article, be sure to ask for feedback from people you trust. Ask them to put themselves in the role of a reader of your target publication. If they are unfamiliar with the publication, share the results of your publication analysis with them. Depending on your purpose and role, you might choose one of the peer-review activities in the chapters in Part Two. You can also review the advice for effective peer review in Chapter 4.

View an Article

The articles that follow were published in the *Indiana Daily Student*, the student newspaper at Indiana University. Paired with photos, the articles make use of font formatting and visual elements to set a mood, call attention to key points, and convey information.

For more examples of articles, see pages 22, 52, 219, and 290 and the e-Pages for *Joining the Conversation*.

Checklist for Writing Articles	✔ Consider your writing situation and in particular your purpose and role.
	✔ Analyze your target publication, focusing on its readers, the subjects and issues addressed in the publication, typical writing conventions, and typical design conventions.
	✔ Develop and organize your argument.
	✔ Collect information to support your argument.
	✔ Draft, design, and review your article, keeping in mind the results of your publication analysis.

▲ Front page of a student newspaper

Callouts:
- A large headline contrasts with the text and the headlines for individual articles.
- Bylines are set in a bold sans-serif font to differentiate them from main body text.
- Newspaper article is formatted in columns.
- Captioned photos add visual interest and information.
- Pull quotes in a large, sans-serif font highlight key ideas and information in the article.

How Can I Create a Multimodal Essay?

As it has become easier to integrate images, audio, video, and other forms of media into essays, a new genre has emerged: the multimodal essay. Multimodal essays are characterized by their essayistic form and their use of multiple types of media. As essays, they present information in a linear sequence, one idea after another. As multimodal documents, they combine text with images, animation, sound, and/or video to establish a line of argument and support the writer's points.

Multimodal essays began appearing several years ago, most often on Web sites such as CNN.com and Salon, but also in blogs whose writers wanted to make use of images, video, and audio. More recently, publications that have focused traditionally on print have begun developing sophisticated multimodal essays. Increasingly, writing instructors are assigning multimodal essays, sometimes as original documents and sometimes as extensions of more traditional print-based academic essays.

To create a multimodal essay, build on your understanding of how to compose an academic essay, and then learn how to use digital composing tools to create a document that helps you accomplish your writing goals and address your readers' expectations.

Build on Your Experiences Writing Academic Essays

The processes writers typically use to compose a multimodal essay are similar to those used to compose academic essays. You need to do the following:

- **Choose a written conversation** by reading widely and looking for a match with your interests, knowledge, and experiences.
- **Listen in on the conversation** by locating sources — including multimodal sources as well as those that are primarily textual — and reading them critically.
- **Reflect on the conversation** by taking notes and evaluating information, ideas, and arguments.
- **Decide how you'll contribute to the conversation** by focusing on a particular role and choosing a main point.
- **Support your main point** with reasons and evidence.
- **Organize your argument.**
- **Draft, revise, and edit your document** with your purpose, readers, and context in mind.

You can read more about the processes involved in choosing, listening in on, and reflecting on a written conversation in Part One. You can read more about the processes associated with particular roles — observing, reporting, analyzing, evaluating, problem solving, and advocating — in the relevant chapters in Part Two.

Consider Your Writing Situation

In comparison with traditional essays, multimodal essays have emerged quite recently as a distinct genre. As a writer, you'll have a great deal of freedom about how to pursue your purpose, adopt your role, address your readers, and adapt to the context in which your essay will be written and read. Perhaps the best example of this is the wide range of materials you can use as evidence in your essay. You should consider not only the information, ideas, and arguments found in your sources but also how your readers will respond to your sources. If your goal is to inform your readers, for example, you might find that one type of medium is more effective than another because it contains more information.

Context also plays an important role in your choice of evidence. If you know that your readers are likely to be reading your essay on a device with a small screen or a slow connection, you might choose an audio clip or an image rather than a video clip because it will open more quickly. Similarly, if you are uploading your essay to a course management system, you might have to work within particular file size limitations. If you cannot upload a large file, you might choose smaller images or use a smaller, lower-quality audio clip instead of a larger video file. Or, rather than importing the video into your essay, you might upload it to YouTube and link to it from the essay.

Even though your readers might not have encountered multimodal essays before, they will have some expectations about design and writing conventions. At a minimum, they will expect you to provide a linear document that contains one or more types of media; uses fonts, colors, shading, borders, and rules consistently and effectively; and is designed to be viewed on a computer screen or tablet. If you develop a lengthy essay, such as the multimodal essay created by Tanya Patel of the University of Texas at Austin (see page 573), your readers will also expect you to provide navigation tools, such as tables of contents and page links, that will allow them to move easily from one part of the essay to another.

Develop and Organize Your Argument

As with most other types of documents, you'll need to spend time choosing a main point, selecting reasons to accept your main point, choosing appropriate evidence, and making decisions about organization. With the exception of issues related to digital media, you'll find that these decisions are nearly identical to those you'll face as you work on various types of academic essays. You can read more about the composing strategies associated with particular writing roles in Part Two.

Collect and Work with Sources

Multimodal essays, by definition, rely on sources such as images, animations, video clips, audio clips, and data files. Like academic essays, they also draw on information, ideas, and arguments from written sources and field research. As you work on your multimodal essay, your first concern should be identifying sources that can be used to support your main point and illustrate the positions and approaches taken by other writers. Then consider how you can use nontextual sources to bring your essay to life. Each of these concerns will shape your decisions about three key issues: choosing among media sources, deciding how to place and stage media sources, and determining whether you should embed a source or link to it.

CHOOSE AMONG MEDIA SOURCES

In composing your multimodal essay, you will have many options about the types of sources you can include in your essay. As you consider your options, give some thought to the effect each type of source will have on your ability to achieve your writing goals, address the expectations of your readers, and adapt to the context in which your document will be read. Think about the differences, for example, between presenting part of a written transcript of an interview, linking to an audio clip of the interview, and embedding a video clip of the interview into your essay. Each has its advantages. A written transcript can be skimmed, while readers will need to spend more time opening and listening to an audio or video clip. In contrast, the audio and video clips would allow the reader to pick up on the speaker's tone of voice or facial expressions, neither of which can be conveyed clearly through a transcript. Similarly, consider the trade-offs between presenting a concise, well-designed table and embedding a spreadsheet containing raw data that a reader could open and work with. Better yet, think about the advantages of including the table *and* the spreadsheet — you'll not only allow your readers to view your conclusions as you've presented them in the table but also give them a chance to work with the data and come to their own conclusions.

PLACE AND STAGE MEDIA SOURCES

As you decide which sources to include in your essay, keep in mind not only how well the sources will help you achieve your goals and meet your readers' expectations but also how they will appeal to your readers and how your readers might interact with them. If your readers are actively engaged with your essay — navigating its contents, viewing images and other illustrations, following links to related sources, and so on — they are more likely to find themselves intrigued with and influenced by your line of argument.

Among the most important design decisions you'll make as you create your multimodal essay is where you'll place each media source and how you'll call attention to it. In most cases, you'll want to introduce the source before the reader encounters it in the text. In this sense, the placement of media sources follows the general guidelines for placing illustrations found on page 551. You should refer to the source in the body of the text, position the source near where it is mentioned, and provide some sort of caption or figure title to help readers see the connection between it and its mention in the text.

Your decisions about how you'll call attention to a media source — that is, how you'll stage it — will depend on how central the source is to the points you are making in your essay. If the source is incidental to the essay — if it is, for example, little more than additional information that provides a modest amount of extra support for a point — then you need not stage it in a way that calls it to the attention of your readers. A photograph of a speaker, for example, might do little more than allow readers to connect a face to a name. In this case, the photo might simply be set off in the margin of the document or aligned along the right side of a paragraph. In contrast, if the media source is a critical part of your essay, you'll want to ensure that your readers pay attention to it. A video source might be placed so that it takes up the complete width of the page, and a detailed caption or figure title might provide information that would lead the reader to view or listen to it.

IMPORT OR LINK TO MEDIA SOURCES

Multimodal essays can include complete files downloaded from media sources, as would be the case if you placed a photograph in your essay, or they can link to media sources, as you might do if you wanted your readers to play a YouTube video. When you import a file into your essay, the file is literally saved within your essay. In contrast, when you link to a file, as you might do if you used the "embed code" that YouTube provides for its videos, the link sends your readers to a source on a Web site or some other sort of network location.

Your decisions about importing a file versus linking to it will depend on factors such as design, the length of time you want your essay to be available, concerns about file size, the software you will use to create your essay, and copyright restrictions (see p. 488).

- **Design.** Importing sources gives you the highest degree of control over the appearance and behavior of the media source, while linking allows you to minimize the file size of your essay and often allows you to ensure that all media elements will play properly when they are opened.

- **Availability.** If you are creating an essay that will continue to be available for readers for a lengthy period of time, as might be the case if you are publishing your essay on a Web site or in a blog, you need to ensure that your media sources will be available even if they disappear from the site where you found them. In this case, importing the media source would be the best choice. In contrast, if your essay will be available only for a short time, as might be the case with a class assignment, your sources will probably be available long enough for your essay to be read and reviewed. In this case, linking would be a reasonable option.

- **File size.** One of the biggest disadvantages of importing media sources into your essay is the resulting increase in file size. If you import a video file, for example, your file might become so large that it would be impossible to send as an e-mail attachment or difficult to download from a Web site. In contrast, if you link to your media sources, the overall size of your essay will be quite small, making it easy to distribute.

- **Software.** Your choice of composing tools (see the next section) can also affect whether you use linking or importing. Some software programs, including most word-processing programs and multimedia presentation tools, can import a wide range of sources, from images to audio to video to data files. In contrast, Web editing programs, such as Adobe Dreamweaver, allow only linking. Although you can certainly save your media files on a Web site, they will be separate from your essay, and you will need to ensure that they can be viewed with a Web browser.

Choose Composing Tools

Your decision about the composing tool you'll use to create your multimodal essay will affect not only *what* you can do in terms of composing, designing, and distributing your essay but also *how you think about* the essay itself. The capabilities of a particular software program allow you to envision particular types of documents. For example, if you decide to use a multimedia presentation program such as Keynote or PowerPoint, you'll most likely think of your essay as a series of pages that readers will move through in a linear manner, rather than jumping around as they might on a Web site. The same will be true if you choose a word-processing program, such as Word or Google Docs. In contrast, if you choose a graphics program such as Adobe Photoshop or Corel Draw or a multimedia presentation program such as Prezi, the idea of distinct pages might not be a major consideration. In this sense, as rhetorician Kenneth Burke has written, a way of seeing is a way of not seeing. The features and capabilities of a particular composing tool will direct your attention to some possibilities even as they obscure others.

Keep Burke's observation in mind as you consider the wide range of software programs that can be used to create a multimodal essay:

- word-processing programs, such as Apple Pages, Google Docs, Microsoft Word, or OpenOffice Writer

- multimedia presentation programs, such as Apple Keynote, Google Slides, Microsoft PowerPoint, or OpenOffice Impress

- Web development tools, such as Adobe Dreamweaver or Google Sites

- publishing tools, such as Adobe InDesign or Microsoft Publisher

- graphics programs, such as Adobe Illustrator or Photoshop, Corel Draw or PhotoPaint, or OpenOffice Draw

As you choose your composing and design tools, consider how their distinctive features will help you accomplish your goals as a writer. A word-processing program might be a better choice than a multimedia presentation program if, for example, you plan to rely more heavily on text than on images and video. In contrast, a multimedia presentation program offers more options for including multimedia elements than do most word-processing or Web development programs. Keep in mind as well the expectations that your readers might have about how to use particular programs. Chances are good that they'll read your essay quite differently if they view it as a Web page or a Prezi document than they will if it is distributed as a word-processing document.

⚐ TECH TIP: COMPOSE YOUR ESSAY WITH A MULTIMEDIA PRESENTATION PROGRAM

Microsoft PowerPoint and other multimedia presentation programs, such as Apple Keynote, Google Slides, or OpenOffice Impress, offer a set of tools that are well suited to integrating multimedia sources with text. The Insert Toolbar in Power-Point, for example, allows you to add images, audio, video, and other media sources along with tables, textboxes, and links. To get started, create a new presentation, and then click on the Insert menu in the command ribbon.

▲ **PowerPoint Insert toolbar**

Using a multimedia presentation program to create a multimedia essay invites you to think of the program not as a set of bulleted slides, but as a group of pages that can be filled with various types of media. If you look at each page as a blank canvas, you can see how you might design an essay containing pages that look like those you might find in a magazine or on the Web.

Develop a Consistent Design

If your multimodal essay uses pages, ensure that they are designed in a way that helps your readers view each page as part of a larger essay. If you've watched a Power-Point presentation, you've probably seen this idea in action. Even though each page

Why Should We Care about the Environment?

We should care because we feel a connection with other living things. As we learn more about this sense of connectedness, we come to realize how important it is that we view the earth not as a set of resources to be exploited but rather as a community.

Yet we so often treat the earth as something that only we inhabit. To some extent, this reflects an unfortunate notion that intelligence can be measured only in human terms. This has proven to be a significant obstacle to efforts to find a way to preserve

Text, a video, and images are used on a multimedia presentation slide.

might have radically different content — a bulleted list of information on one page, a video on another, and an image on yet another — they use the same color scheme, headers and footers, fonts, and background colors.

Regardless of the composing tool you choose, you can ensure a sense of continuity across your essay by using a consistent color scheme and font scheme, using background images consistently (or not at all), and placing recurring information, such as page numbers and navigation tools (see the following section), in the same place on each page. You can view how this is accomplished in the example multimodal essay on page 573.

Create Navigation Tools

Although they are linear documents, multimodal essays often include navigation tools that allow readers to move quickly from one part of the document to another. In this sense, they share a number of similarities with Web sites. As you create your essay, consider including the following types of navigation tools.

- **Next and Previous buttons or links** allow readers to move from one part of an essay to another.

- **Internal links** help readers move from one page to a related page.

- **External links** help readers open related documents.

- **Tables of contents** allow readers of longer multimodal essays to move directly to a particular part of the essay.

- **Essay maps** help readers visualize the essay as a set of concepts, sections, or pages. You can click on part of the map to navigate to a particular point within the essay.

- **Menus** can appear on each page, listing major sections within the essay.

- **Headers and footers** provide information about the document, helping readers recognize which part of the essay they are reading and providing access to links to, for example, a works cited list and an "About This Essay" page.

View a Multimodal Essay

The following examples are drawn from the multimodal essay written by Tanya Patel of the University of Texas at Austin. Tanya developed her essay using Wix (a free Web program) and Adobe Photoshop. Note her use of text, illustrations, color, headings and subheadings, and menus to clearly convey her argument about the danger of using cell phones while driving.

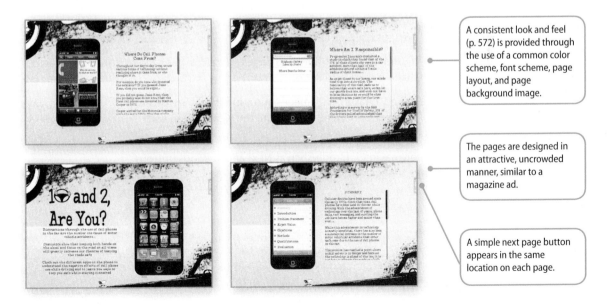

A consistent look and feel (p. 572) is provided through the use of a common color scheme, font scheme, page layout, and page background image.

The pages are designed in an attractive, uncrowded manner, similar to a magazine ad.

A simple next page button appears in the same location on each page.

Checklist for Creating Multimodal Essays

✔ Use your experiences writing academic essays as a foundation for your work on a multimodal essay.

✔ Reflect on your purpose and role, the expectations of your readers, and the context in which your essay will be written and read.

✔ Develop and organize your line of argument by choosing a main point, reasons, and supporting evidence. Consider your role as you plan, and consult other sections of this book that focus on composing processes related to that role.

✔ Choose your composing tools, keeping in mind their appropriateness for your writing situation and their tendency to drive design decisions in particular directions.

✔ Develop an appropriate and consistent design for your document, paying particular attention to the following:

- Consistent use of fonts, colors, shading, borders, and rules

- Readable fonts for headings and subheadings (such as 16-point Times New Roman or Verdana)

- A readable body font designed for on-screen reading (such as 11-point Calibri or Georgia)

- The placement of titles, text, and illustrations, with illustrations labeled and located near relevant text passages

- If used, transitions between pages (dissolves, page flips) that are quick and not distracting

- If used, background images and sounds that are chosen to enhance rather than obscure the elements on each page

✔ Create navigation tools such as Next and Previous buttons, links, menus, and tables of contents.

How Can I Create a Web Page?

A few years ago, the number of documents available on the Web grew larger than those available in print. Not surprisingly, writing courses have begun to pay more attention to how to write and design Web pages. These assignments range from creating a single page that will become part of a larger site to designing an entire Web site. The following discussion focuses on single Web pages.

Consider Your Purpose and Role

As you consider your purpose and role in creating a Web page, you must reflect not only on what you hope to accomplish — informing or persuading your readers, for example — but also on how you can work with the complex array of design, navigation, and media elements that you might use to achieve your purpose. Web pages can engage readers in ways that print documents cannot — they can link directly to related pages, allow visitors to access video and audio files, and support communication among the Web site's readers and writers. This wealth of organization, navigation, and design options, however, carries significant composing and design challenges, such as keeping your readers focused on reading your page instead of following links to other sites.

Consider Reader Expectations

Given the wide range of individuals with access to the Web, writers must anticipate the needs of a much more diverse group of readers than is the case with documents distributed in print or via e-mail. Therefore, writers tend to provide a significant amount of guidance about the purpose of a Web page and the Web site on which it appears. As they consider their readers' needs, they are likely to reflect on their own experiences surfing the Web. Writers know that readers of Web pages want to get to the point quickly and locate the information they need without a great deal of effort. They understand that readers interested in judging the credibility or reliability of a site will look for links to information about its authors and publishers. They know that readers want to be able to anticipate where a link on a page will lead them if they follow it. And writers know that readers expect the media elements on the page to contribute in some meaningful way to its purpose. In other words, they know that their readers expect a well-written, well-designed page that is worth the time they invest in finding and reading it.

Plan Your Page

Developing an effective Web page requires careful planning. The most important concerns to pay attention to during planning include content — the words, images, and other elements you'll include on your page — and the links and other navigation tools your readers will use to find their way to related pages elsewhere on the Web site.

CREATE CONTENT

Web pages can include textual information, images, audio, video, animations, linked files, and applications, among other types of material. As you consider your purpose and role, think about what you want your readers to know, do, or believe after they've visited your page. Your decisions about the content that will be available on your page — including your decision about how to create it — should reflect your understanding of your writing situation.

CHOOSE NAVIGATION TOOLS

Your choice of navigational tools will depend on the size and complexity of the site on which your page appears and the navigational tools that the site designers have made available to you. To help readers navigate a Web site, developers typically create menus that appear on each page, and they often provide page headers, page footers, site maps, tables of contents, and search tools. As you design your Web page, you can include these tools on your page or, in the case of tables of contents, link to them.

As you consider how to help readers move around your page, decide whether you should provide a page menu. Page menus serve as a table of contents for a Web page and are often used on longer Web pages. In addition, you should think carefully about how you will place and design links to related pages. In most cases, links made in the text of a Web page are signaled to readers through the use of underlines and color. Links within the text can also be identified by the use of small icons. When links are made with images or the opening frame of a video clip, writers often provide a caption or a flag that appears when a mouse is hovered over the image or clip. Ideally, the flag will provide information that will help readers decide whether they want to follow the link.

Design Your Page

Over the past decade, the appearance of Web pages has grown similar to that of magazines, with a heavy use of images and other illustrations. Writers typically design a Web page with many of the same considerations they apply to the pages in a magazine, choosing a color scheme that is consistent with other pages on the site, formatting headings and subheadings consistently across pages, and using borders, shading, and rules in a manner similar to that of many print publications. Writers of Web pages, however, must also address the placement and appearance of navigation menus and digital illustrations, such as audio and video clips, animations, embedded applications, and downloadable files.

Your design decisions should reflect your purpose — what you hope your readers will know, believe, or want to do once they've read your page. You should also take into account the overall design of the Web site on which the page will appear and the text and media elements you will include on your page.

ENSURE YOUR PAGE IS CONSISTENT WITH THE OVERALL DESIGN OF THE SITE

Web designers often refer to the importance of a consistent "look and feel." A design that is consistent across all the pages on a site helps readers associate a particular design style with a site. This familiarizes them with the placement of navigation tools, types of information, and other material that the Web site's designers want them to find.

Because one Web page is usually as easy to visit as another, you should avoid different designs on the pages of a given Web site. Different page designs can lead readers to think they've left one site and jumped to another. If you need to differentiate your page from others on the site, use subtle variations in its overall design, such as differences in color or the placement of text or media elements on the page. Keep the following principles in mind as you design your page:

- **Simple is better.** Less is more. Don't try to cram too much on a single page.

- **Keep important information on the screen.** Readers often jump to another Web page if they don't find what they're looking for on the screen. Although it's relatively easy to scroll down a page, few readers are willing to scroll down more than one screen to find the information they're seeking.

- **Avoid overuse of graphics.** Large images can increase load time — or the time it takes for a browser to open a Web page. More important, research suggests that readers of Web pages are drawn to textual information as opposed to graphical information — a behavior that is strikingly different from readers' typical behavior with print documents. Perhaps because so many Web sites use images largely as decoration rather than as sources of information (for example, news photographs, diagrams, and charts), readers typically look first at text on a Web page.

As you begin to design your page, browse the Web for pages that attempt to accomplish a purpose similar to your own. Evaluate their page designs, making note of features and layouts that you might want to use.

DESIGN PAGE ELEMENTS

An important part of the overall look and feel of a Web site is the appearance and placement of specific elements on its pages. The following are some of the most common elements that are displayed on Web pages.

- **Headings** display titles and subtitles on a page and are typically fairly brief.

- **Body text** is used to display ordinary text, such as the text found in paragraphs.

- **Images and other media elements** are commonly found on Web pages and include icons, buttons, photographs, animations, audio files, and video files. The program you are using to create your page will allow you to specify borders, descriptive titles (informational flags), and various horizontal and vertical alignments.

- **Page backgrounds** can range from a simple white background, to a repeating (tiled) image, to a single image that acts as a watermark. Your design decisions should take into account the impact of a background color or image on the readability of text and the emotional tones that the color or image conveys.

- **Links** to other Web pages, to locations elsewhere on the page, and to other Internet resources should be clearly distinguishable from other text on the page.

- **Navigation tools** should be displayed on your page in a manner that is consistent with the overall look and feel of the Web site. Avoid changing the background color or shifting the location, for instance, of a navigation menu. Consistently displaying navigation tools will make it easier for your readers to locate them.

DESIGN YOUR PAGE

After you've considered the overall look and feel of the Web site, begin designing your page. It's easy to start by sketching your design on a piece of paper or in a graphics editing program. Once you've sketched out a design, ask yourself whether it conforms to the overall look and feel of the Web site on which your page will appear. If it doesn't, revise your design. Once you've decided that your sketch will provide a good foundation for designing your page, decide how you'll control the layout of the page. Depending on the tool you use to create your page, you might be able to choose from a set of templates, some of which are designed to suit different types of content (for example, a page built to display news headlines or a page designed around large chunks of text). If you prefer to place each design element yourself to fit your content, most Web editing programs will allow you to do so.

Create Your Page

Web developers create pages using a variety of software tools. The easiest and most straightforward options are free online tools such as Google Sites (sites.google.com) and Zeeblio (zeeblio.com). You can also use word-processing programs, such as Microsoft Word, which allow you to save documents in the HTML format used by Web pages. If you know HTML and CSS — the coding language and style definition specifications used to create Web pages — you can also create Web pages with tools ranging from simple text-editing programs such as NotePad to specialized Web editing programs such as Dreamweaver.

⬏ TECH TIP: CREATE A WEB PAGE WITH A WORD-PROCESSING PROGRAM

Word-processing programs offer a number of advantages to people new to Web site development. These programs are often familiar, inexpensive, and relatively easy to use. They allow you to place and format images, video, and audio clips. They are particularly good at formatting text. And saving a document as a Web page can be done easily using the Save As command. Word-processing programs have a number of disadvantages — they're designed primarily to edit print documents and are not nearly as easy to use as free Web tools such as Google Sites — but they work quite well for simple Web sites and individual Web pages.

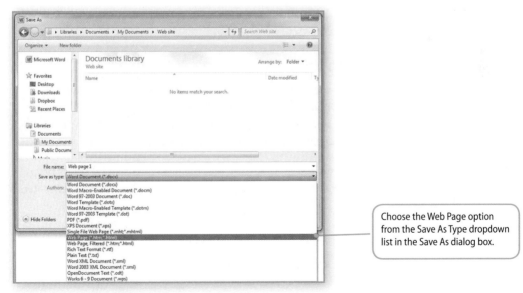

Choose the Web Page option from the Save As Type dropdown list in the Save As dialog box.

▲ **Microsoft Word Save As dialog box**

To create an attractive, functional Web page using a program such as Microsoft Word, you need to know only a small number of features and commands. The following commands can be found in the Insert ribbon in Microsoft Word:

- **Insert Hyperlink.** Links allow you to move from one Web page to another or to move to a location on the current page.

- **Insert Pictures.** You can place a picture within or alongside a passage of text. You can also use pictures as a page banner.

- **Insert Table.** You can use tables to display information, act as a container for menu items, or control the layout of your page. You can add more columns or rows as you edit the table.

- **Insert Textbox.** Textboxes are like sidebars (see p. 548). They can be placed within other passages of text or along the sides of a Web page.

▲ **Microsoft Word Insert toolbar**

To view your Web page, open the folder containing your page file, and double-click on it. It should open in your default Web browser, such as Chrome, Firefox, Internet Explorer, Opera, or Safari. To make changes to your page, edit the file in your word-processing program or Web editing program, save it, and then click on the Reload or Refresh button in your browser.

Put Your Page Online

If you've created your page using a tool such as Google Sites, your page is already online. If you've used Dreamweaver or a word-processing program, you will need to add your page and any associated media files to your Web site. You will find guidance, usually in the form of help pages, from the Web site provider that is hosting your site.

Once your page is online, test it. Make sure that the page opens and displays properly, that links work, and that media elements open properly on different computers and devices. If you are satisfied with the results of your work, share the URL with the people you want to view your page. In a few days, you'll also find that it will be available through search sites such as Google and Bing.

View Web Pages

The following figures show pages from Megan Martinez's Web site about returning military veterans finding green jobs.

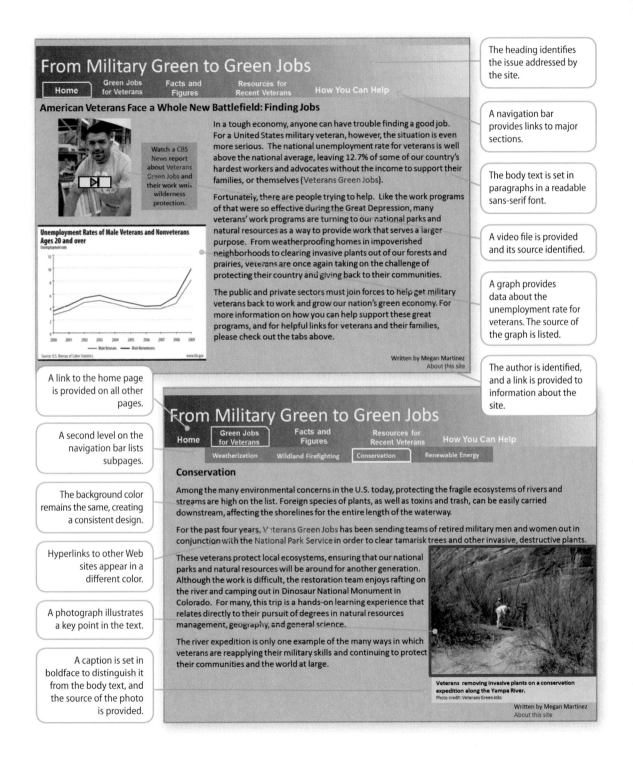

From Military Green to Green Jobs

| Home | Green Jobs for Veterans | Facts and Figures | Resources for Recent Veterans | How You Can Help |

American Veterans Face a Whole New Battlefield: Finding Jobs

Watch a CBS News report about Veterans Green Jobs and their work with wilderness protection.

In a tough economy, anyone can have trouble finding a good job. For a United States military veteran, however, the situation is even more serious. The national unemployment rate for veterans is well above the national average, leaving 12.7% of some of our country's hardest workers and advocates without the income to support their families, or themselves (Veterans Green Jobs).

Fortunately, there are people trying to help. Like the work programs of that were so effective during the Great Depression, many veterans' work programs are turning to our national parks and natural resources as a way to provide work that serves a larger purpose. From weatherproofing homes in impoverished neighborhoods to clearing invasive plants out of our forests and prairies, veterans are once again taking on the challenge of protecting their country and giving back to their communities.

Unemployment Rates of Male Veterans and Nonveterans Ages 20 and over
Unemployment rate

The public and private sectors must join forces to help get military veterans back to work and grow our nation's green economy. For more information on how you can help support these great programs, and for helpful links for veterans and their families, please check out the tabs above.

Source: U.S. Bureau of Labor Statistics
www.bls.gov
— Male Veterans   — Male Nonveterans

Written by Megan Martinez
About this site

From Military Green to Green Jobs

| Home | Green Jobs for Veterans | Facts and Figures | Resources for Recent Veterans | How You Can Help |

| Weatherization | Wildland Firefighting | Conservation | Renewable Energy |

Conservation

Among the many environmental concerns in the U.S. today, protecting the fragile ecosystems of rivers and streams are high on the list. Foreign species of plants, as well as toxins and trash, can be easily carried downstream, affecting the shorelines for the entire length of the waterway.

For the past four years, Veterans Green Jobs has been sending teams of retired military men and women out in conjunction with the National Park Service in order to clear tamarisk trees and other invasive, destructive plants.

These veterans protect local ecosystems, ensuring that our national parks and natural resources will be around for another generation. Although the work is difficult, the restoration team enjoys rafting on the river and camping out in Dinosaur National Monument in Colorado. For many, this trip is a hands-on learning experience that relates directly to their pursuit of degrees in natural resources management, geography, and general science.

The river expedition is only one example of the many ways in which veterans are reapplying their military skills and continuing to protect their communities and the world at large.

Veterans removing invasive plants on a conservation expedition along the Yampa River.
Photo credit: Veterans Green Jobs

Written by Megan Martinez
About this site

Annotations:

The heading identifies the issue addressed by the site.

A navigation bar provides links to major sections.

The body text is set in paragraphs in a readable sans-serif font.

A video file is provided and its source identified.

A graph provides data about the unemployment rate for veterans. The source of the graph is listed.

The author is identified, and a link is provided to information about the site.

A link to the home page is provided on all other pages.

A second level on the navigation bar lists subpages.

The background color remains the same, creating a consistent design.

Hyperlinks to other Web sites appear in a different color.

A photograph illustrates a key point in the text.

A caption is set in boldface to distinguish it from the body text, and the source of the photo is provided.

Checklist
for Developing
Web Pages

✔ Reflect on your writing situation, paying particular attention to your purpose and role as well as your readers' expectations.

✔ Plan your page. Focus on its content and navigation tools.

✔ Design your page. Focus on ensuring that your design is consistent with the design of the site on which it will appear and on the appearance and placement of elements on the page. Pay attention to the following:

- A readable body font designed for on-screen reading (such as 11-point Verdana or Georgia)

- Headings and subheadings formatted in fonts and colors that distinguish them from body text and show the relative importance of levels of headings

- Labels, captions, and pop-up flags (titles) used to help readers understand links and images

- Information presented in brief, readable chunks, using bulleted and numbered lists whenever possible

- Color used to set a mood, highlight information, and help readers understand the function of text and illustrations on the site

- Illustrations placed near the passages that refer to them

- Images kept as small (in kilobytes) as possible, while being clear and easy to see

✔ Create your page. Choose a Web development tool such as Google Sites, a dedicated Web editing program such as Dreamweaver, or a word-processing program.

✔ Put your page online.

✔ Test your page.

✔ Distribute the page's URL.

In Summary: Working with Genres

* **Choose the right genre** (p. 558)

* **Write articles** (p. 560).

* **Create multimodal essays** (p. 565).

* **Create Web pages** (p. 575).

18 Presenting Your Work

Writers are frequently asked to share their work with others. A presentation might accompany a formal written document, such as a report or a proposal, or it might take the place of a written document. Traditionally, presentations have included an oral component — anything from a casual talk to a formal address. Today, however, writers can present their work in the form of a recorded talk, a set of multimedia slides, or a print or digital portfolio. In this chapter, you'll find discussions of strategies for presenting your work in face-to-face and online settings.

How Can I Make an Oral Presentation?

Writers are often asked to make a presentation, lead a discussion, or share their thoughts through speaking rather than writing. The ability to present your ideas through an oral presentation is an important skill that you'll use not only in your courses but also throughout your professional and personal life.

Making an effective oral presentation involves much more than simply taking what you've written and reading it aloud. When you're physically present to share your ideas, your ability to connect personally with your audience is affected by your choice of words, your physical appearance, your use of gestures and other forms of nonverbal communication, your ability to maintain eye contact, and variation in your tone of voice. In addition, your connection with your audience is affected by their ability to follow your line of argument. As you prepare your presentation, remember that most people find it more difficult to understand complex information, ideas, and arguments when they hear them than when they can read them (and reread them). Therefore, be sure to focus on how you can help your readers follow your points and see you as a credible presenter.

Consider Your Purpose, Role, and Audience

When you make an oral presentation, your most important goals are engaging your audience and keeping them interested in your ideas. As you plan your presentation, ask what you want to accomplish, what your audience expects to hear, and how you can balance your purpose with their needs and interests. The answers to these questions will shape everything in your speech from language choices to visual aids.

Narrow Your Scope

It is important to consider how much your audience knows about your topic. With their knowledge and expertise in mind, focus on a few key points and decide how much detail you'll need to provide to help them follow your line of argument. If you have already drafted a written document, use it as the basis for your presentation, but don't try to cover every point and every piece of supporting evidence you've included in your document.

Draw on your thesis statement (see p. 499), reasons and evidence (see p. 502), and conclusions to create a brief overview of your presentation that you can use in your introductory remarks. This "preview statement" will help your audience understand your line of argument and the organization of your presentation right from the start.

Create a Bare-bones Outline

Once you've developed a focus for your presentation and determined its main point and general organization, you can create an outline (see p. 512). It's a good idea to begin with a basic outline that includes the following:

- an opening line that captures the attention of your audience

- a statement of your main point — typically in the form of a thesis statement

- a sentence establishing your credibility and purpose so that your audience can see that you care about and understand the issue, either through personal experience or through research, and that they can trust what you have to say

- two to four key points

- evidence to support your key points

- transition statements to guide your audience through your talk

- a conclusion that reinforces your audience's understanding of the main ideas they should take away from your talk

- a closing line or an invitation to ask questions that makes it clear to your audience that you have finished your presentation

Think about Language

In an oral presentation, you'll use spoken language to connect personally with your audience. Through your choice of words, metaphors, imagery, and turns of speech, you'll engage your listeners in your argument and ideas. Keep your purpose and role in mind as you decide how to address your audience. For example, if you are attempting to solve a problem, your goal might be to engage your audience personally with the problem. You might talk about how the problem affects "us" and ask them to consider what "we" should do to address it.

As you consider your language choices, keep in mind that spoken language is usually more casual than written language. If you adopt the formal tone of your academic research essay, you might sound stiff and unnatural. Remember as well the power of repetition in oral presentations. You'll help your audience follow your line of argument by stating important points more than once and in different ways. Finally, consider the role of emotional appeals in your presentation (see p. 415). To connect personally with your audience and to engage your audience with your issue, you should explore the use of vivid descriptions, surprising statistics, and humor. Don't rely heavily on emotional appeals, however. To maintain your credibility, you'll want to balance emotional appeals with logic by presenting sound reasoning and support for your argument (see p. 416).

Prepare Speaker's Notes

Although many speakers write their presentations word for word, this strategy usually does not produce outstanding results. It's better to develop a set of speaker's notes to prompt yourself as you present your points. Using notes, instead of a word-for-word speech, will force you to speak directly to your listeners. Many seasoned speakers use note cards for their speaker's notes, as they are easy to hold in one hand and are not as distracting as fluttering paper. As you prepare your notes, make sure that they are easy to read so that you can view your next point with a quick glance. Your speaker's notes should include the following information:

- your opening line, written out in full, to get you started in case your mind goes blank because of nervousness
- your preview statement
- any statements that you need to give word for word, such as carefully worded statements about a controversial point or clear descriptions of a complex concept
- your supporting points and reminders of important evidence, including direct quotes, statistics, and names of important people
- transition sentences from one part of the presentation to the next
- memory prompts for any parts of your presentation that you've found yourself forgetting as you practice
- reminders to use a visual aid, such as a chart

Engage with Your Audience

When you give an oral presentation, *how* you say something is almost as important in getting your message across as *what* you say. The following techniques will help you polish your delivery.

- **Maintain eye contact with your audience.** Eye contact communicates that you know your topic and that you care about making sure the audience understands your arguments.

- **Vary the pitch of your voice.** Speaking in a monotone is the fastest way to put your audience to sleep. When you mention a startling statistic, raise your pitch. To demonstrate weight and importance, go to a lower register in your voice. Practice using vocal variety to make sure that it sounds natural.

- **Speak loudly.** You might feel as though you're yelling, but the audience will let you know (by looking surprised) if you are too loud. Speakers rarely are.

- **Articulate every word clearly.** Consonants are often dropped in casual conversation, so try to make them clearer than you would in normal speaking.

- **Slow down.** Most presenters speak too quickly. Slow down your normal rate of speaking to give the audience time to process your words. As you practice, note where you tend to speed up, and add a comment (such as "Slow down!") to your speaker's notes.

View Speaker's Notes

The following speaker's notes are from an oral presentation on the use of steroids by adolescent girls involved in sports.

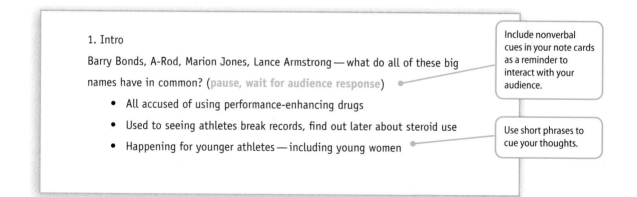

1. Intro

Barry Bonds, A-Rod, Marion Jones, Lance Armstrong — what do all of these big names have in common? (pause, wait for audience response)

- All accused of using performance-enhancing drugs
- Used to seeing athletes break records, find out later about steroid use
- Happening for younger athletes — including young women

Include nonverbal cues in your note cards as a reminder to interact with your audience.

Use short phrases to cue your thoughts.

2. Establish credibility & preview

Use brief reminders about nonverbal communication. Format your nonverbal cues in a different color so you don't accidentally speak them out loud.

- My background as an athlete
- Explain why I care about the topic

SLOW DOWN!

Preview:

Write your preview statement word for word in your notes.

(1) First, I am going to talk about the positive impact that competitive athletics can have on young women.

(2) Then, I'll go over some of the negative consequences of competitive athletics on these young women, including steroid use.

(3) Finally, I want to talk about what parents and coaches can do to help create a positive athletic experience for these young women.

Include your source citations. Refer to your sources to establish your credibility.

3. Positive impact of competitive athletics on young women

- President's Council on Physical Fitness and Exercise — ways sports impact young athletes

For the body:

- Less risk of heart disease and certain cancers as adults
- Improves:
  - Immune system
  - Posture
  - Strength

Use internal transition cues to provide time for you to switch to your next note card as your audience thinks about the point.

  - Flexibility
  - Endurance

Internal transition: Also improves mental health

✔ Determine the presentation's purpose.

✔ Narrow your presentation's scope to between two and four key points.

✔ Write a preview statement.

✔ Choose supporting evidence for your key points.

✔ Create a basic outline of your presentation.

✔ Prepare speaker's notes that you can read easily and quickly.

✔ Consider how the size and physical arrangement of the room will affect your ability to interact with your audience.

✔ Practice your presentation, and ask for feedback from your practice audience.

✔ Arrive early to ensure adequate time for setup.

✔ During the presentation, observe and respond to your audience.

✔ Vary the pitch of your voice, speak loudly, and clearly articulate your words.

Checklist for Preparing and Delivering Oral Presentations

How Can I Create a Multimedia Presentation?

As a student, you've probably seen more than a few multimedia presentations. You've probably also become far too familiar with how easily these kinds of presentations can go badly. If so, you're not alone. Search the Web for phrases such as *death by PowerPoint* and *PowerPoint boredom*, and you'll find thousands of pages that discuss — often quite humorously — efforts to ban the use of programs such as PowerPoint and Keynote.

Fortunately, PowerPoint boredom is a curable condition. Whether you are speaking in front of a group, presenting a recorded talk online, or simply sharing a set of slides, you can create multimedia presentations that engage your audience and might even bring them around to your point of view. With care and planning, you can use multimedia presentation tools to illustrate points using more than spoken words alone, allowing your audience to follow your argument more easily and better understand complex ideas.

Consider Your Context, Audience, Purpose, and Role

During a multimedia presentation, slides containing text or graphics are projected on a screen, and in some cases, audio, video, or animations are played. Multimedia presentations can also include links to the Web and embedded applications, such as spreadsheets. As you consider whether and how you might use multimedia during a presentation, focus in particular on the setting in which your audience will see your presentation. Most often, multimedia presentations are made in person, typically in lecture halls or meeting rooms that are equipped with projection equipment and public address systems. At other times, though, these presentations are given in more intimate settings where the presentation is viewed on a laptop screen or using a portable LCD projector. In some cases, multimedia presentations are created for delivery via the Web, allowing a larger audience to access the presentation. Web-based multimedia presentations can be designed so that the speaker either appears in a smaller video window next to the presentation slides or provides a voice-over for each slide. More often, however, Web-based presentations consist only of the slides, and no audio or video is provided.

A strong multimedia presentation does one of two things. If it is used to accompany an oral presentation in front of a group of listeners, it should highlight your points without stealing the show. If it serves as your only point of contact with your audience — that is, if it will be viewed on a computer, tablet, or smartphone — your presentation needs to stand on its own. In this sense, context — and in particular the setting in which your presentation is delivered and any time limits you might have to work within — has important implications for how you pursue your writing goals and meet your audience's expectations.

Once you understand the context for your presentation, consider how it will shape your efforts to achieve your purpose, adopt your role, and meet the expectations of your audience. If you are giving a talk as you make your presentation, you can use many of the techniques that are used during an oral presentation, such as observing and responding to your audience, varying the pitch and loudness of your voice, using gestures, and establishing eye contact with members of the audience. You can also invite questions and encourage discussion among members of your audience. If you are preparing a presentation that will be viewed on the Web, put yourself in the place of someone who will be encountering your ideas for the first time. Ask yourself what you'd find confusing, surprising, or interesting. Better yet, ask some friends to read a draft of your presentation. Observe their reactions to each slide, and ask them how you might improve the presentation.

Develop Your "Talking Points"

Regardless of the setting in which your presentation will be delivered, you'll need to consider how you'll convey your main point to your audience. Much as you would do with other genres, you'll need to develop a series of key or supporting points and choose evidence to support them. Unlike in written genres, such as articles and multimodal essays, you'll need to make your points quickly. You'll also need to repeat them often enough to get your ideas across clearly, yet not so frequently that you begin to bore your audience. Striking this balance is the key to connecting with your audience. Fortunately, multimedia presentations can make use of some powerful tools for creating that connection.

The distinguishing feature of a multimedia presentation is the wide array of sources you can use to engage with your audience. A presentation on recent changes in education policy, for example, might include video clips in which students, teachers, parents, and community members discuss the effects of those policies or the reasons leading to their development. A presentation on social networking might include links to social-networking sites, a chart illustrating the growth in use of such sites over the past decade, or screenshots showing a range of purposes for which such sites are used.

The sources you choose should support your points or allow you to distinguish your ideas from those advanced by others. If your presentation slides are intended to accompany an oral presentation, your sources should complement rather than compete with what you have to say. You've probably seen more than your fair share of presentations in which speakers have read their slides aloud and offered little or nothing beyond the words on the slide. It is far more effective to use your slides to expand on or illustrate — not simply repeat — what you are saying out loud. If, however, you expect your audience to view your presentation online without a recording of what you are saying, you might create some slides that convey your key points clearly and concisely in writing.

As you choose sources to support your talking points, make sure they will be consistent with any time limits you might face. A video clip might be compelling and highly persuasive, but if it is too long, it will crowd out other points you want to make.

As you might do with a multimodal essay (see p. 565), consider how the differences among various types of sources — such as images, audio clips, video clips, tables, and charts — can help you achieve your purpose. An image projected on a screen while you talk is more likely to complement your words than will a video clip, particularly one that has a sound track. On the other hand, a video clip can convey far more information than can most images. If you are developing a presentation that will be viewed on a computer, tablet, or smartphone, the video clip might be more effective in getting your points across to your audience.

As you decide which sources to include in your presentation, keep in mind the needs, interests, knowledge, experiences, and backgrounds of your audience. Choose sources carefully. Images and video clips that one audience might view without a great deal of concern could be offensive to another. If your subject matter requires exposing your audience to disturbing images or explicit language, as might happen if you are addressing issues such as gun violence or censorship, warn your audience. If you are uncertain about the potential impact of a source, consult your instructor, a librarian, or a friend or classmate who might be similar to the audience you are trying to reach.

Choose Composing Tools

The program you choose to create your multimedia presentation will have a strong effect on its organization and design. Conventional multimedia presentation programs, such as Apple Keynote, Google Slides, Microsoft PowerPoint, and Open-Office Impress, organize presentations as a collection of slides ordered in a linear sequence from a cover slide to a closing slide. If you don't specify a particular layout, these programs use default slides consisting of a heading and a bulleted list. In contrast, a multimedia presentation program such as Prezi (prezi.com) allows you to create "zooming" presentations that can be useful for creative purposes such as digital storytelling, while Capzles (capzles.com) arranges slides along a timeline, which works well when your points have a chronological or sequential structure.

Your choice of composing tool will affect not only how you conceptualize your presentation but also the kinds of multimedia sources you can include and how they will appear. Conventional programs such as PowerPoint offer the greatest flexibility in the types of sources that can be included in a presentation. They also offer a wide range of tools for linking to sites and various types of media on the Web. If you decide to use a less conventional program, however, you need to consider not only that program's capabilities, which might surprise and intrigue your audience, but also its limitations in handling various types of sources.

You'll also find that some multimedia presentation programs provide features that can help you during a presentation. The "presenter view" tools in conventional

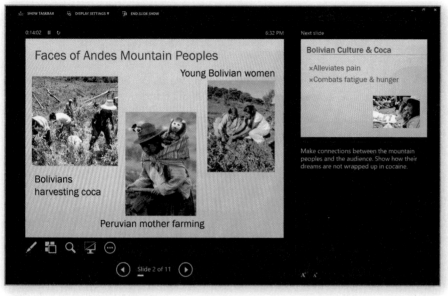

▲ **Presenter view in PowerPoint**

presentation programs allow you to see information that is not projected on the screen, such as notes on the current slide and small images of upcoming slides. These tools can remind you of important ideas that are related to but not displayed on the slide and can help you keep track of where you are in your presentation. Essentially, they serve the same function as the speaker's notes you might use during an oral presentation (see p. 586).

Develop a Consistent Design

Over the past two decades, audiences in settings ranging from business meetings to lecture halls seem to have been subjected to more poorly designed multimedia presentations than there are drops of water in the ocean. Perhaps you, too, have been at some of these presentations. If so, you'll be aware of the benefits of the following design guidelines:

- Choose a color scheme that reflects the purpose and tone of your line of argument. Use bright colors, for example, for a lighthearted topic. Use neutral colors for a serious presentation.
- Be consistent in your choice of fonts, colors, and page layout.

- Use readable fonts, such as 44-point Corbel for headings and 28-point Calibri for body text. Avoid elaborate script fonts, which are often unreadable from a distance, or overly playful fonts like Curlz, which can come across as unprofessional.
- Keep text to a minimum: a general rule is six words per bullet point, six bullet points per slide, and no more than six slides of all text in a row.
- To enhance the readability of slides, use either a light background with dark text or a dark background with light text, and a minimum of text effects (such as shadows or flashing text).
- Use audio, video, and animation with moderation. Generally, clips should run no longer than one minute each.
- Avoid the use of slow or overly complex transitions between slides.
- Avoid the use of distracting sound effects on slides or during slide transitions.

Organize Your Presentation

The organizing pattern (see p. 506) you select for your presentation should help you achieve your purpose and meet the expectations of your readers. It should also be consistent with your line of argument. If you are giving a presentation to an audience, as opposed to creating a presentation that will be read in digital form, you should consider other factors as well, such as your audience's inability to refer back to what you've already presented if they get confused or can't recall something you said earlier. As a result, you might find it useful to summarize key ideas or information at various points in the presentation, to forecast what you'll be talking about in the next part of your presentation, to be open to questions from the audience, and even to ask for questions at particular points.

You can learn more about organizing patterns and strategies for organizing your presentation in Chapter 15.

Practice and Revise Your Presentation

Even experienced presenters find it useful to practice their presentations. They understand how difficult it can be to get everything right the first time. Practicing allows you to ensure that you don't leave out important information and ideas, that the embedded media and links you've included in your presentation display properly and function as expected, and that any animations and other special effects work as intended.

Practicing in front of a group of classmates or friends also allows you to determine whether your overall line of argument makes sense, whether you've organized your reasons and evidence effectively, and whether the sources you've chosen are appropriate. It can also help you learn whether your equipment is working properly and whether your presentation will fit within any time limits you've been given.

Give or Distribute Your Presentation

If you are making a presentation to an audience, you can draw on the same set of techniques used in effective oral presentations, including maintaining eye contact, varying the pitch of your voice, speaking loudly enough to be heard clearly, and slowing down so that your audience can follow your argument (see p. 586). In addition, make sure that you can advance your slides easily — either by using a slide clicker, which is similar to a computer mouse, or by standing close enough to your computer or tablet to advance the slides manually — and that you are facing your audience. In case your equipment fails — for instance, if a laptop loses power or an LCD display fails to work properly — be sure that you have a backup plan. You could bring printouts of your presentation, for example, or create a handout summarizing your points.

If your presentation will be viewed in digital format, make sure that you've removed any notes that you don't want your audience to see; ensure that the format in which you've saved the file can be read on a wide range of computers, tablets, and smartphones; and choose a means of distributing the file. You can distribute a file by placing it on a Web site, uploading it to a blog or social-networking site, attaching it to an e-mail message, sharing it through a service such as DropBox, or saving it on a flash drive and giving it to people you want to view it. If you've uploaded the file, open it and check its appearance. If necessary, revise the presentation, save it to a new file, and replace the file you uploaded. Do the same with files that you plan to attach to e-mail or put on a flash drive.

View a Presentation

The following figures show slides from a multimedia presentation designed by Elizabeth Leontiev, a first-year student who had worked on a writing project that addressed the role of coca leaves and tea in Bolivian daily life.

Title is formatted in a clear, eye-catching font.

Coca Is Not The Enemy

Presented by:
Elizabeth Leontiev

The name of the presenter is clearly identified.

Fonts are large and easy to read.

Faces of Andes Mountain Peoples

Captions for each photograph help the audience understand the issue.

Photographs personalize the presentation.

Bolivians harvesting coca

Peruvian mother farming

Bolivian women harvesting

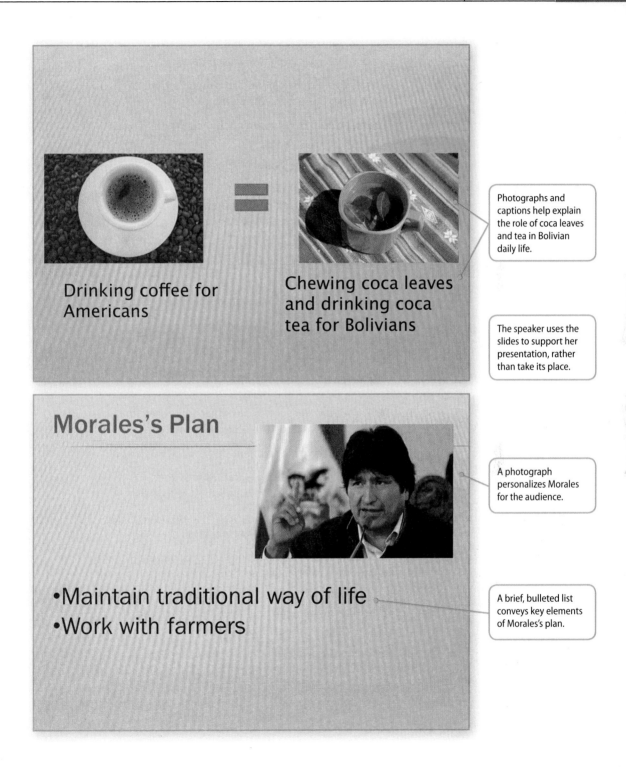

Drinking coffee for Americans

Chewing coca leaves and drinking coca tea for Bolivians

Photographs and captions help explain the role of coca leaves and tea in Bolivian daily life.

The speaker uses the slides to support her presentation, rather than take its place.

Morales's Plan

A photograph personalizes Morales for the audience.

- Maintain traditional way of life
- Work with farmers

A brief, bulleted list conveys key elements of Morales's plan.

Checklist for Creating Multimedia Presentations

✔ Consider your purpose, role, audience, and context.

✔ Create an outline of your presentation, focusing on the line of argument you want to present to your audience.

✔ Identify points that would benefit from multimedia illustrations.

✔ Collect and work with sources that will illustrate or support those points.

✔ Choose a multimedia presentation program that is consistent with your context, purpose, role, and audience.

✔ Follow effective design principles regarding color scheme, fonts, and page layout, paying particular attention to the following:

- Consistent use of fonts, colors, shading, borders, and rules
- Readable fonts for headings and subheadings
- A readable body font designed for viewing on a screen
- If used, transitions between pages (dissolves, page flips) that are quick and not distracting
- If used, background images and sounds that are chosen to enhance rather than obscure the elements on each page

✔ Use multimedia elements in moderation.

✔ To ensure that your slides are readable and well designed, preview your presentation on a screen similar in size to the one you will be using during your talk.

✔ Face your audience as you make your presentation.

✔ Use multimedia elements to advance your line of argument, pointing out important information and illustrations on slides.

✔ Create a backup plan in case your equipment fails. Consider using slide printouts or a handout as a backup.

✔ If you are distributing your presentation in digital format, ensure that it displays properly on computers, tablets, and smartphones.

How Can I Work on a Group Presentation?

Group presentations have become common not only in writing and writing-intensive classes but also in business, nonprofit, and government settings. The extent of collaboration can vary widely: each member of the group might be assigned to work on a different section of the presentation, or the whole group might work together — electronically or in person — to plan, design, draft, polish, revise, and edit the entire presentation. To prepare to work collaboratively on a group presentation, become familiar with the purposes, processes, and potential pitfalls of working with a team. Learning how to work together while you are a student can help you succeed on projects long after you've completed your degree.

Working Together: Develop Guidelines for Group Work

Most writers can look back at a group project and find something they didn't like about the experience. They might have been in a group dominated by an ineffective leader. They might have had to do far more than their fair share on a project. At the last minute, they might have been left in the lurch by someone who failed to deliver a critical part of the project. Whatever the reason, some writers prefer to work alone. Yet group work can be productive and satisfying, and most experienced writers can point to a wide range of situations in which working with other writers significantly improved their work on a writing project.

To get ready to work with other writers, reflect on your experiences with group work. Then, working with the members of your group, develop a set of guidelines that would improve the quality of group work. To carry out this activity, follow these steps:

1. Individually, spend five minutes brainstorming (see p. 32) or freewriting (see p. 33) about your experiences with collaborative work. List both positive and negative experiences.

2. As a group, discuss your experiences. Each person should note the advantages and disadvantages of collaborative work.

3. As a group, identify the most significant challenges to working together effectively.

4. As a group, create a list of guidelines that would address these challenges.

Once you've completed the activity, share your guidelines with other groups in the class. As a class, create a list of guidelines for collaborative work in your course.

Understand the Purposes of Working in a Group

Asking a group to work together reflects a set of beliefs about the value of collaboration. In corporate settings, for example, working together might be a means not only of ensuring that a project results in useful work but also of building a sense of togetherness and commitment among team members. In an academic setting, a group project allows students to carry out a project that a single student would find difficult to produce alone, helps them learn more about a subject, and familiarizes them with the collaborative processes they might encounter in their professional lives. In this sense, collaborating on a project might be as important as — or even more important than — making a presentation or producing a document.

Understand Potential Problems and Develop Solutions

Recognizing — and taking steps to avoid — potential pitfalls can increase the likelihood that a collaborative project will succeed. Common problems encountered during group work range from individual concerns about participating in a group to behaviors that undermine the group's effectiveness. If you want to collaborate successfully, be aware of these problems and learn how solve them.

- **Some people prefer to work alone,** and they make those feelings all too clear, often to the point of insulting their classmates. Remind such people of the reasons the group is working together and the danger their attitude poses to the long-term success of the project.

- **Some people worry about losing a sense of individual worth.** Assure them that their contributions not only are important but also will be recognized as such — if not formally, then by other members of the group.

- **Some individuals will try to dominate a group,** perhaps believing that the project will fail unless they take control. To avoid this problem, make sure at the outset of the project that everyone's ideas are heard and respected, and explain that developing a plan for the project is not a process of arguing for the superiority of a particular set of ideas so much as it is the synthesis of useful ideas.

- **Some members will find it difficult to schedule or attend group meetings.** Ensure that meeting times and locations accommodate everyone's needs. If you can't do so, have the group discuss the problem with the instructor.

- **Some members of a group will use meeting time unproductively** — at least in the eyes of other members of the group. This can cause problems, particularly when it is difficult to find time to meet or if meeting time is limited. To address this issue, be sure the group establishes and sticks to an agenda for each meeting.

- **Some group members will want to work only on what they feel capable of doing well.** In nonacademic settings, where a strong emphasis is often placed on the effectiveness of the final document, this is usually not a problem. In academic settings, however, where the goals of most collaborative projects include learning new skills and acquiring new knowledge, it is important that all members of a group take on new challenges.

- **Some members of a group won't contribute as much as others — and some won't contribute at all.** In collaborative projects for a class, you'll find that some members refuse to participate. Perhaps they assume that they can't make much of a contribution, or perhaps they're trying to save time by not participating. Regardless of their intentions, their lack of participation causes hurt feelings and might affect the overall quality of the project. To avoid these problems, establish ground rules about how to address unequal participation.

- **Some members of a group will resent the extra time required to coordinate work on a project.** Remind these people of the reasons for working together and the benefits of doing so.

- **As the group works on a project, disagreements will arise.** As you develop ground rules for working together, consider how you'll address disagreements. Strategies include voting, discussing until consensus emerges, and seeking guidance from an instructor or a supervisor.

Establish Ground Rules

At the beginning of a project, spend time discussing potential difficulties and establishing ground rules. These can include guidelines for

Working Together: Establish Ground Rules for a Group Project

In your writer's notebook, develop a set of ground rules for your group by responding to the following prompts. Share your responses with the members of your group, and agree on a formal set of rules.

1. Meetings will be held at [location] on [dates and times].

2. Discussions will be [moderated by the same person at each meeting, moderated by a different person at each meeting, unmoderated], and notes will be taken by [the same person at each meeting, a different person at each meeting].

3. When disagreements arise, they will be resolved by _____.

4. The following members of the group will take the lead on the following activities: [list names and activities].

5. To ensure equitable contributions by each group member, we will _____.

6. Group members who do not contribute equitably will face the following consequences: [list consequences].

7. Group members who drop out of the project will face the following consequences: [list consequences].

- selecting meeting times and places
- conducting discussions
- resolving disputes
- determining individual contributions to the project
- ensuring equitable contributions from group members
- defining the consequences for inadequate participation

Ground rules can take various forms, ranging from an informal agreement among group members to a detailed statement signed by each member.

Create a Plan

Once ground rules have been established, develop a plan for completing the project. Plans do not have to be highly detailed, particularly at the beginning stage of the project. However, they should define the overall goals of the project and identify key steps that must be taken to achieve those goals. An effective plan will define deadlines for the completion of each step, identify who is responsible for specific activities associated with completing a given step, and suggest strategies for carrying out those activities.

How Can I Develop a Portfolio?

Portfolios are collections of written documents, reflections on the development of those documents, and related materials such as sources, notes, outlines, and brainstorming. They are typically, but not always, distributed via the Web. Widely used digital portfolio tools (often referred to as e-Portfolios) include the Blackboard e-Portfolio tool (available as part of the Blackboard Learn course management system), the Bedford/St. Martin's e-Portfolio tool (bedfordstmartins.com/eportfolio), and the Writing Studio's free e-Portfolio tool (writing.colostate.edu). Some writers use programs such as PowerPoint or Dreamweaver to create portfolios that can be presented on a flash drive or some other form of offline storage. Still others use free Web tools such as Google Sites (sites.google.com) and Zeeblio (zeeblio.com) to create Web sites to present their portfolios.

Most of these tools allow you to add documents, develop a table of contents, and choose a design template. Some tools, such as Google Sites, Zeeblio, and the Writing Studio's e-Portfolio tool, allow you to make a wide range of design choices, such as choosing color and font schemes, designing custom page banners, and editing the

HTML code on individual pages. As you create a portfolio, you should consider a number of issues that affect design, including your purpose for sharing your work and the expectations of your readers.

Consider Your Writing Situation

Portfolios are sometimes created to showcase a writer's work, as might happen when you are seeking a job or wish to share your work with friends and family. Portfolios are also created in response to class assignments and institutional assessment plans. Some colleges and universities, for example, ask students to create portfolios so that they can measure the overall writing ability of their students.

Readers expect your portfolio to clearly communicate its purpose and content as well as to make it easy to locate and view the documents you've provided. They also expect you to make it easy to get in touch with you. As a result, a well-designed portfolio should provide a table of contents (or something similar) and your contact information. In an e-Portfolio, this information might consist of a navigation menu or a set of links on the main page. In a print portfolio, this information might appear on the first or second page.

Select Your Materials

Your choice of materials will depend on your purpose, your readers' expectations, and the context in which your portfolio will be read. If you are responding to an assignment for a writing course, pay particular attention to the specific requirements of the assignment. Some instructors, for example, will want you to include not only the final draft of an assignment but also your rough drafts, outlines, notes, sources, and any feedback

Working Together: Create a Plan for a Group Project

In your writer's notebook, develop a plan to complete your project. Then share your plan with the members of your group, and develop a group plan.

1. The overall goal of this project is _____.

2. This project will require completing the following steps: [Fill out this information for each step.]

Step:

_____

Deadline:

_____

Ideas for completing the step:

_____

Responsible group member:

_____

you've received from classmates. Your instructor might also ask you to include a reflective statement that looks back over your work and writing process. This often takes the form of a letter or brief essay. In an e-Portfolio, you could also share your reflections through video or audio clips. If you are highlighting your writing skills for a potential employer, you might want to show only your best work — or you might want to show two or three drafts that indicate how you revised and improved a draft over time.

A writing portfolio typically includes some of or all the following materials:

- your contact information (e-mail address, phone number, and/or mailing address)
- an introduction to the portfolio that addresses its purpose and contents
- a reflection on the documents in the portfolio, on your growth as a writer, and on your goals as a writer
- final drafts of documents
- rough drafts of documents, often with comments from instructors or other writers
- sources used in a particular writing project, along with any notes or source evaluations
- planning notes, freewriting and other forms of idea generation, and maps or outlines
- your comments on the work of other writers
- grades and comments from instructors

Choose a Publishing Tool

As with other types of documents, your choice of tools for composing and publishing your portfolio will affect not only how you present your materials but also your understanding of what is possible to present. If you create a print portfolio, you can collect and bind your work, place all your work in a folder, or simply clip it together and share it with a reader. If some of your work turns out to be difficult to include in a print portfolio, as might be the case with note cards or pages in a journal, you might photograph or scan them, print them, and include them with the rest of your work. If you create an e-Portfolio, you have many other options. You can distribute an e-Portfolio as

- a single word-processing or PDF file
- a collection of word-processing or PDF documents
- a PowerPoint or Keynote presentation

- a Web site or blog
- work in an e-Portfolio tool such as the Bedford e-Portfolio

Each of these tools offers possibilities quite different from what you can accomplish with a print portfolio. Even more important, the possibilities associated with each of these tools — and the experiences each tool can offer your readers — differ strikingly. Some tools will allow you to use video and audio clips, while others will give you more control over the kind of navigation menus and links you can create. Some programs, such as PowerPoint and Keynote, will make it relatively easy to use page transitions and animations or to switch easily from one color scheme to another. Your decisions about the tool you use to create your portfolio should reflect your purpose and an awareness of a particular tool's capabilities.

Organize and Design Your Portfolio

The organization and design of your portfolio should reflect your writing goals and your readers' expectations. If you are submitting work for an assessment portfolio that your college has required you to complete, you might have few options when it comes to organization and design. You'll simply be following a template. If you are working on a class project, you might have more freedom, but you'll certainly want to review the assignment carefully for guidance about organization and design. In contrast, if you are working on a personal portfolio, your decisions will be guided by your goals for the project and your awareness of your readers' needs and interests, the time they are likely to put into reading your work, and their technological sophistication. It might be tempting, for example, to upload a folder filled with HTML files to DropBox, iCloud, or SkyDrive, but you should do so only if you are sure your readers will be able to access the files and open them with a Web browser.

As you organize and design your portfolio, keep the principles of simplicity and consistency in mind. You should choose a single organizing pattern, such as chronology or definition (see Chapter 15), that allows you to accomplish your goals and that your readers will find reasonable. You should also develop a consistent look and feel for your portfolio, focusing in particular on issues such as color and font scheme, page layout, and navigation tools. It is likely, of course, that the individual documents in your portfolio will have their own distinctive designs. Readers will expect this, and if the design of these documents is essential to their effect you should not redesign them. However, if you are working with a set of essays in which your design decisions are less important than what you've written, you might consider reformatting them so that they follow the design you've chosen for the portfolio as a whole.

You should also spend some time thinking about how your readers will work with your portfolio. If you are creating a print portfolio, you might use a table of contents to help readers see how your portfolio is organized. You might also attach colored tabs to pages to help readers find the start of each document. If you are creating an e-Portfolio, you might think about providing navigation tools, such as tables of contents and menus, and about using hyperlinks to help readers move from one part of the e-Portfolio to another. (See p. 580 to learn more about hyperlinks.)

Your design decisions should help your readers work easily and quickly with the materials you've included in your portfolio. In general, simple, uncluttered designs that use readable fonts and consistent colors will allow your readers to view your portfolio without distraction.

Introduce and Reflect on Your Work

Most portfolios provide you with an opportunity to introduce your work. Your introduction should provide a framework within which your readers can understand your work. By focusing on particular issues, such as your desire to address the needs of your audience or your ability to use sources effectively, you can direct your readers' attention to areas in which you demonstrate strengths as a writer. Similarly, your introduction can direct your readers' attention to areas in which you hope to improve, allowing them to offer feedback and advice that might help you become a stronger writer.

Reflections are often included with a portfolio, and in particular in portfolios that are assigned in a writing class. If you are working on a class portfolio, be sure to review your portfolio assignment for guidance on reflection. Generally, it is useful to set aside time to write about changes in your composing processes and your growth as a writer. Your reflections can help you decide how you might share your development as a writer with your readers.

It is also a good idea to consider the strengths and weaknesses demonstrated by the materials you've included in your portfolio. Describe the areas in which you are strong and the areas in which you could improve. Then look for evidence from your materials, and either quote it or provide a link to it in your reflective statement. As in other types of writing, providing evidence to support your conclusions will increase the effectiveness of your reflections.

View Pages from a Portfolio

The following portfolio was created by a first-year writing student who wanted to highlight his best work over the course of two semesters of writing classes.

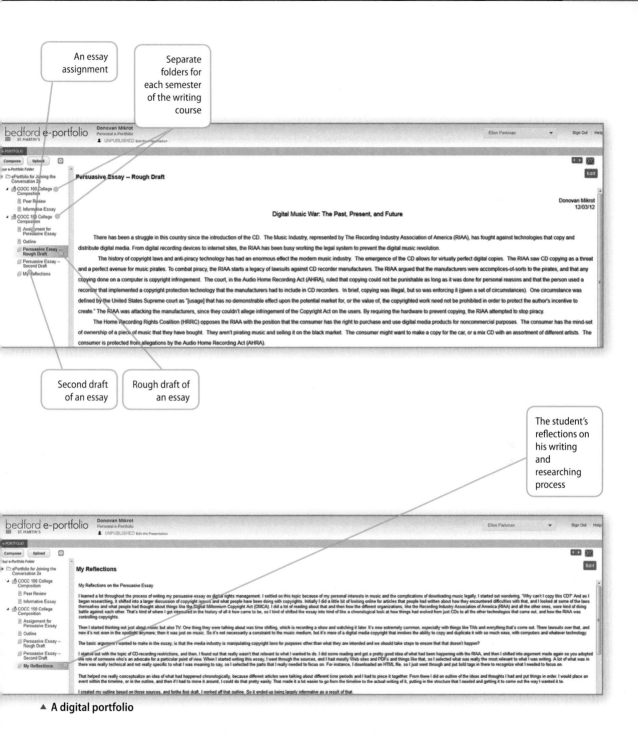

An essay assignment

Separate folders for each semester of the writing course

Second draft of an essay

Rough draft of an essay

The student's reflections on his writing and researching process

Persuasive Essay -- Rough Draft

Edit

Donovan Mikrot
12/03/12

Digital Music War: The Past, Present, and Future

There has been a struggle in this country since the introduction of the CD. The Music Industry, represented by The Recording Industry Association of America (RIAA), has fought against technologies that copy and distribute digital media. From digital recording devices to internet sites, the RIAA has been busy working the legal system to prevent the digital music revolution.

The history of copyright laws and anti-piracy technology has had an enormous effect the modern music industry. The emergence of the CD allows for virtually perfect digital copies. The RIAA saw CD copying as a threat and a perfect avenue for music pirates. To combat piracy, the RIAA starts a legacy of lawsuits against CD recorder manufacturers. The RIAA argued that the manufacturers were accomplices-of-sorts to the pirates, and that any copying done on a computer is copyright infringement. The court, in the Audio Home Recording Act (AHRA), ruled that copying could not be punishable as long as it was done for personal reasons and that the person used a recorder that implemented a copyright protection technology that the manufacturers had to include in CD recorders. In brief, copying was illegal, but so was enforcing it (given a set of circumstances). One circumstance was defined by the United States Supreme court as "[usage] that has no demonstrable effect upon the potential market for, or the value of, the copyrighted work need not be prohibited in order to protect the author's incentive to create." The RIAA was attacking the manufacturers, since they couldn't allege infringement of the Copyright Act on the users. By requiring the hardware to prevent copying, the RIAA attempted to stop piracy.

The Home Recording Rights Coalition (HRRC) opposes the RIAA with the position that the consumer has the right to purchase and use digital media products for noncommercial purposes. The consumer has the mind-set of ownership of a piece of music that they have bought. They aren't pirating music and selling it on the black market. The consumer might want to make a copy for the car, or a mix CD with an assortment of different artists. The consumer is protected from allegations by the Audio Home Recording Act (AHRA).

My Reflections

Edit

My Reflections on the Persuasive Essay

I learned a lot throughout the process of writing my persuasive essay on digital rights management. I settled on this topic because of my personal interests in music and the complications of downloading music legally. I started out wondering, "Why can't I copy this CD?" And as I began researching, it shifted into a larger discussion of copyright issues and what people have been doing with copyrights. Initially I did a little bit of looking online for articles that people had written about how they encountered difficulties with that, and I looked at some of the laws themselves and what people had thought about things like the Digital Millennium Copyright Act (DMCA). I did a lot of reading about that and then how the different organizations, like the Recording Industry Association of America (RIAA) and all the other ones, were kind of doing battle against each other. That's kind of where I got interested in the history of all it how came to be, so I kind of shifted the essay into kind of like a chronological look at how things had evolved from just CDs to all the other technologies that came out, and how the RIAA was controlling copyrights.

Then I started thinking not just about music but also TV. One thing they were talking about was time shifting, which is recording a show and watching it later. It's now extremely common, especially with things like TiVo and everything that's come out. There lawsuits over that, and now it's not even in the spotlight anymore; then it was just on music. So it's not necessarily a constraint to the music medium, but it's more of a digital media copyright that involves the ability to copy and duplicate it with so much ease, with computers and whatever technology.

The basic argument I wanted to make in the essay, is that the media industry is manipulating copyright laws for purposes other than what they are intended and we should take steps to ensure that that doesn't happen?

I started out with the topic of CD-recording restrictions, and then, I found out that really wasn't that relevant to what I wanted to do. I did some reading and got a pretty good idea of what had been happening with the RIAA, and then I shifted into argument mode again so you adopted the role of someone who's an advocate for a particular point of view. When I started writing this essay, I went through the sources, and I had mostly Web sites and PDFs and things like that, so I selected what was really the most relevant to what I was writing. A lot of what was in there was really technical and not really specific to what I was meaning to say, so I selected the parts that I really needed to focus on. For instance, I downloaded an HTML file, so I just went through and put bold tags in there to recognize what I needed to focus on.

That helped me really conceptualize an idea of what had happened chronologically, because different articles were talking about different time periods and I had to piece it together. From there I did an outline of the ideas and thoughts I had and put things in order. I would place an event within the timeline, or in the outline, and then if I had to move it around, I could do that pretty easily. That made it a lot easier to go from the timeline to the actual writing of it, putting in the structure that I needed and getting it to come out the way I wanted to be.

I created my outline based on those sources, and forthe first draft, I worked off that outline. So it ended up being largely informative as a result of that.

▲ **A digital portfolio**

Checklist for Developing Portfolios

✔ Reflect on your writing situation, paying particular attention to the purposes of the portfolio, your readers' expectations, and the context in which your portfolio will be read.

✔ Select materials for your portfolio.

✔ Choose a tool to compose and publish your portfolio.

✔ Choose an organizing pattern for your portfolio.

✔ Develop a simple, consistent design for your portfolio. Pay particular attention to

- Font scheme

- Color scheme

- Page layout

- Navigation tools

✔ Create an introduction that calls attention to particular aspects of your portfolio.

✔ Reflect on the materials presented in your portfolio, calling attention to key issues and offering evidence to support your conclusions.

In Summary: Presenting Your Work

✴ **Make oral presentations** (p. 584).

✴ **Create multimedia presentations** (p. 589).

✴ **Work on group presentations** (p. 599).

✴ **Develop a portfolio** (p. 602).

19 Using Sources Effectively

Using evidence from sources can strengthen your document and show how knowledgeable you've become about the conversation you're joining. In this chapter, you'll learn how to integrate sources into your document and how to work with numerical information, images, audio, and video.

Much of the information in this chapter is based on MLA style, which is commonly used in the humanities. See Chapter 22 for guidelines on APA style, which is used in many social sciences.

How Can I Use Sources to Accomplish My Purposes as a Writer?

Your sources can help you introduce ideas, contrast the ideas of other authors with your own, provide evidence for your points, align yourself with an authority, define concepts, illustrate processes, clarify statements, set a mood, provide examples, and qualify or amplify a point. You can present information from sources in several ways:

- as a quotation, paraphrase, or summary
- as numerical information
- as illustrations such as images, audio, video, and animations

As you draft your document, consider how your use of sources might lead your readers to view your issue in terms that are most favorable to your purposes. By selecting source information carefully, you can make your points more directly than you might want to make them in your own words. Calling opponents of a proposal "inflexible" and "pig-headed," for example, might signal your biases too strongly. Quoting someone who uses those terms, however, allows you to get the point across without undermining an otherwise even and balanced tone.

The following are some of the most effective ways to use information, ideas, and arguments from sources as you contribute to a written conversation about a subject.

Introduce a Point

You can use a quotation, paraphrase, or summary to introduce a point to your readers.

Quotation Used to Introduce a Point

"When I came around the corner, a black bear was standing in the middle of the trail," said Joan Gibson, an avid hiker. "We stared at each other for a moment, wondering who would make the first move. Then the bear looked off to the right and shambled up the mountain. I guess I wasn't worth the trouble." Joan Gibson's story, like those of most hikers who encounter bears in the woods, ends happily. But the growing encroachment of humans on rural areas once left largely to wildlife is causing difficulties not only for people who enjoy spending time in the wide-open spaces but also for the animals that make those spaces their home.

Paraphrase Used to Introduce a Point

A *New York Times* article recently reported that human-bear encounters in Yosemite National Park, which had been on the decline during most of the last decade, have more than doubled in the past year (Spiegel A4). Although no humans have been injured and only one incident resulted in a decision to destroy a bear, park officials point to the uptick in encounters as a warning sign that . . .

Your choice of a quotation or paraphrase will frame the point you want to make, calling your readers' attention to a specific aspect of an idea or argument and laying the groundwork for a response. Think about how the following quotation leads readers to view a public debate about education reform as a battle between reformers and an entrenched teachers union.

> "The teachers union has balked at even the most reasonable proposals for school reform," said Mary Sweeney, press secretary for Save Our Schools, which has sponsored a referendum on the November ballot calling for funding for their voucher plan. "We believe the November election will send a wake-up call about the need to rethink their obstructionist behaviors."
>
> If Sweeney and supporters of Referendum D are successful, the educational landscape in . . .

Phrases such as "balked at even the most reasonable proposals" and "their obstructionist behaviors" place the blame for the problem on the teachers union.

In contrast, note how the following quotation frames the debate as a question of how best to spend scarce education funds.

> "In the past decade, state and local funding of public education in real dollars has declined by 7.2 percent," said Jeffrey Allister, state chair of the governor's Special Commission on Education Reform. "Referendum D, if passed, would further erode that funding by shifting state dollars to private schools." As the state considers the merits of Referendum D, which would institute the first statewide voucher program in the United States, opponents of the measure have . . .

Phrases such as "funding of public education in real dollars has declined" and "further erode that funding" call attention to the financial challenges faced by schools.

Contrast Ideas

When you want to indicate that disagreement exists on a subject, you can use source information to illustrate the nature and intensity of the disagreement. The following example uses partial quotations (see p. 617) to highlight differences in proposed solutions to a problem.

Solutions to the state's higher education funding shortfall range from traditional approaches, such as raising taxes, to more radical solutions, among them privatizing state colleges and universities. Advocates of increased taxes, such as Page Richards of the Higher Education Coalition, argue that declines in state funding of higher education "must be reversed immediately or we will find ourselves in a situation where we are closing rural community colleges and only the wealthiest among us will have access to the best education" (A4). Those in favor of privatizing higher education suggest, however, that free-market approaches will ultimately bring about "a fairer situation in which the poor, many of whom have no interest in higher education, are no longer asked to subsidize higher and higher faculty salaries and larger football stadiums" (Pieters 23).

Base your choices about how to contrast ideas on the clarity and length of your sources and on the effects you hope to achieve. If you want to express complex ideas as concisely as possible, you might use paraphrase and summary. If you want to convey the emotional qualities of an author's position on a subject, use quotations.

Provide Evidence

Documents that consist of a series of unsupported assertions amount to little more than a request for the reader's trust. Even when the writer is eminently trustworthy, most readers find such documents easy to dismiss. In contrast, providing evidence to support your assertions increases the likelihood that your readers will accept your main point. Note the differences between the following passages.

Unsupported Assertion

> No evidence is provided to support the writer's assertion.

Given a choice between two products of comparable quality, reputation, and cost, American consumers are far more likely to purchase goods that use environmentally friendly packaging. Encouraging the use of such packaging is a good idea for America.

Supported Assertion

> Summaries of the results of two studies provide evidence for the assertion made in the first sentence.

Given a choice between two products of comparable quality, reputation, and cost, American consumers are far more likely to purchase goods that use environmentally friendly packaging. A recent study by the High Plains Research Institute found that the shelf life of several biodegradable plastics not only exceeded the shelf life of the products they were used to package but also cost less to produce (Chen and Lohann 33). In addition, a study by the Consumer Products Institute found that, when made aware that products were packaged in environmentally friendly materials, consumers were more likely to buy those products (271).

Similarly, visual sources can lend support to an assertion. An assertion about the unintended consequences of military action, for example, might be accompanied by a photograph of a war-torn street or a wounded child.

Align Yourself with an Authority

Aligning yourself with an authority — such as a subject-matter expert, a scientist, a politician, or a religious figure — allows you to borrow someone else's credibility and status. Start by making an assertion, and follow it with supporting information from a source, such as a quotation, paraphrase, or summary.

> Although voice recognition appears to be a promising technology, challenges associated with vocabulary, homonyms, and accents have slowed its widespread implementation. "The computer right now can do a very good job of voice recognition," said Bill Gates, cofounder and chairman of Microsoft Corporation (59). "It certainly will re-define the way we think of the machines when we have that voice input" (Gates 59).

Define a Concept, Illustrate a Process, or Clarify a Statement

Writers commonly turn to information from sources when that information is clearer and more concise than what they might write themselves. For example, to define a concept, you might quote or paraphrase a dictionary or an encyclopedia. To help readers understand a complex process, such as the steps involved in cellular respiration, you might use an illustration.

Writers also use information from sources to clarify their statements. A writer might explain a point by providing examples from sources or by using quotations or paraphrases to back up an assertion.

> Studies have found connections between weight loss and coffee intake. This doesn't mean that drinking a couple of cups of coffee each day leads to weight loss. However, three recent studies reported that individuals who increased their coffee intake from fewer than three cups to more than eight cups of coffee per day experienced weight losses of up to 7% over a two-month period (Chang; Johnson and Salazar; Neiman). "It may be that increased caffeine intake led to a higher metabolic level, which in turn

led to weight loss," noted John Chang, a senior researcher at the Centers for Disease Control. "Or it might be that drinking so much coffee depressed participants' appetites" (232).

Set a Mood

You can also choose quotations and illustrations with an eye toward establishing an overall mood for your readers. The emotional impact of images of a celebration at a sporting event, an expression of grief at a funeral, or a calming mountain vista can lead your readers to react in specific ways to your document. Similarly, a striking quote, such as "The screams of pain coming out of that room will stay with me as long as I live," can evoke a particular mood in your readers.

Provide an Example

It's often better to *show* with an example than to *tell* with a general description. Examples provide concrete evidence in your document. Featured writer Caitlin Guariglia uses an example from a well-known film to illustrate a point in her essay about her family's relationship with food.

> And the obsession with eating! My grandmother feeds us constantly. My dad and I always laugh at that scene in *Goodfellas* where the mobsters show up at two in the morning after killing someone, and one mobster's mother whips up a full pasta meal for them. We know that my grandmother would do the same thing: "Are you hungry? Here, sit, eat!" Grandma holds interventions over pasta. If she is unhappy with something someone in the family is doing, she invites everyone over for pasta, and we hash it out together.

Amplify or Qualify a Point

You can use amplification to expand the scope of a point. In her analytical essay, featured writer Ali Bizzul uses information from a source to broaden her discussion of the dangers football players face when they add bulk.

> NFL offensive linemen who weigh less than 300 pounds are often described as "undersized," so it's no surprise that young football players are getting the message that bigger is better — and bulking up. A study of high school linemen in Iowa showed that 45% were overweight and 9% were severely obese by adult standards; in comparison, only 18% of other young males were overweight. Even more troubling, a

study in Michigan revealed that among football players from ages 9 to 14, 45% could be considered overweight or obese (as cited in Popke, 2008).

Qualifications, in contrast, allow you to narrow the scope of a statement, reducing the possibility that your readers might misunderstand your meaning. Ali Bizzul makes it clear that deaths related to weight gain are a rare occurrence in football.

Although such fatalities are unusual, a growing number of doctors believe that use of dietary supplements increases the risk of heatstroke among football players.

How Can I Integrate Sources into My Draft?

You can integrate information, ideas, and arguments from sources into your draft by quoting, paraphrasing, summarizing, presenting numerical information, and using illustrations. As you do so, be sure to distinguish your ideas and information from those found in your sources.

Identify Your Sources

You should identify the sources of information in your document for several reasons. First, doing so fulfills your obligation to document your sources. Second, it allows you (and your readers) to recognize the boundaries between your ideas and those borrowed from sources. Third, it can help you strengthen your document by calling attention to the qualifications or experiences of the person whose ideas you are incorporating.

USE ATTRIBUTIONS AND IN-TEXT CITATIONS

Whenever you quote, paraphrase, or summarize, distinguish between your ideas and the information you obtained from your sources by using attributions — brief comments such as "according to" or "as the author points out" — to alert your readers that the point is not your own.

Writers who use the MLA or APA documentation system also provide citations — or acknowledgments of source information — within the text of their documents to indicate where borrowed material ends. These citations, in turn, refer readers to a list of works cited or a list of references at the end of the document.

Note the following examples, which use attributions and in-text citations.

Attributions identify the author of the quotations.

MLA Style

Pamela Coke argues, "Education reform is the best solution for fixing our public schools" (22).

"Education reform is the best solution for fixing our public schools" (Coke 22).

MLA-style in-text citations include the author's name and exact page reference.

APA Style

Pamela Coke (2008) has argued, "Education reform is the best solution for fixing our public schools" (p. 22).

"Education reform is the best solution for fixing our public schools" (Coke, 2008, p. 22).

APA-style in-text citations include the author's name, publication date, and exact page reference.

When you acknowledge material you've borrowed from sources, try to vary the wording of your attributions. Be aware, however, that the verbs in attributions can convey important shades of meaning. For example, saying that someone "alleged" something is quite different from saying that someone "confirmed" something. The form your attributions take will depend on your use of citation style. MLA recommends present tense ("the author points out"), while APA recommends past tense ("the author pointed out") or present perfect tense ("the author has explained").

Some Common Attributions

according to	claims	expresses	reports
acknowledges	comments	inquires	says
affirms	confirms	interprets	states
alleges	declares	muses	suggests
asks	denies	notes	thinks
asserts	describes	observes	wonders
assumes	disputes	points out	writes
believes	emphasizes	remarks	

You can learn more about text citations in Chapter 21 (MLA style) and Chapter 22 (APA style).

PROVIDE A CONTEXT

Skilled writers know the importance of providing a context for the source information they include in their documents. It's not enough to simply put text within two quotation marks and move on. Such "orphan quotations" — quotations dropped into a paragraph without any introduction — are confusing. Worse, paraphrases and summaries inserted without context can easily be mistaken for plagiarism.

To provide a clear context for your source information, establish why the quotation, paraphrase, or summary is reliable by identifying the source's credentials. In addition, indicate how it relates to your main idea and what it contributes to the point you are making. If you don't, readers will wonder why it's there.

> However, Wechsler et al. (2003) analyzed trends at schools using social norms marketing and revealed that the campaigns did not necessarily decrease student drinking; in some cases, schools even reported higher alcohol consumption, according to seven criteria that measured whether students drank, how much, and how often. The team, from the Harvard School of Public Health's College Alcohol Study, suggested that because social norms marketing was first developed at a small school that wasn't very diverse, it might not be as suitable for schools with many different kinds of people. As the researchers explained, "Individual students' drinking behaviors align more closely to the drinking behaviors of their immediate social group rather than to the overall student population at a given school" (p. 492).

Description of the findings

Attribution identifies the source as experts.

The writer follows APA style; parenthetical citation identifies the page number where the quotation was found.

Quote Strategically

A well-chosen quotation can have a powerful impact on your readers' perception of your main point and on the overall quality of your document. Quotations can also add a sense of immediacy by bringing in the voice of someone who has been affected by a subject or can lend a sense of authority to your document by conveying the words of an expert. Quotations can range in form from brief partial quotations to extended block quotations. As you integrate quotations, you might need to modify them to suit your purpose and to fit the flow of your sentences. When you do, be careful to punctuate them properly.

USE PARTIAL, COMPLETE, OR BLOCK QUOTATIONS

Quotations can be parts of sentences (partial), whole sentences (complete), or long passages (block). When you choose one type of quotation over another, consider the length and complexity of the passage as well as the obligation to convey ideas and information fairly.

Partial quotations can be a single word, a phrase, or most of a sentence. They are often used to convey a well-turned phrase or to complete a sentence using important words from a source, as in the following example.

Quotation marks
indicate the borrowed
phrase.

Source information,
including the page
number containing
the quotation, is
clearly identified.

Weitzman (2004) notes that by changing the "contextual forces," such as the availability of alcohol, that encourage students to drink, this approach more strongly emphasizes policies that directly put a stop to excessive drinking — unlike the social norms marketing approach, which relies on influencing individual behavior (p. 187).

Complete quotations are typically one or more full sentences and are most often used when the meaning of the passage cannot be conveyed adequately by a few well-chosen words, as in the following example.

> I smiled when I read Elizabeth Gilbert's memoir *Eat, Pray, Love*. Gilbert writes, "The Neapolitan women in particular are such a gang of tough-voiced, loud-mouthed, generous, nosy dames, all bossy and annoyed and right up in your face just trying to friggin' *help* you for chrissake, you dope — *why they gotta do everything around here?*" (78).

Block quotations are extended quotations (usually more than four typed lines) that are set off in a block from the rest of the text. In general, use a colon to introduce the quotation, indent the entire quotation one inch from the left margin, and include source information according to the documentation system you are using (such as MLA or APA). Since the blocked text indicates that you are quoting directly, you do not need to include quotation marks.

> Instead of cutting education funding, states should provide more money for schools, especially now when jobs are scarce and even trained workers are eager to return to school. Patrick Callan, president of the National Center for Public Policy and Higher Education, observes:
>
> > When the economy is good, and state universities are somewhat better funded, we raise tuition as little as possible. When the economy is bad, we raise tuition and sock it to families, when people can least afford it. That's exactly the opposite of what we need. (qtd. in Lewin)

Parenthetical citation
indicates that this
material was quoted
in another source. In
block quotations, the
citation information
is placed after
the period.

MODIFY QUOTATIONS APPROPRIATELY

You can modify quotations to fit your draft. It is acceptable, for example, to delete unnecessary words or to change the tense of a word in a partial quotation so that it fits your sentence. Keep in mind, however, that writers have an obligation to quote sources accurately and fairly. You should indicate when you have added or deleted words, and you should not modify quotations in a way that distorts their meaning.

The most useful strategies for modifying quotations include using an ellipsis mark (. . .) to indicate deleted words, using brackets ([ ]) to clarify meaning, and using "sic" to note errors in a source.

Modify a direct quotation using an ellipsis mark. When only part of a passage relates to your writing project, you might want to quote only that part in your document. To indicate that you have changed a quotation by deleting words, use three spaced periods, called an ellipsis mark (. . .). If you don't, your readers will assume that the quotation you are presenting is identical to the text found in the source.

Original Passage

Under Congressional Republicans, however, funding to encourage community and national service through the Corporation has dropped in both nominal and real dollars. This year, the Republican FY 2007 Labor–Health and Human Services–Education appropriations ("LHHS") bill cuts these efforts $77 million (9 percent) below FY 2006 and $112.5 million (12 percent) below FY 2004, when the Corporation's funding was at its peak. In real terms, support for these volunteer programs will have been slashed 20 percent in the last four years. The result has been cuts in participation in all three national service programs.

Source: U.S. House of Representatives, Committee on Appropriations — Democratic Staff. *House Republicans Slash National Service.* September 12, 2006, p. 2.

Quotation Modified Correctly Using Ellipsis Marks

"Under Congressional Republicans . . . , funding to encourage community and national service through the Corporation has dropped in both nominal and real dollars. . . . In real terms, support for these volunteer programs will have been slashed 20 percent in the last four years. The result has been cuts in participation in all three national service programs" (U.S. House of Representatives, Committee on Appropriations — Democratic Staff 2).

> Three periods indicate that material was deleted from within a sentence.

> Four periods indicate the deletion of one or more full sentences.

Modify a direct quotation using brackets. To modify a direct quotation by changing or adding words, use brackets ([ ]). If you don't, readers will assume that the quotation you are presenting is identical to the text found in the source.

The following example shows the use of brackets to change the tense of a verb in a partial quotation.

Original Quotation

"They treated us like family and refused to accept a tip."

Modified Quotation

Brackets indicate that the tense of a word has been changed.

> It's a place where the staff treats you "like family and refuse[s] to accept a tip," said travel writer Melissa Ancomi.

Modify quotations using "sic."   If a passage you are quoting contains a misspelled word or an incorrect fact, use the word "sic" in brackets to indicate that the error occurred in the original passage. If you don't, your readers might think that the mistake is yours.

Quotation Modified Correctly Using "Sic"

> "George W. Brush's [sic] interest in faith-based initiatives strongly shaped his national service agenda" (Vincent 221).

PUNCTUATE QUOTATIONS CORRECTLY

Use the following rules for punctuating quotations:

- Use double quotation marks (" ") around partial or complete quotations. Do not use quotation marks for block quotations.

- Use single quotation marks (' ') to indicate quoted material within a quotation.

    > "The hotel manager told the guests to 'make yourselves at home.'"

- Place commas and periods inside quotation marks.

- Place question marks and exclamation points outside quotation marks if the punctuation pertains to the entire sentence rather than the quotation. In the following example, the original quotation is not a question, so the question mark should be placed after the quotation mark.

    > But what can be gained from following the committee's recommendation that the state should "avoid, without exceptions, any proposed tax hike"?

- Place question marks and exclamation points inside quotation marks if the punctuation pertains to the quotation itself.

    > Dawn Smith asked a critical question: "Do college students understand the importance of avoiding running up the debt on their credit cards?"

- Place colons and semicolons outside quotation marks.

    > Many college students consider themselves "free at last"; all too often, however, they find that freedom has its costs.

- When citation information is provided after a partial or complete quotation, place the punctuation mark (comma, period, semicolon, colon, or question mark) after the parenthetical citation.

> "Preliminary reports have been consistent," Yates notes. "Without immediate changes to current practices, we will deplete known oil supplies by mid-century" (335).

- At the end of a block quotation, place the final punctuation before the parenthetical citation.

- Use three spaced periods (an ellipsis mark) to indicate an omission within a sentence.

> According to critic Joe Robinson, Americans are overworked: "Ask Americans how things are really going and you'll hear stories of . . . fifty- and sixty-hour weeks with no letup in sight" (467).

- Place a period before the ellipsis mark to indicate an omission at the end of a sentence.

> The most recent information indicates, says Chen, that "we can expect a significant increase in costs by the end of the decade. . . . Those costs, however, should ramp up slowly" (35).

Checklist for Quoting

✔ Identify the source of the quotation.

✔ Punctuate the quotation appropriately.

✔ Use ellipsis marks, brackets, and "sic" as necessary.

✔ Check each quotation against the source to be sure you aren't introducing errors or misrepresenting the source.

✔ Use transitions and attributions to integrate the quotation effectively into your draft.

✔ Ensure that the source is cited in your works cited or references list.

Paraphrase Information, Ideas, and Arguments

A paraphrase is a restatement, in your own words, of a passage from a source. Paraphrases can be used to illustrate or support a point you make in your document or to illustrate another author's argument about a subject. Writers choose to paraphrase rather than quote when a paraphrase would present the point more clearly or concisely than would a quotation from a source. Writers also choose to use paraphrases to add variety to a document — particularly when a large number of quotations have already been used—or when they find that the original passage would alter the tone or style of their document. For example, a writer of an article about a band that was purposefully pushing the boundaries of contemporary music might want to note that an important music reviewer had written, "I found this 'concert' to be a complete waste of my time." If the writer had already quoted more compelling statements from several other reviewers, however, the writer might use a paraphrase to indicate that the reviewer had found little in the band's most recent concert to recommend their music.

ENSURE THE ACCURACY AND FAIRNESS OF EACH PARAPHRASE

Your notes are likely to include a number of paraphrases of information, ideas, and arguments from your sources. Before you integrate a paraphrase into your document, make sure that it is an accurate and fair representation of the source. Reread the source, and double-check your paraphrase against it. Then revise the paraphrase as necessary so that it fits the context and tone of your document. Be sure that you have conveyed the meaning of the passage but that the wording and sentence structure differ from those in the original passage. (See pp. 62–63 for more on paraphrasing.)

INTEGRATE EACH PARAPHRASE INTO YOUR DOCUMENT

Use author attributions and transitions to help readers distinguish your ideas, information, and arguments from those drawn from your sources. Be sure to cite the source in the text and in your works cited list or references list (see Chapters 21 and 22).

In the following example, note how one writer lets readers know where his statement ends and where the support for his statement, in the form of a paraphrase, begins.

> The writer's idea

As digital music and video gained popularity, inventors assumed that the same rules would apply to the new hardware and software they developed for digital files. Instead, the DMCA lets music, computer, gaming, and other companies restrict technology and research that could potentially be used to get around their DRM — including research that would help address computer security (Electronic Frontier Foundation).

> Source of paraphrase (in this case, a Web document) is cited per MLA style.

✔ Identify the source of the paraphrased material.

✔ Compare the original passage with your paraphrase. Make sure that you have conveyed the meaning of the passage but that the wording and sentence structure differ from those in the original passage.

✔ Use transitions and attributions to integrate the paraphrase smoothly into your draft.

✔ Ensure that the source is cited in your works cited or references list.

Checklist for Paraphrasing

Summarize Sources

A summary is a concise statement, written in your own words, of the information, ideas, and arguments found in a source. When you integrate a summary into your draft, review the source to make sure your summary is an accurate and fair representation. In addition, be sure to identify the source and include a citation.

You can summarize an entire source, parts of a particular source, or a group of sources to support your ideas.

SUMMARIZE AN ENTIRE SOURCE

Writers frequently summarize an entire work. In some cases, the summary might occupy one or more paragraphs or be integrated into a discussion contained in one or more paragraphs. In other cases, the summary might be as brief as a single sentence.

In her analytical essay about the health risks faced by overweight athletes, featured writer Ali Bizzul offers a brief, "nutshell" summary of another source.

> In an editorial in the medical journal *Neurosurgery*, three sports-medicine specialists noted that after a 1994 federal law exempted dietary supplements from regulation by the Food and Drug Administration, heat-related injuries among football players began to rise (Bailes, Cantu, & Day, 2002).

The entire source is summarized; because it is a summary, not a direct quotation, page numbers are not necessary.

SUMMARIZE SPECIFIC INFORMATION AND IDEAS FROM A SOURCE

You can also use summaries to convey key information or ideas from a source. In the following example, the writer of an essay summarizes a section of a book about college admissions. His summary is highlighted in yellow.

Summary is intro-
duced with the
author of the book,
title, and specific
source of the ideas.

Bill Paul, author of *Getting In: Inside the College Admissions Process*, a book that tells the stories of several students applying to an elite Ivy League institution, shares three suggestions for students who want to get into a college. Paul bases these suggestions on his discussions with Fred Hargadon, who in 1995 was dean of admissions at Princeton. Hargadon suggested that the best way students can enhance their chances for acceptance into the college of their choice is to read widely, learn to speak a second language, and engage in activities that interest and excite them and that also help them develop their confidence and creativity (235-49).

Per MLA style, exact
pages are cited.

SUMMARIZE A GROUP OF SOURCES

In addition to summarizing a single source, writers often summarize groups of sources. Such collective summaries (often introduced by phrases such as "Numerous authors argue . . ." or "The research in this area seems to indicate that . . .") allow you to establish a point briefly and with authority. They are particularly effective at the beginning of a document, when you are establishing the nature of the conversation you are joining, and can serve as a transitional device when you move from one major section of the document to another.

When you summarize a group of sources, separate the citations with a semicolon. MLA guidelines require including author and page information, as in the following example.

> Several critics argue that the Hemingway code hero is not always male (Graulich 217; Sherman 78; Watters 33).

In APA style, the author and the date of publication must be included.

> The benefits of early detection of breast cancer have been well documented (Page, 2011; Richards, 2013; Vincent, 2012).

Checklist for Summarizing

✔ Identify the source of the quotation.

✔ Ensure that you have summarized the source in your own words. Make sure that you do not merely string together a series of close paraphrases of key passages.

✔ Use transitions and attributions to integrate the summary smoothly into your draft.

✔ Ensure that the source is cited in your works cited or references list.

Present Numerical Information

If it suits your subject, you might use numerical information, such as statistics, in your document. You can present this information within sentences. Or you might use tables, charts, or graphs, as featured writer Ellen Page did in her informative essay about the use of DDT in preventing malaria.

If you use tables, charts, or graphs, you still need to accurately and fairly present the numerical information in your document and clearly identify the source of the data, just as you would for textual information. For more information about using tables, charts, and graphs, see page 549.

Use Images, Audio, and Video

Including images in your print document or adding images, audio, or video files to your electronic document can enhance its effectiveness. Use caution, however, when taking images and audio or video files from other sources. Simply copying a photograph or an audio or video file into your document might be a form of plagiarism.

One student writer carefully documented the source of the image she used in her informative essay. Because she was writing an academic essay — rather than a document intended for publication and wide distribution — she did not seek permission to use it. (In contrast, the publisher of this book sought and received permission to publish that image.)

If you are creating an electronic document, such as a Web page or a multimedia presentation, use the following guidelines to integrating digital illustrations:

- Make a link between your document and a document that contains an image, a sound clip, or a video clip — rather than copying the image and placing it in your document.
- If it isn't possible or appropriate to create a link to another document, contact the owner of the image, sound clip, or video clip for permission to use it.
- If you cannot contact the owner, review the fair-use guidelines discussed on page 488 for guidance about using the material.

As you would for any sources you cite in your document, make sure you fairly present images, audio, or video and identify the author or creator.

Only by investing in educating their citizens during hard economic times will states see the benefits of having educated workers and business owners — and higher-earning taxpayers — in the state during better times. For this reason, higher education should be a top priority in even trimmed-down state budgets so that students and their families won't face drastic increases in tuition.

At the same time, students still ultimately bear the responsibility for finding the best path to an affordable college education. Students and their families are a necessary part of the solution. They should be willing to apply to a variety of schools, including those they can afford more easily without financial aid. Many students and their families are now considering less expensive routes to a college degree, such as enrolling in public universities or community colleges in their home states (Saleh). Out of eighty-seven college freshmen surveyed at Colorado State University, 80% were likely to recommend community college to a sibling or friend concerned about tuition costs (Tillson). When asked about the benefits of attending community college, students responded that they saw it as "easier to afford" and appreciated that it "makes it easier to work and attend school at the same time" (see Fig. 1). The survey shows that students today are giving community colleges serious thought as an alternative to a four-year university.

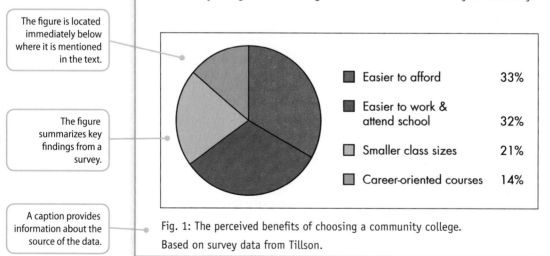

Easier to afford	33%
Easier to work & attend school	32%
Smaller class sizes	21%
Career-oriented courses	14%

Fig. 1: The perceived benefits of choosing a community college. Based on survey data from Tillson.

A parenthetical reference to the figure is provided.

The figure is located immediately below where it is mentioned in the text.

The figure summarizes key findings from a survey.

A caption provides information about the source of the data.

▲ A chart presenting information in an essay

the most promising alternatives in development is hydrogen—an abundant fuel that is environmentally safe, is far more versatile than gasoline or diesel, can be used to create electricity and fuel internal combustion engines, and produces no waste. Because of these attributes, some experts have argued that a hydrogen economy—an energy system that uses only a hydrogen-oxygen reaction to create energy and electricity—could solve many fuel-related problems, from global warming to America's dependence on foreign oil (Crabtree, Dresselhause, and Buchanan 39). At first glance, hydrogen appears to be the perfect choice. However, three barriers stand in the way of widespread hydrogen usage: as a fuel, it is expensive to produce, difficult to store, and complicated to distribute.

The key to a hydrogen economy is the fuel cell, which uses hydrogen gas and oxygen to produce electricity. In a way, a fuel cell is like a battery, but it never requires charging and it produces only electricity, heat, and water vapor (see Fig. 1). The U.S. Department of Energy (DOE) explains that hydrogen fuel cells use electrode plates to separate hydrogen's protons and electrons, diverting the stream of electrons to create electricity. A "stack" of fuel cells is scalable, so the same basic structure has many different uses ("Hydrogen Fuel"). In theory, stacks of hydrogen fuel

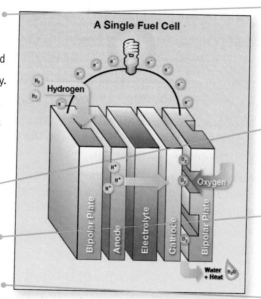

Fig. 1: Simplified model of a fuel cell. United States Department of Energy, "Hydrogen Fuel Cells."

The figure is located next to where it is referred to in the text.

A parenthetical reference to the figure is provided.

Text is "wrapped" around the figure and caption (see Chapter 16).

The figure illustrates a complex process that would be too difficult to describe using text alone.

A caption provides information about the source of the figure.

▲ An image providing an overview of a complex process

How Can I Ensure I've Avoided Plagiarism?

Because plagiarized material will often differ in style, tone, and word choice from the rest of your document, your readers are likely to notice these differences and wonder whether you've plagiarized the material — or, if not, why you've written a document that has so many stylistic inconsistencies. If your readers react negatively, it's unlikely that your document will be successful.

You can avoid plagiarism by quoting, paraphrasing, and summarizing accurately and appropriately; distinguishing between your ideas and ideas in your sources; and identifying sources in your document.

Quote, Paraphrase, and Summarize Accurately and Appropriately

Unintentional plagiarism usually occurs when a writer takes poor notes and then uses the information from those notes in a document. As you draft, do the following:

- Look for notes that differ from your usual style of writing. More often than not, if a note doesn't sound like your own writing, it isn't.

- Place quotation marks around any direct quotations, use ellipses and brackets appropriately (see pp. 619–620), and identify the source and the page or paragraph number of the quotation.

- Make sure that paraphrases differ significantly in word choice and sentence structure from the passage being paraphrased, and identify the source and page or paragraph number from which you took the paraphrase.

- Make sure that summaries are not just a series of passages or close paraphrases copied from the source.

Distinguish between Your Ideas and Ideas in Your Sources

Failing to distinguish between your ideas and ideas drawn from your sources can lead readers to think other writers' ideas are yours. Examine how the following writer might have failed to distinguish his ideas from those of Joel Levine and Lawrence May, authors of a source he used in his essay.

Failing to Credit Ideas to a Source

According to Joel Levine and Lawrence May, authors of *Getting In*, entrance exams are an extremely important part of a student's college application and carry a great deal of weight. In fact, a college entrance examination is one of the two most significant factors in getting into college. The other, unsurprisingly, is high school grades.

Because the second and third sentences fail to identify Levine and May as the source of the information about the second important factor affecting admissions decisions — high school grades — the passage implies that the writer is the source of that information.

As it turns out, the writer actually included the necessary attribution in his essay.

Giving Credit to the Source

According to Joel Levine and Lawrence May, authors of *Getting In*, entrance exams are an extremely important part of a student's college application and carry a great deal of weight. In fact, they claim that a college entrance examination is "one of the two most significant factors" in getting into college (the other, unsurprisingly, is high school grades).

> The attribution "they claim" credits the source of the information to Levine and May.

> Quotation marks are used to indicate a partial quotation.

You can use attributions to distinguish between your ideas and those obtained from your sources. As you draft your document, use the name of an author or the title of the source you're drawing from each time you introduce ideas from a source.

Examples of Attribution

According to Scott McPherson . . .

Jill Bedard writes . . .

Tom Huckin reports . . .

Kate Kiefer observes . . .

Bob Phelps suggests . . .

In the words of William Hochman . . .

As Shirley Guitron tells it . . .

Shaun Beaty indicates . . .

Jessica Richards calls our attention to . . .

Check for Unattributed Sources in Your Document

Writers sometimes neglect to identify the sources from which they have drawn their information. You should include a complete citation for each source you refer to in your document. The citation should appear in the text of the document (as an in-text citation, footnote, or endnote) or in a works cited list, references list, or bibliography.

The following examples use MLA style for citing sources; more detailed information about the sources appears in a list of works cited at the end of the document. In the first example, the writer uses a combination of attribution and parenthetical information; in the second example, the writer provides only a parenthetical citation.

> MLA-style in-text citations include the author's name and exact page reference.

Gavin Miller argues, "We must explore emerging energy technologies before we reach a peak oil crisis" (322).

"We must explore emerging energy technologies before we reach a peak oil crisis" (Miller 322).

How Should I Document My Sources?

In addition to citing your sources within the text of your document, you should provide complete publication information for each source you've used. Fully documenting your sources can help you achieve your purposes as a writer, such as establishing your authority and persuading your readers. Documenting your sources also helps you avoid plagiarism, gives credit to others who have written about a subject, and creates a record of their work that your readers can follow and build on.

Choose a Documentation System

The documentation systems most commonly used in academic disciplines are the following:

- **MLA.** This style, developed by the Modern Language Association, is used primarily in the humanities — English, philosophy, linguistics, world languages, and so on. See Chapter 21.

- **APA.** Developed by the American Psychological Association, this style is used mainly in the social sciences — psychology, sociology, anthropology, political science, economics, education, and so on. See Chapter 22.

- *Chicago.* Developed by the University of Chicago Press, this style is used primarily in history, journalism, and the humanities.

- **CSE.** This style, developed by the Council of Science Editors (formerly the Council of Biology Editors), is used mainly in the physical and life sciences — chemistry, geology, biology, botany, and so on — and in mathematics.

Your choice of documentation system will be guided by the discipline or field within which you are writing and by any documentation requirements associated with your writing project. If your project has been assigned to you, ask the person who assigned it or someone who has written a similar document which documentation system you should use. If you are working on a project for a writing class, your instructor will usually tell you which documentation system to follow.

Your choice of documentation system will also be guided by the genre you have chosen for your document. For example, while academic essays and articles appearing in scholarly journals typically use a documentation system such as MLA or APA, newspaper and magazine articles often do not; instead, they identify sources in the main text of the document rather than in a works cited or references list. If you write an electronic document that cites other online sources, you might simply link to those sources.

Provide In-Text References and Publication Information

The specific format of your in-text citations will depend on the documentation system you are following. If you use MLA or APA style, you will refer to sources in the text of your document using a combination of attributions and parenthetical information and will include a list of sources at the end of your document. The works cited list (MLA) or references list (APA) includes the following key publication information about each source:

- author(s) and/or editor(s)
- title
- publication date
- publisher and city of publication (for books)
- periodical name, volume, issue, and page numbers (for articles)
- URL and access date (for online publications)

Each documentation system creates an association between in-text citations and the works cited or references list. See Chapters 21 and 22 for documentation models.

In Summary: Using Sources Effectively

* Use sources to support your points (p. 610).

* Indicate the boundaries between source material and your own ideas (p. 615).

* Modify direct quotations carefully (p. 617).

* Use paraphrases to present ideas more clearly or concisely than is possible through direct quotation (p. 621).

* Revise paraphrases to fit your tone and style (p. 621).

* Summarize entire sources, parts of sources, or groups of sources (p. 623).

* Integrate numerical information appropriately (p. 625).

* Integrate images, audio, and video responsibly (p. 625).

* Check for unintentional plagiarism (p. 628).

* Document your sources (p. 630).

20 Revising and Editing

⏩ When writers revise and edit, they evaluate the effectiveness of their drafts and work to improve them. Although the two processes are related, they focus on different aspects of a document. Revising involves assessing how well a document responds to a specific writing situation, presents a main point and reasons to accept that point, and uses evidence. Editing includes evaluating and improving the expression — at the sentence and word levels — of the information, ideas, and arguments in the document.

What Should I Focus on When I Revise?

Revising involves rethinking and re-envisioning what you've written. It focuses on such big-picture issues as whether the document you've drafted is appropriate for your writing situation; whether your thesis statement is sound and well supported; whether you've properly integrated sources into your document; whether you've organized and presented your information, ideas, and arguments clearly and effectively; and whether you've made appropriate decisions about genre and design.

Consider Your Writing Situation

As you revise, ask whether your document helps you achieve your purposes. If your assignment directed you to inform readers about a particular subject, for instance, consider whether you've provided appropriate information, whether you've offered enough information, and whether that information is presented clearly. If your purpose is to convince or persuade your readers, ask whether you have chosen appropriate reasons and evidence and presented your argument as effectively as you can. You'll find revision suggestions for specific types of assignments in Chapters 5 through 10.

In addition, review your readers' needs, interests, backgrounds, and knowledge of the subject. During revision, imagine how your readers will react to your document by asking questions such as these:

- Will my readers trust what I have to say? How can I establish my credibility?
- Will my readers have other ideas about how to address this subject? How can I convince them that they should believe what I say?
- Will my readers find my evidence appropriate and accurate? Is my selection of evidence consistent with their values, beliefs, and experiences?

Finally, identify your requirements, limitations, and opportunities (see p. 31). Ask yourself whether you've met the specific requirements of the assignment, such as length and number of sources. Evaluate your efforts to work around limitations, such as lack of access to information. Think about whether you've taken full advantage of your opportunities and any new ones that have come your way.

Consider Your Argument and Ideas

As you revise, ask how well you are conveying your argument and ideas to your readers. First, check the clarity of your thesis statement. Is it phrased in a way that is compatible with the needs and interests of your readers? Second, ask whether your reasons will help your readers understand and accept your thesis statement. As you make this assessment, keep in mind your primary role as a writer — such as advocate, reporter, or interpreter.

- **Writing to reflect.** Have you created a dominant impression of your subject or indicated the significance of your observations for readers? (See Chapter 5.)

- **Writing to inform.** Is the level of detail you've provided consistent with your readers' knowledge of the subject? Have you clearly defined any key concepts and ideas? (See Chapter 6.)

- **Writing to interpret or analyze.** Are your analyses clear and accurate? Have you provided appropriate and sufficient background information to help your readers follow your reasoning? (See Chapter 7.)

- **Writing to evaluate.** Have you clearly described the subject, defined your evaluative criteria, and provided a clear rationale for your judgments? (See Chapter 8.)

- **Writing to solve problems.** Have you clearly defined the problem, considered alternative solutions, and discussed your proposed solution? (See Chapter 9.)

- **Writing to convince or persuade.** Have you made a clear overall point, provided reasons, and presented evidence to support your reasons? (See Chapter 10.)

Consider Your Use, Integration, and Documentation of Sources

Think about how you've used source information in your document. Review the amount of evidence you've provided for your points and the appropriateness of that evidence for your purpose and readers. If you are arguing about an issue, determine whether you've identified and addressed reasonable opposing viewpoints.

As you do so, determine whether you've presented information, ideas, and arguments from your sources accurately and fairly. Be sure that quotations are accurate and appropriately documented. Ensure that paraphrases and summaries represent the source reasonably and fairly. Although fairness can be difficult to judge, ask whether you've achieved it. For example, writing that an author "ridiculed" a particular idea might enhance the impact of a passage. If the author was only raising questions about the idea, however, using that term would be unfair both to your source and to the idea itself.

Ask yourself, as well, how effectively you've introduced the work of other authors. Begin by considering your use of attributions in terms of your purpose and role.

By characterizing the contributions particular sources are making to the overall conversation, you can frame their arguments — and yours — in a way that helps you achieve your goals. You can also show how particular sources approach your issue, helping your readers better understand how your contribution advances the conversation.

Then consider the relationship you are trying to establish with your readers. Readers appreciate clear identification of the source of a quotation, paraphrase, or summary. (For more information about quoting, paraphrasing, and summarizing, see Chapter 19.) Readers also appreciate some variety in how evidence from sources is introduced. To make your writing stand out, vary the words and phrases that identify the sources of the information, ideas, and arguments you use in your document.

Common Attributions	More Specific Attributions
The author wrote . . .	The author expressed the opinion that . . .
The author said . . .	The author denied this, noting . . .
The author stated . . .	In response, the author observed that . . .

It's also important to review your works cited or references list for completeness and accuracy. Remember that lack of proper documentation can reduce your document's effectiveness and diminish your credibility. You can learn more about integrating sources in Chapter 19. For guidelines on documenting your sources, see Chapters 21 and 22.

Consider the Structure and Organization of Your Document

Your readers should be able to locate information and ideas easily. As you read your introduction, ask whether it clearly and concisely conveys your main point and whether it helps your readers anticipate the structure and organization of your document. Reflect on the appropriateness of your organizing pattern (see p. 506) for your purpose and readers. If you've used headings and subheadings, evaluate their effectiveness.

Make sure your document is easy to read. Check for effective paragraphing and paragraph structure (see p. 520). If you have several small paragraphs, you might combine paragraphs with similar ideas. If you have a number of long paragraphs, break them up and add transitions. Finally, ask whether your conclusion leaves your readers with something to think about. The most effective conclusions typically provide more than just a summary of your argument.

Consider Genre and Design

Consider both the genre — or type — of document that you are writing and your use of design principles and elements (see Chapter 16). If your assignment gave you a choice of genre, ask whether the genre you've selected is appropriate, given your purpose and readers. For example, would it be more effective to reach your readers via an informative Web site, an opinion column, or a brochure? Would it be more effective to publish your document as a blog entry or as a letter to the editor of a magazine or newspaper? Regardless of the type of document you're writing, make sure that you've followed the conventions associated with it, such as level of formality, accepted sources of evidence, and organization.

Take a careful look, as well, at how you've designed your document (see Chapter 16). Does it resemble what your readers will expect? For example, if you're writing an academic essay, have you double-spaced your lines, used a readable font, and set wide margins? If you're creating a Web site, have you made it easy for your readers to find their way around? Have you consistently formatted your headings and subheadings? Have you used design principles and elements to achieve your purpose and consider your readers?

What Strategies Can I Use to Revise?

You can draw on several strategies for reviewing and improving your document. As you use them, keep track of your ideas for revision by writing comments on sticky notes or in the margins of print documents, by using the Comment tool in word-processing documents, or by creating a to-do list in your writer's notebook.

Save Multiple Drafts

You might not be happy with every revision you make. To avoid wishing that you hadn't made extensive revisions to a draft of your document, save a new copy of your draft before every major revising session. You can add a number to your drafts' file names, such as Draft1.doc, Draft2.doc, and so on; add the date, such as

Draft-April6.doc and Draft-April10.doc; or use some other naming system that works for you. What's important is that you save multiple versions of your drafts in case you don't like the changes you've made.

Highlight Your Main Point, Reasons, and Evidence

As you revise, make sure that your main point (usually expressed as a thesis statement), reasons, and evidence are fully developed. An effective way to do this is to identify and examine each element in your draft, both individually and as a group of related points. If you are working with a printed document, use a highlighter, colored pens or pencils, or sticky notes. If you are working on a digital document, use a highlighting tool to mark the text. You might use different colors to highlight your main point, reasons, and evidence. If you are focusing solely on the evidence in your document, use different colors to highlight evidence from different sources (to help you check whether you are relying too heavily on a single source) or to differentiate the types of evidence you are using (such as quotations, paraphrases, summaries, and numerical data).

When you have finished highlighting your draft, review it to determine whether your reasons support your main points as effectively as you had hoped and whether the evidence you've provided to support your reasons is sufficient and varied. If you have relied too heavily on a particular source, for example, your readers might wonder why they shouldn't simply read that source and ignore your document. If you've provided too little evidence, they'll question the basis for your conclusions.

Challenge Your Assumptions

It's easy to accept ideas and arguments that you've worked so hard to develop. But what would a reader with fresh eyes think? Challenge your main point, reasons, and evidence by using one of the following strategies. Keep track of your challenges by using the Comment tool in your word-processing program.

PUT YOURSELF IN THE PLACE OF YOUR READERS

As you read, pretend that you are one of your readers. Try to imagine a single reader — or, if you're ambitious, a group of readers. Ask questions they might ask. Imagine concerns they might bring to their reading of your document. A reader interested in solving a problem might ask, for example, whether a proposed solution is cost-effective, is more appropriate than alternative solutions, or has unacceptable side effects. As you revise, take these questions and concerns into account.

PLAY DEVIL'S ADVOCATE

A devil's advocate raises reasonable objections to ideas and arguments. As you review your document, identify your key claims, and then pose reasonable objections to them. Make note of these potential objections, and take them into account as you revise.

PLAY THE "SO WHAT?" GAME

As you read your document, ask why readers would care about what you are saying. By asking "So what?" questions, you can gain a better understanding of what your readers are likely to care about and how they might respond to your arguments and ideas. Make note of your responses to these questions, and consider them as you revise.

Scan, Outline, and Map Your Document

Use the following strategies to review the structure, organization, and design of your document:

- **Scan headings and subheadings.** If you have used headings and subheadings, they can help you track the overall flow of your ideas. Ask whether the organization they reveal is appropriate for your writing situation and your role as a writer.

- **Scan the first sentence of each paragraph.** A quick reading of the first sentence of each paragraph can reveal points at which your ideas shift. As you note these shifts, think about whether they are appropriate and effective.

- **Outline your document.** Create a topical or sentence outline of your document (see p. 515) to assess its structure and organization. This strategy, sometimes called a reverse outline, helps you identify the sequence of your points and the amount of space you've devoted to each aspect of your document. If you are viewing your document in a word-processing program, use the Styles tool to assign levels to headings in your document; then view it in Outline view.

- **Map your document.** On paper or in a graphics program, draw a map of your document. Like an outline, a map can help you identify the organization of your points and the amount of evidence you've used to support them. As you review the organization and structure of your document, reflect on whether it is appropriate given your purpose, readers, argument, and available information.

Ask for Feedback

After spending long hours on a project, you might find it difficult to identify problems that your readers might have with your draft. You might read the same paragraph eight times and still fail to notice that the evidence you are using to support a point actually contradicts it. Or you might not notice that your document's organization could confuse your readers. You can ask for feedback on your draft from a friend, relative, colleague, or writing center tutor. It's generally a good idea to ask for help from someone who will be frank as well as supportive. You should also be specific about the kinds of comments you're looking for. Hearing "it's just fine" from a reviewer will not help you to revise. You can learn more about engaging in a peer review in Chapter 4.

Checklist for Revision

✔ Review your writing situation. Does your document help you achieve your purposes? Does it address your readers' needs, interests, knowledge, and backgrounds? Is it well adapted to the context in which it will be read?

✔ Consider your writing assignment. Does your document address the writing assignment's requirements? Does it effectively work around limitations and take advantage of opportunities?

✔ Evaluate the presentation of your ideas. Does your document provide a clear and appropriate thesis statement? Do your reasons and evidence support your thesis statement, and are they consistent with your primary role as a writer?

✔ Assess your use, integration, and documentation of sources. Have you offered adequate support for your points, considered reasonable opposing viewpoints, integrated and acknowledged your sources, and distinguished between your work and that of other writers? Have you used variety in your introduction and attribution of sources? Have you documented your sources appropriately?

✔ Examine the structure and organization of your document. Is the introduction clear and concise, does it convey your main point, and does it help your readers anticipate the structure of your document? Is the organization of the document easy to follow? Are paragraphs easy to read? Are transitions effective? Does the conclusion provide more than just a summary of the document?

✔ Evaluate genre and design. Does the genre you've chosen help you accomplish your purpose? Have you followed the style and design conventions associated with the type of document you've created?

What Should I Focus on When I Edit?

Editing involves assessing the effectiveness, accuracy, and appropriateness of the words and sentences in a document. Before you begin to edit, remember that editing focuses on your document's words and sentences, not on its overall structure or ideas. If you're uncertain about whether you've organized your document as effectively as possible or whether you've provided enough support for your argument, deal with those issues first. In the same way that you wouldn't start painting a house until you've finished building the walls, hold off on editing until you're confident that you're finished revising.

Focus on Accuracy

You risk damaging your credibility if you provide inaccurate information in your document. To reduce this risk, do the following:

- **Check your facts and figures.** Your readers might think that you're deliberately misleading them if you fail to provide accurate information. As you edit, return to your original sources or your notes to check any facts and figures.

- **Check every quotation.** Return to your original sources or consult your notes to ensure that you have quoted each source exactly. Make sure that you have noted any changes to a quotation with ellipses or brackets and that those changes haven't altered the original meaning of the passage (see pp. 619–620). Be sure to cite each source both in the text and in a works cited or references list (see Chapters 21 and 22).

- **Check the spelling of every name.** Don't rely on electronic spelling checkers, which provide the correct spelling for only the most common or prominent names.

Focus on Economy

Editing for economy involves reducing the number of words needed to express an idea or convey information. Often you can achieve greater economy in your writing by removing unnecessary modifiers, removing unnecessary introductory phrases such as *there are* and *it is*, and eliminating stock phrases (see pp. 522–523). Editing for economy generally makes it easier for your readers to understand your meaning, but you should use care; your readers still need to understand the point you are trying to make (see Chapter 16).

Focus on Consistency

Editing your document for consistency helps you present information and ideas in a uniform way. Use the following techniques to edit for consistency:

- **Treat concepts consistently.** Review your document for consistent treatment of concepts, information, ideas, definitions, and anecdotes.

- **Use numbers consistently.** Check the documentation system you are using for its guidelines on the treatment of numbers. You might find, for instance, that you should spell out the numbers zero through nine and use Arabic numerals for numbers larger than nine.

- **Treat your sources consistently.** Avoid referring to some sources using first names and to others using honorifics, such as *Dr.*, *Mr.*, or *Ms.* Also check that you have cited your sources appropriately for the documentation style you are using, such as MLA or APA (see Chapters 21 and 22). Review each reference for consistent presentation of names, page numbers, and publication dates.

- **Format your document consistently.** Avoid any inconsistencies in your use of fonts, headings, and subheadings and in your placement and captioning of images, tables, charts, and other illustrations (see Chapter 16).

Focus on Style

Your readers will judge you — and what you have to say — not only on what you say but also on how you say it. Edit for matters of style by choosing the right words, using active and passive voice appropriately, adopting a consistent point of view, rewriting complex sentences, varying your sentence length and structure, providing transitions, and avoiding sexist language.

Focus on Spelling, Grammar, and Punctuation

Poor spelling doesn't necessarily affect your ability to get your point across — in most cases, readers will understand even the most atrociously spelled document — but it does affect what your readers think of you. If you ignore spelling errors in your document, you'll erode their confidence in your ability to present ideas or make an argument. The same goes for grammar and punctuation. If your sentences have subject-verb agreement problems or don't use the appropriate punctuation, readers might not trust that you have presented your facts correctly. As you put the finishing touches on your document, keep a dictionary and good grammar handbook close by.

What Strategies Can I Use to Edit?

Thorough editing involves making several passes through your document to ensure that you've addressed accuracy, economy, consistency, style, spelling, grammar, and punctuation. The following tips can make that process both easier and more productive.

Read Carefully

As you've worked on your document, you've become quite familiar with it. As a result, it can be easy to read what you *meant* to write instead of what you actually wrote. The following strategies can help you read with fresh eyes:

- **Set your document aside before you edit.** If time permits, allow a day or two to pass before you begin editing your document. Taking time off between revising and editing can help you see your document more clearly.

- **Pause between sentences for a quick check.** Avoid getting caught up in the flow of your document by stopping after you read each sentence. Slowing down can help you identify problems with your text.

- **Read aloud.** Reading your document aloud can help you find problems that might not be apparent when it's read silently.

- **Read in reverse order.** To check for problems with individual sentences, start at the end of your document and read the last sentence first, and then work backward through the document. To check for problems at the word level, read each word starting with the last one in the document. Disrupting the normal flow of your document can alert you to problems that might not stand out when you read it normally.

Mark and Search Your Document

Use the following marking and searching strategies to edit for accuracy, economy, consistency, and style:

- **Mark your document.** As you read, use a highlighter pen or the highlighting tool in your word-processing program to mark errors or information that should be double-checked. Consider using different colors to highlight specific types of problems, such as sexist language or inconsistent use of formal titles.

- **Use the Find and Replace tools.** Use your word-processing program to edit concepts, names, numbers, and titles for consistency and accuracy. Once you've identified a word or phrase that you'd like to check or change, you can search for it throughout your document. If you are referring to sources using a parenthetical citation style, such as MLA or APA, use the Find tool to search for an opening parenthesis. If you discover that you've consistently misspelled a word or name, use the Replace tool to correct it throughout your document.

- **Use the Split Window tool.** Some word-processing programs allow you to split your window so that you can view different parts of your document at the same time. Use this tool to ensure that you are referring to a concept in the same way throughout your document or to check for consistent use of fonts, headings, subheadings, illustrations, and tables.

Use Spelling, Grammar, and Style Tools with Caution

Most word-processing programs provide tools to check spelling, grammar, punctuation, and style. Used with an awareness of their limitations, these tools can significantly reduce the effort required to edit a document.

Spelling checkers have two primary limitations. First, they can't identify words that are spelled correctly but misused — such as *to/two/too*, *their/they're/there*, and *advice/advise*. Second, spelling checkers are ineffective when they run into a word they don't recognize, such as proper names, technical and scientific terms, and unusual words. To compound this problem, spelling checkers often suggest replacement words. If you accept suggestions uncritically, you might end up with a paper full of incorrect words and misspelled names.

The main limitation of grammar, punctuation, and style checkers is inaccurate advice. Although much of the advice they offer is sound, a significant proportion is not. If you are confident about your knowledge of grammar, punctuation, and style, you can use the grammar- and style-checking tools in your word-processing program to identify potential problem areas in your document. These tools can point out problems you might have overlooked, such as a subject-verb agreement problem that occurred when you revised a sentence. However, if you don't have a strong knowledge of grammar, punctuation, and style, you can easily be misled by inaccurate advice.

If you have any doubts about advice from your word-processing program's spelling checker, consult an up-to-date dictionary. If you have concerns about the suggestions you receive from the grammar-, punctuation-, and style-checking tools, consult a good grammar handbook.

Ask for Feedback

One of the biggest challenges writers face is reading a draft of their own work as a reader rather than as the writer. Because you know what you're trying to say, you'll find it easy to understand your draft. And because you've read your document so many times, you're likely to overlook errors in spelling, punctuation, and grammar. After you've edited your document, ask a friend, relative, or classmate to proofread it and to make note of any problems.

✔ Ensure that your document is accurate. Check facts and figures, quotations, and the spelling of names.	**Checklist for Editing**
✔ Edit for economy. Strive to express your ideas and argument concisely yet clearly.	
✔ Ensure that your document is consistent. Use concepts, numbers, and source information consistently. Check your document for consistent use of formatting and design.	
✔ Improve your style. Strive for economy, use appropriate words, check your verbs, rewrite overly complex sentences, vary sentence length and structure, and remove sexist language.	
✔ Check for correct spelling, grammar, and punctuation. Use your word-processing program's spelling, grammar, punctuation, and style tools; consult a grammar handbook and a dictionary; and ask someone to proofread your draft.	

In Summary: Revising and Editing

* Focus on the big picture when you revise by keeping your writing situation in mind (p. 634).

* Revise more effectively by saving multiple drafts; highlighting; challenging your assumptions; scanning, outlining, and mapping your document; and asking for feedback (p. 637).

* Focus on accuracy, economy, consistency, style, spelling, grammar, and punctuation when you edit (p. 641).

* Take advantage of editing strategies (p. 643).

PART FIVE

Documenting Sources

Using MLA Style

Modern Language Association (MLA) style, used primarily in
the humanities, emphasizes the authors of a source and the
pages on which information is located in the source. Writers
who use the MLA documentation system cite, or formally
acknowledge, source information within their text using
parentheses, and they provide a list of sources in a works
cited list at the end of their document. The works cited list
also indicates the medium of the source (print, Web, film,
manuscript, and so on).

Caitlin Guariglia, *Mi Famiglia*, page 150

Jennie Tillson, *Death, Taxes, and College Tuition*, page 367

Vince Reid, *The Changing Face of Online Gaming*, page 422

For more information about MLA style, consult the *MLA
Handbook for Writers of Research Papers*, Seventh Edition.
Information about the *MLA Handbook* can also be found at
www.mla.org.

CITATIONS WITHIN YOUR TEXT

ENTRIES IN YOUR WORKS CITED LIST

How Do I Cite Sources within the Text of My Document?

MLA style uses parentheses for in-text citations to acknowledge the use of another author's words, facts, and ideas. When you refer to a source within your text, provide the author's last name and specific page number(s) — if the source is paginated. Your reader can then go to the works cited list at the end of your document to find a full citation.

1. Basic format for a source named in your text Most often, you will want to name the author of a source within your sentence rather than in a parenthetical citation. By doing so, you create a context for the material (words, facts, or ideas) that you are including, and you indicate where the information from the author begins. When you are using a direct quotation, paraphrase, or summary from a source and have named the author in your sentence, place only the page number in parentheses after the borrowed material. The period follows the closing parenthesis.

> According to Tattersall, when early humans emerged from the dense forests to the adjacent woodlands, their mobility and diet were forced to change dramatically (45).

When you are using a block (or extended) quotation, the parenthetical citation comes after the final punctuation and a single space (see p. 618).

If you continue to refer to a single source for several sentences in a row within one paragraph — and without intervening references to another source — you may place your reference at the end of the paragraph. However, be sure to include all of the relevant page numbers.

2. Basic format for a source not named in your text When you have not mentioned the author in your sentence, you must place the author's name and the page number in parentheses after the quotation, paraphrase, or summary. Again, the period follows the closing parenthesis.

> It would have been impossible for early humans to digest red meat, as their stomachs lacked the necessary acids to break down the muscle and tissue before delivery to the intestines (Tattersall 46).

3. Entire source If you are referring to an entire source rather than to a specific page or pages, you do not need a parenthetical citation.

Author Jhumpa Lahiri adapted the title for her book of stories, *Unaccustomed Earth,* from a line in the first chapter of Nathaniel Hawthorne's *The Scarlet Letter.*

4. Corporate, group, or government author Cite the corporation, group, or government agency as you would an individual author. You may use abbreviations for the source in subsequent references if you add the abbreviation in parentheses at the first mention of the name.

The Social Security Administration (SSA) estimates that a twenty-year-old has a three in ten chance of becoming disabled before he or she reaches retirement age (4). If a worker does become disabled, SSA assigns a representative to review the case individually (7).

5. Unknown author If you are citing a source that has no known author, such as the book *A Woman in Berlin,* use a brief version of the title in the parenthetical citation.

The narrator pays particular attention to the culture of rape in Berlin during World War II, calling it a "collective experience" and claiming that German women comforted one another by speaking openly about it — something they never would have considered during peacetime (*Woman in Berlin* 147).

6. Two or more works by the same author For references to authors with more than one work in your works cited list, insert a short version of the title between the author and the page number, separating the author and the title with a comma.

(Sacks, *Hallucinations* 77)

(Sacks, *Mind's Eye* 123)

7. Two or more authors with the same last name Include the first initial and last name in the parenthetical citation.

(F. McCourt 27)

(M. McCourt 55)

8. Two or three authors Include the last name of each author in your citation.

In the year following Hurricane Katrina, journalist and activist Jane Wholey brought together a group of twenty New Orleans middle schoolers in an effort to reimagine their school system's food environment from the ground up (Gottlieb and Joshi 2).

9. Four or more authors Use only the last name of the first author and the abbreviation "et al." (Latin for "and others"). There is no comma between the author's name and "et al."

> (Johnson et al. 17)

10. Literary work Along with the page number(s), give other identifying information, such as a chapter, scene, or line number, that will help readers find the passage.

> One prominent motif introduced at the opening of *Beloved* is bestiality, exemplified in Sethe's being described as "down on all fours" at the first appearance of her dead daughter's ghost (Morrison 27; ch. 1).

11. Work in an edited collection or anthology Cite the author of the work, not the editor of the collection or anthology. (See also item 28 on p. 657.)

> In his satirical essay "A Presidential Candidate," Mark Twain outlines his plan to thwart the opposition, insisting that "if you know the worst about a candidate, to begin with, every attempt to spring things on him will be checkmated" (3).

12. Sacred text Give the name of the edition you are using, along with the chapter and verse (or their equivalent).

> It is still very sage advice to "withhold not good from them to whom it is due, when it is in the power of thine hand to do it" (*King James Bible,* Prov. 2.27).

> The Qur'an points to the bee and its natural ability to produce honey as proof of God's existence ("The Bees" 16.68).

13. Two or more works cited together Use a semicolon to separate entries.

> Byron Bancroft Johnson founded the American League in 1901 by raiding the National League for its best players, offering them competitive salaries to jump leagues (Appel 3; Stout and Johnson 8).

14. Source quoted in another source Ideally, you should track down the original source of the quotation. If you must use a quotation cited by another author, use the abbreviation "qtd. in" (for "quoted in") when you cite the source.

> When Henry Ford introduced the Model T, he insisted on making it a practical and affordable family car, maintaining that "no man making a good salary will be unable to

own one — and enjoy with his family the blessing of hours of pleasure in God's great open spaces" (qtd. in Booth 9).

15. Source without page numbers Give a section, paragraph, or screen number, if numbered, in the parenthetical citation.

First-time American mothers and fathers both have aged an average of three to four years since 1970 (Shulevitz, par. 4).

If no numbers are available, list only the author's name.

It is adults, not children, who present the greatest challenge in gift-giving, as adults tend to long for intangibles — like love or career success — that are harder to pin down (Rothman).

How Do I Prepare the List of Works Cited?

MLA-style research documents include a reference list titled "Works Cited," which begins on a new page at the end of the document. If you wish to acknowledge sources that you read but did not cite in your text, you may include them in a second list titled "Works Consulted."

The list is alphabetized by author. If the author's name is unknown, alphabetize the entry using the title of the source. If you cite more than one work by the same author, alphabetize the group under the author's last name, with each entry listed alphabetically by title (see item 21 on p. 655).

All entries in the list are double-spaced, with no extra space between entries. Entries are formatted with a hanging indent: the first line of an entry is flush with the left margin, and subsequent lines are indented one-half inch.

In longer documents, a list of works cited may be given at the end of each chapter or section. In electronic documents that use links, such as a Web site, the list of works cited is often a separate page to which other pages are linked. To see works cited lists in MLA style, see pages 155, 373, and 428.

Print Books

16. One author List the author's last name first, followed by a comma and the first name. Italicize the book title and subtitle, if any. List the city of publication and the publisher, separated by a colon; then insert a comma and the publication year. End with the medium "Print" and a period.

> Martenson, Chris. *The Crash Course: The Unsustainable Future of Our Economy, Energy, and Environment*. Hoboken: Wiley, 2011. Print.

17. Two or three authors List all the authors in the same order as on the title page, last name first for only the first author listed. Use commas to separate authors' names.

> Gable, Walter, and Carolyn Zogg. *The Seneca Army Depot: Fighting Wars from the New York Army Homefront*. Charleston: History Press, 2012. Print.

18. Four or more authors Provide the first author's name (last name first) followed by a comma, and then the abbreviation "et al." (Latin for "and others").

> Heartney, Eleanor, et al. *After the Revolution: Women Who Transformed Contemporary Art*. New York: Prestel, 2013. Print.

19. Corporate or group author Write out the full name of the corporation or group, and cite the name as you would an author. This name is often also the name of the publisher.

> National Geographic. *Great Empires: An Illustrated Atlas*. Washington: Natl. Geographic, 2012. Print.

20. Unknown author When no author is listed on the title or copyright page, begin the entry with the title of the work. Alphabetize the entry by the first word of the title other than *A*, *An*, or *The*.

> *The Kingfisher History Encyclopedia*. New York: Macmillan, 2012. Print.

21. Two or more books by the same author Use the author's name in the first entry. Thereafter, use three hyphens followed by a period in place of the author's name. List the entries alphabetically by title.

> Hitchens, Christopher. *Arguably: Essays by Christopher Hitchens*. New York: Hachette, 2012. Print.

> ---. *God Is Not Great: How Religion Poisons Everything*. New York: Hachette, 2009. Print.

> ---. *Mortality*. New York: Hachette, 2012. Print.

How do I cite books using MLA style?

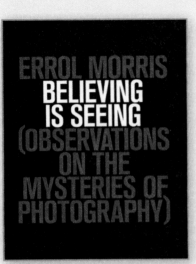

When citing a book, use the information from the title page and the copyright page (on the reverse side of the title page), not from the book's cover or a library catalog. Consult pages 654–658 for additional models for citing books.

```
  ┌─ A ─┐ ┌──────────────── B ─────────────────┐
```
Morris, Errol. *Believing Is Seeing (Observations on the Mysteries of Photography).*
```
     ┌── C ──┐┌── D ──┐ ┌ E ┐┌ F ┐
```
New York: Penguin, 2011. Print.

A   **The author.** Give the last name first, followed by a comma, the first name, and the middle initial (if given). Omit titles such as "MD," "PhD," or "Sir"; include suffixes after the name and a comma (O'Driscoll, Gerald P., Jr.). End with a period.

B   **The title.** Give the full title; include the subtitle (if any), preceded by a colon. Italicize the title and subtitle; capitalize all major words. End with a period.

C   **The city of publication.** If more than one city is given, use the first one listed. Insert a colon.

D   **The publisher.** Give a shortened version of the publisher's name ("Harper" for HarperCollins Publishers; "Harcourt" for Harcourt Brace; "Oxford UP" for Oxford University Press). Do not include the words "Publisher" or "Inc." Follow with a comma.

E   **The year of publication.** If more than one copyright date is given, use the most recent one. Use "n.d." if no date is given. End with a period.

F   **The medium consulted.** For a printed book, insert "Print" and end with a period.

22. Editor(s) Use the abbreviation "ed." or "eds."

> Bradley, Adam, and Andrew DuBois, eds. *The Anthology of Rap*. New Haven: Yale UP,
> 2011. Print.

23. Author with an editor Include the name of the editor (first name first) after the title. Use the abbreviation "Ed." (meaning "Edited by").

> Solomon, Golda. *Medicine Woman of Jazz*. Ed. M. Stefan Strozier and Kyle Tourke. New
> York: World Audience, 2012. Print.

24. Translated book List the author first and then the title, followed by the name of the translator and publication information. Use the abbreviation "Trans."

> Paz, Octavio. *The Poems of Octavio Paz*. Trans. Eliot Weinberger. New York: New
> Directions, 2012. Print.

25. Edition other than the first Include the number of the edition and the abbreviation "ed." (meaning "edition") after the title.

> MacQueen, Norrie. *The United Nations, Peace Operations and the Cold War*. 2nd ed.
> New York: Pearson, 2011. Print.

26. Republished book Indicate the original date of publication after the title.

> Davidson, Bruce. *Subway*. 1986. New York: Aperture, 2011. Print.

27. Multivolume work Include the total number of volumes and the abbreviation "vols." after the title.

> Gates, Alexander, and Robert P. Blauvelt. *Encyclopedia of Pollution*. 2 vols. New York:
> Infobase, 2012. Print.

If you have used only one of the volumes in your document, include the volume number after the title. List the total number of volumes after the publication information.

> Lyubimov, Alexander V., ed. *Encyclopedia of Drug Metabolism and Interactions*. Vol. 3.
> Hoboken: Wiley, 2012. Print. 6 vols.

28. Work in an edited collection or anthology Begin your citation with the author. Surround the title of the selection with quotation marks. Follow this with the title of the anthology or collection in italics, the abbreviation "Ed." (meaning "Edited by"), and the names of the editor(s) (first name first) as well as publication information. Then give the inclusive page numbers for the selection or chapter. End with the medium.

> Hayden, Thomas. "How to Hatch a Dinosaur." *The Best American Science and Nature Writing 2012*. Ed. Dan Ariely and Tim Folger. New York: Houghton, 2012. 35-43. Print.

If you are using multiple works from the same anthology, you may include the anthology itself in your list of works cited and cross-reference it in the citations for individual works. Do not include the medium in the cross-referenced entries.

> Gears, Jeff. "'The Great Machine Doesn't Wear a Cape!': American Cultural Anxiety and the Post-9/11 Superhero." Pustz 250-61.

> Lewis, A. David. "The Militarism of American Superheroes after 9/11." Pustz 223-36.

> Pustz, Matthew, ed. *Comic Books and American Cultural History: An Anthology*. New York: Continuum, 2012. Print.

29. Foreword, introduction, preface, or afterword Begin with the author of the part you are citing and the name of that part. Add the title of the work; "By" or "Ed." and the work's author or editor (first name first); and publication information. Then give the inclusive page numbers for the part. End with the medium.

> Mika, Mike. Introduction. *The Art of Video Games: From Pac-Man to Mass Effect*. By Chris Melissinos and Patrick O'Rourke. New York: Welcome, 2012. 10-11. Print.

If the foreword or other part has a title, include the title in quotation marks between the author and the name of the part.

> Kaplan, Jacob. "Not to Be Forgotten." Foreword. *Chicago Cable Cars*. By Greg Borzo. Charleston: History Press, 2012. 9-12. Print.

30. Sacred text Include the title of the version as it appears on the title page. If the title does not identify the version, place that information directly after the title.

> *Holy Bible, 1611 King James Version*. Grand Rapids, MI: Zondervan, 2011. Print.

31. Dissertation or thesis Cite as you would a book, but include an appropriate label such as "Diss." or "MA thesis" after the title. Add the school and the year before any publication information.

Adams, Claire E. *Effects of Mindfulness on Body Image, Affect, and Smoking in Women.* Diss. Louisiana State U, 2011. Ann Arbor: ProQuest, 2011. Print.

Sources in Print Journals, Magazines, and Newspapers

32. Article in a journal Enclose the article title in quotation marks. After the journal title, list the volume number, add a period, and insert the issue number, with no space. Then insert the year of publication in parentheses, a colon, and inclusive page numbers. Include the issue number regardless of whether the journal restarts its pagination for each issue or each volume. End with the medium.

Linesch, Debra, et al. "An Art Therapy Exploration of Immigration with Latino Families." *Art Therapy: Journal of the American Art Therapy Association* 29.3 (2012): 120-26. Print.

33. Article in a monthly or bimonthly magazine After the author's name and title of the article, list the title of the magazine, the date (use abbreviations for all months except May, June, and July), and inclusive page numbers. End with the medium.

Honan, Mat. "Kill the Password: Why a String of Characters Can't Protect Us Anymore." *Wired*. Dec. 2012: 47-53. Print.

34. Article in a weekly or biweekly magazine Give the exact date of publication, inverted.

Labash, Matt. "The Day the Twinkie Died." *Weekly Standard* 10 Dec. 2012: 29. Print.

35. Article in a newspaper If the name of the newspaper begins with *The*, omit the word. If the newspaper is not a national newspaper (such as the *Wall Street Journal*, *Christian Science Monitor*, or *Chronicle of Higher Education*) or if the city of publication is not part of its name, add the city in square brackets after the name of the newspaper: "[Salem]." List the date in inverted order, and if the masthead indicates that the paper has more than one edition, give this information after the date ("natl. ed.," "late ed."). Follow with a colon and a space, and then list the page numbers (use the section letter before the page number if the newspaper uses letters to designate sections). If the article does not appear on consecutive pages, write only the first page number and a plus sign (+), with no space between. End with the medium.

Guynn, Jessica. "Facebook Won't Stop at 1B Users." *Baltimore Sun* 6 Dec. 2012: A12. Print.

How do I cite articles from periodicals using MLA style?

Periodicals include journals, magazines, and newspapers. This page gives an example of a citation for a print magazine article. Models for citing articles from journals and newspapers are on page 659.

If you need to cite a periodical article you accessed electronically, follow the guidelines below and see also item 56 on page 665 and item 65 on page 669.

┌── A ──┐ ┌─────── B ───────┐ ┌ C ┐┌ D ┐┌ E ┐┌ F ┐┌ G ┐
Thompson, Clive. "Unsaving the Planet." *Wired* 20.3 (2012): 42. Print.

A   The author. The author. Give the last name first, followed by a comma, the first name, and the middle initial (if given). Omit titles such as "MD," "PhD," or "Sir"; include suffixes after the name and a comma (O'Driscoll, Gerald P., Jr.). End with a period.

B   The article title. Give the full title; include the subtitle (if any), preceded by a colon. Enclose the title and subtitle in quotation marks, and capitalize all major words. Place a period inside the closing quotation mark.

C   The periodical title. Italicize the periodical title; exclude any initial "A," "An," or "The"; capitalize all major words.

D   The volume number and issue number. For journals, include the volume number, followed by a period (no space) and the issue number.

E   The date of publication. For journals, give the year in parentheses, followed by a colon. For monthly magazines, don't use parentheses; give the month and year. For weekly magazines and newspapers, don't use parentheses; give the day, month, and year, in that order. Abbreviate the names of all months except May, June, and July.

F   Inclusive page number(s). For numbers 100 and above, give only the last two digits and any other preceding digits if different from the first number (22-28, 402-10, 1437-45, 592-603). Include section letters for newspapers, if relevant. End with a period.

G   The medium consulted. For print journals, magazines, and newspapers, insert "Print" and end with a period.

36. Unsigned article Begin with the title of the article. Alphabetize by the first word other than *A*, *An*, or *The*.

> "Cloud Nein? Is Global Drought Really Getting Worse?" *Economist*. [London]
>   1 Dec. 2012: 37-38. Print.

37. Editorial Include the word "Editorial" after the title.

> "Defending the Insanity Defense." Editorial. *Los Angeles Times* 28 Nov. 2012: A17.
>   Print.

38. Letter to the editor Include the word "Letter" after the title.

> Goggin, Michael. "Wind Energy Reliable and Safe Alternative." Letter. *Columbus*
>   *Dispatch* 6 Dec. 2012: A11. Print.

39. Review After the author and title of the review, include the words "Rev. of" followed by the title of the work under review; a comma; the word "by" or "ed." (for a book) or "dir." (for a play or film); and the name of the author or director. Continue with publication information for the review.

> Oshinsky, David. "Sporty Jews." Rev. of *Jewish Jocks: An Unorthodox Hall of Fame*, ed.
>   Franklin Foer and Mark Tracy. *New York Times* 30 Nov. 2012: BR49. Print.

40. Published interview Begin with the person interviewed. If the published interview has a title, give it in quotation marks. If not, write the word "Interview." If an interviewer is identified and relevant to your project, give that name next. Then supply the publication data.

> Baldwin, Alec. "Happy Landing, Mr. Baldwin." Interview by Todd S. Purdum. *Vanity Fair*
>   Aug. 2012: 49-52. Print.

Print Reference Works

41. Entry in an encyclopedia, dictionary, thesaurus, handbook, or almanac Unless the entry is signed, begin your citation with the title of the entry in quotation marks, followed by a period. Give the title of the reference work, italicized, and the edition (if available) and year of publication. If the work is arranged alphabetically, you may omit the volume and page numbers.

> "Ringtone." *Webster's American English Dictionary*. 2011. Print.

If a reference work is not well known, provide all of the bibliographic information.

> Murray, Michael T., and Joseph Pizzorno. "Insomnia." *The Encyclopedia of Natural Medicine*. 3rd ed. New York: Atria, 2012. Print.

42. Map or chart Generally, treat a map or chart as you would a book without authors. Give its title, the word "Map" or "Chart," and publication information. For a map in an atlas, give the map title (in quotation marks), followed by publication information for the atlas and page numbers for the map. If the creator of the map or chart is listed, use his or her name as you would an author's name.

> *Thomas Guide: Los Angeles County*. Map. Chicago: Rand, 2011. Print.

> "Greenland." Map. *Atlas of the World*. 19th ed. London: Oxford UP, 2012. 154. Print.

43. Government publication In most cases, cite the government agency as the author. If there is a named author, editor, or compiler, provide that name after the title. Use the abbreviations "Dept." for department, "Cong." for Congress, "S." for Senate, "H." or "HR" for House of Representatives, "Res." for resolution, "Rept." for report, "Doc." for document, and "GPO" for Government Printing Office.

> United States Dept. of Health and Human Services. *Addiction Counseling Competencies: The Knowledge, Skills, and Attitudes of Professional Practice*. Washington: GPO, 2012. Print.

If you are citing from the *Congressional Record*, the entry is simply *Cong. Rec.* followed by the date, a colon, the page numbers, and the medium.

44. Brochure or pamphlet Format the entry as you would for a book (see p. 656).

> UNICEF. *Legacies*. London: UNICEF UK, 2012. Print.

Field Sources

45. Personal interview Place the name of the person interviewed first, words to indicate how the interview was conducted ("Personal interview," "Telephone interview," or "E-mail interview"), and the date.

> Caplan, Nigel. Personal interview. 20 June 2013.

46. Personal survey Place the title of the survey first, followed by the location of the survey if it was conducted in a particular city or state, the date the survey was first distributed, and an indication of how the interview was conducted ("Telephone survey," "E-mail survey," "Web survey," "Mail survey," or "Face-to-face survey").

> "Survey of Student Satisfaction with Academic Advising." Middlebury College. 22 Apr. 2012. E-mail survey.

47. Unpublished letter If the letter was written to you, give the writer's name, the words "Letter to the author" (no quotation marks), and the date the letter was written. End with the form of the material: use "MS" (meaning "manuscript") for a handwritten letter and "TS" (meaning "typescript") for a typed letter.

> Cortinez, Veronica. Letter to the author. 17 Jan. 2013. TS.

If the letter was written to someone else, give that name rather than "the author."

48. Lecture or public address Give the speaker's name and the title of the lecture (if there is one). If the lecture was part of a meeting or convention, identify that event. Conclude with the event data, including venue, city, and date. End with the appropriate label ("Lecture," "Panel discussion," "Reading").

> Wood, James. Porter Square Books, Cambridge. 11 Dec. 2012. Reading.

Media Sources

49. Film or video recording Generally begin with the title of the film or recording. Always supply the name of the director (following the abbreviation "Dir."), the distributor, and the year of original release. You may also insert other relevant information, such as the names of the performers or screenplay writers, before the distributor. End with the medium ("Film," "DVD," "Blu-ray disc," "Videocassette"). For DVDs, Blu-ray discs, and videocassettes, include the original release date.

> *The Hobbit: An Unexpected Journey*. Dir. Peter Jackson. Perf. Martin Freeman and Ian McKellen. New Line Cinema, 2012. Film.

> *On the Waterfront*. Dir. Elia Kazan. 1954. Criterion Collection, 2013. DVD.

50. Television or radio program Include the title of the program, the network or station, the call letters and city (if any), the date on which the program aired, and the medium ("Radio," "Television"). If there are relevant persons to name (such as the author, director, host, narrator, or actor), include that information after the title.

If the program has named episodes or segments, list those in quotation marks. If the material you're citing is an interview, include the word "Interview" and, if relevant, the name of the interviewer.

> "Inside Amazon: Secrets of an Online Mega-Giant." *Nightline*. Host Neal Karlinsky. ABC. WMAR, Baltimore, 26 Nov. 2012. Television.

> "The Key to Zen for Tony Bennett: 'Life Is a Gift.'" *Talk of the Nation*. Host Neal Conan. Natl. Public Radio. WBUR, Boston, 20 Nov. 2012. Radio.

> Romney, Mitt. Interview by Brian Williams. *NBC Nightly News*. NBC. WWMT, Kalamazoo, 8 Dec. 2012. Television.

51. Sound recording Begin with the name of the person whose work you want to highlight: the composer, the conductor, or the performer. Next list the title, followed by the names of other artists (composer, conductor, performers), with abbreviations indicating their roles. The recording information includes the manufacturer and the date. End with the medium of the recording ("CD," "LP," "Audiocassette," "Audio-tape," "MP3 file").

> Stoltzman, Richard. *Mozart: Clarinet Concerto, Clarinet Quintet*. English Chamber Orchestra. RCA Red Seal, 2011. CD.

If you wish to cite a particular track on the recording, give its performer and title (in quotation marks), and then proceed with the information about the recording. For live recordings, include the date of the performance between the title and the recording data.

> Peter, Paul & Mary. "Puff, the Magic Dragon." *Live in Japan, 1967*. Rec. 16 Jan. 1967. Rhino Records, 2012. MP3 file.

52. Live performance Generally, begin with the title of the performance. Then give the author and director; the major performers; and the theater, city, and date. End with "Performance."

> *The Book of Mormon*. By Matt Stone and Trey Parker. Dir. Casey Nicholaw and Trey Parker. Perf. Gavin Creel and Jared Gertner. Bank of America Theater, Chicago. 11 Dec. 2012. Performance.

53. Work of art Give the name of the artist; the title of the work (italicized); the date of composition; the medium of composition; the name of the collection, museum, or owner; and the city. If you are citing artwork published in a book, add the publication information for the book and the medium of publication ("Print") at the end.

> Perez, Enoc. *Marina Towers, Chicago*. 2012. Oil on canvas. Corcoran Gallery of Art,
> Washington.

54. Advertisement Provide the name of the product, service, or organization being advertised, followed by the word "Advertisement." Then provide the usual publication information.

> New York Lottery. Advertisement. *New York Post* Aug. 2012: 13. Print.

55. Cartoon Treat a cartoon like an article in a newspaper or magazine. Give the cartoonist's name, the title of the cartoon if there is one (in quotation marks), the word "Cartoon," and the publication data for the source.

> Bish, Randy. "NHL Standstill." Cartoon. *Pittsburgh Tribune-Review* 7 Dec. 2012: 37.
> Print.

Electronic Sources

56. Article from an online database or subscription service Cite it as you would a print article, and then give the name of the database in italics, the medium consulted ("Web"), and the date you accessed the article. (See also item 32 on p. 659.)

> Sander, Libby. "How 4 Colleges Take on Veterans' Issues, in Research and Real Life."
> *Chronicle of Higher Education* 59.4 (2012): 17-25. *Academic Search Premier*. Web.
> 4 Feb. 2013.

57. Short work from a Web site Include the author (if available), the title of the document in quotation marks, and the title of the Web site in italics. Then give the sponsor or publisher followed by a comma, the date of publication or last update followed by a period, the medium ("Web"), and the access date. (See also p. 668.) Do not include URLs in works cited entries.

> Snelling, Sherri. "Why Laughter Is Crucial for Caregivers." *Next Avenue*. PBS, 2012.
> Web. 10 Dec. 2012.

58. Academic course or department Web site For a course page, give the name of the instructor, the course title in italics, a description such as "Course home page," the course dates, the department, the institution, the medium, and your date of

How do I cite articles from databases using MLA style?

Libraries subscribe to services such as LexisNexis, ProQuest, InfoTrac, and EBSCOhost that provide access to databases of digital texts. The databases provide publication information, abstracts, and the complete text of documents in a specific subject area, discipline, or profession. (See also Chapter 12.)

Klugman, Joshua. "The Advanced Placement Arms Race and the Reproduction of Educational Inequality." *Teachers College Record* 115.5 (2013): 1. *ProQuest Education Journals*. Web. 7 Feb. 2013

A   **The author.** Give the last name first, followed by a comma, the first name, and the middle initial (if given). Omit titles such as "MD," "PhD," or "Sir"; include suffixes after the name and a comma (O'Driscoll, Gerald P., Jr.). End with a period.

B   **The article title.** Give the full title; include the subtitle (if any), preceded by a colon. Enclose the full title in quotation marks, and capitalize all major words. Place a period inside the closing quotation mark.

C   **The periodical title.** Italicize the periodical title; exclude any initial "A," "An," or "The"; capitalize all major words.

D   **The volume number and issue number if appropriate.** For journals, give the volume number, and then insert a period (no space) and the issue number.

E   **The date of publication.** For journals, give the year in parentheses, followed by a colon. For monthly magazines, don't use parentheses; give the month and year. For weekly magazines and newspapers, give the day, month, and year.

F   **Inclusive page number(s).** Include section letters for newspapers, if relevant. If no pagination is given, use "n. pag."

G   **The name of the database.** Italicize the name of the database, followed by a period.

H   **The medium consulted.** Use "Web" followed by a period.

I   **The date of access.** Use the day-month-year format; abbreviate all months except May, June, and July. End with a period.

access. For a department page, give the department name, a description such as "Home page," the institution, the date of the last update, the medium, and the date of access.

> Long, Jacqueline. *CLST 273/WSGS 297: Classical Tragedy with a Focus on Women's Studies and Gender*. Course home page. Fall 2012. Classical Studies Dept., Loyola U Chicago. Web. 7 Oct. 2012.

> Dept. of English. Home page. East Carolina U, 2012. Web. 3 Jan. 2013.

59. Personal Web site If the site has no title, give a description such as "Home page."

> Beal, Timothy. Home page. Harper, 2011. Web. 24 Nov. 2012.

60. Message posted to a newsgroup, electronic mailing list, or online discussion forum Cite the name of the person who posted the message and the title (from the subject line, in quotation marks); if the posting has no title, add the phrase "Online posting." Then add the name of the Web site (italicized), the sponsor or publisher, the date of the message, the medium ("Web"), and the date you accessed the posting.

> Biesanz, Jeremy. "Tanaka Personality Dissertation Award." *Social Psychology Network*. Scott Plous, Wesleyan U, 6 Feb. 2012. Web. 3 Dec. 2012.

61. Article or page on a wiki Because the material on a wiki is likely to change, include your date of access.

> "Sustainability." *Wikipedia*. Wikimedia Foundation, 9 Dec. 2012. Web. 22 Dec. 2012.

62. Blog To cite an entry or a comment on a blog, give the author of the entry or comment (if available), the title of the entry or comment in quotation marks, the title of the blog (italicized), the sponsor or publisher, the date the material was posted, the medium, and the access date.

> Marcotte, Amanda. "War Isn't a Male Value." *The XX Factor*. Washington Post, 29 Jan. 2013. Web. 6 Feb. 2013.

63. E-mail message Cite the sender of the message; the title (from the subject line); a phrase indicating the recipient of the message ("Message to"); the date of the message; and the medium ("E-mail"). (Note that MLA's style is to hyphenate the word *e-mail*.)

How do I cite works from Web sites using MLA style?

You will likely need to search the site to find some of the citation information you need. For some sites, all of the details may not be available; find as many as you can. Remember that the citation information you provide should allow readers to retrace your steps electronically to locate the sources. Consult pages 665–670 for additional models for citing Web sources.

Holt, Wythe. "Utopian Communities." *The American Revolution*. National Park Service, 13 May 2003. Web. 20 Dec. 2012.

A **The author of the work.** Give the last name first, followed by a comma, the first name, and the middle initial (if given). Omit titles such as "MD," "PhD," or "Sir"; include suffixes after the name and a comma (O'Driscoll, Gerald P., Jr.). Insert a period. If no author is given, begin with the title.

B **The title of the work.** Give the full title; include the subtitle (if any), preceded by a colon. Enclose the title and subtitle in quotation marks, and capitalize all major words. Place a period inside the closing quotation mark.

C **The title of the Web site.** Give the title of the entire site, italicized. If there is no clear title and it is a personal home page, use "Home page" without italicizing it. End with a period.

D **The name of the sponsoring organization.** Look for the sponsor's name at the bottom of the site's home page. If no publisher or sponsor is available, use "N. p." Follow with a comma.

E **The date of publication or most recent update.** Use the day-month-year format; abbreviate all months except May, June, and July. If no date is given, use "n.d." End with a period.

H **The medium consulted.** For works found online, use "Web" followed by a period.

G **The date you accessed it.** Give the most recent date you accessed the site. End with a period.

Zhang, Xudong. "Commentary on Mo Yan's 'Change.'" Message to Prof. Kristin Ross. 17
Apr. 2012. E-mail.

McMann, Lillian. "Ideas for Final Paper." Message to Carla Chavez. 25 Jan. 2013.
E-mail.

64. Online book Cite an online book as you would a print book; then give title of
the database or Web site (italicized), the medium ("Web"), and the access date (see
also item 16 on p. 654).

Sunderland, Jane. *Language, Gender and Children's Fiction*. New York: Continuum, 2011.
Google Book Search. Web. 4 May 2012.

65. Online periodical article Provide the author, the title of the article (in quotation
marks), and the name of the Web site (in italics). Then add the publisher or sponsor,
the date of publication, the medium ("Web"), and your date of access (see also items
32–40 on pp. 659–661).

Gold, Jenny. "'Life Specialists' Help Young Patients Cope with Illness." *Washingtonpost*
.com. Washington Post, 3 Dec. 2012. Web. 17 Dec. 2012.

Campos, Paul. "Too Many Lawyers? Who Says?" *Salon.com*. Salon Media Group, 29 Nov.
2012. Web. 29 Jan. 2013.

66. Online film or video clip (See also item 49 on p. 663.)

"Great Barrier Reef Loses More Than Half Its Coral Cover." *The Guardian*. Reuters, 2 Oct.
2012. Web. 4 Feb. 2013.

67. Online image Treat maps, charts, advertisements, and other visual documents you find online as you would the print versions, but include the Web site
(italicized), sponsor or publisher of the site, the medium ("Web"), and your date of
access. For a work of art found online, omit the medium of composition, and after
the location, add the title of the Web site or database (italicized), the medium consulted ("Web"), and your date of access. (See also item 42 on p. 662 and items 53–55
on pp. 664–665.)

"Grand Canyon National Park, Grand Canyon Village, Arizona." Map. *Google Maps*.
Google, 6 Feb. 2013. Web. 6 Feb. 2013.

Thompson, Bob. *Tree*. 1962. Natl. Gallery of Art, Washington. *National Gallery of Art*.
Web. 30 Mar. 2012.

IBM. Advertisement. *New Yorker.* Condé Nast, 2012. Web. 14 Dec. 2012.

68. DVD, Blu-ray disc, or CD-ROM Treat a work published on DVD, Blu-ray disc, or CD-ROM as you would a book, noting "DVD," "Blu-ray disc," or "CD-ROM" as the medium.

Lewis, Michael. *Moneyball: The Art of Winning an Unfair Game.* Cologne: Random House Audio, 2011. CD-ROM.

69. Computer software or video game Cite computer software as you would a book. Provide additional information about the medium on which it is distributed ("CD-ROM," "Xbox 360," and so on) and the version.

Cross of the Dutchman. Leeuwarden: Triangle Studios, 2012. CD-ROM.

70. Other online sources For other online sources, adapt the guidelines to the medium. Include as much information as necessary for your readers to easily find your source. The example below is for a radio program available in an online archive.

"Why Legos Are So Expensive — And So Popular." *All Things Considered.* Host Robert Siegal. Chicago Public Radio. WBEZ, Chicago. 13 Dec. 2012. Web. 17 Jan. 2013.

Using APA Style

American Psychological Association (APA) style, used
primarily in the social sciences and in some of the natural
sciences, emphasizes the author(s) and publication date of a
source. Writers who use the APA documentation system cite,
or formally acknowledge, information within their text using
parentheses and provide a list of sources, called a references
list, at the end of their document.

To see student essays formatted and documented in APA
style, use one of the following examples in Part Two:

> Ellen Page, *To Spray or Not to Spray: The Issue of DDT Use for
> Indoor Residual Spraying*, page 201
>
> Ali Bizzul, *Living (and Dying) Large*, page 262
>
> Dwight Haynes, *Making Better Choices: Two Approaches
> to Reducing College Drinking*, page 313

For more information about APA style, consult the *Publication
Manual of the American Psychological Association*, Sixth Edition.
Information about this publication can be found on the
APA Web site at www.apa.org.

CITATIONS WITHIN YOUR TEXT

ENTRIES IN YOUR REFERENCES LIST

● PRINT BOOKS

● SOURCES IN PRINT JOURNALS, MAGAZINES, AND NEWSPAPERS

● PRINT REFERENCE WORKS

● FIELD SOURCES

● MEDIA SOURCES

● ELECTRONIC SOURCES

● OTHER SOURCES

How Do I Cite Sources within the Text of My Document?

APA uses an author-date form of in-text citation to acknowledge the use of another writer's words, facts, or ideas. When you are summarizing or paraphrasing, provide the author's last name and the year of publication either in the sentence or in parentheses at the end of the sentence. You may include a page or chapter reference if it would help readers find the original material in a longer work. When you are quoting, the citation in parentheses must include the page(s) or paragraph(s) (for sources that do not have pages) in which the quotation can be found.

Although APA requires page numbers only for direct quotations, your instructor might prefer that you include a page or paragraph number with every source you cite in your document. If you're not certain of the requirements for your project, ask your instructor for guidance.

1. Basic format for a source named in your text Place the publication year in parentheses directly after the author's last name. Include the page number (with "p." for "page") in parentheses after a direct quotation.

> Jennings (2012) pointed out that humans are poor students of probability, meaning that we're prone to "develop paranoid nightmare-inducing phobias about the unlikeliest things (plane crashes, strangers kidnapping our kids) while ignoring far more pressing risks (heart disease, car accidents)" (p. xiv).

> According to Jennings (2012), humans have a tendency to fear the most unlikely phenomena, while brushing off more apparent dangers.

Note that APA style requires using the past tense or present perfect tense to introduce the material you are citing: *Jennings argued* or *Jennings has argued*.

2. Basic format for a source not named in your text Insert a parenthetical note that gives the author's last name and the year of the publication, separated by a comma. For a quotation, include the page or paragraph number of the source.

> Psychoneuroimmunology, a new field of medicine, "studies the ways that the psyche — the mind and its content of emotions — profoundly interacts with the body's nervous system and how both of them, in turn, form an essential link with our immune defenses" (Mate, 2011, p. 5).

> Psychoneuroimmunology is a new field of medicine that examines the link between human emotion and physiology and how that unity affects health and immunity over the course of a life (Mate, 2011).

3. Two authors List the last names of both authors in every mention in the text. If you mention the authors' names in a sentence, use the word "and" to separate the last names, as shown in the first example. If you place the authors' names in the parenthetical citation, use an ampersand (&) to separate the last names, as shown in the second example.

> Tannenbaum and Marks (2012) indicated that "many of [MTV's] most important founders came from radio backgrounds, which freed them from abiding by the existing rules of the television industry" (p. 14).

> MTV was largely founded by individuals with radio expertise, which allowed the network to operate outside the constraints of the television industry (Tannenbaum & Marks, 2012).

4. Three, four, or five authors In parentheses, name all the authors the first time you cite the source, using an ampersand (&) before the last author's name. In subsequent references to the source, use the last name of the first author followed by the abbreviation "et al." (Latin for "and others").

> Those who suffer from body dysmorphic disorder (BDD) are preoccupied with one or more areas of the body they feel are imperfect or deformed (Wilhelm, Phillips, & Steketee, 2013). As a result, they tend to engage in compulsive rituals to improve or conceal the perceived flaw (Wilhelm et al., 2013).

5. Six or more authors In all references to the source, give the first author's last name followed by "et al."

> While their study suggests that female Operation Enduring Freedom and Operation Iraqi Freedom soldiers are just as resilient to combat-related stress as are male soldiers, Vogt et al. (2011) submitted that further research is needed to evaluate gender differences in the long-term effects of stress postdeployment.

6. Corporate, group, or government author In general, cite the full name of the corporation, group, or government agency the first time it is mentioned in your text. If you add an abbreviation for the name in square brackets the first time you cite the source, you can use the abbreviation in subsequent citations.

A new international treaty has been signed to help combat the illicit trade of tobacco products (World Health Organization [WHO], 2013). This protocol will not only establish a global tracing system to reduce and eliminate illicit tobacco trade but will also play an important role in protecting people around the world from a serious health risk (WHO, 2013).

7. Unknown author Sources with unknown authors are listed by title in the list of references (see item 18 on p. 679). In your in-text citation, shorten the title as much as possible without introducing confusion. Add quotation marks to article titles, and italicize book titles.

While life expectancy in general has improved for those living in developed countries, the improvement has been far more drastic for men — a phenomenon that is closing the gender gap in longevity ("Catching Up," 2013).

8. Two or more works by the same author in the same year After organizing the works alphabetically by title, insert a lowercase letter after the publication year ("2013a" or "2013b").

Garfield (2012b) noted that our evolution as a society is consistently reflected in how we map our world: from the origins of triangulation and the fixing of longitude to aerial photography and, now, GPS and satellite navigation.

9. Two or more authors with the same last name Use the authors' initials in each citation.

While both R. Cohen (2012) and L. Cohen (2012) have presented stark and sincere biographies free of bias, L. Cohen has introduced a new concept to the genre by chronicling three worthy subjects at once.

10. Two or more works cited together List the sources in alphabetical order, and separate them with semicolons. If you are referring to two or more sources by the same author, order those sources chronologically and give the author's last name only once ("Gharib, 2010, 2012").

Rather than encourage exploration into more difficult and inaccessible energy stores, our new awareness of the finite nature of the earth's resources should incite a change in lifestyle that no longer strains the limits of our environment (Dietz & O'Neill, 2013; Klare, 2012).

11. Source cited in another source Ideally, you should track down the original source of the information. If you cannot find the original, mention its author and indicate where it was cited.

> Slater posited that the rise in online dating services has led to a decrease in commitment, as this technology fosters the notion that one can always find a more compatible mate (as cited in Weissmann, 2013).

12. Source with no page numbers Many visual documents, such as brochures, and electronic sources, such as Web sites and full-text articles from databases, lack page numbers. If the source has numbered paragraphs, indicate the paragraph number. If the paragraphs are not numbered, include the section heading and indicate which paragraph in that section contains the cited material.

> Doig (2012) examined the rise in tactical urbanism, a kind of city planning newly employed by big government to take small bits of unusable public space and re-create them as parks, gardens, and other areas designed for public use (para. 3).

13. E-mail, letters, and other personal communication Give the first initial(s) and last name of the person with whom you corresponded, the words "personal communication," and the date. Don't include personal communication in your references list.

> (C. Soto, personal communication, May 13, 2012)

14. Web site For an entire Web site, give the URL in parentheses in your text, and don't include it in your references list. To cite a quotation from a Web site, give the paragraph number and include the source in your references list.

> The Library of Congress (http://loc.gov) offers extensive online collections of manuscripts, correspondence, sound recordings, photographs, prints, and audiovisual materials spanning decades of American history.

> The Environmental Protection Agency (2013) combats climate change by evaluating policy options that "range from comprehensive market-based legislation to targeted regulations to reduce emissions and improve the efficiency of vehicles, power plants and large industrial sources" (para. 2).

How Do I Prepare the References List?

The references list contains publication information for all sources that you have cited within your document, with two exceptions. Entire Web sites and personal communication, such as e-mail messages, letters, and interviews, are cited only in the text of the document.

Begin the list on a new page at the end of the document, and center the title "References" at the top. Organize the list alphabetically by author (if the source is an organization, alphabetize it by the name of the organization; if the source has no known author, alphabetize it by title). All of the entries should be double-spaced with no extra space between entries. Entries are formatted with a hanging indent: the first line is flush with the left margin, and subsequent lines are indented one-half inch. Only the initial word and proper nouns (names of people, organizations, cities, states, and so on) in a source title and subtitle are capitalized.

In longer documents, a references list may be given at the end of each chapter or section. In electronic documents that use links, such as Web sites, the references list is often a separate page to which other pages are linked.

For examples of references lists in APA style, see pages 208, 267, and 319.

Print Books

15. One author List the author's last name followed by a comma and the first initial. Insert the date in parentheses and italicize the title. Follow with the place of publication and the publisher, separated by a colon.

> D'Angelo, J. (2012). *Ethics in science: Ethical misconduct in scientific research.* Boca Raton, FL: CRC Press.

16. Two or more authors List the authors in the same order as the title page does, each with last name first. Use commas to separate authors and use an ampersand (&) before the final author's name. List every author up to and including seven; for a work with eight or more authors, give the first six names followed by three ellipsis dots and the last author's name. (Do not use an ampersand in such cases.)

> Gibbs, N., & Duffy, M. (2012). *The president's club: Inside the world's most exclusive fraternity.* New York, NY: Simon & Schuster.

How do I cite books using APA style?

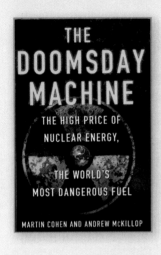

When citing a book, use the information from the title page and the copyright page (on the reverse side of the title page), not from the book's cover or a library catalog. Consult pages 677–680 for additional models for citing books.

A ─────────── B ── C ───────────────

Cohen, M., & McKillop, A. (2012). *The doomsday machine: The high price of nuclear*

─────── C ─────── D ── E ───

energy, the world's most dangerous fuel. New York, NY: Palgrave Macmillan.

A   **The author.** Give the last name first, followed by a comma and initials for first name and, if any, middle name. Separate initials with a space (Leakey, R. E.). Separate the names of multiple authors with commas; use an ampersand (&) before the final author's name.

B   **The year of publication.** Put the most recent copyright year in parentheses, and end with a period (outside the closing parenthesis).

C   **The title and, if any, the subtitle.** Give the full title; include the subtitle (if any), preceded by a colon. Italicize the title and subtitle, capitalizing only the first word of the title, the first word of the subtitle, and any proper nouns or proper adjectives. End with a period.

D   **The place of publication.** If more than one city is given, use the first one listed. Use an abbreviation for U.S. states and territories; spell out city and country names for locations outside the United States (Cambridge, England). For Canadian cities, also include the province. Insert a colon.

E   **The publisher.** Give the publisher's name. Omit words such as "Inc." and "Co." Include and do not abbreviate such terms as "University," "Books," and "Press." End with a period.

17. Corporate or group author Write out the full name of a corporate or group author. If the corporation is also the publisher, use "Author" for the publisher's name.

American Pharmacists Association. (2012). *Drug information handbook: A comprehensive resource for all clinicians and healthcare professionals*. Hudson, OH: Author.

18. Unknown author When no author is listed on the title or copyright page, begin the entry with the title of the work. Alphabetize the entry by the first significant word of the title (not including *A, An*, or *The*).

The book of Aquarius: Alchemy and the philosopher's stone. (2011). Charleston, SC: Forgotten Books.

19. Two or more books by the same author(s) Give the author's name in each entry and list the titles in chronological order.

Macintyre, B. (2011). *Operation mincemeat: How a dead man and a bizarre plan fooled the Nazis and assured an Allied victory*. New York, NY: Broadway Paperbacks.

Macintyre, B. (2012). *Double cross: The true story of the D-Day spies*. New York, NY: Crown Publishers.

20. Translated book List the author first, followed by the year of publication, the title, and the translator (in parentheses, identified by the abbreviation "Trans."). Place the original date of the work's publication at the end of the entry.

Alighieri, D. (2011). *Divine comedy, Cary's translation, complete* (H. F. Cary, Trans.). Auckland, New Zealand: Aeterna Publishing. (Original work published 1805).

21. Edition other than the first Note the edition ("2nd ed.," "Rev. ed.") after the title.

Rosa, A. & Eschholz, P. (2012). *Models for writers* (11th ed.). Boston, MA: Bedford/ St. Martin's.

22. Author with an editor Include the editor's name and the abbreviation "Ed." in parentheses after the title.

Newport, M. T. (2011). *Alzheimer's disease: What if there was a cure?* (P. Hirsch, Ed.). Laguna Beach, CA: Basic Health Publications.

23. Work in an edited collection or anthology, including a foreword, introduction, preface, or afterword Begin the entry with the author, the publication date, and the title of the chapter or selection (not italicized). Follow this with the word "In," the names of the editors (initials first), the abbreviation "Ed." or "Eds." in parentheses, the title of the anthology or collection (italicized), inclusive page numbers for the chapter or selection (in parentheses, with the abbreviation "pp."), and the place and publisher.

> Gherovici, P. (2011). Bulimia: Between phobia and addiction. In Y. G. Baldwin, K. R. Malone, & T. Svolos (Eds.), *Lacan and addiction: An anthology* (pp. 93-110). London, England: Karnac Books.

> Mate, G. (2012). Foreword. In L. Rowntree & A. Boden (Eds.), *Hidden lives: Coming out on mental illness* (pp. 1-2). Victoria, British Columbia: Brindle & Glass.

24. Sacred text Treat as you would a book (see items 15–18 on pp. 677–679).

> *Holy Bible: King James version.* (2011). New York, NY: American Bible Society.

25. Dissertation or thesis Give the author, date, and title before identifying the type of work (doctoral dissertation or master's thesis). End with the name of the database and the identifying number, or the URL.

> West, R. (2012). *Hostility toward the unattractive: Challenging current "sexual harassment" law* (Doctoral dissertation). Available from Dissertation.com. (http://www.dissertation.com/book.php?method=ISBN&book=1612339417)

26. Two or more sources by the same author in the same year List the works alphabetically, and include lowercase letters (*a*, *b*, and so on) after the dates.

> Roach, M. (2013a). *Gulp: Adventures on the alimentary canal.* New York, NY: W. W. Norton.

> Roach, M. (2013b). *My planet: Finding humor in the oddest places.* White Plains, NY: Reader's Digest.

Sources in Print Journals, Magazines, and Newspapers

27. Article in a journal paginated by volume Most journals continue page numbers throughout an entire annual volume, beginning again at page 1 only in the first volume of the next year. After the author and publication year, provide the article title, the journal title, the volume number (italicized), and the inclusive page numbers.

Leaf, J. B. Oppenheim-Leaf, M. L. Leaf, R., Courtemanche, A. B., Taubman, M., McEachin, J., . . . Sherman, J. A. (2012) Observational effects on preference selection for three children on the autism spectrum. *Journal of Applied Behavior Analysis, 45*, 473-483.

28. Article in a journal paginated by issue Some journals begin at page 1 for every issue. Include the issue number (in parentheses, not italicized) after the volume number.

Thompson, R. J., Mata, J., Jaeggi, S. M., Buschkuehl, M., Jonides, J., & Gotlib, I. H. The everyday emotional experience of adults with major depressive disorder: Examining emotional instability, inertia, and reactivity. *Journal of Abnormal Psychology, 121*(4), 819-829.

29. Article in a magazine The author's name and the publication date (year and month for monthly magazines; year, month, and date for weekly or biweekly magazines) are followed by the title of the article, the magazine title (italicized), and the volume number (also italicized) and the issue number, if any. Include all page numbers.

Sifferlin, A. (2012, November 29). Predicting obesity at birth. *Time, 180*(22), 34-35.

Fecht, S. (2012, December). Reef in a box. *Popular Science, 281*(6), 16.

30. Article in a newspaper List the author's name and the complete date (year first). Next give the article title followed by the name of the newspaper (italicized). Include all page numbers, preceded by "p." or "pp."

Mestel, R. (2012, March 4). Genetically engineered salmon moves closer to FDA approval. *Los Angeles Times*, p. A17.

31. Unsigned article Begin with the article title, and alphabetize in the references list by the first word in the title other than *A, An*, or *The*. Use "p." or "pp." before page numbers.

RNA-only genes: The origin of species? (2012, April 28). *The Economist, 388*(8592), p. 40.

32. Editorial Include the word "Editorial" in square brackets after the title.

Affirm gays' right to marriage [Editorial]. (2012, December 14). *The Dallas Morning News*, p. B12.

How do I cite articles from print periodicals using APA style?

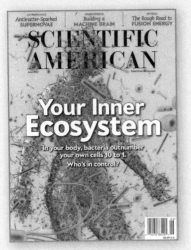

Periodicals include journals, magazines, and newspapers. This page gives an example of a citation for an article in a magazine. Models for citing articles from journals and newspapers are on pages 680–683. If you need to cite a periodical article you accessed electronically, follow the guidelines below and see pages 685–687.

┌──── A ────┐ ┌── B ──┐ ┌──── C ────┐
Kaiser, D., & Creager, A. N. H. (2012, June). The right way to get it wrong.

┌──── D ────┐ ┌ E ┐ ┌ F ┐
Scientific American, 306(6), 70-75.

A **The author.** Give the last name first, followed by a comma and initials for first and middle names. Separate the names of multiple authors with commas; use an ampersand (&) before the final author's name.

B **The year of publication.** Put the year in parentheses and end with a period (outside the closing parenthesis). For magazines and newspapers, include the month and, if relevant, the day (2012, April 13).

C **The article title.** Give the full title; include the subtitle (if any), preceded by a colon. Do not underline, italicize, or put the title in quotation marks. Capitalize only the first word of the title, the first word of the subtitle, and any proper nouns or proper adjectives. End with a period (unless the article title ends with a question mark).

D **The periodical title.** Italicize the periodical title, and capitalize all major words. Insert a comma.

E **The volume and issue number, if relevant.** For magazines and journals with volume numbers, include the volume number, italicized. For magazines and for journals that start each issue with page 1, include the issue number in parentheses, not italicized. Insert a comma.

F **Inclusive page number(s).** Give all of the numbers in full (248-254, not 248-54). For newspapers, include the abbreviation "p." or "pp." for page and section letters, if relevant (p. B12). End with a period.

33. Letter to the editor Include the words "Letter to the editor" in square brackets after the title of the letter, if any.

> Gonzalez Hernandez, L. (2012, November 23). Stores should close on holidays [Letter to the editor]. *Newsday*, p. A24.

34. Review After the title of the review, include the words "Review of the book . . ." or "Review of the film . . ." and so on in square brackets, followed by the title of the work reviewed. If the reviewed work is a book, include the author's name after a comma; if it's a film or other media, include the year of release.

> Kakutani, M. (2012, December 11). Recalling lives altered, in ways vivid and untidy [Review of the book *Dear Life: Stories*, by Alice Munro]. *The New York Times Book Review*, p. C1.

> Fleming, J. (2012, October 27). American stage's 'Wit' is good medicine [Review of the play *Wit*, 1995]. *The Tampa Bay Times*, p. C3.

When the review is untitled, follow the date of the review with the bracketed information.

> Travers, P. (2012, September 10). [Review of the motion picture *The Master*, 2012]. *Rolling Stone, 11*(1154), 63.

Print Reference Works

35. Entry in an encyclopedia, dictionary, thesaurus, handbook, or almanac Begin your citation with the name of the author or, if the entry is unsigned, the title of the entry. Proceed with the date, the entry title (if not already given), the title of the reference work, the edition number, and the pages. If the contents of the reference work are arranged alphabetically, omit the volume and page numbers.

> Wade-Matthews, M., & Thompson, W. (2011). String quartet. In *The encyclopedia of music: Musical instruments and the art of music-making*. Leicester, England: Anness.

36. Government publication Give the name of the department, office, agency, or committee that issued the report as the author. If the document has a report or special file number, place that in parentheses after the title.

Veterans Affairs Department. (2012). *Federal benefits for veterans, dependents, and survivors 2012*. Washington, DC: Government Printing Office.

37. Brochure or pamphlet Format the entry as you would a book (see items 15–18 on pp. 677–679); insert "n.d." if there is no publication date.

UNESCO. (n.d.). *The world heritage brochure*. Paris: Author.

Field Sources

38. Personal interview Treat unpublished interviews as personal communications, and include them in your text only (see item 13 on p. 676). Do not cite personal interviews in your references list.

39. Unpublished survey data Give the title of the survey first, followed by the date the survey was distributed, and the words "Unpublished raw data."

The University of Iowa graduation exit survey. (2012, April 22). Unpublished raw data.

40. Unpublished letter Treat unpublished letters as personal communications, and include them in your text only (see item 13 on p. 676). Do not cite unpublished letters in your references list.

41. Lecture or public address Provide the name of the speaker, followed by the full date of the presentation and the title of the speech if there is one. End the entry with a brief description of the event and its location.

Russell, E. (2011, February 13). *Drawing on Darwin: Evolutionary history and the use of science in history*. University Lecture series at Carnegie Mellon University, Pittsburgh, PA.

Media Sources

42. Film or video recording List the director and producer (if available), the date of release, the title, the medium in square brackets ("Motion picture," "DVD," or "Blu-ray disc"), the country where the film was made, and the studio or distributor.

Cronenberg, D. (Director). (2012). *Cosmopolis* [Motion picture]. United States: Alfama Films.

43. Television or radio program List the director, writer, producer, host, or reporter (if available); the broadcast date; the title, followed by "Television" or "Radio" and "broadcast" or "series episode" in square brackets; the name of the series; and the city and name of the broadcaster. For an episode in a series, include the producer of the series before the series name.

> Levis, K. (Writer/producer), & Ernst, A. (Producer). (2012, July 24). Alaska gold [Television series episode]. In D. Fanning (Executive producer), *Frontline*. Boston, MA: WGBH.

> Ashbrook, T. (Host). (2012, December 20). Who owns your digital life? [Radio broadcast]. In K. Shiffman (Executive producer), *On point*. Boston, MA: WBUR.

44. Sound recording List the author of the song; the date; the song title, followed by "On" and the recording title in italics; the medium in square brackets; and the production data. If the song was recorded by an artist other than the author, add "Recorded by" plus the artist's name in square brackets after the song title and the recording year in parentheses after the production data.

> Jones, N. (2012). Good morning. On *Little broken hearts* [CD]. New York, NY: Blue Note Records.

Electronic Sources

45. Article with a DOI A DOI (digital object identifier) is a unique number assigned to specific content, such as a journal article. If a DOI is available, include it; you do not need to provide a database name or URL.

> Hughes, V. (2012). Stress: The roots of resilience. *Nature, 490*(7419), 165-167. doi:10.1038/490165a

46. Article without a DOI If no DOI is available, give the URL for the journal's home page.

> Varvil-Weld, L., Turrisi, R., Scaglione, N., Mallett, K. A., & Ray, A. E. (2013). Parents' and students' reports of parenting: Which are more reliably associated with college student drinking? *Addictive Behaviors, 38*(3), 1699-1703. Retrieved from http://www.journals.elsevier.com

47. Online periodical article An article published online is unlikely to have page numbers. Include the URL for the site from which the article was retrieved.

> Barnes, W. B., & Slate, J. R. (2013). College readiness is not one-size-fits-all. *Current Issues in Education*. Retrieved from http://cie.asu.edu/ojs/index.php/cieatasu/article/view/1070

How do I cite online articles using APA style?

Many periodical articles can be accessed online, either through a journal or magazine's Web site or through a database. (See also Chapter 12.)

Russell, V., & Curtis, W. (2013, January). Comparing a large- and small-scale online language course: An examination of teacher and learner perceptions. *The Internet and Higher Education, 16,* 1-13. doi:10.1016/j.iheduc.2012.07.002

A   **The author.** Give the last name first, followed by a comma and initials. Separate the names of multiple authors with commas; use an ampersand (&) before the final author's name.

B   **The date of publication.** Put the year in parentheses and end with a period (outside the closing parenthesis). For magazines and newspapers, include the month and, if relevant, the day (2012, April 13).

C   **The article title.** Give the full title; include the subtitle (if any), preceded by a colon. Do not underline, italicize, or put the title or subtitle in quotes. Capitalize only the first word of the title, the first word of the subtitle, and any proper nouns or proper adjectives. End with a period.

D   **The periodical title.** Italicize the periodical title, and capitalize all major words. Insert a comma.

E   **The volume number and issue number.** For magazines and journals, include the volume number, italicized. For magazines and for journals that start each issue with page 1, include the issue number in parentheses, not italicized. Insert a comma.

F   **Inclusive page number(s).** Give all of the numbers in full (317-327, not 317-27). For newspapers, include the abbreviation "p." or "pp." for page numbers and, if relevant, section letters (p. B12).

G   **The DOI or URL.** Give the unique digital object identifier (DOI), if available; you do not need to provide a retrieval date, database name, or URL. If there is no DOI, include the words "Retrieved from" and the URL of the journal or magazine home page.

48. Web document For a stand-alone Web source such as a report, or a section within a larger Web site, cite as much of the following information as possible: author, publication date, document title, and URL. If the content is likely to be changed or updated, include your retrieval date.

Scirica, C. (2012, September 14). *Could banning large soft drinks be effective in the fight against obesity?* Retrieved from http://www.massgeneral.org/about /newsarticle.aspx?id=3743

United States Mint. (2012). *How coins are made.* Retrieved from http://www.usmint .gov/faqs/circulating_coins/index.cfm?action=coins

49. Online book Cite the electronic version only if a print version is not available or is hard to find.

Robinson, K. (n.d.). *Beyond the wilderness*. Retrieved from http://onlineoriginals.com /showitem.asp?itemID=113

50. E-mail message or real-time communication Because e-mail messages and real-time communication, such as text messages, are difficult or impossible for your readers to retrieve, APA does not recommend including them in your references list. You should treat them as personal communication and cite them parenthetically in your text (see item 13 on p. 676).

51. Message posted to a newsgroup, electronic mailing list, or online discussion forum List the author, posting date, and the title of the post or message subject line. Include a description of the message or post in square brackets. End with the URL where the archived message can be retrieved. Include the name of the group, list, or forum if it's not part of the URL.

Skambis, K. (2011, October 27). Re: Welcome to the lung connection: Living with lung disease [Online discussion list comment]. Retrieved from http://connection .lungusa.org/discussions/welcome-to-the-lung-connection-living-with-lung -di/2011/07/25/1-welcome-to-the-lung-connection-living-with-lung

52. Article or page on a wiki Because the material on a wiki is likely to change, include a retrieval date.

Diabetes. (n.d.). *WikiHealth*. Retrieved March 22, 2013, from http://www.wikihealth .com/Diabetes

How do I cite works from Web sites using APA style?

You will likely need to search the Web site to find some of the citation information you need. For some sites, all of the details may not be available; find as many as you can. Remember that the citation you provide should allow readers to retrace your steps electronically to locate the sources. Consult pages 685–689 for additional models for citing Web sources.

———— A ———— ———— B ———— ———— C ————

Lamont, M., & Sun, A. (2012, December 10). *How China's elite universities will have*

— C — ———————— D ————————

to change. Retrieved from http://chronicle.com/article/How-Chinas-Elite

——— D ———

-Universities/136173/

A   **The author of the work.** Give the last name first, followed by a comma and initials. Separate the names of multiple authors with commas; use an ampersand (&) before the final author's name. If the source has no author, list the title first and follow it with the date.

B   **The date of publication.** Put the year in parentheses and include the month and day, if available. If there is no date, use "n.d." in parentheses. End with a period (outside the closing parenthesis).

C   **The title of the work.** Give the full title, italicized; include the subtitle (if any), preceded by a colon. Capitalize only the first word of the title, the first word of the subtitle, and any proper nouns or proper adjectives.

D   **Retrieval information.** Include a retrieval date if the material is likely to be changed or updated, or if it lacks a set publication date. (Because this commentary has a set publication date, the retrieval date is not necessary.) End with the URL.

53. Blog To cite an entry on a blog, give the author (or screen name, if available), the date the material was posted, and the title of the entry. Include the description "Web log post" in square brackets and the URL. To cite a comment on a blog, use the description "Web log comment."

> Rubin, G. (2012, October 17). Does waiting in a line drive you crazy? Here's why [Web log post]. Retrieved from http://www.happiness-project.com/happiness _project/2012/10/does-waiting-in-a-line-drive-you-crazy-heres-why/

54. Podcast Give the name of the producer, the date of the podcast, and the title. Include a description in square brackets and the URL.

> Goldsmith, J. (Producer). (2012, December 23). Joss Whedon — The Avengers Q&A [Audio podcast]. Retrieved from http://www.theqandapodcast.com/2012/12 /joss-whedon-avengers-q.html

55. Online video post Give the name of the creator, the date it was posted, and the title. Include a description in square brackets and the URL.

> Neistat, C. (2012, November 3). Staten Island hurricane destruction [Video file]. Retrieved from https://www.youtube.com/watch?feature=player_embedded&v =Wr9594oKZNQ#

56. Computer software or game Sometimes a person is named as having rights to the software or game: in that case, list that person as the author. Otherwise, begin the entry with the name of the program or game, and identify the source in square brackets after the name as "Computer software" or "Computer game." Treat the organization that produces the software or game as the publisher. If you're referring to a specific version that isn't included in the name, put this information last.

> Rosetta Stone Spanish (Latin America) Level 1 [Computer software]. Arlington, VA: Rosetta Stone.

Other Sources

57. General advice about other sources For citing other types of sources, APA suggests that you use as a guide a source type listed in its manual that most closely resembles the type of source you want to cite.

Acknowledgments

Page 18: Editorial Image, LLC/PhotoEdit.

Page 19: Courtesy of Montana Conservation Corps. Reproduced by permission.

Page 20: Courtesy of Veterans Green Jobs. Reproduced by permission.

Page 21: (Top) Reprinted with the permission of the Center For Energy Workforce Development. (Bottom) U.S. Department of Labor, VETS.

Page 22: Lana Zinger and Andrea Cohen. "Veterans Returning from War into the Classroom: How Can Colleges Be Better Prepared to Meet Their Needs." Reproduced by permission of Dr. Lana Zinger.

Pages 24–25: Courtesy of Veterans Green Jobs. Reproduced by permission.

Pages 52–55: Courtesy of the *State & Local Energy Report*; Photos: Veterans Green Jobs.

Page 56: Courtesy of Veterans Green Jobs. Reproduced by permission.

Page 57: Courtesy of Sierra Club. Photo: Veterans Green Jobs.

Page 71: Courtesy of The Pew Research Center.

Pages 73–74: Bill Doe and BG James "Spider" Marks. "Guest Commentary: Green Jobs for Veterans." From the *Denver Post*. Courtesy of Veterans Green Jobs.

Page 100: John Crawford. "Preface" from *The Last True Story I'll Ever Tell*. Copyright © 2005, 2006 by John Crawford. Used by permission of Riverhead Books, an imprint of Penguin Group (USA), LLC.

Page 101: (Top) Experiencing War: Stories from the Veterans History Project, American Folklife Center, Library of Congress. (Bottom) Liam Corley. "Brave Words: Rehabilitating the Veteran–Writer." From *College English*, Volume 74, Number 4, March 2012. Copyright © 2012 by the National Council of Teachers of English. Reprinted with permission.

Pages 105–112: Cheryl Strayed. "What Kind of Woman Are You?" From *Wild: From Lost to Found on the Pacific Crest Trail*. Copyright © 2012 by Cheryl Strayed. Used by permission of Alfred A. Knopf, Inc. an imprint of the Knopf Doubleday Publishing Group, a division of Random House, LLC. All rights reserved.

Pages 114–117: David Sedaris. "Keeping Up." From *When You Are Engulfed in Flames*. Copyright © 2008 by David Sedaris. By permission of Little, Brown and Company. All rights reserved.

Pages 120–131: James Mollison. *Where Children Sleep*. Copyright © James Mollison. Published in 2010.

Salvatore Scibona. "Where I Learned to Read." From *The New Yorker*, June 13, 2011. Copyright © 2011 by Salvatore Scibona. Reprinted by permission of William Morris Endeavor Entertainment LLC.

Firoozeh Dumas. "Waterloo." From *Funny in Farsi*. Copyright © 2003 by Firoozeh Dumas. Reprinted by permission of the author.

Elvia Bautista. "Remembering All the Boys." Copyright © 2006 by Elvia Bautista. From the book *This I Believe: The Personal Philosophies of Remarkable Men and Women* edited by Jay Allison and Dan Gediman. Copyright © 2006 by This I Believe, Inc. Used by permission of Henry Holt and Company, LLC. All rights reserved. Screenshot: This I Believe Web site. Copyright © 2005–2013 by This I Believe, Inc. Used with permission.

Page 160: Allianz SE, Germany.

Page 161: (Top) Briana Pastorino, Loma Linda University Health. (Bottom) Courtesy of Disabled Sports USA. Archer photo: Courtesy of Arizona Disabled Sports; Skier photo: Courtesy of © Tyler Stableford Photography. Reproduced by permission.

Pages 165–170: George Chauncey. "The Legacy of Antigay Discrimination." From *Why Marriage? The History Shaping Today's Debate over Gay Equality*. Reproduced with permission of Basic Books via Copyright Clearance Center.

Pages 172–174: Courtesy of AVG Technologies USA, Inc. Reproduced by permission.

Pages 176–179: "Animal Welfare and Autism Champion," a feature article on Temple Grandin from the Colorado State University Web site, April 2008, is reprinted by permission of Temple Grandin. Photo: Copyright © Rosalie Winard.

Page 183: Courtesy of the Colorado State University Libraries. Reproduced by permission.

Page 189: Courtesy of World Health Organization. Copyright © World Malaria Report, 2010, by permission. http://www.who.int/malaria/world_malaria_report_2010/en/.

"Concussion in Sports." Centers for Disease Control and Prevention. Reproduced by permission.

"Preparing Your Pets for Emergencies Makes Sense." Ready.gov/FEMA.

"World DataBank." Courtesy of The World Bank.

Page 214: Alison Gopnik. "Why Play Is Serious." Copyright © courtesy of Professor Alison Gopnik, reproduced by permission. Originally appeared in *Smithsonian*, July–August 2012. Photo: © Jessica Hische/Blend Images/Getty.

Index

Missing something? To access the online material that accompanies this text, visit **bedfordstmartins.com/conversation**. Students who do not buy a new book can purchase access at this site.

Inside the Bedford Integrated Media for *Joining the Conversation*

Chapter 5: Writing to Reflect

John Crawford, "The Last True Story I'll Ever Tell" (memoir)

Ashleigh Alexis Bryant, "Library of Congress Veterans History Project" (interview)

Liam Corley, "'Brave Words': Rehabilitating the Veteran-Writer" (journal article)

Salvatore Scibona, "Where I Learned to Read" (literacy narrative)

Firoozeh Dumas, "Waterloo" (memoir)

Elvia Bautista, "Remembering All the Boys" (audio essay)

Chapter 6: Writing to Inform

Allianz, "Cycling" (infographic)

Loma Linda University Medical Center, "Loma Linda University Medical Center's Orthotics and Prosthetics Team Gives Brazilian Athlete Ability to Walk" (press release)

Disabled Sports USA, "I Can Do Anything" (Web site)

The Centers for Disease Control, "Concussion in Sports" (Web site)

FEMA, "Preparing Your Pets for Emergencies Makes Sense" (brochure)

The World Bank, "World DataBank" (map)

Chapter 7: Writing to Analyze

Alison Gopnik, "Why Play Is Serious" (magazine article)

UC Berkeley, "Scientists Tap the Genius of Babies and Youngsters to Make Computers Smarter" (webcast)

Alliance for Childhood, "Crisis in the Kindergarten" (professional report)

Chicago Tribune, "The Drone Future" (news analysis)

Adriana Barbaro and Jeremy Earp, "Consuming Kids: The Commercialization of Childhood" (documentary film)

Marlene Zuk, "Misguided Nostalgia for Our Paleo Past" (analytical essay)

Chapter 8: Writing to Evaluate

Glenn Derene, "15 Gadgets vs. One Personal Trainer" (online article)

Georgia Department of Public Health, "The Hype and Hope of Mobile Health" (government blog)

CNET.com, "Nike+ Fuelband vs. FitBit Ultra – Prizefight" (video review)

LIFT, "oneLIFT 2012 Impact Report" (progress report)

EnviroMedia Social Marketing and the University of Oregon, "Greenwashing Index" (ratings Web site)

U.S. Department of Education, "College Scorecard" (comparison tool)

Chapter 9: Writing to Solve Problems

Robert Lemos, "Defending Your Identity" (magazine article)

Dave Johnson, "How to Prevent Identity Theft" (online news article)

Federal Trade Commission, "Identity Theft" (government Web site)

Jim Trainum, "Get It on Tape" (guest editorial)

Atul Gawande, "Suggestions on Becoming a Positive Deviant" (advice)

Cynthia Graber, "Fare Start" (audio report)

Chapter 10: Writing to Convince or Persuade

Ruth E. Sternberg, "Arts at the Core" (professional article)

American Music Conference, "Reverse Economics?" (case history)

NAMM Foundation, "Keep Music Education Strong" (brochure)

Michelle Obama, "Who Are You Going to Be?" (speech)

Cyrus Habib, "Show Us the Money" (opinion column)

SPARK Movement, "Our Letter to LEGO" (open letter)